Psychology & Christianity Integration

Seminal Works that Shaped the Movement

Edited by

Daryl H. Stevenson
Brian E. Eck
Peter C. Hill

Christian Association for Psychological Studies, Inc.
Batavia, Illinois

CAPS
INTERNATIONAL

Psychology & Christianity Integration:
Seminal Works that Shaped the Movement

Edited by Daryl H. Stevenson, Brian E. Eck, and Peter C. Hill

Celebrating 50 Years of the Christian Association for Psychological Studies

Copyright © 2007 Christian Association for Psychological Studies, Inc.
P.O. Box 365, Batavia, Illinois 60510
www.caps.net

Softcover ISBN 978-0-9792237-0-9
Hardcover ISBN 978-0-9792237-1-6

Printed in the United States of America
1 2 3 4 5 6 7

Publisher's Cataloging-in-Publication Data
Psychology & Christianity integration : seminal works that
shaped the movement / edited by Daryl H. Stevenson,
Brian E. Eck, Peter C. Hill.
p. cm.
Includes bibliographical references and index.
LCCN 2006940282
ISBN-13: 978-0-9792237-0-9 (softcover)
ISBN-10: 0-9792237-0-9 (softcover)
ISBN-13: 978-0-9792237-1-6 (hardcover)
ISBN-10: 0-9792237-1-7 (hardcover)

1. Christianity--Psychology. 2. Psychology and
religion.   I. Stevenson, Daryl H. II. Eck, Brian E.
III. Hill, Peter C., 1953- IV. Title: Psychology and
Christianity integration.

BR110.P79 2007   261.5'15   QBI07-600016

Cover design by: Sue Baxter, DAYSEVENDESIGN

Dedication

This book is dedicated to those who have gone before us, who plowed the ground and planted the seeds of the integration movement; to those who will come next, who will expand and diversify the movement; and finally to our students, who have challenged, questioned and inspired us.

Acknowledgements

The editors wish to say thanks to the following individuals who assisted in the production of this book.

Lisa Brown, Kristina Lucking, and Brianne Baier from Azusa Pacific University.

Ruth Rorem, Jennifer Wilkerson, Lauren Maltby, Richie Bollinger, and Carissa Dwiwardani from Biola University.

Claire Mellis, Don Latva and Russ Law from Christian Printing Service.

A special thanks to Katie Kopp for her outstanding work on the index.

Editors

Daryl H. Stevenson, PhD, completed his clinical psychology degree at Biola University's Rosemead School of Psychology and is Professor of Psychology at Houghton College in New York. For twenty-five years he has supervised senior psychology interns and taught courses in Psychology and Christianity, Personality, Abnormal, and Work Team Dynamics. In 1999, he was awarded Houghton's Teaching Excellence Award, and has served as Chair of both the Psychology Department and the Division of History and Social Science. He has presented papers and workshops at CAPS conferences, and has served as the academic representative on the International CAPS Board of Directors, President of CAPS (1999-2000), column editor for the former *CAPS Report* newsletter, and consulting editor for the *Journal of Psychology and Christianity*.

Brian E. Eck, PhD, completed his clinical psychology degree from Biola University's Rosemead School of Psychology. He is Professor and Chair of the Psychology Department at Azusa Pacific University (APU) in California and is also a licensed psychologist in clinical practice in Covina, CA. He serves as Managing Editor of the *Journal of Psychology and Christianity* and has served in roles for CAPS-East, CAPS-West, and the CAPS International Board of Directors. He has published numerous articles and given numerous conference presentations and workshops. At APU he regularly teaches courses on integration, the psychology of religion, the history of psychology, and clinical practice.

Peter C. Hill, PhD, completed his social psychology degree from the University of Houston. A prominent figure in the integration literature, Hill has been Editor of the *Journal of Psychology and Christianity* since 1989, an active member in both CAPS (where he received the Distinguished Member Award in 1998) and APA Division 36 (serving as President in 2000-2001), co-author of *The Psychology of Fundamentalism* (with Hood and Williamson in 2005), and co-editor of *Measures of Religiosity* (with Hood in 1999) as well as *Baker's Encyclopedia of Psychology and Counseling* (with Benner in 1999). Hill has taught regularly an undergraduate integration course, produced numerous other scholarly works, and delivered many conference presentations. Currently, he serves as the undergraduate psychology department chair at Biola University in California.

Advisory Board

Contents

Preface v

Introduction 1
    Daryl H. Stevenson

Section I. Historical and Theoretical Integration...17
   Introduction
   Suggestions for Further Reading

   Chapter 1: Perspectives on the Integration of Psychology and Theology.....................21
             S. Bruce Narramore

   Chapter 2: Moving Through the Jungle: A Decade of Integration................................33
             Gary R. Collins

   Chapter 3: The Search for Truth in the Task of Integration...38
             James D. Guy, Jr.

   Chapter 4: Christ, the Lord of Psychology 42
             Eric J. Johnson

   Chapter 5: The Interface of Theology and Psychology..58
             J. Harold Ellens

   Chapter 6: The Tension Between Psychology and Theology:
             An Anthropological Solution..68
             Hendrika Vande Kemp

   Chapter 7: Sola scriptura: Then and now...75
             James R. Beck

   Chapter 8: John Wesley and Psychology..82
             H. Newton Malony

Section II. Science and Faith Reconciliation 93
   Introduction
   Suggestions for Further Reading

   Chapter 9: Integration of Faith and Science—The Very Idea 96
             Nicholas Wolterstorff

   Chapter 10: Christian Perspectives on the Sciences of Man...102
             C. Stephen Evans

   Chapter 11: Psychology's Two Cultures: A Christian Analysis......................................113
             Mary Stewart Van Leeuwen

   Chapter 12: Implications for Integration from a New Philosophy of Psychology as Science.......126
             Peter C. Hill

Chapter 13: A Constructive Relationship for Religion with the Science and Profession of Psychology: Perhaps the Boldest Model Yet..136
Stanton L. Jones

Section III. Perspectives on Personhood 155
Introduction
Suggestions for Further Reading

Chapter 14: Biblical Teaching on Personality 159
H. D. McDonald

Chapter 15: The Concept of the Self as the Key to Integration..170
C. Stephen Evans

Section IV. Levels and Types of Integration...177
Introduction
Suggestions for Further Reading

Chapter 16: The Task Ahead: Six Levels of Integration of Christianity and Psychology 180
Robert E. Larzelere

Chapter 17: The Task of integration: A Modest Proposal..187
Steve Bouma-Prediger

Chapter 18: Integration and Beyond: Principled, Professional, Personal.......................196
Siang-Yang Tan

Section V. Models of Integration 205
Introduction
Suggestions for Further Reading

Chapter 19: Sacred and Secular Models of Psychology and Religion 208
John D. Carter

Chapter 20: On Living in Athens: Models of Relating Psychology, Church, and Culture...............217
Alvin C. Dueck

Chapter 21: Integrating the Integrators: An Organizing Framework for a Multifaceted Process of Integration 227
Brian E. Eck

Section VI. Applied Integration 239
Introduction
Suggestions for Further Reading

Chapter 22: The Incarnation as a Metaphor for Psychotherapy 244
David G. Benner

Chapter 23: Consecrated Counseling: Reflections on the Distinctives of Christian Counseling 250
Rodger K. Bufford

Chapter 24: A Blueprint for Intradisciplinary Integration 261
Everett L. Worthington, Jr.

Chapter 25: The Psychotherapist as Christian Ethicist: Theology Applied to Practice.........................268
Alan C. Tjeltveit

Chapter 26: Integration in the Therapy Room: An Overview of the Literature 277
　　　　　M. Elizabeth Lewis Hall and Todd W. Hall

Chapter 27: Psychotherapeutic Virtues and the Grammar of Faith 292
　　　　　Robert C. Roberts

Chapter 28: Dealing with Religious Resistance in Psychotherapy 303
　　　　　S. Bruce Narramore

Chapter 29: An Exploration of the Therapeutic Use of Spiritual Disciplines in
　　　　　Clinical Practice 312
　　　　　Brian E. Eck

Section VII. Integrative Research 327
Introduction
Suggestions for Further Reading

Chapter 30: Lying in the Laboratory: Deception in Human Research from Psychological,
　　　　　Philosophical, and Theological Perspectives 330
　　　　　Rodney L. Bassett, David Basinger, and Paul Livermore

Chapter 31: National Collaborative Research on How Students Learn Integration:
　　　　　Final Report 342
　　　　　Randall L. Sorenson, Kimberly R. Derflinger,
　　　　　Rodger K. Bufford, and Mark R. McMinn

Chapter 32: Please Forgive Me: Transgressor's Emotions and Physiology During
　　　　　Imagery of Seeking Forgiveness and Victim Responses 352
　　　　　Charlotte vanOyen Witvliet, Thomas E. Ludwig, and David J. Bauer

Chapter 33: Being a Good Neighbor: Can Students Come to Value Homosexual Persons? 366
　　　　　Rodney L. Bassett, Marika VanNikkelen-Kuyper, Deanna Johnson, Ashley Miller,
　　　　　Anna Carter, and Julie P. Grimm

Postscript: What's Next? 375

Index 379

Preface

On June 6, 1946, one of the most high profile organizations in twentieth century America was chartered. Its status has grown in American culture to be a major influence on how we spend our leisure time and hard-earned dollars, how we express our competitive attitudes, who we emulate as icons of fashion and style, and what we count as important in our lives. The National Basketball Association (NBA) has grown to symbolize the hubris, wealth, and pride of American sport.

It was no surprise that 50 years later the NBA wanted to select a list of the "50 Greatest Players" of all time to celebrate the league's 50th anniversary. A blue-ribbon panel of sport media, former players, coaches, and team executives (50, of course) was selected to consider the players' statistics and to exercise judgment and wisdom from their knowledge of the game. Having done their work, NBA Commissioner David Stern unveiled the definitive list of the 50 Greatest Players in NBA history on October 29, 1996 at a press luncheon in New York City. But the debate continued about whether the 50 selected were actually THE best. Fans, pros, coaches, and the media-at-large had their ideas, and shortly after the list emerged, new stars cut and slashed their way into hearts and record books. Tim Duncan, Kobe Bryant, LeBron James, and Dwayne Wade were not included on the list, nor even considered, because they had not yet made their appearances.

The problem with picking a list where "greatest" or "best" are the criteria, is that it creates a moving target that is never exactly correct, as judged somehow by a consensus of knowledgeable people. A quick Google search of "top 10," "top 50," or "best 100" leads to uncountable lists. The Travel Channel frequently highlights the "10 best…" beaches of the world, roller coasters, opulent yachts, weekend getaways, and exotic hotels. It makes for good TV, but few know who the judges were. Every year new books hit the stands at Borders and Barnes & Noble, gathering the best of something, such as Cirian Parker's *The Thinkers 50: The World's Most Influential Business Writers and Leaders*. The Internet, of course, has sites listing the Top 50 web sites, virtually all of which you and we have never visited. Whether the venue is the Olympics, academics, executive talent, or frog-jumping contests, we like to identify the best, to venerate the leaders among the masses, and to sort through the myriad to single out those that bubble to the top.

Compared to the NBA's 50th year celebration, the Christian Association for Psychological Studies (CAPS) conducted a much quieter one for its 50th birthday in 2006. If you do that Google search, you will not find a definitive Top 50 list of the "best Christian psychologists," and there is no listing of the best research or most readable works on the integration of psychology and Christian theology over the last 50 years. To our knowledge, no one has attempted such lists and for good reasons.

The seeds of this celebratory volume were sown on February 16, 2005 when Steve Allison, the CAPS International Conference Coordinator, sent some planning ideas to a small group for the April 2006 convention. The theme was going to be a celebration of the 50th anniversary of our CAPS organization. Selecting a list of the best Christian psychologists never was a viable idea, but a more plausible "nutty idea," as Steve put it, was to publish a volume of the "best of the best" written about integration of psychology and Christian theology over the last half century. Clearly, the idea resonated with the group, and when the concept was presented to the International CAPS Board of Directors two months later, the informal ground-swell of support achieved official sanction. From that beginning, the Board recruited an editing team, established a target date for completion, and provided the assurance of financial backing to sustain the effort through to publication.

Exactly how this volume took shape was the responsibility of the editors, and from the start, we knew the ideal of collecting the "best of the best" psychological-theological scholarship would be elusive, just as the definitive list of best basketball players proves to be endlessly debatable, in spite of the fact that there are statistics to guide the choices. Who could have possibly read enough to claim competency or even familiarity with that literary landscape? And further, given the broad and often controversial understanding of the term "integration" over the last half century, what are the parameters that allow a theoretical, applied, or research piece to be considered? What would be the criteria for either inclusion or exclusion?

Steve Allison's "nutty idea" of isolating the "best of the best" of the articles and chapters in the psychological integration literature proved to be a bit unrealistic. We did not, however, give up on developing a very special anthology. For the same reasons that basketball coaches would not necessarily want on their team the five best players in terms of statistics, athleticism, or skill (even if they could be indubitably identified), we saw the value of selecting a group of "players" (articles and chapters, in our case) which could achieve our goal. In basketball, the goal is to achieve a play-er synergy, which requires assessing how they work together to accomplish the goal of winning against all comers. When celebrating 50 years of integrative scholarship is the game, the criteria for the "best" may mean ascertaining how the selected articles and chapters best work together to achieve the goal of conveying the movement's *Zeitgeist*. For those 50 years, the psychology-theology integration discussion has been embodied in CAPS' mission. This volume has evolved, then, into our attempt to identify and select the best works for the good of the team. Together they provide an accurate window on the movement. Just as assembling a team of the five absolutely best basketball players does not always result in a well-honed team that wins every game, we have draft-ed (to extend our basketball analogy) works that provide dimension to our team: some historical analysis, theoretical grounding, expert observations, empirical data, and application.

As editors, we knew there was potential for some grumblings and unhappiness over the canon we humbly selected. It was possible that some scholars would do a slow and quiet burn for being omitted, but we take heart in assuming that they understand the constraints of a single volume. We were bolstered by knowing that no current volume provided earlier-published works with a comprehensive overview under one cover. Earlier efforts to gather significant articles and book chapters dealing with aspects of psychology/mental health and religion/Christian faith (for example, Fleck & Carter, 1981; Malony, 1983, 1991; Jones, 1986; Roberts & Talbot, 1997; McMinn & Phillips, 2001) brought together substantive thinking by multiple authors, had somewhat differ-ent purposes, and only one (McMinn & Phillips) is still available in print. There seemed to be space in the landscape for a fresh collection of key resources.

Culling the massive literature for memorable and substantive works that have shaped our collective thinking requires more than an enthusiastic trio. Multiple minds and the input from many would give guidance and some degree of empirical validation. But how should this effort be organized and executed?

Since 2002, seminars and papers on teaching the undergraduate integration course were pre-sented at the International CAPS Conferences (Stevenson & Eck, 2002; Entwistle, Stevenson, & White, 2004, Stevenson et al, 2005; Eck, Tisdale, & Stevenson, 2006). Part of that effort was to establish and maintain an informal email network of instructors in colleges and universities who teach a course or courses in explicit integration, primarily to undergraduates. Presumably, if any particular interest group was familiar with the literature, it would be those instructors. Nearly 60 are now part of this list, called the Integration Instructors' Network (IIN), and so we turned to will-ing members of that list for help. Other internationally known scholars who merited a say in what we were planning were solicited through email in June 2005 for their input.

Following the invitation to be part of what became the Advisory Board for this volume, 31 busy practitioners and scholars responded affirmatively to our request for their nominations of up to 15 of the "most significant article or book chapter contributions to the integrative literature over the last half century. Which ones really ought to be in a volume that highlights the best of the last 50 years?"

After blindly submitting our own lists, we sat back and waited for the avalanche of data to come pouring in, and it did! Long lists, sometimes with annotations, and short lists with as few as three offerings, arrived through the summer and fall. However, the dream of having controversial decisions taken out of our hands never materialized fully through the frequency analysis. The final tally gave us a consensus core of integration articles on which to build this collection, but the elegant empirical results we hoped for, of a consensus set of two or three dozen articles and book chapters, never quite emerged. There were some clear preferences for particular articles, but hundreds of articles were mentioned by one scholar, and one alone, demonstrating the wide scope of interest by 34 scholars. This was not a major surprise, since there is reason to anticipate this, and because that result is supported by previous information about what IIN instructors ask their students to read (Stevenson, 2004).

In retrospect, we asked tough duty of our participants. Some lamented that we did not ask for whole books, for that would have been easier for many, but it was clearly not in line with this single-volume project. Others had particular people in mind who "really ought to be" in this volume, but no single article came to mind for them. It was the body of one's scholarship, and not a discrete piece of writing, that came to their minds. A few works, therefore, were the choice of the frequently-mentioned scholars whom we approached to select what they considered their most appropriate work for our purposes.

In spite of all our efforts to allow free-wheeling empirical data to shape this anthology, we had to make some hard decisions. Given the nature of the task to commemorate CAPS' 50 years, we used additional criteria for an article's inclusion. We selected scholarly works that:

o are seminal and exemplary of integrative scholarship.

o are written by key people who shaped the movement.

o are accessible to students and professionals.

o have broad appeal to Christians in the psychological and pastoral professions.

o uniquely shape or trace the history of the last 50 years of integration's development.

These decisions have implications. The articles that emerged are recognized as seminal, important, and formative of integrative thought. They are not evenly balanced between theory, research, and practice, and they are not drawn evenly from the previous five decades. Also, not all the included articles and chapters are exemplars of *doing* integration. Some are what we labeled *balcony* articles, while others are *main floor* players. This rough distinction became a way for us to distinguish between important summary articles that stand off, observe, and assess the state of affairs (for example Narramore, 1973 and Collins, 1983, this volume). They talk *about* integration and the contextual factors surrounding it. Other articles or chapters are *main floor* or frontline examples of integration thinking and research in action (for example MacDonald, 1986, and Witvliet, et al., 2002, this volume). Both types of articles have value toward gaining a perspective on the state of integrative thought.

Presenting over thirty articles in a volume requires an organizing scheme. Wanting to allow the results to suggest a scheme, if possible, or to modify our preliminary categories, our scheme was imposed after the frequency analysis had been completed. Our seven section scheme was mostly rationally-derived from an earlier content analysis of 20 syllabi submitted by instructors who teach an undergraduate explicit integration course (Stevenson & Eck, 2002). We assumed that multiple syllabi from instructors with widely disparate graduate school backgrounds, and with further diversity stemming from various college and university theological traditions, personal theological commitments, instructor age, teaching experience, and geographical locations, would lead to a general consensus about what seemed to be the key topics and content that "ought to be covered" in a general introductory course in integration.

It made sense that the consensual scheme should generalize to organizing principles suitable for this volume. So, six categories emerged in the earlier content analysis, with the seventh, integration research, being added by the editors. The seven categories that structure the presentation, then, are (1) Historical and Theoretical Integration (2) Faith and Science Reconciliation, (3) Perspectives on Personhood, (4) Levels and Types of Integration (5) Models of Integration, (6) Applied Integration, and (7) Integrative Research. Each of these sections begins with an introduction that serves as an advanced organizer.

As with all anthologies, this book is not meant to be read straight through in a burst of energetic, non-stop reading. It is not even meant to be read in linear fashion, from front to back. It should be sampled over time as you are drawn to sections that address your particular interest and curiosity, guided by the seven section introductions. Should you want to expand beyond what is here, the annotated *Suggestions for Further Reading* lists will provide some guidance.

As editors, we take responsibility for the content and focus of this volume. We would however, like to extend special thanks to three groups. First, we are grateful to the members of the International CAPS Board of Directors, and particularly to Paul Regan, Executive Director, for offering enthusiastic and unfailing support from the start. They entrusted the task to us and then stood back. We have done our best not to let them down.

Secondly, we were pleased with the active response of our Advisory Board members and are indebted to them for their serious and gracious effort to think deeply and long about three things: the initial list of important sources that they believed were among the best; the suggested further readings for each subsection; and their speculations about the future direction of integration. Some of them will not even see their choices and ideas emerge here from the empirical process, but that does not diminish the important function that all have served in their capacity as members of the Advisory Board.

Finally, we extend our heartfelt gratitude to an exclusive third group--our wives, Gudy, Enid, and Carol—who have had to share us with our offices and computers more than is typical over these months. No project gets completed without carving out time from those who want to share it with us. They accepted the constraints and understood the importance of the work to us, freeing us to persevere. Their support is always crucial and always felt.

May a new generation of seasoned and student scholars continue to engage in the general integration enterprise contoured in these pages. We hope that these scholars, like those sustained for more than 50 years by kingdom-building inspiration, continue to find a home in CAPS for the 50 years to come.

References

Eck, B., Tisdale, T., & Stevenson, D. H. (2006). *Teaching integration courses: Models, methods, & mentors*. Presented at the International CAPS Conference, Cincinnati, OH, March 11.

Entwistle, D. N., Stevenson, D. H., & White, S. (2004). *Teaching the undergraduate integration course*. A seminar presented at the International CAPS Conference, Ft. Lauderdale, FL, March 26-29.

Fleck, J. R., & Carter, J. D. (Eds.). (1981). *Psychology and Christianity: Integrative readings*. Nashville: Abingdon.

Jones, S. L. (1986). *Psychology and the Christian faith: An introductory reader*. Grand Rapids, MI: Baker.

Malony, H. N. (Ed.). (1983). *Wholeness and holiness: Readings in the psychology/theology of mental health*. Grand Rapids, MI: Baker.

Malony, H. N. (Ed.). (1991). *Psychology of religion: Personalities, problems, possibilities*. Grand Rapids, MI: Baker.

McMinn, M. R., & Phillips, T. R. (Eds.). (2001). *Care for the soul: Exploring the intersection of psychology and theology*. Downers Grove, IL: InterVarsity.

Roberts, R. C., & Talbot, M. R. (Eds.). (1997). *Limning the psyche: Explorations in Christian psychology*. Grand Rapids, MI: Eerdmans.

Stevenson, D. H. (2004). *Integration in the classroom: Who is reading what, and why?* A paper presented at the International CAPS Conference, Ft. Lauderdale, FL, March 26-29.

Stevenson, D. H. (2005). *Teaching integration and integration in our teaching*. A four hour seminar on concepts and activities presented with eight others. International CAPS Conference, Dallas, TX, April 7.

Stevenson, D. H., & Eck, B. (2002). *Teaching the integrative concepts course in the undergraduate curriculum*. Presented at the International CAPS Conference, Chicago, IL. April 12.

Introduction: The Nature of Integration and Its Historical Context

Daryl H. Stevenson
Houghton College

Two new-born, spotted twin fawns playfully pranced across the lawn and stopped in the sparse bushes a dozen yards away. The movement to my extreme left drew my immediate attention as I was relaxing in my recliner. At first I rolled left and leaned closer to the screened window to get a better look. With eyes now inches from the screen and straining to clear up the blur so I could see the unusual surprise visitors across the yard, I moved my head and eyes and then backed away from the screen so the details of the scene could become clearer. As I leaped up and out of the chair quickly, the pair and their mother were spooked by my movement, and they bounded off into the wooded thickets.

Many readers will be familiar with this common visual experience looking through a window screen. While our tendency is to approach objects of interest—to get in there for a better look—we enhance our perspective only as we move back and allow the integrated and multiple visual pathways to merge synergistically in the dynamic of the movement. Paradoxically, the closer my eye moved toward that scene, and the more I remained still as I tried to look through the screen grid, the more blurry and restricted was my perspective. Retreating from the screen allowed an integration of apertures to provide the clues to the whole scene. Getting closer to the minute, single apertures—sthe small voids where sight is totally unobstructed—actually restricted the view. Under normal circumstances we cannot physically achieve complete, unobstructed, and ideal clarity by viewing through one aperture in the screen.

Thinking integratively appears to be much like this. While all metaphors and analogies break down, two principles are demonstrated here that are useful as we explore the nature and task of integration. Keeping these in mind can help us hold our anxieties at bay while we naturally want to see the world "as it is."

The first principle is that one cannot eliminate the restricting biases that both shape and obscure our vision. We are forced to live with them but there are ways to minimize or manage them. That is, we cannot achieve pure vision to view the world. We always need to filter our perception through a grid of control beliefs, experiences, and commitments. It was this fact that Paul speaks about in his Corinthian letter: "Now we see but a poor reflection as in a mirror; then we shall see face to face. Now I know in part; then I shall know fully. . . ." (I Corinthians 13:12, NIV). This is fundamentally a theological statement about the effects of our finitude, our fallen world, and our coping in it.

A second principle this analogy suggests is the importance of a plurality of ideas as a way to sharpen our perspective on truth. So, we draw upon the first principle to lend veracity to the second. While it is tempting to declare that there is one view, God's view, we will never fully know God's view, for it is obscured from us. Some believers conclude that multiple notions of truth must be in conflict and therefore contain some degree of error that contaminates the truth. However, just as iron on iron forges a more useful tool than the original iron ingot, multiple ideas sharpen each other in their interplay. Pushing the screen analogy a bit further, single apertures provide only a small portion of the true visual picture compared to the perception that results from dynamic eye movement. In the same way, single, isolated ideas account for some cognitive information, but when added to the mix of many through the dynamic of reflection and argument, something creative and more wonderful emerges. That is the basis of true scholarship.

The message should be clear as we apply the analogy to scholarship: the more thinking we do using multiple ideas, the more intentional we are in causing the big picture *Gestalt* to emerge. Consequently it is more likely that the incomplete becomes more complete. Integration of psychology and Christian theology allows us to reduce the gap between ignorance and complete (although unattainable) knowledge.

In the following sections of this essay, I address the over-worked and often misunderstood concept of integration (as used in our context), document the origin of the term, explain some of the diverse thinking that is ascribed to integration, contrast the concept with the psychology of religion, and attempt to explain integration's task which, in turn, leads to a methods discussion. Finally, all this is placed into historical context as we briefly analyze the 50 years of CAPS' development.

The Concept of Integration

Historically, the concept of integration, as it applies to psychology and theology, is slippery and elusive at best. I intend to be more specific in explaining (perhaps addressing is a better word) the essence of integration, for this book is, after all, dedicated to a 50-year movement captured by that one word. Yet in doing so, I risk trivializing the vast complexity of the literature that has developed over the decades, risk under-estimating the significant differences among the disciplines, and risk over-estimating my ability to find some high ground from which to declare an inclusive perspective. I take some comfort in knowing that there are many prominent articles provided for follow up in this volume and in the *Suggestions for Further Reading* in each of the seven sections. Clearly, there are pitfalls and likely criticisms, since all facets and aspects of the term cannot possibly be treated here. Further, others have tried to clarify and explain before (e.g., Collins, 1983, Faw, 1998, Ellens, 1997, among many) but not in the same way that I have in mind. So, my aim is not to solve this confusing muddle for all time but to sharpen our thinking substantially, particularly for readers fairly new to this topic.

Evolution of the Term

Vande Kemp (1986) documented the first known use of the term in an article by Fritz Künkel in 1953. This German immigrant to the United States wrote an article entitled, "The Integration of Religion and Psychology," in the short-lived journal, the *Journal of Psychotherapy as a Religious Process*, published between 1953 and 1957. Künkel could not have imagined what he was setting in motion by his use of that term. Integration has been the preferred and most convenient label used over the past 50 years to cover a wide range of thought, although other terms such as relationship, psychotheology, synthesis, interaction, dialogue, interface, and mutual illumination (c.f. Collins, 1983; Ellens, 1997) have been put forth at various times as possibly more desirable terms. Integration is the term, however, that has persisted.

There is no evidence that Künkel's use of the term influenced the Dutch Reformed founders of the Christian Association for Psychological Studies (CAPS) shortly thereafter, but it is reasonable to suppose that there might have been some awareness of this journal since its circulation grew to about 700, with nearly 100 library subscriptions (Vande Kemp, 1986). Even if there were some awareness, there is no reason to think that Künkel and the CAPS founders shared a similar conception, undergirding theology, or psychological perspective. *The Journal of Psychotherapy as a Religious Process* was highly influenced by Otto Rank's therapy model, with devotees often writing about applying Christian insights to that modality.

CAPS was one of several organizational efforts launched in the late 1940s and 50s to open dialogue about faith, religion, and mental health. Today it is the lone survivor of those early efforts and is identified with conservative Protestant Christianity. It started as a project of truth-seeking Dutch Reformed pastors, theologians, and mental health professionals eager to bring their Christian worldview to bear upon the psychological maladies of their day. Later in this essay I will trace that history more closely.

Integration Today

Integration is a general term used by Christian scholars around the world. It is short-hand for the broader concept of "integration of faith and learning," and the phrase derives from a model of scholarship rooted in the Dutch Reformed tradition. In their volume, *Scholarship and Christian Faith: Enlarging the Conversation*, Jacobsen and Jacobsen (2004) critique these origins, and identify several other traditions that practice Christian scholarship, such as Anabaptist, Wesleyan, Lutheran, and Pentecostal, but without ascribing the label "integration" to them. They see these outside the integration tradition and argue for a larger conversation regarding Christian scholarship.

A broader, more pluralistic meaning of the term, however, appears to be attached to the concept when the particular arena of scholarship is psychology and Christian theology. Although the Dutch Reformed influence has remained as one of multiple traditions that CAPS members bring to conference discussions or to the pages of the CAPS journal, the integration model based on Arthur Holmes' (1975, 1977) and Nicholas Wolterstorff's (1984) body of work has a more focused and circumscribed meaning than the term generally in use today among the CAPS constituency.

With many meanings developed over time and place, the simple but unfulfilling explanation of integration is to say that it is complex, that there are many views which are sometimes competing, and that there is no unity among scholars who claim to be integrative. Knowing that there are many Christian theological traditions and psychological perspectives raises the question about whose theological and psychological perspectives are being integrated. That is where many people see the quagmire coming and just give up. Surely accepting these qualifiers can lead to no further clarity, they say. But even acknowledging the pitfalls and constraints, there can be a positive, meaningful, and working understanding of integration that is suitable for getting most people on the same page. That does not mean getting everyone doing the same thing or thinking exactly the same way, but we must clarify what Christian integrative thought means and what co-laborers are trying to accomplish. Dialogue in the context of having generally shared goals and with mutual understanding of assumptions (not always shared, however) are required of any scholarly endeavor, for scholarship is communal. There are no Lone Ranger scholars, because scholarly thought is inherently built upon others' ideas and are related back to the community for critique and expansion (Jacobsen & Jacobsen, 2004).

Integration Broadly and Narrowly Conceived. There are micro and macro meanings that have grown attached to the term integration. It may be used more loosely—that is, more broadly conceived—and it may apply inclusively to the many who dabble in relating some aspect of religious faith and overall human well-being. Practitioners of Christian Science or the Church of Scientology, conceivably, could qualify here. There are scholars, psychologists or otherwise, who consider themselves integrative but then others who flatly deny that these scholars meet their particular criteria for being integrative. The two groups have differing litmus tests. At issue is whether we can say that anyone interested in relating psychological understanding with some form of religion or spirituality is integrative. On a macro, inclusive level, we might be tempted to say, "Of course." We then would say, "Welcome to the integrative family, where we all have some interest in relating these areas of our lives," although we might secretly harbor prejudice against those who vary much from our more dearly-held perspective. However, this is not how the term integration is generally used as defined here and as historically situated within CAPS.

As we mentally slide along a continuum from broadly conceived to narrowly conceived at the other end, we can imagine zooming past other intermediate positions held by serious, rigorous, intellectual, and well-trained Christian psychologists. As the meaning behind the term becomes increasingly more specific and narrowly conceived, it has more qualifying assumptions, and thus is more exclusive to those who accept those assumptions. Basic epistemological assumptions, for example, might include a personal God who created the universe, a humankind that can know God personally, and a human capacity for reason to seek truth in a sinful, fallen world.

The model of scholarship I am calling integration, more narrowly conceived, has historically been tied to the particularities of an encompassing Christian worldview. That worldview affirms certain propositional truths on which to build the integration project. While discussing the difference between "Christian scholarship" and "Christian studies,"[1] the Jacobsens (2004) suggest that only persons of owned faith can achieve deep reflection and creativity, and therefore any work that requires such scholarship should best be considered an insider's task. Christian studies, however, amounts to a description, and can be achieved even by unbelieving outsiders. To allow just anyone to be viewed as an integrator severely pales the term's meaning.

One example of a more narrowly conceived formulation is John Carter's quite well known typology based on models of relationship between psychology and Christian theology (Carter, 1977). These were derived from Niebuhr's classic typology outlined in *Christ and Culture* (1951). Carter reworks and re-labels several of the original types into four models, with corresponding secular and sacred aspects to each. The secular psychology-*against*-religion position, and the corresponding sacred model, Scripture-*against*-psychology, are anti-integrationist by definition. The second model is the psychology-*of*-religion (not to be confused with the sub-discipline of the same name) and its flip side, the Scripture-*of*-psychology perspective. Third is the secular psychology-*parallels*-religion model, with its counterpart, Scripture-*parallels*-psychology. The *of* and the *parallels* models represent two idealized, but sub-integrative, positions that *only* demonstrate a "relationship," in this view. The last model, psychology-*integrates*-religion and the Scripture-*integrates*-psychology, is the only true integration model for Carter. It has specific assumptions associated with it and thus portrays a more micro, narrowly conceived, silo. Still, other scholars see justifiable biblical warrant for accepting the alternative models,[2] and so not all scholars accept the narrowness of the *integrates* definition suggested by Carter.

Carter's analysis hinges on a Reformed view and has been highly influential in the formative thinking of many who initially pursue their curiosity about integrative issues. This typology, at its best, begins to open up scholarly interest in the greater complexities of Christian integrative scholarship, or, at its worst, provides a false sense of arrival.

Integration versus Psychology of Religion. The contrast between these two sub-disciplinary fields are characterized here and pushed somewhat toward their extremes in an effort to clarify them, although in daily practice these distinctions are not always so rigid or apparent.

The psychology of religion is a much older sub-discipline than narrowly conceived integration. It has its own journals such as the *Journal for the Scientific Study of Religion* and the *International Journal for the Psychology of Religion.* Committed Christian intellectuals publish good work in these journals, but their work may not be integrative in nature, as I am framing it.

Since Leuba (1896), Starbuck (1901), and James (1902), mainstream psychology has viewed the scientific exploration of religious variables as a worthy pursuit, just like any other aspect of human experience. Studying religion as the independent variable may be practiced from any religious persuasion, including agnostic and atheistic world views. Viewing religious phenomena through the eyes of empirical scientific psychology teaches us much about these behaviors, and we might learn these new insights in a course at any secular western-culture college or university.

Psychology of religion experienced some professional disrepute in the 1930s and 40s, but was resurgent in the 1950s, largely due to Gordon Allport's (1950) *The Individual and His Religion.* Psychologists of religion look through the disciplinary eyes of psychology to view and attempt to understand religious phenomena. They use the scientific method to unveil aspects of human experience associated with religion and spirituality. In the intervening years, the psychology of religion has continued to flourish as part of mainstream psychology, in part through the influence of the American Psychological Association's Division 36, Psychologists of Religion.

The wider culture's increasing interest in our personal, spiritual, non-empirical side has fed the popularity of research and thought about our spirituality. It would be natural to assume this is just an expansion of integrative research. But psychology and theology integration, more narrowly conceived, is often viewed by psychologists of religion as only a discrete and small portion of their larger field, if they regard it at all. If a reference to integration appears in their scholarly work, it is probably a function of that scholar's Christian worldview (e.g., Malony, 1991; Paloutzian, 1996). It is much more likely, however, that integration is simply not a topic of discussion for many psychologists of religion, for it assumes a worldview that many guild members find antithetical to scientific inquiry. Still, integrators join the APA's Division 36, hold leadership positions, and actively support its purposes because their interests are generally compatible and parallel, although not always converging and mutually affirming.

This characterization of psychology of religion stands in contrast to integration. The first is informed by a method that venerates scientific inquiry and may be practiced by "outsiders," while the latter is a mindset, a way of thinking from a particular worldview that is practiced by "insiders." The two often cross paths in our evangelical journals (with differences sometimes indistinguishable, and frequently unacknowledged), and they cross-pollinate each other within the thinking of evangelical scholars. The two most acknowledged journals for dialogue on integration issues are the *Journal of Psychology and Christianity* (published since 1982 by CAPS) and the *Journal of Psychology and Theology* (published since 1973 by the Rosemead School of Psychology at Biola University). These journals deal in some way with secular psychology and religious/theological issues as they relate to theory, research, or practice from a more narrowly conceived view of integration. Integrators, often from an evangelical perspective, assay psychology through religious eyes of faith, which is the reverse of psychologists of religion.

The Task of Integration

Now that we have some greater demarcation of these two overlapping spheres of scholarly endeavor, we may push on to the heart of this essay. Various authors have gathered multiple statements in their quest to bring some order to understanding integration as more narrowly conceived. Faw (1998), for example, provides seven representative definitions to show that the term is understood somewhat differently depending on the questions one is trying to resolve, but few stray from the core notion. Although each author uses different words, a summary of their thought leads to the essential core finding: integration is the task of searching for the unity of truth, seeing things whole from a Christian perspective, and holistically attempting to relate elements of an objective real world given by God at creation. It is fundamentally a discovery, not a human creation; an illumination by multiple perspectives, not a cloudy amalgamation; an understanding of what is, not inventing what ought to be. Thus, integration is a mindset that inspires and directs activity and is not an achievable end-point in itself. Entwistle (2004) characterizes well this integrative mindset:

> Integration is *a priori*, a thing that we discover when we are uncovering the fundamental unity that God created, however much it might currently appear to be *dis*-integrated. On the other hand, *integration* is also something we do as we create ways of thinking about, combining, and applying psychological and theological truths. ... If Christ lays claim to all of one's life... then integration becomes not just feasible, but imperative" (italics in original) (p. 19).

Another way to think about integration is to recognize that users must distinguish the *noun* and *verb* qualities in everyday use. It is important to do so, or at least to be mindful of the difference. Integration is both something that *is* (the *a priori* seamless whole of the created universe), and it is something that we *do* (the here and now process of discovering God's truths through various kinds of research and writing). Both are legitimate and require the other. Any book, chapter, or article that purports to be integrative is understood by insiders to be an attempt to expand our knowledge of truth. Yet, enough epistemological humility is required to consider the possibility that the ideas may be wrong in light of the reality we want to unveil. Integrationists attempt to unveil what is, with full acceptance that the whole truth, limited by our humanness, will not be fully grasped. Recall that St. Paul reminded us of our finitude in his letter to the Corinthians.

The How of Integration

Perhaps more elusive than the *what* of integration (that is, the task) is the *how* (the method). Scholars have wrestled with the how, perhaps more frequently than the what, because it appears that is where we need to roll up our sleeves and get to work. "Just show me how to do it and I can get started! No more talk *about* it!" This is a common and understandable request from those emphasizing the verb qualities over the noun qualities. But the *how* must follow the *what*, just as any method must be informed by the purpose that drives it. As a classroom instructor, for example, I use methods and techniques that flow from my philosophy of education. It makes no sense to use methods that have discontinuity from my philosophical perspective.

The perspective that goals inform the behavior (or method, in this case), was among others championed by Alfred Adler (1927), an Austrian psychiatrist and one of the founding theorists and practitioners of personality theory and psychotherapy. He adopted the teleological position that current behavior is directed by future goals. What is it that directs behavior and motivates how we live? Adler believed it was the drive to fulfill our cognitively-cast future goals. [Others who developed teleological perspectives included McDougall's (1923) hormic psychology and Tolman's (1932) purposive behaviorism.] Thus, do not ask an Adlerian *how* to plan to do anything unless the goal is clear. An Adlerian would likely ask you what are you trying to do, and once that goal is clear, they believe you will find a way to do it.

This teleological perspective is a useful concept for integration, although it certainly is not the end of the issue. My brief point is to blunt the argument that we must find the particular *how*, and then all agree on it, before we can move forward with the task. In my judgment, that is not the way it works. In similar fashion, many psychotherapists are taught to have a goal in mind for the therapy process rather than learn the right and perfect words to say in a given situation or session. Therapy moves forward with creative and even elegant dialogue that serves the interest of the therapeutic goal.

Integrative scholars need to know what they are trying to accomplish, not just what they should say or do at any moment. Know what you want to accomplish and you will find a way to do it. And knowing that goal, one can figure out ways to help in the broad scholarly effort, and it will be done by scholars from many Christian sub-cultures and differing psychological specialties. Such an approach succeeds only in an atmosphere of tolerance and respect.

Key Markers of Integration

Integration begins with and is driven by a Christian worldview that affirms the limited, necessary, but sufficient core Christian beliefs. Monsma (1994) has suggested such beliefs as:

- a sovereign God who created and actively upholds the universe
- a moral order of things which humans can basically know
- human beings as image bearers of God
- an original goodness in humans at creation but who are now corrupted
- a savior in Jesus Christ, who empowers persons to live in harmony with the moral order

Holding these beliefs leads toward a "Christian mind" (Blamires, 1963; Gill, 1989; Noll, 1994) and an integrative mindset. One's theological understanding intentionally shapes the rationale on the front end of research for what issues or problems are chosen for study. Clinical psychology, for instance, attracts believers who seek ways to channel their Christian control beliefs (Wolterstorff, 1984) into sound psychological practice in the consulting and counseling rooms. They select topics for research that interest them, just as all researchers do, but their curiosity about a topic is typically generated by deeply held religious conviction, which may be deemed irrelevant by many other researchers.

Once a topic is chosen, integrative reflection on the problem will shape the nature of the data-collection and might even lead one to question the assumptions of the means and mechanisms of the classical scientific research process itself. Traditional instruments and techniques might be followed, or some new method that stretches the boundaries of "normal science" (Kuhn, 1971) could be indicated and thus justified by the complex nature of the problem. One key in decision-making for integrators is the degree of trust they place in the traditional textbook definition of good science. Integrationists are not in harmony here, for one's theological tradition and psychological training influences their decisions (Evans, 1976).

On the back end of a study, integrative thinking shapes the results at the point of interpreting the data, drawing conclusions, and making claims. It is no longer tenable to think that we are objective and unscathed by our personal commitments, because science *is* what scientists *do*. That is, science is not a monolithic entity that stands outside human influence, but is the product of erring, imperfect humans following general rules of procedure to the best of their ability. Some feel more warranted than others in breaching those rules, leading them to conclusions that are shaped by their own personal schemas or worldviews. Integrators generally value acknowledging at the outset the nature of their worldview and attempt to be consistent throughout the process of scientific inquiry, including their conclusions and claims.

Ultimately then, rigorous integrative thought embeds our metaphysical propositions, our methods, our empirical data, and our interpretative claims in the context of our Christian worldview to draw us closer to the truth as we believe God created it. Integration will be approached from multiple theological and psychological perspectives. Our theologies are enhanced and not diminished, made inferior, or watered down by psychology as some Christian anti-integration critics might fear. Our psychologies are also not diminished, but rather expanded by the added truth that theology brings to studying human nature and which secular anti-integration psychologists will miss. Since our mandate is to seek the truth, the integration enterprise is not just feasible but, as Entwistle concludes, imperative.

Brief Analytical History of CAPS

We turn now to the soil in which this integration movement took root and flourished. Without stable institutions to provide or support a steady flow of ideas and scholars, no intellectual movement can survive. Serious integrative thought has been a central mission of CAPS and the Christian graduate programs that have emerged since the 1960s. Certainly not all integrative work is conceived or written by graduate school-affiliated scholars or by CAPS members. But CAPS is the oldest organization and the flagship for psychologists and psychologically-minded professionals who think about serious scholarship. Among sister liberal arts disciplines, it was also one of the first to create a professional home for believers.[3]

It is not just a curiosity or aberration that the history of the organization runs parallel to the increasing amount of published work. New thinking may first get stimulated at CAPS conferences (which may be international, regional, or local meetings) or possibly through CAPS' *Journal of Psychology and Christianity (JPC)*. The doctoral programs such as those at Fuller, Biola, George Fox, Wheaton, Regent, Azusa Pacific, and Seattle Pacific, plus the many masters programs at Christian universities and seminaries across the country, have also been a source of creative thought and research.

The tradition this volume celebrates and which is embodied in the purposes and practices of CAPS, followed an evolution that bears closer scrutiny. All organizations form through the confluence of important figures, intellectual trends, and historical developments. Once formed, organizations evolve and mature over their lifetimes.

One way to think about the growth of CAPS is through a broad Eriksonian scheme (Erikson, 1950), which leads us to think in terms of general stages of development. As we shall see, the organization clearly owes its birth and infant sustenance to the Dutch Reformed tradition which helped develop a sense of trust in the possibility of working out a complete integration of psychological understanding with a Reformed worldview. The archives and personal testimony of major figures shed light on subsequent stages displaying a childhood break from parental rules, then a stormy adolescence but with consolidation of values, and to some extent, a mature identity achievement. Longtime inside observers have no illusions about CAPS being a fully wise, mature adult at 50. In keeping with Erikson's lifespan stages, CAPS has not yet accomplished a full-capacity, full-fledged generativity and productivity, and no acceptance of its own demise. The following sections convey a brief analytical account of the development so far, using dates that appear to be significant transition points.

Birth and Infancy: 1954-1964

The history of CAPS is not co-terminous with the history of integrative thought, whether broadly or narrowly defined, as Vande Kemp (1986), Serrano (2006), and many others effectively argue. The broader more macro notion of integration as described earlier may be applied to many in the decades prior to the 1950s. Christian Science (Mary Baker Eddy), the Emmanuel Movement (Gifford, 1998), the New Thought Movement (Phineas Parkhurst Quimby), Alcoholics Anonymous (Kurtz, 1979), and the pastoral care movement (Holifield, 1983), to name a few, were very different in their religious commitments and their proximity to modern psychological thought, but all these movements were drawing together religious understanding, emotional and physical health, and mature functioning. Where there were scholars with more conservative religious commitment teaching and writing about integration, they did so in relative isolation. The exceptions would be the church fathers and Protestant reformers who had much to say about spiritual and emotional well-being stemming from the *sola scriptura* debates (Beck, 1997).

By the 1950s, according to Neftali Serrano[4] (2006), some Christian groups and fringe groups had weighed in on the issue of integration with the exception of conservative or evangelical Christians. The early 20th century schism that more crisply separated the Christian church into liberal and fundamentalist wings pitted conservative theology versus modern psychology (Narramore, 1973). Disengagement by the conservatives from worldly secularist thinking, particularly in psychology, did not allow rapprochement until the 1950s, which was likely the biggest reason for the delay in integration being taken up by evangelicals.

As we have seen, it was not the evangelicals who formally established CAPS in 1956, but rather, a group of men associated with the culturally-rich Dutch Reformed enclaves in North America. The first conference was in 1954, and entitled, "The First American Calvinistic Conference on Psychology, Psychiatry, and Religion," (Serrano, 2001, p.146). Klaire Kuiper, a psychiatrist and medical director of the Bethesda Sanatorium, in Denver, Colorado, initiated the call. He sent a letter to 18 colleagues and interested parties to invite them to:

> a conference bringing together representatives of the various disciplines bearing on the study and application of psychology for the purpose of sharing our thinking on basic problems, evaluating the literature, and reinterpreting established facts consistently with the Reformed system of thought generally (from Kuiper's letter, quoted by Serrano, 2001, p. 54).

To understand who those colleagues were, and why this endeavor was limited to those in the Dutch Reformed tradition, one must understand the Dutch Reformed influence on the first and second generation Americans of Dutch descent. To explain fully that influence requires much more space than is available here, but the essence of that history is the pervasive nature of Dutch Reformed theology on all life as articulated originally by Abraham Kuyper (1837-1920).

Kuyper had been a pastor, theologian, journalist, philosopher, and prime minister of the Netherlands, and he embodied for the Dutch what it meant to be an integrated churchman, politician, and citizen. He became a key figure whose example was used widely, both in the Netherlands and in the American Dutch cultural enclaves, toward which immigrants gravitated, to support the fundamental notion that Christianity should influence "every sphere of life." That phrase became the mantra of many in that tradition because it evidenced in simple words the conviction that society and culture should be grounded in Christian thought. But not just any Christian thought would do; it needed to be a distinctly Calvinist system of thought, which would lead to a distinctively "Calvinistic dynamic psychology" (Serrano, 2001, p.37). The goal of the conference was to initiate an intellectual project to make a significant, transformative contribution in mental health, just as they had done in their schools, hospitals, and churches.

Virtually every recipient of Kuiper's January 8, 1954 letter expressed optimism and enthusiasm. The proposal was essentially to establish an "integration think-tank," although probably no one used that phrase at the time. Early conferences were dominated by philosophically and theologically-oriented papers, delivered by prominent theologians, educators, and pastors in addition to mental health professionals. The clear emphasis was to work out a view of psychology and personhood embedded in Calvinistic theology.

The Dutch Reformed tradition had a more fully developed Christian worldview than most Protestant denominations, a theology that mandated impact and transformation of all of life, and a history of engagement with society. There was every reason to believe that the integration project on which these men embarked would be successful in time. Fellowshipping with like-minded scholars and professionals and developing applications to ameliorate human emotional suffering emerged as an important by-product of the original philosophical and theological impetus for the gathering.

Kuiper's 1954 invitation letter proved to be a positive valence for those who recognized the need for bringing together serious Christian worldview thinking with an understanding of human nature and personhood. In the first three years, the new organization attracted 40-60 participants and began to experience the pains of expanding both in numbers and agenda. In the first decade, the membership numbers grew to 161 attendees at the 1965 convention (Serrano, 2001). While numbers were growing modestly, and as the prominent figures of the movement and CAPS itself matured, changes were inevitable.

Childhood: 1964-1974

We might characterize this second stage as a childhood break from the parental values. As the first decade came to a close, the fledgling CAPS organization was still heavily influenced by a Dutch Reformed epistemology, but also was fighting for survival as an organization. The third-generation Dutch community was more Americanized, and whether to expand beyond the Dutch community dominated the Board of Directors discussions. Minutes from meetings during the mid-sixties include hints of a newer, younger generation that was championing various causes, including pushing for a more progressive interpretation of the Scriptures, expanding membership to other Protestant groups, calling for more practical conference presentations that would appeal to practitioners, asking for some inclusion of empirical research (especially applied research), and desiring a move toward nationalization.

There were, of course, counter-calls for remaining true to orthodoxy and the original purposes of CAPS, and the Executive Secretary at the time, William Hiemstra, felt the pinch of balancing the need for growth and his allegiance to the old guard gentlemen with whom he had served since the beginning. In the end, the progressives prevailed. Regional groups were started in several areas during Hiemstra's watch, eventually completing nationalization. Invited speakers such as O. Hobart Mowrer, David Busby, and Vernon Grounds were also beginning to be drawn from outside the Dutch culture (Serrano, 2001).

A new ground-swell of openness in the late 1960s and early 1970s led to CAPS bifurcating into a smaller, more progressive-thinking group of Dutch-heritage professionals, and a larger, more conservative group, also of that heritage. A wedge was growing and a new plurality of ideas marked that period. J. Harold (Hal) Ellens, Ron Rottschafer, Don Postema, and William Kooistra were leaders of this progressive group, and although the Board generally continued to be dominated by Reformed conservatives, Ellens eventually gained enough support to be named the Executive Secretary in 1974 (Serrano 2001).

Additionally, the grass-roots call for a more clinical focus stemmed from CAPS becoming more of a professional organization devoted to its clinical members, leaving many non-clinical members behind. The Dutch Reformed members, especially those who were more theologically conservative, became more closely tied with American evangelicalism through their shared Christian values, but the groups differed in that evangelicals had no specific communal theological and cultural mindset. Evangelicalism had been, and continues to be today, more loosely organized than the Dutch tradition. It is not tied to ethnic, language, or national boundaries, and it had no unifying Christian worldview from which everything emanates. This "evangelicalization" has had a very significant role in the direction that CAPS took after decade two.

American evangelicalism traced its history along a radically different path than the Dutch Reformed tradition. Mark Noll (1994) identifies evangelicals as not being characterized for their thinking but rather for their piety. He argues that for evangelicals the life of the mind and the life of faith were out of balance. Carter and Narramore (1979) and more substantially Marsden (1980), have illuminated this disjuncture as being rooted in the evangelicals response to the de-Christianization of American culture during the modern period. The liberal wing of the church in the late 19th century found secular modernism to be a path to solving the ills that plagued the human condition. That led to a social gospel church that desired to meet people at their point of need without imposing the claims of Christ. The fundamentalist reaction was to create a distance from the modern secularist ideals that threatened to dilute the faith to a watery porridge. Fundamentalists, and the evangelicals who evolved from that most conservative position, retreated from the culture, including the academy, with corresponding loss of confidence that the world might be transformed by secular knowledge. Serrano (2001) explains:

> This cultural conflict caused a cultural retreat on the part of fundamentalists that continued to pervade American evangelical thinking about culture, life, and religion.... American evangelical religion, in its efforts to emerge from fundamentalism attempted to adopt a more open stance to culture, and yet hung on to the fundamentals of the faith as its restraint from falling too far into culture.... Therefore there has always been an inherent tension within evangelicalism in America about how far one should stray into these gray areas of Christian application (p. 124).

Against this historical backdrop we find in CAPS a convergence of these two traditions: the conservative Dutch Reformed, with their optimism rooted in the Calvinistic worldview that the world can be won over, and the evangelicals, whose fundamentalist heritage often reduced Christianity to its bare essentials, which lacked a full-orbed theological worldview, but which placed an emphasis on helping the individual to achieve a moral way to live and to gain salvation. That convergence, argues Serrano (2006), is what re-directed the CAPS integration project as envisioned by the founders, so that by the middle 1970s, CAPS was transitioning to a greater evangelical base, with profound effects on its future. The natures of psycho-theological integration and of CAPS as an organization, were changing.

Adolescence: 1975-1987

A stormy adolescence, on the way toward coming of age, characterized the beginning of the third decade for CAPS, now under the leadership of Hal Ellens of Michigan. In the mid 1970s CAPS was still marked by its Dutch Reformed roots, but an increasing evangelicalization was in process.

Craig Ellison, of California, was a member of the CAPS National Advisory Committee in 1973 and was asked to aid the progress of growth in the west by creating a conference for Christian counselors and other clinicians. The West Coast Conference of Christian Psychologists/Counselors was held that year, attracting over 200 participants. This group decided to organize into the Western Association of Christians for Psychological Studies (WACPS), and by doing so rejected affiliation with CAPS. The WACPS was more conservative, evangelical, and clinically-minded, while CAPS, though experiencing growing pains of greater inclusiveness, was still largely Dutch Reformed. The chief reasons for remaining separate in the early years of attempted merger boiled down to some mistrust on both sides about the other organization's statement of faith and guiding mission. Theological traditions rose up to shape the language and, in particular, there were some tensions over the nature of the statement of faith contained in Article II of the CAPS constitution. In 1973, CAPS rejected WACPS' initial proposal, believing the changes would alter the interdisciplinary nature of CAPS and move it toward the more clinical focus of WACPS.

Article II of the CAPS constitution was the statement of faith to which all members give assent when joining. From CAPS' founding, the Dutch Reformed wording stated: "The Association shall be based on the Bible as interpreted in the historic Reformed Creeds." Hal Ellens, who gave CAPS unfailing and energetic leadership through these years of merger, consolidation, and expansion, did not identify as an evangelical and was initially opposed to altering the creedal statement of Article II. However, being a willing progressive who pushed for any changes that would make CAPS a stronger and better organization, he pushed for compromise. By 1974 the new Article II language read as follows: "The basis for this organization is the belief in the Lordship of Jesus Christ and that through God's Word, the Bible, and through communion of Christians, the Holy Spirit guides us as members of the helping professions in achieving personal growth of self and others" (Serrano, 2001, p. 110). Clearly the shift in emphasis demonstrates CAPS' greater openness and ecumenism. It was a key shift in identity and focus, one that has forever changed CAPS.

Ellison, who served on both boards, desired to see both organizations merge and he worked tirelessly to that end. He was the visionary who, through sheer energy and commitment, shepherded the negotiation process over several years until final consummation of the merger in 1979. Subsequently, the CAPS membership increased by over 400, and began a membership profile that remains today with the CAPS West Region being the largest in the organization. As CAPS nationalized, other regions were created. By the early 1980s, there were regions in the East, Southeast, Southwest, Rocky Mountains/Plains, Midwest, as well as West. However, in 2003, the Rocky Mountain/Plains Region was dissolved and absorbed by neighboring regions.

The period following the merger brought unprecedented professionalism and growth. This included expanding the CAPS Bulletin into a peer-reviewed journal in 1982 (*Journal of Psychology and Christianity*), edited by Hal Ellens; establishing an endowment to help underwrite the journal; creating regional and local gatherings during the year between national conferences; securing approval to be a continuing education provider for the American Psychological Association (1984), and later a CEU provider for the National Board of Certified Counselors (1991); and establishing a code of ethics for clinical practice.

The early 1980s marked a growth in CAPS other than just in membership. During these years, CAPS revisited some of the issues that the founders held important. There was a renewed valuing of the pastoral care professional through the creation of a representative seat on the International Board and the dedication of a special issue of the journal in 1984 to Pastoral Issues.

There were also controversial issues that needed to be worked through. One issue was identifying the range of acceptable theological and psychological perspectives that could be represented within conference presentations and forums. With its acceptance of greater diversity regarding issues like homosexuality, and the lively debate that resulted, CAPS accepted that there was no single Christian position nor agreement on such issues, despite the more conservative evangelical influence. CAPS remains a Christian community for those in the helping and academic professions, does not take polemical stands on divisive issues, and allows issues a fair and balanced Board or conference hearing. The mid 1980s was a period which demonstrated commitment to this credo.

Young Adulthood: 1987-1994

By 1987, Hal Ellens was prepared to retire. He had his hand on the tiller through the most tumultuous years, and left the helm of the organization as it enjoyed unprecedented enthusiasm, strength, and vigor. In spite of often holding minority views during theological and scriptural discussions with his more conservative friends, Ellens valued the open and fair exchange of ideas. As of this writing he remains an active and prolific writer and editor of broad theological, biblical, and philosophy of science works. He is an active CAPS member, conference presenter, and generous benefactor of the organization he helped shape over these 50 years. Hal Ellens was present at the very first meeting at Calvin College in 1954 and has partly watched and largely shaped the metamorphosis that results in the CAPS of today.

Though some welcomed Ellens' decision to step down as Executive Secretary (in the early 1990s the title changed to Executive Director), his retirement was cause for others to fear. A less flexible and tolerant Executive Secretary might have allowed CAPS to slip back from the broader interdenominational, international, and evangelical values it now held. Some worried that the next Executive Secretary might not be so tolerant, especially if the new one came from the Dutch Reformed stock from which all previous leaders had come. Concerned that the perceived gains might be lost, Robert King, Jr., retired Navy aviator and now Christian psychologist, willingly accepted the Board's invitation to fill the position. This was the same Californian Bob King who had written a letter to Craig Ellison in 1977 to register his opinion that CAPS and WACPS should not merge for all the theological reasons mentioned earlier (Serrano, 2001). Time had covered those cracks of dissension, and by 1987, CAPS was moving ahead with the direction it had set nearly a decade before.

Under Bob King, and with the faithful help of his wife Mary, CAPS continued to serve its constituency which first crested the 2000 member mark in 1990. By this time, about 75% of the membership was clinically trained (Allison, 2006). The terms Christian counseling and Christian counselors were ever more in use to indicate the inclusiveness CAPS hoped to cultivate. In the early 1990s, King led Board discussions regarding how to navigate the challenges CAPS faced as another proprietary organization provided a Christian alternative for clinically-minded CAPS members. The leadership decided to stay the course as a not-for-profit association that serves its constituency through quality conferences, professional/academic publications, some membership perks, and collegial community. As much as anything, that challenge to CAPS' viability led to the strongest sense of identity achievement to that point.

Other events at that time also contributed to a stronger organizational identity. By 1988, Hal Ellens had also stepped down as Editor in Chief of the CAPS *Journal* and Peter Hill was selected to guide it forward. As of this writing, Hill remains in that capacity and has overseen an increasingly expanded, high quality publication that is one of the foremost integration journals. By 1996, over 250 libraries worldwide subscribed to the *Journal of Psychology and Christianity* (Allison, 2006).

Another key to CAPS' increasingly professional identity by this period was the creation of the Masters Christian Counseling videotapes series by recognized senior professionals Siang-Yang Tan, Bruce Narramore, and Ev Worthington. By 1994, stability in CAPS identity had been achieved and Bob King, now beyond retirement age, decided to step down. Randolph K. Sanders, a Christian psychologist in practice in the San Antonio, Texas area, was invited by the Board to be the new Executive Director. Bob King continued as Managing Editor of the *JPC* until his resignation in 1997, after he contracted cancer and shortly before his death.

Identity Achievement: 1994-2006

As Randy Sanders became Executive Director, his wife Bette also became an integral part of the professional staff, and together they served for the next 11 years. Sanders' modest, self-effacing, optimistic, consensus-building style was just what CAPS needed to meet the challenges. The significant problem in that day was growing the membership, which had slipped due to multiple factors. In addition to the new alternative organization for less professionally-trained Christian clinicians, many academicians had felt somewhat ignored or side-stepped, due to the heavy clinical and pastoral emphasis of the CAPS conference programs. New initiatives to address these issues included: the 2000 Andrew Connection, whereby those who brought new members into the fold—see John 1:40-42—received a financial incentive; hiring the Meeting Management Group of Tampa, Florida to manage CAPS conventions; a new logo and expanded journal pages; working out cooperative membership and conference display arrangements with the North American Christian Association of Social Workers; lowering student fees and giving representation on the Board; and increasing the emphasis on academic issues at conferences starting in 2001. This latter initiative meant that several specially-invited "distinguished scholars" were included in the program track to attract academics who might otherwise seek other conference venues for their scholarly outlets and collegial relationships.

Through the 1990s, the *JPC* continued to be a major effort by CAPS to expand the integrative literature. Hill's leadership sought to bring a balance among clinical, research, and theological papers. He also affirmed an earlier move by his predecessor Ellens to devote two issues per year to probe more deeply topics of special interest to an increasingly broad constituency, a format still in effect today. Guided by guest editors, topics have included Religious Values in Psychotherapy (1991), Forgiveness (1992), Multicultural Counseling (1992), Children's Issues (1993), Behavioral Medicine from a Christian Perspective (1995), Homosexuality (1996), Psychology Within the Christian Tradition (1998), Psychology and the Holy Spirit (1999), and Psychology and Wesleyan Theology (2004). Perhaps the most widely referenced special issue is the now classic Integration Revisited (1996), which shared reflections on the state of integration by major scholars like John Carter, Stephen Evans, Stan Jones, Hendrika Vande Kemp, and Mary Stewart VanLeeuwen.

The special issue format allowed more depth of coverage for topics of interest to clinicians and, to a lesser extent, academicians. The wide range of topics comports with the broad evangelical expansion in interest and conception of what counts as integration. Critics might lament the loss of its original moorings to the Dutch Reformed tradition, with resulting loss of coherence and a more scattered approach to scholarship and practice. Enthusiasts might laud the Christian exploration into topics that confront practitioners daily but without losing hope that a larger *Gestalt* will some day be more perceived and understood.

During the most recent two decades, there has been a postmodern influence on the integration project initiated in the mid 1950s. Gone for the most part is the hope of achieving a neatly wrapped, monolithic structure of the world shaped through Christian Reformed theology. Like personality theory more broadly, there are fewer scholarly attempts now at a grand Christian scheme and more efforts at understanding integration through more limited domains. Integration's pastiche carries the promise of probing new fronts, exposing new areas for empirical exploration, and breaking new therapeutic ground—all of which would have probably baffled many of the CAPS founders. With no clear anchor in the Reformed tenets of faith and its Christian worldview, the founders would likely say that no real progress can be made. The progressive voices, on the other hand, tout the interdenominational, international, and evangelical fervor that allows scholars of many perspectives to address the issues they care about deeply. Is a meta-integration of all these directions near? It is not even on the horizon and for some, would not be desirable.

Further Growth: 2006 –

CAPS continues to evolve its identity, a fact that shows in the selection of a new Executive Director who is not a psychologist. Following Randy Sanders' retirement from the role in 2005 after stellar and humble service, Paul Regan became the first non-psychologist to hold the Executive Director position. With a doctorate in organizational development and management, his talents were soon applied to the tired structure of the organization that had been slower in change management than was good for it. A new management team was assembled to revitalize the organization's marketing and communication. Steve Allison was hired from within the organization as a part-time conference coordinator and manager. The Web site was revamped, the new e-publication (CAPS *Connect!*) was created to replace the hardcopy *CAPS Report*, and the continuing education responsibilities were outsourced. At the 50th anniversary conference, the Board introduced a reorganization plan for regions and regional directors which will provide more accountability, continuity, parity of compensation methods, and standardized procedures across the organization (Allison, 2006).

CAPS' full history is not yet complete. In its 50th year, it is like a maturing adult, with more hope of things to accomplish. While mental health practice, pastoral and spiritual care, and modern scientific methods continue to change, there will be no less of a need for quality research and thought based on Christian values and worldviews. The masthead on the Web site explains: CAPS has "a rich heritage, a bright future." We have seen the former and expect the latter.

Notes

1. Douglas and Rhonda Jacobsen provide a helpful analysis of the distinction. Christian studies may be completed from the outside—it is essentially descriptive—and can be done by anyone. But that is not true of *Christian scholarship*, they say: "The purpose of Christian scholarship is not description but reflection—to reflect on the world from the perspective of faith and to reflect on one's own faith from the perspective of scholarship. This is an insider's task. The questions are existential, and the answers need in some sense to be vetted by one's religious colleagues as well as by one's scholarly peers. Thus it is the faith orientation of the scholar that makes the work Christian." (Jacobsen & Jacobsen, 2004, p. 152).

2. Interestingly, in the five "idealized" models described in *Christ and Culture*, and from which Carter borrowed heavily for his models, Niebuhr assumed that all the various positions had some degree of biblical warrant. He gave examples of groups that held that view, but he also acknowledged which model fit best with his own theology. Carter was even more clear about which of his models was true-blue integration, and he more strongly implied that the others were deficient, sub-integrative efforts to relate psychology and Christian theology. Carter's "integrates" model fits well with my use of the phrase "integration narrowly conceived" but it is not necessarily the definitive model of integration more narrowly conceived.

3. Other groups of scholars have developed their own professional organizations during this time, so this was not a unique period for psychologists. A few sample organizations and their establishment dates, according to their Web sites, are: American Scientific Affiliation (1941), North American Association of Christian Social Workers (1954), The Conference on Faith and History (1968), Association of Christians Teaching Sociology (1976), Society of Christian Philosophers (1978), Christian Business Faculty Association (1980), Affiliation of Christian Biologists (1990), Christians in Political Science (1991), and the Society for the Study of Psychology & Wesleyan Theology (1999).

4. I am deeply indebted to Neftali Serrano for his analysis of the establishment and early years of CAPS. Serrano's doctoral dissertation at Wheaton College entitled, *A History of the Christian Association for Psychological Studies, 1956-1978* is substantially and understandably more detailed than his journal article, *Conservative Christians in Psychology: A History of the Christian Association for Psychological Studies (CAPS), 1954-1978*, published in the winter 2006 issue of the CAPS' *Journal of Psychology and Christianity (JPC)*. Both are worth reading for a more thorough sense of the people, trends, and historical developments during the 20th century in North America that led to CAPS' creation. Serrano acknowledges his personal placement in this flow of history and how this impacts his interpretation of facts and events. His account and general theses were sanctioned by at least one who was present in that period and in those early meetings. Hal Ellens, whose personal experience, involvement, and dedication to CAPS are exceeded by no one, remarked after a Serrano conference presentation: "Neftali Serrano has it right" (personal conversation, April 11, 2006). Another author, Steve Allison, has carried the analysis forward to the modern period in his historical review, *The Christian Association for Psychological Studies: A History (1979-2006)*, also published in the winter 2006 *JPC* special issue. Allison, Brian Eck, Peter Hill, and I all served overlapping terms on the CAPS International Board of Directors during the 1980s and into the current century. I have drawn liberally from all their insights and knowledge of CAPS over the life of the organization, and I especially urge interested readers to consult the Serrano and Allison accounts directly.

References

Adler, A. (1927). *The practice and theory of individual psychology*. New York: Harcourt, Brace, & World.

Allison, S. H. (2006). The Christian Association for Psychological Studies: A history (1979-2006). *Journal of Psychology and Christianity, 25*, 305-310.

Allport, G. W. (1950). *The individual and his religion: A psychological interpretation*. New York: Macmillan.

Beck, J. R. (1997). *Sola scriptura*: Then and now. *Journal of Psychology and Christianity, 16*, 293-302.

Blamires, H. (1963). *The Christian mind*. London: William Clowes & Sons.

Carter, J. D. (1977). Secular and sacred models of psychology and religion. *Journal of Psychology and Theology, 5*, 197-208.

Carter, J. D., & Narramore, S. B. (Eds.). (1979). *The integration of psychology and theology: An introduction.* Grand Rapids, MI: Zondervan.

Collins, G. R. (1983). Moving through the jungle: A decade of integration. *Journal of Psychology and Theology, 11*, 2-7.

Ellens, J. H. (1997). The interface of psychology and theology. *Journal of Psychology and Christianity, 16*, 5-17.

Entwistle, D. N. (2004) *Integrative approaches to psychology and Christianity: An introduction to worldview issues, philosophical foundations, and models of integration.* Eugene, OR: Wipf & Stock.

Erikson. E. H. (1950). *Childhood and society.* New York: Norton.

Faw, H. W. (1998). Wilderness wanderings and promised integration: The quest for clarity. *Journal of Psychology and Christianity, 26*, 147-158.

Gifford, S. (1998). *The Emmanuel Movement: The origins of group treatment and the assault on lay psychotherapy.* Boston: Howard.

Gill, D. W. (1989). *The opening of the Christian mind: Taking every thought captive to Christ.* Downers Gove: InterVarsity.

Holifield, E. B., (1983). *A history of pastoral care in America.* Nashville: Abingdon.

Holmes, A. (1975). *The idea of a Christian college.* Grand Rapids: Eerdmans.

Holmes, A. (1977). *All truth is God's truth.* Grand Rapids: Eerdmans.

Jacobsen, D., & Jacobsen, R. H. (2004). *Scholarship & Christian faith: Enlarging the conversation.* New York: Oxford University Press.

James, W. (1902). *The varieties of religious experience: A study in human nature.* New York: Random House.

Jones, S. L. (1986). *Psychology and the Christian faith: An introductory reader.* Grand Rapids, MI: Baker.

Kuhn, T. S. (1971). *The structure of scientific revolutions.* (2nd. ed.). Chicago: University of Chicago Press.

Kurtz, E. (1979). *Not-God: A history of Alcoholics Anonymous.* Center City, MN: Hazelden Educational Services.

Leuba, J. H. (1896). A study in the psychology of religious phenomena. *American Journal of Psychology, 5*, 309-385.

MacDougall, W. (1923). *An outline of psychology.* New York: Schribner.

Malony, H. N. (Ed.). (1983). *Wholeness and holiness: Readings in the psychology/theology of mental health.* Grand Rapids, MI: Baker.

Malony, H. N. (Ed.). (1991). *Psychology of religion: Personalities, problems, possibilities.* Grand Rapids, MI: Baker.

Marsden, G. M. (1980). *Fundamentalism and American culture: The shaping of twentieth-century evangelicalism, 1870-1925.* Oxford: Oxford University Press.

Monsma, S. V. (1994). Christian worldview in academia. *Faculty Dialogue, 21*, 139-147.

Narramore, S. B. (1973). Perspectives on the integration of psychology and theology. *Journal of Psychology and Theology, 1,1*, 3-18.

Niebuhr, H. R. (1951). *Christ and culture.* New York, NY: Harper and Row.

Noll, M. (1994). *The scandal of the evangelical mind.* Grand Rapids: Eerdmans.

Paloutzian, R. F. (1996). *Invitation to the psychology of religion* (2nd ed.). Boston: Allyn & Bacon.

Serrano, N. (2001). *A history of the Christian Association for Psychological Studies: 1954-1978.* Unpublished doctoral dissertation, Wheaton College, Wheaton, IL.

Serrano, N. (2006). Conservative Christians in psychology: A history of the Christian Association for Psychological Studies (CAPS), 1954-1978. *Journal of Psychology and Christianity, 25*, 293-304.

Starbuck, E. D. (1901). *The psychology of religion: An empirical study of the growth of religious consciousness.* New York: Scribner.

Tolman, E. C. (1932). *Purposive behaviorism in animals and men.* New York: Century.

Vande Kemp, H. (1984). *Psychology and theology in Western thought, 1672-1965.* White Plains, NY: Kraus.

Vande Kemp, H. (1986). An early attempt at integration: *The Journal of Psychotherapy as a Religious Process. Journal of Psychology and Theology, 14*, 3-14.

Weatherhead, L. D. (1951). *Psychology, religion, and healing.* Nashville: Abingdon.

Wolterstorff, N. (1984). *Reason within the bounds of religion.* (2nd ed.) Grand Rapids, MI: Eerdmans.

Section I
Historical and Theoretical Integration

Integration is nothing new, for it pre-dates the human record. In another sense, integration is an emerging field of study in the 20th century. We account for this apparent discrepancy by suggesting the dual nature of the term integration developed in the Introduction. Our Christian *a priori* understanding leads to the assumption that all creation is a seamless whole, and thus integration just is. There is nothing that stands outside of this creation except God, all is touched by God, and all is ontologically sacred. It is also true that scholars proactively seek to make sense of the world as we know it and some even ground their activities on their perceived mandate of Genesis 1: 28 (i.e., a reference to being in charge of and subduing the earth, implying the duty to understand and master it). In this sense then, integration must be fought for, honed from competing ideas, inferred out of data, and forged through experience.

In the limited space devoted here to broad issues of historical context and theoretical foundations, we present eight articles that ground the integration movement for the sections to come. Some take stock of the historical impediments and debates about integration, others emphasize integration's grander *a priori* theological nature, and still others clearly provide a window on active Christian scholarship that moves us forward. These works vary widely in purpose, seek to make different arguments or observations (sometimes competing), are based on somewhat divergent theological traditions of the authors, and require different psychological and theological levels of sophistication by readers.

This section's first article is the dedicatory editorial written by S. Bruce Narramore (1973) for the inaugural issue of the *Journal of Psychology and Theology (JPT)*. Pre-dating CAPS' *Journal of Psychology and Christianity (JPC)* by nine years, the *JPT* was launched with the vision of being a unique publication that will publish theoretical and theological papers from a variety of positions, contain applied papers with relevance to the pastor and practitioner, and build a body of research data relating to readers' interests. The article, *Perspectives on the Integration of Psychology and Theology*, leads this grouping of articles because Narramore effectively and succinctly pointed out the key problems in bringing the disparate parties together to work out ways of shaping an integrated literature that is faithful to the uniqueness of the two disciplines.

Narramore reflects on the relevant history that led to that historic 1973 publication launch and traces the conflicts between the century-old discipline of psychology and the historical development of the Christian church in North America. He describes four deficiencies that have hindered previous efforts at creating a Christian psychology and then surveys barriers to integration efforts. Narramore details some key reasons why modern psychology and the liberal church found more common ground and why modern psychology and the conservative Christian church have been slow in warming to each other. Neither liberal nor conservative Christians were drawing from the Scriptural resources to address the personal human needs of men and women of faith or applying them to a serious study of psychology. That, says Narramore, was now going to change, and the *JPT* was going to be a central place where many of these issues will be worked out among the community of believing mental health practitioners and academic scholars.

Ten years later, Gary Collins (1983) was invited by the editors to take stock of the first 40 issues of *JPT*. His report, *Moving Through the Jungle: A Decade of Integration*, attempts to organize the body of material these issues contain. His efforts produced no discernible scheme, he reports, due to the wide diversity of topics. Listing just 17 widely varying topics helps to make his point: "we may be settling for a shotgun approach, moving in various directions at the same time, but with few clear goals ...."

The remainder of his article conveys a renewed plea for focus on seven areas that Collins uses to challenge the readership in their future efforts. First, he calls for clarifying the goals, by which he means pondering more deeply about what we mean by integration and thinking hard about what integration efforts should accomplish. Second, Collins challenges *JPT* readers and particularly contributors, to resist a drift from evangelicalism, retain fidelity to that view, and improve the theological sophistication in articles by encouraging theologically-trained authors to publish. Third, Collins asks his readers to sharpen their assumptions of both the theological and psychological underpinnings and to alter the methods, claims, and applications that derive from them. Fourth, he argues for greater emphasis on the practical applications that would serve well the professional readership. Fifth, Collins asks for articles that promote competent and balanced analyses of world events, American phenomena such as the Moral Majority, and a host of other contemporary topics. His sixth plea is the need to drill down deeper into topics of general readership interest, and one way to do that is to publish more special topic issues presenting differing perspectives. Finally, the seventh key point Collins shares is a reminder that we must be honest and fair in declaring our biases, we must "think Christianly," and we must realize our integration starts with a profoundly personal Christian worldview.

James Guy, Jr. (1980) addresses the central problem of epistemology in *The Search for Truth in the Task of Integration*. Unlike many far-ranging articles that sweep across a diverse landscape of issues, Guy is principally concerned with just one: the nature of knowing truth. Can humankind fully know and understand truth? His tact is to argue that humankind cannot exhaustively know all truth, which brings him into apparent contention with statements made previously by Collins in an earlier book. In raising this challenge, to which Collins later replied, the two scholars are doing what good scholarship calls for. It demonstrates exactly Guy's main thesis about the nature of knowing truth. It cannot be apprehended in its fullness, but the crucible of interchange and controversy are "catalysts for growth, bringing excitement and joy rather than fear and defensiveness." Thus we "need not be troubled by a variety of integrative models ... nor by the diversity of therapeutic ... techniques and goals ...." Christian psychologists may adopt any model or orientation as they seek to work out a personal integration within the scope of their life's calling.

Eric Johnson's (1997) article, *Christ, the Lord of Psychology*, post-dates Guy's article by 17 years, and may illustrate the increasing levels of sophistication Christian psychologists had gained in thinking about integration's nature, meaning, purpose, and process. The article requires some degree of philosophical and theological sophistication to grasp the depth of the argument. While Johnson begins with an assumption very compatible with Guy's, he develops a dense treatment of the biblical concept of the kingdom of God. All of psychology and everything else should be brought under the lordship of Christ. Integration is more than a theoretical, abstract notion. Since Christianity is theocentric, all kingdom psychology necessarily involves recognizing God's centrality. Integration, then, is viewed fundamentally as praxis—living out our mandate as kingdom members. He proceeds to expand on six aspects within which kingdom psychology plays out. For those asking *how* to do integration, here is an answer.

It is significant that the word integration is not in the title of J. Harold Ellens' (1997) article, *The Interface of Psychology and Theology*, for he argues that integration is not the best term to describe this relationship. From his unique perspective as one of CAPS' founders, Ellens maintains that the term integration is problematic because it implies that two realms, the natural and the supernatural, are in need of uniting. Further, he believes the evangelical influence encouraged an asymmetrical relationship between psychology and theology, giving preference to theology. He asserts that such a view was never the goal of the founders. From his strong commitment to the Reformed tradition, he posits a theological view that affirms the ultimate unity of God's truth, the equal standing of both psychological science and theological science in the discussion, and the ontological view that there is no sacred/secular split.

Arguing vigorously that "interface for mutual illumination" is better semantically since both sciences contribute to greater understanding of the other, Ellens lays out three operational principles before explicating his model with four levels of interface between psychology and theology: theory development, research methodology, database development, and operational application.

Hendrika Vande Kemp's (1982) scholarly work, *The Tension Between Psychology and Theology: An Anthropological Solution*, explores the apparent violation of sacred boundaries and the tensions over territoriality. In a previous companion article not presented here (Vande Kemp, 1982), she traces the roots of the term *psyche*, its evolution into the term *psychology*, and the consequent abandonment of the *soul* by modern psychology, leaving it to the theologians to clarify. In the present article, she continues her argument through considering the historical debate over the nature of the person, and in particular, the nature of what is humanly psychological and humanly spiritual. Of concern are several perpetual questions of integration: What is the relationship between mental health and salvation? Are there spiritual illnesses as well as mental illnesses? How does illness spring from unconscious? Clearly, she says, mental and spiritual health diverge in psychopathology.

Drawing from a range of writers, across time and training, she concludes that the integrator's task is not to create a Christian psychology based on biblical anthropology, nor to construct a psychologically-sophisticated theology. To do so does violence to the psychological and the spiritual, which serve as catalyst for the other. There is to be no amalgamation resulting in the loss of either's identity, and no imperializing battles over which is more significant. To use her analogy, the two disciplines "must walk hand in hand, as parents of a child destined to become spiritually sanctified and psychologically whole." Much as Ellens had argued, Vande Kemp asserts that wisdom calls each to "a relationship of mutual cooperation and respect."

Another aspect of the tension in the Christian community relative to psychology and theology is analyzed by James Beck (1997). His article, *Sola Scriptura: Then and Now*, details clearly the historical debate on the proper use of knowledge from non-biblical sources. Should Scripture be the absolutely exclusive source of teaching, rejecting the many potential sources of distortion and contamination, or may believers legitimately use non-biblical sources, but with primacy given to Scripture?

Using two historical cases studies, one from early church fathers of the second and third centuries and one from the Reformation period, Beck illustrates that the modern anti-integration and pro-integration discussion renews an old theme. Both camps affirm the Reformation principle of *sola scriptura* (scripture only), but Beck explains that they disagree on what it means. In the end, Beck points out that holding Scripture in exclusivity may be easier to assert than actually do, and that there are powerful reasons to use new knowledge under the authority of the Bible.

The final article in this section could be considered a case study of Beck's second *sola scriptura* interpretation that allows new knowledge to be used under biblical authority. *John Wesley and Psychology*, by Newt Malony (1999), provides a study of an important figure in Christian history. Wesley's life and thought have implications for modern Christians in the psychological disciplines. Malony shows the multiple dimensions of Wesley's example as he used secular scientific knowledge for helping persons find health and happiness, modeled both struggle with religious doubt and triumph in God's grace through cognitive self-mastery, and demonstrated compassionate concern for the physical and emotional suffering of the very needy and poor. He believes Wesley can be considered a psychological theologian whose life and teachings encourage ministry to self and others in very practical ways.

Readers cannot expect to cover the full gamut of history and theory in these eight articles, but they should gain a richer foundation for understanding the integration movement's location in the milieu of scholarly ideas.

Suggestions for Further Reading: Historical and Theoretical Integration

Collins, G. R. (1977). *The rebuilding of psychology: An integration of psychology and Christianity*. Wheaton, IL: Tyndale.

> As one of the original books on integration from an evangelical perspective, Collins reviews and evaluates the nature and assumptions of modern psychology and proposes moving psychology to a new foundation that is based on the assumptions that come from a Christian worldview perspective.

Evans, C. S. (1989). *Wisdom and humanness in psychology: Prospects for a Christian approach*. Grand Rapids, MI: Baker.

> Suggesting that the empirical model of science as an objective and value-neutral enterprise is inappropriate for psychology, the author aims to demonstrate the possibility and viability of a distinctive Christian psychology.

Farnsworth, K. E. (1995). *Whole-hearted integration: Harmonizing psychology and Christianity through word and deed*. Grand Rapids, MI: Baker.

> Emphasizes that integration must not be primarily cognitive (critical integration) but should be worked out in daily living, which he calls embodied integration.

Jacobsen, D. & Jacobsen, R. H. (2004). *Scholarship & Christian faith: Enlarging the conversation*. New York: Oxford University Press.

> Critiques the integration model of scholarship as being primarily Reformed in commitment and argues for expanding the notion of Christian scholarship to include other theological traditions.

Jaki, S. (1999). *Bible and science*. Front Royal, VA: Christendom Press.

> Provides a historical examination of the interaction between contributions of the Bible and of science, with many foundational theological and philosophical issues briefly discussed.

John Paul II (1998). *Fides et ratio: Encyclical letter on the relationship between faith and reason*. (http://www.vatican.va/holy_father/john_paul_ii/encyclicals/documents/hf_jp-ii_enc_15101998_fides-et-ratio_en.html)

> Difficult but rewarding reading, but contains unique and profound insights not found anywhere else.

Jones, S. L. (Ed.). (1986). *Psychology and the Christian faith: An introductory reader*. Grand Rapids, MI: Baker.

> Provides a diverse group of cross-disciplinary scholars' views on topics that tend to parallel traditional introductory psychology texts; Jones' own chapter one is particularly useful as an introduction.

Jones, S. L. & Butman, R. E. (1991). *Modern psychotherapies: A comprehensive Christian appraisal*. Downers Grove, IL: InterVarsity Press.

> Provides some of the most comprehensive and balanced coverage of therapeutic psychology from a Christian perspective; a new edition coming out shortly.

Kirwan, W. T. (1984). *Biblical concepts for Christian counseling: A case for integrating psychology and theology*. Grand Rapids, MI: Baker.

> Trained in both psychology and theology, his chapter two in particular is very useful as he compares the psychological focus on thinking, feeling, and acting with the biblical concepts of knowing, being, and doing.

Sorenson, R. L. (2004). *Minding spirituality*. Hillsdale NJ: Analytic Press.

> This now-standard volume relates psychoanalysis, religion, and spirituality in ways that transcends most of the typical integration literature.

Vande Kemp, H. (1982). The tension between psychology and theology: The etymological roots. *Journal of Psychology and Theology, 10*, 105-112.

> First of two companion articles (the second is included in this volume), it addresses the historical term psyche and the derivation of how psychology became soul-less in the modern period.

Wolterstorff, N. (1984). *Reason within the bounds of religion*. (2nd ed.). Grand Rapids, MI: Eerdmans.

> Fairly brief but dense treatment of integration by one of the foremost Christian philosophers of our time, resulting in rewarding reading.

Perspectives on the Integration of Psychology and Theology

Bruce Narramore
Rosemead Graduate School of Psychology

As editor of the *Journal of Psychology and Theology,* the author sketches the main purposes of this new publication. A statement of the goals of the editorial committee is followed by a brief evaluation of the present status of efforts to integrate biblical and psychological truth, a survey of some factors that have hindered the progress of integrative endeavors, and some suggestions for potentially fruitful areas of study and interaction.

In this first issue of the *Journal of Psychology and Theology* it is important to pause a moment and consider our objectives. This Journal is a unique professional publication. While its content will overlap a variety of psychological and theological periodicals, its major focus and commitment are distinct.

Recent years have seen a proliferation of new data, theories, and methods in psychology. At many points the concepts and data of this developing psychological science are impinging on areas traditionally dealt with by the church. In many quarters the whole process of "curing sick souls" is moving from the church to the doorsteps of psychologists and other mental health professionals. Increasingly, our society is looking to psychology to shed new light on the basic issues of human existence. Questions on the nature of man, society, and the universe are being directed more to the secular psychological community than to the church.

Most of us view this trend with mixed emotions. On the one hand we sense the great potential in a scientific study of man. We know that objective data and well constructed theories may deepen our understanding of man, God's most complex creation. We are also aware that the church has sometimes failed to minister to the emotional needs of its constituents; and we realize the church has often failed to speak clearly to vital psychological issues. Undoubtedly the new insights of psychology can help us in these areas.

On the other hand, the rapid growth of the psychological sciences and professions may also be viewed as an encroachment on the ministry of the church. We sense a veiled threat (or sometimes obvious) to the authority of the Scriptures, the reality of the supernatural, and the role of the Christian ministry.

These mixed feelings touch a wide range of concerned Christians. The man on the street, for example, sees in psychology new insights that may provide relief from personal discomfort and despair. He gains new hope for "victory" through the application of psychological concepts or techniques. At the same time he may also sense a slight feeling of guilt at turning outside the church for professional help. He may have been told his problems are entirely spiritual and that what he really needs is more faith, or a deeper commitment, not psychotherapy.

Ministers too, are caught up in this conflict. Confronted by a variety of deep emotional entanglements of parishioners, they sense the need for a deeper understanding of the human personality. At the same time they feel the Bible should contain all answers to man's dilemma. If they look toward psychology they may feel a sense of disloyalty to the Scriptures.

Christian psychologists and related professional workers also have mixed feelings. They know their disciplines hold much truth; and they hope to apply this truth in the framework of their Christian faith. Yet, at the same time, they are aware of many barriers to this application. They face some clear differences of opinion with their secular community, and their Christian brothers are sometimes extremely resistant to any attempts to relate psychological principles to the Christian life.

But the minister and psychologist are not the only ones caught up in this conflict. The theologian, the physician, and the student of psychology and scripture all share concerns for the whole man. They know they cannot minister effectively if they neglect the contributions of related disciplines.

But how do we go about this integration? In what way can the psychologist, minister, physician, or theologian effectively relate his Christian view of life to the secular study of psychology? And in what ways can the Christian church draw on the insights of psychology to build a more effective ministry?

The *Journal of Psychology and Theology* hopes to aid a large group of evangelical Christians in this process of integration. To reach this end, the Journal will serve as a forum for exchanging ideas and information relating to the integration of psychology and scripture.

The Journal will contain research studies aimed at gradually building a body of objective data relating to our interests. This is a foundation for building any sort of cohesive approach to the problems that confront us. Theoretical papers will be another major focus of concern. If we are to further an integrative understanding of man, we must set in motion a regular stream of verbal interactions in this area. In addition to theory and data, each issue of the *Journal of Psychology and Theology* will contain applied papers dealing with the practical applications of biblical and psychological concepts to the work of the church in general and to the therapeutic process in particular.

This is our goal in abbreviated form. We hope the *Journal of Psychology and Theology* will provide an interdisciplinary forum for the integration of biblical and psychological truth. In doing this our publication policy is very broad. Both theoretical, research and applied papers will be accepted for publications. Articles relating to academic psychology will be presented along with papers of relevance to the local pastor interested in psychology. Papers from a variety of theoretical and theological positions will be published. While the Rosemead Graduate School of Psychology is committed to an historical, evangelical theology, papers will not be limited to this specific view. Although the bulk of articles will represent current evangelical thinking, the editors believe authors from varying positions may have a good deal of stimulating thinking to add to our integrative efforts. The criteria for these articles, then, will be their challenging nature to the evangelical rather than their doctrinal accuracy.

In summary, here is our major goal. We hope the *Journal of Psychology and Theology* will serve as a forum for the integration and application of psychological and biblical information. To accomplish this goal, we will publish articles dealing with the three areas of (*a*) data, (*b*) theory, and (*c*) application. We will also keep Journal content sufficiently broad to appeal to a multidisciplinary readership and to inform these readers through provocative articles of interest to the evangelical community.

The Present Status of Integrative Efforts Between Psychology and Christianity

As we present this first issue, another need comes to light. This is the need to put our current thinking in an historical perspective. Why is it that nearly one hundred years after the founding of modern psychology we have only scattered attempts at integrating our Christian faith with psychological theory and data?

Over the past 40 years we have an increasing number of Christians who are psychologists. We have also had a large number of ministers and theologians with interests in psychology. Many of these men have been productive. Some have initiated psychology majors in our Christian colleges. Others have entered private practice and started psychological clinics. Still others have written helpful books and articles on psychology from a Christian perspective. Through these efforts the role of a "Christian psychologist" has gained a certain respectability within the Christian community. From the evangelical community, men like Collins (1969), Hyder (1971), Narramore (1960), Nelson (1960), and Tournier (1962) have written books directed to the Christian layman or pastor. These men combined some aspects of biblical and psychological truth to offer insight and guidance to Christians looking for help in personal living.

On a somewhat different level, other authors have tried to find parallels between biblical truth and various schools of psychological thinking. Tweedie (1961), for example, did this with Frankl's Logotherapy. Pfister (1948) and Barkman (1965) have attempted the same thing with psychoanalytic theory. And, more recently, Drakeford (1967) has taken a similar approach with a more directive "Reality Therapy" orientation.

From the theological or ministerial side of the fence, men like Adams (1970), Hiltner (1949), Hulme (1956, 1970), LaHay (1966), Oates (1962), and Roberts (1950) have offered similar publications. Although varying greatly in both their biblical positions and their psychological sophistication, all of these have played a part in bringing psychology to the attention of the church. To focus briefly on their contributions, we summarize as follows. All of these men have contributed to (*a*) gradually reducing the church's fear of psychology, (*b*) making some distinctions between spiritual and emotional maladjustments, (*c*) removing the stigma of seeking professional help for personal problems, (*d*) giving the layman increased insights into human behavior, (*e*) encouraging ministers and theologians to give attention to the whole person (including the emotional side of life), and (*f*) encouraging younger Christians to view the discipline of psychology as a potential field for Christian service. From the extreme defensiveness and isolation of the 40s, men like this have helped the Church come a long way.

But we still have far to go. Nearly all of our past efforts suffer from the same four deficiencies: (*a*) They lack objective, scientific data, (*b*) they lack clearly defined theological and philosophical underpinnings, (*c*) they lack a general theory of behavior, and (*d*) they lack a well thought out theory of personality. One of the few exceptions to this is the book *What, Then, Is Man*, authored by a group of Lutheran psychologists and theologians (Meehl et al., 1958). This book makes a good start on promoting a healthy dialogue on some basic issues of integration.

Without an explicit philosophical position, objective data, and a general behavior theory, it is impossible to have a system of psychology. Since we lack these basic elements, we cannot accurately say there is such a thing as "Christian psychology." There are many Christian psychologists, but until we gain further data and refine our theoretical thinking, it will be impossible to have a systematic Christian view of psychology. Even at this I suspect we may not have one generally accepted psychology for the Christian. Instead, we might expect several well thought out views of man in accordance with biblical truth and current psychological knowledge.

But let's back up a bit. Why is it that centuries after the reformation and nearly 100 years after the founding of modern psychology the Christian church still has not gathered any significant bank of psychological data? Why have we failed to carefully examine the underlying philosophical positions of secular psychology ad suggest some biblical alternatives? And why have we not developed either a definitive Christian theory of personality or a general theory of behavior? In fact, why is it that in many corners of the evangelical church there remains considerable suspicion and distrust of psychological theory and data? And to look at the other side of the coin, why do many secular psychologists have serious quarrels with religion in general and evangelical Christianity in particular? Why is it that such mutual fear and skepticism exist?

If we are to have a meaningful interdisciplinary dialogue we must go beyond our past fears, prejudices, and misunderstandings. We must clearly see the issues at hand and begin to attack them one by one. To date the Christian has been generally fearful of psychology. At the same time the average secular psychologist has had his share of bad attitudes toward religion.

In discussing the mutual anxieties of psychologists and theologians when in each other's presence, Paul Barkman (1965) gives an interesting description. He writes:

> Rather typically, if a psychologist (of psychoanalytic orientation) were to listen to a theologian (of Calvinist orientation) discuss theology, the psychologist might be quite puzzled to find himself described as 'an unregenerate soul resists the Holy Spirit with worldly wisdom because of a depraved nature and an impenitent spirit.' (Unless, of course, the psychologist were a minister's son— which many of them are.) To this he might reply that the theologian has 'a parabolic personality trait disturbance with an unresolved oedipal complex, who is engaging in projection of repressed hostility toward a castrating father figure.' The theologian might return home proud of his testimony, puzzled and a little shaken, and say to his wife. 'Today I met a psychoanalyst!' The psychologist might well go home to his wife proud of his educative function, somewhat anxious and perplexed, and using his wife as a therapist say, 'Today I met a preacher!' (pp. 9-10)

Barkman here picks up an attitude that has hindered integration. I would like to go further and suggest several reasons for our past failure to establish a distinctively Christian psychology. The first few of these reasons arise out of the 20th Century historical development of the Christian church, especially the effect of the liberal—conservative splits of the 1920s. These reasons include: (*a*) The Christian's fear of the naturalistic explanation of psychology; (*b*) the Christian's fear of the deterministic emphasis of psychology; (*c*) the Christian's difference with secular psychology's view of man; (*d*) the Christian's differences with a secular view of sex and some bad experiences with psychology; and (*e*) the Christian's fear of emotions, especially sex, aggression, and intimacy. The other barriers lie more at the feet of the non-Christian community. Among these are (*a*) The psychologist's superficial understanding of

Christianity; (*b*) the psychologists' identity problem and his overconcern with objective scientism; (*c*) the psychologist's blindness to spiritual truth and his unconscious fear of spiritual issues like death and hell; and (*d*) realities of time. Let's consider each of these barriers.

The Historical Development of the Christian Church

During the great theological divisions of the twenties most denominations split into "liberal" and "conservative" elements. Each group went its own way. On the one hand, the evangelical wing of the church focused on concepts like personal salvation, scriptural inerrancy, heaven and hell, and human depravity. On the other hand, the liberal church chose to minister to the social needs of man. Both wings were concerned for the individual. For the fundamentalist their concern was primarily for salvation. For the liberal the emphasis was a social gospel. In reacting to what they felt was the fundamentalist's negative emphases on hell, depravity, personal salvation, and inerrancy of scripture, the liberal wing of the church began to focus more on human potential and social action. They rebelled against the fundamentalists' "pessimistic" view of man and began to hold out hope that through human effort workable solutions to man's dilemmas would be found. As this segment of the church moved further from a focus on biblical theology and personal salvation it turned increasingly to sociology, psychology, and politics as alternate means of ministering to the needs of man.

At the same time, the "conservative" wing of the church reaffirmed its commitment to the authority of scripture and renewed its focus on personal salvation through the redemptive work of Christ. In doing so, this wing of the church largely disassociated itself from areas of political or social concern exhibited by the "liberals." The conservative church had a great deal of social outreach but they limited it largely in terms of medical health services, help for the down and outers, and assistance to members of local congregations.

In the 1920s, a significant movement was unknowingly begun in the Christian church. A man by the name of Anton Boisen (1926) published an article challenging the church to become involved in the emotional ills of man. In issuing this challenge, Boisen said,

> We have therefore this truly remarkable situation—a church which has always been interested in the care of the sick, confining her efforts to the types of cases

(physical) in which religion has least concern and least to contribute, while in those types in which it is impossible to tell where the domain of the medical worker leaves off and that of the religious worker begins (mental problems), there the church is doing nothing. (p. 9)

Boisen soon became a spokesman for those encouraging the church to minister to the emotional needs of society. By 1930 this new emphasis gained so much ground *The Council for Clinical Pastoral Training* was formed. This organization functioned to stimulate and coordinate new efforts at training ministers to cope with the personal problems of parishioners. Soon many seminaries were asking students to take short term internships in mental hospitals as a means of becoming sensitive to the psychological needs of people.

To all this the liberal church reacted favorably. Here was a way to minister to the inner needs of man. Psychology offered hope for the present world, not a "pie in the sky" brand of Christian faith. In the thirties and forties, liberal pastoral counseling was strongly influenced by the therapeutic teachings of Sigmund Freud. A distinct emphasis began to move throughout the pastoral counseling movement.

Rather than being viewed as sinful, people with problems were seen as sick. Feelings of guilt and remorse were no longer seen as Christian virtues. Instead, they were the results of inhibited upbringings which resulted in overly strict superegos (consciences). The goal of the pastor-counselor was no longer viewed as leading parishioners to accept God's forgiveness of their sins. Instead, the goal was to relax the strictness of this harsh superego so the person could be freed to enjoy his life. Well known liberal theologians like Harry Emerson Fosdick (1943) took up the banner of this new view of man. In his book *On Being A Real Person* Fosdick endorsed the psychoanalytic view that neuroses arose not from a lack of responsibility but from an overly strict conscience. He wrote:

> Indiscriminate praise of conscientiousness is psychologically dangerous. Many people worry themselves into complete disintegration over mere trifles, and others have consciences so obtuse that they can get away with anything. (p. 133)

This thinking fit well with the liberal doctrine of man. A person with emotional problems was not necessarily a depraved sinner. Instead, he was a victim of his environment. The solution to his ailments did not necessarily lie in a spiritual new birth and consequent growth. Instead, it lay in an anthropocentric growth process which needn't be concerned with supernatural phenomena.

During the 1940s a new influence came into American psychology and was soon heartily endorsed by the liberal pastoral counseling movement. This was the "non-directive" or "client-centered counseling" of Carl Rogers (1942). Raised in what he describes as a "strict religious environment," Rogers later attended Union Theological Seminary. His writings reflect a strong rejection of the idea that man is basically sinful. Instead, he focuses on the innate tendency toward growth and actualization. Given a healthy environment, man will throw off his negative reactions and develop into a healthy, fully functioning person. Based on these underlying presuppositions Rogers' therapeutic method centered on providing the client a warm, accepting, non-judgmental atmosphere. Rather than giving directive advice to a person in need of outside guidance, Rogers' "client-centered therapy" encouraged the client to seek his own solutions. The counselor was no longer an expert or a guide. Instead, he was an accepting friend who listened empathetically to the struggles of another human being. This counseling method had great appeal to the liberal church. Once again, it fit in with a positive view of the nature of man and his potential.

But neither psychoanalytic nor client-centered therapy had much room for biblical insight or directive counsel. As the pastoral counselor began to rely largely on these secular theories, the idea that man was a spiritual being in need of salvation and spiritual counsel gradually slipped into the background. As a matter of fact, a counseling approach that gave much attention to specific biblical teaching seemed somehow suspect and unscientific. In the minds of the intellectual liberals, any strong reliance on scriptural teaching smacked of authoritarianism and the "fundamentalist mentality." Liberal theology was believed to have progressed beyond this narrow view!

In recent years, one final force has pressed into the mental health picture of the liberal church. This is the influence of existential philosophy and psychology. After two world wars, many continental theologians began to rethink their views on the goodness and potentials of man as well as God's revelation to man. Søren Kierkegaard (1944) began to focus on existential encounters as sources of true meaning in life. Later existentialists developed this thinking and propounded the idea that man had to struggle to find personal meaning and identity in the midst of a confusing and meaningless world.

This thinking is now playing a significant role in the personal ministry of the liberal and neo-orthodox wings of the church.

To bring us up to date, let's briefly summarize these main psychological influences on the liberal church. In the twenties there was a needed awareness to the inner emotional needs of man prompted first by the influence of Anton Boisen. Since this wing of the church was in the process of rejecting the traditional theological view of man, it was immediately receptive to the influence of psychoanalytic writings which portrayed man as a sick individual needing psychological help rather than a sinner needing grace. After twenty years of this influence, the client-centered therapy of Carl Rogers came on the scene and was heartily endorsed. Finally, in recent years, the influence of the existentialists has brought a focus on the need to find subjective, personal meaning out of an existential crisis encounter.

Each of these influences, the psychoanalytic, the Rogerian, and existentialist, has one thing in common: they have very little room for a theology which focuses on sin, personal salvation, and biblical absolutes. In other words, the focus on personal adjustment and mental hygiene has been largely divorced from the teachings of the Bible and placed within the framework of a secular psychology. This is the great weakness of the liberal church. They have no hope of developing a biblically sound perspective of psychology since they have forsaken the authoritative teachings of the Scriptures. While discussing this development and the fact that many professional psychologists are now dissatisfied with their traditional psychotherapeutic approaches, Hobart Mowrer (1961) asks, "Has evangelical religion sold its birthright for a mess of psychological pottage?" In other words, Mowrer, a secular psychologist, is aware that much of the church has lost its potentially helpful contributions to psychology. Instead of standing on the Scriptures and offering some alternative perspectives, many Christians have merely jumped indiscriminately on the current psychological bandwagon.

While the liberal church was busy adopting a basically secular approach to personal adjustment and psychology, the evangelical church took a different tact. It steered clear of psychology. The pastoral counseling of the typical conservative minister was often limited. And when he did counsel, it was usually following a conversion or in periods of death, grief, or special hardship. While many evangelical ministers were sensitive and supportive, the bulk of their ministry was of a directive, Bible teaching nature that failed to cope with many of the hidden wishes and frustrations of emotional living. The typical conservative minister was 20 or 30 years behind his liberal churchman in being aware of the contributions of psychology to the understanding of men.

The Fear of Naturalistic Explanations

A primary reason for the evangelical's failure to encounter psychological science concerned the influence of the *supernatural*. Psychology, of course, was deeply committed to naturalistic explanations. If it were to build a science of behavior, it would have to have a set of laws. It would have to be able to accurately predict behavior given all the influential variables. This left no room for supernatural influences.

This stance brought threat and apprehension to the evangelical. If psychology could explain and modify human behavior without reference to spiritual principles, the whole concept of the supernatural was in question. This is the very turn the liberal church took in adopting the naturalistic views of a secular psychology. Although few would voice this fear. it seems clear that part of the uneasy anxiety suffered by evangelical Christians in the presence of psychology is traceable to his fear of losing the influence of the supernatural.

The Fear of Determinism and Irresponsibility

Another conservative fear was that when people understood the causes of behavior, man would no longer feel responsible for his actions. Psychotherapy, especially psychoanalytically oriented therapy, was seen as an attempt to set men free of their inhibitions and turn them into impulsive, irresponsible sinners. Although this attitude is a gross misrepresentation of most psychological theory, it has persisted even until today in a criticism common to the anti-psychological stance of many Christian writers. Jay Adams states:

> The idea of sickness as the cause of personal problems vitiates all notions of human responsibility. This is the crux of the matter. People no longer consider themselves responsible for what they do wrong. Instead they blame society— 'ours is a sick society,' they say. Others specifically blame grandmother, mother, the church, a school teacher, or some other particular individual for their actions. Freudian psychoanalysis itself turns out to be an archeological expedition back into the past in which a search is made for others on whom to pin the blame for our behavior. The fundamental idea is to find out how others have

wronged us. It should not be difficult to see how irresponsibility is the upshot of such an emphasis and how many of the domestic and world wide problems we face in our time are directly related to it. (pp. 5-6)

While many practicing psychologists certainly have been guilty of allowing clients to avoid responsibility, this is due more to their personal therapeutic deficiencies than to the falsity of most psychological theory. Take psychoanalytic theory, for example. It has been most severely criticized as promoting irresponsible acting out and immediate gratification of all desires. In contrast to this, Waelder (1960), a well respected analyst, writes:

> A psychoanalytic approach to education, finally, does not mean that children should get what they want when they want it. Rather it means an attempt to find for each situation the proper balance between satisfaction and frustration, in the light of the general principle that we have to search for the optimal ingredients of healthy development, vis., love and discipline; how to love without pampering and how to discipline without traumatizing. (p. 254)

Suffice it to say, psychology's emphasis on determinism and the Christian's fear that psychological explanations will lead to irresponsibility have been major barriers to attempts at integration.

The Fear of Humanistic Views of Man

The influence of Rogers and similar theoreticians was also rejected by the evangelicals. This was apparently due both to his emphasis on the nature of man and to his therapeutic method. To a doctrinally oriented, Bible teaching movement, the idea of sitting quietly and empathizing with the needs of parishioners was difficult enough to swallow. Add to this the view that man is essentially good and you can see how out of line with the traditional evangelical approach Rogers' views would be. They were entirely out of keeping with the counseling approach that had a ready verse for every human need. The evangelical church was not yet ready for a deep look at the inner emotional needs of man. In discussing the church's frequent failure to apply its theology to human experience, William Hulme (1956) writes:

> The successors of the great churchmen of the past have too often communicated the doctrines of the church in a legalistic fashion that had little relation to the

dynamics of the human personality. The result is an overintellectualized religion that is unable to reach the deep emotional conflicts of life. Such a religion plays into the hands of those who would rather rationalize than resolve these conflicts. (p. 8)

The Fear of Sex

The centrality of sexual impulses to Freudian theory was a red flag to conservative churchmen. They feared that therapeutic approaches emphasizing the inhibitions of sexual feelings as basic to neuroses would lead to a lowering of standards and a movement from a biblical position. This was a sign that psychology was "of the devil" and had nothing to offer a biblical Christian. Without going into depth, it is obvious that this view had some truth. On the other hand, it may have been overdone. The high view of sexuality endorsed in Scripture has certainly not been accepted by an unsaved world. At the same time, it is equally apparent that many Christians have been guilty of promoting a repressive, unrealistic view of sex. This conflict served to place almost insurmountable barriers between some Christians and the discipline of psychology.

The Christian's Fear of Feelings

Feelings can be frightening. Intense love, moods of depression, outbursts of anger, and needs for support are carefully avoided by many people. For Christians especially, there is the fear that love will turn to lust, or discouragement to despair. In earnestly desiring to live the Christian life, everyone builds facades to hide their inner selves. Christians are told they should be happy, so they smile (even though they hurt inside). They are told Christians should be loving so they try to love (even though they feel quite differently). And they are told Christians should be saintly so they put on an outward show of piety.

From the day of their conversion Christians begin learning the rules of their Christian subculture. They are taught how to act, think, and feel in order to live the 'victorious life." In one group or denomination the "key" is found in an external set of legalistic actions. In another culture the sign of spiritual maturity is to be found in an aggressive witness. If a person is really "filled with the Spirit" he will show it by his soul-winning efforts. For other groups the sign of spiritual success is the "baptism of the Spirit." Speaking in tongues becomes a sure indication of spiritual blessing or maturity.

These and other emphases in various Christian cultures lead the Christian follower to try to mold his lifestyle in accordance with the standards and ideals of his unique subculture. In doing this, many are forced to put on the expected external trappings at the expense of an honest encounter with their true emotions.

An example of this negation of emotion is found in the prevalent parallel between a railroad train and the Christian life. We are told the engine is fact (the Bible), the next car is faith (trust in God's Word), and the caboose is feeling. The train of the Christian life must obviously be pulled by fact and followed by faith. The train (Christian experience) will run with or without the caboose (feeling).

In fact, major decisions in life should be based on the Word of God. But this simple analogy tends to picture feelings as kind of a nuisance factor in the Christian life. The impression is sometimes given that we would be better off without emotions. They just lead to subjective feeling-oriented decisions which muddy the waters of consistent Christian living.

Another common manifestation of this fear of feelings and intimacy is found in one of our favorite hymns. We are told, "Are you weary, are you heavy-hearted? Tell it to Jesus alone." In other words, don't share your problems with another person. Instead, hold it in, hide your needs and "tell it to Jesus alone." What a contrast this isolationistic view of the Christian life is to the following passages.

> "Bear ye one another's burdens, and so fulfill the law of Christ" (Galatians 6:2).
>
> "Confess your faults one to another, and pray one for another, that ye may be healed. The effectual fervent prayer of a righteous man availeth much" (James 5:16).
>
> "Wherefore, comfort yourselves together and edify one another, even as also ye do" (1 Thessalonians 5:11).

This fearful avoidance of feelings in the Christian life has encouraged many to erect or maintain rigid barriers against deep involvement and has caused others to approach Christian service as an obligation rather than the natural result of living a fulfilling life. In the area of psychology, it has caused many to anxiously steer clear of any involvement for fear of contaminating a pure, "objective," intellectualized theology with the "subjective" content of inner human nature.

Summary of the Christian Fears

We can now see why the church has largely failed to make distinctive contributions to psychology. Instead of ministering to the inner emotional needs, the evangelical church has focused primarily on the need for personal salvation, doctrinal orthodoxy, and moral purity. Its social emphasis was largely in the realm of physical medicine. A series of important conflicts with psychology have held the evangelical back from the potential contributions of psychology.

The liberals have failed because they moved from their biblical moorings and adopted an essentially secular psychology. Neither group is actively applying the vast resources of Scriptural teachings to the daily personal needs of the average m an or to the academic study of psychology.

Psychology's Failure to Participate in Integrative Efforts

But we cannot lay the failure to develop a sufficiently integrated view of man entirely at the feet of the Christian community. Psychologists too, have played their part in isolationism. Let's look at some reasons for the hesitancy of psychologists to join with Christians in an effort to gain a broadened view of man.

Superficial Understanding of the Christian Faith

As a starter, few psychologists theorizing about the nature of man are actively religious. Many have had only superficial contact with biblical Christianity, while others have had very negative encounters. Take the psychotherapist who has counseled a number of Christian patients, each suffering from a deep sense of worthlessness and guilt. These clients naturally relate these feelings to their Christian experience. They think their guilt and condemnation come directly from the Lord. And what is the therapist to conclude? His natural response is that religion is a destructive force that causes people to feel worthless and guilty. Add to this a brief encounter with the term "total depravity" and our psychologist is sure that religious faith attempts to sabotage positive mental health by instilling deep feelings of guilt and fear.

The Psychologist's Identity Problem

But there are other reasons for psychological skepticism about a theological encounter. As a discipline, psychology still is rather young. In contrast to the natural sciences, psychology has had a hard time finding its niche. The inner workings of the mind have a tint of the subjective, an alien word to experimental scientists. As a matter of fact, even now some people argue that psychology is still somewhat less than science. To overcome its identity problem, psychology has had to make determined efforts to establish itself in the mainstream of the scientific world. To do this it had to emphasize major tenets and methods of objective science. These, of course, included a rigid adherence to the scientific method and to naturalistic assumptions about the universe.

Based on this philosophy, graduate training programs ignore the possibility of supernatural phenomena. Trained in these types of programs, a prospective scientist cannot easily escape adopting a similar attitude toward supernatural phenomence. The religious devotee is seen as either naïve, dependent, unscientific, and possibly as all three! Otto Fenichel (1945), a staunch supporter of orthodox psychoanalysis, says:

> Scientific psychology explains mental phenomena as a result of the interplay of primitive physical needs—rooted in the biological history—and the influences of the environment on these needs. There is no place for any third factor. (p. 5)

Unclear Perceptions

Still another difficulty is the fact that certain perceptions on truth and reality are not open to the unbeliever. The apostle Paul writes:

> Even so the things of God knoweth no man, but the spirit of God. Now we have received, not the spirit of the world, but the Spirit who is of God; that we might know the things that are freely given to us of God. Which things also we speak, not in the words which man's wisdom teacheth, but which the Holy Spirit teacheth, comparing spiritual things with spiritual. But the natural man receiveth not the things of the Spirit of God; for they are foolishness unto him, neither can he know them, because they are spiritually discerned. But he that is spiritual judgeth all things, yet he himself is judged of no man. For who hath known the mind of the Lord, that he may instruct him? But we have the mind of Christ. (1 Cor. 11-16)

Paul makes the clear point that there is a wisdom which the person who does not possess a personal relationship with Christ cannot possess. It is impossible for the unregenerate person to comprehend some aspects of the truth. In spite of great personal sensitivity and insight, the non-Christian psychologist has a limited vision on the condition of man. Some conflict in views of the nature of man and his functioning are clearly due to this lack of perception of the non-Christian person. At this point we should add a word of caution. Some Christians have a way of writing off every difference of opinion with a non-Christian to his "lack of spiritual discernment." While this is often true, sometimes the misunderstanding is as much our fault as it is our unsaved friend's. We tend to clutter up the Christian message with our own brand of Christian subculture and cloud over a clear picture of biblical truth. In these cases we need to help our non-Christian colleague cut through these externals to the core ideas of Bible truth.

Realities of Time

But these factors alone do not account for the hesitancy of psychologists to join in an integrative encounter. The practical realities of time and competence make it difficult for the average man to master his chosen discipline effectively, let alone take the time to really see the viewpoints and teaching of a related profession. Even well meaning, open-minded men are limited in their ability to dialogue intelligently with colleagues in other disciplines.

The Unique Challenge for Christian Psychology

This concludes our survey of some of the barriers to effective integration. But where do we go from here. If we are going to push ahead for a comprehensive understanding of the human part of God's creation, we must have a group of committed Christian professionals who are willing to invest their time and efforts in furthering the integration of psychology and scripture. To do this effectively will require both the delineation of areas for study and a certain set of personal attributes and attitudes. We must begin by identifying the potential contributions of a psychological study from a Christian point of view. Without attempting to be comprehensive, let me suggest a number of areas that need to be explored. These issues must be dealt with if we are to develop a meaningful Christian viewpoint on psychology and its applications.

The Challenge of Theory

Consider first the theoretical issues. Several of these have traditionally divided psychologists and theologians. Determinism and personal responsibility are key examples. Any acceptable Christian view of man will have to include a satisfactory resolution of arguments centering around determinism, choice, and responsibility. All respectable scientists acknowledge the lawfulness of behavior, and most adhere to some form of determinism. The theologian, on the other hand, in spite of some theoretical debates on election and predestination, is essentially committed to a view of human responsibility. How are we to reconcile these seemingly conflicting views?

Of no less concern is the mind-body question. Can man and his mental functions be reduced entirely to the physiological? Or do we reject the assumptions of this materialistic monism? Similarly, how are we to view conversion? Can we accede to a psychological explanation of this phenomenon? Or can we move closer to clarifying the interrelations of divine intervention, conditioning processes, and inner attitudes? And what about the guilt problem? Are we to view guilt as a "divinely given rebuke or conscience warning light"? Or is it merely an "introjected parent" or "conditioned response"?

And what about miracles and faith healing? The Bible clearly reports these occurrences. Psychologists explain them away as psychological phenomena, a kind of spontaneous remission based upon an infantile belief in magic. Some theologians likewise try to dismiss these present day events by dispensationalizing them out of existence. But does this really resolve the problem? Can't we come to some more definitive thinking on these issues?

After surveying a number of pastors and psychologists, Meehl (1958, p. 5) concludes, "We are prepared to state firmly that he who does not come to terms with such theoretical problems as determinism, guilt, original sin, materialist monism, conscience, and conversion cannot even begin to work out a cognitive reapproachment between Christian theology and the secular sciences of behavior." After nearly fifteen years these still appear to be among the most basic issues facing us today.

The Challenge of Data

Now let's turn to the area of objective data. What are some areas that need more careful study? Certainly we need to study the effects of spiritual conversion. We know the process of regeneration makes important inner changes. But shouldn't we expect to find them manifested in demonstrable overt behavior? And what about the sanctification (growth) process? Are believers, in fact, evidencing superior adjustment to their non-Christian counterparts? Or is the sole effect of the Christian life an insurance policy for eternity?

The influences of different variables in the development of morality should be a prime area of study. Mature morality is a major goal of Christian training. Yet we are all aware of gross failures in this area and the large percentage of drop-outs among second generation Christians. What accounts for these successes and failures? Can we really write this off as solely a matter of spiritual dedication?

The attitudes and belief systems of Christians are also a rich potential field of study. The present state of research here is very inconclusive. Sanua (1969) writes:

> A number of empirical studies, which do not support the general belief that religion is the fountainhead of all moral tenets of our society, have been reviewed in this paper. According to Allport (3) religious instruction seems to include a contradictory set of beliefs. He stated that 'most religious persons tend to internalize the divisive role of religion, whereas only a small minority are able to accept the unifying bond, moral and ethical principles underlying religion.' Thus, on the one hand, religious leaders advocate love of all mankind and the equality of men as being children of God, while, on the other hand, certain religious teachings hold that only those who possess the 'truth' may be saved.
>
> As a result, religious education as it is being taught today does not seem to ensure healthier attitudes, despite its emphasis on ethical behavior. This should raise a major point of discussion among religious leaders to determine whether possibilities exist to remedy this failure to communicate the ethical aspects of religion rather than its ritual. (p. 1211)

Can we go beyond this view and design carefully controlled studies of various religious groupings to come to a clearer understanding of the results of Christian life and training? Although these studies pose some difficult methodological problems, they seem essential to clarifying certain distorted images people hold of Christians and finding out to what extent they differ from their unsaved counterparts.

Outcome studies on "Christian psychotherapy" also are important. The many variables of this interpersonal process and the general finding that the therapist's theoretical orientation is less important than the process variables raise serious questions about the ability to come to definitive conclusions. Yet if we are claiming some sort of superiority for "Christian counseling," it's about time we stopped to see if claims are backed by solid data.

Another area for study is the effectiveness of various forms of Christian ministries. What personal, organizational, and strategic variables account for our failures and successes? Studies could be done in local churches, missionary organizations, educational institutions, and a wide variety of other settings. In relationship to this we need longitudinal studies of vocational fulfillment and success in different Christian ministries. Some mission boards have nearly a 50 percent drop out rate over the first two terms of service. Can we devise more effective screening processes through objective research? Or does our reliance on the Holy Spirit rule out this approach to personnel selection?

The Challenge of Application

And what about pragmatics? Out of our research and theorizing can we find effective ways of ministering to a world in need? Can we offer suggestions for maximizing the effectiveness of worship services? Is the new "Body Life" emphasis producing more mature believers? Can we improve our Christian education system? Can we train our Christian workers more efficiently? Can we improve our counseling skills? And can we devise educational or counseling programs that will make a sizeable dent in the problem of the disintegrating American family?

These and other questions come to our attention. We could double or triple this list with little effort. Some of the problems are large and some are small. Some are largely abstract and theoretical while others have an immediate relevance to Christian living. But all are within the domain of the Christian psychologist and concerned minister or theologian. They are issues that have not been satisfactorily resolved for most of the Christian world, let alone the secular professional. Perhaps here, in these areas, we have a portion of the unique calling of the Christian psychologist. I am convinced that God has some specific plans for Christians in the field of psychology. These plans must fit into His overall ministry in the world. If we fail to address these issues, the Church will continue to limit its effectiveness in some very vital areas.

The Personal Challenge

But it is not enough to merely delineate specific problem areas. If we are to be most effective we must pursue our task with a basic set of personal and professional attitudes. The human factor will be a major determinant of the success of our endeavors. As Christians, we must recognize that it is impossible to segment our lives into the sacred and the secular. The very vocations we select, the problems we choose to tackle, and the theoretical framework of our efforts are all influenced by our personal lives in general and our relationships to God in particular.

The first essential attitude for effective integration is a respect for the complete inspiration and authority of the Scriptures. Without using the Bible in a narrow-minded, prejudicial way, we must acknowledge it as God's objective, accurate revelation to man. When our human views (contaminated by our limited perceptions) come into conflict with the Bible we must place our allegiance in the Scripture. This does not mean we naively close our eyes to apparent conflicts. There are times we may need to re-evaluate our theological positions. If we are honest we must all admit there is a good bit of cultural dogmatism in all of our beliefs. We must be willing to get beyond this and make clear studies of seeming conflict areas. Once we are sure of a biblical teaching we must refuse to try to twist and distort clear teachings of the Scriptures to fit our human thinking or our psychological theories,. As psychologists we should be most alert to the universal tendency to project our own needs, conflicts, and biases onto our Scriptural interpretations. We should also be aware of the fact that our distinctive is our credence in God's inerrant Word. If we fail to base our work on this we are building on an inadequate foundation and will have a psychology essentially no different from the secular psychologist.

Second, we must have an attitude of commitment to the scientific method and rigorous academic study. We must not allow ourselves to be second rate professionals because of our Christian stand. For too long Christians have copped out on rigorous study and research by claiming all the truth they need to know is contained within the Bible. While all the truth necessary to understand salvation and God's basic dealings in the universe are there, there is certainly much more truth we need to know. If we are to develop a significant body of integrative truth, we must hold out high standards for our professional endeavors.

Third, we need a personal commitment to Jesus Christ. If we are to be motivated to pursue an in-depth study of the nature of man, we must see a spiritual purpose in our work. We must see ourselves as servants of God called to understand the workings of creation. In many unique ways those of us ministering in the various areas of psychology have the opportunity of leading others into deeper spiritual truth. Unless we keep a vision of God's plan of salvation for the human race we will reverse our priorities and our professional endeavors will become sterile intellectual exercises that actually serve to defend against inner spiritual and emotional needs instead of becoming part of the redemptive plan of God. This is probably one of the most common pitfalls of the evangelical. In working for academic and professional respectability we minimize our personal spiritual lives and short-circuit God's total involvement in our lives.

Finally, we need an attitude of respect for both the Christian and the secular community. As Christians we will lose our effectiveness if we develop a superior or paranoid attitude toward the world. If we degrade the data of our science and set ourselves outside the scientific method we are doomed to failure. An isolationistic attitude may maintain our doctrinal purity but it will cause us to fail to grab hold of a large portion of God's general revelation.

Likewise, if we as psychologists set ourselves against our theologians we handicap our studies. We must get beyond our personal vocational interests, our personal spiritual experiences, and our personal prejudices to avail ourselves of rounded truth. Even within the evangelical community we continue to have divisions. Theologians often see psychology as an inferior source of truth when compared to the Bible (which I believe we must acknowledge if we're honest). But with this attitude often comes a certain sense of superiority and disdain for psychological endeavors. On the other hand, we psychologists like to think of ourselves as more broad minded, open, and scientific (which I think many theologians must admit if they are honest). But with this we adopt a certain sense of superiority at not being so "narrow minded" as the theologian. Similarly, the scholar and academician tend to look with disdain on their applied brethren. They are viewed as less rigorous and scientific. At the same time the practitioner (be he ministerial, medical, or psychological) often has a certain bias toward his academic colleague. He may accuse him of being impractical and insensitive to human need.

If we can lay aside our personal prejudices (way of defending against our unconscious feelings of inferiority) and develop a truly cooperative attitude, we will soon be a long way along the road of integration.

Summary

The evangelical church has a great opportunity to combine the special revelation of God's word with the general revelation studied by the psychological sciences and professions. The end result of this integration can be a broader (and deeper) view of human life. Historically we have failed to have sufficient dialogue and interaction. Currently we are in a position to gather relevant objective data, seek well-constructed theoretical views, and find improved techniques for applying our biblical and psychological data. To do this we need a group of committed professional people who can mix a personal piety with a commitment to the authority of the Word of God and to high quality professional endeavors. The editorial staff of the *Journal of Psychology and Theology* is happy to have a part in this process and encourages you to join with us in this effort. Your studies and publications will determine just how far our efforts will proceed.

References

Adams, J. (1970). *Competent to counsel.* New Jersey: Presbyterian and Reformed Publishing Company.

Barkman, P. (1965). *Man in conflict.* Grand Rapids, MI: Zondervan Publishing House.

Boisen, A. (1936). Challenge to our seminaries. *Christian Work*, p. 120.

Colling, G. (1964). *Search for reality.* Wheaton: IL. Key Publishers.

Drakeford, J. (1967). *Integrity therapy.* Nashville, TN: Broadman Press.

Fenichel, O. (1945). T*he psychoanalytic theory of neurosis.* New York: W. W. Norton & Company, Inc.

Fosdick, H. (1943). *On being a real person.* New York: Harper & Row Publishers.

Hiltner, S. (1949). *Pastoral Counseling.* New York: Abingdon Press.

Hulme, W. (1956). *Counseling and theology.* Philadelphia, PA: Fortress Press.

Hyder, O. (1971). *The Christian's handbook of psychiatry.* Old Tappan, NJ: Fleming H. Revell Company.

Kierkegaard, S. (1944). *Concept of dread.* Princeton, NJ: Princeton University Press.

LaHaye, T. (1966). *Spirit controlled temperament.* Wheaton, IL: Tyndale House Publishers.

Meehl, P., Klann, R., Schmieding, A., Breimeier, K., & Schroeder-Slomann, S. *What, then, is man?* St. Louis, MO: Concordia Publishing House.

Miller, K. (1967). *A second touch.* Waco, TX: Word Books.

Mowrer, H. (1961). *The crisis in psychiatry and religion.* Princeton, NJ: D. Van Nostrand Company, Inc.

Narramore, C. (1960). *The psychology of counseling.* Grand Rapids, MI: Zondervan Publishing House.

Nelson, M. (1960). *Why Christians crack up.* Chicago: Moody Bible Institute.

Oates, W. (1962). *Protestant pastoral counseling.* Philadelphia, PA: The Westminster Press.

Pfister, O. (1948). *Christianity and fear: A study in history and in the psychology and hygiene of religion.* London: George Allen and Unwin Ltd.

Roberts, D. (1942). *Psychotherapy and a Christian view of man.* New York: Charles Scribner's Sons.

Rogers, C. (1942). *Counseling and psychotherapy: New concepts in practice.* Boston: Houghton Mifflin Company.

Sanua, V. (1969). Religion, mental health, and personality: A review of empirical studies. *American Journal of Psychiatry, 125,* 9.

Tournier, P. (1962). *Guilt and grace.* New York: Harper and Row.

Tweedie, D. (1961). *Logotherapy and the Christian faith.* Grand Rapids, MI: Baker Book House.

Waelder, R. (1960). *Basic theory of psychoanalysis.* New York: International Universities Press.

2

Moving Through the Jungle:
A Decade of Integration

Gary R. Collins
Trinity Evangelical Divinity School

Moving into the field of integration has been compared to the challenging but pioneering task of clearing away brush at the edge of a jungle. Building on the work of early leaders in the psychology-religion dialogue, it is suggested that in future issues of the Journal writers should work at clarifying our goals for integration, retaining our evangelical theology, sharpening our assumptions, focusing on the practical, evaluating emerging trends, sharpening the focus of each issue, and admitting the personal implications of integration.

Several years ago, near the time when the *Journal* began publication, I discussed integration with a seminary colleague who is well known as an evangelical theologian. My friend suggested,

> Christians in psychology are pioneers. Much of the scholarly work in theological and biblical disciplines is a refinement of what already has been discovered, a retreading of well traveled paths, and an avoidance of investigative routes that others have found to be "deadends." In contrast, those who want to integrate psychology with theology or biblical studies are carving new pathways. Such people are like explorers standing at the edge of a jungle with a machete, but with no real sense of where or even how to cut through the brush.

The imagery is picturesque (and I suspect my mind has added a few embellishments over the years) but the point is basic: Integration is a new field, and the people who read or write in journals such as this one often are still "finding their way." We are still refining methodology, deciding which issues are important, determining what needs to be done, and sometimes evaluating whether the effort is worth all of our work, or even possible.

Like the laborer with the machete, however, there is value in stopping periodically to examine our work, to see where we have failed or made progress, and to ponder our next moves.

Such self-examination should start with a reminder that the relationship between psychology and religion has been studied for decades—long before the *Journal* began publication. Freud, Jung, James, Hall, Fromm, Allport, Mowrer, and a host of lesser known people pondered the psychology-religion interface, before most of us were born. The theological and psychological perspectives of these early pioneers were diverse, and "integration" was rarely a goal in their work. Most sought to understand—and sometimes to explain away—religious attitudes and behavior. Nevertheless, their exploratory efforts can give insight into useful methodology, the influence of assumptions, the selection of issues to be considered, and the practical implications of our work. Carefully written critiques which summarize, evaluate, and help readers learn from the work of others have appeared in the *Journal* but, to avoid the mistakes of others and to clarify issues for future investigation, it is essential that we know more about the historical roots of the psychology-theology interaction.

In preparing this article, I reviewed all forty issues of the *Journal* thus far. I had planned to categorize the articles under headings such as "historical overviews," "integration theory," "psychopathology," "pastoral counseling," and "articles on the self," but after a couple of frustrating hours, I abandoned the project. The articles which have appeared in this publication are so diverse that they almost defy classification. Reports of research and historical evaluations have been interspersed with literature reviews and papers on such diverse topics as spiritual conflict, nouthetic counseling, homosexuality, the mental health of Jesus, communication theory, feminism, holiness, demon possession, loneliness, urban ministries, cognitive theory, hypnosis, grace, inner healing, counselor education, systems theory, and masturbation. It could be argued that such diversity is healthy especially in these early stages of our work. Psychology is a complex field concerned with numerous issues, and it is not surprising that the *Journal* covers a variety of topics.

Is it possible however, that we are too diverse? The forty journals on my desk leave me with the feeling that we may be settling for a shotgun approach, moving in various directions at the same time, but with few clear goals, in spite of the carefully stated "publications policy" which appears on the back cover of each issue.

So where do we go from here? The editors' invitation to prepare an evaluation of the *Journal*'s first decade has stimulated me to make several observations about the task of integration and the future of this publication. I emphasize that these are only the opinions of one person, and they are not listed in any special order of importance.

Clarifying our Goals

On the front cover, each issue of this journal is described as "An Evangelical Forum for the Integration of Psychology and Theology." Fleck and Carter (1981) have noted that there is no particular significance to the term "integration." The word has been used, especially in evangelical circles, to describe the relationship between psychology and Christianity, but it does not imply the fusion of two fields into a third discipline, the reduction of psychology to "nothing but" religion (or vice versa), or the lining up of psychological terms alongside somewhat similar Christian concepts and calling the result "integration." Some have suggested that other terms would be better; that it would be more precise to talk about the "synthesis," "interaction," "dialogue," or "interface" between psychology and Christianity. These newer terms may be more accurate, but they have not come into wide use and it now seems unlikely that we ever will shift to a new terminology. We are left, then, with the difficult task of defining integration both conceptually and operationally.

Integration is an emerging field of study. It seeks (a) to discover and comprehend truth about God and his created universe by using scientific methods (including empirical, clinical, and field observations) and the hermeneutically valid principles of biblical interpretation, (b) to combine such findings, when possible, into systematic conclusions, (c) to search for ways of resolving apparent discrepancies between findings, and (d) to utilize the resulting conclusions in a way which enables us to more accurately understand human behavior and more effectively facilitate the changes which help individuals move towards spiritual and psychological wholeness. All will not agree with this statement of purpose, but surely there is value in pondering

what we mean by integration and considering what our integrative efforts should seek to accomplish.

In a thoughtful book published several years ago, Crabb (1977) wrote about "spoiling the Egyptians," taking insights from psychology and making use of those concepts which are compatible with Christian presuppositions and scriptural teaching. In his analysis, however, Crabb did not describe how we go about this task. Like many others, including me, he has written about the need for integration but has said little about the process and methodology of integrating Christianity and psychology. In contrast, Farnsworth's recent article (1982) on the "conduct of integration" is a move in the direction of considering how we approach the integrative task.

In the coming decades, I suggest that we could benefit from additional articles on the meaning, purposes, and methodology of integration. We are unlikely to make significant progress in this field if we have only foggy ideas about these basic issues. We cannot reach the goals of integration if we do not know what the goals are, or if we are not even sure that our integration work is worth doing.

Retaining Our Theology

This journal exists as "an evangelical forum" for integrating psychology and theology. Regretfully, the term "evangelical" has become confused during the past decade. It would be difficult to find a definition which all would accept but surely one foundation of evangelicalism is an acceptance of the Bible as the authoritative Word of God. Evangelicals who write about psychology and religion differ from Freud, James, Ellis, and others, in that we accept the Scripture as God's only written revelation to the human race. The Bible is more than an interesting piece of literature. It is a book of truth which teaches us about God, gives unique insights into human nature, and makes personal claims on our lives.

Since the founding of the *Journal* I have been listed as a "contributing editor." This means that I am asked, at times, to review and critique submitted articles before the editorial committee makes a final decision concerning publication. Within recent years I have noted that some of these articles reflect a drift away from the evangelical position which makes the *Journal* unique.

Surely, no one would like to see this publication move to a narrow fundamentalist position, but neither would it be beneficial to have this become a journal of psychology and religion-in-general. To their credit the editors have kept the *Journal* on a course which might be described as "broadly evangelical." I would hope that this distinctive would be maintained.

One way to retain the present theological perspective is to have more articles written by persons who are theologically trained. That is a difficult goal to accomplish. Few people have dual training and it appears that psychologists and others in the professional helping disciplines are more interested in integration than are theologians. Perhaps readers of the *Journal* should insure its greater circulation among theologians. We need more articles like Smith's controversial appraisal of integration (1975). We could benefit from the input of people like McQuilkin (1975) and others who are active in organizations such as the Evangelical Theological Society.

In the meantime, those who might tend to be critical of periodic theological or hermeneutical naivite in the *Journal* should ponder how they could do better or how they could help psychological writers to be more sophisticated theologically.

Sharpening Our Assumptions

In the first issues of this journal and in two subsequent publications (Collins 1973, 1977, 1981) I proposed that productive integration must start with a consideration of the assumptions in which psychology and theology are constructed. Some readers challenged the proposal that psychology should be rebuilt on biblically based assumptions but there has been little criticism of the idea, proposed by a number of writers, that all scholarly activity is based on presuppositions which must be acknowledged, described, and clarified. Several years ago, Wertheimer (1972) wrote that psychologists simply cannot avoid making at least implicit statements concerning a number of semiphilosophical issues: Such issues involve almost every psychological question or investigation, and where psychologists stand on them is shaped by or shapes their psychological thinking in many important ways.

Wertheimer identified ten fundamental presuppositional questions which every psychologist should consider: (a) Are humans masters or victims of their fate? (b) Are humans basically good or basically evil? (c) Should our research focus on holistic issues or on the smaller elements which make up the whole? (d) Is behavior best explained by physiology or by psychological "mental" explanations? (e) Should we look at behavior subjectively or objectively? (f) In explaining behavior is it better to search the past or to concentrate on the present? (g) Are personality, capabilities, and behavior influenced more by nature or by nurture? (h) Do we aim for theories which are simple or complex? (i) In our research should we strive for precision or for a broader richness? (j) Should we concentrate more on theory or on data collection?

Wertheimer notes correctly that these issues have existed for centuries. They represent ends of continua and not "either-or" categories. They also are issues which should be considered in detail from a Christian perspective.

Sharpening our assumptions must be a continual process, discussed at least periodically within the pages of the *Journal*. But it is not a process which should consume so much attention and effort that we never turn to the research, or to the practical applications which grow out of the assumptions.

Focusing on the Practical

Considering the present widespread interest in Christian counseling (including pastoral counseling), it is surprising that no nationally recognized, high quality evangelical counseling journal exists. Christian counselors must get information from secular journals, books, or occasional articles in *Leadership* or *Christianity Today*.

The *Journal of Psychology and Theology* does publish practical articles, and the "publications policy" clearly indicates that applied papers are welcome. Nevertheless, the major emphasis in the *Journal* appears to be theoretical. I suspect that relatively few pastors or full time professional care givers find the articles to be of practical help in their counseling work. It would be helpful to see more of an applied perspective in this publication.

But what is the major purpose of the *Journal*? Clearly it is not intended to be a "how-to-do-it" guidebook. If we had more emphasis on the practical, there would be less room for theoretical articles or for research reports. Even now it is possible that the editors receive few well-written manuscripts that are both practical in emphasis and sound in psychological and theological scholarship. Instead of more practical emphasis in this publication, perhaps there is need for a new periodical with an applied emphasis which would stand alongside the present *Journal*.

Even if most practical articles were to be published elsewhere, in one applied area the *Journal* must take leadership. We must give more attention to the previously mentioned issue of integration methodology, How do we do integration? What skills and methods are involved? Who is qualified to work in this area" What are the dangers or sources of error? Must we develop techniques that differ from the established methods in psychology and theology? Most of us agree that assumptions are important, and many recognize the value of integration, but how we approach the integrative task could be a major emphasis of this *Journal* in the coming decade.

Evaluating the Trends

The field of psychology is so diverse and popular that fads and emerging trends appear often in both professional and nonprofessional circles. Some of these contemporary movements fade quickly, but others persist, exert a major influence, and merit careful, fair evaluation. Carter's analysis of the Gothard seminars (1974), his appraisal of nouthetic counseling (Carter, 1975), and the Alsdurf and Malony (1980) critique of Stapleton's "inner healing," are examples of critiques written from psychological and theological perspectives.

It is difficult for any one person to be aware of all psychologically-oriented trends, and it is even harder to know how these movements should be evaluated. What is happening at present, for example, in the field of community psychology and how could this movement be critiqued? How do we evaluate the boom in lay counseling, the emergence of church counseling centers, the growing self-help movement, or the interest in cross-cultural psychology? This is neither a political nor a social psychology publication, but is there room in the *Journal* for competent and balanced analyses of social issues such as the influence of the Moral Majority, the anti-nuclear movement, the electronic church, the apparent increase in mate beating, the interest in occult phenomena, or the emergence of psychology among Christians in non-American cultures?

I hesitate to make predictions about future trends, but it appears that religious experience may become an issue of increasing interest. At the turn of the century, the early pioneers in this field wrote about the psychology of conversion, faith healing, and worship. These still are significant issues, and so are glossolalia, parapsychology, demon possession, and altered states of consciousness. During the past decade articles have appeared dealing with many of these topics, but few are of an "overview and critique" nature.

Articles designed to help readers keep abreast of emerging trends might be interspersed with articles suggesting methodology for evaluation. How do we evaluate religious experience or new movements from a psychological and theological perspective? College students are not the only people who might like an answer to that question.

Sharpening the Focus

The second issue of the *Journal* (April 1973) was a special issue commemorating the work of Paul

Tournier at the time of his 75th birthday. A forthcoming issue is planned which will focus on psychology and missions (Fall, 1983). Between these two issues there have been no clear special emphases. Each issue is a collection of articles, usually on a variety of unrelated topics.

Clearly this reflects an editorial policy which has worked well in the past, but would there be value in devoting, say, half the articles in each future issue to a special topic? Other journals do this and for me, at least, it adds interest. In addition to missions, could there be issues of the *Journal* devoted to topics such as Christian theories of counseling, the psychology of worship, values, sex counseling, parapsychology, spiritual maturity, pastoral psychology, the nature of peprsons, or psychological perspectives on hermeneutics and apologetics.

I realize that this is easier to propose than to accomplish. It is easy for a critic to say what should be in a journal; it is much more difficult for editors to find appropriate high quality articles. *The Counseling Psychologist* advertises coming special issues in advance, solicits relevant articles, and appoints a guest editor for each issue. As a staff decision, *Leadership* editors decide on the topic for each issue and invite qualified writers to prepare articles. These are printed alongside unsolicited manuscripts. Could the *Journal* develop similar policies?

Perhaps this is the point to make a comment about research. It is my impression that the overall quality has not been good. The desire to include empirical research in this *Journal* is admirable, but surely no research is better than poor research. The quality in the future should be better and sharper.

Admitting the Personal

Integration can be an aloof intellectual enterprise, mentally challenging but personally irrelevant. Carter and Narramore (1979) challenge this impersonal perspective with the proposal that in addition to

the relating of secular and Christian concepts ... integration is also a way of living and a way of thinking. In fact, it seems to us that very little conceptual integration is possible without a degree of personal integration.... It is far too easy to ensconce ourselves securely behind the walls of our theological or psychological professionalism in order to avoid facing the truth about ourselves and consequently being open to new perspectives.

As Christians our aim must not be simply to pursue isolated intellectual understanding. The clear message of Scripture is that God intervened in history to change lives.... Integrative efforts come alive when we recognize their eternal aspect and see our work as part of humanity's God-ordained task of reconciling men to God, themselves, and others. (pp. 117-118, 121)

This viewpoint is not typical of the unbiased perspective which most professional journals seek to attain. Total objectivity is impossible, however, and it is more honest intellectually to admit our values and to state them openly than to pretend that we are completely objective or neutral.

Most of the writers in this journal would claim to be Christians and as such we cannot deny the personal relevance and spiritual implications of our integrative work. This, of course, does not need to be stated in every article, but perhaps it should be mentioned occasionally and remembered frequently.

In his perceptive volume on the Christian mind, British critic Harry Blamires (1978) proposed that we need to "think christianly," viewing all issues from a Christian perspective and in terms of the human being's "eternal destiny as the redeemed and chosen child of God" (p. 42). Blamires assumes that there is nothing that one can experience, however "trivial, worldly, or even evil," which cannot be thought about "christianly."

Is it possible that we who work in this field and read the *Journal* can learn to "think christianly" and "think psychologically" about our academic interests, our counseling, our world, and our personal lives? Such thinking, if done carefully, can give rise to high quality articles which will continue to enrich the pages of the *Journal*, and will contribute to the continuing movement through the jungle of psychology-theology issues.

References

Alsdurf, J., & Malony, H. N. (1980). A critique of Ruth Carter Stapleton's ministry of "Inner healing." *Journal of Psychology and Theology. 8*(3), 173-184.

Blamires, H. (1978). *The Christian mind.* Ann Arbor, MI: Servant. (Originally published, 1963)

Carter, J. D. (1974). The psychology of Gothard and Basic Youth Conflicts Seminar. *Journal of Psychology and Theology, 2*(4), 249-259.

Carter, J. D. (1975). Adams' theory of nouthetic counseling. *Journal of Psychology and Theology, 3*(3), 143-155.

Carter, J. D., & Narramore, S. B. (1979). *The integration of psychology and theology: An introduction.* Grand Rapids, MI: Zondervan.

Collins, G. R. (1973). Psychology on a new foundation: A proposal for the future. *Journal of Psychology and Theology, 1*(1) 19-27.

Collins, G. R. (1977). *The rebuilding of psychology: An integration of psychology and theology.* Wheaton, IL: Tyndale.

Collins, G. R. (1981). *Psychology and theology: Prospects for integration.* Nashville, TN: Abingdon.

Crabb, L. J., Jr. (1977). *Effective biblical counseling.* Grand Rapids, MI: Zondervan.

Farnsworth, K. E. (1982). The conduct of integration. *Journal of Psychology and Theology. 10*(4), 308-319.

Fleck, J. R., & Carter, J. D. (Eds.). (1981). *Psychology and theology: Integrative readings.* Nashville, TN: Abingdon.

McQuilkin, J. R. (December 30, 1975). *The behavioral sciences under the authority of Scripture.* Paper presented at Evangelical Theological Society. Jackson, MS.

Smith, C. R. (1975). What part hath psychology with theology? *Journal of Psychology and Theology, 3*(4), 272-276.

Wertheimer, M. (1972). *Fundamental issues in psychology.* New York: Holt, Rinehart and Winston.

3

The Search for Truth in the Task of Integration

James D. Guy, Jr.
Graduate School of Psychology
Fuller Theological Seminary

The task of integrating psychology and Christian theology can be spoken of as the search for truth concerning the nature of mankind and our existence. God is the source of all truth, and truth is revealed to us through both general and special revelation. The crucial issue is whether or not mankind can fully know and understand this truth. The model for integration proposed by Collins is an example of a system which assumes that we can fully and accurately discover and interpret truth. This assumption leads Collins to imply that one true model for integration may exist as well as one true set of therapeutic assumptions, techniques, and goals. Careful examination of biblical data, as well as recognition of numerous conflicting theories about the truth, may lead one to conclude that we cannot fully discover and understand truth with total accuracy. The implications of this fact for the task of integration are considered in detail.

The task of integrating psychology and Christian theology is too broad and diverse to adequately define or limit its parameters. Because of its expansive nature there are multiple ways of approaching the problem. For the purposes of this discussion, the task of integrating psychology and Christian theology will be spoken of simply as the search for truth concerning the nature of humanity and our existence. In this search, the disciplines of psychology and theology serve as tools which aid in the discovery of this truth. As such, they complement, enrich, and inform each other within the total process of discovery and systematization. This interaction hopefully results in a higher level of insight and understanding concerning the nature of humanity and the nature of our relationships with God and other persons.

Rather than proposing a specific model for the integration of psychology and theology, I have chosen to direct my comments towards some of the basic, foundational considerations which underlie the formation of specific integrative models. These personal reflections are offered to encourage further dialogue and discussion concerning the presuppositions involved in the task of integration.

The Search for Truth

If the integration of psychology and theology is to be regarded as the search for truth concerning human nature, an initial question logically emerges regarding the etiology of that truth. Most, if not all, involved in the task of integration identify God as the source of truth (Carter & Mohline, 1976; Collins, 1977; Jeeves, 1960; Lambert, 1961; Meehl, Klann, Schmieding, Breimeier, & Schroeder-Slomann, 1958). A commonly held presupposition is typically stated in the following manner: God exists, and he is the source of all truth (Collins, 1977). Choosing to avoid the numerous philosophical issues concerning the nature and existence of truth, most models of integration assume that this is a basic, self-evident premise. This implies that truth is absolute and eternal, being grounded in the changeless nature of God. However, it is important to note that in identifying a single source of truth, it does not follow that there is a single means of revelation. Furthermore, one source of truth does not necessitate nor guarantee harmony in the perception or interpretation of that truth. Though there may be a single source of truth, there may be several means of revealing it, as well as many ways of perceiving and interpreting it. The obvious impact of these factors upon the task of integration is quite profound.

If integration is conceptualized as the search for truth concerning human nature, and God is identified as the source of this truth, the next logical issue involves the revelation of this truth. It has traditionally been held that God reveals this truth to us through both general and special revelation, with both nature and the Bible serving as expressions of representations of this truth. The disciplines of psychology and theology are attempts to discover and systematize truth by means of the study of the natural sciences and biblical revelation.

Can We Know the Truth?

These basic presuppositions lead to a central issue: Are we capable of knowing this truth? Are we capable of totally discovering, accurately perceiving, and correctly systematizing this revealed truth concerning the very nature of humanity and our existence? More specifically, can the person involved in the integration of psychology and theology realistically hope to discover absolute truth and obtain accurate insight and knowledge about human nature?

The way in which this question is answered has a profound impact upon the task of integration. The answer shapes and determines the direction of study and the model which is to be constructed. It is at this crucial point that I feel a number of current scholars may have made a serious error. To explore the full impact of this question, it will be necessary to develop the issues in more detail.

As a professor in a major evangelical seminary, an author of several books on integration, and a popular conference speaker, G. Collins is regarded by many as a spokesman and leader in the task of integrating psychology and theology within a conservative evangelical framework. In his recent book, *The Rebuilding of Psychology: An Integration of Psychology and Theology* (1977), he sets forth a model based upon the assumption that we can, indeed, know the truth. Collins begins with the basic premise that God exists and is the source of all truth. This he feels is true by definition. He then suggests that a corollary exists which logically emerges from this premise. Man, who exists, can know the truth (1977, p. 152). Collins states that the truth of this corollary is self-evident within the truth of the premise. For support, Collins points to John 8:31-32, "You shall know the truth, and the truth shall set you free," and John 16:13, "He (the Holy Spirit) shall guide you into all truth," as God's promise that Christians can know the truth about the nature of humanity and our existence (1977, pp. 126-128). For these reasons, Collins concludes, we (at least Christians) can know the truth. The implications of this position for the task of integration will be discussed later.

There may be a number of serious difficulties in this position. First of all, the statement "Man, who exists, can know the truth," is not a corollary emerging from the premise "God exists and is the source of all truth." In geometry, a corollary is a logical truth which is self-contained within the premise. It becomes true automatically when the truth of the premise has been established. It is "an immediate inference from a proved proposition" (Webster, 1977). In this case, however, the existence of God does not necessitate the existence of man, nor does the fact that God is the source of all truth establish the fact that man can know this truth. Therefore, the statement "Man, who exists, can know the truth" is not, in fact, a corollary, but it is a separate presupposition. As such, it can be either true or false, regardless of the validity of the basic premise.

As noted above, Collins cited John 8:31-32 and John 16:13 in support of his position that God has promised that man can know the truth. However, study of the Greek text reveals that the truth spoken of in both of these references is the truth of the gospel message which leads to freedom from the bondage of sin, and into the victory of eternal life (Thayer, 1889). Jesus appears to have been referring to spiritual wisdom which leads to salvation, rather than empirical accuracy which leads to complete truth and understanding of human nature and our existence. Therefore, it appears that these texts may not support the premise that we are able to know absolute truth in the integration of psychology and theology. Quite to the contrary, the Bible seems to indicate that we are incapable of discovering and systematizing total truth. We are a limited creation; though we were created in the image of God, we were not given the ability to know the mind of God (Isaiah 55: 8-9). Our created limitations hinder us from knowing truth as God knows it. Furthermore, because of the Fall and the constant degenerative effects of sin, our created capacities for knowledge have been further hindered and restricted. Sin has handicapped our ability to know the truth. As a result we see dimly, through a fog, and truth appears distorted and confused (1 Corinthians 13:12).

Experience provides evidence that we cannot know total truth with complete accuracy. General revelation is one source of revealed truth which can be studied in an attempt to discover the truth about human nature. By studying nature through the disciplines of science, we make many hypotheses concerning truth as it is revealed in the patterns of nature. Unfortunately, because of our limitations, we are unable to fully know the truth due to errors in observation and interpretation (Barbour, 1968, Salisbury, 1965). We may misperceive the truth due to personal unique biases. Or the cultural context may distort and introduce error into our observations. Human limitations may lead to miscalculation, unsuitable or inadequate measuring techniques, or errors in interpretation and systematization. It does not appear that we are able to fully or accurately perceive and interpret truth as it is revealed through nature, due to our created limitations and the effects of sin.

The results of these limitations are readily apparent in the history of science. Mankind knows relatively little about "truth" as it is revealed through nature. The existence of numerous, conflicting hypotheses about truth attest to this fact. Constantly changing theories suggest that we may be unable to know the truth in a total, all-inclusive sense. At the very least, it can be said that up to this present time we have been unable to discover and systematize absolute truth through our study of nature.

Special revelation is a second source of revealed truth, and we may attempt to know the truth through the study of the Bible. The Scriptures reveal ultimate truth about mankind and our existence, as does nature. Theology is an attempt to systematize and conceptualize this truth (Barbour, 1968; Meehl et al., 1958; Oates, 1958; Salisbury, 1965). Attempts to know the truth as it is revealed through the Bible are prone to the same errors and inaccuracies found in the observation and interpretation of truth as it is revealed through nature (Jeeves, 1960). Many of the same tools of observation and systematization are used, and the interpretation of biblical truth is subject to many of the same errors of bias, cultural influence, and miscalculation and misinterpretation (Meehl, et al., 1968). Therefore, we may be capable of only partial knowledge of truth as it is revealed through the Bible. While the Holy Spirit may give wisdom which leads to salvation and a meaningful life, our attempts to observe and interpret truth contained in the biblical data may continue to be plagued with error. Therefore, it can be concluded that we probably cannot totally and accurately know the truth as it is revealed through special revelation.

The results of this problem are again quite apparent. There are numerous, conflicting theories about truth as it is revealed in the Bible. Constantly changing interpretations indicate that, while the Bible does contain truth, we may be unable to fully know it due to errors in observation and interpretation. Each person's theology is uniquely their own, shaped by their own bias and culture (Allport, 1950).

This line of reasoning leads to the following conclusion. The existence of numerous, conflicting, and constantly changing theories about truth, as it is revealed through both general and special revelation, suggests that efforts to observe and interpret revealed truth are plagued with error and inaccuracy. Therefore, it appears that we are unable to fully know the truth since our knowledge is partial, at best.

Implications

In proposing that we can know truth, one is forced to deal with the existence of a great diversity and plurality among theories concerning this truth which are evident in both psychology and theology.

Collins does this by suggesting that this great diversity of theories indicates the presence of error. In his striving to formulate a model of absolute truth, all presuppositions and theories which have limitations and some degree of error are cast aside (1977, pp. 70-90). As a result, Collins suggests that empiricism, relativism, naturalism, and operationalism must be rejected because they are only partially true. The presence of error seems to invalidate their usefulness in discovering and understanding total truth.

The implications of this model for the integration of psychology and theology are quite significant. If the truth about human nature and our existence can be known, and if the Bible is to be the primary and authoritative source of this truth, the basis for the integration of psychology and theology must lie in the observation and interpretation of the biblical data. Collins suggests that the Bible should be the source of all therapeutic assumptions, techniques, and goals (1977, pp. 126-132). The implication is that it may be possible for the Christian psychologist to discover one "true" set of therapeutic assumptions, techniques, and goals. This suggests the existence of one true model for the integration of psychology and theology which can be discovered and known with certainty and accuracy.

If, on the other hand, one rejects the notion that we can know the truth, the implications for the task of integration are quite different. First of all, diversity need not be regarded as an enemy. Because we are unable to fully and entirely know truth, all of our hypotheses and theories concerning this truth will be inaccurate and only partially true. However, partial error does not invalidate partial truth. The limitations of a given theory do not cancel its validity. All theories about truth must be regarded as partial conceptualizations of that truth. Because they are human theories about God's truth, they will be distorted by our limitations and errors. Yet, they still have value, and they still represent or reflect ultimate truth. With this view, diversity and conflict among various theories about truth actually bring about a process of growth and development. Plurality, with its controversy and debate, may result in higher levels of accuracy in the observation and interpretation of the truth. Numerous conflicting and changing theories about truth tend to bring refinement and elimination of error. While we will never totally know the truth in our present state, this diversity will enrich and inform our efforts at gaining more accurate notions about that truth.

Toleration and affirmation of diversity make it unnecessary to construct a hierarchy of truth such as the one proposed by Collins. Because we are unable to know the truth and our attempts to do so are prone to error, the conclusions of theology are prone to the same errors as those made when formulating the conclusions of science. Neither set of theories about truth needs to have ultimate authority over the other (Lambert, 1961; Stace, 1952). Assumptions about the truth as it is revealed in the Bible need not be regarded as authoritative over the assumptions of science. If God is, indeed, the source of all revealed truth, any apparent contradiction is the result of error in observation or interpretation of that truth in the disciplines of science or theology, or both (Langford, 1966; Meehl, et al., 1958). Because error is probable in either field, diversity can be viewed as a stimulus for growth and development—a process which hopefully will result in higher levels of accuracy and understanding in the search for truth.

If we are unable to fully discover and accurately interpret the truth about human nature and our existence, the search for one "true" model of integration will be quite fruitless. All scholars involved in the task of integration will be prone to make errors. No single model will achieve total omniscience. Therefore, numerous and conflicting theories may be legitimate and desirable, leading to higher levels of truth and accuracy. Both psychology and theology will provide clues to enable those involved in the task of integration to formulate theories about this truth. Each model will contain some degree of truth, and dialogue and controversy will tend to refine that truth and decrease the amount of error. There will be no single model of integration, nor will there be one set of therapeutic assumptions, techniques, or goals which are totally accurate and true. Christian psychologists are free to adopt any one of a variety of models and orientations as they seek to work out a personal integration within the scope of their own private ministries.

Conclusion

To recognize that man is unable to fully know the truth is to risk some degree of skepticism. However, in the search for truth such a realization is necessary in order to avoid illusion and fantasy. Dialogue amidst this uncertainty serves as a catalyst for greater accuracy and understanding in conceptualizing truth. When dialogue is silenced, growth ceases.

Christian psychologists need not be troubled by the variety of integrative models found in the literature today, nor need they be troubled by the diversity of therapeutic assumptions, techniques, and goals. As professionals, they must recognize that all models, including their own, contain a degree of error. As Christians, they must search both the

Scriptures and their hearts as they seek to better understand the truth which is revealed through special revelation. As scientists, they must search nature with hopes of gaining new insights into the truth revealed through general revelation. Finally, they must be willing to allow their personal models to be informed by those of others. This process will regard controversy and diversity as catalysts for growth, bringing excitement and joy rather than fear and defensiveness.

While these observations may appear overly simplistic to some, a review of the current literature in the field of integration will reveal that these comments may indeed be warranted. Elements of intolerance and authoritarianism have appeared which tend to silence meaningful dialogue. Amidst the diversity, conflicts, and turmoil which result from the imperfection of our observations and interpretations of the truth as God has revealed it, let us strive together to affirm each other in our attempts to gain a more accurate understanding of the truth. Let's not confuse the fact that we are unable to know total truth with the fact that we can know greater degrees of truth than we presently know. Herein lies the value of diversity and dialogue.

References

Allport, G. W. (1950). *The individual and his religion: A psychological interpretation.* New York: Macmillan.

Barbour, I. G. (1968). *Science and religion.* New York: Harper and Row.

Collins, G. R. (1977). *The rebuilding of psychology: An integration of psychology and theology.* Wheaton, IL: Tyndale House.

Jeeves, M. (1960). *Contemporary psychology and Christian belief and experience.* London: Tyndale.

Lambert, J. (1961). *Science and sanctity.* London: Faith Press.

Langford, J. (1966). *Galileo, science, and the church.* Ann Arbor, MI: University of Michigan Press.

Meehl, B., Klann, R., Schnieding, A., Breimeier, K., & Schroeder-Slomann, S. (1958). *What, then, is man?* St. Louis, MO: Concordia.

Oates, W. (1958). *What psychology says about religion.* New York: Association.

Carter, J. D., & Mohline, R. J. (1976). The nature and scope of integration: A proposal. *Journal of Psychology and Theology, 4*(1), 3-14.

Salisbury, F. (1965). *Truth by reason and by revelation.* Salt Lake City, UT: Deseret.

Stace, W. T. (1952). *Religion and the modern mind.* New York: Lippincott.

Thayer, J. (1889). *Thayer's Greek-English lexicon.* Grand Rapids, MI: AP&A.

Webster's new collegiate dictionary. (1977) Springfield, IL: Merriam.

4

Christ, The Lord of Psychology

Eric L. Johnson
Northwestern College

The lordship of Christ over all of a Christian's life is an assumption basic to Christianity. The acknowledgement of his lordship in psychology is especially problematic today because of the pervasive naturalism and neo-positivism of modern psychology. Nevertheless, an understanding of the kingdom concept in Scripture suggests that Christians are inevitably called to work towards the expression of Christ's lordship in psychology. This occurs as the Christian pursues psychological knowledge and practice *before God*, aware that all true truth about human nature is an expression of God's mind, that sin and finitude limit one's ability to grasp the truth, that the Scriptures are needed to properly interpret human nature, and that kingdom activity involves a faithful response to Christ's lordship in one's work with others and one's knowing of human nature.

When Paul the apostle first came into contact with Jesus Christ, he was asked by Jesus, "Why are you persecuting me?" and Saul responded, "Who are you, Lord?" (Acts 9:5, New American Standard Bible). The voice answered, "I am Jesus the Nazarene, whom you are persecuting," and Saul responded, "What shall I do, Lord?" (Acts 22:7-10). Saul addressed Christ as "Lord" immediately and this practice continued throughout his life. In all his letters, as well as the rest of the New Testament, the term "Lord" was used to refer to Jesus. Acknowledging Christ's lordship involved repudiating all former gods and submitting to Christ's absolute supremacy over all life (Harris, 1986), and entering into a certain authority relationship with Christ in which the Christian lived in submissive but active obedience to his master: "It is the Lord Christ whom you serve" (Col. 3:24). Consequently, everything the Christian does is to be done in Jesus' name to the glory of God (Col. 3:17; 1 Co. 10:31). Submitting to the authority of Christ in all of one's life was a distinguishing mark of an early Christian and seems fundamental to Christianity.

The Offense of Christ's Lordship Over Psychology

The purpose of this article is to explore how Christ's lordship relates to the field of psychology. This is a task fraught with difficulties today because the naturalism and neo-positivism that pervade psychology preclude any such use of religion within psychology. Most psychologists would argue that psychology and psychotherapy are disciplines or activities that are relatively neutral with regard to religious issues. As any introduction text suggests, psychology, like any good science, ought to be as objective as possible and all findings and theories should be capable of verification by any interested and knowledgeable party (cm. Atkinson, Atkinson, Smith, & Bem, 1990; Kalat, 1993; Wade & Tavris, 1993); therefore, specifically Christian beliefs have no place in the science of psychology. Similarly, while modern psychotherapists acknowledge that the counselor's values cannot be kept out of therapy (Corey, 1991; George & Cristiani, 1990), it is assumed, nevertheless, that the counselor ought not to teach certain beliefs or "direct their clients toward the attitudes and values *they* judge as being 'right'" (Corey, 1991).

In such a context, the concept of the lordship of Christ simply does not make sense. Yet, as many have suggested in recent years, modern psychology and psychotherapy are not nearly as neutral or objective as is popularly assumed. Rather, they are historically-conditioned disciplines and sets of practices that have arisen within the last 100-150 years. In appreciation for their contributions to modern life and awareness, it must not be overlooked that psychology and therapy are situated in a particular time and place in the history of humankind. Therefore, to understand them best, one must locate them within their historical context. As both a molder and reflector of 20th century attitudes towards human nature, modern psychology and therapy share the positivism, relativism, individualism, and secularity that dominate modern thought (Buss, 1979; Danziger, 1990; Evans, 1989; Farnsworth, 1985; Gross, 1978; Lasch, 1979; Toulmin & Leary, 1985; Vander Goot, 1986; Yankelovich, 1981). Modern psychology and therapy are simply modern versions of psychology and therapy (though they are versions that have been usually successful in laying clam to being the only authoritative approach to studying human nature and treating personal problems in the 20th century; Danziger, 1979). As a result, the Christian need not conclude that "only one show can play in this town." Who says that Christ's lordship has no place in psychology? Who set up the rules here? B. F. Skinner? Jean Piaget? Hans Eysenck? Why must I share their assumptions about the extent of Christ's lordship? Perhaps there are different ways of understanding ourselves as Christian psychologists than that prescribed by the reigning secular powers in psychology.

The King and the Kingdom

The belief in Christ's lordship over the believer is rooted in a theme that pervades the Scriptures from beginning to end: the kingdom of God. To better understand how psychology might be brought under the lordship of Christ, I will first examine the nature of the kingdom of God.

God, the King of All

The God of the Hebrew Scriptures presented himself as more than the deity of a small tribe in Palestine; he revealed himself to be the God of the universe. In the beginning it was the God of Israel who created the heavens and the earth. The first humans were accountable to him and essentially obligated to fulfill his commands.

Later, in the Psalms, the theme of his universal lordship is clearly sounded. The Psalmist declared that Yahweh is a great king over all the earth (47:2). He called upon the kingdoms of the earth to sing praises to the Lord (68:32) and shout joyfully before King Yahweh (98:6), and he called upon his hearers to say among the nations that the Lord reigns and that he will judge the peoples (96:10). "For You are Yahweh most High over all the earth; Thou art exalted far above all gods" (97:9). The Hebrews were taught that all the peoples of the world were supposed to live for Yahweh since he is the King of the universe and the King of all.

Rebellious Subjects

However, the Scriptures also teach that God's authority is being contested throughout the world. The fall of humankind occurred through the deceit of an enemy of God who tempted God's image-bearers into rebellion. Much of the rest of the Old Testament presents a contrast between those who submit to Yahweh and those who serve other gods. Consider the conflict between Moses and the leaders of Egypt, the conquest of Canaan, the continual fighting against the Philistines, and the context between Yahweh and Elijah on one side and Baal and his priests on the other. Many of the Old Testament narratives are set up as conflicts between God's servants and his enemies.

The New Testament likewise asserts that there is massive opposition to God's lordship on the earth. This is first demonstrated in attacks upon God's Son. Not too long after the Christ's birth, a pagan King attempted to destroy him (Matt. 2:13-18). Much later, as he entered upon his adult ministry, the devil showed Jesus all the kingdoms of the world and said he would give them to Jesus if he would worship the devil and not God. Christ's response was an Old Testament quote: "You shall worship the Lord your God, and serve Him only" (Matt. 4:8-10). Christ was eventually opposed by the rulers of the Hebrew people, God's chosen; and the New Testament record of the human opposition to God climaxes in the putting to death of God's Son by both Romans and Jews.

John sometimes used the term *world* to denote humanity as rebellious and hostile to God. He quoted Jesus as saying that the world hated Jesus (John 15:18) and did not know God (John 17:25). John also wrote that this world has a ruler besides God to whom it submits (1 John 5:18) who was being defeated through Christ's redemptive actions (John 12:31; 16:11). Paul also recognized a cosmic rebellion. He wrote about "this present evil age" (Gal. 1:4) or "this world" (Eps. 2:2) which is controlled by the "prince of the power of the air, of the spirit that is now working in the sons of disobedience" (Eph. 2:2). Furthermore, he understood that all of humankind participated in this opposition (Rom. 1-3; Eph. 2:1-3). Apart from God's grace, all oppose God. Becoming a Christian then involves being delivered from this "domain" of darkness (Col. 1;13).

The Coming Kingdom

It is into this context that the Son of God entered, declaring, "The time is fulfilled, and the kingdom of God is at hand; repent and believe in the gospel" (Matt. 1:44f). He came to bring in a new kingdom which was really an old kingdom; He came to bring in the reestablishment of God's lordship over his image-bearers. The good news he preached was that God's reign was returning in a definitive way on the earth; justice and righteousness would finally prevail and God's servants would prosper forever. This preaching included a call to his hearers to repent of their sinful ways and believe in this message of his coming reign. Certain virtues were said to be characteristic of those in the Kingdom (Matt. 5:3,5,20; 18:3,4,23fl; 13:44; 25:31-46). Such virtues demonstrate God's reign over his people through their godlikeness and show that this kingdom is presently a spiritual realm manifested in the hearts and lives of God's people. Importantly, God is revealed to be a King who desires to avoid judgment and to bring his rebellious subjects back to sanity, submission, love, and forgiveness (Luke 15:11; John 3:16; Matt: 1-10).

Yet, Ridderbos (1962) points out that the underlying theme of Jesus' teaching on the kingdom is not primarily the salvation of humans; it is the manifestation and vindication of the divine glory. It is God's kingdom, implying that he is its focus as well as its source. The kingdom therefore is not simply the fruit of human activity, but the accomplishment of God's redemptive power within human life. Christ's kingdom parables often have an individual at the center of the action: a man sowing seed (Matt. 13:37), a landowner (Matt. 21:33-41), a king and a marriage feast for his son (Matt. 22:1fl), and a man and his servants (Matt. 25:14). God is this central figure; he is the king who, having final authority, is ordering the events of his kingdom.

The coming of the kingdom will apparently happen in three stages. The complete coming of the kingdom will happen in the future (Matt. 13:33; 26:29; cm. Matt. 5:5). There will be a consummation of the kingdom that will occur when he returns to earth a second time, in the millennium (Stage 2: Acts 1:6,7; Rev. 20:4) and then forever (Stage 3). Yet, the kingdom was also being established during Christ's first coming (Stage 1: Matt. 1:14); Christ could say that the kingdom of heaven was forcefully asserting itself in his ministry, manifested through his miracles (Matt. 11:12; Ridderbos, 1962). However, only after his death and resurrection could Christ make the claim that "All authority has been given me in heaven and on the earth" (Matt. 28:18). Only then did he become the *Lord* Jesus Christ, highly exalted by God, so that in the end "every tongue should confess that Jesus Christ is Lord, to the glory of God the Father" (Phil. 2:9,11). In that day, he will be called King of Kings and Lord of Lords (Rev. 19:16).

The Kingdom and the New Creation in Paul

Although Paul used the term *kingdom* far less frequently than did Jesus, the concept undergirded his theology. As previously mentioned, he viewed Christ as Lord. In Col. 1:13 Paul stated that God "delivered us from the domain of darkness, and transferred us to the kingdom of His beloved Son." However, Paul more often expressed a contrast between two ages or two worlds, than two kingdoms (Vos, 1972). He wrote of a present age loved by sinners (2 Tim. 4:10) of which Satan is the god (2 Co. 4:4), which he contrasted with the age to come (Eph. 1:22). He also wrote of being crucified to this world (Gal. 6:14) and being a part of the new creation (Gal. 6:15; 2 Co. 5:17). Paul's understanding of history appears to have been shaped by a contrast between a present, evil existence and a coming, new existence in which Paul was already participating. Because the believer is "in Christ"

(Paul's most important soteriological phrase), he or she has already received a foretaste of the coming redemption (Rom. 6:1-11) and is participating now in the coming divine world order.'

However, as many writers have pointed out (Ladd, 1974; Ridderbos, 1975; Vos, 1972), according to Paul, while God's ultimate victory has been guaranteed, human history is the playing out of a serious conflict between two ages which continues throughout this stage. There is a tension between what God has already accomplished (and is accomplishing), and the evil, sin, and weakness that remains the experience of those in the kingdom who suffer persecution from others and from within. Perfect redemption awaits. Nevertheless, in this age God in Christ is bringing about his reign on the earth through his people.

The Kingdom and Psychology

The kingdom of God is especially important for this essay because the concept is essentially historical. The kingdom is a dynamic, historical movement of God existing throughout this era in various forms, overcoming evil and extending the reign of God through saved humanity. As an historical process its progress is uneven; much like any social movement, it is characterized by advances and setbacks. However, God will ultimately prevail and bring all things to an end in which he is finally vindicated and glorified. Because the kingdom is an historical process, the concept of the kingdom helps Christians to understand their place in the world and how they are to live during this period.

The modern roots of psychology demonstrate the relevance of this perspective for Christians in psychology. Many of the major figures in early modern psychology were individuals raised more or less within Christian or Jewish families whose life journey involved a moving away from this religious orientation, including such notables as G. Stanley Hall, William James, John Dewey, J. B. Watson, B. F. Skinner, Sigmund Freud, Carl Jung, Karen Horney, Erich Fromm, Jean Piaget, Carl Rogers, and Abraham Maslow. The writings of these individuals, without exception, make clear that they saw their work and the field of psychology as offering more sound alternatives to traditional Judeo-Christian forms of meaning-making. And part of what drove them was likely the excitement that comes with being a cultural revolutionary. Though there are exceptions, much of modern psychology's research and theory-building has grown up within this implicit post-religious dynamic.

Being a Christian in psychology, then, is more than a theoretical enterprise, involving the relating of abstract, a-temporal propositions through "integration." Modern psychology is an historical phenomenon, shaped by psychological, cultural, and religious factors. Throughout the past 100 years, unbelieving individuals in psychology have been living out their lives in largely unconscious yet fundamental opposition to God, and the field of psychology has been shaped to some extent by this underlying anti-spiritual agenda. To cite one contemporary example, most Americans are religious, as well as most people across the world. Religion is very important in the lives of most human beings. Why then has so little attention been paid to religion in the introductory psychology textbooks? It is to people's advantage to reckon with the contextual, spiritual realities within which they work. The kingdom concept provides people with theological justification for such considerations, and alerts them to the fact that all intellectual activity is a dynamic, culturally-embedded, spiritually-charged, kingdom-related enterprise.

But how are individuals to understand psychology as kingdom-activity, activity that is an expression of God's reign on the earth? Surely this would at least include doing one's best and conducting oneself ethically. Doubtless, such quality and integrity does glorify God. However, doing psychology to God's glory involves much more. Many non-Christians advocate honesty and quality. The main difference is that Christianity is necessarily theocentric; *that* is why Christians do what they do. God is the greatest being in the universe and the center of the Christian's life. Consequently, doing kingdom psychology necessarily involves recognizing his centrality within the practice of the discipline. Therefore, I will consider six components of the context within which kingdom psychology operates: the King's mind, the King's mind in creation, the influence of sin and creation grace, the kingdom documents, and the servant's response to the King.

The Mind of the King

God knows all things (1 John 3:20; Heb, 4:13). He sees all that people do (Matt. 6:8), even inside the human heart (Jer. 20:12). Bavinck (1918/1951) argues that God's knowledge is not gained through observations or experience but is eternal. His knowledge existed before the world was formed (Eph. 1:4,5; 2 Tim. 1:9), therefore no one can add to his knowledge (Isa. 41:13ff). With regard to the creation, his exhaustive knowledge of its form is due to the fact that he formed it. God knows all possible things as well. He knows what will happen in history (Isa. 46:100) because he ordained it (Eph. 1:11); but he also knows what could have happened, as well as all things that human imagination can construct

(Plantinga, 1993). Third, God knows what should be. In a disordered world, there is a gap between what exists and what is the ideal state of affairs. God knows how he intended his creation to be, and so he alone is able to reveal his ideal for it.

In Christian thought, God's understanding of the creation is distinguished from the creation, yet the creation is an exact expression of that understanding (Frame, 1987; Stoker, 1973; Van Til, 1969). Christians interested in human beings therefore have a two-fold primary goal: to understand human nature (a) as it is and (b) the way God does. Yet this is a single goal. Knowing something means knowing it the way God does because God's interpretation of something logically precedes one's own understanding (Van Til, 1969). Since God knows a thing perfectly and comprehensively in all its characteristics, significance, and relations with other things (Stoker, 1973; Van Til, 1969), a science is valid to the extent that it recognizes God's understanding of a thing. Put another way, for any proposition p, p is true if and only if God believes it (Plantinga, 1993). A Christian, then, assumes that humans and God can agree about many things, and it is the agreement between the divine mind and the created order *and* the human mind which constitutes true knowledge.[1]

Psychology, then, in the Christian framework, is not an independent activity that operates apart from God; it is dependent upon God's mercy to illuminate human understanding and reveal things about human nature through human reflection, research, and creative insight. The Christian psychologist submits to God's lordship in his or her thoughts and beliefs. The assumption that God's mind is the epistemological goal has value for four reasons. First, it directs people to God at the heart of their knowing. Their knowledge of things is not done in a vacuum; it is relational. In knowing, people have to do with God. Therefore, humans should seek knowledge prayerfully. Second, this assumption constitutes an ideal for which people can and should cognitively strive; it gives individuals something to work towards by providing an ideal for human knowledge. While people can never know human nature exhaustively (the way God does), they can know something about it and they can get closer to God's understanding of it (Van Til, 1969). Third, people have limited access to information about what human nature should be like. Empirical methods can reveal the consequences of certain conditions or behaviors, but they cannot clearly tell people how to evaluate those consequences. They also cannot provide trans-cultural criteria for human maturity and mental health. Yet psychology and especially psychotherapy inevitably assume some normative goals regarding human nature. Because God's mind includes what people should be, science and therapy should be informed by God's understanding of the human *telos*, and not simply human nature as it is.

The fourth value of taking God's mind as one's knowledge ideal is that people need to know the significance of a thing and its relation to other things and to God ultimately, in addition to knowing the thing itself (O'Donovan, 1986). God alone knows the significance of all things, and so the goal is to know God's understanding of a thing's significance. For example, to know that aggression has at least some genetic component is very important knowledge; but to know the significance of that information is another matter. A fact and its significance are found in the mind of God, and some of that mind is revealed in Scripture. So, the Christian's epistemological goal is to understand more of all that God thinks about something.[2]

Getting closer to the whole truth about a thing is the explicit goal of science, but the fulfillment of this aim really depends upon one's religious framework. Much of Western science appears content to study phenomenological facts, regardless of God and the ultimate significance of those facts. However, science does not have to limit itself to this. Science in the kingdom cannot be so neatly cut off from all of life and from God's purposes for the creation. Of course, holding that human beings can know what God knows does not mean that they *do* know what God knows. This important problem, however, must be left to others with more competence and space than I have to deal with it.

Creation: Out of the King's Mind

The second component of the context for kingdom psychology is the object of that science: human nature. The Scriptures reveal that all the creation (including human nature) has order, and that order proceeds from and testifies to God (O'Donovan, 1986). God created all things and continues to hold them together by the word of his power (Gen. 1; Col. 1:17; Heb. 1:3). Jesus Christ is that Word of God (John 1:1-14; cm. Prov. 8:12-36). The Word of God, then, is the source of the inherent lawfulness and order that is found throughout the creation (Frame, 1987), and it is that Word which is the creation's intelligibility, expressed in its structure and development, that is the focus of the scientist. Therefore, whenever the scientist encounters the creation, he or she will encounter some of the glory, wisdom, and power of God (Psa. 19:1-3; Rom. 1;20). This witness is evident within the human as well: one's conscience (Rom. 2:12-13) and joy (Acts 14:17) testify of

God. All of creation is a sacrament (Torrance, 1969) since every aspect of God's creation points beyond itself to its maker and witnesses to God and his wonder. Because God made everything, every fact, every relation between every fact, and every context within which the facts and their relations are situated, both in general and in specific, historically-contingent contexts are what they are because of where they are in the plan of God (Stoker, 1973). As Spier put it (1954),

> Everything created possesses meaning. In other words the creation is not self-sufficient. Nothing exists by itself or for itself. Everything exists in a coherence with other things. And every aspect of reality points beyond itself towards the other aspects of reality. The creation does not contain any resting point in itself, but it points beyond itself toward the Creator. (p. 20)

To ignore or leave out this component in science is to misunderstand the creation. Stoker (1973) wrote "No area, no fact can be objectively, correctly, and truly interpreted unless it be seen in its absolute dependence upon God" (p. 59). But how can that be? Many unbelievers discover many things without even acknowledging God. Stoker, however, distinguished between the "horizontal meaning-moment" and the "vertical meaning-moment" of a thing. The horizontal is the meaning of a thing that makes it different from other things, for example, that which makes a tree a tree and not a butterfly. This dimension of meaning can often be studied by any competent human being. The vertical meaning-moment is its God-createdness and divine significance, and to appreciate this dimension of meaning requires faithful knowing.

However, though distinguishable, these two aspects of meaning are united in the mind of God. and so they should be united in the minds of God's servants. To leave out the vertical dimension is to leave out what is arguably the most important feature of any fact: its God-relation. Obviously an unbeliever can know much about a particular species of tree: the shape of its leaves, the type of bark it has, its fruit; but to leave out the Maker of the tree is to miss the preeminent fact of the tree. Suppose someone were to say that he or she knew who the founder of operant conditioning was, that he had worked for the government during World War II, that he did most of his research on rats, that he wrote a novel that illustrated his views on human conditioning, and that his name was Albert Bandura. Could one say that that person knew who the founder of operant conditioning was? Similarly, to leave God out of one's understanding of something is to miss what is most important.

This is especially relevant in psychology where the subject matter is so clearly and directly related to God. In such areas the witness of God helps to shape the content of human understanding of the topic itself. How can one understand human beings in God's image without reference to God, that which is being imaged? How can people properly understand things like human motivation, agency, or self-esteem without reflecting upon human-relatedness to God? So, recognizing God is required for the most comprehensive psychology.

The Tendency to Obscure the King's Mind

That humans see things in biased ways has become a truism in social psychology (Nisbett & Ross, 1980). These biases are due to prior learning and training, as well as a pervasive proclivity to see things in ways that enhance one's positive self-assessment (Myers, 1980). However (perhaps related to this self-serving bias), it is apparent that humans also have a bias against God and all that pertains to him. This bias leads people to resist seeing things his way, insofar as such truth bears on their relationship with and accountability to him; so that the closer the topic is to this vertical dimension, the religious core of human existence (Jones, 1986), the more the truth is obscured. Consequently, the human sciences and especially religion are the most affected; mathematics and physics appear to be hardly affected at all.[3] In psychology, this motive alters perception research very little, but distorts judgments about maturity and abnormality significantly more, since such judgments are more closely connected to one's relation with God. This tendency to obscure the truth has been termed "the noetic effects of sin' (Nash, 19188; Westphal, 1990).

Though Christians have been set free fundamentally from the power of sin through Christ, they are by no means exempt from its influence. In fact, a perverse side-effect of being reconciled to God can be a false self-confidence that leads them to act as if they have an immunity from error and self-serving bias. The results of such attitudes in the church are as disastrous as they are evident. Yet having been freed from the need to defend themselves, Christians, of all people, should be aware of the sinful resistance of the human mind to the truth (as well as the limitations of the human mind due to the finitude of human beings). This awareness should foster the kind of humility that leads the Christian to submit to the truth wherever found, to weight confidence according to the evidence, to seek new knowledge, and to relinquish false beliefs in the light of further evidence.

A Gift from the King: Creation Grace

But if sin is so distorting, how is it that non-Christians know so much that is true? To begin with, the human race is continuing to fulfill the Lord's creation mandate (Van Til, 1959), given in Genesis 1, to subdue the earth. Science is one way fallen humans continue (unwittingly) to obey their God. However, ultimately all good things come from God (James 1:17), and since he is the source of all knowledge and wisdom, whatever any has must have come from him. Isaiah states that God "instructs and teaches" the farmer the skills of farming (28:24-29). God continues to teach his image-bearers. This mercy partially but significantly restrains the noetic effects of sin, allowing God's image-bearers to understand countless facets of his creation, in spite of their alienation from him. This goodness of God to those who continue to resist his purposes has been termed *common grace* (Murray, 1977; C. Van Til, 1972; H. Van Til, 1959). However *creation grace* is used here to underscore its unity and continuity with God's goodness in creation. Nevertheless, this grace is unmerited, given to sinners who live independently of the giver. Moreover, creation grace is given to lead to redemptive grace (Rom 2:4; O'Donovan, 1986), and so is subordinate to it.[4] The unbeliever should be humbled by God's goodness and turn to him to be reconciled. Regardless, as a result of the goodness of the Lord of psychology, non-Christians in the past century have discovered many important aspects of human nature. Though sin continues to obscure some of the most important aspects, non-Christians are enabled to discern much of God's mind in the creation order, and those in God's kingdom will be eager to celebrate God's goodness wherever it appears.

The Kingdom Documents

Especially in light of the obscuring motive of sin, people are fortunate that the interpretation of God's mind in creation does not occur in a textual vacuum. God has revealed truth verbally in the Old and New Testaments. For all its perspicuity, the mind of God in creation is not as clear as his spoken word (Crabb, 1981). The verbal revelation found in the Bible furnishes the inspired substance of a Christian world view as well as the king's revealed will for his subjects' thought, heart, and life. Together with the Spirit, they provide divinely inspired "spectacles" (Calvin 1556/1960) without which people are unable to see the rest of God's word in creation the way it really is. Moreover, the Scriptures are a normative good for the soul. One is commanded to receive them and enter experientially into their truth, for one's own good. While admittedly not written in scientific, technical speech, these documents present themes of tremendous importance to psychology from the standpoint of the kingdom (Johnson, 1992). It is only by becoming thoroughly imbued with a scriptural view of human nature that Christians will be able to offer a real alternative to contemporary, secular psychology that is more consonant with God's views.

Down through the ages, Christians have differed in their views of how to relate the Scriptures (and faith and theology) to philosophy and other academic disciplines. One approach was to see God's word in creation and the Scriptures as fundamentally distinct. Such dualism assumed that truth could be discovered by one's reason (or the practice of science) apart from the revealed truth of the Scriptures, and this approach can be seen in some of the early church fathers as well as later teachers as profound as Aquinas. However, Christians like Aquinas believed there was still a fundamental relation between truth delivered by reason and by revelation through faith. In the modern period, reason's autonomy is radicalized into a liberation from faith, so that reason's (and science's) autonomy has become an unquestioned assumption of modern epistemology (Schaeffer, 1968a; Van Til, 1969). Faith was relegated to subjective opinion, whereas knowledge was (and is) considered fact confirmed by reason (or research).

Currently, evangelical perspectivalism (e.g., Jeeves, 1976; Myers, 1978) largely affirms the religious autonomy of psychology. This position recognizes the importance of religious belief, but argues that good science requires the bracketing of one's faith-beliefs and placing them on a different epistemological level. Certain versions of the concept of integration have also fostered a separation between faith and other forms of knowing. These versions assume the relative independence of theoretical thought in the sciences from faith/theology and imply that the Christian's primary intellectual task is to integrate their religious beliefs with disciplines that have already been developed. However, in such versions, the introduction of faith into the formation of knowledge inevitably becomes a second order process. Psychology is first created by (mostly) those outside the kingdom (who cannot see things theocentrically); and only then is it related to the Christian faith. The problem is that such versions of integration allow faith to be brought into the project too late to be of much formative assistance. Moreover, though appreciative of the effects

of creation grace, such approaches are relatively naive about the noetic effects of sin.

Another ancient approach to the relation of faith/Scripture/theology to philosophy and other disciplines has emphasized the oneness of God's word in creation and Scripture, the dependence of all theoretical thought on issues of faith, and the ultimate unity of human thought in the mind of God. This position maintains that one's ultimate faith-beliefs form a special class of knowledge—beliefs that logically precede and provide the foundation for all other knowledge. Christian thinkers as diverse as Augustine, Bonaventure, Pascal, Kuyper, C. Van Til, Dooyeweerd, and Plantinga argue (in different ways) that everyone possesses faith-beliefs of some sort and these faith-beliefs may legitimately shape what constitutes other knowledge in one's epistemological project.

A word dualism which separates God's word in creation and Scripture must in some way be overcome if one is to develop a vision of human nature that reveals the unity of these two forms of divine discourse that are already united in God. From the Christian standpoint God's mind is the ultimate concern of all science. Moreover, Christ is the Word of God, the singular expression of God's mind. Consequently, he is the integration of the created and revealed rational orders. God's mind revealed in creation and in Scripture is a harmonious unity expressed through Christ, in whom are hidden all the treasures of wisdom and knowledge (Col. 2:3). It is, then, misguided to allow a secular understanding of one aspect of God's word (the creation order) to develop autonomously (especially since it is largely produced by those working on a non-kingdom agenda), and then seek to relate it to the other, post-facto.[5] To gain greater consonance with God's mind, it is necessary to do psychology by dialectically relating the two aspects of the one Word continuously, from the start (using a hermeneutical circle, Palmer, 1969). This should foster the realization of Christ's lordship in psychology more thoroughly than a dualistic approach does, by allowing biblical teachings to suggest potentially fruitful courses of research, theory-building, and counseling, and by permitting a more radical critique of secular models in modern psychology, ultimately leading to greater validity in psychology. (The program of Christian psychology does not reject integration, but it also does not see integration as the sole task of the Christian.)

Kingdom Responses to the Expression of God's Mind

The final component of a kingdom psychology is the Christian himself or herself. The Christian is called upon to respond to God and the revelation of his mind as a kingdom member.

Kingdom knowing and fearing the Lord. The book of Proverbs contains the provocative claim that the fear of Yahweh is the beginning of knowledge (1:7) and wisdom (9:10). Before one can know anything in the comprehensive sense that will be discussed in this section, one must humbly acknowledge and revere the Maker of all things. Von Rad (1972) wrote that the wise men of Israel did not posit a separation between faith and knowledge because they could not even conceive of any reality not controlled by Yahweh. Knowing was an ethical and religious activity for the sage, conducted under the authority of the Lord of life. Moreover, this teaching of Proverbs suggests that the elders of Israel saw that the fundamental danger in the search for knowledge was beginning wrongly, beginning with pride and a neglect of God (Von Rad, 1972). Von Rad goes on to say that

> Faith does not—as is popularly believed today—hinder knowledge; on the contrary, it is what liberates knowledge, enables it really to come to the point and indicates to it its proper place in the sphere of varied, human activity. In Israel, the intellect never freed itself from or became independent of the foundation of its whole existence; that is its commitment to Yahweh. (p. 68)

Of course someone might argue that this teaching of Proverbs is referring to common sense knowledge or moral wisdom like Proverbs, not the sort of scientific reasoning in psychology. However, the wise of Israel were not ignorant of scientific understanding. Solomon, for example, was known for having an immense knowledge of animals and birds (1 Kings 4:29-34). But more fundamentally, Proverbs is explicitly addressing the starting point of knowing. Why would the fear of God be disposed of at some higher, more abstract level of reasoning? If anything, it would seem to be even more important there, to keep one from arrogance. The expression "the fear of God" is simply a short-hand way of describing the inherently theocentric, kingdom context of all legitimate knowing activity.

This use of the fear of God suggests that a Christian's response in science must be one of obedience. According to Frame (1987), knowledge for the Christian goes hand in hand with obedience. "Neither is unilaterally prior to the other, either temporally or causally. They are inseparable and simultaneous" (p. 443). Similarly O'Donovan (1986)

states "Knowledge of the natural order is moral knowledge, and as such it is coordinated with obedience. There can be no true knowledge of that order without loving acceptance of it and conformity to it ... (p. 87). Christians obey God by following him in their truth-seeking wherever he leads.

Declare "the Lord reigns." Simply pondering some of the mysteries in nature (for example, how infants are formed in the womb: Psa. 139:13-15), inevitably produces joyful praise in Christians. The wonder and glory of the creation provokes a response of awe, and an appreciation of the beauty and complexity of the creation as well as its Creator. Given that the tasks of the research scientist, teacher, or counselor include reflecting on such beauty, it would seem appropriate that he or she regularly slip into heart-felt worship throughout the course of a day's activities. Such praise is at least part of what it means to live in God's kingdom.

The absence of such praise in modern psychology provides further evidence that this world is alienated from its maker. Today the Lord of the universe has been banished from his creation and relegated to church buildings and funerals. The Christian is called upon to declare the praises of God among the nations (Psa. 18:49; 57:9; 96:3; 108-3; 96:10). Practicing psychology in the kingdom then inevitably includes sincere declarations of praise and acknowledgements of his lordship.

Contending for the King. Kingdom psychology also involves contending against that which is opposed to the King. While God is seeking all to join his side, his will continues to be resisted on earth. Human history consists of a fundamental communal struggle which will endure until Jesus comes again (Berkhof, 1979; Plantinga, 1990; Schaeffer, 1968b). During this era Christians are called to participate in this supernatural conflict. The Christian psychology teacher, student, researcher, and counselor are clearly implicated in the contest. The field of psychology is not neutral; it belongs to God. Yet, modern psychology demonstrates a pervasive alienation from its master; God is not in any of its theories or practices. It is a set of systems almost completely secular in its ultimate beliefs, interpretations, and conclusions.

Paul recognized this context at the level of knowledge. In 1 Corinthians 1-3 he distinguished between two kinds of knowing; the wisdom of the world or of men (1:20; 2:5, 3:19) and fleshly knowing (3:3) on the one hand, and the wisdom of God (1:21) and words taught by the spirit (2:13) on the other. He warned the Colossians not to be taken captive (a war metaphor) "through philosophy and empty deception, according to the tradition of men, according to the elementary principles of the world, rather than according to God" (Col. 2:8). Apparently they were exposed to certain errors that Paul saw were heretical. He told them to avoid capture by the thinking of the old age (truth that comes strictly from fallen human sources) and to be rooted in Christ who is the source of the new wisdom. You died with Christ, he wrote, to the elementary teachings of the world (2:20); live new in Christ, confident that your new self "is being renewed to a true knowledge according to the image of the One who created him" (3:10). The kingdom has a new wisdom and to participate in the kingdom means to submit to that wisdom and reject the wisdom of this age/world (Dennison, 1985). In 2 Corinthians 10:3-6, Paul makes quite explicit the challenge facing the believer.

> For though we walk in the flesh, we do not war according to the flesh, for the weapons of our warfare are not of the flesh, but divinely powerful for the destruction of fortresses. We are destroying speculations and every lofty thing raised up against the knowledge of God, and we are taking every thought captive to the obedience of Christ ...

Paul called his readers to resist unbelief wherever it appeared and to examine every thought, in order to submit all rebel thoughts to the "obedience of Christ." For the Christian psychologist this would include wrestling with the theories and interpretations of research that make up modern psychology and sifting out the ungodly speculations and prideful independence that are woven into the modern version of the discipline, often so subtly that little that is directly subversive will be apparent to the untrained eye. However, assumptions like humans are no more than organisms or computer-like thinking machines, humans are largely not responsible for their behavior, morality is biology, the highest goal of therapy is self-determined happiness, and normality cannot be absolutely determined, pervade the writings of modern psychology. The kingdom psychologist is called upon to pull out such threads in the tapestry of psychology and reweave the discipline with God's assumptions.

Abraham Kuyper, theologian, founder of the Free University of Amsterdam, and prime minister of Holland (1904-1908) gave much thought to the constrictive place of the Christian in the world. He argued (1898) that thinking minds have been separated into two distinct camps because of *regeneration*, the change in the Christian due to Christ's sal-

vation. According to Kuyper, as the power of regeneration is realized, it leads necessarily to the formation of two kinds of science: one founded on unbelieving principles and inevitably misshapen by sin, and the other founded upon faith in God and submissive to Scripture. He believed that the regenerate and unregenerate are working on essentially two different projects, each going in different directions. Religiously speaking there cannot be any ultimate unity of science because the existence of God's kingdom has created a different set of sciences (kingdom-sciences?) that are conducted to bring glory to God and that are shaped by different assumptions and a different agenda than are sciences created by the non-Christian. The assumptions of the two groups may so differ that even what constitutes grounds for argument may not be shared. Following Augustine, he believed that regeneration leads inevitably to a fundamental antithesis between the city (or kingdom) of God and the city of Man.

Yet Kuyper (1898) recognized that unbelievers can obtain truth. He wrote that scientists practicing the two types of science will not differ in measuring or observing, likewise logic and language are formally the same for both groups. Consequently, many theories and interpretations of data will be valid. (His work on common grace is more extensive than perhaps anyone in the church's history, H. Van Til, 1959. Unfortunately, most of it remains in Dutch.) However, Kuyper believed that the noetic effects of sin predispose unbelievers to obscure the truth at key points, thus resulting in sciences that are proceeding in a non-theocentric direction.

According to Kuyper, then, part of contesting for God's truth in his kingdom involves identifying the truth used in the service of other gods and claiming it for its true source and owner. However, a great difficulty remains: How does the believer discern what is valid as he or she contends for the faith within psychology? This task is incredibly difficult in the present situation, given the profound social pressures and constraints on Christians at the academic power centers of modern culture to think secularly and suppress Christian interpretation. This context can lead to compromises with secular thinking, a result termed *synthesis* (Runner, 1982). Through education and exposure to non-Christian thought, before and after becoming a Christian, the believer inevitably mixes truth and error. However, Runner argues Christians are called to the task of purifying, or reforming, their thinking from secular or pagan influence to increasingly closer conformity to the word of God in creation and Scripture. Part of our task as kingdom-psychologists would therefore include self-criticism, so that we resist our own tendency towards synthesis with non-Christian thought, even while we take advantage of all that is truly good in secular psychology.

What are some psychological topics that should be contended for as Christians interact with those in modern psychology? Because of different assumptions, some topics would be nearly futile to discuss (e.g., sin or the Holy Spirit). However, conversation could occur (and has) on a variety of other subjects, including topics like an emphasis on personhood across the disciplines (Van Leeuwen, 1985), values in counseling (Tjeltveit, 1989), the positive contributions of one's family and social tradition to self formation, the importance of narrative for moral development (Vitz, 1990), ethical criteria for establishing abnormality and psychological well-being, the influence of individualism and capitalism on the counseling profession (Dueck, 1995), the validity of evil and guilt, the reality of volition and the impact of human choice on neurochemistry, and the value of religion for psychology (Jones, 1994).

It should be underscored that the Lord desires that this conflict not be engaged with worldly weapons of slander and arrogance, but kingdom "weapons" of love, humility, and respect for all God's image-bearers. The kingdom is not antithetical to a principled pluralism that listens respectfully to and learns from others, from the standpoint of the faith.

Cooperating with those outside the kingdom. Related to the previous point, many Christian psychologists are working in areas that are relatively uncontentious: e.g., the construction of achievement tests, vision research, treatment of mental retardation, or employee adjustment. Such work usually involves cooperative activity with non-Christians. Though obvious, it should be stated explicitly that such activity, when conducted by faith, consists in a faithful participation in God's creation grace and is legitimate and valuable kingdom work. Such endeavors are no different than teaching at a public school or working in the health services. Christians ought to cooperate fully with all who are working with creation grace. Wariness is only justified when the activity threatens the higher good of redemptive grace.

Developing a Christian psychology. As part of the Christian's response to God's mind in creation, he or she is called to be re-creative. Christian psychologists have more to do than parasitically sift the writings of their secular colleagues. The Christian faith has its own agenda that may or may not resemble the agenda of any secular psychology. Within the kingdom of God, the Christian psychological community is set free to chart new territory in psychology. By becoming immersed in Scripture and the Christian tradition, Christian psychologists may be enabled to discover new facts and theories, devising new lines of research to more accurately understand human nature the way it really is, the way God sees it. Christian psychologists are free to take more seriously the reality of human choice and personal responsibility; agape love, hope, joy, humility, and other distinctively Christian virtues; sin and its development, guilt, and hypocrisy; the demonic; biblically-influenced definitions of abnormality and maturity; spiritual formation according to grace; the indwelling and power of the Holy Spirit; the development of saving faith; the impact of union with Christ on one's self-understanding, self-efficacy, and locus of control; and theocentric motivation; to name a few. Doing so would likely lead to a body of research and theory that is qualitatively distinct from the production of modern psychology. Christians in psychology must do more than simply contribute to the field of psychology as it is. They have an obligation to God and his people to work towards a psychology that is thoroughly consistent with a Christian framework, regardless of its acceptability by secularists. Because of its difficulty, this part of the task has been little realized thus far; however, some promising work has been done in various quarters (e.g., Adams, 1979; Anderson, 1990; Benner, 1988; Crabb, 1988; Evans, 1989; Narramore, 1984; Oden, 1990; Powlison, 1988; Roberts, 1990, 1993; and others).

Integrating within the kingdom. None of this means that integration is unnecessary. However, it should be seen as secondary, rather than primary; subordinate to the task of developing a framework, body of research theory, and practice more submissive to God's whole mind than what is acceptable to modern psychology. This priority suggests a shift from traditional notions of integration which have viewed it as fundamentally interdisciplinary rather than intercommunal. The kingdom psychologist does not seek to integrate faith with psychology, for psychology, as all of life, is an expression of faith. Rather, the goal is to figure out how to make use of psychological work produced by different faith communities (e.g., the modern). The problem is not a category problem as much as a translation problem (cf. MacIntyre, 1988). This type of problem requires one to work at understanding what that community means before translating or reconceptualizing their psychological work into what Christians mean (as opposed to the traditional view which accepts a text's meaning as relatively unproblematic). When integration is seen as the primary duty, a fateful (dualistic) step has already taken place: a rift has occurred between faith and reason/science that integration then attempts to bridge. Though strangely compatible with modernity, this view of integration unfortunately undermines the interpretive role a Christian framework should play in one's thought. In addition, it increases the probability that Christians may unwittingly synthesize unexamined secular assumptions into their belief-system. Lastly, it limits the Christian's creativity, making it impossible to move conceptually beyond the work of other communities.

Nevertheless, having said all that, the research and theory of those outside God's kingdom should be received thankfully as due to his creation grace, to the extent that it accurately reflects the created order. This perspective is especially necessary today since the majority of good psychological research is being done by non-Christians. Consequently, integration, properly conceived, remains an important task.

Integration within the kingdom involves at least five steps. The first step is simply the activation of one's Christian evaluative framework (including faith-beliefs like the Christian story—creation, fall, redemption, and consummation—and other beliefs that relate to human nature, e.g., personhood). Activating this world view schema is a prerequisite for Christian critical thinking; otherwise, one's faith beliefs form a ghetto in one's mind, providing no evaluative influence on the secular material one reads. Second, the attempt is made to understand the finding or concept that is the focus of integration. This understanding will involve reference to the ultimate framework of the author/school in order to adequately interpret its full sense. Third, the finding or concept should be assessed in terms of its compatibility with the Scriptures as well as whether it meets other validity criteria, including theoretic support, statistical procedures, research design, sampling, empirical evidence, and so forth. Problems like sampling or extreme heterodoxy (e.g., the assertion that all humans have a god-self within), would undermine confidence in the finding and could necessitate its outright rejection. This step has long been recognized as essential for Christians in psychology (e.g., Crabb, 1977). If the concept passes this test, its degree of theoretic complexity and, correspondingly, the level of integration that is involved (Larzelere, 1980) will need to be assessed. Simple physiological facts require little in the way of reinterpretation (perhaps simply acknowledging their createdness), whereas therapeutic facts may

require a more radical transformation. Lastly, depending upon these prior judgments, the task of Christian translation or reconceptualization follows. This step entails making sense of the original finding or concept according to a Christian evaluative framework and grammar.

As a first example, consider the relation of positive illusions and mental health. Self-deception has been found to result in better adaptiveness and greater overall happiness, which has led some to conclude that some self-deception is essentially good (Taylor, 1989). A Christian can appreciate such correlations, however, and still recognize that self-deception is usually an evil, so that the good consequences of such cognitive activity are only relatively good, but do not necessarily bring glory to God. Here, integration involves a reassessment of the moral evaluation of a finding. Contrary to positivism, such moral evaluations are a part of psychology (as evidenced by secular evaluations of self-deception like Taylor's). As another example, the naturalistic orientation of locus of control (LOC) research has led to the assumption that there are but two LOC orientations that form the ends of a continuum: internal and external. However, a sophisticated Christian understanding is necessarily more complex. God can be viewed as the ultimate source of one's goodness with that knowledge serving to increase one's sense of self-efficacy. A Christian can then be both strongly external and internal in relation with God. In this example, integration involves the assumption of modern LOC concepts along with the recognition of a Christian's unique, dependent relation with the Creator, which results in more complicated LOC schemata (Stephens, 1985).

Maslow's concept of self actualization requires even greater care in integration. From a distance, the notions of self-actualization and sanctification appear somewhat similar. However, upon closer examination, one sees that Maslow's notion was expressed within a linguistic community and naturalistic framework in which the self is seen as the supreme, orienting principle in human life (Maslow, 1954, 1970).[6] For the Christian, however, relationship is prior, preeminently one's relationship with God. Because God is the center of the universe, Christians throughout the ages have believed that the highest motivational state of which a person was capable necessarily involved experiencing one's Creator/Redeemer. While one may recognize similarities between the peak experiences of true Christians and non-Christians, Maslow himself did not believe dogmatic religion was compatible with self-actualization. Christians, too, should be careful not to equate formal similarity with actual identity. Baboons and humans have many similarities, but the differences are quite profound and are the reason they are grouped in different families. Overlooking such differences should not be tolerated in biology. The problem is even more serious with psychological concepts like self-actualization because considerations regarding the ultimate motivation principle of human life are so dependent on socially-constructed formulations that involve fundamental world view, moral, and theological commitments. Translation here may require leaving the term self-actualization to the humanists. The integrative task will lead the Christian community to learn from Maslow's research regarding the highest form of human life that modern humans outside Christ attain and to note similarities with Christian experience; yet one may need to label the Christian correlate as Christ-actualization or something similar, communicating the inherent theocentric relational base of the highest level of human motivation from a Christian standpoint, and attempt to describe its unique features.

Because of God's creation grace, the vast majority of the theory and research of non-Christians will be valuable. Rarely will any seriously proposed psychological finding or theory have no truth-value. When error is found, it is usually a parasite on truth. Consequently, along with any modification, the translation will require the preservation of whatever conceptual material is deemed valid. (It should be added that throughout the integrative process, there is always a need to be open to having one's evaluative framework corrected within certain theoretic, theological, and epistemological bounds).

Not everyone in the kingdom, however, agrees about the value of integration. Those in the biblical counseling movement question the merit of receiving insights from non-Christians regarding the soul, particularly psychotherapeutic insights (Adams, 1973; Bobgan & Bobgan, 1987; Ganz, 1993; MacArthur & Mack, 1994; e.g., Master's College does not have a psychology major). Admittedly, their primary concern is counseling; and it is here that their criticisms are the most compelling. They have sounded a needed alarm in the kingdom about the lordship of Christ in counseling, particularly in their concern that a secular confidence in the self or human strategies is replacing faithful confidence in the power of God to bring healing to the soul. The biblical counseling movement has seized upon what are arguably two of the most important issues in human life: who shall be Lord and how shall one change into his likeness? However, out of reaction to the synthesis of many well-meaning Christian

therapists; and because of an extreme emphasis on the antithesis and sin; poor, unsympathetic scholarship; and in some cases a lack of biblical charity (e.g., Bobgan & Bobgan, 1989), their critique of modern psychology and integration has greatly oversimplified the interpretation of secular psychology texts and led to much confusion among God's people. Though there are differences in this group (e.g., Adams, 1986 has acknowledged that psychology can be legitimate), their general approach borders on the fundamentalistic and reactionary. They are guilty of not taking seriously enough God's creation grace and seem largely ignorant of the ways God has designed genuine knowledge-formation to proceed in a pluralistic culture. Non-Christian bias has influenced the content and practice of modern psychology, but it is also the case that God has revealed so much about the brain, learning, human development, motivation, social influences, forms of abnormality, and even helpful counseling practices through the labors of secular psychologists. The Lord reigns, and he uses even those who oppose him to bring glory to him (Van Til, 1972). In full agreement with biblical counseling's demand for an increasingly theocentric orientation, kingdom psychologists should, nevertheless, gratefully use God's gifts to non-Christians, through the Christian critical thinking process known as integration, in a subordinate way that reconceptualizes the truth under the authority of God and his word.

Viewing humans multidimensionally and hierarchically. Humans are extraordinarily complex: "The inward thought and the heart of a man are unsearchable" (Psa. 64:6). Only God has exhaustive knowledge of human beings. To know human nature as fully as possible, it is necessary to explore it from many different vantages, including the biological (genetic, hormonal, neurological, morphological), environmental (physical, interpersonal, economic, cultural), behavioral, cognitive, affective, motivational, volitional, biographical, characterological, ethical, and religious; and using many different methods, including observational, case study, cross-cultural, narrative, discursive, deconstructive, and phenomenological. Many of these perspectives and methods have obviously been explored and used in modern psychology. Yet because of the complexity of the task and because of neo-positivist and naturalistic assumptions that limit the explicit use of values within the discipline, modern psychology has neglected some perspectives and been unable to provide an overall evaluative framework within which to interpret, place, and relate the myriads of facts that have been found thus far. However, knowing things like God knows them requires seeing as much of their multidimensional complexity as possible and also means understanding them in their hierarchical interrelations. All perspectives on human nature are important, but some are more important than others, for example, the specifically human and especially the religious dimensions. As an example, biological and behavioral findings need to be interpreted within a larger person-centered framework that recognizes human choice and responsibility, and this framework, in turn, should be interpreted within a theocentric framework in which all humans are understood before God. Progress in the articulation of such an interpretive framework can be seen in the work of Evans (1989), Farnsworth (1985), and Van Leeuwen (1985).

Working toward the King's mind. Lastly, kingdom psychologists are to attempt to realize God's understanding of the human *telos* (or goal) through their activities within the field; God knows what humans should be like. Through Scripture, experience, and research people can come to an understanding of God's desires and ideals for humankind. Serving the Lord requires the Christian psychologist to implement God's revealed values and norms in his or her own life, to help others become what God desires them to be, and to do what he or she can to bring in justice for those who suffer. Consequently, Christians in psychology will by faith be drawn closer to God's will in their personal lives: dealing ethically with others, avoiding biblically-defined immorality and deceit, and helping others self-sacrificially (what Farnsworth, 1985, has termed "embodied integration"). Going further, the Christian researcher might be drawn to do research that focuses on the needs of the poor or handicapped; while the psychology teacher would avoid condoning homosexual behavior when teaching on sexual orientation, and yet foster awareness of the sin of homophobia. Envisioning the human *telos* for his counselees, the Christian psychotherapist would counsel according to God's understanding of human maturity by wisely and lovingly, but inevitably, seeking to foster a deeper, richer relationship between God and their clients, as appropriate. Also, it would seem that therapists in the kingdom would not allow financial considerations alone to dictate caseload but would reach out to those who have no insurance and cannot pay middle-class rates (Dueck, 1995).

Obviously, this kind of work has been done for decades. However, a distinction should be made between kingdom activity that deals in redemptive grace: done in and for the church within an explic-it Christian context; and kingdom activity that deals in creation grace: ministry to others that does not address the religious core of their life, at least not directly, done within a broader cultural context than the church. The former type of kingdom activity includes developing a Christian psychology, teaching psychology at Christian institutions, counseling Christians, assessing and counseling of missionaries, writing to the Christian community, and training families or lay counselors in churches, all with overt reliance upon the Bible and the Holy Spirit. Kingdom activity that deals in creation grace, on the other hand, includes things like helping parolees stay employed, assessing the educational needs of learning-disabled children, doing vocational counseling, teaching at secular institutions, counseling disaster victims, helping families learn to communicate, writing for the secular community, or administering medication to alleviate depression without an ongoing, explicit acknowledgement of the Bible or God's presence. Such work fundamentally is a good that testifies of God's goodness and manifests God's love through Christians to their neighbors.

Yes, as I indicated above, there is an underlying unity between creation and redemptive grace in that the former is given to lead to the latter. Creation grace kingdom activity ultimately serves God's redemptive purposes because it points to the One who is the Savior of all (1 Tim. 4:10). Moreover, Christians need to be strategically placed and wisely involved in the life of post-Christian culture. Christians ought to be prayerfully committed to this type of work, so long as it does nothing to contradict the program of redemptive grace.

The problem is that Christians in psychology may unwittingly work with non-Christians in ways that go against the agenda of redemptive grace and God's creation order. For example, a counselee might seek to alleviate guilt feelings he suffers because of his ongoing extra-marital affair. To help the counselee quell his conscience without addressing the sin would, from a Christian standpoint, be unethical and anti-redemptive. Living in the kingdom requires psychologists to do all they do for God's glory, even if it goes counter to the ethical norms of non-Christians. According to the fundamentally individualistic, secular counseling community, counselors must work within the value-system of the counselee. However, in some cases, the clients' difficulties are a function of the pathology of their values. With such persons, the best thing the kingdom-minded counselor could do would be to help them find better values: the values of the kingdom. Of course, this must be done with integrity, wisdom, and respect for the counselee. Moreover, this may have economic implications, for a respect for the client will sometimes lead to the recommendation that a client find another counselor who shares more of his or her values. Nevertheless, the kingdom-oriented counselor cannot contribute to a client's journey away from the kingdom. Much counseling about issues relating to moral choices, motivation, guilt, purpose in life, interpretation of stress, and self-acceptance has an essentially religious core. Great care must be exercised by Christian psychologists that they not directly or passively confirm counselees in a non-theocentric direction. Whether acting primarily with Christians or non-Christians, the kingdom psychologist seeks to help others move as much in the direction of God's mind regarding human normality and maturity as possible and to do as little as possible that would unwittingly promote movement further away from God.

The believing psychologist is called upon to participate in the kingdom of God. The secular powers that basically control psychology's standards, journals, and educational institutions will make such work difficult; it makes even the understanding of such a task difficult, especially for those trained in such a context. However, the Christian psychologist who is participating in the kingdom of God will be moved to call into question the asssumptions of this age and resist conformity to it, and seek transformation by the renewing of the mind, heart, and life, to joyfully serve the Lord of psychology.

Notes

1. Plato believed that there were various "Ideas," or "Forms," universal concepts that really existed. In contrast, the world was filled with inferior copies of these Ideas. According to Plato, the goal for human knowledge was to understand the Ideas, the universal truths untainted by their instantiation in this world. Superficially, it may look as if the position being outlined here is platonic. Both positions assume some extra-empirical reality that is at the basis of human knowledge. However, there are at least four differences. First, Plato's Ideas were in some way ultimate, standing even over god. For Plato, God wa subject to the Ideas as much as humans were, for he used them as a model in forming the world (Timacus). Christianity assumes that God is ultimate. Second, Plato was referring to universal concepts. God's mind includes much more than universal concepts. As discussed above, God's mind includes the knowledge of all that is,both universal and particular, as well as all that could be and all that should be. Third, the Ideas are impersonal, ultimate principles. However, I have been talking about God's mind. This is a personal reality; it is God himself in his knowledge. Fourth, while God's mind is the extra-empirical source of truth (and so is similar to the Ideas), there is no reason for the Christian to disparage empirical knowledge the way

that Plato did. Humans encounter God's mind through empirical reality, as well as through reason and the Scriptures, all mediated by the Spirit of God. So the creation is a primary means through which one comes to know God's mind.

2. The possibility of knowing things as they really are is contested at the present time (let alone the possibility of knowing God's mind!); first, by those who believe absolute knowledge is impossible (skepticism); and second, by those who have been influenced by Kant (which includes most Western thinkers). Kant (1781/1965) believed that humans could never know a thing as it truly was; only how it appeared to them according to the categories of thought that they project on to the world. Kant did not deny that there was a real world, he simply denied that humans could ever be sure they know it as it really was. But this position poses an interesting problem for the Christian: if Kant is correct then people cannot be sure about anything they believe, including their knowledge of God.

Recently some Christians have pursued a very different tack, attempting to give an account of true beliefs as knowledge that results from the working of reliable belief producing mechanisms (Alston, 1991; Plantinga, 1993). Plantinga (1983) earlier argued that of the whole set of beliefs one has, some are "basic." That is they are assumed in one's thinking and cannot be proven to be true to everyone else's satisfaction, for example a belief in God's existence. Not everyone will agree with that belief; nevertheless, the Christian may hold that belief, given all that he or she knows to be true. Some of what the Christian knows to be true includes the teaching of the Scriptures understood by the Holy Spirit, and the experience of God working in his or her life. More recently, Plantinga, 1993, 19940 has attempted to describe how humans form true beliefs, asserting that they can assume that their cognitive equipment is generally reliable (all things being equal) because it was designed by God for the purpose of obtaining knowledge about things.

Given such Christian assumptions, it is thoroughly plausible that God knows all things, that humans made in his image can truly know some of those things (Plantinga, 1994), and that they should therefore strive to "duplicate' God's thoughts (Frame, 1987). Hume and Kant might not be satisfied with this set of beliefs but the Christian is warranted in holding it.

The Scriptures themselves legitimate such an approach to knowledge for they provide a profound knowledge "test case" (at least a Christian would think so!). The authors of the Scriptures take a common-sense approach to their own knowledge claims. They assume that what they say about God and about human beings is from God, is true, and should be believed; because God is Lord it must be believed. If in fact God has revealed things about himself and human nature through the spoken or written words of humans, then knowledge about God and humans in the Bible is obtainable; and by analogy if true knowledge is obtainable in one book (albeit a very special book), it is obtainable elsewhere. To believe that the Bible has obtainable truth is to indirectly legitimize other sources of information about God's world.

Contemporary Kantians might argue that to posit God's mind is wholly unuseful for epistemology because even if there was such a mind humans would never have any guarantee that they had agreed with it; positing God's mind gives people nothing except perhaps unwarranted self-confidence. However, this criticism is meaningful only in a Kantian universe. The Christian begins by assuming God. It is appropriate for Christians to assume that God's mind is the source of all truth because that is the actual case, given all the evidence that Christians have at their disposal. Just because a Kantian does not find that compelling is not sufficient reason for a Christian to avoid believing in the epistemological ideal of God's mind.

3. Therefore, while Christians in all disciplines are bidden to take them captive to the obedience of Christ (2 Cor. 10:5), the promise of a distinctively Christian mathematics is much less evident than that of the human sciences, and most obviously religion.

4. O'Donovan (1986) asserts that the creation order, distorted through the fall, is vindicated and most fully realized through redemption. Creation grace then is necessarily subordinate to and fulfilled in redemptive grace, both proceeding from the one good will of God.

5. This, of course, also means that theology cannot be done in an experiential or creation vacuum either. The further removed God's word in Scripture is from God's word in creation, the less relevant to one's life it seems.

6. This is not to equate self-actualization with a crude narcissism. That there is qualitative difference between the two processes is beyond doubt. Nevertheless, Maslow's view of human maturity and the people he selected as exemplars both preclude the possibility that orthodox Muslims, Jews, or evangelicals be seen as self-actualizing. It also seems beyond doubt that Maslow's concept is as much an expression as it is a documentation of 20th century American individualism.

References

Adams, J. (1973). *Competent to counsel.* hillipsburg, NJ: Presbyterian and Reformed.

Adams, J. (1979). *More than redemption: A theology of Christian counseling.* Phillipsburg, NJ: Presbyterian and Reformed.

Adams, J. (1986). *How to help people change.* Grand Rapids, MI: Zondervan.

Alston, W. P. (1991). *Perceiving God.* Ithaca, NY: Cornell University Press.

Anderson, R. S. (1990). *Christians who counsel: The vocation of wholistic therapy.* Grand Rapids, MI: Zondervan.

Atkinson, R. L., Atkinson, R. C., Smith, E. E., & Bem, D. (1990). *Introduction to psychology* (10th ed.). San Diego, CA: Harcourt Brace Jovanovich.

Bavinck, H. (1951). *The doctrine of God* (W. Hendriksen, Trans.). Grand Rapids, MI: Eerdmans.

Benner, D. G. (1988). *Psychotherapy and the spiritual quest.* Grand Rapids, MI: Baker.

Berkhof, H. (1979). *Christ: The meaning of history.* Grand Rapids, MI: Baker.

Bobgan, M., & Bobgan, D. (1987). *The psychological/The spiritual way: Are Christianity and psychotherapy compatible?* Minneapolis, MN: Bethany.

Bobgan, M., & Bobgan, D. (1989). *Prophets of psychoheresy.* Santa Barbara, CA: EastGate.

Buss, A. R. (1979). The emerging field of the sociology of psychological knowledge. In A. R. Buss (Ed.), *Psychology in social context* (pp. 1-23). New York: Irvington.

Calvin, J. (1960). *Institutes of the Christian religion* (F. L. Battles, Trans.). Philadelphia: Westminster. (Original work published 1556)

Corey, G. (1991). *Theory and practice of counseling and psychotherapy.* Pacific Grove, CA: Brooks/Cole.

Crabb, L. J., Jr. (1977). *Effective biblical counseling.* Grand Rapids, MI: Zondervan.

Crabb, L. J., Jr. (1981). Biblical authority and Christian psychology. *Journal of Psychology and Theology, 9,* 305-311.

Danziger, K. (1979). The social origins of modern psychology. In A. R. Buss (Ed.), *Psychology in social context* (pp. 27-46). New York: Irvington.

Danziger, K. (1990). *Constructing the subject: Historical origins of psychology research.* Cambridge, England: Cambridge University Press.

Dennison, W. D. (1985). *Paul's two-age construction and apologetics.* Lanham, MD: University Press of America.

Dueck, A. C. (1995). *Between Jerusalem and Athens: Ethical perspectives on culture, religion, and psychotherapy.* Grand Rapids, MI: Baker.

Evans. C. S. (1989). *Wisdom and humanness in psychology: Prospects for a Christian approach.* Grand Rapids, MI: Baker.

Farnsworth, K. E. (1985). *Whole-hearted integration: Harmonizing psychology and Christianity through word and deed.* Grand Rapids, MI: Baker.

Frame, J. (1987). *The doctrine of the knowledge of God.* Phillipsburg, NJ: Presbyterian and Reformed.

Ganz, R. (1993). *Psychobabble: The failure of modern psychology and the biblical alternative.* Wheaton, IL: Crossway Books.

George, R. L., & Cristiani, T. S. (1990). *Counseling: Theory and practice* (3rd ed.). Englewood, Cliffs, NJ: Prentice Hall.

Gross, M. (1978). *The psychological society.* New York: Simon and Schuster.

Harris, M. J. (1986). Lord. In G. W. Bromiley (Ed.), *International standard Bible encyclopedia* (Vol. 3) (pp. 157-158). Grand Rapids, MI: Eerdmans.

Jeeves, M. (1976). *Psychology and Christianity: The view both ways.* Downers Grove, IL: InterVarsity Press.

Johnson, E. L. (1992). A place for the Bible within psychological science. *Journal of Psychology and Theology, 20,* 346-355.

Jones, S. L. (1986). Relating the Christian faith to psychology. In S. L. Jones (Ed.), *Psychology and the Christian faith* (pp. 15-33). Grand Rapids, MI: Baker.

Jones, S. L. (1994). A constructive relationship for religion with the science and profession of psychology: Perhaps the boldest model yet. *American Psychologist, 49,* 184-199.

Kalat, J. W. (1993). *Introduction to psychology* (3rd ed.). Pacific Grove, CA: Brooks/Cole.

Kant, I. (1965). *Critique of pure reason* (N. K. Smith, Trans.). New York: St. Martin's Press. (Original work published 1781)

Kuyper, A. (1898). *Sacred theology.* (J. H. DeVries, Trans.). New York: Charles Scribner's & Sons.

Lasch, C. (1979). *The culture of narcissism: American life in an age of diminishing expectations.* New York: Warner Books.

Ladd, G. E. (1974). *A theology of the New Testament.* Grand Rapids, MI: Eerdmans.

Larzelere, R. E. (1980). The task ahead: Six levels of integration of Christianity and psychology. *Journal of Psychology and Theology, 8,* 3-11.

MacArthur, J. F., Jr., & Mack, W. A. (1994). *Introduction to biblical counseling.* Dallas, TX: Word.

McIntyre, A. (1988). *Whose justice? Which rationality?* Notre Dame, IN: University of Notre Dame.

Maslow, A. H. (1954). *Motivation and personality.* New York: Harper & Brothers.

Maslow, A. H. (1970). *Religions, values, and peak experiences.* New York: Viking Press.

Murray, J. (1977). Common grace: In *Collected writings of John Murray: Vol. 2, Systematic theology.* Edinburgh, Scotland. The Banner of Truth Trust.

Myers, D. G. (1978). *The human puzzle: Psychological research and Christian belief.* New York: Harper & Row.

Myers, D. G. (1980). *The inflated self: Human illusions and the biblical call to hope.* New York: Seabury Press.

Narramore, S. B. (1984). *No condemnation: Rethinking guilt and motivation.* Grand Rapids, MI: Zondervan.

Nash, R. (1988). *Faith and reason.* Grand Rapids, MI: Zondervan.

Nisbett, R., & Ross, L. (1980). *Human inference: Strategies and shortcomings of social judgment.* Englewood Cliffs, NJ: Prentice-Hall.

Oden, T. (1990, October). *What psychologists can learn from the historic pastoral care tradition.* Paper presented at the Rech Conference. Wheaton College, Wheaton, IL.

O'Donovan, O. (1986). *Resurrection and moral order: An outline for evangelical ethics.* Grand Rapids, MI: Eerdmans.

Palmer, R. E. (1969). *Hermeneutics.* Evanston, IL: Northwestern University Press.

Plantinga, A. (1990). *The twin pillars of Christian scholarship* (Stob Lectures, 1989-1990). Grand Rapids, MI: Calvin College and Seminary.

Plantinga, A. (1983). Reason and belief in God. In A. Plantinga & N. Wolterstorff (Eds.). *Faith and rationality: Reason and belief in God* (pp. 16-92). Notre Dame, IN: University of Notre Dame.

Plantinga, A. (1993). *Warrant and proper function.* New York: Oxford University Press.

Plantinga, A. (1994). Divine knowledge. In C. S. Evans & M. Westphal (Eds.), *Christian perspectives on religious knowledge* (pp. 40-65). Grand Rapids, MI: Eerdmans.

Powlison, D. (1988). Crucial issues in contemporary biblical counseling. *The Journal of Pastoral Practice, 9,* 191-218.

Ridderbos, H. (1962). *The coming of the kingdom.* Philadelphia: Presbyterian and Reformed.

Ridderbos, H. (1975). *Paul: An outline of his theology.* (J. R. DeWitt, Trans.). Grand Rapids, MI: Eerdmans.

Roberts, R. C. (1990). Parameters of a Christian psychology. Unpublished manuscript.

Roberts, R. C. (1993). *Taking the word to heart: Self and other in an age of therapies.* Grand Rapids, MI: Eerdmans.

Runner, H. E. (1982). *The relation of the Bible to learning.* Jordan Station, Ontario: Paideia Press.

Schaeffer, F. (1968a). *Escape from reason.* London: InterVarsity Press.

Schaeffer, F. (1968b). *The God who is there.* London: Hodder & Stoughton.

Spier, J. M. (1954). *An introduction to Christian philosophy.* (D. H. Freeman, Trans.). Philadelphia: Presbyterian and Reformed.

Stephens, M. W. (1985). Locus of control. In D. G. Benner (Ed.), *Baker encyclopedia of psychology* (p. 653). Grand Rapids, MI: Baker.

Stoker, H. (1973). Reconnoitering the theory of knowledge of Prof. Dr. Cornelius Van Til. In E. R. Gechan (Ed.), *Jerusalem and Athens* (pp. 25-72). Phillipsburg, NJ: Presbyterian and Reformed.

Taylor, S. E. (1989). *Positive illusions.* New York: Basic Books.

Tjeltveit, A. C. (1989). The ubiquity of models of human beings in psychotherapy: The need for rigorous reflection. *Psychotherapy, 26,* 1-10.

Torrance, T. F. (1969), *Theological science.* Oxford, England: Oxford University Press.

Toulmin, S., & Leary, D. E. (1985). The cult of empiricism in psychology, and beyond. In S. Koch & D. E. Leary (Eds.), *A century of psychology as science* (pp. 594-617). New York: McGraw-Hill.

Vander Goot, M. (1986). *Narrating psychology or how psychology gets made.* Briston, IN: Wyndam Hall.

Van Leeuwen, M. (1985). *The person in psychology.* Grand Rapids, MI: Eerdmans.

Van Til C. (1969). *A Christian theory of knowledge.* Phillipsburg, NJ: Presbyterian and Reformed.

Van Til, H. (1959). *The Calvinistic concept of culture.* Grand Rapids, MI: Baker.

Vitz, P. (1990). The use of stories in moral development: New psychological reasons for an old education method. *American Psychologist, 45,* 709-720.

Von Rad, G. (1972). *Wisdom in Israel* (J. D. Martin, Trans.). Nashville, TN: Abingdon.

Vos, G. (1972). *The Pauline eschatology.* Grand Rapids, MI: Eerdmans.

Wade, C., & Tavris, C. (1993). *Psychology* (3rd. ed.). New York: HarperCollins.

Westphal, M. (1990). Taking St. Paul seriously: Sin as an epistemological category. In T. P. Flint (Ed.), *Christian philosophy* (pp. 200-226). Notre Dame, IN: University of Notre Dame Press.

Yankelovich, D. (1981). *New rules: Searching for self-fulfillment in a world turned upside down.* New York: Random House.

5

The Interface of Psychology and Theology

J. Harold Ellens
University of Michigan

This article discusses the semantic issues in such terminology as the integration and interface of psychology and theology and defines principles for their interdisciplinary relationship as sciences. It suggests models for theology illumining psychology and vice versa. This project is illustrated by observations upon the efforts of CAPS to wrestle with these issues. This inevitably unfolds some of the story of the author's fifteen-year pilgrimage as Editor of *JPC* and Executive Director of CAPS and his endeavor to relate the sciences of psychology and theology, psychological experience and spirituality, emotional health and biblical faith. It claims that the relationship of psychology and theology is less a matter of integration of the two into each other's framework, scientifically or intuitively, and more a matter of their interface for mutual illumination as sources of insight in which God's truth is revealed.

Responding to the invitation to write this article on the interface of psychology and theology, I do so with three purposes in mind. I wish to present an articulate perspective upon the relationship between the disciplines of psychology and theology. In that connection I will describe in some degree my personal odyssey in the pursuit of this interface of sciences and their applications during my forty years of work in both scientific theology and clinical psychology. This latter inevitably requires me to comment upon that part of the interdisciplinary pilgrimage of American scholarship which was pursued by the Christian Association for Psychological Studies over the first forty years of its existence, and particularly during my fifteen years as the Executive Director and as the Editor of the *Journal of Psychology and Christianity*, including the years it was known as the *CAPS Bulletin*.

In that regard, it is the first claim of this article that psychology and theology, as discreet disciplines, are both sciences, in an equivalent sense, through which it is possible and necessary to discern the world of created reality. Thus, they are equivalently windows through which to read God's self-revelation in the material world of humans and things. So both are essential scientific lenses through which the transcendent world of God's reality may be discovered. Therefore, no one can claim to be serious about his or her scientific endeavors in these two fields if the investigative enterprise does not assume and involve an exhaustive process of illumining psychological models and perspectives with the scientific insights of theology and illumining theological models and perspectives with the scientific information of psychology.

The second claim made here is that the scientific underpinnings of theology, such as biblical interpretation, text analysis, linguistic studies, cultural data, literary-historical evaluations, archaeological investigations, and philosophical reflections, all of which are scientifically crucial to theology-formation, is an enterprise upon which all the tools of human inquiry must be brought to bear in order to distill from the text the full range of cognitive and affective import, which the text carries and offers the inquirer. Among these tools are historical criticism, literary criticism, form criticism, redaction criticism, and textual criticism proper. Lately, some scholars such as Howard Clark Kee have attempted to bring sociological perspectives to biblical studies as the primary source of theology. Gerd Theissen has written on the psychological aspects of Pauline thought. The science and models of psychology must be employed as a lens through which to see any text, sacred or secular, and the theological concepts which they drive. Inevitably that will afford fresh and productive new dimensions of insights.

When the Christian Association for Psychological Studies was established forty years ago, it was the clear intent of its founders that the believing community should explore in a systematic way the manner in which our actual ontological relationships with God, as well as our psychological perception, experience, or projection of that relationship interfaces with our state of health. The assumption which I believe lay behind that concern was the conviction that the interface was definitive for our psychological and spiritual well-being as humans, together with the suspicion that that interface might also have much to do with our physical well-being. Moreover, it became clear from the kinds of papers which were read at the convocations of CAPS during its first two decades that it was the mind of the association that sometimes the nature of our personal religion or spirituality, our posture before the face of God, creates or expands psychological pathology and spiritual disfunction, while frequently our real or perceived relationship with God, the Bible, our faith tradition, and/or theology enhances health in body, mind, and spirit.

It was not the concern of the founders to drag the psychologically aware community, or indeed any part of the communities of faith and science, into questionable processes of mysticism, subjective pietism, para-psychology, spiritism, or the occult. It was very much the opposite; namely, to explore why it seemed to be at least heuristically and perhaps even empirically evident that wholistic health involves the self-actualization of the full range of grand potentials for growth with which God has invested humans by creating us in God's own image in body (soma), mind (nous), psyche (psyche), and spirit (pneuma).

There was a corollary implication at the center of this charter for the scientific psycho-spiritual pilgrimage of CAPS. It was the notion, less formally defined perhaps than the first motivation for establishing such a community of inquiry, that if we could understand how religious faith interfaces with human health, theology with psychology, we would also see, conversely, how the psychological insights we have about the dynamics of human health and illness illumine the messages in the text of the Bible and hence should contribute to the content and shape of theology. In retrospect, that seems to have been a fruitful set of objectives and intuitive assumptions, which have become the focus of inquiry for a wider world of scholarship today. In any case, it was largely that two-sided trajectory of CAPS' pilgrimage which became the channel for my personal and scholarly quest for the majority of my life and work.

Exposition

When I came to the position of Executive Director of The Christian Association for Psychological Studies in 1974 the scene was verdant, in both the evangelical and the progressive or mainline Christian communities, with a luxuriant growth of models for exploring and conceptualizing the relationship between our faith and work, our religion and our profession, our theological and psychological sciences, our confessions and our careers as practitioners in the social sciences and clinical arts. On the one hand, such evangelical psychologists as H. Newton Malony, John Carter, Bruce Narramore, and others were beginning to write on these issues. On the other hand, such progressive scholars as

Seward Hiltner, Don Browning, James Lapsley, LeRoy Aden, Colin Brown, Wayne Oates, Liston Mills, and others were producing a spate of sturdy volumes treating the interface of psychology and religion. Anton Boisen had, in many generative ways, parlayed his own serious psychoses into a series of models and proposals regarding the interface of psychology and theology which had sturdily set the stage for these later scholars. The work of William James had, of course, provided a useful framework of thought in the context of which to do the kind of work we were seeking to do. Whether one worked in his light or against his notions, he was the unavoidable rock to which one anchored or on which one was honed to a finer edge.

There were two interesting negative characteristics in that phase of the inquiry which I have spent my professional life endeavoring to heal. The first was that the evangelical community did not speak to or read the works of the progressive, then referred to as the liberal, community. Neither did the mainline scholars read the evangelicals or dialogue with them. Moreover, the second problem was that the evangelicals generally came to this inquiry into the relationship between theology and psychology from the side of scientific psychology, having been trained primarily as professional psychologists, mostly at the doctoral level. On the other hand, the progressives came to the inquiry from the side of scientific theology, having been trained primarily as professional theologians teaching in pastoral care departments at seminaries. Therefore, the evangelicals did not trust the progressives because they thought they did not know scientific psychology and were working mainly with an intuitive popularization of the field. The progressives did not trust the evangelicals because they thought they did not know scientific theology and were working mainly with an intuitive and primitive Sunday School religion, or the dogmatic categories and language of fundamentalism.

They were both in error, of course. Actually such scholars as Seward Hiltner, Don Browning, Peter Homans, and the like, were heavily trained in psychoanalytic and psychodynamic psychology. Moreover, Professor Malony is an ordained Methodist minister with a standard theological education who spent most of his teaching life addressing the issue which the evangelicals called the integration of psychology and spirituality. His evangelical colleagues were mostly well-informed persons who, even if they had little formal theological training, were biblically and spiritually reasonably well-informed and at least consummately honest. Moreover, it must be said for the evangelicals that they began to read the positions of and take seriously the dialogue with the progressives before the latter began to take them seriously. Don Browning was one of the progressives who by 1980 recognized that his colleagues needed to be reading the evangelical publications as thoroughly as the evangelicals had begun to read theirs. Today, it seems to me, the dialogue between the two communities runs on apace so that the names, evangelical and progressive, which once distinguished them, are becoming less and less useful at the levels of academic, clinical, and research operations.

However, there was a central problem in the framework within which the evangelical community generally tended to conceptualize the relationship between faith and practice and between theology and psychology, and in the language used to express that relationship. Evangelical scholars have tended even to this time to describe the problem as that of the integration of theology and psychology. Two aspects of this language and its implied conceptual model are problematic. First, to think of the issue as that of integration suggests that the two components to be integrated in a unified model are in some way inherently disparate. Second, the categories of theology and psychology must be conceived of as being commensurate as scientific enterprises, not merely as a discussion between psychology and religion. Regarding the latter, it must be noted that religion is a psychospiritual practice which has a cultural character and cultic expression. It is a sociological process as well as an expression of a philosophico-theological worldview. Psychology and theology, on the other hand, are scientific and academic disciplines which express themselves, as sciences, in academic, clinical, and research operations.

Thus the religious counterpart of the discipline of psychology is the science of theology. So even if the issue were to be formulated as a problem of integration, it should at least be structured as the integration of theology and psychology as scientific disciplines and of psychological and theological worldviews. Addressing such matters as the integration of faith and life, of pastoral care and clinical practice, or of one's religion and vocation are different though not unrelated matters.

Nonetheless, the word integration remains problematic because it suggests a model in which two disparate entities, psychology and theology, essentially alien to each other, must be lined up or force-fitted to each other in order to insure decent or responsible work in the helping professions or in theological understanding. There is a difference, of course, between the science of theology and that of psychology. Each has its own universe of discourse, each its own paradigms, arena of inquiry, database, objectives, and controls within the framework of scientific inquiry. Both depend upon empirical and heuristic data and methods. Each has its own forming and informing history, and each depends upon theory formation which must respond with integrity to the scientific constraints upon theory development and testing, and each must respond with integrity to its respective database. However, as science, both psychology and theology operate with essentially the same general models of method, coherence, and objectivity.

My perception has been consistently that what we really have always sought in the quest to understand the relationship between the scientific disciplines of psychology and theology, together with the relationship of their applied arts and the worldviews they afford us, is an interface of mutual illumination. This I argued with some vigor in my Finch Lectures in 1980 and in my 1982 publication, *God's Grace and Human Health* (pp. 19-36, 94-115). The question whether integration or interface of mutual illumination is the better term is an epistemological problem on the theoretical science level, a structural problem on the applied science level, and a problem of psychodynamic dissonance or harmony on the experience level.

There is also a theological problem which may be implied in the integration paradigm and for many evangelicals lurks only slightly below the surface of conscious thought; namely, that the truth value of data produced by psychology has a lesser valence than the truth value of the insights of theology or the message of the text of the Bible. To put it simply, there may be the assumption or the claim that the truth of the Bible is more truthful than the truth of psychology; more important divine revelation. I have vigorously contested this position, as have the scholars from the progressive community generally, largely on the theological grounds that God reveals the divine self in nature and in grace, in Scripture and in creation, in faith and in work; and with equal valence since all truth is God's truth and God does not speak with a forked tongue.

The Reformed tradition, for example, in which I have always stood, consistently has held out for the notion of God's two books of creation and the Bible, even though the tradition used the terms of general and special revelation, respectively. Under the rubrics of this spiritually and scientifically rich Calvinist tradition, scientific inquiry into theology and spirituality stands on equal footing with scientific inquiry into the natural and social sciences, and vice versa. Both are seen as equivalent inquiries into God's self-revelation. The world of truth is not conceived schizophrenically as divided into sacred and secular, in that sense. The immanent and transcendent categories of reality are not seen as alien to each other or in any sense discontinuous. Most of all, this material world is not seen, as it generally is in fundamentalism, as alien to God's life but rather as God's dwelling place, God's home with us, God's own design, domain, and delight.

Perhaps there is, therefore, a second theological problem implied in the integration model; namely, the notion that the revelation in creation is not merely different in value from that of Scripture, but that what we see through the science of theology and what we see through the science of psychology represent two radically different realms of ontological reality, specifically the world of the natural and of the supernatural. These terms have become largely nonfunctional in the thought world of the progressive community, though there has been an increase in such terminology as "material and transcendent worlds" and the like, as the positivism of enlightenment thinking has come under fire in recent decades. The rise of transcendental psychologies and the resurgence of transcendental theologies in the progressive community is a corollary to this post-enlightenment mindset.

The insights of the postmodern era regarding the impossibility of achieving a valueless scientific objectivity are crucial here, namely, the realization that all scientific theory development is born, in the first place, out of assumptions which are to some degree driven or shaped by one's religious, theological, or value-laden predisposition. All the data one acquires, therefore, are not strictly speaking empirical data or objective rationality but rather the formulations of *Reason Within the Bounds of Religion* (Wolterstorff, 1976).

A Model of Mutual Scientific Illumination

To speak of a model of interface between two scientific enterprises or operational categories which offers mutual illumination between them is to suggest what may be called a perspectival model. This way of looking at the matter and of speaking of it would have found agreement from Seward Hiltner and most of the progressive community of scholars. There are three principles, I think, which such a model must reflect if it is to be a thorough-going expression of scientific and psycho-spiritual integrity.

First, theology and psychology are both sciences in their own right, stand legitimately on their own foundations and, when read carefully, are two equivalent sources of illuminating truth. Speaking theologically or religiously, they are two equivalent sources of God's self-revelation in creation and Scripture, as I noted above. Conversely, speaking psychologically, they are two equivalent subjects of scientific study, assessment, and description. They are not alien in any inherent sense. When they seem at odds, paradoxical, or disparate in some way it must always be because of a dysfunction on one of three counts. Either we have failed to do scientific theology well enough or we have failed to investigate the science of psychology thoroughly enough. Or, second, we have distorted the science of the theological or natural world by arbitrary dogmatism, not properly constrained by sound investigation of God's word/scientific truth in creation or in the Bible. Or, third, we have drawn erroneous conclusions in either of those investigations and not allowed each of the scientific disciplines to illumine the other adequately, honestly, or thoroughly.

Wherever truth is found, it is truth, God's truth, having equal warrant with all other truth. Some truth may have greater weight than other truth in a specific situation, but there is no difference in its warrant or valence as truth (Ellens, 1982, p. 24). If you have just been hit by a car and are bleeding from the jugular, the truth about blood pressure and arterial closure may be significantly more important at that moment than any product of theological science. There are undoubtedly other circumstances in which the opposite is the case. In any case, truth is truth, regardless of who finds it, where, or how.

Egbert Schuurman, at that time a professor of philosophy at Eindhoven Institute of Technology and lecturer at the Free University of Amsterdam, published in 1980 a work entitled *Technology and the Future: A Philosophical Challenge* and in that same year another book, *Reflections of the Technological Society*. These were only slightly preceded by the work of the distinguished Benedictine priest, Stanley L. Jaki, *The Road of Science and the Ways to God* (1978) and soon followed by Jaki's (1980) *Cosmos and Creator*. In these seminal works the authors developed the claim that, given the nature of human mind and personality, it is imperative to recognize that the mutual illumination of all scientific disciplines is essential to a full-orbed and honest achievement in any of them. These signal volumes were followed rapidly by a rich flow of useful interdisciplinary studies during the last decade and there seems to be no indication that this fecund quest will in any way abate in the century, indeed millennium, before us.

Second, the criterion of soundness in theory development or operational application of the illumination the sciences of psychology and theology bring to each other is not the effectiveness with which our psychological insights fit in with our theological worldview or our theological insights fit in with our psychological worldview, but rather whether they make discernible claims upon each other in a way that either requires modification of the other or makes the thoroughgoing understanding of the other more evident. Perhaps one could say that it has to do with the way in which one enlarges or resolves problems in the internal coherence of the other. Psychological data, insights, paradigms, or worldviews may be helpful in illumining a biblical text and/or theological proposition by enlarging the perception of the internal coherence of the text or proposition, resolving problems in the coherence of the text or proposition, or disturbing the supposed coherence of the text or proposition in a way that leads to an enlarged understanding of what the coherent message of the text or proposition is; as well as illumining the degree to which all of these conform to and account for the data about God and humans which arises in the database.

Comparably, theological data, insights, paradigms, or worldviews may be helpful in illumining the internal coherence or lack thereof in the living human document; namely, the patient in the clinical process or under research analysis, in a way that will discernably enhance the formulation of psychological models and propositions, clinical procedures, and the healing progress of that patient; as well as illumining the degree to which the psychological project coheres with the imperatives of the data about humans (and God) which arises in the database. Such theological illumination may resolve problems or impasses in the process of the therapy, or may disturb the presumed progress only to lay bare deeper needs, coherence, or incoherence in the living human document (Gerkin, 1984). Similarly, theological light may illumine the process of *theoretical* work in psychology, enhancing the understanding of the living human document about which both sciences are concerned to take accurate account.

Third, the responsible function of the perspectival model of that interface which provides mutual illumination between the psychological and theological sciences requires an incarnational posture on the part of the scientist or practitioner. That is, for the illumination to take place, the person who brings the lights of psychology to theology and the biblical text or those of theology to psychology and the living human document must believe that each respective science has legitimate light to bring to bear and that that light is the light of truth incarnated in the understanding possessed by the scholar. This implies that the scholar

perceives herself or himself as a midwife of the truth not merely a manipulator of insights or data.

In describing the operational application of these three principles to the enterprise of bringing theological illumination to the science and practice of psychology in my above-mentioned book, I enunciated eight biblical insights significant to the full understanding of the living human document: the patient in therapy (1982, pp. 27-36). These were the biblical theology of 1) human personhood, of 2) alienation, of 3) sin, of 4) discipline, of 5) grace, of the 6) wounded healer, of 7) mortality, and of 8) celebration.

These I followed with twelve practical applications of biblical theology to the psychotherapeutic setting. This is neither the time nor situation to explicate these in detail, but I list them for the sake of the completeness and symmetry of this article. They have to do with the biblical illumination of the 1) identity of the patient before God, the 2) certification of the patient's destiny as self-actualization of the Imago Dei, the 3) assurance the patient can derive from the radical nature of grace, the 4) inherent dignity of the patient as a creature of God despite his or her illness, the 5) assurance of the therapist that his or her task is not to take ultimate responsibility for the patient but to incite a finite growth process, the 6) affirmation of the patient's self-esteem in his or her certification as person before the face of God, the 7) permission to give up situation inappropriate or neurotic anxiety in a world where grace and providence reign, the 8) affirmation of transference and countertransference as sources of energy that can be employed for healing, 9) God's inviolable goodwill and not threat as the context of all of life in health or illness, 10) growth as the objective and purpose of existence, 11) freedom from the need on the part of the therapist and the patient to play God in therapy or in life, and the 12) recognition that mortality is acceptable, that is, that theology offers the opportunity for relief from the ultimate panic that stands as a specter behind all pathology. Because God is God and grace is grace, it is perfectly acceptable, even delightful, to age, wrinkle, watch one's youthfulness fade, and embrace the finitude of life; the messages of our culture to the contrary, notwithstanding!

A Formal Model of Scientific Interface

The biblical story is a paradigm of the human psychological odyssey and as such asserts an inherent union of experience in our history and, metaphorically at least, in God's history (see Miles, 1995). This idea has been explicated helpfully as well by John Cobb (1969, 1982) and the process theologians. The import of this centers in the realization that life for

God, as Spirit, however mythically or ontologically we conceive of it, and the life of the human psyche cut across each other at such substantive levels as to effect the description and definition of both. Presumably the only thing we can know about God or the meaning and content of our God-talk is what we can understand through the perceptions and projections of the human person. So any theology about God, us, and the world is heavily dependent upon the cognitive and affective apperceptive processes of human beings. Thus to employ theology for insights regarding any reality requires the employment of a useful and warrantable anthropology and, therefore, a sound psychology. Conversely, to employ a proper psychology in the pursuit of truth also requires a useful and warrantable anthropology and, therefore, I claim, a sound theology.

Psychology and theology are, thus, inevitably interlinked regardless of what the immediate focus or concern of either is. Hence, whether we are exploring a biblical document or the living human document, the mutual illumination of psychology and theology is imperative because a properly enlightened anthropology is required for both. Moreover, the mutual illumination undoubtedly takes place precisely in the anthropology which is formed or forming in, which functions in, and which informs each discipline. Since both disciplines deal with the psychospiritual domains, either of these which ignores the other is not adequately serious about itself.

So one must come at each of these two disciplines with an eye to the other. This is likely to be true regarding the science which explores any other facet of the cosmos, as well, of course. Theology is barren without a comprehensive appreciation of creation, and creation ultimately can only be understood theologically, that is, in terms of its ultimate transcendent source, nature, meaning, and destiny. The natural and social sciences must inquire finally of theology and theology must listen and speak to the natural and social sciences in order to make sense of itself.

Psychology and theology exercise the stewardship of their mandates by collecting data, formulating theories for accounting for the data, and applying the interpreted data to operational concerns in their respective disciplines. Theory development in this process depends upon the *weltanschaung*, the *pou sto* from which one comes to the scientific enterprise. That means that behind the theory development and data collection or interpretation is a faith assumption, a belief regarding the nature and function of reality (see Wolterstorff, 1976). Thus, all scientific activity from data collection to theoretical or operational

interpretation of the data has significant theological or spiritual as well as psychological import.

To this end, CAPS, from its outset forty years ago, began to publish its own work in the form of the annual *Proceedings* of the CAPS conventions. These volumes are still of great value and indicate the profundity of the investigations undertaken by the participants in that dialogue in those early years. Frequently, I note that studies done more recently for CAPS conventions or published in *JPC* are not alert to that early work and replow the same ground, often in less profound ways. In 1974 we moved from the publication of the *Proceedings* and began to bring out a quarterly magazine style journal known as *The CAPS Bulletin*. As founding editor of that organ, I continually looked forward to the time when a more standard professional journal could be established and the opportunity came for that in 1982. By decision of the National Board of CAPS, I was instructed to begin publishing the *Journal of Psychology and Christianity* which is endowed and has flourished since then, under my editorship until 1988 and since then from the hand of the very able academic and research psychologist, Dr. Peter Hill of Grove City College.

The consistent objective of these endeavors has been to develop working models of the interface of the sciences of psychology and theology at both the theoretical and operational levels. Thus I attempted to give conscious circumspect leadership to the CAPS community in developing a formal model of what we were trying to do in our search for a more complete understanding of how these disciplines work in their interaction in the faith, professional work, and life of concerned Christian scientists. In 1982 I published such a proposed model and have continued to refine it since then in such works as *The Church and Pastoral Care* (Aden & Ellens, 1988), *Christian Counseling and Psychotherapy* (Ellens, 1987), *Counseling and the Human Predicament* (Ellens, 1989), and *Christian Perspectives on Human Development* (Aden, Benner, & Ellens, 1992).

In this process it has seemed increasingly clear to me that there are four levels at which scientific and operational disciplines interface. These are the levels of theory development, research methodology, database development, and operational application (see Figure 1).

The first three categories do not differ in their function from one discipline to the next. The fourth category is similar in function for all disciplines but the arena in which the function is executed differs from the 1) psychological clinic to the 2) pastoral care setting to the 3) formulation and teaching of

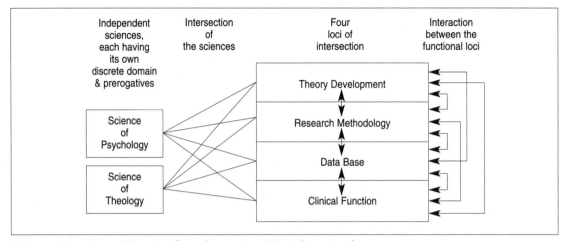

Figure 1. Levels at which scientific and operational disciplines interface.

theological or psychological constructs in the academy to the 4) research labs and libraries. The crucial issue regarding the interface and mutual illumination which psychology and theology afford each other in this model is the recognition that each of these disciplines comes to the work at each of the four levels with its own independent parlance, prerogatives, perspectives, and purposes, but all encounter each other at each level of the model in the anthropology which is functioning or forming at that level in the mind and worldview of the scientist.

In fact, one can go a step further and demonstrate that it is in the theological or psychological personality theory which is functioning or forming in that anthropology that the interface and mutual illumination takes place (see Figure 2). It is in that notion of the nature and function of the human person who does science, experiences conceptualization of aspects and functions of the cosmos, and relates to God that the various disciplines meet to bring their illuminating insights to bear on all the others. It is that sense of the operative nature of humanness, particularly the epistemology operating in one's anthropology and theory of the human person, which is at stake in how theology illumines the psychological address to the living human document and psychology illumines the theological address to the biblical document or theological proposition. Our anthropology, properly illumined affords us our understanding of how God is and speaks to us. In sum, therefore, I see theology and psychology as different perspectives or frames of reference, with differing fields of discourse, dealing with the same subject matter; namely the function of the living human document which is sometimes described in the textual documents of the Bible (see Figure 3). In this living human document and its cosmic context can be

seen the reflections of the face and heart of God. The illumination which psychology can bring to theology, thus, is the light it offers about the nature and function of the living human document as author, context, initial audience, interpreter, subsequent audience, and modifiable object of theological concepts. The illumination theology can bring to psychology is the light it offers about the nature and function of the theological data as modifier, context, in that sense author, audience, and interpreter of the living human document.

A Look Toward the Future

A continuing fruitful struggle to understand and employ the potential of the sciences and practice of psychology and theology for mutual illumination is imperative for at least two concrete reasons. First, the recent data regarding the etiology of psychopathology is moving us more and more toward the inevitable conclusion that at least 80% of everything we see in the clinic derives from genetic and/or biochemical sources rather than environmental influences. When that is combined with the government statistics on the generally relative ineffectiveness of its own costly prison rehabilitation programs and attempts to train the so-called hard-core unemployed, one is forced to ask to what extent these latter conditions are driven by the former. If there should prove to be some significant correlation between biochemical-based psychopathology and the limits of a person's potential for rehabilitation or social function, as I think we shall find, we are faced in the field of psychology with an enormous problem of both a theological and ethical nature. The theological problem is the classical problem of determinism and personal freedom. The ethical problem is that of whether the state or some external entity such as the medical profession can or should, for example, take responsibility for such

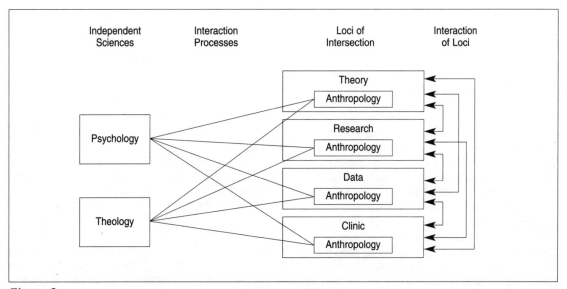

Figure 2.
The anthropological concept that is forming or functioning in each locus of intersection is the actual junction element that constitutes the site of intersection.

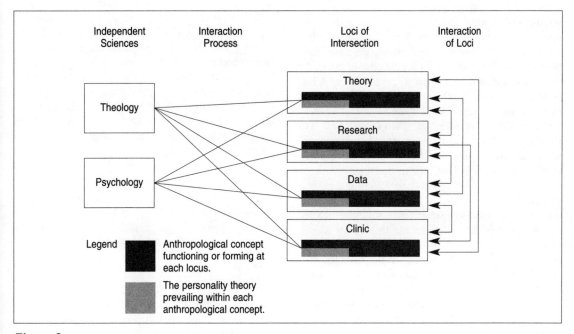

Figure 3.

forced medication of the persons involved as to render them amenable to rehabilitation and social function, for their own good and that of society. Thus it is clear that theology and psychology are thrown inextricably together in this applied and operational arena as well as in that of theoretical scientific investigation.

Second, the converse of this interface for mutual illumination, namely, the light psychology can bring to theology, is just as crucial and perhaps more tractable. Psychology has been able to develop a number of standardized paradigms for understanding the living human document and these paradigms have proven useful cross-culturally. Therefore, it may be assumed that they are also applicable cross-generationally and from one millennium to another. That is, our current models for understanding human beings are likely to be applicable when we use them to view persons from a thousand years ago or from biblical times, provided we can secure a substantial amount of information about those persons.

One might be able, for example, to note that Tertullian was a lawyer by training and that he was meticulously preoccupied with the precise and subtle nuances of the meaning of words and expressions, that he tolerated no variance or margin of flexibility in the denotation or connotation of the words he used in formulating his early Christian creedal statements, that he was inordinately legalistic in his theological and church political notions, and that when the church of North Africa moved toward vesting its authority in the bishops and their Apostolic Succession instead of following his rigid formulations and proposals, he left the Orthodox Church for the Montanists (Jackson & Gilmore, 1950, pp. 305-308). Having noted these things and presumably developing a similar but more extended body of knowledge about him, his history and function, we could successfully employ our diagnostic categories of today, with their implied psychological models for understanding the living human document, and draw appropriate conclusions regarding Tertullian's health and pathology. We might conclude, for example, that he was suffering from at least a mild case of compulsivity and paranoia. In such a case, it would be important to have made this psychological assessment in order to understand what he wrote, intended, and meant by his theological works; and how we should take them, and perhaps even how seriously we should take them as part of the early formulations of what has become the Christian tradition.

Similarly, it is possible today to bring the insights and models of psychology to bear upon a biblical text or theological construct, assessing the nature and function of the author, of the implied or stated intended audience, of the real audiences in the church's history which interpreted the text, together with their interpretations, and thus assess the reasons, healthy or pathological, for the constructs that were expressed in the text and in subsequent theological uses of it. That is to say, in addition to all the other text-critical paradigms which are legitimately applied to the text of Scripture and of theological traditions, surely we must apply the paradigms for understanding how humans function, what they tend to say, why they say what they say the way they say it, and what messages mean as seen through standardized psychological paradigms when applied in a given context. Psychology is another lens through which it is possible to see any text and understand dimensions of it and the way it

reflects the living human documents behind it and, therefore, reflects and interprets God who stands behind and created the living human document. Neither humans nor God can be adequately understood if one does not employ this lens.

Conclusion

I have made the claim and CAPS has spent forty years in quest of the trust that psychology properly done before the face of God will reveal that face through living human documents and thus illumine theology in essential ways. I have made the further claim, also confidently pursued for four decades by CAPS, that theology properly done before the face of God will reveal that face in the text of Scripture and thus have light to bring to psychology. I make the final claim that as each is a lens to see deeply into its own scientific arena, so each in bringing light to the other discipline is a lens to assist in seeing the face of God in that other science more clearly, by seeing the face of that science's own living human documents more clearly, in the clinic or behind the biblical-theological text.

Without such bifocal spectacles properly adjusted on our seeking scientific eyes, looking at both psychology and theology, we shall have our view of God distorted and thus inevitably our view of humans and humanness as well. Conversely, if we have our theological or psychological anthropology distorted because we have not properly illumined each with the other, we shall not see God rightly in creation or in the Scripture, to our great and unnecessary confusion and loss.

References

Aden, L., & Ellens, J. H. (Eds.) (1988). *The church and pastoral care*. Grand Rapids, MI: Baker.

Aden, L., Benner, D. G., & Ellens, J. H. (Eds.) (1992). *Christian perspectives on human development*. Grand Rapids, MI: Baker.

Cobb, J. B. (1969). *God and the world*. Philadelphia: Westminster.

Cobb, J. B. (1982). *Process theology as a political theology*. Philadelphia: Westminster.

Ellens, J. H. (1982). *God's grace and human health*. Nashville: Abingdon.

Ellens, J. H. (1987). Biblical themes in psychological theory and practice. In D. G. Benner (Ed.), *Christian counseling and psychotherapy*. Grand Rapids, MI: Baker.

Ellens, J. H. (1989). A psychospiritual view of sin and sickness: The nature of human failure. In L. Aden and D. G. Benner (Eds.), *Counseling and the human predicament: A study of sin, guilt, and forgiveness*. Grand Rapids, MI: Baker.

Gerkin, C. (1984). *The living human document*. Nashville, TN: Abingdon.

Jackson, S. M., & Gilmore, G. W. (Eds.). (1950). *The new Schaff-Herzog encyclopedia of religious knowledge* (Vol. XI), Grand Rapids, MI: Baker.

Jaki, S. (1978). *The road of science and the ways to God.* Chicago: University of Chicago Press.

Jaki, S. (1980). *Cosmos and creator.* Edinburgh: Scottish Academic Press.

Miles, J. (1995). *God: A biography.* New York: Knopf.

Schuurman, E. (1980). *Reflections of the technological society.* Toronto: Wedge.

Schuurman, E. (1980). *Technology and the future: A philosophical challenge.* New York: Radix.

Wolterstorff, N. (1976). *Reason within the bounds of religion.* Grand Rapids, MI: Eerdmans.

The Tension Between Psychology and Theology: An Anthropological Solution

Hendrika Vande Kemp
Graduate School of Psychology
Fuller Theological Seminary

Having traced the etymological roots of the tension between psychology and theology (Vande Kemp, 1982), the author discusses the presence of a twentieth-century "psychology without a soul." Some aspects of the depth-psychological tradition are examined in their documentation of unconscious processes and their assertion of the presence of both soul and spirit. The author argues for a trichotomic anthropology which differentiates, at least for clinical and pastoral purposes, between the spiritual and the psychological.

As indicated in an earlier article (Vande Kemp, 1982), a suspiciousness often exists between Christian psychologists and theologians parallel to the tension between Christian and secular psychologists. Underlying this tension there appears to be a battle over territoriality and the implication that sacred boundaries are being violated, and sacred territory defaced. To address a possible root of this problem, the etymological roots of the term *psyche* were traced, along with its transformation into the term *psychology*. This was followed by an examination of the shift in the definition of *psychology* and the range of its subject matter. Significant in this development was the fact that the "new" psychology, when it emerged, included an inescapable awareness of the realm of the unconscious and its processes. As Jung (1933, p. 203) stated in *Modern Man in Search of a Soul*, "We can no longer deny that the dark stirrings of the unconscious are effective powers—that psychic forces exist which cannot, for the present at least, be fitted in with our rational world-order."

Psychology Without a Soul

All of the previous discussion concerning the ambiguity of the term *psychology* would remain a mere matter of semantics if we were not interested in the processes of saving and healing "souls," And this becomes rather confusing to the therapist who realizes that psychology, which literally denotes "the science of the soul," has become a science "without a soul." As Drakeford (1964, p. 3) points out, "The word 'soul' lost its place in the psychologist's vocabulary, as he left to the theologian the task of clarifying the troublesome word."

Thymotology or Psychology?

Considering this abandonment of the soul by psychology, Watson (1968, pp. 9-10) suggested that it might be appropriate to rename our science "thymotology," since it was concerned with thought, emotion, and conscious experience rather than the immortal soul. While a secular psychologist might easily settle for the suggestion of a more accurate name for our science, Christian psychologists are gravely concerned because psychology has chosen to banish the immortal soul from its realm. The recognition that psychology was a science "without a soul" came early for these observers. While we have already reviewed the changing connotations of *psychology*, one explicit statement excluding the soul is worthy of citation, as it was made by William James (1890/1950, Vol. 1, p. 344):

> It [the soul] *is at all events needless for expressing the actual subjective phenomena of consciousness as they appear ...* The unity, the identity, the individuality, and the immateriality that appear in the psychic life are thus accounted for as phenomenal and temporal facts exclusively, and with no need of reference to any more simple or substantial agent than the present thought or "section" of the stream.

While James banished immortality and the soul from his early psychology, in later years "James progressed from a feeling of the probability of immortality to a genuine belief" (Perry, 1935, Vol. 2, p. 385). His later position is clear in *The Varieties of Religious Experience* (James, 1902/1961, p. 164), where he opposed the "no-soul" doctrine of Buddhism, the skepticism of Hume, and, by analogy, the no-soul version of modern psychology (of which many other statements are quoted by Arnett, 1904, pp. 354-356). This opposition is echoed and re-echoed by Christians of the twentieth century. One of the first to do so explicitly was Gruender (1911), whose book bore the appropriate title, *Psychology Without a Soul: A Criticism*. Gruender criticized the materialism and positivism of Structuralism and early Functionalism (exemplified by Titchener and James) and argued for the soul's substantiality, simplicity, spirituality, and immortality, thus reasserting all the qualities previously denied by James. Rank (1931/1950) echoed these sentiments in *Psychology and the Soul*, noting that "although psychology may be a natural science, its spiritual basis defies explanation in terms of natural science or of psychology, because the psyche is neither a mere function of the brain nor a sublimation of instinct" (p. 5).

In describing twentieth-century psychology, Allport (1950, p. v) claimed that "psychology without a soul became its badge of distinction." That same year Fromm (1950, p. 6) also commented that "psychology thus became a science lacking its main subject matter, the soul," which was associated with the higher human powers such as love, reason, conscience, and values. A quarter century later Tart (1975) used the same argument to introduce transpersonal systems of psychology: "Yet much of the agony of our time stems from a spiritual vacuum. Our culture, our psychology, has ruled out man's spiritual nature, but the cost of this attempted suppression is enormous" (p. 5).

As one reads these comments, it becomes readily apparent that writers at times speak of the soul as the mental, the psychological, the contents of the unconscious. Others speak of the soul as the spiritual side of our being. At times the terms are used interchangeably; occasionally they overlap. The soul is certainly, and perhaps always has been, difficult to define. And scientific, philosophical, and theological definitions have always had to compete with the natural language, the definitions of the general public. Though Zilboorg (1941) and others may decry the older meanings which cling to "psyche," the richness of tradition may still have something to teach psychology. Ulanov and Ulanov (1975) make this case for the soul in *Religion and the Unconscious*:

> That does not for a moment persuade those who have met the soul in their work in depth psychology, or religion, or any other discipline that deals with human interiority, that the soul is simply a remnant of a looser time in

human intellectual enterprise or a continuing mark of superstition or easy credulity, sooner or later to be replaced by the discoveries and determinations of more tough-minded scientists. Unquestionably, the word has been used awkwardly, inexactly, has been part of the easy currency of the crackpots and charlatans of the interior life, in which the world always abounds. Nonetheless, "soul" describes very well, with a rich tradition of experience as well as speculation behind it, the organizing principle of life, that which the body gives up when it turns from a living organism into a cadaver. (p. 82)

Intrapersonal and Transpersonal Perspectives

Those of us in the Christian tradition sincerely affirm something beyond the physical, a realm of the spiritual, which *must* be included in a definitive anthropology. Depth psychologists are also in agreement that there is more to humanity than body and mind, that the nonphysical aspect includes something beyond conscious processes. There is a dimension described as the unconscious which has been revealed in a number of different guises. The "preconscious' and "unconscious" of Freud (1933), the "individual" unconscious and "collective" unconscious of Jung (1912/1916), and more recently the "individual," "generic," and "collective" unconscious of Kahler (1957), modeled on Neumann's (1954) differentiation between the "collective unconscious" and the "mass unconscious."

Neumann's history of consciousness is especially interesting in that he adopts a "recapitulation theory" in which "ontogenetic development may ... be regarded as a modified recapitulation of phylogenetic development" (p. xx). Throughout the centuries in the evolution of Western culture, "the conscious system has absorbed more and more unconscious contents and progressively extended its frontiers" (p. xviii). In this developmental sequence (postulated as well in the psychology of Jaynes [1976], and much earlier in the work of Carus [1848]), Neumann recognizes a tendency which is deeply troubling to Christian theologians: With the increasing differentiation of consciousness from unconsciousness we are less inclined to take seriously the spiritual forces outside of us.

> Contents which are primarily transpersonal and originally appeared as such are, in the course of development, taken to be personal. The secondary

personalization of primary transpersonal contents is in a certain sense an evolutionary necessity, but it constellates dangers which for modern man are altogether excessive. It is necessary for the structure of personality that contents originally taking the form of transpersonal deities should finally come to be experienced as contents of the human psyche. But this process ceases to be a danger to psychic health only when the psyche is itself regarded suprapersonally, as a numinous world of transpersonal happenings. If, on the other hand, transpersonal contents are reduced to the data of a purely personalistic psychology, the result is not only an appalling impoverishment of individual life—that might remain merely a private concern—but also a congestion of the collective unconscious which has disastrous consequences for humanity at large … The relation of the ego to the unconscious and of the personal to the transpersonal decides the fate not only of the individual but of humanity. The theater of this encounter is the human mind. (Neumann, 1954, pp. xxiii-xxiv)

Concern that this intrapersonal focus is psychopathological in nature comes from both Christian and secular psychologists as they emphasize not only the importance of the collective unconscious but also the critical nature of the spiritual, the part of "the depth" that brings us into contact with the transpersonal. And it is, I think, the expression of this concern on the part of many depth psychologists (rather than the omission of the spiritual realm, which is common to so much of twentieth-century psychology), that leads to so much of the tension between psychology and Christian theology. It is this that leads to disputes over territoriality, the relationship between psyche and spirit, and that between salvation and mental health.

A New Trichotomy: Spirited Psychology and Ensouled Theology

Especially important in this debate are the questions raised by the biblical psychologists of the nineteenth century: "Does human nature consist of body and soul only, or of body, soul, and spirit? And if the latter, what is the relationship between spirit and soul?" For the sake of simplicity, Berkhof's (1938) historical summary of the debate between dichotomists and trichotomists is restated here:

It is customary, especially in Christian circles, to conceive of man as consisting of two, and only two, distinct parts, namely, body and soul. This view is technically called *dichotomy*. Alongside of it, however, another made its appearance, to the effect that human nature consists of three parts, body, soul, and spirit. It is designated by the term *trichotomy*. The tri-partite conception of man originated in Greek philosophy, which conceived of the relation of the body and spirit of man to each other after the analogy of the mutual relation between the material universe and God. It was thought that, just as the latter could enter into communion with each other only by means of a third substance of an intermediate being, so the former could only enter into mutual vital relationships by means of a third or intermediate element, namely, the soul. The soul was regarded as, on the one hand, immaterial, and on the other, adapted to the body. In so far as it appropriated the *nous* or *pneuma*, it was regarded as immortal, but in so far as it was related to the body, it was carnal and mortal. The most familiar but also the crudest form of trichotomy is that which takes the body for the material part of man's nature, the soul as the principle of animal life, and the spirit as the God-related rational and immortal element in man. The trichotomic conceptions of man found considerable favor with the Greek or Alexandrian Church Fathers of the early Christian centuries … During the nineteenth century trichotomy was revived in some form or other by certain German and English theologians, as Roos, Olshausen, Beck, Delitzsch, Auberlen, White, and Heard, but it did not meet with great favor in the theological world. (pp. 191-192)

One recognizes a trichotomic view in the psychology of the romantic philosophers. As Ellenberger (1970, p, 205) puts it, "Van Schubert distinguished three constitutive parts of the human being: *Leib* (the living body), soul, and spirit." Troxler took this a step further, distinguishing between *leib* and *korper*, or soma and body, as well as soul and spirit. The soul was responsible for intellectual knowledge (and thus incorporated mind) while the spirit opened the person to the divine light (Ellenberger, 1970, p. 206). Already we see here a trichotomy more complex than that described by Berkhof: The nature of the soul is something other than an animate principle, and its function more than intermediary. There was something more complex about the fully functioning human being than the spiritual component. But just how this other component was related to the spiritual was confusing. Fechner (cited in Lowrie, 1946) summarized this ambiguity in *Ueber die Seelenfrage* (1861):

> Now it is in point to say what I understand by the words spirit and soul. It is notorious that almost every one conceives differently the relation of spirit and soul, and doubtless many conceive it in a way one cannot comprehend. Perhaps a few words on this subject, if not absolutely necessary, may be useful.
>
> For illustration, take a circle, divide it by a perpendicular line into right and left halves, then horizontally into upper and lower. One usage is to call the whole circle indifferently spirit or soul; another to all the right half spirit, the left half soul, a third, to call the upper part spirit, the lower part soul.
>
> In the first sense spirit and soul as a whole are opposed to the body as a whole. In the second sense the spirit is the active principle, masculine, creative, generative ... while the soul is the desiring, the receptive, the womanly side....
> In the third sense the spirit is the higher, the soul the lower—no longer a queen but a maidservant. (pp. 133-134)

The first of these is of course the familiar dichotomous position generally recognized as "biblical," which lies at the base of the endless controversies over the mind-body relation. The latter two are versions of trichotomous positions. In the second we recognize the familiar Jungian distinction between anima and animus, based on the ancient Eastern principle of the *Yin* and *Yang*. In the third we have a restatement of the early Christian trichotomy which is articulated in a somewhat different manner by Weidner (1912):

> The spirit and soul of man are to be distinguished as primary and secondary, but not with the view that the spirit and soul are substantially one and the same. Two passages in this connection, claim special consideration, 1 Thess. 5:23 and Heb. 4:12.

> There is no natural soul between spirit and body, but only a life of the soul that proceeds from the spirit itself. The spiritual or understanding soul and the bodily soul are in their essence and nature one. The one thing we must stress is that the soul is of one nature with the spirit.
>
> The soul proceeds from the spirit.... The true view is that the soul, whether it be called substance or potentiality, is not the spirit itself, but another nature conditioned by the spirit, although standing incomparably nearer to it than to the body. Possibly it is best to say, the spirit and soul are of one nature, but of distinct substances. (pp. 14-16)

Pathology: Psychological or Spiritual?

It is essentially this version of trichotomy that is articulated by many contemporary depth psychologists who are forced to confront the unconscious in all its complexity and, through their clinical experience, find that it manifests itself in two forms which are at times distinct, at other times indistinguishable: Spirit and soul. Such a version of trichotomy may be found in Frankl, who divided individual functioning into three factors: Physical, psychological, and spiritual (Tweedie, 1961). Here, we are spiritual beings who have a psyche. Consciousness grows out of unconscious spirituality, which also gives rise to love, conscience, and esthetic appreciation. The spirit may be masked by the psyche, in that neuroses and psychoses interfere with the free expression of spirituality.

This raises perpetually recurring critical questions in the dialogues concerning integration: What is the relationship between mental health and salvation? Are there spiritual illnesses as well as mental illnesses? How does illness spring from the unconscious? An early response to these questions came from Carus (1846) in his history of the unconscious. Carus asserted that "the unconscious is basically sound and does not know disease; one of its functions is 'the healing power of Nature'" (cited in Ellenberger, 1970, p. 208). Twentieth-century psychology has cast considerable doubt on Carus' assertion, especially the neo-Jungian group: "In quite general terms, it can be stated that forces excluded from the conscious mind accumulate and build up a tension in the unconscious, and that this tension is quite definitely destructive" (Neumann, 1969, p. 49). And equating such destructiveness with the "spiritual" aspect of persons creates considerable difficulty, unless the simple equation of sickness and sin is affirmed.

Ulanov and Ulanov (1975) address some of these issues in their discussion of soul (by which they mean spirit) and psyche. They claim, as did Weidner (1912), that it is the spirit which lies behind, and is the source of a healthy psyche: "The psyche enables one to be a person and to become a self. The soul offers the psyche that wishing, desiring, hoping, giving, altogether attentive willingness to be one's own self, one's own person, in relation to the multiple worlds of otherness" (p. 96). They claim that "the soul, unlike the psyche, cannot be defeated by sickness, whether of the body or the psyche, though it is certainly seriously affected by it. Neurosis is not sin, after all, nor is health the state of grace" (pp. 91-92). In fact, for the Ulanovs the critical difference between spirit and psyche is that "the soul [spirit] can make use even of illness in ways that the psyche cannot" (p. 91). Hillman (1975) makes the same point:

> Pathologizing, so says spirit, is by its very nature confined only to soul; only the psyche can be pathological, as the word psychopathology attests. There is no "pneumapathology," and as one German tradition has insisted, there can be no such thing as *mental* illness (*Geisteskrankheit*), for the spirit cannot pathologize.... *The psyche does not exist without pathologizing.* Since the unconscious was discovered as an operative factor in every soul, pathologizing has been recognized as an inherent aspect of the interior personality. (pp. 69-70)

Thus, while it is true, as White (1960) asserts, that "religion can no more exclude from the psyche what, by general consent, belongs to the psyche than psychology can exclude from the psyche what traditionally is ascribed to the soul" (p. 13), there is a clinical rationale for distinguishing between the psychological and the spiritual. The realms diverge in psychopathology, and to treat psychological pathologizing as a spiritual problem constitutes a dangerous scotoma in one's therapeutic world view. Certainly it is true that the spiritual processes of justification, regeneration, and sanctification enable the person to pursue psychological wholeness. But there is also a necessity to approach the psyche on its own terms, in its own language and modes:

> We have lost the third, middle position which earlier in our tradition, and in others too, was the place of soul: a world of imagination, passion, fantasy, reflection, that is neither physical and material on the one hand, nor spiritual and abstract on the other, yet bound to them both. By having its own realm psyche has its own logic—psychology— which is neither a science of physical things nor a metaphysics of spiritual things. Psychological pathologies also belong to this realm. Approaching them from either side, in terms of medical sickness or religion's suffering, sin, and salvation, misses the target of soul. (Hillman, 1975, pp. 67-68)

Two Distinct Disciplines

Although there is no need to challenge the exegetical scholarship that led the dominant Christian tradition to conclude that a biblical anthropology is essentially dichotomous, such an anthropology is also limited to its own culture and time. It is no mere coincidence that a distinct discipline of psychology emerged late in the nineteenth century at a time when philosophers and theologians and physiologists were each, in their own way, beginning to attend to the unconscious mind and its processes. But this was, in itself, also no mere historical accident. If the historians of the unconscious have given us a correct analysis, the unconscious was not only a new concept but also a new phenomenon: Only at that time in history had consciousness sufficiently differentiated itself from the unconscious for depth psychology to have an object of study different from that of the theologian, philosopher, or psychologist of perception.

Perhaps the most shattering insight of depth psychology was the recognition that previous notions of rationality (which are foundational to our theologies) were woefully inadequate, having accounted only for conscious interests of the ego. As Hartmann (1939/1958) pointed out, rationality must include mental functions such as dreams and fantasy as well as the more respected logic and intellect. Theology was thus pointed back to the richness of the mythological tradition (and the mythopoeic function of the unconscious), while psychology was forced to penetrate more deeply into the rich inner world. This leads us to support a view of the psychical world such as that expressed by Maher (quoted by Arnett, 1904, p. 356):

> *Mind* designates the animating principle as the subject of consciousness, while soul refers to it as the root of all forms of vital activity. Spirit is of narrower extension than mind, indicating properly a being capable of the *higher*

rational or *intellectual* order of conscious life.

In modern consciousness these functions are increasingly differentiated, and psychic life is accordingly more complex. And the insights of depth psychologists are new because they are studying a different dimension of personhood from that which has been the focus of classical, traditional, systematic theologies, even though this new dimension interacts with the spiritual world of the depths. And just as spirit and psyche are distinct. theology and psychology should remain distinct in their identities and goals. Thus, Ulanov and Ulanov (1975) argue against reductionism by either discipline, and claim that "we cannot ... make any easy equation between psychic health and the sanctification of the soul" (p. 89).

Conclusion

Thus, the task of integration is neither to construct a "Christian psychology" based entirely on biblical anthropology, which leaves out all the enriching aspects of the psyche, nor to construct a psychologically sophisticated theology, which would still ignore the unique issues of psychopathologizing and genuine soul-making. Rather, it is to construct a model which allows the process of soul-making (or mental health) to meet in the depths with the processes of sanctification, leading to a person who is both spiritually and psychologically whole. In the depths, processes of intrapersonal integration (assimilation and accommodation) are constantly taking place. It is here that a spiritual decision is assimilated through dreams, fantasies, and imaginative processes of the psyche. Here too spiritual growth is accommodated, leading to a restructuring of the person which facilitates further psychological growth. Each function—psychological and spiritual—serves as a catalyst for the other, but they are not substitutes for each other. When either is neglected, the other suffers in response. Thus, psychology and theology walk hand in hand, as parents of a child destined to become spiritually sanctified and psychologically whole. When the parents divorce, or engage in other forms of conflict, the child is pulled in one direction or another, personifying "psychology without the spirit" and "theology without a soul." Psychology without a spirit tends to lose its soul as well, becoming the objectivist science with which we are so familiar. Theology without a soul results in an impoverished life of the spirit, a religious life filled with intellectual understanding and assent, but no personal experi-ence of God's promises. The wisdom of the mystics and the insights of the depth psychologists call each of them back from a reductionist perspective, that has no room for the other, to a relationship of mutual cooperation and respect.

References

Arnett, L. D., (1904). The soul, a study of past and present beliefs. *American Journal of Psychology, 15*(2), 121-200; 15(3), 347-382.

Berkhof, L. (1938). *Systematic theology.* Grand Rapids, MI: Eerdmans.

Carus, C. G. (1846). *Psyche, zur Entwickslungsgeschichte der Seele.* Pforzheim: Flammer Und Hoffman.

Delitzsch, F. (1966). *A system of biblical psychology.* Grand Rapids, MI: Baker. (Originally published, 1855)

Drakeford, J. W. (1964). *Psychology in search of a soul.* Nashville, TN: Broadman.

Ellenberger, H. F. (1970). *The discovery of the unconscious: The history and evolution of dynamic psychiatry.* New York: Basic.

Fechner, G. T. (1861). *Ueber die Seelenfrage: Ein Gang durch die Sichtbare Welt um die unsichtbare zu finden.* Leipzig: Amelang.

Freud, S. (1933). [*New introductory lectures on psychoanalysis*] (W. J. H. Sprott, Trans.). New York: Norton.

Fromm, E. (1950). *Psychoanalysis and religion.* New Haven, CT: Yale University.

Gruender, H. (1911). *Psychology without a soul: A criticism.* St. Louis, MO: Joseph Gumniersback.

Hartmann, H. (1961). [*Ego psychology and the problem of adaptation*] (D. Rapaport, Trans.). New York: International Universities. (Originally published, 1938)

Hillman, J. (1975). *Re-visioning psychology.* New York: Harper & Row.

James, W. (1950). *The principles of psychology* (2 Vols.). New York: Dover. (Originally published, 1890)

James, W. (1961). *The varieties of religious experience.* New York: Collier-Macmillan. (Originally published, 1902)

Jaynes, J. (1976). *The origins of consciousness in the breakdown of the bicameral mind.* Boston, MA: Houghton Mifflin.

Jung, C. G. (1916). [*Psychology of the unconscious*] (B. M. Hinkle, Trans.). New York: Moffatt Yard. (Originally published, 1912)

Jung, C. G. [*Modern man in search of a soul*] (W. S. Dell & C. F. Baynes, Trans.). New York: Harcourt, Brace & World.

Kahler, E. (1957). *The tower and the abyss: An inquiry into the transformation of the individual.* New York: Braziler.

Lowrie, W. (Ed. and trans..). (1946). *Religion of a scientist: Selections from Gustav Th. Fechner.* London: Kegan Paul, Trench, Trubner.

Neumann, E. (1954). *The origins and history of consciousness.* Princeton, NJ: Princeton University.

Neumann, E. (1969). [*Depth psychology and a new ethic*] (E. Rolfe, Trans.). New York. Harper. (Originally published, 1949)

Perry, R. B. (1935). *The thought and character of William James* (2 Vols.). Boston, MA: Little, Brown & Co.

Rank, O. (1961). [*Psychology and the soul*] (W. D. Turner, Trans.). New York: A. S. Barnes. (Originally published, 1931)

Tart, C. T. (Ed.). (1975). *Transpersonal psychologies.* New York: Harper & Row.

Tweedie, D. F., Jr. (1961). *Logotherapy: An evaluation of Frankl's existential approach to psychotherapy.* Grand Rapids, MI: Baker.

Ulanov, A., & Ulanov, B. (1975). *Religion and the unconscious.* Philadelphia, PA: Westminster.

Vande Kemp, H. (1982). The tension between psychology and theology: The etymological roots. *Journal of Psychology and Theology, 10*(2), 105-112.

Watson, R. I. (1963). *The great psychologists: Aristotle to Freud* (2nd ed.). Philadelphia, PA: Lippincott.

Weidner, F. (1912). *The doctrine of man: Outline notes based on Luthardt.* Chicago: Wartburg.

Zilbourg, G., & Henry, G. W. (1941). *A history of medical psychology.* New York: Norton.

Sola Scriptura: Then and Now

James R. Beck
Denver Conservative Baptist Seminary

The current debate among Christian counselors regarding the value and/or the danger of integration has prompted all parties involved to discuss the role of Scripture relative to other forms of knowledge. This article discusses two historical precedents for this current debate: the struggle among second and third century apologists regarding how the church should view ancient Greek philosophy and the Protestant assertion of the principle of *sola scriptura* during the Reformation era as an alternative to the Roman system which afforded equal authority to both Scripture and tradition. The article explores how these earlier debates among Christians are similar to and different from the current debate among Christian counselors.

A host of sincere people has recently raised a number of Protestant Reformation themes in an attempt to keep modern evangelical Christianity in close connection with its historic roots. The Cambridge Declaration outlines these themes (*sola scriptura, solus Christus, sola gratia, sola fide, soli deo gloria*) as the standards by which the evangelical church can measure current praxis against true, historic Christianity (Christians United for Reformation, 1996). *Sola scriptura* heads the list because it highlights the need to have questions of authority clearly defined before the other components of biblically anchored faith can be determined. The Cambridge Declaration insists that many modern trends and influences, including psychology and therapeutic technique, have threatened the commitment of evangelicals to the principle that Scripture alone must be our authority.

This famous battle cry of the Protestant Reformation has also appeared with vigor and force in the current debate among Christian counselors regarding the relative place of Scripture and other forms of knowledge, principally psychological knowledge, in counseling ministries. Since the rise of the Christian counseling movement, evangelical Christians have striven to understand how they should or should not utilize the vast amount of information about human behavior that has been generated by the social science of psychology and its related discipline of psychotherapy. Evangelicals are divided in their opinions on this matter.

A significant group of people strenuously object to the use of findings from the psychological disciplines. They argue that this psychological knowledge is, in fact, representative of a new, secular religion that is competing for the minds and affections of people. MacArthur (1991) writes, "Unfamiliarity with the Spirit's sanctifying work has opened the door for the church's current obsession with psychology. Psychological sanctification has become a substitute for the Spirit-filled life" (p. 105). Thus those who would be faithful to the Bible must shun the use of these findings and rely instead solely upon the Bible and what it teaches. In addition, opponents of the integration enterprise have alleged that advocates of integration have mishandled, abused, and otherwise distorted Scripture in their attempt to bolster their claim that material from psychology can be legitimately used by Christian professionals in their work with people. Bulkley (1993) asserts that the Christian public is deceived by the claims of Christian psychology because its advocates quote Scripture out of context, distort the true meaning of the Bible, deny the teachings of the Bible, or otherwise add to or delete from the Bible's message. Regarding modern evangelicalism, one writer claims that an interest in using psychological science has nearly ruined the church. "While still professing that God's revelation in Scripture is sufficient for salvation, it has nearly, if not virtually, abandoned it in favor of modern psychological theories and techniques for sanctification" (Kistler, 1995, p. 279).

Another large group of evangelicals argues that it is very possible for Christians to be faithful to historic, biblical Christianity while at the same time utilizing reliable findings from the discipline of psychology. The name most frequently attached to this position is integration. Pro-integrationists have proposed various models to guide and direct this endeavor (Carter & Narramore, 1979; Farnsworth, 1985; Jones & Butman, 1991). Integrationists differ from those who oppose the movement on several scores. Integrationists argue that all truth has God as its source and therefore cannot be feared or shunned; that Scripture is totally and completely sufficient regarding the establishment and maintenance of fellowship with God (salvation and sanctification); that the special revelation we have in the Bible serves as a guide for exploring general revelation; and that Scripture itself gives us precedents for how God-honoring believers used knowledge from sources other than the Bible to serve God.

Both camps, those who favor integration and those who oppose it, would affirm the value and importance of the Reformation principle of *sola scriptura*. These two groups would disagree, however, as to what the phrase actually means. Anti-integrationists argue that the *sola scriptura* principle requires us to use no other knowledge than what we glean from Scripture in our work with distressed people. Pro-integrationists counter by asserting that the *sola scriptura* principle refers only to the knowledge we need about God, God's will for people, and God's plan of salvation and sanctification for them.

Anti-integrationists have consistently implied in their writings that their position on the matter is the only true and historic Christian position regarding the use of knowledge derived from non-biblical sources. Such an implication is incorrect since we can find disagreement on this very issue throughout the history of the church. Spanning back over the centuries one can identify two major examples of this disagreement among Christians found first, among second and third century Christian apologists and later in the Protestant Reformation era itself. This article will review those two historical examples in the hope that we can better understand the context of the current *sola scriptura* debate.

Second and Third Century Apologists

As the church began to spread throughout the Roman empire, it became necessary for educated and skilled leaders to defend Christianity in the intellectual arenas of the day (Timothy, 1973). For example, a critic named Celsus wrote in his *True Discourse* that Christianity was not a new ethic but simply one borrowed from existing philosophies, that Christianity's attack on idolatry was not new but was anticipated by Greek philosophers, and that Christians disparaged reason (Latourette, 1953). Christian apologists had to respond to these vitriolic attacks that were made against Christians; and they had to demonstrate that the Christian religion was not only anchored in history, it was also morally superior to any other alternative religious system. In the process then of creating an effective apologetic for Christianity, these early church fathers were forced to deal with Greek philosophy. The apolo-

gists were very critical of the personal morals of the philosophers and the errors and inconsistencies in pagan thought (Grant, 1988). This apologetic approach thus shares much in common with current attacks on psychology by Christians who claim it cannot be legitimately used by believers.

The apologists asked, How did philosophy compare with the teachings of the Bible? Should Christians jettison any and all use of Greek thought forms because they had pagan, pre-Christian origins? Or could they be used under the authority of revealed truth in the Bible? The apologists differed in their attitude toward pre-Christian thought. The "relation of truth to speculative thought in the mid-second century may have varied in different places just as the relation of truth to the Bible varied since the New Testament canon was not fixed" (Story, 1970, p. xxi). Chief among those who adopted a very negative attitude toward Greek philosophy and its potential use by Christians was Tertullian.

Tertullian of Carthage, c150-225

Many authorities believe Tertullian was a lawyer who converted to Christianity as an adult. He is a prominent example of the North African school of theology and is best known as the first of the great Latin church fathers. He abandoned writing in Greek quite early in his career to write most of his works in Latin. His contribution to the development of the Christian doctrine of the Trinity is widely praised; in fact, he coined the word "trinity."

Greek philosophy was much older than was Christianity. Tertullian's attitude toward it was not positive as the following quotation from his *De praescriptione haereticorum* indicates.

> It is this philosophy which is the subject matter of this world's wisdom, that rash interpreter of the divine nature and order. In fact, heresies are themselves prompted by philosophy.... Wretched Aristotle! who taught them dialectic, that art of building up and demolishing, so protean in statement, so far-fetched in conjecture, so unyielding in controversy, so productive of disputes, self-stultifying, since it is ever handling questions but never settling anything: What is there in common between Athens and Jerusalem? What between the Academy and the Church? What between heretics and Christians? ... Away with all projects for a "Stoic," a "Platonic" or a "dialectic" Christianity! After Christ Jesus we desire no subtle

theories, no acute inquiries after the gospel. (Bettenson, 1943, pp. 9-10)

Tertullian was not plain-spoken; his prose was colorful, vigorous, and polemical, if not pugnacious. He called Plato in one place the "Patriarch of heretics" and labeled the serene death of Socrates as nothing but "a forced or affected composure" (Neve, 1946, Vol. 1, p. 93). "For Tertullian there are no positive connections between the faith of Christians and the philosophy of the Greeks" (Dueck, 1995, p. 153). He viewed Greek philosophy as rash and worldly, a pernicious influence toward evil, a discipline that seduces people from the truth, and a major source of heresy (Morgan, 1928).

Yet our analysis of Tertullian and his attitude toward Greek philosophy cannot end with a mere review of his rhetorical statements. A careful reading of Tertullian reveals that he frequently used Stoic and Platonic elements in building his theology. "Others have shown that he borrowed extensively from the very philosophers whom he blamed for having given rise to heresy" (Gonzalez, 1993, p. 148). Tertullian knew that Greek philosophy was the teaching of men and was by itself untrue as opposed to Christianity which was from God and was true. Nonetheless, his mind was saturated "with Stoic thought," he produced a "Christianized Stoicism," and "he was especially fond of the writings of Plato and the Stoics" (Morgan, 1928, pp. 11, 12). How do we account for this internal inconsistency in the thought and writings of Tertullian?

Gonzalez (1993) proposes that Tertullian posed Athens and Jerusalem as polar opposites but not in the manner in which reason and faith are opposites. Instead, Gonzalez asserts that Athens and Jerusalem represent two types of reason. Athens stands for dialectical reason that guides itself by itself and Jerusalem represents historical reason that uses facts. Ayers (1979) argues that Tertullian's attacks on Greek philosophy must be understood in the context in which they were made: Tertullian's attacks on heresy. In fact, the famous Athens-Jerusalem remark is made in a major work on heresy. "To be sure he insists that the rule of faith should serve as the dominant norm for the Christian's thought, but this does not mean that all philosophy must be rejected" (Ayers, 1979, p. 27). He only rejected the philosophy that Gnostics used to bolster their heresy.

Positive Apologetic Views of Greek Philosophy

Other second and third century Christian apologists were much more receptive to the careful use of Greek philosophy under the guidance of the superior revelation of Scripture. If current anti-inte-

grationists find Tertullian to be their patron saint, pro-integrationists are very likely to resonate heartily with the work of Justin Martyr, Clement of Alexandria, and Athanasius.

Justin Martyr, who wrote his *Apology* around 150 A.D., exhibited a very positive view toward ancient Greek philosophies.

> Whatever has been uttered aright by any men in any place belongs to us Christians; for, next to God, we worship and love the reason (Word) which is from the unbegotten and ineffable God; since on our account He has been made man, that, being made partaker of our sufferings, he may also bring us healing. For all the authors were able to see the truth darkly, through the implanted seed of reason (the Word) dwelling in them. For the seed and imitation of a thing, given according to a man's capacity, is one thing; far different is the thing itself, the sharing of which and its representation is given according to his grace. (Bettenson, 1943, pp. 8-9)

It is not hard to detect that Justin Martyr is quite optimistic about how Christians can benefit from the study of knowledge that predates the New Testament, especially Platonists and the Stoics (Droge, 1993). He rejected Greek religion, but he felt Greek philosophy had much to contribute. He saw in Plato the truths that God is "Transcendent, as well as immutable, impossible, incorporeal, and nameless" (Ferguson, 1993, p. 306). He was not attempting to reconcile Christianity to Greek philosophy because he was convinced that Christianity embodied truth in its fullness. Christianity corrects and completes what is elsewhere incomplete but still useful. As an apologist he argued,

> If therefore, we agree on some points with your honored poets and philosophers, and on other points offer a more complete and supernatural teaching, and if we alone produce proof of our statements, why are we unjustly hated beyond all others? (Falls, 1948, p. 35)

Indeed, "We can understand why Justin Martyr, that 'philosopher in the mantle of a Christian,' would speak of Socrates as having practically been a Christian" (Neve, 1946, vol. 1, p. 21).

Another example of an early Christian apologist who wrote with positive attitudes toward the disciplined use of pre-Christian knowledge is Clement of Alexandria. Clement was very influential in the

development of early Christology. He felt that training in philosophy was excellent preparation for the
mind. He noted that Plato urged his followers to be
students of nature just as Scripture did in Proverbs
6:6, 8 (Ferguson, 1991). The Greek mysteries were
profane and unholy. Greek religion was bankrupt
and foolish to worship "gods" who were mere
humans in origin and immoral at that. Yet some
philosophers knew a great deal of truth (Plato,
Antisthenes, Xenophon, Socrates, Cleanthes,
Pythagoras) in that they recognized the majesty of the
true God (Butterworth, 1979). In philosophy we can
find sufficient truth to lead us to investigate more fully
the truth that is found most completely in the Bible.

It is possible to trace this line of reasoning in subsequent centuries of church history. Only one
example will be mentioned, namely that of Philip
Melanchthon (1497-1560), the great theological colleague of Martin Luther. He, like Justin and Clement
in earlier centuries, felt that the study of philosophy
was valuable for Christians. He is well known for
saying that an uneducated theology is an "Illiad of
ills" (Keen, 1988, p. 66). Moral philosophy has a
positive contribution to make to the education and
preparation of the Christian. He wrote,

> Nor do I wish to mix them together, as
> a cook mixes a stew, but I wish to help
> the theologian in the economy of
> method…. It seems to me that it is a
> help in leading life to choose a role that
> does not have a zeal for disputes as its
> goal, but the inquiry of truth, and which
> also loves moderate views, and does not
> seize upon the praises of the unlearned,
> deceptive arguments and absurd views.
> (Keen, 1988, p. 68, 69)

Regarding Melanchthon, he "did not observe the
distinction between secular and sacred texts,
between Athens and Jerusalem in Tertullian's
image. This ability to combine the classical and the
biblical, and later the patristic traditions is a key to
understanding his work and his contribution to the
reformation" (Keen, 1988, p. 4). Melanchthon
secured for future generations a place for secular
learning and the various natural sciences by giving
them an auxiliary place next to and governed by
the pure doctrine of the church (Seeberg, 1964).

Sola Scriptura: A Reformation Battle Cry

The second great example of how the church has
wrestled with the roper use of knowledge from
non-biblical sources in our theology and ministry
comes directly out of the Protestant Reformation.

The Reformers did not direct massive amounts of
energy toward the issue of how to use or not use
ancient Greek philosophy, although the problem
did arise at times in connection with how to evaluate the Scholasticism of the Middle Ages. Instead,
the Reformers aimed their attention at the relationship between church tradition and Scripture. In this
instance, the issue was not focused on knowledge
gathered previous to the revelation contained in the
New Testament but knowledge gathered subsequent to inscripturation. Here the struggle did not
concern knowledge generated by non-Christians or
pre-Christians but by Christians themselves.

Roman Catholic theology had come to grant
authority to both Scripture and tradition. Both were,
in turn, under the authority of the church. At the
time the Protestant Reformation began to unfold in
the sixteenth century, this system of dual authority
had been in place for a considerable length of time
and was, in fact, related to the existence within the
church of many theological problems that the
Reformers desperately wanted to change. So it
became necessary for them to address the issue
early in the reformation process.

Martin Luther and *Sola Scriptura*

One can find pre-Reformation rumblings of theological insistence on *sola scriptura*. For example, in
1324 Marsilius of Padua wrote a treatise entitled
Defensor Pacis, a work that resulted in papal condemnation from both John XXII in 1327 and Gregory
XI in 1378. "Marsilius can be said to have held a doctrine of *sola scriptura* as far as politics was concerned" (Willis, 1984, p. 282). Marsilius was used by
Cranmer and Hooker in the sixteenth century English
Reformation as an important source and authority for
their work. John Wyclif also gives hints of *sola scriptura* convictions when he rejected various portions
of earlier Scholastic theology that did not conform to
Scripture. These examples notwithstanding, Martin
Luther is the prominent name attached to the development of the *sola scriptura* Reformation emphasis.

In order to understand better Luther's attitude
toward tradition, it is helpful to review his attitudes
toward philosophy in general and Greek philosophy
in particular as discussed in the previous section of
this article. He attacked Scholastic Theology's practice of building upon Aristotelian philosophy, but he
did not attack philosophy as a discipline. He felt that
good philosophy could be used as "an ordering
principle by which the biblical revelation was clearly set forth" (George, 1988, p. 58). His very famous
statement at Worms ("Unless I am convicted by
Scripture and plain reason, I cannot and I will not

recant") indicates that he was not opposed to philosophy or reason in general, as long as it was utilized under the authority of Scripture.

In 1519 Eck forced Luther to affirm the conviction of John Hus that the authority of the general church councils and the pope must be rejected. This conviction launched Luther into the development of a *sola scriptura* doctrine that found expression in his 1520 *Babylonian Captivity of the Church*: "What is asserted without the Scriptures or proven revelation may be held as an opinion, but need not be believed" (George, 1988, p. 80-81). Luther taught that Scripture is the *norma normans* (determining norm) but not the *norma normata* (determined norm). In other words, the Bible is the guide or rule by which all other teaching is evaluated; even the church itself is derived from Scripture and is subject to the authority of Scripture. The Bible has authority because of itself, not because the church forwards authority to it. The then current Roman system of two streams of authority (tradition and Scripture) under the rule of the church was clearly under attack. To medieval teachings about Scripture (its authority, perfection, soteriological necessity and redemptive sufficiency) the Reformers now add the principle of *sola scriptura* (Muller, 1993).

Luther's proclamations triggered an intense discussion of the canon of the Bible. The Roman system asserted that the canon was set and stable because the church had so recognized it. Luther argued, by way of contrast, that the church was merely attesting the authenticity of the canon but was not granting to it its authenticity. The Bible, declared the Reformers, was self-authenticating and did not need the church to make it so.

The principles of *sola scriptura, sola gratia*, and *sola fide* were all taken up by other Reformers such as Zwingli and Calvin. Zwingli claimed that *sola scriptura* had its roots in Augustine who wrote. "Lo here you have the Scripture as master and teacher and guide, not the Fathers, not the misunderstood Church of certain people" (George, 1988, p. 126-127). Calvin became a systematic expositor of these basic Reformation themes.

The resulting Reformation doctrine is well expressed by sections of the Belgic Confession (1561):

> We believe that these Holy Scriptures fully contain the will of God and teach sufficiently all that man must believe if he is to be saved. (Article 7) (Vanderwaal, 1978, p. 7)
>
> Neither may we consider any writings of men, however holy these men may have been, of equal value with those divine Scriptures ... (Article 7) (Greidanus, 1970, p. 1)

The Reformers did not jettison tradition; they merely made it subordinate to the authority of Scripture. The authority of all councils and theologians is subordinate to and derived from Scripture; even the authority of church officials comes from Scripture and not from the office itself (McGrath, 1988). The church was clearly not more authoritative than Scripture in the convictions of the Reformers.

The magesterial Reformers did not espouse *nuda scripture* (only the Bible and nothing but the Bible). For example, their exegesis of Scripture is in the tradition of those who came before them, for the most part.

> It is thus entirely anachronistic to view the *sola scriptura* of Luther and his contemporaries as a declaration that all of theology ought to be constructed anew, without reference to the church's tradition of interpretation, by the lonely exegete confronting the naked text. (Muller, 1993, p. 51)

Likewise, many of the Reformers wished to retain some aspects of tradition in their theological system. Infant baptism ("though apostolic, was not expressly taught in Scripture," Pelikan, 1984, p. 265) is one example of a teaching with more of an anchor in tradition than in Scripture that many Reformers retained.

Mainstream Reformation thought thus did not dispense with tradition; it merely brought it under the authority of the Bible. Scripture was an infallible rule for making theological judgments. Scripture judged the church and tradition but that did not mean the church and tradition had no role. Other information could be used and should be used by believers and those willing to submit non-biblical material to the scrutiny of the Bible. It was necessary for us to make use of non-biblical material in order to function well in the world. "It is equally anachronistic to assume that Scripture functioned for the Reformers like a set of numbered facts or propositions suitable for use as ready made solutions to any and all questions capable of arising in the course of human history" (Muller, 1993, p. 51-52).

The Radical Reformation and Sola Scriptura

Some radical Reformers in the Anabaptist tradition wanted to rid the church of an attachment to tradition but wished to retain some room for the role on an "inner light" that could help reveal God's will to us. However, most of the radical reformers took the *sola scriptura* principle to its logical extreme, something Reformers in the Magesterial Reformation did not do. The radicals attempted to obey only Scripture without any heed to convention or tradition. People were seen running nude through the streets of Amsterdam because of Isaiah 20:2-3, preaching from the rooftops because of Matthew 10:27, or masquerading as children because of Matthew 10:2-4 (George, 1988). Some radicals began to advocate polygamy by "drawing upon patriarchal precedent" (Pelikan, 1984, p. 265). This understanding of the radicals regarding the meaning of *sola scriptura* did not represent the majority view among reformers, however.

Roman Catholic Response to Sola Scriptura Teaching

The Roman Catholic church responded to Reformation teaching about the primacy of Scripture with vigor. The Council of Trent addressed much of its energy toward a refutation of *sola scriptura*. Roman Catholic theologians charged that a complete detachment from tradition would put such doctrines as the Trinity and the Person of Christ at great risk since both of these doctrines were forged at the great church councils at Nicea and Chalcedon. Those who stood in the Reformation tradition responded that Protestants had no intention of dismantling the theological structures that the early church had constructed, although they asserted that the work of the great church councils was only reliable and authoritative to the degree that it fully conformed to Scripture and was derived from it. Protestants retained the Apostle's Creed and the great formulations of Nicea and Chalcedon as expressions of the "true intentions of Scripture against heretical deviations" (George, 1988, p. 82). These creeds were coinherent with the Scripture although Scripture had priority.

Another major Roman Catholic attack on *sola scriptura* revolved around the Protestant trend of writing and following their own creeds. If Reformers were going to be consistent, they would have to forego the adding of new tests of faith; after all, if Scripture is sufficient as a rule of faith how can anyone add a new Confession of Faith or a new creed to which all clergy must conform? The Reformation leader Bellarmine responded that Protestant creeds were indeed norms but that they were subject to another, higher norm: that of Scripture.

Roman Catholics also charged Reformers with removing tradition and the church from the sphere of authority along with Scripture and merely substituting individual interpretation as a new source of authority that in actuality paralleled Scripture. Catholic theologians pointed out that by allowing such a high place for the role of individual interpretation, Protestants were opening themselves up to the development of heresy much the same as had occurred with the Arians centuries earlier. Individual interpretation certainly did begin to introduce disagreements, especially over the nature of the Lord's supper. Many of those disagreements among those sixteenth century Reformers regarding the true meaning of the Lord's Supper endure to the present time. As soon as the authority of the church to interpret Scripture was removed, unity became the first victim and diversity of theological thought began to rule the day among Protestants.

Both the Reformers and Roman Catholic theologians agreed to reject any and all human reason and custom when it disagreed with the teachings of Scripture. But they disagreed on whether there are truths not found in Scripture or deducible from it that must be believed as a condition for salvation. The tradition which was handed down from the Apostolic Age retained its authority for Roman Catholics but lost its authority for Reformers.

Conclusion

These two historical illustrations bear some similarities to twentieth century struggles while at the same time sustaining substantial differences from them. For example, the struggle of early church fathers regarding the proper place of Greek philosophy and the Reformers' struggle against tradition as an equal authority along with Scripture both deal with non-biblical sources of human knowledge: in the former instance, human knowledge produced by non-Christians before the revelation of the New Testament and, in the latter instance, human knowledge produced by Christians after the production of the New Testament. Critics of Christian psychology focus their attention primarily on recent knowledge produced by non-believers and assert that we should not use that material. Integrationists argue that we can use that information when it is used under the authority of the Bible in a way similar to that advocated by those who favor Christian liberal arts education.

Furthermore, the early church illustration gives us examples of someone such as Tertullian who could argue vigorously against the use of any non-biblical material but who could not succeed in actually doing it and of those who could use non-biblical material while still being faithful to Scripture. The Reformation example gives us a picture of advocates of *sola scriptura* who believed in the primacy of Scripture rather than in its absolute exclusivity, as well as a picture of those who tried to apply the principle of *sola scriptura* in an absolute sense and failed at the task.

References

Ayers, R. H. (1979). *Language, logic, and reason in the church fathers: A study of Tertullian, Augustine, and Aquinas.* New York: Georg Olms Verlag.

Bettenson, H. (Ed.). (1943). *Documents of the Christian church.* New York: Oxford University Press.

Bulkley, E. (1993). *Why Christians can't trust psychology.* Eugene, OR: Harvest House Publishers.

Butterworth, G. W. (Trans.). (1979). *Clement of Alexandria.* Cambridge, MA: Harvard University Press.

Carter, J. D., & Narramore, S. B. (1979). *The integration of psychology and theology: An introduction.* Grand Rapids, MI: Zondervan.

Christians United for Reformation (1996). *The Cambridge Declaration.* Anaheim, CA: Author.

Droge, A. J. (1993). Justin Martyr and the restoration of philosophy. In E. Ferguson (Ed.), *The early church and Graeco-Roman thought* (65-81). New York: Garland Publishing, Inc.

Dueck, A. C. (1995). *Between Athens and Jerusalem.* Grand Rapids, MI: Baker Books.

Falls, T. B. (Trans.). (1948). *Saint Justin Martyr.* Washington, DC: The Catholic University of America Press.

Farnsworth, K. E. (1985). *Wholehearted integration: Harmonizing psychology and Christianity through word and deed.* Grand Rapids, MI: Baker Book House.

Ferguson, E. (1993). *The early church and Graeco-Roman thought.* New York: Garland Publishing, Inc.

Ferguson, J. (Trans.). (1991). *Clement of Alexandria, Stromateis, books one to three.* Washington, DC: The Catholic University of America Press.

George, T. (1988). *Theology of the reformers.* Nashville, TN: Broadman Press.

Gonzalez, J. L. (1993). Athens and Jerusalem revisited: Reason and authority in Tertullian. In E. Ferguson, (Ed.), *The early church and Graeco-Roman thought* (pp. 147-155). New York: Garland Publishing, Inc.

Grant, R. M. (1988). *Greek apologists of the second century.* Philadelphia: Westminster Press.

Greidanus, S. (1970). *Sola scriptura: Problems and principles in preaching historical texts.* Toronto: Wedge Publishing Foundation.

Jones, S. L., & Butman, R. E. (1991). *Modern psychotherapies: A comprehensive Christian appraisal.* Downers Grove, IL: InterVarsity Press.

Keen, R. (Trans.). (1988). *A Melanchthon reader.* New York: Peter Lang.

Kistler, D. (Ed.). (1995). *Sola scriptura: The Protestant position on the Bible.* Morgan, PA: Soli Dei Gloria Publications.

Latourette, K. S. (1953). *A history of Christianity.* New York: Harper & Row.

MacArthur, J. (1991). *Our sufficiency in Christ.* Dallas: Word Publishing.

McGrath, A. A. (1988). *Reformation thought.* Oxford: Basil Blackwell.

Morgan, J. (1928). *The importance of Tertullian in the development of Christian dogma.* London: KeganPaul, Trench, Trubner & Co., Ltd.

Muller, R. A. (1993). *Post-Reformation reformed dogmatics* (Vol. 2). Grand Rapids, MI: Baker Book House.

Neve, J. L. (1946). *A history of Christian thought* (Vols. 1-2). Philadelphia, PA: The Muhlenberg Press.

Pelikan, J. (1984). *The Christian tradition: A history of the development of doctrine,* Vol. 4. Chicago: The University of Chicago Press.

Seeberg, R. (1964). *Textbook of the history of doctrines.* Grand Rapids, MI: Baker Book House.

Story, C. I. K. (1970). *The nature of truth in the Gospel of Truth and in the writings of Justin Martyr.* Leiden: E. J. Brill.

Timothy, H. (1973). *The early Christian apologists and Greek philosophy.* Assen: Van Gorcum.

Vanderwaal, C. (1978). *Search the scriptures.* Vol. 1. St. Catharines, Ontario: Paideia Press.

Willis, J. R. (1984). *A history of Christian thought.* Vol. 2. Smithtown, NY: Exposition Press.

John Wesley and Psychology

H. Newton Malony
Fuller Theological Seminary

John Wesley was the founder of the Methodist movement. As a significant figure in Christian history, Wesley has import for modern Christian psychology in at least four ways: (1) his contention that the findings of science could be used by Christians for the glory of God and the alleviation of human suffering; (2) his personal example of how difficult it is to put faith into practice in daily living; (3) his teachings about the grace of God and the possibility of Christian perfection; and (4) his concern for social justice and the welfare of the poor. This essay discusses these issues and demonstrates how a study of Wesley can influence modern Christian psychology.

John Wesley was the 18th Century Anglican priest whose ministry led to the establishment of the Methodist movement in England, Wales, Scotland, and the United States. Widely read in matters of public health, medicine, natural science, and social policy, as well as in the literature of the Christian tradition, Wesley is of unique interest to modern Christian psychology for several reasons.

First, Wesley became convinced that secular knowledge could be used to the glory of God (English, 1991; Wesley, 1751, 1760). He struggled with how to incorporate the discoveries of Sir Isaac Newton into his ministry (Wesley, 1777b). This issue is similar to that faced by those who would integrate modern psychology and Christian theology (Malony, 1986a). Wesley provides an example of a paradigm that can still be used.

Second, for much of his life, Wesley struggled personally with religious doubt, uncertainty, and temptation. His persistent search for assurance of God's love can serve as a reminder of the difference between verbal affirmations and the inner difficulty persons might have in following a counselor's encouragement to apply religion to their daily life.

Third, because of his own triumph over his doubts, Wesley came to have a unique understanding about the grace of God and the process of spiritual development. His teachings on these issues view God's grace as like a seed that can grow with proper intention (Wesley, 1777a).[1] Wesley's ideas are very similar to the insights of today's cognitive-behavioral psychologists about the ways to achieve self-mastery (Myers, 1993, p. 424ff).

Lastly, although Oxford educated and from a privileged family, Wesley had a strong passion for social justice and was deeply concerned about the welfare of the poor. The last letter he wrote (February 14, 1791—one week before he died) was to William Wilberforce encouraging him in his efforts to end slavery in the British empire (cf. Colson, 1987). He published a home health-care manual that went through thirty-six editions (Malony, 1996; Wesley, 1751). He balanced a burden for personal salvation with an ethical concern for justice. This approach ties Wesley to the Hebrew prophets of eighth century B.C.E. and the teachings of Jesus. It provides a worthy example of compassionate concern which today's Christian psychologists would do well to emulate (Malony, 1986b).

John Wesley (1704-1791)

A brief survey of his life will help locate John Wesley in Christian history. His ministry led to the establishment of the Methodist movement in England, Wales, Ireland, Scotland, and the United States. His life spanned every decade of the eighteenth century. Like his father, Samuel, and his brother, Charles, Wesley became a priest in the Church of England. A graduate of Oxford, Wesley often preached but never functioned as a parish priest. Instead, he became a teacher of Greek and Hebrew at Lincoln College.

Although an ordained person, Wesley never felt sure of his own salvation and sought to cover up his doubts by over-zealousness. It might be conjectured that some of his pietistic compulsivity had its roots, in part, in his own psychological anxiety.[2] He preached faith, but was unsure of it himself. Out of a desire to assuage his own doubts about God's presence in his life, Wesley decided to leave Oxford in the mid-1730s and accept an invitation to become the chaplain of Georgia, a newly organized settlement in the new world. Troubled by his father's death and his own insecurity, Wesley entered into this new venture in hopes of converting the Indians and of "saving his own soul," as he wrote to a friend at Oxford.

Underneath his concern for the Indians was an interest in "folk medicine." Wesley thought that Indian medicine had not been contaminated by Western ideas, which focused on expensive medications that only the rich could afford. Later in his life, this interest in medicine became a passion for the welfare of the poor for whose sake he wrote a home health-care manual to be discussed in the final section of this article (Wesley, 1751).

An experience on the boat trip over to Georgia became very important to Wesley's Christian experience. The ship almost sank during an Atlantic storm. While Wesley was leading prayers in the bowels of the ship, a group of Moravian Christians remained on deck singing hymns as they continued going about their duties. Wesley was dumbfounded by their courage. He asked their leader how they had been able to remain calm in the midst of the storm. "Our people are not afraid to die," he was told. He was deeply impressed with the confident faith he saw in these unlettered Moravian Christians because it was so different from his own doubt and fears.

The conversion of the Indians was much more difficult than Wesley anticipated, and he had little chance to study their folk medicine. More importantly, however, was his experience with Sophie Hopkins, one of three women with whom Wesley was to have unfortunate experiences during his lifetime. He returned to England in the spring of 1738 feeling a failure both in romance and in evangelism.

For the next month, Wesley moped around London, feeling depressed and a failure. During this time he consulted periodically with the Moravian leader, Peter Bohler, over why he did not feel God's forgiveness for his sins. Bohler advised Wesley to "preach faith until he had it." On the night of May 24, he wandered into a Moravian prayer meeting on Aldersgate street where they were studying Luther's commentary on the book of Romans. He remembered the confidence the Moravians had shown during the Atlantic storm and hoped that he could reclaim his faith. During the meeting Wesley had a profound religious experience. The assurance of faith became real. He felt his "heart strangely warmed." He wrote that, for the first time in his life, he "did know his sins forgiven" (Wesley, 1738, p. 99). This sense of renewed faith became the passion of his life.

Within a few weeks of this experience, George Whitefield asked Wesley to take over his ministry of preaching in the fields near Bristol. Wesley decided to accept the invitation. After the response to his first sermon, Wesley became excited about the possibility that a similar revival might occur in Britain. Thus began almost fifty years of traversing the British Isles—preaching in the open air to those who would not come to church. It is estimated that, during his lifetime, Wesley traveled over 40,000 miles per year—first on horseback and then in a special coach with a writing desk and book shelves. There was a great response to his preaching, particularly among those who felt alienated from the Church of England. Some historians have judged Wesley to have saved Great Britain from the ravages of the French Revolution.

One of the reasons for his impact was what happened after his preaching. When he ended his revivals, he organized converts into class meetings. He anticipated the insights of social psychology about the importance of social support. Class members met weekly for encouragement and instruction. Each meeting began with the question "What is the state of your soul?" Wesley wrote directions for these class meetings and prepared materials from the classics for leaders to use in their preparation (Williams, 1960, p. 136; also see Outler, 1964, p. 180).

Wesley was a practical, rather than a systematic, theologian. His journal (reflecting his own Christian experience); his sermons (directed toward conversion and right thinking about spiritual growth); his books (concerning science as well as theology); his letters (often written to public figures about the affairs of the day); and his tracts (published as a means for influencing the average person) have left a rich legacy from which to infer Wesley's deep involvement in the pragmatic issues of Christian living. Because of his central focus on personal experience Wesley had been accused of having no interest in theology, but such a statement is far from the truth. He had strong doctrines of creation, salvation, assurance, and perfection—all worked out in the fire of his own, and his followers' life experience. His goal was always to make things "pure and simple by a lover of mankind and of common sense"— an appellation he often added to the titles of his books and tracts (cf. Wesley, 1760).

John Wesley on the Christian Response to Science

A critical question for Christians is, "What shall be their attitude toward the findings of contemporary social/behavioral science, particularly those theories which ignore or deny the power of religion?" John Wesley addressed this question. Although living a century before the establishment of psychology as a science, Wesley was very involved in religious responses to the laws of mechanics proposed by Sir Isaac Newton (English, 1991; Haas, 1994a, 1995). Newton conceived of his scientific theories as the discovered laws of God. Many low-church leaders agreed with him and embraced the Newtonian world-view with enthusiasm. Yet, other high-church persons were suspicious that Newton's laws of the "Book of Nature" might supersede the revealed truths of the "Book of the Bible." Initially, Wesley embraced this point of view because he feared that such thinking might lead to deism or atheism (Hendricks, 1983). He felt that there was a danger that a mechanistic world view would result in perceiving God as an impersonal force rather than as a personal redeemer (cf. White, 1896, p. 128). However, Wesley later changed his mind and, like Augustine and St. Thomas Aquinas before him, came to believe that logical reasoning, seen in science, could reveal the laws of God in nature (Haas, 1994b; cf. Wesley, 1744b). Yet he also remained convinced that the Bible still contained the truths that could lead to personal salvation. Further, in an almost post-modern manner, Wesley frequently emphasized "the littleness (or *incompleteness*) of all human knowledge" (Wesley, 1784a, p. 337, parenthesis mine). In another sermon, "God's approbation of His works" (1782), he asserted "How small a part of this great work of God is man able to understand" (p. 206; cf. also in the sermon "The case of reason impartially considered, 1781).

Having conceived of Newton's ideas as posing no threat to matters of personal redemption, Wesley set out to study them for himself and digest them for the average person. He wrote a five volume work entitled *A Survey of the Wisdom of God in the Creation or a Compendium of Natural Philosophy* (1777b/1809). "Natural philosophy" was a synonym for "natural science" at this time. Wesley's prime interest, as stated in the introduction, was to summarize the theories of "the great Newton" (Wesley, 1784b). In the publishing of these volumes, Wesley affirmed Newton's contention in the founding of the Royal Academy of Science that discovering the laws of God could be put to use in the alleviation of human suffering. Once again, Wesley's pragmatic motivation can be seen. The study of science was, for him, a means for making life better—physically as well as spiritually. He was convinced that much suffering was caused by violating God's physical laws (cf. Wesley, 1751). Wesley conceived of nature as a harmonious divine creation whose laws, if followed, would help persons live fulfilled lives.

Wesley's model of the relationship between science and religion is a useful paradigm for contemporary psychology/theology integration. In a sense, it represents the contention that "all truth is God's truth." It provides a basis for saying that learning the laws of human behavior, determined by psychology, would be both useful and God-given. Those laws can be learned and applied with the confidence that they were put here in creation by God and can be used for the benefit of persons.

An intriguing example of Wesley's openness to science can be seen in his interest in the healing possibilities of static electricity which he had first seen in a public demonstration by Benjamin Franklin. Wesley seemed eager to embrace new ideas, particularly if they accorded with his conviction that a given discovery was part of God's plan for helping persons find health and happiness. Wesley's use of electricity for curing disease is an example of how psychological integrators can creatively apply science for human good.

Although most persons thought of static electricity as good entertainment, Wesley joined a handful of physicians in perceiving the healing possibilities of electric shock treatment. Wesley's interest led him to write *The Desideratum, or Electricity Made Plain and Useful by a Lover of Mankind and of Common Sense* (1760). This volume, coupled with the placement of electrical machines in all of his free clinics and his recommendations that "electrifying" would cure or help over 35 illnesses, led Wesley to be judged to be one of three most notable electrotherapists in the eighteenth century (Hill, Schiller, & Tyerman, 1981). His awareness of the psychosomatic underlay of many illnesses and his theological rationale for the use of electricity represent a valid combination of science and religion.

The static electricity machine, a replica of which can be seen in the museum of the mother church of Methodism on City Road in London, consists of a suspended hollow glass tube through which runs a metal bar that is attached to a handle for rotating the cylinder. A leather pad covered by a piece of black silk rubs against the cylinder as it is turned, thus creating a buildup of static electricity which can be discharged by grasping a metal ball attached through a metal arm to inside the cylinder. The strength of the charge could be controlled by the number of turns of the cylinder. Electricity could be discharged *into* a person by grasping the ball or discharged *through* a person by holding one hand on the ball and the other hand on another piece of metal.

Of primary interest, however, is the theological rationale Wesley gave for his interest in the therapeutic use of electricity. He called electricity the "elixir of life" provided by God for use as a "nonnatural remedy." Wesley decided that, in creation, God had made electricity the basic source of all human movement (Wesley, 1760). Note how this idea went beyond the Newtonian laws of mechanics that had postulated a static universe where movement was determined solely by mass, force, and gravity. Wesley felt that there was a deficiency or overabundance of electricity in almost every physical malady. For example, in mania there was too much and in depression there was too little electricity in the human body. Restoring the electrical balance was the key to restoring creation to the state God intended originally.

Wesley called these efforts to harness electrical current a "non-natural" way of capturing again the healing power of creation. The very discovery of a way to do this, that is, through a machine, was not natural; it was manufactured. But it was part of God's provision for restoration after the fall when creation had lost its original health (Malony, 1995). In his book, Wesley justified this approach thusly:

> We know that the Creator of the Universe, is likewise, the Governor of all Things therein. But we know likewise, that he governs by *second Causes*: and that accordingly it is his Will, we should use all Probable Means he has given us to attain every lawful End. (1760, p. 29, italics mine)

These "second causes" were the ways that human investigators divined to control and direct the forces of nature for making human life more fulfilling.

What is innovative about Wesley's conjecture is its affirmation of technology and science as a God-intended means for benefiting humankind. Science, understood in this way, was God's way of restoring creation. God provided a means, through science, to redeem the world in spite of human sin.

Few divines have affirmed the importance of scientific discovery and application so strongly. Wesley provides a firm basis for today's integration of faith and science, or psychology and theology. Many of the non-religious, or secular, models of psychology could be affirmed as God-given, from this point of view. In this regard, it is important to remember that the Methodist slogan, originally attributed to Wesley, has always been "Let us join the sound mind and the warm heart (Wesley, 1744a), that is, let us unite our Christian experience with the use of reasonable thinking. The Wesleyan movement should always be thought of as a product of the Enlightenment rather than an off-shoot of the Protestant Reformation. Methodism has never been suspicious of science or secular education (Wesley, 1744b, 1745). In fact, one recent book written by a Methodist scholar was entitled *Loving God with One's Mind* (Trotter, 1987). In America, Methodism established over 200 colleges and universities, all of which had strong departments of science. As Haas (1995, p. 234) stated, for Wesley, "Science correctly understood was to serve the cause of Christ rather than to be feared."

John Wesley's Personal Difficulty in Accepting God's Love

Another perennial problem faced by Christian psychologists is "whether and when to include religion in their counseling." As one who had great difficulty in feeling confident of God's love, Wesley provides a good personal example of the possibilities and pitfalls of applying the recommendations he received. Of course, John Wesley never went to a psychologist for counseling but he did seek counsel, particularly from his brother Charles and from other Christian leaders, such as the Moravian Peter Bohler. More importantly, he constantly engaged in "self modification," as the behaviorists might term it. His strong efforts to find assurance of God's love were definitely action oriented. Some even accused Wesley of deliberate works-righteousness.

From the year 1709, when he was but a young boy, Wesley was considered as destined for a special role in life. At that time he jumped safely from the second floor of his burning home and was called thereafter by his mother "a brand plucked from the burning." He was caught between the grandiose expectations of his mother and the sympathetic indulgence of his father who, although supportive of holy habits and regular sacramental worship, told his son that the real test of faith was the "inner witness of the heart." While there are no indications that Wesley showed any evidence of psychological distress prior to age twenty-two, when he elected to follow his father's encouragement to become a priest, thereafter his obsessive compulsiveness became apparent. At that time he entered into a life-long effort to obtain an inner emotional certainty of his salvation through strenuous behavioral piety. His account of this decision, written some years after the fact attests to this frantic approach to attain religious assurance:

> When I was about twenty-two, my father pressed me to enter into Holy Orders. At the same time, the providence of God directing me to Kempis' *Christian Pattern*, I began to see that true religion was seated in the heart (note: the inner spiritual witness) and that God's law extended to all our thoughts as well as words and actions (note; the compulsivity). I began to alter

the whole form of my conversation and to set in earnest upon "a new life." I set apart an hour or two a day for religious retirement. I communicated (took the sacrament) every week. I watched against all sin, whether in word or deed. I began to aim at, and pray for, inward holiness (note: the attempt to combine outer actions with inner feelings). So that now, *doing so much and living so good a life*, I doubted not but I was a good Christian. (Wesley, 1738; italics in original; parentheses added)

This quote, from one of Wesley's accounts of his 1738 Aldersgate experience, clearly demonstrates his life-long dilemma. It can be seen that he wanted desperately to feel inwardly assured of his salvation but he was not content to accept this as a gift of God. He compulsively attempted to earn this inward witness by good behavior. His Moravian confidant, Peter Bohler, told Wesley to "preach faith until you have it; then you will preach faith because you have it." This Wesley did. Even in the midst of his worst depression the month before his Aldersgate experience, Wesley continued to preach faith in parishes around London and to regularly engage in pious actions—as if what he proclaimed with his mouth he felt in his heart.

Interestingly, going to the Moravian prayer meeting on the night of May 24, 1738 was not one of these pious behaviors. As he stated, "I went very unwillingly." As often happens in such situations, desperate psychological splitting occurred and Wesley's problem was resolved by an over-identification with one side of his dilemma (cf. Kallstad, 1974). His report testifies to this process:

> About a quarter before nine, while he was describing the change which God works in the heart through faith in Christ, I felt my heart strangely warmed. I felt I did trust in Christ, Christ alone for salvation; and an assurance was given me that he had taken away *my* sins, even *mine*, and saved *me* from the law of sin and death. (Wesley, 1738, italics in original)

The Aldersgate experience only partially resolved Wesley's dilemma. The inner assurance he had always sought was short-lived. This experience, long touted as a dramatic turning point, did not result in as much peace of mind as historians have claimed. Wesley's *Journal* is filled with references to fluctuations in his mood during the two years *after*

Aldersgate (Outler, 1964, p. 14). It is likely that biographers have made too much of the Aldersgate experience. In all his writings, Wesley only mentioned it one other time. The road between 1738 and Wesley's death in 1791 was filled with periods of doubt as well as exultation. He continued to put much effort into seeking to make the inner peace he experienced at Aldersgate a fact of everyday life. There is a painting in the museum on City Road in London which pictures him in a semi-coma on his death bed with his arms raised high. According to an apocryphal story that as he was dying, Wesley was asked to raise his arms in response if he still felt assured of his salvation.

Wesley's religious experience is similar to that of Peter, the disciple. It did not follow a straight line but ebbed and flowed. The experience of the average person is probably very akin to that of Wesley and Peter. Redemptive truths are easily confessed but are only spasmodically felt. Counselors would do well to remember the difficulties persons experience in making the truths of the mind become the truths of daily life. As will be seen in the next section, Wesley's life experience with faith and doubt significantly impacted his theological reflections.

John Wesley's Doctrine of the Grace of God and the Possibility of Christian Perfection

The question of whether assurance of God's love came all-at-once, as in Aldersgate-type experiences, or was a feeling that became stronger over an extended period of time became an important issue in Wesley's teachings. Although he remained convinced that the faith of *adherence* (the practice of the *means* of grace—worship, prayer, good works) would lead to the faith of *assurance* (inner certitude; religious *feelings* of certainty), Wesley still treasured dramatic episodes such as Aldersgate, during which a strong sense of security arose all at once (cf. Outler, 1964, p. 51ff). He taught his followers to expect them but came to realize that the enthusiastic behavior of those who had such experiences could become problematic.

On the one hand, the behavior which accompanied Aldersgate-type experience in Wesley's followers became excessive at times. All of the behaviors reported by today's charismatic Christians were reported by Methodists in the eighteenth century. These included speaking in tongues, dancing, barking, faintings, and jerkings. Wesley tried to control these expressions through such sermons as "On enthusiasm" (1750) and "The witness of the Spirit" (1746). While he retained a conviction that faith must become personal through subjective experience, he became troubled by these behaviors. He felt that the behaviors that resulted from personal experience should be seen in good works such as the fruit of the Spirit in Galatians, or in acts of mercy and justice such as seen in Hosea and Amos. Where witness to the Holy Spirit could be seen only in strange behavior, he felt this led to pride and grandiosity. As he stated:

> Truly, when I saw what God had done among his people between forty and fifty years ago … I could expect nothing less than that all these would have lived like angels here below … But instead of this, it brought forth wild grapes—fruit of quite contrary nature … It brought forth enthusiasm, imaginary inspiration, ascribing to the all-wise God all the wild, absurd, self-inconsistent dreams of a heated imagination. (1788)

The reputation of Methodists became tainted with the reputation of being "enthusiasts" who sought more emotional highs than pious behavior. Anglicans repudiated Wesley's claim that his was simply an evangelistic society within the Church of England. As an illustration of how these reactions to personal experience influences public reaction, one mental hospital reported in the early 1790s that during the past year it had admitted ninety-three patients for "madness and Methodism."

In his attempts to control the outbreak of these charismatic reactions, Wesley was significantly influenced by Jonathan Edwards' *Treatise on Religious Affects* (1746/1959). Edwards normalized subjective experience. Wesley agreed with his taxonomy of the emotions that should accompany spiritual experience. Although he disagreed strongly with Edwards' "quietism" which disconnected any expectation or seeking for personal experiences of assurance, he nevertheless thought enough of Edwards' treatise that he published an "extract" of his book—leaving out all of the Calvinistic theology in which human initiative was absent (Wesley, 1773).

Wesley was never fully successful in controlling these excesses and, in fact, an even more troubling concern became the claims of some of his followers that they had been "sanctified" by the visitation of the Holy Spirit and that they had attained a blessed state of sinlessness. This was in addition to their sense of assurance of God's love or any other feelings that their hearts had been "strangely warmed." This concerned Wesley greatly. Although he was convinced that growth toward perfection was possible, he did not think it occurred spontaneously in one experience. He parted with the Moravians over

this issue. He was troubled by their pompous claims of sinlessness. He felt such assertions bordered on antinomianism—outrageous claims that persons could do what they wanted now that they had attained a new state of grace. On the basis of scriptural teaching and his own experience, Wesley felt that such claims were premature (Outler, 1964). He wrote a tract entitled "Cautions and directions given to the greatest professors in the Methodist Societies" (1762) in which he stated his disapproval of any "profession" of sinless sanctification.

Nevertheless, Wesley was convinced that "sinless perfection" was possible "in this life." In the most famous of Wesley's tracts, entitled "A plain account of Christian Perfection as believed and taught by the Rev. Mr. John Wesley from the year 1725 to the year 1777" (1777a), Wesley proposed that "perfection should be sought at least five minutes before death." To be perfect meant, to Wesley, giving complete, undivided attention to seeking and following the will of God. He contended that this was possible because God's grace was a gift to people at the time of their conversion. This grace of God was like a seed that is planted in the heart of the believer. God intended the seed of grace to grow like a plant and all Christians should make the development of grace to be the goal of their lives. Wesley felt that this development could, like a plant with excellent fruit, reach a time of perfection when believers' lives were completely governed by God.

Wesley's doctrine of perfection united justification and sanctification. Justification of persons to God occurred at the time of conversion but sanctification came about over a lifetime. Although Wesley put great emphasis on human agency after conversion, he retained a strong doctrine of God's power and initiative in justification. In conversion, humans, through their free will, did not just "cooperate" with God. Instead they acted out of the "prevenient," or pre-existing, grace of God which God had implanted inside them in creation (Cannon, 1946, p. 114). After conversion, however, spiritual development depended heavily on human effort. Wesley felt that God's power was self-limited by human response. In the same vein, he felt that human response was real and that change was possible. He suggested that Christians should work toward becoming perfect in this life—at least "five minutes before death." The setting of a specific time was in response to Luther's contention that we should expect perfection, or a "fully righteous body," no sooner than five minutes *after* death (cf. Cannon, 1946, p. 242ff).

This difference between Wesley and Luther reflects a radical distinction in their views of the human being. Luther felt that human beings did not really change after conversion. They remain sinners who are saved by God's grace. God looks at them through the sinlessness of Jesus Christ. Prior to death God considers them righteous for Christ's sake. After death persons will be made truly righteous because God will clothe them with new righteous bodies. Grace, for Luther, is a change in God's perception; a new way of looking at persons. Grace, for Wesley, was an active ingredient implanted in the human heart, something inside persons as well as in God's perception.

As can be seen, Wesley's understanding resulted in a positive view of human capacity. According to Wesley, God expects humans to change through the working of the Holy Spirit in their hearts. There is a tradition, that continues to this day, of asking Methodist ministers, at the time of their ordination, if they intend to "go on to perfection in this life." They must answer "Yes." Lutheran ministers are asked no such question.

Although dissimilar to Lutheran tradition, Wesley's understanding of growth in grace leading to perfection embodies a view of human agency that would be compatible with much in contemporary cognitive/behavioral psychology (cf. Ellis, 1962; Beck, Rush, Shaw, & Emery, 1979). Therapy, from this point of view, involves helping people change their behavior by distinguishing between rational and irrational thinking, a la Ellis, and by reversing negative thinking, a la Beck, et al. Like Wesley, these authors presume that thoughts and intentions are the key to personal change. Further, Wesley, but not Luther, would have had much in common with many contemporary "faith development" theorists such as James Fowler (1981) who conceived of spiritual growth as occurring along a series of stages that eventuate in an optimal level of religious perception and understanding. While Wesley would probably view perfection as more behavioral than would Fowler, he would agree on the centrality of cognition and intention. Both would be very optimistic about the possibility of humans developing spiritually. They would both see the value in unique single experiences as well as intentional daily effort.

John Wesley's Compassionate Concern for Justice and the Welfare of the Poor

Yet another question with which Christian counselors have to deal is "How much should I become involved with the environment in which my clients live?" For Wesley, this question was phrased in this form, "Since I am an evangelist who is primarily concerned with the spiritual redemption of people,

should I be concerned with their physical and social circumstances?" He answered a definite "Yes!" A dominant feature of John Wesley's life was his compassionate concern for justice and the welfare of the poor. Although from a privileged social class, Wesley had a strong social conscience. He continued throughout his life to be sensitive to the plight of those less fortunate. He serves as a worthy example for religious help-givers in every generation, such as modern Christian psychologists, who should feel called to be involved in all areas of life, not just helping them solve problems in weekly counseling sessions in the confines of their offices.

In addition to the numerous letters he wrote to public officials, such as the letter to Wilberforce on slavery noted earlier, Wesley made statements about social justice wherever he preached. When speaking at Stoke-on-Trent, he noted the low wages of potters and made public recommendations that pottery owners pay them a living wage. When he preached at Penzance he spoke out against smuggling after hearing that citizens were changing the lighthouse in an effort to cause shipwrecks. After the ships crashed on the rocks, these upstanding citizens joined the outlaw pirates in plundering ships to the utter disregard of loss of life and goods.

However, it is in matters of healthcare that Wesley's concern for the disadvantaged can be most clearly seen. Had he not become a priest, Wesley would likely have become a physician. He had a sincere desire to help people handle the sufferings of life—physical as well as spiritual. Quite early in his adulthood he had become disillusioned with the treatment afforded the poor. He observed that physicians shied away from offering services to those who could not pay for them.

Wesley was an avid reader and writer. He rose from sleep at 4:00 AM each morning and worked tirelessly preparing sermons, reading Scripture, digesting the classics, composing pamphlets, studying medicine, making judgments about current affairs and writing books. He was probably as well informed on the medicine of his day as many physicians. Here we see the seeds of Wesley's boldness in publishing a home health-care manual for the poor entitled *Primitive Physick: Or an Easy and Natural Method of Curing Most Diseases* (1751). This volume became the most popular home health-care manual of the eighteenth century and went through over thirty printings in Britain and America. Wesley contended that most, if not all, of his recommended ingredients could be found in a woman's kitchen and most of the treatments he recommended had gone through "experimentation" over many generations (cf. Malony, 1996).

In the book, Wesley gathered together cures for 288 illnesses. He arranged the names of the illnesses in alphabetical order and listed three to four cures for each one. He recommended trying the first and if that didn't work to try the second, etc. Beside each of the cures that he had personally tried, Wesley put a "T" and beside those that always worked he put an "I" (for Infallible). While a number of the cures were quaint, others of them were as reputable as any used by regular doctors. Out of concern for cost, Wesley suggested that most of the ingredients for the treatments could be found in a woman's kitchen.

The reaction of the medical community was generally negative. Typical was the judgment of one of the queen's physicians who called Wesley a quack in *Lloyd's Evening Post*. Wesley responded with the following letter: "Dear Sir, My bookseller informs me that since you published your remarks on *Primitive Physick*, there has been a greater demand than ever. If, therefore, you please to publish a few further remarks you would confer a favor on your Humble Servant" (Hill, 1958, p. 121). In an uncannily modern comment, Wesley defended his "dabbling" in medical affairs by stating, "Neither Jesus nor His disciples derived their authority from the national licensing corporation of their day … Licensing bodies may be set up as social safeguards or as protection for private interests … unrecognized authority may bypass them or sweep them aside" (Hill, 1958, p. 15).

Out of a concern for the health-care which he felt that the poor were *not* receiving, Wesley reflected on providing free health care in clinics in London and Bristol in this manner: "For more than twenty years I had numberless proofs that regular physicians do exceedingly little good. From a deep conviction of this I have believed it my duty within these four months past to prescribe such medicines to 600-700 of the poor as I knew were proper for their several disorders. … Now, ought I to have let one of these poor wretches perish because I was not a regular physician? To have said, 'I know what will cure you, but I am not of the College; You must send for Doctor Mead?' Before Dr. Mead had come in his chariot the man might have been in his coffin" (Hill, 1958, p. 15). Wesley was so offended by what he considered British physicians' money obsession that he took matters into his own hand and provided free care for the poor.

It is possible to relate Wesley's concerns about health to many of the foci of modern health psychology (Malony, 1996). Wesley, just as health psychologists, was interested in the promotion of health, the prevention and treatment of illness, the identification

of the causes of illness, and the improvement of the health care system. He recommended breathing pure air, eating temperately, exercising abundantly, getting plenty of sleep, having good bowel movements, and controlling the emotions. He based his admonitions on the biblical teaching that the body was the temple of the Holy Spirit (1 Cor. 6:19).

Wesley wrote many pamphlets calling for environmental change in housing, wages, community services, etc. He was convinced that many illnesses were provoked by trauma of stressful social conditions. He was very sensitive to psychosomatic illnesses and chided physicians who prescribed drugs when they should be listening with compassion. One of the entries in his personal journal recounted the story of a woman who had a chronic stomach ache over the death of her son but to whom doctors kept giving medications as if her problem was physical (Hill, 1958, p. 22).

Finally, he deplored the conditions of the hospitals and wrote out a long list of recommendations for people to use in the treatment of their loved ones when they were sick. Many of these concerns about health and social welfare resulted from his observations of the deplorable conditions in which common people lived. He is credited with coining the saying "Cleanliness is next to Godliness." His admonitions to the leaders of his societies had many references to health issues. Among them was one which stated "Don't stink above ground" (cleanliness) and another "Kill yourself a little every day" (dieting)! One commentator wrote this about Wesley's concern with health: "More than any other major figure in Christendom, John Wesley involved himself with the theory and practice of medicine and with the specific principles and practices of ideal physical and mental health" (Vanderpool, 1986, p. 320).

Wesley combined his evangelistic concern for salvation with a sensitivity to how life situations and physical environments caused disease and suffering. His example is worthy of emulation by Christian care-givers who might be tempted to think that people could overcome any physical conditions if they had the proper attitude or applied their faith to their predicaments. He attended to issues of social injustice and welfare apart from concern for salvation in a way that Christian counselors could use as an example. As noted, many of his concerns parallel those of modern community and health psychology. Christian counselors should resist the temptation to think that they fulfill their roles when they give good advice or encourage religious faith. People are often burdened down in a way that only material assistance can assuage. It is important to be sensitive to the fact that conditions under which people function can overwhelm any profit they might get from hours of counseling.

Conclusion

This article has considered the life and work of the eighteenth century divine, John Wesley. Known primarily for his role as the founder of the Methodist movement, Wesley also evidenced deep involvement in improving the health and circumstance of common people. Four aspects of his life and teaching were considered to have import for modern Christian psychology: (1) his reactions to the scientific discoveries of his day, (2) his personal dealings with doubts about God's love, (3) his teachings about grace and spiritual growth, and (4) his concern for justice and welfare. He provides modern psychologists with a model for relating faith with science. He exemplifies the way many people struggle with applying religion to their daily lives. His theological reflections about religious enthusiasm and the grace of God are very helpful in understanding human experience. His sensitivity to the importance of the influence of the environment and the need to be socially concerned is inspiring. Many of his persuasions parallel contemporary psychological approaches to problem solving and the importance of perception in human behavior. Overall, John Wesley should be considered a practical, psychological theologian whose life and teachings can be very informative and influential for those who would integrate their Christian faith with modern psychology.

Notes

1. Most of the works of Wesley cited in this article were published in 1831 with T. Jackson as editor. This multivolume set was republished by Zondervan in 1958. Original publication dates will be the only dates used in the text.

2. Outler noted that when he visited Moravian settlements in Germany after his Aldersgate experience, they barred Wesley from the Holy Communion because they considered him to be a perturbed individual (1964, p. 14). Note that this was *after* the experience of assurance which supposedly assuaged his doubts.

References

Beck, A. T., Rush, A. J., Shaw, B. F., & Emery, G. (1979). *Cognitive therapy of depression.* New York: Guilford Press.

Cannon. W. R. (1946). *The theology of John Wesley.* Abingdon Press: Nashville, TN.

Colson, C. (1987). *Kingdoms in conflict.* New York: Harper.

Edwards, J. (1959). A treatise concerning religious affections. In J. E. Smith (Ed.), *The works of Jonathan Edwards:* Vol. 2 (pp. 93-462). New Haven, CT: Yale University Press. (Original work published 1746)

Ellis, A. (1962). *Reason and emotion in psychotherapy.* Secaucus, NJ: Citadel Press.

English, J. C. (1991). John Wesley and Isaac Newton's "System of the World." *Proceedings of the Wesley Historical Society, 48,* 71.

Fowler, J. W. (1981). *Stages of faith: The psychology of human development and the quest for meaning.* San Francisco: Harper & Row.

Haas, J. W., Jr. (1994a). Eighteenth century evangelical responses to science: John Wesley's enduring legacy. *Science and Christian Belief, 6,* 83-102.Haas, J. W., Jr. (1994b). John Wesley's eighteenth century views on science and Christianity: An examination of the charge of antiscience. *Church History, 63,* 378-392.

Haas, J. W., Jr. (1995). John Wesley's vision of science in the service of Christ. *Perspectives on Science and Christian Faith, 47,* 234-243.

Hendricks, M. E. (1983). John Wesley and natural theology. *Wesleyan Theological Journal, 12,* 12-13.

Hill, A. (1958). *John Wesley among the physicians: A study in eighteenth century medicine.* London: Epworth.

Hill, A., Schiller, F., & Tyerman, L. (1981). Reverend Wesley, Doctor Marat, and their electrical fire. *Clio Medica, 115,* 159-176.

Kallstad, T. (1974). *John Wesley and the Bible: A psychological study.* Stockholm: Almquist & Wiksell.

Malony, H. N. (1986a). From Galileo to Whitehead: Century-specific questions of current import to science and faith. In H. N. Malony (Ed.), *Integration musings: Thoughts on being a Christian professional* (pp. 9-20). Pasadena, CA: Integration Press.

Malony, H. N. (1986b). Micah 6:8. In H. N. Malony (Ed.), *Integration musings: Thoughts on being a Christian professional* (pp. 193-196). Pasadena, CA: Integration Press.

Malony, H. N. (1995). John Wesley and the eighteenth century uses of electricity. *Perspectives on Science and the Christian Faith, 47,* 244-254.

Malony, H. N. (1996). John Wesley's "Primitive Physick": An 18th century health psychology. *Journal of Health Psychology, 1*(2), 147-159.

Myers, D. G. (1993). *Exploring psychology* (2nd ed.). New York: Worth.

Outler, A. C. (Ed.). (1964). *John Wesley.* New York: Oxford University Press.

Trotter, F. T. (1987). *Loving God with one's mind.* Nashville, TN: Board of Higher Education and Ministry of the United Methodist Church.

Vanderpool, H. Y. (1986). The Wesleyan-Methodist tradition. In R. L. Numbers & D. W. Amundsen (Eds.), *Caring and curing in the western religious traditions* (pp. 317-353). New York: Macmillan.

Wesley, J. (1958). Journal for May 24. In T. Jackson (Ed.). *The works of the Reverend John Wesley, A.M.* (3rd ed., Vol. 1, p. 103). Grand Rapids, MI: Zondervan. (Original work published 1738)

Wesley, J. (1958). The character of a Methodist. In T. Jackson (Ed.). *The works of the Reverend John Wesley, A. M.* (3rd ed., Vol. 8, pp. 339-347). Grand Rapids, MI: Zondervan. (Original work published 1744a)

Wesley, J. (1958). An earnest appeal to men of reason and religion. In T. Jackson (Ed.), *The works of the Reverend John Wesley, A.M.* (3rd ed., Vol. 8, pp. 1-45). Grand Rapids, MI: Zondervan. (Original work published 1744b)

Wesley, J. (1958). A further appeal to men of reason. In T. Jackson (Ed.), *The works of the Reverend John Wesley, A.M.* (3rd ed., Vol. 8, pp. 46-135). Grand Rapids, MI: Zondervan. (Original work published 1745)

Wesley, J. (1958). The witness of the Spirit. In T. Jackson (Ed.), *The works of the Reverend John Wesley, A.M.* (3rd ed. Vol. 5, pp. 111-122). Grand Rapids, MI: Zondervan. (Original work published 1746)

Wesley, J. (1958). On enthusiasm. In T. Jackson (Ed.), *The works of the Reverend John Wesley, A.M.* (3rd ed., Vol. 5, pp. 467-478). Grand Rapids, MI: Zondervan. (Original work published 1750)

Wesley, J. (1751). *Primitive physick: Or an essay and natural method of curing most diseases.* London: J. Palmar.

Wesley, J. (1760). *The desideratum, Or electricity made pure and simple by a lover of mankind and of common sense.* London: Bailliere, Tindall, and Cox.

Wesley, J. (1958). Cautions and directions given to the greatest professors in the Methodist Societies. In T. Jackson (Ed.), *The works of the Reverend John Wesley, A.M.* (3rd ed., Vol. 7, p. 22). Grand Rapids, MI: Zondervan. (Original work published 1762)

Wesley, J. (1958). An extract from a treatise concerning religious affections. In T. Jackson (Ed.), *The works of the Reverend John Wesley, A.M.* (3rd ed., Vol. 4, p. 103). Grand Rapids, MI: Zondervan. (Original work published 1773)

Wesley, J. (1958). A plain account of Christian perfection as believed and taught by the Rev. Mr. John Wesley from the year 1725 to the year 1777. In T. Jackson (Ed.). *The works of the Reverend John Wesley, A.M.* (3rd ed., Vol. 9, pp. 366-445). Grand Rapids, MI: Zondervan. (Original work published 1777a)

Wesley, J. (1809). *A survey of the wisdom of God in the creation or a compendium of natural philosophy in five volumes.* London: J. Fry and Co. (Original work published 1777b)

Wesley, J. (1958). The case of reason impartially considered. In T. Jackson (Ed.), *The works of the Reverend John Wesley, A.M.* (3rd ed., Vol. 6 pp. 350-360). Grand Rapids, MI: Zondervan. (Original work published 1781)

Wesley, J. (1958). God's approbation of His works. In T. Jackson (Ed.), *The works of the Reverend John Wesley, A.M.* (3rd ed., Vol. 6, pp. 206-214). Grand Rapids, MI: Zondervan. (Original work published 1782)

Wesley, J. (1958). The imperfection of human knowledge. In T. Jackson (Ed.), *The works of the Reverend John Wesley, A.M.* (3rd ed., Vol. 6, pp. 337-349). Grand Rapids, MI: Zondervan. (Original work published 1784a)

Wesley, J. (1958). On the gradual improvement of natural philosophy. In T. Jackson (Ed.), *The works of the Reverend John Wesley, A.M.* (3rd ed., Vol. 13, pp. 482-487). Grand Rapids, MI: Zondervan. (Original work published 1784b)

Wesley, J. (1958). On God's vineyard. In T. Jackson (Ed.). *The works of the Reverend John Wesley, A.M.* (3rd ed., Vol. 7, pp. 202-213). Grand Rapids, MI: Zondervan. (Original work published 1788)

White, A. D. (1896). *A history of the warfare of science with theology in Christendom.* New York: D. Appleton.

Williams, C. W. (1960). *John Wesley's theology today.* New York: Abingdon.

Section II
Science and Faith Reconciliation

Psychologists have been trained in an age of science. Standard definitions in Psychology 101 emphasize psychology's scientific basis for the study of behavior and mental processes and, for many psychologists, this is the only model of training received all the way through graduate school. It should therefore come as little surprise that empirical research is often viewed as the ultimate test of our ideas and it is not unusual for professional journals to accept only empirically based articles. Furthermore, we attend sessions at professional conferences, including CAPS' own international and regional conferences, where empirical data is often afforded a privileged position.

However, Christian psychologists are also a people of faith who take the claims of Christianity and the authority of scripture seriously. They find themselves perched precariously on a boundary between commitments to empirical forms of knowing and to other forms of knowledge, including revealed knowledge. So, Christians, particularly those in the academy, must reconcile their allegiance to a faith-based revealed form of knowing, yet not sacrifice their commitment to a discipline that uses a radically different epistemology. As Evans points out in the second article in this section, surely no one wants to be unscientific, for science, so it seems to many, gives us perhaps our best shot at gaining an accurate understanding of the real world.

At the very heart of integration we find issues of epistemology. Just how are we to go about doing our work? On what basis should we make claims of knowledge? To compound matters further, it is not simply a matter of epistemological preference, for with each method of knowing comes other important philosophical considerations and assumptions: what is the nature of the individual, is one free to choose or are actions totally determined, to what extent is one changeable, and just how much about one is even potentially knowable? It is not just Christian psychologists who must wrestle with these issues, however, for the discipline as a whole has increasingly questioned and debated the philosophical basis of psychology. No longer, as pointed out in several of the following articles, do psychologists uncritically accept the positivist position that science is a totally objective enterprise, free of value, and where postulates and hypotheses are determined only in terms of statistical probabilities to understand contingent relationships. Instead, philosophers and historians of science have made a convincing case that much scientific inquiry does not hold to this objective ideal.

Articles dealing with such questions in the integration literature over the past 50 years have been many, but five appear to stand out. In the first article reprinted in this section, Nicholas Wolterstorff (1984), in his article, *Integration of Faith and Science—The Very Idea*, proposed that the compelling force behind the integration movement is not so much the influence of scholarly developments in psychology, theology, or philosophy of science as much as it is "a real existential feeling of tension and conflict between two things that we care about, and the consequent desire to bring them together in some acceptable fashion." Despite this uneasiness, Wolterstorff maintained that it is difficult for Christian psychologists to place a scientific discipline like psychology into a Christian perspective, largely due to a cluster of Cartesian assumptions that helped produce the narrow positivistic vision of science. Arguing that the dominance of a Cartesian picture of science is beginning to disintegrate, Wolterstorff challenged the Christian to take advantage of a new found methodological pluralism and participate in "the nitty-gritty of actual psychological explorations."

C. Stephen Evans' (1976) classic article, *Christian Perspectives on the Sciences of Man*, is presented next as a useful taxonomy for considering how the Christian can respond to the prevalence of scientism in Western society. Scientism is "the tendency to make scientific procedures and theories epistemologically and metaphysically ultimate." One's responses to the following three theses, according to Evans, can help articulate one's view of what comprises proper science: 1) *the unity of science thesis* ("the belief that all sciences employ the same basic methodology, that of the natural sciences interpreted positivistically, in which deterministic causal explanations are empirically derived for predictive purposes"); 2) *the completeness of science thesis* ("the belief that there are no areas of reality which are not amenable to scientific investigation, at least in principle"); and 3) *the ultimacy of science thesis* ("the belief that science gives us the ultimate truth about the reality it investigates"). By analyzing responses collectively to these three theses, the Christian psychologist can fit into one of the following categorical types with regard to her views of science. The *Capitulator*, the first type described by Evans, agrees with all three theses. The *Limiter of Science*, of which there are two types according to Evans, either disagrees with only the second thesis (a *Territorialist*) or the third thesis (a *Perspectivalist*). The *Humanizer of Science* rejects only the first thesis. All positions, argues Evans, have both strengths and limitations, though the author himself cautiously recommends either a Perspectivalist Limiter position or a moderate Humanizer view.

In her 1988 article, *Psychology's 'Two Cultures': A Christian Analysis*, Mary Stewart Van Leeuwen pointed out that Christians can be found, perhaps even in a roughly equal distribution, in both the traditional positivistic culture of science as well as a post-positivistic, humanistic culture. Drawing upon the conclusions of two empirical studies reported in the 1980s in the *American Psychologist*, demonstrating that most psychologists (especially behavioral and experimental psychologists) fail to acknowledge that epistemic values do in fact operate in the context of theory justification, she argues that both cultures competing for disciplinary control have serious limitations. Van Leeuwen proposes that Christians consider yet a third approach, "one in which their control beliefs enable them to steer the line between reductionism and self-deification in psychological anthropology, and between positivism and skepticism in psychological epistemology." She encourages Christian psychologists to take seriously a philosophical and methodological pluralism that accounts for the reality of human reflexivity which will make "*social* scientific theorizing an inescapably moral endeavor." Christian psychologists must adapt and use their complete arsenal of tools to investigate not only those aspects of human behavior that are outside human awareness and control as finite and sinful creatures, but also those aspects whereby intelligible accounts of human action as image bearers can be articulated.

Peter Hill's (1989) article, *Implications for Integration from a New Philosophy of Psychology as Science*, while largely compatible with Van Leeuwen's fundamental thesis, attempts to place such an alternative approach onto even surer philosophical footing. He proposes a *realist* theory of science drawn from the little known (among psychologists) writings on epistemology by Roy Bhaskar and as applied to psychology by such respected scholars in the field as Peter Manicas and Paul Secord. Rooted in a perspective of ontological realism but epistemological relativism, the realist perspective questions the traditional positivistic insistence that causal laws of human behavior *must* manifest themselves in empirical regularities. Such an insistence, Hill argues, assumes that human behavior is by nature a closed system, which is contrary to a Christian understanding of the person. Thus, prediction of human behavior, which assumes total regularity of a closed-system variety, cannot be the sole litmus test for the accuracy or veracity of a theory. Instead, Hill proposes a realist account of science that places a greater emphasis on explanation, rather than prediction, as a proper goal of science, claiming that "once it is understood that the substantive domain of psychology is the underlying structure of behavior, and not empirical regularities, the importance of methodological pluralism takes on a new, brighter light."

The final article in this section, *A Constructive Relationship for Religion with the Science and Profession of Psychology*, by Stan Jones (1994), is arguably among the top few integration articles, in terms of importance, written in the past half century. This article is set apart by the fact that it was published in the *American Psychologist*, the flagship journal of the American Psychological

Association (APA). Prior to this article, the topic of religion (including integration) had been virtually ignored in APA publication materials. Since its publication, the APA has published a number of books and articles (in APA owned journals) stressing the centrality and predictive importance of religious faith in psychological functioning. The extent to which these developments can be traced to the publication of Jones' article is unclear; however, the excellence with which Jones articulated an integrative perspective provided a gold-standard introduction to a larger psychological audience. Jones provides a bold and convincing proposal for how religion can be a constructive partner with both the science and practice of psychology. It is readily apparent some twelve years later that Jones' objective "to stimulate a greater awareness within the psychological community of the importance and pervasiveness of religious beliefs and commitments to the scientific and professional objectives of contemporary psychology" was hugely successful.

We believe these articles represent the very best of integration efforts with a special focus on science and faith reconciliation over the past 50 years. It is our hope that their reintroduction to readers will spur further development in integrative thought.

Suggestions for Further Reading: Science and Faith Reconciliation

Barbour, I. G. (1990). *Religion in an age of science*. San Francisco: Harper Collins.
Arguing that there is a place for religion in an age dominated by science, the author explores five challenges by science to which contemporary Christianity must respond to remain a viable and effective source of fulfillment and hope.

Barbour, I. G. (2000). *Religion and science: Historical and contemporary issues*. San Francisco: Harper.
After a historical review of the interaction between science and religion, Barbour reviews the contemporary dialogue between religion and the methods & theories of science and ends with reflections on human nature, process theology & philosophy, and the natural world.

MacKay, D. M. (1974). *The clock work image*. Downers Grove, Illinois: InterVarsity.
This small, often referenced book examines Christian and scientific views of the universe.

Manicas, P. T., & Secord, P. F. (1983). Implications for psychology of the new philosophy of science. *American Psychologist, 38*, 399-413.
Salient features of changes in the philosophy of science since the positivist era are identified and their implications for doing psychology as a scientific discipline are discussed.

Myers, D. G., & Jeeves, M. A. (1987). *Psychology through the eyes of faith*. San Francisco: Harper & Row.
Classic beginning reader providing insights on human nature from introductory psychology topics and with reflections on how those connect with Christian belief.

Polkinghorne, J. (1998). *Belief in God in an age of science*. New Haven, CT: Yale University Press.
Theologians and scientists (including psychologists) will find much in this rather short and thought-provoking book by a theologian-scientist.

Ratzsch, D. (1986). *Philosophy of science: The natural sciences in Christian perspective*.Downers Grove, IL: InterVarsity.
Offers a concise summary of the philosophy of science in its traditional and contemporary forms, the limitations and challenges of science, and an exploration of possible ways for relating science and religious belief.

Reichenbach, B. (1998). The new integrationists of science and religion. *Christian Scholar's Review, 27* (3), 338-352.
Reviewing the alleged conflict between religion and science this article reviews integrative efforts in the areas of scientific method, subject matter, and goals.

Sire, J. (1997). *The universe next door: A basic worldview catalog* (3rd ed.). Downers Grove, IL: InterVarsity.
Essential worldviews text for undergraduates and graduate students to help them understand some of the necessary philosophical issues before they begin to think about integration.

Van Leeuwen, M.S. (1982). *The sorcerer's apprentice: A Christian looks at the changing face of psychology*. Downers Grove, IL: InterVarsity.
Evaluates the failures of modernistic science and argues for a more human science.

Integration of Faith and Science—
The Very Idea

Nicholas Wolterstorff
Calvin College

Christians in contemporary academic psychology are troubled by the assumptions of determinism and the inherent goodness of man which operate in psychology and introduce conflicts between psychology and christian faith. Various strategies used by psychologists to resolve these conflicts are described and judged to be inadequate. A christian psychological model of the person capable of suggesting theories and research programs is needed. External criticism of psychological theories cannot substitute for the reconstruction of psychology in terms of christian "control beliefs." The process of reconstructing psychology in terms of christian convictions must take account of the new image of science forming upon the wreckage of the Cartesian consensual vision of how science ought to be conducted.

Why suddenly all this talk among psychologists about the integration of faith and learning?

A decade ago you would have heard little about it; two decades ago, almost nothing. Psychologists are not alone in this; Christians in all the academic disciplines have expressed the same concern. We are participants in a remarkable movement.

I submit that the fundamental reason Christians in academic scientific psychology begin to talk about the integration of faith and psychology is that, when they work in contemporary psychology, there are things there that bother them. There are developments there that make them feel uneasy. It appears to them that their christian faith is in tension with certain developments in psychology. So they begin to ask: How can we get these two things together? They are not about to give up their faith, nor psychology. So they ask how the tension can be released. My thesis is that this spreading concern for integration is not the result of the writings of theorists in ivory towers. Neither is it the result of a calm concern to bring integration where previously there was peaceful but segregated coexistence. It is the result of a real existential feeling of tension and conflict between two things that we care about, and the consequent desire to bring them together in some acceptable fashion.

Exposition

What is it that characteristically bothers the Christian about contemporary academic psychology? What is it that prompts these attempts at integration? No doubt a lot of different things, but speaking now as someone who surveys psychology from the outside, whose profession is that of philosopher rather than psychologist, if we dig beneath the surface we find one or the other of two roots of tension at work.

Very often what disturbs us about psychology is its deterministic assumptions. The model of the person which is tacitly or explicitly at work is one according to which the life of a human being is totally determined by his external environment and his internal drives. The reason this disturbs us is that it is not evident that this is compatible with the biblical emphasis on responsibility nor with the biblical assumption of human creativity.

There is a second root of tension as well. In much contemporary psychology it is assumed that if only the individual can be freed from external influence and from internal inhibition, then that individual will blossom out into a loving, caring, healthy individual. What disturbs us about this is that we find it difficult to see how this assumption that human beings are inherently good can be combined with the biblical emphasis on sin.

Once these two roots of tension are brought to light one feels that they are themselves at cross-purposes with each other; one suspects that they are to be found at work in different streams of contemporary psychology. Yet in such developmental theorists as Piaget and Kohlberg one finds a curious and fascinating blend of the two assumptions: we are both determined and inherently good.

What disturbs the Christian about contemporary psychology is obviously not little things here and there. What bothers us is that there are fundamental models of the person at work which seem quite

© *Journal of Psychology and Christianity*, 1984, *3*(2), 12-19. Used by permission.

alien to the christian model of the person. In the one case the model of the person at work is that of something wholly determined and hence not free and responsible in any authentic sense. In the other case the model of the person at work is that of someone who would be good if he could be free, but who in fact finds himself constantly imposed upon and constrained.

What have we typically done to ease the tension? What have we characteristically done to calm the disturbance? What have been our typical strategies of integration?

Methods of Integration

Sometimes we are persuaded on reflection that *something has to give*, that the tension we feel is real and not merely apparent and accordingly that to release it we must give something up. Often what we decide to give up so as to release the tension is some facet of our understanding of the christian faith. We engage in what I in some of my writings have called *harmonizing*: We revise our understanding of the faith so as to harmonize it with our scientific convictions. I well remember the christian philosopher who, in a lecture he gave at my college, introduced his talk by remarking that since determinism was a standard assumption of the human sciences, and since Christians should not allow themselves to be forced into beating a hasty retreat as they have so often done in the past, he proposed to begin exploring ways of construing the christian faith along deterministic lines. That was a flamboyant example of harmonizing. In the same way, someone would be engaged in harmonizing if, after observing that a standard assumption of contemporary human science is that the individual is potentially good and would in fact *be* good if freed from baleful influence, he undertook to reinterpret the christian faith so that it taught nothing in conflict with this. In all such cases it is assumed that there really is tension, that accordingly something must give, and that it is the understanding of the faith that must give. Harmonizing is one familiar strategy of integration.

An obvious alternative is to assume that nothing has to give in either science or faith, that the conflict proves, upon close analysis, to be only apparent, not real, that the felt tension has no basis in fact. We do not have to revise our faith in any significant way, nor our psychology. What has to be revised is the belief that there is a genuine conflict here. An illusion must be eliminated.

This strategy comes in various versions. One version is what Stephan Evans (1977) has called com-patibilism. The compatibilist says that there is no problem. Human behavior is entirely determined but also we are responsible and free. These are both true, two truths, if you will: a bit of mystery here perhaps, but no real contradiction. Or if the other assumption is in the forefront of attention, the compatibilist says that the root of evil is that the innocent individual is in one way or another "put upon." If he were not, he would blossom forth in love and charity. On the other hand, it is true that there are within us dark impulses of hostility. Two truths, mysterious perhaps that they should both be true, but so it is. When doing science we speak as scientists; when engaged in religious activities we speak as religious people. There are simply two languages, each with its own frame of reference, speaking about one complex reality; difficulty arises only if we try to cross the languages.

I judge that most of us do not rest easy with compatibilism. We do not relish mysteries very much, at least not those which we in our hearts suspect to be mysteries of our own making. Accordingly, most of us who are convinced that the felt tension has no solid basis in fact seek to release that felt tension in a different way. We do it by insisting that the *scope* of psychology and the *scope* of faith must both be delimited so as to prevent these from getting into each other's hair. We follow the strategy of *delimitation*. The psychologist, we say, does indeed discover that we are creatures of stimulus and response. He does indeed discover that our actions are determined by our environment and by our inner drives, but we need not suppose that this is true for *all* our actions: nothing in psychology proper shows that. Any psychologist who generalizes in that fashion is going beyond the proper scope of psychology. In addition to the realm of determination there is a realm of freedom: nothing that psychologists have discovered should lead us to think otherwise. Alternately, psychology does indeed show that if we free a person from the bondage of internal inhibition and external influence, allowing him to grow and mature, love will flow forth, but we need not suppose that this is true across the board. If some psychologist claims that it is, he is going beyond his competence as psychologist and speaking as philosopher. There is more to human existence than that of which psychology informs. It is in this more that we come up against the dark fact of sin.

These are the strategies of the *delimiters*. They delimit the scope of psychology and of christian faith. They suggest that when we grasp the scope of psychology and faith, our feelings of tension are released. Nothing in science or faith has to be given up so as to release the tension. Only something in our *understanding* of them has to give, specifically in our understanding of their scope.

These are the three main strategies we have followed for our practice of integration, that of the *harmonizers*, who insist that something has to give in our understanding of the faith, and those of the *compatibilists* and *delimiters*, both of whom insist that nothing has to give except our conviction that there is real conflict.

It is the delimiters who are the most prominent. I could not count the number of times that christian psychologists have said to me that there is no problem in accepting radical behaviorism, provided we do not follow Skinner in thinking that it applies to everything. When Skinner goes off into radical claims he is not speaking as a psychologist. He has drifted into philosophy!

This response of the christian delimiter is mindless. It may be true that some of our actions are conditioned in exactly the manner that Skinner understands operant conditioning to work, and that others of our actions are not. It may be true that sometimes when we remove inhibitions and domination from some aspect of a person's life, that aspect of that person's life begins to flower, without this being true across the board. However, if you as a psychologist say that operant conditioning as Skinner understands it holds for some human behavior but not for all, *and then do not go on to give a more comprehensive theory which explains that remainder, which points out the borderline between the two, and which shows how this remainder fits with that area of conditioning*, this response of delimitation is empty of theoretical content. Until you do provide that more comprehensive theory, people will try to make use of Skinnerian theory across the board for you have given nothing else either for thought or for research. Albert Bandura has earned the theoretician's right to say that Skinner's operant conditioning theory applies only to a certain area of human life, because he has proposed a more comprehensive theory which provides a limited place for operant conditioning as Skinner understands it, and offers a theoretical account of very much of the rest of human behavior as well. Furthermore, Bandura's alternative theory has suggested to him a host of fruitful and suggestive research projects. By contrast, the christian delimiter who says that the Christian cannot accept Skinner's claim that his theory applies to all human behavior, but that otherwise there is no conflict, gives us no suggestions whatever as to alternative research programs. Consequently, we know what sort of research he will do if he does research: he will do Skinnerian operant conditioning research.

What I mean to suggest is that the delimitation strategy for integration comes to nothing unless it is backed up by an alternative *psychological* model of the person which is more comprehensive than the determinist model and more comprehensive than the self-realizationist model. I am suggesting in turn that that model will come to nothing, will not even be a *psychological* model, unless it actually suggests theories to us and is supported and implemented by a research program. The model must also be faithful to the biblical vision, for if it is not, though we may have a psychological model, we do not have a *Christian* psychological model.

A Philosophical Insight

My own profession is that of philosopher. With respect to psychology, I have done nothing more than dip into it. The deepest dip I took occurred when I was writing my book, *Education for Responsible Action*. The question addressed in the book was how we can effectively and responsibly shape how students and others act in order to answer the question. I scouted through whatever psychological literature I could find that was relevant to the topic. In perusing this literature I found several different psychological models of the person at work. I found none that I could embrace as a Christian. All seemed to me deficient. I felt I had no choice but to use a theological-philosophical model of the person and pick and choose, in terms of that model, among the results reported in the psychological literature, hoping to arrive at a coherent picture. What was needed was a *psychological* model which was faithful to the theological model but went beyond it by actually giving a comprehensive theory of psychological dynamics, founded on and suggestive of a program of research. I am not aware that anything of the sort has emerged.

My impression is that christian psychologists generally stand on the outside of on-going psychology when they make their criticisms. If and when they do research, they participate in the research programs suggested by the very theories that they find unsatisfactory. Until you have an alternative theory supported by and suggestive of research, the extant theory will hold the field. Particularly will this be true if criticism comes to little more than saying that the extant theory does not hold for everything. Radical behaviorism is clearly in its decline, but not because of the external criticisms of Christians.

I have suggested that in much of psychology there is a deterministic model of the person at work, and that in a good deal of the rest of psychology, there is a self-realization model at work. I have further suggested that the Christian must struggle toward the formulation of an alternative model which is both biblically faithful and is genuinely a psychological model in that it comprises theories which are supported by and suggestive of research projects. Let me now bring out the assumption which lies beneath this recommendation. Our christian faith should function as guide and critic in our practice of psychology and other disciplines. Sometimes when there is a felt tension between psychology and christian faith, the tension is genuine and what should give way is not our understanding of the christian faith but our psychological convictions. Sometimes the struggle toward integration should take the form of *psychological revisionism*. Sometimes the Christian is absolutely right to be bothered in a deep way by developments in psychology. Sometimes what he or she should do in response is struggle to reconstruct psychology, allowing his christian conviction to function as what *Reason within the Bounds of Religion* (Wolterstorff, 1976) calls "control beliefs."

Consider again that christian philosopher who came to my department and pointed to the felt tension between the determinism of the contemporary psychologist's model of persons and the traditional understanding of persons in the christian faith. My response was the opposite of his. I agreed something has to give, but what should give is the psychology, not the faith, for as a Christian, I am fully persuaded that we are free and responsible agents before God and our fellows. What is there about contemporary psychology that forces me to knuckle under this point? Have they proved their deterministic claims? What are the proofs? What are the deterministic laws? It is psychology, not my faith, that must be reformed at the point of tension.

There are many christian scholars who are reluctant to follow this advice. They are reluctant to practice psychology in christian perspective, preferring instead to look at psychology as customarily practiced in christian perspective. Why the reluctance to make our faith rather than our psychology determinative? One reason is that many of us in the twentieth century who are Christians do not see the world through biblical eyes. In some abstract way we hold to the tenets of the christian faith, but our faith is hardly operative when we actually deal with human beings. Then other frameworks of conviction shape our vision, so we do not, in any way, sense and feel a conflict.

There is also the longing for professional prestige, and the sense of intimidation which often accompanies that. christian scholars often feel intimidated by the members of their profession. If you want to gain professional prestige you have to go along with the academic consensus and make your peace with that. The psychological factor of intimidation must not be discounted in explaining why many christian psychologists feel nervous and reluctant in the face of my advice.

There is a third reason for uneasy feelings when I talk about the gospel functioning as critic and guide, a third reason for feeling uneasy when I say that one's christian convictions should function as control beliefs in the practice of psychology. Following this advice sounds like inserting faith where it has no business being inserted. We work with a certain vision of science, and of the proper business of the scientist, and according to that vision one's faith is simply irrelevant to the proper conduct of a science. I want to explore briefly this vision of a true science with which so many of us operate, by going back to the French Renaissance philosopher Descartes who formed our modern understanding of knowledge rationality, and science.

Descartes and Positivism

Descartes was impressed with the diversity of human opinion. Reflecting on his education in one of the best schools of France, he highlighted the fact that his teachers disagreed with each other. A twentieth century student would have reveled in this diversity. Descartes was persuaded that it was the sign of something amiss in his education. What was amiss was that the sciences had not yet been set on their proper foundation.

Do you see what a fateful assumption this was? Descartes was assuming that a true science will gain the consensus of all rational persons, and not in some eschatological future but right here and now and every step of the way. True science is consensus science. Descartes' vision was that in the midst of this enormous diversity of human opinion it is possible to erect a great tower, a tower of science, a tower built on rational consensus, a tower to which each of us can add our small brick, a tower which from generation to generation will show progress, a tower from which all personal idiosyncrasy has been eliminated and which is objective, impartial, consensual. In short, Descartes assumes that (1) in the construction of a science we must confine ourselves to that on which we can gain rational consensus. Let me now go on to list five other assumptions which Descartes made, assumptions equally as influential as that first. Descartes assumes:

(2) There are within us common shared capacities for the acquisition of knowledge and that if we use these in the right way we will achieve the consensus needed for science. Method is of prime importance.

(3) In mathematics and mathematical physics, scientists are already using the right method since in these sciences there is already for the most part the desired consensus. These sciences then are paradigms of rationality.

(4) To find out the proper method for using our knowledge-acquiring capacities, we should extract from mathematics and physics the method that they are using and use this method across the board.

(5) The proper method is axiomatic, starting with certitude. Others, later, would relax Descartes' rigorism and allow inductive reasoning, but all would share Descartes' lust for grounding our scientific beliefs in certitude.

(6) Science properly conducted will never conflict with the christian faith. Correspondingly, to insert one's faith into the process of building up a science is to pollute that process with the very diversity and lack of consensus that we are struggling to eliminate. We must practice methodological atheism.

This cluster of Cartesian assumptions has been profoundly formative of our way of thinking about theorizing. Why has psychology been so much in the grip of the model of the physical sciences? Because we have adopted Descartes' conviction that in those sciences we are in the presence of the finest flowering of human rationality. Is there not consensus in these sciences? Here the right method has been found. Why have we thought that in the practice of the sciences we have to keep faith out? Because we have adopted Descartes' conviction that the project of a science is a consensus project, a here and now consensus, not an eschatological consensus. In the sciences one confines oneself to what any rational person would consent to: The christian faith most emphatically does not satisfy that condition.

The Dissonance

When we confront contemporary academic psychology with the Cartesian picture in mind we feel some dissonance. The picture tells us that between science responsibly conducted and faith properly understood there will never be conflict. Yet we feel tension. The thing to notice, however, is that most of us resolve the felt tension without giving up the Cartesian picture of science. If we are harmonizers, we revise our understanding of the christian faith, we

conclude that we must have understood it incorrectly at some point. If we are compatibilists we say that everything is in order as it is. If we are delimiters, we say that we must have drawn mistaken conclusions about the scope of extant theories. Our image of science remains that of a consensus enterprise. Faith does not gain so much as a handhold within it.

This whole Cartesian picture of genuine science has come crashing down in the last 25 years. Let me sketch out quickly some of the shattering developments. Karl Popper has argued that science proceeds neither in deductive nor inductive fashion. It matters not at all, says Popper, how you get your theories, whether by induction or whatever; what matters is only whether or not your theories have been falsified. If they have not been falsified, you are entitled to hold on to them whether or not other scientists happen to agree with you. Consensus, as Popper sees it, is at best an eschatological hope rather than an initiating insistence. Various followers of Popper such as Imre Lakatos have gone beyond their master and pointed out how slithery is the notion of falsification. Strictly speaking, theories are rarely falsified. What rather happens is that anomalies turn up, which make holding the theory increasingly *ad hoc* but rarely impossible. The full picture which emerges from the Popper school is that the rationality at work in science is very different from what the Cartesian tradition thought it was: Lakatos has gone so far in repudiating the consensus vision as to say that science advances by way of a plurality of tenaciously held-to theories.

Another line of thought comes from such as Kuhn and Feyerabend who argue that what often happens, even in such paradigm sciences as mathematics and physics, is not rational by anyone's understanding of rationality. Non-rational shifts in paradigms occur and, worse yet, just plain old fashioned stubbornness, jealousy, and rhetorical persuasiveness. Whatever may have yielded consensus in these sciences, one cannot simplistically say that it was rationality working at its highest pitch. All the while these new theories and analyses of science were emerging, physics and mathematics themselves were on the move into dark bewildering terrain. New and profoundly perplexing developments have taken place right within them.

Likewise, the Marxists have had their say, arguing that our faculties for the acquisition of belief and knowledge are not the common property of humanity, neutral and impartial, but are corrupted and polluted by our social situations. Psychologists of all sorts have argued that even perception is polluted by beliefs and expectations, not to mention indigenously human distortions of our sensory mechanisms. Continental thinkers have insisted that the physical sciences must not be taken as the paradigm for all science since, while their goal is nomological explanation, the goal of the human sciences is something quite different: interpretation resulting in understanding (*Verstehen*). Let us not forget, moreover, the philosophers who have argued that Cartesian foundationalism is untenable as a theory of knowledge, or of rationality.

Conclusion

For all these and yet more reasons, the Cartesian picture of science has collapsed in the last quarter century. We live and work in the midst of the wreckage. No comprehensive picture has yet emerged to take its place. Neither am I able to offer to you a comprehensive picture, though I think I do see what has to be said of a number of issues. Let me mention just one of those. I think that as we struggle to form a new image of science we shall have to give up the vision of science as a consensus enterprise, other than in some ultimate eschatological sense. We shall have to give up the notion that one must limit oneself to saying what every rational person would agree on. We must instead begin to see science as the articulation of a person's view of life, in interaction of course, with the world and with our fellows. Did Skinner win consensus on his deterministic model of the person before he set about doing his research in that framework? Did Carl Rogers win consensus on his self-realization model before he

began his work? Of course not. We have to begin taking seriously the actual pluralism of the academy and stop overlooking or excusing it. The traditional assumption was that pluralism in the academy is proof that things were not being done right, that at least one of us was not acting in fully rational fashion; at least one of us was not rightly using the right methods. We shall have to scrap this picture. The responsible pursuit of science does not yield consensus but pluralism; we see things differently, without that fact itself being the sign of irrationality on anyone's part. The central beliefs with which we each unavoidably operate do not enjoy consensus.

My plea is that in this pluralism of the academy the christian psychologist occupies his or her rightful place. Occupy it as a Christian who sees the world in the light of the gospel, but occupy it also as a psychologist, not as one who surveys the scene from outside and now and then makes some clucking noises, but as one who participates in the nitty-gritty of actual psychological explorations. Do not just be a critic. Be a creative initiator, faithful in your thinking as in your doing the gospel of Jesus Christ.

References

Evans, C. S. (1977). *Preserving the person*. Downers Grove, IL: InterVarsity Press.

Wolterstorff, N. (1976). *Reason within the bounds of religion*. Grand Rapids, MI: Eerdmans.

Wolterstorff, N. (1980). *Education for responsible action*. Grand Rapids, MI: Eerdmans.

10

Christian Perspectives on the Sciences of Man

C. Stephen Evans
Wheaton College

For the Christian working in the social and behavioral sciences there are often conflicts between faith and discipline. This essay focuses on some of these tension points.

The Problem

The tension between faith and reason, secular learning and Christian belief,[1] has historically been localized in various arenas. In the time of Copernicus and Galileo physics seems to have been the primary locus of controversy. In the nineteenth and early twentieth centuries biology seems to have been the main sore spot. Today, in my judgment, the sciences of man, particularly psychology, sociology, anthropology, and also brain psychology[2] are the crucial battlegrounds, and thus ought to be a central point of concern for Christian educators.

That this is so may seem surprising. Would not one expect the humanities to be the center of tension? It is there where the most explicit overlap between thought and faith occurs. In literature and philosophy, the questions about God, values, and the meaning of human existence are likely to be central. Just for that reason, however, I believe that the tension in the humanities is likely to be less. Although particular writers and philosophers may espouse non-Christian views, at least the questions which occupy Christian thought are respectable to the humanist, even if his answers differ. And generally the lack of scientific pretension can plausibly lead to a tolerance for opposing viewpoints so that even the Christian answers are given a respectable hearing. On the whole, with important exceptions, the humanities presuppose a conception of man as personal—a valuing, though not always rational, agent—a perspective on man which is congruent with Christian thought.

This is by no means the case in the sciences which deal with man. At the risk of over-generalization, and consciously ignoring some definite counter-movements, it is fair to say that the rise of the social sciences in the twentieth century has been marked by the demise of the person. That is, there is a definite tendency to avoid explanations of human behavior which appeal to the conscious decisions of persons in favor of almost any non-personal factors. Let us take an example. In ordinary life it is perfectly conceivable that a convert to a religion, if asked why he is a believer might reply, "Because I have chosen to be a believer." If pressed, he might offer reasons why he chose, but he would insist that those reasons were not coercive. Ultimately his own free choice is at the root of the matter. Perhaps the one point of agreement which would unite Skinner, Durkheim, Freud, and Marx, to take a few representative greats, would be that this explanation of behavior is almost certainly scientifically invalid. And it is important to see that the falseness of the proferred explanation does not necessarily stem from the dishonesty of the proferrer. No, the problem with the explanation is that it does not explain; it is not the logically proper type of explanation. Beyond this the aforementioned scientist would diverge. To explain the decision to become a believer, Skinner would speak of operant conditioning with its related concepts, Durkheim of the degree of social cohesion and the nature of the authority bonding the various groups which have shaped the individual's identity and world, Freud of unconscious and presumably biologically grounded forces, and Marx would speak of the material and economic self-interests of the social class of the believer. In the interpretation of the explanation proferred by the believer himself, such categories as rationalization, ideology, and reinforced verbal-behavior would emerge. In none of this would any recognizable correlate of the person as a valuing, cognitively aware, responsible agent appear. Yet this latter perspective is surely a central aspect of a religion which wishes to talk of sin and righteousness, knowing God, and—I would even argue—loving God.

Why is it that such personalistic categories as choices, purposes, and reasons are absent from these sciences of man? The answer is deceptively simple and complex. Briefly, it is because social scientists have wanted to be *scientists*. The complexity arises when one tries to explain how the particular conception of what it means to be scientific, which underlies that simple explanation, arose and gained wide-spread acceptance. In essence, I suppose, however, that one commonly offered explanation does give at least part of the story, and that is that social scientists simply emulated natural scientists. Physics and biology were genuine sciences, so if one wishes to be a scientist one must use the sorts of methods and concepts employed by physicists and biologists.

Here, certain erroneous views about the history of these sciences come into the picture, views which were popularized but not invented by John Stuart Mill and Auguste Comte. One is the myth of pure empiricism. According to this tale, modern science emerged when men began to use their eyes and ears, to look about the world and gather observations, as opposed to ignorant but pious medievals, who were so busy reading ancient texts and slavishly submitting to authorities that they never bothered to look around and discover such obvious facts as that a body in motion travels in a straight line at a constant speed unless acted upon by a force. This empiricist myth is one factor which has made many social scientists blind to the importance of philosophical presuppositions in their work. "We scientists have nothing to do with philosophical speculation. We deal with facts, which are derived from our observations of how things really are." This is no doubt the source of the confusion over determinism, which many social scientists somehow see as an hypothesis or theory verified by their observations, rather than an assumption which makes their work possible. This empiricist myth, combined with the questionable notion that scientific observations can only be made of physical objects, is also no doubt a source of physicalistic biases in the social sciences.

A second erroneous view of the history of the natural sciences which has had important implications for social scientists concerns the notion of causality. Best expressed in Comte's "law of three stages," this is the idea that the development of science is contingent on the rejection of personal and "abstract" types of causality in favor of efficient, mechanical causality. On Comte's view, the thunder which primitive man regarded as caused by Thor's angry toss of his hammer, and which might be explained by a slightly more sophisticated Aristotelian-type philosopher as a result of a "sonic principle" inherent in storm clouds, is at last explained scientifically by analyzing the event as the mechanical result of antecedent conditions discovered by observation. The key to scientific success lies in giving up "anthropomorphic" modes of explanation for mechanical types.[3] Of course someone might observe that rejecting personal-type explanations of non-personal events like thunder is one thing; rejecting personal-type explanations for the actions of persons is quite another. However, to press this at this point would be to beg the important questions.

To argue that these myths are myths is beyond the scope of this article. However, it is safe to say that a growing consensus of historians and philosophers of science would agree that both are at least highly misleading and open to question.[4] While almost no one would deny the importance of empirical observation in science, one must have an equally sharp sense for the theory-laden character of most if not all observation. As for causality, Kuhn and Toulmin have documented the extent to which what is seen as a genuine causal explanation and what is regarded as a mere verbal solution is a function of changing historical "paradigms" or "ideals of natural order." These considerations should give pause to social scientists eager to model their disciplines on the natural sciences, on the grounds of the methodological unity of science.[5]

However, the more basic question is not, perhaps, "What game is being played by physical scientists?" but "Should social scientists be playing the same game?" To argue analogically from the success of the physical sciences begs the question. Corresponding success in the social sciences can be expected only if the reality being studied is basically similar, which is the point at issue. Arguing from the success of the social sciences themselves may be open to question on two counts. First, some would question how successful these sciences have been. Are the lack of powerful, universally accepted explanatory theories to be dismissed as the result of the relative youthfulness of the sciences involved? Second and more serious is the contention that the success of these sciences is relative to assumptions about the nature of science which are internal to the sciences in question. Thus, success in prediction of behavior is a measure of scientific adequacy, only given the assumption that the aim of a science dealing with man is prediction. Toulmin (1961, Chaps. 1-3) has argued that the aim of any science is not prediction but intelligibility or understanding. This raises the crucial question as to what it is to understand a person or a person's behavior.

The tension between our ordinary view of man which employs what we have called personalistic categories to interpret and explain human behavior and the image of man which seems to emerge from but perhaps actually underlies the social sciences is made peculiarly problematic by one other factor— the prestige of science in today's world. To be scientific in one's view is still *de rigeur* in most circles, academic or otherwise. Certainly no one wishes to be regarded as unscientific. Thus in any conflict between common sense and science there can be no question of who is right. In sophisticated circles this scientism—the belief that all truth is scientific truth and that the sciences give us our best shot at knowing "how things really are"—becomes explicit. The following quotation from D. M. Armstrong (1970) may be regarded as a representative statement of a belief which is often tacit in the statements of "tough-minded" intellectuals of a naturalistic bent.

> I think that the best clue we have to the nature of mind is furnished by the discoveries and hypotheses of modern science concerning the nature of man....
>
> What reason have I, it may be asked, for taking my stand on science? ... Why this "scientism?"
>
> It seems to me that the answer to this question is very simple. If we consider the search for truth, in all its fields, we find that it is only in science that men versed in their subject can, after investigation that is more or less prolonged ... reach substantial agreement about what is the case....
>
> I conclude that it is the scientific vision of man, and not the philosophical or religious or artistic or moral vision of man, that is the best clue we have to the nature of man. And it is rational to argue from the best evidence we have. (pp. 68-69)

Let us summarize our conclusions so far. There is a prima facie conflict between the conception of man as responsible agent which is implicit in Christian theology as well as much of our everyday awareness of persons, and the conception of man implicit in the dominant tradition in several of the social sciences. The de-personalizing scientific view of man seems to be necessitated by a certain conception of what makes a discipline a science, which in turn is based on a particular interpretation of the history and character of the natural sciences, emphasizing empirical observation of physical events and deterministic modes of causality. This tension is aggravated by the prevalence of scientism in western culture, the tendency to make scientific procedures and theories epistemologically and metaphysically ultimate.

Possible Responses

It should be apparent even to the thoughtful layman at this point that the real enemy is scientism and not social science *per se*. With this demon exorcised, various possibilities for integrating Christian conceptions of man and the sciences of man immediately present themselves. No doubt points of tension would remain, but tension can be creative as well as destructive. It is therefore tempting at this point to launch into yet another philosophical attack on the ghost of positivism and hope that the remainder of the problem will solve itself.

We shall resist this temptation, however, for several reasons. The most important of these is that some would urge that the positivistic scientism which is the source of most of the trouble is not something *added* to the social sciences but is part and parcel of their chief concepts and procedures. This claim cannot be dismissed without a thorough airing, which would require detailed examination of the particular social science under indictment. This is a job beyond the scope of this article and probably beyond the present competence of the writer.

We shall therefore proceed directly to analyze some possible responses to the social sciences as previously delineated without attempting to decide in advance what is science and what is scientism. These responses are best conceived of as Weberian "ideal types," perhaps somewhat analogous to the five views of Christ and culture portrayed by Niebuhr in his book by that title. They are not necessarily mutually exclusive and perhaps no single individual is a perfect representative of any of them. If asked which is *the* Christian view of the social sciences, the correct answer is all and none. All represent possible bases for a reasonably coherent Christian response to the social sciences; none is exclusively Christian in the sense that non-Christians could not hold views which are either identical or closely analogous. Despite their ideal character, I think that recognizable aspects of these responses can be identified among thoughtful people, including social scientists themselves, who have reflected on the social sciences.

These possible responses can be logically delineated by analyzing their views on three theses, which, taken collectively, produce the problem. These three are

1) The unity of science thesis
2) The completeness of science thesis
3) The ultimacy of science thesis

1) By the unity of science thesis, I mean the belief that all sciences employ the same basic methodology, that of the natural sciences interpreted positivistically, in which deterministic causal explanations are empirically derived for predictive purposes. 2) By the completeness of science thesis, I mean the belief that there are no areas of reality which are not amenable to scientific investigation, at least in principle. 3) By the ultimacy of science thesis, I mean the belief that science gives us the ultimate truth about the reality it investigates, both the nature of that reality and the ultimate explanation of the occurrences.

I shall analyze four possible responses to the crisis of the social sciences. These are described by asking which, if any, of these three theses are rejected. (Other logically possible views which reject more than one of these three theses can be viewed as combinations of the four I discuss.) These four views fall into three basic categories which I shall term, with admitted prejudice, the Capitulators, the Limiters of Science, and the Humanizers of Science. The second category, the Limiters of Science, comes in two types which we shall designate as the "Territorialists" and the "Perspectivalists," using the latter term in a different sense from that employed by Arthur Holmes (1969, Chaps. 5-6) in his discussions of metaphysical perspectives.

1. Capitulators accept all three theses.

2.A. Limiters of Science who are Territorialists reject thesis (2), the completeness of science thesis.

2.B. Limiters of Science who are Perspectivalists reject thesis (3), the ultimacy of science thesis.

3. Humanizers of Science reject thesis (1), the unity of science thesis.

We shall discuss each of these positions in more detail.

Capitulators

The Capitulatory position is the one for which I have least sympathy, as evidenced by the prejudicial name I have assigned it. Nevertheless, I regard it possible to hold this position and still to be intellectually coherent and genuinely Christian. It is worthy of respect as well as critical analysis.

Basically, the position of the Capitulators is that this is indeed a mechanistic universe, and there is no reason to think that human behavior is any exception. The idea that there are "gaps" in the scientific chain of causes in which "spiritual" or "mental" reality might reside is a weak foundation for a Christian understanding of man. No, the Capitulators say, let there be no weak, defensive, holding actions, in which a person-of-the-gaps is gradually enfeebled and diminished. True, scientific explanations of human behav-

ior, whether concerned with physiological, psychological, or socio-cultural mechanisms, are as yet far from complete. But this ignorance is merely a sign of the complexity of the subject and finiteness of the scientists, and it is sure to diminish in time.

In what sense can such a view be Christian? The point of integration here is the creative sovereignty of God. Proponents of such a view will stress the biblical concept of God as the one who continuously maintains in being every aspect of the created order. There is no biblical warrant, they will assert, for the view that God determines the outcome of some events, while leaving others undetermined. Man himself, the Capitulators will say, is seen in Scripture as "dust," part of the created order. Hence there is no biblical warrant for asking him to be the great exception to the laws of the created order.

Here, the critic will ask, "But what of the biblical picture of man as free and responsible agent?" What happened to freedom and responsibility in such a deterministic framework? Here a variety of responses emerge. One might be simply to take the bull by the horns and deny that man is in any sense free and responsible. Such a hard-nosed response is rare, however.

A more typical response is to assert that freedom and responsibility are really compatible with deterministic explanation. "Man is both free and determined." This may mean several things. It may simply amount to intellectual doubletalk, a dishonest attempt to have one's logical cake and eat it too. That is, it may simply be equivalent to asserting that A and not-A are both true. Called to question on his determinism, this type of Capitulator willingly admits that freedom is "also" true but fails to give any account of how it is compatible with determinism, although a sense of paradox is plainly present.

A more honest attempt to hang on to both freedom and determinism is found in the individual who asserts that both are true, but who admits his inability to reconcile them. After all, why should the whole of reality be intelligible to our feeble human reason. The whole business is an admitted paradox, a mystery or enigma, but it is one which we cannot escape affirming. This sort of intellectual modesty is in my view a perfectly legitimate stance, provided that it is the outcome of honest intellectual struggle, rather than an evasion of it. But it seems to me that the Capitulator who takes this line is really on the way towards becoming a Limiter of Science of some sort. For what he is really doing is asserting that there are some kinds of truths or aspects of reality which are not intelligible to the human intellect and thus not amenable to scientific inquiry.

The most consistent and sophisticated way of reconciling determinism and freedom is based on a careful analysis of the concepts of freedom and responsibility. Why must we assume that freedom and causal determinism are incompatible? Do we mean by a free event merely one that is random or uncaused? Is our ability to predict a person's behavior inconsistent with our holding him responsible for what he does? The answer to both questions seems to this sort of Capitulator to be negative. A free act, one for which a person is to be held responsible, is simply one which is caused by the character or will of the person in question. When someone holds a gun to my ribs and asks for my money, my response is hardly a free one. But in many cases I am under no such compulsion. The causes of my behavior lie within my own psyche, or personality, or brain. I am responsible for the act since I originated it. Though God may ultimately determine the outcome since he maintains and controls the whole created order, nevertheless within that created order persons exist and their choices and decisions are part of the means whereby God accomplishes his ends. The critic may here interpose that freedom requires that the person "could have chosen differently." Our reconciler of freedom and determinism replies that indeed he could have chosen differently. That is, he could have chosen differently *if* he wished to, *if* his character had been different, *if* his genes had been different, etc. Thus the thesis that "he could have chosen otherwise" is interpreted in such a way that it is compatible with the thesis: "Given the chain of causes, his choice is determined."

When developed along these lines, the Capitulatory position is powerful and attractive, and it provides a coherent framework for a Christian who wishes to integrate his faith and the findings of the social sciences. Nevertheless, there are some hard questions that must be asked of it, primarily concerning the analyses of freedom and responsibility which have been offered. In this deterministic framework, is the operative concept of responsibility really that necessary for moral responsibility? In this framework are men not responsible for their acts in precisely the same sense in which machines (computers?) are responsible for their "behavior," or in which an apple tree is responsible for producing the fruit which it does? Does the notion of moral freedom demand not merely that the person could have done otherwise *if* some things had been different (his genes, his background, his character), but that the person has at least some alternatives among which he may choose, even if nothing about the causal nexus prior to that point of decision had been

different? When we hold a person morally responsible do we not say to him, "You could have done otherwise *even given* your past and present." When we ourselves deliberate about an act, do we not necessarily presuppose that the alternatives we consider are genuine alternatives? These are the questions that the Capitulator who wishes to reconcile freedom and determinism must answer.

Limiters of Science

Next we shall consider the response of the Limiters of Science, the category which comes in two species. What all Limiters have in common is a conviction that not all truths about the human person (and reality in general) are scientific truths. While basically accepting thesis (1), the unity of science thesis, the Limiters feel that the naturalistic scientific method carries with it definite limitations which cannot and must not be transgressed. Limiters differ, however, over just what are these limits and how they should be drawn. Territorialists conceive the limits in terms of regions of reality, types of entities that science is incapable of dealing with. They therefore deny thesis (2), the completeness of science thesis. Perspectivalists, on the other hand, do not deny that science can legitimately treat any and every region of reality. They see the limits of science as limits of outlook or perspective. Although the scientist may have something to say about everything, he does not tell the whole story about some things (perhaps not anything). The scientific method is a commitment to a certain way of seeing things, which enables one to see some important things. But it is not the only possible such perspective; to gain a view of man as he really is, to gain metaphysical truth one must not look only or even mainly to science. Perspectivalists therefore deny thesis (3), the ultimacy of science thesis.

Territorialists.

The classic example of territorialism is Descartes' mind-body dualism. Descartes made his peace with mechanistic science and human freedom by a dualistic ontology. Reality is composed of two radically different sorts of stuff, *res extensa* and *res cognitans*. In the material realm mechanistic explanations are complete. But the human mind, Descartes said, was not a material thing but a spiritual reality, attached to a body but occupying no specific spatial location. The contents of the mind were said to be essentially private, available only to introspection and beyond the reach of a science which can only deal with publicly observable, spatial entities.

Territorial tendencies are also found in some of the neo-Kantian and idealist conceptions of the dual realms of nature and spirit. Nature is the realm of necessity where events are governed by universal laws. The world of the spirit is, however, the world of freedom; the realm of the unique event which resists law-like explanation. This is only one strain in idealist thought, however, and it is over-ridden by Humanizers of Science influences. Hence we shall treat them more fully later on.

Since the advent of mechanistic science, dualistic types of views have been perhaps dominant in orthodox Protestant thought. Many Protestant theologians have followed Descartes in seeing man as body *plus* soul, or body *plus* spirit. The biblical bases of such a view are well-known, although it is controversial to what extent such dualistic views are Hebraic or Greek in origin. Paul speaks of the body as a tent which we live in, or a suit of clothes (1 Cor. 5:1-4)· He also says that to be absent from the body is to be present with the Lord(1 Cor. 5:6-7), implying that personal existence may continue apart from the body. Christ says we are not to fear those who can kill the body, but he who can destroy *both* body and soul(Matt. 10:28). Implicit in the whole biblical account is a conception of man as *more* than just dust, and this something more is frequently referred to as soul or *spirit*.

When applied to the social sciences, dualistic views hold some rather harsh implications. Though perhaps reticent to do so because of the prestige of science, it would seem that a consistent dualist ought to charge naturalistically inclined social scientists with trespassing on a forbidden domain. While physiology as a science of the human *body* may seem legitimate, the notion of a science of man which ignores the soul, that intellectual valuing center of activity which represents the real person or at least the center of the real person, is a flagrant contradiction of terms. The success of the sciences which have dispensed with a non-physical soul must be regarded as essentially circular. Having begun from a perspective which essentially defines spiritual reality out of existence, the social scientist completes his circle of explanation by announcing that nowhere in his investigation did he discover such a reality or feel the need to postulate it. The territorialist is therefore at least implicitly a militant critic of the social sciences.

Territorialism, however, is not without its own problems. Chief among these is putting humpty-dumpty together again after he has been fragmented. That is, having sundered the man from his body, or culture from nature, the dualistic thinker has great difficulty in understanding the evidently intimate relationship between his discrete regions.

Mind-body dualists have traditionally seen the relationship of mind to body and vice versa as one of causal interaction. Causal interaction, however, does not seem adequate to account for the peculiarly intimate relationship which I have to my body. A threat to my body is a threat to *me*. The multitude of intimate relationships between physiological and mental happenings, discovered by modern brain research, while perhaps compatible with dualism, do not seem congenial to it.

A second problem with dualism is the extent to which it appears to rest on a priori claims. Since the position of the territorialist is that empirical science cannot really investigate the mind, he cannot really offer empirical support for his contentions. His main appeals are to our immediate intuitive awareness of the mental and to a variety of philosophical arguments designed to show the radically non-physical character of the mind. Many of the arguments are formidable and dualism has had able champions in the twentieth century (Campbell, 1957; Ducasse, 1960). Nevertheless, the *Zeitgeist* has definitely been against the dualist. To many, including many philosophers, dualism just does not seem a live option. Even a philosopher, while seeking to transcend such cultural biases, must inevitably find some options more promising and worthy of an investment of critical energy than others. Philosophies are partially, if not completely, philosophies of their age. The biblical basis of dualism has also been challenged by many thinkers today, including some prominent evangelical thinkers (Reichenbach, 1973; 1974; Dooyeweerd, 1960). Nevertheless, the claims of dualism have by no means been disposed of and it remains a possible perspective from which critically to analyze the sciences of man.

Perspectivalism.

Our second type of Limiter of Science is the thinker who denies the ultimacy of science. In contrast to the dualist, he may stress the unity of man. He may admit that to some extent, it is true to say that man is his body, or man is a complex of socio-cultural relationships. However, the perspectivalist stresses that this unitary reality can be seen from different viewpoints, and when seen from these multiple viewpoints, different aspects appear. Science is limited not by what sorts of objects can be studied, but by what can be said about the objects it studies.

In relationship to the biblical conception of man, the Perspectivalist is likely to stress the different functions and purposes of the biblical and scientific accounts. The Bible is not a scientific textbook; it tells us who did it and why rather than what and how. As man is a part of the created order, it is no cause for alarm that scientists have begun to describe man and explain his behavior as part of that order. Such scientific accounts have their value but they cannot replace, because they do not compete with accounts which view man as a moral agent made in the image of God.

One excellent example of a perspectivalist would be the French Catholic, Gabriel Marcel (1956; 1962; 1964). While emphasizing the unity of the person and the body, Marcel nonetheless argues that scientific accounts necessarily perceive the person as part of an objective order, a set of problems to be solved. Concrete or lived-experience of the person, however, is of an entirely different order. In such experience, the person is seen as presence, not as object, and the difficulties encountered are mysteries to be explored, rather than problems to be solved. To support this mystery/problem distinction Marcel gives a critique of scientific method, attempting to show that it is grounded in an *attitude* towards the world, an attitude of mistrust which precludes perception of the fully personal, and which, if extended beyond the realm of science, results in a total dehumanization of existence.

Another example of a perspectivalist is D. M. MacKay, a British brain researcher and computer scientist. There are some elements in MacKay's thought which tend towards a Capitulationist view. In a lecture delivered at Wheaton College in July, 1975, MacKay (1975) stressed the thesis that God does not determine the outcome of some events while leaving others undetermined. And in his published work, MacKay asserts (1974, p. 78) that in principle a super-scientist who knew all about our brain-cells could successfully predict the outcome of decisions we have not yet made, so long as he did not inform us of his prediction.

However, the general thrust of MacKay's work is certainly Perspectivalist. MacKay (1974, pp. 36-37) uses the analogy of an "electric sign-board" to illustrate his view of the limits of science. An electrician giving an electrical account of the sign might describe the sign completely and speak only of light-bulbs, electrical circuits, etc. In his own terms, his exploration is complete, and what he describes is identical with the sign. Yet nowhere in his account do we have any reference to what the sign says, to its message or significance. The account given by the electrician is not flawed as an electrical account, it simply reflects the limitations which are an inherent part of his perspective. To say more, we must take another vantage point. Trying to claim that the scientific perspective on man tells us all there is to know

is a reductionistic fallacy which MacKay (1974, p. 42) labels "nothing-buttery." Clearly the limits of science are not limits of territory.

> No part of the world of observable events is outside the boundary of scientific study. However little the scientist may make of some of these from his professional standpoint, he is certainly entitled to try. His conclusions, however limited in scope, may be of real help in appropriate circumstances. The limitations will show up rather in the restricted kinds of description his language allows him to make of the events he studies, and the kinds of point he will be obliged to miss (theoretically) in consequence. (p. 36)

A secular philosopher whose view of the relationship of scientific to "everyday" explanations and accounts is very similar to MacKay's is Gilbert Ryle. In his book *Dilemmas*, Ryle (1954) uses the analogy of an accountant's report on a college to illustrate the way in which an account may "cover everything" but nonetheless fail to say what is essential.

Quite obviously, within the general category of Perspectivalism, a range of viewpoints would be possible. These could be arranged in a continuum from those on one extreme who would take a pragmatic or fictionalist interpretation of science, denying that scientific theories have any truth value, to those who would take a realistic interpretation of science, but would argue that personalistic or theological accounts are needed to complement this scientific truth. This range of viewpoints illustrates one of the key problems which Perspectivalism faces. Alternate accounts of the same phenomena inevitably raise the question as to whether or not one or more of the accounts may not be superfluous. It is difficult to see just how man's actions can be both free *and* mechanistically determined, unless freedom is re-interpreted as Capitulators are wont to do. Thus the Perspectivalist must ask, "Is the scientific account true? What sort of 'truth' does it possess? How can these alternate stories about man be put together to form a coherent picture?" The Perspectivalist must clearly show why the differing accounts are needed, highlighting both their differences and the ways in which they are related. for it must not be forgotten that these alternate accounts are accounts of the *same* reality.

Humanizers of Science

The last critical position we shall consider questions thesis (1) of our original triumvirate, the unity of science thesis. While not questioning the right of the sciences to explore every sort of phenomenon, they question the idea that the methods and procedures of the natural sciences, conceived positivistically, are normative for all sorts of sciences. Perhaps the truly scientific mode of procedure is not to follow a rigid set of methods which has been legislated in an *a priori* fashion, but rather to discover and adopt methods peculiar and appropriate to the particular subject matter under investigation. This tradition goes back at least to Aristotle, who held that different subject areas required different methods of investigation, different sorts of explanations, and even allowed different degrees of certainty.

It is in this category that we must place the multitude of counter-movements to the dominant academic trends in the sciences which deal with man. In psychology these counter-trends have been designated by Abraham Maslow (1968) as "third-force" psychology, meaning that it is an alternative both to orthodox Freudian and behavioristic psychologies. Into this group must be placed Maslow himself, Carl Rogers, Gordon Allport, Kurt Goldstein, as well as the original defectors from Freud (Adler particularly), and such neo-Freudians as Erich Fromm. For the most part, what has been designated existential psychology, represented notably by Rollo May, belongs in this group, and the attempts to produce a phenomenological psychology may be perhaps the most typical example of all. Maslow (1968) expresses the fundamental motive of this widespread and diverse movement well.

> Many sensitive people, especially artists, are afraid that science besmirches and depresses, that it tears things apart rather than integrating them, thereby killing rather than creating. None of this I feel is necessary. All that is needed for science to be a help in positive human fulfillment is an enlarging and deepening of the conception of its nature, its goals, and its methods. (p. viii)

Some of the dominant themes in these "humanistic psychologies" have been the unity of the person, the significance of free choices, the crucial place of values in science and in life, the pervasiveness of alienation in modern life, and the need to overcome this condition courageously and re-integrate the person. Such concepts and themes presuppose a view of man remarkably congruent with a Christian conception of man as responsible agent. In fact, some of these humanistic psychologies actually appear to be a form of substitute religion for some of their partisans.

Analogous humanistic movements can be located in other sciences that deal with man. In sociology,

those scientists who stress the importance of the participant-observer method, and who argue that qualitative observations may be as significant as quantitative methods belong in this category. In this field, the humanist's case is often put in terms of the necessity for *Verstehen*, empathetic understanding, to give a true account of human society. The term had wide currency among German idealists who distinguished between the natural sciences and the "sciences of the spirit." These two sorts of sciences differ not only in subject matters but in fundamental aims and methods. Their thinking is reflected to some degree in the work of Collingwood (1956) in the philosophy of history.

This *Verstehen* tradition in sociology certainly has its roots in Max Weber (1947), who borrowed the concept of *Verstehen* from Dilthey, to stress the importance of an awareness of subjective meanings of human acts. Although Weber himself was by no means hostile to naturalistic scientific methods, he stressed the necessity for understanding human acts as they are understood by the agent, at least as a starting-place for a scientific conception of man. An outstanding contemporary sociologist who has written in a manner consistent with Weber, is Peter Berger (1963), although some of Berger's ideas clearly relate more closely to the Perspectival Limiters of Science.

Representatives of the Humanizers of Science can be found in anthropology as well, particularly in the school of British social anthropology. In their work these scientists stress the uniqueness of different cultures and the importance of understanding the conceptual framework of the culture one is studying, of understanding the world as perceived by the members of the society one is investigating.

Among philosophers of science, the Humanizers of Science have some noted representatives. A curious congruence in this field between philosophical schools with rather different ancestries can be noted. On the one hand, phenomenologists such as Alfred Schutz (1967) and Maurice Natason (1962) have stressed the dependence of the human sciences on the experienced meanings which constitute the life-world. Surprisingly, one major group of analytic philosophers heavily influenced by the later "ordinary language" philosophy of Wittgenstein has come to conclusions which are strikingly similar. The most well-known figure in this movement is Peter Winch. In his little book, *The Idea of a Social Science*, Winch (1958) argues that the scientist who deals with man must make his primary goal the understanding of the values and meanings which structures the world as perceived by the persons under study.

The Humanizers of Science can themselves be divided into moderate and extreme factions. The extremists wish to drive the behaviorists, functionalists, etc., completely from the field. Such methods are totally inappropriate from their perspective. The more moderate Humanizers merely talk of supplementing or broadening, or placing in context, the non-personalistic categories employed by their fellow-scientists.

Yet this view, like the others, is not without its problems. Perhaps the key one concerns the preservation of scientific integrity. Can scientific consensus, objectivity, and progress be maintained if quantitative and statistical methods are abandoned? Does not too much of humanistic "sciences" seem merely to be sophisticated linguistic rumination on common-sense everyday perspectives? In daring to talk of the nature of man in normative terms, do not the sciences abandon their scientific character and become adjuncts to competing schools of philosophy? The Humanizers may reply that this has already happened in unconscious fashion, and that they are simply becoming explicitly aware of their presuppositions. But in looking at the writings of such psychologists as Maslow and Rogers, one senses basic confusions over what "science" means to them, and over what is philosophical assumption and what is the fruit of empirical research. The task which the Humanizers must tackle is that of spelling out in clear and unequivocal terms the character, methods, and norms of humanistic sciences of man. Ultimately the proof is in the pudding. The prospects for a humanistic psychology, sociology, etc., lie in the hands of those who will go beyond programmatic statements to produce genuine scientific work.

Some Personal Conclusions

Having surveyed the field and analyzed the options, my own positive contribution will be slender. Each of the four positions I have outlined has its strengths and weaknesses and I find myself drawn and repelled by each in turn. If forced to choose, however, I confess I would opt for either a Perspectivalist Limiter view or else a moderate Humanizer position. I am convinced in fact that these two views are closer than they first appear to be.

The main difference between them may in the last analysis be essentially semantic. It concerns the question, "What sort of intellectual enterprise deserves the essentially honorific title of 'science'?" No one familiar with the power of words and the prestige of science would want to call such a dispute "merely" one of semantics. But the following points should be noted: (1) Moderate humanizers do not deny that there are more restricted methods of investigation which can legitimately and usefully tell us things about man. They merely wish to urge that the scientific picture produced by these methods is fragmented and incomplete and must be supplemented by richer and looser procedures to get a full picture of man.

(2) Perspectivalists do not necessarily deny that the dimensions or aspects of human reality which science, because of its limited perspective, fails to see can be cognitively investigated or reflected upon in some way. They are inclined to say that man can be reflected upon as a moral, religious, and creative being. Concepts can be explored and beliefs formed in the arenas of theology, philosophy, literature, and in everyday life. While these arenas may not be judged sciences, they can nonetheless be penetrated by thought. We can in these matters be learned or ignorant, wise or foolish. We can form our opinions for good and bad reasons, and these can be discussed and examined in the critical marketplace of ideas. I conclude that there is hope for a reconciliation of these two positions.

Having confessed to a predilection for some such reconciled version of 2B and 3, what reasons can be given for the affinity? The view seems attractive because speaking both as a philosopher and a Christian, it seems to accomplish three tasks well:

1) It preserved the personhood of the person; man as free, responsible agent is not reduced to something less than personal.
2) It preserves the unity of man.
3) It preserves the integrity of science.

At this point a critic might interpose, "But aren't you begging all the important questions? Sure, it would be nice to preserve the old, rich conception of what it is to be a person. But suppose that view is just false. Suppose man is simply nothing more than physio-chemical events, or unconscious drives, or a constellation of sociological structures."

An adequate reply to this charge is of course beyond the scope of this article. Nevertheless, I shall try to sketch the outlines of a possible reply. It is at this point that I lean heavily towards a Perspectival view. It seems to me that no adequate scientific reply can be made to this criticism. The final battle-line for the validity of the personal must be fought at the level of philosophical reflection.

What must be said is essentially this. All men (including men of science) are both observers and agents. They could never be observers if they were not sometimes agents and they could never be agents if they were not sometimes observers.[6] As observers we sometimes observe our fellow observers and agents. We observe them in a variety of ways, sometimes very much in the same way that we observe trees and stones and molecules. There is nothing illegitimate about this. It is simply true that sometimes the conscious purposes and beliefs of the observer-agent we are observing are not genuinely causally efficacious. Sometimes persons act in ways which can be predicted if the observer knows something about the brain-physiology, or class structure, or early childhood of the person being observed, even if the person himself is unaware of the importance of these factors. So we ignore the personal character of the person being observed. We try to understand his behavior as we would any other objects in the natural order, and our efforts may succeed. We may even help the person under study gain a new self-awareness, to help him become more personally responsible for his acts.

This type of observing of the other, whose roots are found in our ordinary dealings with one another, (He doesn't really know why he does that, but an objective observer can see...) represents in embryo form the sciences of man. Developed, magnified, governed by rigorous norms and methods, we discover more and more about man as object. The critical question then is, "Can a conception of man which sees him as an object in the natural order, part of a causal mechanism, be the *whole* truth?"

If we radically change our perspective and reflect on what it is to be a person acting, a very different picture emerges. What is crucial is that we do not merely *observe* man acting, but consider what it is to be a person from the viewpoint of the *agent himself*. The person faced with a choice or decision cannot simply step back and *observe* himself making the decision. He cannot simply reflect on his past, or his genes, or his social relationships with a view toward *predicting* his decision. He must *make* the decision. As he deliberates, he must presuppose that he has a choice which he can make well or poorly. That he is free, that some decisions are better (more valuable) than others, are the necessary presuppositions of meaningful choice. While the personalistic conception of man may not emerge as the outcome of an empirical investigation of human actions toward which we take an essentially objective stance, it is the ever-present background which we constantly presuppose when we ourselves act.

So which conception of man must we opt for? Shall we view ourselves purely as objects, or shall we affirm the conception of man which we presuppose in the act of choosing? The answer to this question is implicit in our initial remarks on man as observer-agent. Observing is itself an activity, and it is an activity which can only take place if man engages in other activities as well. Science itself is a human activity which presupposes that the one pursuing the activity is a valuing, and to some extent rational, agent. No true account of man could be derived from science which makes the existence of science itself as a form of human activity unintelligible.

What we are affirming is what Kant termed the "primacy of the practical," and what Kierkegaard would have termed the primacy of existing over knowing. To affirm the primacy of living and doing over objective thinking and knowing is by no means to reject or minimize the importance of objective thinking and knowing. It is simply to note that thinking and knowing are personal activities, and to set them within their proper context, the context of agency. Scientists do not simply happen to be persons in addition to being scientists. Being a scientist is itself a form of the personal, a way of being-in-the-world. The scientist who repudiates the reality of the personal on the basis of his scientific work is involved in what I should call a practical self-contradiction. He interprets his findings in such a way that they contradict the beliefs to which his actions as a scientist necessarily commit him. Even the person who denies the significance of the personal affirms it to the extent that his denial is a significant act.

To live is to choose. To cease to choose is to cease to live. No conception of man, which does not make sense of choosing as seen by the chooser can be finally adequate. Behavioristic science can certainly explain "choices" after a fashion, but these explanations do not make sense of choices from the perspective of the agent. And that perspective cannot be rationally repudiated so long as one continues to *be* an agent. Someone has said that war is too important to be left to generals. So here we might say that the essential truth about personhood is too important to be left to the sciences. Though scientific knowledge may be tremendously important, one does not need to go to psychology textbooks to realize that one is a person, and that to be a person is to be faced with decisions for which one is responsible. Anyone who honestly asks "What shall I do with my life?" possesses the resources to understand what it is to be a person. And a person who possesses this understanding is at least intellectually ready for a confrontation with the Christian revelation, in which the True Person makes himself known. For the biblical account of man's nature, origin, present status, and future potential through God's redemptive activity is throughout an account of persons acting responsibly or irresponsibly in relationship to God and their fellow persons.

Notes

1. The writer regards these disjunctive categories as seriously inadequate, but wishes to employ them in explicating a perceived problem.

2. I shall use terms like "social science" and "sciences of man" in a very broad sense to include all these disciplines, and others to the extent that they share a common desire to develop a scientific conception of man by methods parallel to those employed in the "hard" natural sciences.

3. Here in-house quarrels between mechanistic models proper and more organismic or functionalist types is unimportant. Neither model emphasizes the causal efficaciousness of the conscious choices of personal agents.

4. For moderate criticisms see H. Butterfield (1965), and E. A. Burtt (1955). For more far-reaching criticism see T. Kuhn (1962), and S. Toulmin (1961).

5. Matson (1964) suggests that closer attention to the physical sciences today might actually lead social scientists to be more tolerant and open to non-mechanistic and non-deterministic views of man.

6. This thesis is argued for extensively by John Macmurray (1957, especially chapter 4), and by Stuart Hampshire (1959).

References

Armstrong, D. M. (1970) The Nature of Mind. In *The Mind-Brain Identity Theory*, C. V. Borst, Ed., (pp. 68-69) London: MacMillan.

Berger, P. (1963). *Invitation to Sociology: A Humanistic Perspective*. Garden City; Doubleday and Co.

Butterfield, H. (1965). *The Origins of Modern Science*, rev. ed. New York: The Free Press,

Burtt, E. A. (1955). *The Metaphysical Foundations of Modern Physical Science*, rev. ed. Garden City, NY: Doubleday and Co.

Campbell, C. A. (1957). *On Selfhood and Godhood*. London: Allen and Unwin.

Collingwood, R. G. (1956). *The Idea of History*. New York: Oxford University Press.

Dooyeweerd, H. (1960). *In The Twilight of Western Thought*. (pp. 157-195). Philadelphia, PA: The Presbyterian and Reformed Publishing Co.

Ducasse, C. J. (1960). In Defense of Dualism. In *Dimensions of Mind*, S. Hook, (Ed.). New York: Macmillan.

Hampshire, S. (1959). *Thought and Action*. New York: Viking Press.

Holmes, A. (1969). *Christian Philosophy in the 20th Century*. Nutley, NJ: The Craig Press.

Kuhn, T. (1962). *The Structure of Scientific Revolutions*. Chicago: The University of Chicago Press,.

MacKay, D. M. (1974). *The Clockwork Image* London: InterVarsity Press.

MacKay, D. M. (1975, July 21). Lecture heard by this writer at the International Conference on Human Engineering and the Future of Man, Wheaton College, Wheaton, IL.

Macmurray, J. (1957). *The Self as Agent*. London: Faber and Faber, Ltd.

Marcel, G. (1956). *The Philosophy of Existentialism* New York: The Citadel Press.

Marcel, G. (1962). *Homo Victor*. New York: Harper and Row.

Marcel, G. (1964). *Creative Fidelity* New York: Noonday Press, 1964

Maslow, A. (1968). *Toward a Psychology of Being*. New York: Van Nostrand Reinhold Co.

Matson, F. (1964). *The Broken Image*. Garden City, NY: Doubleday and Co.

Natanson, M. (1962). *Literature, Philosophy, and the Social Sciences*. The Hague: Martinus Nijhoff.

Reichenbach, B. (1973). Life After Death: Possible or Impossible. *Christian Scholar's Review, III, 4*, 232-244.

Reichenback, B. (1974). Re-Creationism and Personal Identity," *Christian Scholar's Review, IV, 4*, 326+.

Ryle, G. (1954). *Dilemmas*. (Chap. V) Cambridge: Cambridge University Press.

Schutz, A. (1967). *The Phenomenology of the Social World*. Evanston, IL: Northwestern University Press.

Toulmin, S. (1961). *Foresight and Understanding*. Bloomington, IN: Indiana University Press.

Weber, M. (1947). *The Theory of Social and Economic Organization*. (pp. 87-123). New York: Oxford University Press.

Winch, P. (1958). *The Idea of a Social Science*. London: Routledge and Kegan Paul.

11

Psychology's "Two Cultures": A Christian Analysis

Mary Stewart Van Leeuwen
Calvin College

In this essay the author analyzes the stance of Christian psychologists with respect to the "two cultures" in contemporary academic psychology—one of them "positivist and scientistic," the other "post-positivist and humanistic."

Psychologists in the Anglo-American tradition suffer from an ironic but seldom-admitted schizophrenia.[1] While claiming progressively greater success in exposing hidden influences on the behavior of their clients and subjects, most have assumed that their own theories and methods can in principle be laundered of any personal, social, or metaphysical agenda to which psychologists themselves, might privately adhere. There have been historical exceptions to this mentality, of course, the chief of which originated with Freud, who (whatever one may think of his biologically reductionist anthropology) understood only too well that the unanalyzed analyst was in danger of muddying, rather than clarifying the therapeutic waters by the operation of his or her own defense mechanisms when confronting patients whose problems struck too close to home. But in general, as a psychologist of Catholic background once put it, "the average psychologist seldom applies his technical knowledge to himself, ostensibly his is the only immaculate perception" (Maloney, 1974).

Self-examination then, has not been a strong point throughout most of psychology's century-long history as a formalized discipline. But even outside the clinical tradition there has been at least one forum in North America in which questions about paradigms, politics and even (although more rarely) metaphysics have regularly surfaced. I refer to the pages of the *American Psychologist*, the official monthly organ of the American Psychological Association, now approaching a half-century of continuous publication. In addition to reports of an empirical or theoretical nature, the *American Psychologist* has a tradition of publishing articles of a "metapsychological" sort—ones in which the paradigmatic *status quo* is not simply taken for granted and elaborated, but examined critically. For this article I have examined a number of articles of the metapsychological sort published in the *American Psychologist* over the past ten years. From these, and from related writings in psychology and its cognate disciplines, the following three points will be developed.

1) Both theoretically and methodologically, Anglo-American psychology is the uneasy home of two competing and progressively more evenly-matched "cultures," the first positivist and scientistic, the second post-positivist and humanistic. There are subcultural themes within each culture which vary across time and constituency, but the broad contours of each and the gulf that separates the two can be clearly documented, as can the strengths and weaknesses of each.

2) Christian psychologists can be found in both cultures, and in each case can give plausible reasons for maintaining that their preferred camp is where thoughtful Christians should cast their lot.

3) Christians now choosing sides in this debate should consider the possibility of a "third way," one in which their control beliefs enable them to steer a fine line between reductionism and self-deification in psychological anthropology and between positivism and skepticism in psychological epistemology. Whether Christians have the wit or the will to develop such a position (let alone have it accepted by the discipline at large) is, of course, another story.

Tracking the Two Cultures

I begin with a pair of companion-articles which appeared in the *American Psychologist*. The first, by one of American psychology's elder statesmen, Gregory Kimble (1984) of Duke University, was entitled "Psychology's Two Cultures." The second, co-authored by Leonard Krasner and Arthur Houts (1984) (from state universities in New York and Tennessee respectively) was "A Study of the 'Value' Systems of Behavioral Scientists." In recent years the

American Psychologist has published several attempts to analyze competing value-systems within its constituency[2] but these two are unique in attempting systematically empirical, as opposed to anecdotal, accounts of these subcultures. That the journal chose to publish two such studies side by side may be seen as a reassertion of empirical values on the part of the editors, a concession to the growing literature critical of value-free conceptions of science,[3] or possibly both.

Kimble (1984) takes his cue from C. P. Snow's 1959 lecture on "The Two Cultures and the Scientific Revolution," in which, as a practitioner of both the sciences and the humanities, Snow (1964) deplored the gap in methods, values, and conceptual language that increasingly deemed to be separating these two major branches of Western culture. "In psychology," Kimble (1984) asserts, "these conflicting cultures exist within a single field, and those who hold opposing values are currently engaged in a bitter family feud" (p. 834). Armed with past analyses of these value conflicts, Kimble (1984) developed what he called the "Epistemic Differential"—a scale in which each of twelve discipline-related value issues is represented in bipolar form. Respondents rank themselves on a scale of 1 to 10 with regard to their position on each issue—for example, scientific vs. humanistic values as motivators of scholarship, belief in the determinism vs. indeterminism of behavior, nature vs. nurture as the predominant shaper of human behavior, and objectivity vs. empathy as the best means of understanding behavior.

Kimble's (1984) responding samples were of three kinds: first, a group of undergraduate students with no previous training in psychology; second, a sample of over half the officers of the various divisions of the American Psychological Association (APA),[4] and third, members of the APA who belonged to only one of four divisions of the Association: Division 3 (Experimental), Division 9 (The Society for the Psychological Study of Social Issues), Division 29 (Psychotherapy) or Division 32 (Humanistic). His scoring procedure allowed a total item score to be assigned to each respondent, from -12 (the most extreme "scientist" position) to +12 (the most extreme "humanistic").[5] Results for the first two groups (heterogenous samples of pre-psychology students and APA officers) showed a roughly normal distribution of scores, with the means in each case very close to the center—that is, showing no clear evidence for the "two cultures" phenomenon.

But once psychologists have sorted themselves into specific APA interest groups, the picture changes dramatically. Factor analysis of these scores isolated six scale items that could be referred to as the "scientist-humanist cluster."[6] On every one of these, members of APA Division 3 (Experimental) had mean scores in the most extreme scientistic direction. Differences among the other three divisions, while still significant, were generally less pronounced, but all three groups were clearly more committed to the humanistic end of the continuum, with average scores in the predicted order: Division 9 psychologists were the most moderate humanizers, and Division 32 the most extreme. The "two cultures" phenomenon in psychology, Kimble (1984) concludes,

> comes about as the result of a birds-of-a-feather phenomenon. People with biases in either the humanist or scientist direction find their way into organizations where these values are dominant. Once they are there a process of socialization takes over. The biases that made the organization attractive in the first place are nurtured and strengthened. In short, the dual processes of selection and emphasis … are the bases for psychology's two cultures. (p. 838)

Kimble's (1984; cf. Kuhn, 1970, pp. 151-152) data also show that there are very few psychologists totally committed to one extreme or the other. Nevertheless, he affirms the general existence of the "two cultures" in psychology, and notes that

> in the very same debate, one group may speak vehemently on points that the other group takes as trivial, or they talk at cross purposes. None of this will come as news to anyone who has attended a session of the APA council of representatives, or participated in a departmental faculty meeting. (p. 838)

The companion study by Krasner and Houts (1984) is simpler in its sampling strategy, but more complex in its measures of values. It compared a sample of psychologists strongly associated with the development of the behavior modification movement[7] with a sample of randomly selected psychologists not identified with that movement, and asked members of each group to complete not one, but *three* different "values" scales. The first of these, a "Theoretical Orientation Survey," originally developed and used elsewhere, was designed to assess disciplinary commitments according to dimensions quite similar to those used in Kimble's (1984) study. The other two scales, designed for this particular study, included an "Epistemological Style Questionnaire" to assess degree of adherence to each of three different scientific "styles"—empiricism, rationalism, and metaphorism—and a 67-item "Values Survey" to assess respondents' views on a wider variety of issues (e.g., degree of ethical constraint appropriate in science, of government involvement in the economy and social services, of science in the solution of environmental and social problems, degree of adherence to a social Darwinist vs. an altruistic social philosophy, and to a theistic vs. an atheistic worldview).[8]

On the first two scales (assessing discipline-related assumptions) the two groups showed, if anything, even clearer differences than occurred in the Kimble (1984) study. Compared to the group of randomly-selected, *non*-behavioral psychologists, those associated with the behavior modification movement were more anti-theoretical, less convinced of the existence of free will, more tied to purely quantitative and behavioral (as opposed to qualitative and self-report) data, more physically reductionistic in their view of human beings, less accepting of the use of metaphor in theorizing, and more convinced that value-free induction was possible in the conduct of psychological research.

On the third, more wide-ranging, "Value Survey Scale" there were *no* significant differences between the two groups on *any* of the issues polled: on the average, behavioral and non-behavioral psychologists leaned equally towards the view that science should be about facts not values, yet mixed this with a strong sense of research *ethics* and a moderate sense of social responsibility regarding the *application* of research findings. Both groups leaned equally (although not militantly) towards atheism rather than theism as a worldview, shunned social Darwinism while sharing a moderately conservative political philosophy, and were moderately against evnironmentalistic legislation even though they supported more government control of health care delivery.

This second study (Krasner & Houts, 1984) thus supports the "two cultures" hypothesis regarding discipline-specific values, but not the idea that these two cultures might be paralleled by ideological polarization in other areas. Nevertheless, when the authors *pooled* the data for both groups and looked for certain inter-item correlations among the various scales, some weak yet significant relationships emerged between discipline-specific and other values:

> Subjects [behavioral *or* non-behavioral]
> who endorsed freedom of inquiry as

opposed to ethical constraints on research, and who favored social Darwinism as opposed to social altruism also favored behavioral as opposed to experiential content emphasis within psychology. Subjects who endorsed the view that science is value-neutral also favored physiological reductionism and quantitative as opposed to qualitative methods in psychology. In contrast, subjects who endorsed the view that science is value-laden favored an intuitive approach to science. (p. 846)

The Two Cultures Compete for Control

To the Christian analyst, perhaps the most intriguing aspect of these studies is not so much what *does* differentiate the "two cultures" in psychology as the failure of the theism/atheism dimension to enter into the picture at all. According to the second of these studies, theism and atheism are no differently distributed among behavioral and non-behavioral psychologists and, moreover, there is no significant correlation between strength of theistic beliefs on the one hand and patterns of *either* disciplinary *or* social values on the other. To a consideration of this point I will return, but for the moment let us consider some reactions to this pair of "two cultures" studies from later issues of the *American Psychologist*. Interestingly, none of the published responses endorsed the positivistic *status quo* which dominates academic psychology—perhaps because that which is in ascendancy generates no sense of defensiveness in its adherents. Actual reactions ranged from pleas for methodological reform to those calling for the wholesale replacement of the traditionally-positivist paradigm by a post-positivist one emphasizing the sociology—and even the politics—of psychological knowledge.

According to the latter, psychology is as much about values as it is about objective facts. Moreover, psychological theorizing reflects the disguised ideology of its creators in ways that these two studies barely began to tap. Social psychologist Rhoda Unger (1985) reported her own research indicating that both socioeconomic background and political allegiance are strongly correlated with psychologists' position on the nature/nurture controversy. More specifically, psychologists from economically privileged backgrounds and/or of conservative political views were much more apt to endorse statements such as "Science has underestimated the extent to which genes affect human behavior"; "Most sex differences have an evolutionary purpose"; "Biological

sex, sex role, and sexual preference are highly related to each other in normal people"; and "A great
deal can be learned about human behavior by studying animals" (pp. 1413-1414). The apparent connection between political conservatism and allegiance to
a more biologically-determinist theory of human
nature is particularly worrisome to feminist psychologists, because, in Unger's (1985) words,

> [It] may account for the consistent reap-
> pearance of biology in controversies
> involving the empowerment of former-
> ly disenfranchised groups. The assump-
> tion of whether a racial or sexual entity
> is a biological or a social group is fun-
> damental to both political and scientific
> paradigms. Thus, a shift from the bio-
> logical position (the study of sex differ-
> ences) to a social position (the exami-
> nation of gender) was a necessary step
> in the development of a new psycholo-
> gy of women. (p. 1414)[9]

But it is not only feminist social psychologists who
advocate the politicization of psychology in a more
leftist direction. In an earlier *American Psychologist*
article titled, "Cognitive Psychology as Ideology,"
Clark University's Edward Sampson (1981) argued
that current cognitive theory, by emphasizing the
mental structures and operations of the individual,
"represents a set of values and interests that repro-
duce and reaffirm the existing nature of the social
order" (p. 730).[10] Taking his cue from the Frankfurt
critical theorists, Sampson (1981) asserted that cognitive psychologists such as Piaget take the existing
object and social worlds as given, and concentrate
only on how the individual person schematizes and
performs mental operations on these. In doing so,
they fail to see how the existing social order may
actually influence what persons *take to be* "given"
and "immutable."

Far from wanting to remedy this situation by
reasserting objectivist ideals, Sampson (1981) recommended "a critical study of psychology *and* society,
a study that is self-conscious about its context [and]
its values ... In this we would no longer spend our
time describing what *is*, thereby participating in its
reproduction; our aims would be more transformative, designed to increase human welfare and freedom. Of necessity, this would require a transformation of society" (pp. 741-742, italics, mine). Thus, to
Sampson (1981, as to Unger, 1985), the problem is
not so much that psychology is politicized as the fact
that a) it has a tradition of *denying* its political
assumptions by dressing them up in "scientific" lan-

guage, and b) the political assumptions it *does* have
are hierarchical and privilege maintaining, rather
than egalitarian, in their underlying intent. But while
this position may be something of an improvement
on the attempt to have one's positivist cake and eat
it too, its adherents offer no clear reasons (other
than phrases such as "It seems a worthy role for the
field") (p. 741) as to why the implicitly-rightist agenda in psychology should be replaced by an explicit-
ly-leftist one.[11]

A more radical variation on this same theme is the
movement social psychologist Kenneth Gergen
(1973) labels "social constructionism."[12] Strong on
the sociology of knowledge thesis, Gergen (1973)
rejects the possibility of mapping social reality in a
historically decontextualized manner and comes
close to defining scientific "truth" in terms of professional consensus at a given point in time. He
believes, with Unger (1985) and Sampson (1981),
that psychology should *consciously* espouse an
advocacy role on the side of the weak and disenfranchised. To this end, he would abandon the
attempt to establish transtemporal laws of social
interaction using the hypothetico-deductive
approach, concentrating instead on the development of bold, general theories whose persuasive
value alone might provoke social reform. But as
with Sampson (1981), although one may approve of
Gergen's (1973, 1982, 1985) concern to make the
value-base of psychology more explicit, it is not
clear how he can simultaneously promote epistemological relativism and a particular ethical agenda,
however laudable the latter may seem.[13]

Moreover, those committed to the more traditional combination of positivist epistemology and evo-
lutionist anthropology have not taken the post-positivist challenge lying down. While conceding that
they may previously have overestimated the continuity between human and animal learning, underestimated the complexity of the human mind, and
paid too little attention to the ethical aspects of their
research, these traditionalists offer paradigms for
psychology that remain unremittingly naturalistic
and scientistic. For example, in a 1981 *American
Psychologist* article, Arthur Staats proposed to unify
psychological theory around a "social behaviorist"
paradigm which acknowledges reciprocal causality
between the person and the environment; in the
end, however, the person is still reduced to a product of the environment (now both internal and
external, immediate and historical) with the result
that such attempts never get beyond a "soft determinist" view of personhood.[14]

Bolder still are attempts to combine a soft-determinist anthropology with an epistemology which views scientific accounts of persons, at least in principle, as both ultimate and complete—even to the point of providing a moral framework. Such attempts hearken back to B. F. Skinner's (1971) "experimental ethics," but with a new, physiologically reductionist twist about which Skinner (1974) could merely conjecture wistfully. For example, the well-known neuroscientist Roger Sperry published in the 1977 *American Psychologist* his "unifying view of mind and brain." This was based on his theory that the mind, while not a separate substance from the brain, emerges from the brain to function as a non-reducible, causally-powerful entity which can then affect the natural world from which it originally evolved. It is not Sperry's emergentism *per se* that is troubling; indeed, at least one philosopher (Hasker, 1974; 1983) has argued that such a position on the mind-brain question is compatible with the anthropological dualism of traditional Christian theology.[15] But Sperry (1977) goes on to claim that since values are inevitably a part of this emergent-mind complex, and since scientists have expert knowledge about the evolution and functioning of the brain (or at least possess the best *methods* for knowing progressively more about these) it follows that scientists are in the best position to dictate ultimate human values. In language worthy of both Carl Sagan and pop Eastern mysticism, he concludes his paper as follows:

> In the eyes of science, to put it simply, man's creator becomes the vast interwoven fabric of all evolving nature, a tremendously complex concept that includes all the immutable and emergent forces of cosmic causation that control everything from high-energy subnuclear particles to galaxies, not forgetting the causal properties that govern brains and behavior at individual levels. For all of these, science has gradually become our accepted authority, offering a cosmic scheme that renders most others simplistic by comparison.... It follows accordingly on the above terms that what is good, right, or to be valued is defined very broadly to be that which accords with, sustains, and enhances the orderly design of evolving nature.... Although man, as part of evolving nature and at the peak of the evolutionary scale, remains the prime consideration, mankind does stand to lose some

> of the uniqueness and "measure of all things" status accorded in some previous systems. A sense of higher meaning is preserved with a meaningful relation to something deemed more important than the human species taken by itself. (pp. 243-244)

Christian Responses to the "Two Cultures" Dispute

If the above summary reflects the current state of psychology, we may seem reduced to choosing between the epistemological *hubris* of positivists and the moral self-righteousness of post-positivists.[16] Faced with such a choice, Christian psychologists might be forgiven for invoking a plague upon both these houses and starting to build one afresh on their own terms, even as they continue to "plunder the Egyptians" for materials worth preserving from each of these competing structures. In point of fact, however, the emergence of such a "third way" has been very slow to develop, at least among confessing Protestants. Why is this the case, and how, in practice, *do* most of these psychologists deal with the two competing cultures?

Let us recall the earlier observation that psychologists' position on the theistic-atheistic dimension was unable to predict adherence to either of the two cultures; indeed, it could not predict responses to any single item from the three "values surveys" used in the second of the "two cultures" studies. On reflection, perhaps this is not so surprising. With regard to social values at least, Christians with an equally high view of biblical authority can be pacifists or just-war theorists, proponents of minimal or extensive government regulation, free-enterprisers or welfare-statists, and separatist or non-separatist with regard to the larger society. Indeed, one study of self-identified evangelical congressmen in Washington isolated at least four different "religious belief packages," each of which was consistently related to voting patterns running the gamut from extreme political conservatism to extreme liberalism. To come even close to predicting an evangelical congressman's vote (the authors concluded) "you need to know how he interprets his religion, not merely how he labels it (see Benson & Strommen, 1981).

What is true of Christians in politics is equally true of Christians in psychology. A minority (as in the political sphere) are thoroughgoing separatists, convinced that the Bible is the sufficient and only valid textbook of human behavior.[17] Most, however, have a higher view of common grace, and are prepared to accept theoretical insights which are compatible with Scripture regardless of their origin. Moreover, *basic* theological differences among evangelicals in psychology appear to be quite minimal, at least as regards the doctrine of persons. None embrace metaphysical determinism, with its total denial of human freedom and moral accountability. Nor do many appear to be "closet humanists" who overemphasize human autonomy to the extent of endorsing narcissistic self-indulgence and/or denying the reality and persistence of sin. (There has, however, been a spate of books—some by Christians with culturally separatist leanings—sounding warnings against other Christians judged to be overly invested in the theories and therapeutic techniques of humanistic psychology.[18]

What *does* seem to account for the apparently even distribution of Christians across psychology's "two cultures" are differences in theological *emphasis* combined with one or more other factors. Among applied psychologists, professional context appears to be one such factor. Thus, for example, those working with *undersocialized* persons (certain types of criminals and substance abusers, overly-indulged adolescents from wealthy homes, etc.) may lean heavily on the doctrine of sin, espouse more traditional views of social authority, and make more use of behavioral techniques of a "top-down" variety (e.g., rewards contingent on progressive behavior change, often within a controlled environment). By contrast, those working with *oversocialized* clients (for example, from abusive, authoritarian, or legalistic homes) are more apt to emphasize the doctrine of grace, the dignity which is part of *imago Dei* and must be valued and cultivated in all persons, and the advocacy role Christians are called to exercise on behalf of socially marginalized groups. Their techniques, predictably, are more likely to be drawn from humanistic psychologies, with Rogerian "active listening" and "unconditional positive regard" high on the list. Whether the theological emphases of each group lead to or result from their respective work settings (or both) is a question which merits further investigation.[19]

Perspectivalism and Its Problems

But among practicing Christians in academic settings, what seems to count is the interaction of theological emphasis with a preferred philosophy of science. By and large Christians seem to agree that worldview considerations do, and should, influence the conduct of psychological research; but they differ regarding the *points* of the research process at which they believe these considerations may operate. Many (perhaps still the majority among evangelicals) hold that religious convictions should operate only in theory—and hypothesis--construction at the *beginning* of the research process, and in the practical application of results at the *end*. With regard to the intermediate steps, however, they still adhere to the belief that the context of theory *justification* can be made—at least in principle—totally value-free. It is claimed that in psychology, as in other sciences, the best means to this end is the assiduous operationalization and quantification of all variables and, where possible, the design and execution of experiments. Crucial to such a stand is adherence to the "unity of science" thesis—the notion that method consists of giving causal, deterministic explanations which are empirically testable.[20]

How is such an approach justified theologically, especially given the earlier observation that no Christian psychologists appear to embrace metaphysical determinism, with its reduction of personhood to a complex of mechanical responses to internal and external, past and present stimuli? It is justified by publicly rejecting anthropological reductionism in principle while simultaneously adhering to the unity of science thesis—that is, by embracing *methodological*, but not metaphysical determinism. On this account, the traditional methods of science yield only one "perspective" on human behavior (a deterministic one) to which others (from the humanities, the arts, and religion) must be added to yield a more complete picture. At the same time, however, it is assumed that the mechanical metaphor is the *only* legitimate one for academic psychologists to use in the study of human behavior—that because psychology threw its lot in with the Newtonian-leaning natural sciences a century ago, there can be no compromising this allegiance today.

Perspectivalists readily concede that the elimination of "bias" (read: "values") in the context of theory justification is a more difficult process in the social than in the natural sciences, because of the complexities that result when human beings study other human beings; indeed, they admit, such methodological purity may never be achieved, and psychologists may perforce have to become more humble about what their efforts can produce in terms of general laws of human behavior. Nevertheless, such purity remains the ideal of all psychologists—Christian or otherwise—committed to the unity of science and the hypothetico-deductive approach. In fact, to at least one Christian perspectivalist adherence to this ideal is part and parcel of concretely visible sanctification. In Donald MacKay's (1984) words:

If we publish results of our investigations, we must strive to "tell it like it is," knowing that the Author is at our elbow, a silent judge of the accuracy with which we claim to describe the world He has created.... If our limitations, both intellectual and moral, predictably limit our achievement of this goal, this is something not to be gloried in, but to be acknowledged in a spirit of repentance. Any idea that it could justify a dismissal of the ideal of value-free knowledge as a "myth" would be as irrational—and as irreligious—as to dismiss the ideal of *righteousness* as a "myth" on the grounds that we can never perfectly attain that ... [Christians must not] forget that, whatever their difficulties in gaining objective knowledge, they are supposed to be in the loving service of the One to whom Truth is sacred, and carelessness or deliberate bias in stating it is an affront. (p. 235)

But according to some critics, the adherents of this "perspectivalist compromise"[21] are both schizophrenic and falsely modest: the former because they disavow reductionism in principle while preserving it in practice of the discipline, the latter because they disguise academic imperialism in the cloak of epistemological humility. That is, the perspectivalist readily confesses the problems of using the hypothetico-deductive approach in psychology, while at the same time demanding loyalty to that approach of all who would call themselves true (yea, even properly Christian) psychologists. Moreover, critics add, perspectivalists' adherence to the unity of science thesis carries with it the assumption that explanation in *natural* science is always deterministic in character, an assumption belied by modern quantum physical theory.[22]

Christian critics of perspectivalism further assert that it sidesteps difficult questions about human nature which it is the responsibility of Christian psychologists to consider. What does it mean that persons are formed in the image of God in a way that accords all human beings the potential for creativity, dominion, and moral responsibility? What does it imply for theory and method in psychology that we are *simultaneously* "dust of the earth" and imagers of God in a way that separates us from the rest of creation? And why (other than for reasons of historical precedent) do perspectivalists hold that psychologists should try to separate these two aspects of human existence, in effect telling their research

respondents to put their transcendent qualities on hold while they are subjected to methods of inquiry originally designed for the study of subhuman phenomena?[23] These are questions to which Christian perspectivalists have given no answers.

Perspectivalists do, however, invoke other theological justifications for a high view of natural science, traditionally conceived. One is the doctrine of creation as espoused by Christians who participated in the formalization of science itself. The Christian worldview of Pascal, Bacon, Newton, Boyle, and many founders of Britain's Royal Society helped make science possible as an independent form of knowledge not beholden to the institutional church, precisely because these men believed in the goodness and the uniformity of God's creation, and in humanity's creational mandate to exercise responsible dominion over the earth. A number of Christian perspectivalists claim to be continuing in this Reformation-based tradition. But at the same time they tend to gloss over the fact that their role-models predate the 19th-century emergence of the social sciences, and that the continuity of the latter with natural science is precisely the issue under debate.[24]

Finally, some perspectivalists appeal to another aspect of the doctrine of sanctification—the Christian mandate to serve one's neighbor—as justification for a positivist philosophy of science. Science has so often been the birthplace of technologies which promote human welfare (from split-brain techniques to therapies for traumatic stress) that it seems subject to a kind of "halo effect" in the eyes of Christians whose theology stresses a service-oriented activism. But such a view, however laudable its motive, implicitly reduces science to technology, and explanation to empirical prediction—a view of *natural* science that its most successful practitioners have routinely rejected (Toulmin, 1961). Moreover, it tends to assume that questions of research *ethics* can be settled on utilitarian grounds alone; as long as one's research is aimed at the greatest good for the greatest number, questions about informed consent, the use of deception, and the infliction of stress are deemed to be secondary. These issues too are often glossed over by perspectivalists.[25]

Enter the Humanizers

Dissatisfactions with the perspectivalist compromise can be summarized as follows: perspectivalists not only adhere to the unity of science thesis, but implicitly demand the same adherence of all others who would call themselves social scientists. In doing so, they are not only clinging to an outdated and inaccurate model of how the *natural* sciences operate, but are additionally producing truncated theories of human functioning by their refusal to consider, at least within the context of their own discipline, any explanations of human behavior other than deterministic ones.

As this debate continues to heat up among Christian psychologists, an article in the 1985 *American Psychologist* by Notre Dame's George S. Howard deserves mention. Drawing on the work of philosopher of science Ernan McMullin, Howard (1985) begins by educating the periodical's readership about the function of *epistemic values* in the conduct of natural science. Epistemic values are those standards employed by scientists to choose among competing theoretical explanations. At least six such values seem to have been regularly operative in the history of science, including not only *predictive accuracy*, but *simplicity, internal coherence, consistency with other theories, unifying power* (the ability to bring together hitherto disparate areas of inquiry), and *fruitfulness* (the capacity to supply metaphorical resources which help to resolve anomalies and extend the knowledge base).[26] For psychologists still of a positivist bent,

> the crucial point of the above analysis is that epistemic values function as values, not as strict rules, to guide the work of science. McMullin, Kuhn, and others demonstrated that theory development in the most mature natural sciences is influenced by the selective application of epistemic criteria. This is, of course, a different picture of the operation of science than a traditional logicist would have chosen to paint. (Howard, 1985, p. 259)[27]

So far, Howard (1985) merely seems to be reinforcing the conclusions of the empirical studies of psychology's "two cultures" described at the beginning of this article: epistemic values *do* operate in the context of theory justification in psychology, just as they do in natural science, even though many psychologists (ironically, those who pride themselves in being most "scientific," such as behavioral and experimental psychologists) refuse to acknowledge this. But Howard (1985) goes a step beyond affirming psychology's continuity with the rest of science on the basis of its adherence to the same epistemic values. Specifically, he believes that these values may have to be *augmented* "to the degree necessary to accommodate our subject matter's unique characteristics" (p. 260). Central among those characteristics, Howard (1985) points out, is

reflexivity, the capacity of persons to "self-reflect," or deliberate about themselves in a given situation, and so gain a measure of autonomy over what might otherwise determine their behavior.

As Howard (1985) points out, in science traditionally conceived, "the notion of rational objectivity … required a lack of reciprocal interaction between observer and object. The scientist was to observe nature, but nature was not to reflect upon itself being observed" (p. 260). There is, of course, a recurrent theme in science fiction about the chemist who sits alone in his laboratory, brooding about what to do with a strange concoction he has produced, when suddenly it occurs to him that the strange concoction is sitting alone in the test-tube brooding about what to do with *him.* But in reality, as far as we know, reflexivity is a privilege (or a problem, depending on one's viewpoint) reserved to human beings: "No quark ever wondered why a physicist wanted to know *that.* No protein ever changed an attitude or two to curry favor with a biochemist. And no beetle ever told an entomologist to bug off" (Bohannan, 1982, p. 25).

To mainstream psychologists, human reflexivity is simply a methodological annoyance—and one which can in principle be overcome by tighter experimental controls: one can keep subjects naive, or even deceived, as to the real purposes of the study, or (tighter still) use such unobtrusive techniques that subjects do not even know that they are being studied. The goal here is to give subjects a handicap in the mutual-observation game, thereby (hopefully) reducing them temporarily to the same level as the "pre-reflexive" entities for which the methods of science were originally designed. Hence the social dynamic is a hermeneutic of suspicion operative: one cannot, according to this approach, ever simply ask respondents to give an account of themselves, because their behavior is actually the product of forces beyond their control and largely beyond their ken.[28]

For Howard (1985), the reality of human reflexivity has first of all an extra-experimental significance: persons are not merely *participants* in psychological research; they are also *consumers* of psychological theories. As such, they can, and do, alter their behavior on the basis of what psychologists proclaim. For Howard,

> possible examples include individuals who actively resist agreeing with others' opinions … because of their knowledge of the results of conformity studies. Or perhaps simply informing depressed clients that depressed people tend to be

more self-critical would make them more aware of their self-derogatory tendencies and aid them in actually reversing these tendencies. (p. 261)

But precisely because public access to the results of psychological research often leads people to "reconstruct" their behavior and self-image accordingly, Howard holds that psychologists have a responsibility not to limit themselves to impoverished models of humanness: by viewing people only as reinforcement maximizers or information processors (for example), psychologists risk becoming "unwitting contributors to a self-fulfilling prophecy wherein humans actually become more like the model" (Howard, 1985, pp. 263-274).

Thus it may be all very well to argue for the exclusion of non-epistemic values from *natural* scientific theorizing; but Howard (1985) argues that the reality of human reflexivity makes *social* scientific theorizing an inescapably moral endeavor: because psychological theories are important "mirrors" by means of which people in Western culture "groom" themselves, and because, moreover, such theories are always underdetermined by empirical data, they can be crafted and disseminated in ways that work to people's benefit *or* detriment. The dominant "man-as-machine" metaphor has been beneficial inasmuch as it has helped to temper justice with mercy in legal decisions regarding the reduced responsibility of brain-damaged persons, or those from an environment so abusive that they are driven to desperate measures to escape it. But the same metaphor has also contributed to a sense of fatalism, "learned helplessness," and a dulled sense of personal accountability in our highly psychologized society. Therefore, Howard concludes, the discipline badly needs innovative theories *and* methods which will at least supplement, if not replace those which have leaned so heavily on examplars drawn from the pre-20th century natural sciences.

Such a conclusion seems to be a reasonable compromise between the outdated positivism of psychology's scientistic subculture and the epistemological skepticism *cum* political partisanship of much of the humanistic one.[30] It should, moreover, be a conclusion attractive to Christians who have found the perspectivalist compromise less than satisfying: not only does it allow for the development of "active agent" theories of social behavior (which are compatible with the biblical notion of accountable dominion as part of the *imago Dei*); it also allows for a research approach in which the deceptive and adversarial stance between researchers and respondents can be replaced by a more honest and

collaborative one—an approach which assumes that at least *sometimes* a hermeneutic of trust can appropriately operate. People may not always know, or be able to say, what they are up to; as finite and sinful creatures, they *are* often prey to forces outside their present awareness and control. But sometimes they *can* give an intelligent account of their actions, one which requires no other explanation beyond itself. A major task (heretofore badly neglected) of psychology is the exploration of *both* types of behavior, as well as the ways in which they interact.

For Christians wishing to take up this challenge, some helpful groundwork has been laid by philosopher Stephen Evans (1977). Recognizing the need to deal with anthropological and epistemological questions simultaneously, he also realizes that Christian psychologists must do even this on an interdisciplinary basis, acknowledging the role that philosophical and theological dimensions inevitably play in their theory-building. With regard to anthropology, Evans (1977) rejects perspectivalism on the grounds that it embraces only a "relational" anthropology, one which holds that there is nothing unique about human beings *per se* (substantially or essentially), but instead locates human significance only in *how* God has chosen to relate to persons in a covenantal fashion. There is a moment of truth in this idea; indeed, it was strongly pushed during the Reformation and beyond as an antidote to human pride: "Nothing in my hands I bring; simply to Thy cross I cling," goes the old pietist hymn. Relational anthropology also seems to allow the perspectivalist to get the best of two worlds: by acknowledging the importance of covenant theology they maintain a Christian identity; at the same time, by asserting that what (if anything) makes humans unique is a strictly empirical, not a revelational question, they spare themselves the embarrassment of seeming like religious fanatics in the eye of their secular colleagues.

But Evans (in press) rightly asserts that the value of relational anthropology to perspectivalists is also its weakness:

If human dignity lies in the fact that God cares about us, or in the possibility of our knowing about him, rather than in some unique human quality, then the theologian [or psychologist] is saved from making any potentially embarrassing claims about the difference between human and other animals.... Nor must the theologian [or psychologist] affirm any non-material soul or spirit as a factor in understanding human behavior ... [But] the advantages of immunity from scientific refutation and a theological barrier to human pride ... are purchased at a price. The price of immunity from scientific refutation is the danger of lack of relevance to contemporary thought forms. What cannot be refuted by science also cannot be supported by science, and may be difficult to relate to science. (pp. 5-6)

Evans (1988) also recognizes that the desire of Christian perspectivalists not to be "embarrassed" by scientific "findings" about the continuity of human and non-human functioning rests on assumptions about the empirical neutrality of science and its independence of metaphysical, religious, and even epistemic values. By contrast, he points to post-positivist scientists and philosophers who hold that in all sciences—but especially the social sciences—metaphysical and religious commitments play not only an inevitable, but a positive role. If this is so, writes Evans, then "we ought to allow our Christian assumptions to interpenetrate our actual work as scientists.... The challenge is to go beyond rejection [of science] and conformism [to the current social science paradigm] to doing scientific work ... within a consciously Christian frame of reference" (pp. 15-16, see Wolterstorff, 1976). By this criterion, the relational anthropology of the perspectivalist could be unapologetically reunited with a substantial anthropology claiming certain biblical "givens" about human nature, such as accountable dominion, sociability, gender identity, the quest for meaning, and a stubborn resistance to truth about one's condition before God.

By this criterion, too, the empiricist, "objective" perspective on personhood could well be supplemented, if not replaced, by an interpretivist, or "hermeneutical" approach, in which "observing and explaining human action is strongly analogous, not to the natural sciences, but to the interpretation of a literary text. In Evans (1988) words, "recognizing a human action involves understanding its meaning; explaining action is inseparable from understanding the reasons for an action. Nor is this a value-free enterprise. Deciding whether a person's reasons are genuine reasons involves, among other things, reflecting on whether the reasons are good reasons. This is so because actions performed for good reasons in many circumstances require no further explanation, while manifestly inadequate reasons are suspected of being rationalizations."[31]

There are, of course, hazards lurking in this approach too. Epistemologically, if persons are more like "texts" than like materials in an experiment, can there be any intersubjectively verifiable criteria by which we can judge our readings of them, and if not, can a hermeneutical psychology be "real" science? Anthropologically, if persons are rule-makers and rule-followers whose being is constituted not by nature but by cultural and linguistic activity, as some versions of the hermeneutic approach hold, then is not such autonomy as they do have merely a collective "social construction" (recall Gergen here) which the individual cannot critically transcend to exercise freedom or moral responsibility? On such a view, how can there be any universal criteria for judging among competing systems of rule-governed behavior? There remains only a profound cultural and moral relativism.[32]

But these problems also afflict the deterministic approach, whether metaphysically or merely methodologically embraced: persons viewed as the products of nature are also "beyond freedom and dignity" (to borrow Skinner's phrase), and since values under such a paradigm are similarly determined, there is no way to rank-order the moral or cultural systems to which such persons belong. Moreover, the permeation of even natural science by values—metaphysical as well as epistemic—renders it a much more 'hermeneutical' endeavor than previously believed; yet theory-adjudication is still possible despite—indeed, even because of—such values. So too in textual interpretation: "Reasoned argument and criticism do succeed in showing that some interpretations are warranted and some are not. To say that an enterprise is hermeneutical does not imply then that it is totally subjective and irrational."[33]

Christians can legitimately use a basic biblical anthropology to navigate such hazards—one which recognizes the impact of nature, culture, and human freedom, but places all of these in the context of creational norms, the reality of sin, and the promise of redemption. As they do so, they can (in Evans', 1988, words) "join the contemporary conversation and participate in scholarly work, but with a healthy irreverence and suspicion of the contemporary scholarly establishments. [They] need to clearly tell an increasingly secular world what Christians think about human beings, and show them the power of such a perspective" (p. 16).

Notes

1. The author would like to acknowledge the help of Calvin College philosophy department colleagues, both regular and visiting, in criticizing earlier drafts of this article, and making suggestions for its improvement.

2. The following is a sampling of such essays published in the *American Psychologist* over the past decade:

George W. Albee, "The Protestant Ethic, Sex, and Psychotherapy," (Vol. 32, 1977, pp. 150-161); Richard C. Atkinson, "Reflections on Psychology's Past and Concerns About Its Future" (Vol. 32, 1977, pp. 205-210); D. L. Bazelton, "Veils, Values, and Social Responsibility" (Vol. 37, 1982, pp. 115-121); Jerome D. Frank, "Nature and Function of Belief Systems: Humanism and Transcendental Religion" (Vol. 32, 1977; pp. 555-559); Frederick. H. Kanfer, "Personal Control, Social Control, and Altruism: Can Society Survive the Age of Individualism?" (Vol. 34, 1979, pp. 231-239); David C. McClelland, "Managing Motivation to Expand Human Freedom" (Vol. 33, 1978, pp. 201-210); S. B. Sarason, "An Asocial Psychology and a Misdirected Clinical Psychology" (Vol. 36, 1981, pp. 827-836); Roger W. Sperry, "Bridging Science and Values: A Unifying View of the Mind and Brain" (Vol. 32, 1977, pp. 237-245).

3. See for example Thomas Kuhn (1970), *The Structure of Scientific Revolutions*, 2nd ed. (Chicago: University of Chicago Press; Imre Lakatos & A. Musgrave, eds. (1970), *Criticism and the Growth of Knowledge* (Cambridge University Press); Ian I. Mitroff (1974), *The Subjective Side of Science* (New York: Elsevier); Michael Polanyi (1958), *Personal Knowledge: Towards a Post-Critical Philosophy* (New York: Harper and Row); Frederick Suppe (1974), *The Structure of Scientific Theories* (Urbana: University of Illinois Press); Stephen Toulmin (1958), *The Philosophy of Science* (London: Hutchinson).

4. As of 1987, the American Psychological Association had 47 different divisions representing a total membership of over 76,000.

5. Each of Kimble's (1984) twelve scale items was set out with the humanistic position described at the right, the scientist position at the left, and the numbers 1-10 between the two. The respondent's score was thus the number of items on which he or she took a position to the *right* of 5, minus the number of items on which the respondent took a position to the *left* of 5, ignoring all responses of 5. Because there were 12 items on the test, these calculations place each subject on a 25-point scale, from -12 (the most extreme scientist position to +12 (the most extreme humanistic position).

6. These items included issues such as importance of scholarly vs. humane values, commitment to determinism vs. indeterminism of behavior, preference for observation vs. intuition as a source of knowledge, commitment to heredity vs. environment as the chief determinant of behavior, and a concept of organisms as primarily reactive or creative.

7. The sampling strategy for inclusion in the behavioral group included the following criteria: a) self-identification of their work as behavior modification during the period 1946-1976; b) citation of the respondent's work in publications on behavior modification in the period 1946-1976; c) at least one publication or presentation (exclusive of dissertations) prior to 1956; d) professional contact with at least one other member of this group.

8. Krasner and Houts' (1984) Theoretical Orientation Survey was first designed and used by Richard W. Coan (1979). See his *Psychologists: Personal and Theoretical Pathways* (New York: Irvington). The term "metaphorism" in their Epistemological Style Questionnaire refers to a preference for theorizing by reducing complex concepts in familiar metaphors —e.g., Freud's "hydraulic" metaphor explaining the interaction of the id, ego, and superego, or Piaget's "equilibrium/disequilibrium" metaphor to explain the way that cognitive development takes place in children.

9. See also Suzanne J. Kessler and Wendy McKenna (1895). *Gender: An Ethnomethodological Approach*. Chicago: University of Chicago Press, for an elaboration of this view.

10. Related critiques can be found in Susan Buck-Morss (1975), "Socioeconomic Bias in Piaget's Theory and Its Implications for Cross-Culture Studies." *Human Development 18*, 35-49, and in Kenneth J. Gergen (1978), "Towards Generative Theory," *Journal of Personality and Social Psychology, 36*, 1344-1360.

11. Note that when social scientists speak of the "politicizing" of their respective disciplines, they may mean a) that extra-disciplinary values *do* in fact play a role, b) that such values *should* play a role, c) that although a) *may* hold, b) should not; or d) that both a) and b) hold, but the content of the predominant extra-disciplinary values should change. A helpful analysis of this debate by a sociologist can be found in Richard Perkins (1985), "Values, Alienation, and Christian Sociology," *Christian Scholar's Review, XV*, 1, 8-27, with a subsequent response by Stephen Evans in Vol. *XV, 3*. See also David Braybrooke (1987), *Philosophy of Social Science*. (Englewood Cliffs, NJ: Prentice-Hall). and C. Stephen Evans (forthcoming), *Psychology as a Human Science: Prospects for a Christian Approach* (Grand Rapids, MI: Baker).

12. See for example Kenneth J. Gergen (1973). "Social Psychology as History," *Journal of Personality and Social Psychology, 26*, 309-320; K. J. Gergen (1982). *Towards Transformation in Social Knowledge* (New York: Springer-Verlag); K. J. Gergen (1985) "The Social Constructionist Movement in Modern Psychology," *American Psychologist, 30*, 3, 266-275. Note also parallels with Paul K. Feyerabend's (1976) *Against Method* (New York: Humanities Press), and with Richard Rorty's (1979) *Philosophy and the Mirror of Nature* (Princeton University Press).

13. It is possible to be a skeptic about the ability of natural science to deliver ultimate truth and still remain anti-skeptical about morality, but Gergen does not make clear his basis for such a distinction. It is also the case that epistemological relativism can be combined with an ethical agenda— but to be consistent, the adherent of such a position has to concede that this agenda has no normative force outside the "language-game" community in which it originated.

14. For a summary of criticisms of "soft determinism" or "compatibilism" (the view that a "free" action is merely an "uncoerced" or "internally-produced" [but still necessarily determined] event, see Richard Taylor (1984), *Metaphysics*, 2nd ed. (Englewood Cliffs, NJ: Prentice-Hall), pp. 48-57. See also C. Stephen Evans (1977), *Preserving the Person: A Look at the Human Sciences* (Downers Grove, IL: InterVarsity Press), and Del Ratzsch (1987). *Philosophy of Science: The Natural Sciences in Christian Perspective*

(Downers Grove, IL: InterVarsity Press).

15. See also Karl Popper & John Eccles (1977), *The Self and its Brain* (New York: Springer), and Wilder Penfield (1975), *The Mystery of the Mind* (Princeton, NJ: Princeton University Press)

16. But it should be noted from the Sperry (1977) quotation that positivists are not lacking in moral self-righteousness either.

17. See for example Jay Adams (1970), *Competent to Counsel* (Grand Rapids, MI: Baker), and Richard Grenz (1976), Nouthetic Counselling Defended, *Journal of Psychology and Theology, 4*, 193-205. For summary of a more inclusive kind of Christian separatism as embodied in the so-called "Christian Reconstructionist' movement, see Rodney Clapp (1987, Feb. 20), Democracy as Heresy. *Christianity Today, 31*, pp. 17-23.

18. See for example David Hunt & T. A. McMahon (1985), *The Seduction of Christianity.* (Eugene, OR: Harvest House). More balanced is Paul C. Vitz' (1977) *Psychology as Religion: The Cult of Self-Worship.* Grand Rapids, MI: Eerdmans. For a secular critique of the "culture of narcissism" in psychology, see Michael A. Wallach & Lise Wallach (1983), *Psychology's Sanctions for Selfishness* (San Francisco: W. H. Freeman).

19. The contrast suggested in this paragraph is based on anecdotal observation only. I know of no systematic study demonstrating these trends, and offer them merely as suggestive.

20. Examples of this "perspectivalist" approach include Rodger Bufford (1981), *The Human Reflex: Behavioral Psychology in Biblical Perspective.* (New York: Harper and Row); Malcolm A. Jeeves (1976), *Psychology and Christianity: The View Both Ways.* (Leicester, UK: InterVarsity Press); D. Gareth Jones (1981), *Our Fragile Brains: A Christian Perspective on Brain Research* (Downers Grove, IL: InterVarsity Press.); Donald M. MacKay (1974), *The Clockwork Image* (London: InterVarsity Press.); (1979), *Human Science and Human Dignity* (London: Hodder and Stoughton); and (1980), *Brains, Machines, and Persons* (Grand Rapids, MI: Eerdmans); David G. Myers (1978). *The Human Puzzle: Psychological Research and Christian Belief* (San Francisco: Harper and Row). See also D. G. Myers (1985, April) "Current Trends in Psychology; Myths and Realities," (Keynote address to the Christian Association of Psychological Studies, Grand Rapids, MI.)

21. The term "perspectivalism," as used in this section of the article, was coined by Stephen Evans. See his *Preserving the Person*, (1977) Ch. 9.

22. See for example, Rom Harre (ed.). (1969). *Scientific Thought, 1900-1960* (Oxford: Clarendon Press), or Ernest Nagel (1961), *The Structure of Science* (London: Routledge and Kegan Paul).

23. For an elaboration of these criticisms see C. Stephen Evans (1984), Must Psychoanalysis Embrace Determinism? *Psychoanalysis and Contemporary Thought, 7*, 339-375. See also Evans' "Healing Old Wounds and Recovering Old Insights: Towards a Christian View of the Person for Today," in Mark Noll and David Wells, eds., (in press), *Christian Faith and Practice in the Modern World:*

Theology from an Evangelical Point of View. Grand Rapids, MI: Eerdmans, and his "Human Persons as Substantial Achievers" (Unpublished Manuscript, St. Olaf College, Northfield, MN). See also Stanton L. Jones, (ed.) (1986), *Psychology and the Christian Faith* (Grand Rapids, MI: Baker), especially the chapters by Jones and Hodges.

24. See for example D. G. Myers (1978), *The Human Puzzle*, Ch. 1, and in particular his appeal to Reijer Hooykaas (1972), *Religion and the Rise of Modern Science* (Grand Rapids, MI: Eerdmans) and to Robert K Merton (1970), *Science, Technology, and Society in Seventeenth Century England* (New York: Fertig).

25. This attitude is most apparent in Jones (1981) *Our Fragile Brains*, but also implicit in the writings of Jeeves, MacKay, and Myers.

26. For an elaboration see Thomas Kuhn (1977), *The Essential Tension* (Chicago: University of Chicago Press), and Ernan McMullin, "Values in Science," in P. D. Asquity & T. Nickles (eds.), (1983), *Proceedings of the 1982 Philisophty of Science Association*, Vol. 2. (East Lansing: Philosophy of Science Association). For a discussion of epistemic values as they relate to psychological theorizing, see Melvin H. Marx & F. E. Goodson (eds.) (1976), *Theories in Contemporary Psychology* (New York: MacMillan), especially the chapter by Goodson and Morgan, pp. 286-299. For an elaboration of the importance of epistemic values to a Christian critique of psychology, see Mary Stewart Van Leeuwen (in press), "Evangelicals and the Social Sciences: A Forty-Year Appraisal," *Journal of the American Scientific Affiliation.*

27. Howard's references to Kuhn and McMullin are those cited in Note 26. See also McMulliin's "Two Faces of Science" (1974, June), *Review of Metaphysics, 27*, 655-676, and "The Ambiguity of Historicism" (1978), in *Current Research in Philosophy of Science* (Philosophy of Science Association, pp. 58-83).

28. See also Van Leeuwen, *The Sorcerer's Apprentice*, Ch. 2 and 3, and also her (1983, Sept.) 'Reflexivity in North American Psychology: Historical Reflections on One Aspect of a Changing Paradigm," *Journal of the American Scientific Affiliation, 35*, 162-167. Classic mainstream treatments of reflexivity as subject "reactivity," to be circumvented by methodological means, include Robert Rosenthal & Robert L. Rosnow (1969), *Artifact in Behavioural Research* (New York: Academic Press), and E. J. Webb, Donald T. Campbell, R. D. Schwartz, & Lee Sechrest (1966), *Unobtrusive Measures* (Skokie, IL: Rand-McNally).

29. See also Gergen (1973), "Social Psychology as History," and two works on the sociology of popular psychological knowledge by Sherri Turkle: (1978), *Psychoanalytic Politics: Freud's French Revolution* (New York: Basic Books), and (1984) *The Second Self: Computers and the Human Spirit* (New York: Simon and Schuster).

30. It could also be argued that, by taking human reflexivity into account, psychological theorists would merely be appealing to the epistemic value of empirical adequacy— i.e., acknowledging that this is an observed, unique, and therefore important characteristic of persons. On such an account, it is not that psychology is differently conducted

than the natural sciences, but that psychologists fail to understand how epistemic values inform *all* the sciences, and should learn to unify their discipline around these values, rather than the outdated unity-of-science thesis.

31. Evans, "Human Persons as Substantial Achievers," pp. 6-7. For a more detailed application, see also Evans' (1984), "Must Psychoanalysis Embrace Determinism?" The basic development of this approach by a philosopher of social science is Peter Winch's (1958), *The Idea of a Social Science*, London: Routledge and Kegan Paul, and its most sophisticated application to psychology is probably Rom Harre & Paul Secord (1972), *The Explanation of Social Behavior* (Oxford: Basil Blackwell). Empirical outworkings of this approach in psychology are exemplified in Van Leeuwen, The *Sorcerer's Apprentice*, Ch. 3 and *The Person in Psychology*, Ch. 11. See also Ronald S. Valle & Mark King (1978), *Existential and Phenomenological Alternatives for Psychology* (New York: Oxford University Press), Braybrook (1987), *Philosophy of a Social Science* (Englewood Cliffs, NJ: Prentice-Hall), Evans (in press), *Psychology as a Human Science*, and George Howard (1986), *Dare We Develop a Human Science?* (Notre Dame, IN: Academic Publications).

32. This is a position which seems to be strongly imp.lied by Peter Winch (1967) in his "On Understanding a Primitive Society," in D. Z. Phillips (ed.), Religion and Understanding (Oxford: Basil Blackwell).

33. Evans (1984), "Must Psychology Embrace Determinism?," p. 362. It should be noted that treating persons as texts will lead to a host of questions hitherto of interest mostly to literary critics. When one speaks of the "meaning" of a texgt, this can mean a) m;eaning for the author, b) meaning for the individual reader, c) meaning for a given historical communinty receiving the text, and/or d) intrinsic meaning (assuming that this can be identified, an assumption with which deconstructionists take issue). Analogous questions can be asked about the "meaning" of individual and group behavior, with parallel debates. On this reading, psychology needs not only to become more hermeneutic in its study of persons, but to become more sophisticated in its understanding of hermeneutical theory as well. My thanks to Lambert Zuidervaart for clarifying these points.

References

Benson, P. L., & Strommen, M. P. (1981) Religion on Capitol Hill: How beliefs affect voting in the U.S. Congress. *Psychology Today, 15*, 3, 46-57.

Bohannan, P. (1982, May). The mouse that roars. *Science, 81*, 25-26.

Evans, C. S. (1977), *Preserving the person: A look at the human sciences*. Downers Grove, IL: InterVarsity Press.

Evans, C. S. (in press). Healing Old Wounds and Recovering Old Insights: Towards a Christian View of the Person for Today. In M. Noll & D. Wells (Eds.), *Christian Faith and Practice in the Modern World: Theology from an Evangelical Point of View*.(Grand Rapids, MI: Eerdmans.

Howard, G. S. (1985). The role of values in the science of psychology. *American Psychologist, 40*, 3, 255-265.

Kimble, G. A. (1984). Psychology's two cultures. *American Psychologist, 39*, 8, 833-839.

Krassner, L., & Houts, A. C. (1984). A study of the "value" systems of behavioral scientists. *American Psychologist, 39*, 840-850.

MacKay, D. M. (1984). Objectivity in Christian perspective. *Journal of the American Scientific Affiliation*, 36, 4, 235.

Mahoney, M. J. (1974). *Cognition and behavior modification*. Cambridge MA: Ballinger. (pp. 289-290).

Sampson, E. E. (1981). Cognitive psychology as ideology. *American Psychologist, 36*, 7, 730-743.

Skinner, B. F. (1948). *Beyond freedom and dignity*. New York: Knopf.

Skinner, B. F. (1974). *About behavorism*. New York: Knopf.

Snow, C. P. (1964). *The two cultures and a second look*. London: Cambridge University Press. (original essay, plus a retrospective commentary)

Staats, A. W. (1981). Paradigmatic behaviorism, unified theory construction methods, and the Zeitgeist of separatism. *American Psychologist, 36*, (3), 239-256.

Toulmin, S. (1961). *Foresight and understanding*. Bloomington, IN: Indiana University Press.

Unger, R. K. (1985). Epistemological consistency and its scientific implications. *American Psychologist, 40*, (12), 1413-1414.

Wolterstorff, N. (1976). *Reason within the bounds of religion*. Grand Rapids, MI: Eerdmans.

12

Implications for Integration From a New Philosophy of Psychology as Science

Peter C. Hill
Grove City College

Attempts to integrate scientific psychology with Christian thought are often based on a mistaken view of the nature of science. Scientific investigation is neither foundationistic, based solely on data, nor a relativistic social enterprise. A new philosophy of science, called simply the realist theory, recognizes the need for interactive levels of stratification to explain even specific behaviors. Thus, the actions of persons may be understood as open-systemic events involving a wide variety of causal structures. Identifying and explaining such structures require a theoretical ingenuity that is philosophically sophisticated, willing to consider fundamental issues, open to methodological pluralism and empirically consistent. Adopting this view of science enhances the opportunity of integration of psychological discovery with Christian insight.

The "integration" literature for psychology and Christianity has begun in recent years to increasingly question and debate the philosophical basis of current mainstream psychology and has raised some very legitimate concerns that are relevant to the task of integration. Some (Van Leeuwen, 1982, 1985; Farnsworth, 1985) have argued that the methods of psychology should be humanized, emphasizing alternative approaches to research including "co-investigation" (Farnsworth, 1985) with the person being studied for a more complete understanding of his/her social behavior. While the merits of empirical methods such as systematic observation, measurement, and experimentation are paid lip-service by Van Leeuwen (1982), these "humanizers-of-science" (Evans, 1977) question the relevance and usefulness of most empirical research.

These concerns reflect the radical change that philosophy of science has undergone during the past three decades. Though positivism has been thoroughly denounced as a legitimate approach to science, alternative views, particularly of the social sciences, have either been slow in arriving or have been incomplete in prescribing proper scientific investigation.

What is proposed here as an alternative understanding of the nature of social science, called the *realist theory of science* (Bhaskar, 1975), provides more than mere quibbles with the prevailing positivistic view. In fact, what is suggested is a radical alternative that questions the very goals and purpose of scientific investigation. And while the particular theory proposed here is yet to be a widely recognized theory of science, the combined efforts of revisionists such as Koch (1959-1963), Scriven (1956), Kuhn (1970), Polanyi (1958), and a host of others in the past few decades should prompt us to recognize that we can no longer talk glibly about integrating faith and science or theology and psychology without first defining our terms. A parallel soul-searching may be occurring in theology, and that is equally relevant to the task of integration. This article, however, is concerned with our understanding of psychology as a science, which has implications for how we should approach the interface of psychology with Christian thought.

The Historical Context

Before discussing three distinct perspectives of science, a brief consideration of the historical context of psychology's claim to be scientific and how that claim has been modified over the past century is in order. Among the most distinguishing characteristics of psychology's historically brief claim of being a science is its "on again-off again" relationship with philosophy (Toulmin and Leary, 1985).

The prevailing stereotype of psychology becoming a science is, of course, attributed to Wundt's establishment of a laboratory in Leipzig, Germany, a century and now also a decade ago. The common understanding of Wundt's "founding" of an independent (from philosophy) experimental psychology is that psychology had finally come of age and could now join the higher and more respected tier of sciences such as physics and biology, both of whom had (supposedly) demonstrated a self-reliance from an initial dependence on philosophy, the mother science.

© *Journal of Psychology and Christianity*, 1989, 8(1), 61-74. Used by permission.

But unlike what is supposed by many, Wundt did not envision a psychology independent of philosophy, but rather saw a mutual interdependence between the two disciplines. Toulmin and Leary (1985) claim that "... the establishment of Wundt's new laboratory was not intended to inaugurate a separate, autonomous field of experimental psychology, independent of all other subjects.... rather, Wundt saw it [the new laboratory] as contributing toward *one* [emphasis theirs] legitimate research program, among others.... and even after he had defined his narrower research program for the experimental study of 'the manifold of consciousness,' he never suggested that this should constitute the entirety of psychology, still less that the results obtained from this new program could be used to build a psychological science free of all more general intellectual connections, either with philosophical arguments or with contemporary theoretical issues in neighboring fields of science" (p. 595).

But by the early 1900s neither psychology nor the general intellectual climate had much regard for philosophical discourse. By the time that Watson had convinced American psychology of the merits of "classical behaviorism," the goal of an independent psychology similar to the status enjoyed by physics, was perceived to be in reach. Watson, by claiming that the only legitimate subject matter was that which was observable and that the complete objectivity of findings must be a central feature of behaviorism, considered the divorce with philosophy now complete (Harre, Gundlack, Metraux, Ockwell, and Wilkes, 1985).

But the neobehaviorism of the 1930s to 1950s once again found itself wedded to philosophy. This time, however, the remarriage was based on *philosophy's* promise to drop its subjective language in favor of a dialect that even Watson may have felt comfortable with. For what psychology listened to was a group of philosophers, the logical positivists, who clearly supported the objectivist agenda so strongly propounded by the behaviorists themselves. In part because of the relative recency (1950s) of this assemblage, as well as the dominating strength of the resulting positivist orthodoxy over American psychology for twenty-plus years, and also its lingering (though less reputable) legacy on psychology today. I refer to this philosophy as the "historically dominant view" and briefly describe in the next section its underlying philosophical rationale, constrained by its emphasis on methodology.

As already noted, since the 1950s, a radical change has taken place in philosophy of science and what seems to be the root issue is the very conception of science itself. Alternative views one and two, also described in the next section, reflect this mutation. Psychology has been slow in taking note of this new philosophical direction, but notification calls (Gergen, 1985; Manicas & Secord, 1983; Rychlak, 1975; Sampson, 1978) are being made.

One of the options under serious consideration by a number of revisionists (Koch, 1981; Robinson, 1976; Royce, 1982; Vande Kemp, 1987) is that psychology should again reconsider uniting itself with the *broader* concerns of philosophy, as opposed to the narrow positivist agenda. Vande Kemp (1987) says that she "... would personally recommend the 'philosophizing' of psychology. Contemporary psychologists would generate much more meaningful research if they were not afraid to align themselves with the old psychology which was undifferentiated from philosophy" (p. 25).

The fact of the matter is that psychology simply cannot be conceptually independent of philosophy. Koch (1981), in the admittedly lengthy quotation that follows, says it better than I.

> Though many of us have generated a vociferous rhetoric of independence in this century (especially those of the behaviorist persuasion), one and all have of necessity presupposed strong, if garbled, philosophical commitments in the conduct of their work. Psychology is necessarily the most philosophically-sensitive discipline in the entire gamut of disciplines that claim empirical status. We cannot discriminate a so-called variable, pose a research question, choose or invent a method, project a theory, stipulate a psychotechnology, without making strong presumptions of philosophical cast about the nature of our human subject matter—presumptions that can be ordered to age-old contexts of philosophical discussion. Even our nomenclature for the basic fields of specialized research within psychology (e.g., sensation, perception, cognition, memory, motivation, emotion, etc.) has its origin in philosophy. Let us note, also, that even during the period when the claim to independence was most aggressively asserted (the neobehavioristically dominated Age of Theory that I have already mentioned), we were basing, and explicitly so, our 'official' epistemology on logical positivism and cognate formulations within the philosophy of science. (p. 256)

What I am suggesting is that the call to reconsider psychology's drive for independence should be taken seriously and one which I hope to show sits well with the major thesis to be developed in this article. It is time now to investigate three different understandings of the very conception of science and then to demonstrate how recent developments in the way science is conceived have major implications for the Christian integrationist.

Three Understandings of Science

The Historically Dominant View:
The Positivist Approach

The positivist understanding of science, long a dominating view, can be summarized by the following. Science is composed of research (often atheoretical) that is "objective" in that it should only test hypotheses that have been designed to be tentative solutions to the questions raised through observation, then subjective bias may creep in. What is thus taken for granted is a Humean conception of causality whereby regular contingent relationships between events is enough evidence for judging a relationship as causal. Regular contingent relationships are understood in terms of statistical probabilities between independent and dependent variables. These observable relationships then make up the "facts" by which hypotheses are tested.

The general conception of the role of theory is that it is often not necessary but when used, must be capable of being "rationally reconstructed" in deductive form to empirical phenomena. That is, for theory to be useful and valid, it must provide a set of asserted postulates consisting of fundamental laws and hypotheses that can through the rules of logic or mathematics (or both), in turn provide experimentally testable theorems (Toulmin and Leary, 1985). Theory is otherwise of little value. This hypothetico-deductive approach, championed by Clark Hull (1943), was the dominant form of conceptualizing the role of theory during the neobehaviorist era. While this description is brief and simplistic, it does highlight the major epistemological model by which recently established alternative views of science can be compared.

Alternative View Number One:
The Paradigmatic Approach

Kuhns' (1970) well-known *The Structure of Scientific Revolutions* has provided the scientific community a service by alerting members to the social nature of their activity. It should be noted that Kuhn's analysis is not a full-blown philosophy of science. His theory is not prescriptive but rather is merely an attempt to describe the process by which he believes knowledge has been historically gathered. In fact, Kuhn carefully refers to himself as a historian and not a philosopher of science. Yet, as will be pointed out, his view has important philosophical implications.

Scientific disciplines, Kuhn maintained, develop their own rules of practice which define not only the questions to be answered but also, at least implicitly, and often explicitly, identify how those questions must be answered. The philosophical underpinnings of Kuhn's contentions did not originate with his influential book. Several philosophers of science, most notably Toulmin (1953), Scriven (1956), and Hansen (1958) were laying the revolutionary foundation before Kuhn's book was originally published in 1962. As Manicas and Secord (1983) point out, however, these works went largely unnoticed by scientific psychology and it was Kuhn's notion of paradigm that finally shook the social scientific community from its philosophical lethargy.

One meaning of paradigm is sociological in that it stands for a community of scientists whereby members corporately share a set of values, beliefs, and methods about their subject matter. The second sense of paradigm refers to an implicit acceptance of models or exemplars as concrete puzzle solutions that may serve as a basis for the solution of other yet-to-be-solved puzzles within normal science.

Kuhn's analysis of the scientific enterprise as fundamentally a puzzle-solving activity has several important implications. First, the boundaries or limits of the puzzle will help determine not only the puzzle's solution but will even influence what will be observed within the puzzle and what will be missed outside the puzzle. Thus there are no truly "objective" observations, but only those defined by the inherent theoretical notions, assumptions, and preconceptions of the puzzle itself.

A second important implication is that despite Kuhn's attempt to deny it in his 1970 postscript, his view of science as a puzzle-solving activity is ultimately relativistic. What determines the boundary of the puzzle are the sociologically defined rules of practice inherent within the prevailing paradigm itself. The question can thus be raised as to whether there is any coherent ontological development as a scientific discipline progresses from one paradigm to another, and eventually to a third paradigm, etc. Answering this question certainly involves a value judgment which Kuhn himself used when he answered in the negative. That is, Kuhn does not see from the history of science any necessarily better representation of what is "really there" in subsequent paradigms than in their predecessors, despite insights that may be gained during the revolutionary change. He argues that since each paradigm is a self-contained puzzle, each will contain only a partial picture of truth.

Kuhn has provided an interesting and, surely to some people, a refreshing analysis of science. Clearly, one rendition, in the spirit of Kuhn, is that scientific progress is but a value judgment and therefore the claims of many scientific disciplines may be exaggerated. And certainly some may feel justified in arguing that our current understanding of the world is not necessarily any closer to an accurate representation of reality than the understandings of previous generations.

Yet Kuhn's analysis is undoubtedly disturbing to others. His idea that science is primarily a social activity, the truth of which is determined through consensus, that data are largely a function of the subjective values and preconceptions of the data-collector, and that any assumption of ontological development is questionable, portrays scientific activity with a skepticism that clearly questions the validity, and maybe even the relevance, of what many work-a-day scientists actually do.

Indeed, whether one finds Kuhn's analysis agreeable or not is in itself a judgment call. I suspect that those who find Kuhn's argument convincing are more likely to settle for uncertainty in drawing conclusions about the nature of reality. The well-known twentieth century philosopher Bertrand Russell maintained that

> ... almost all the questions of most interest to speculative minds are such as science cannot answer.... It is not good either to forget the questions that philosophy asks, or to persuade ourselves that we have indubitable answers to them. To teach how to live without certainty, and yet without being paralyzed by hesitation, is perhaps the chief thing that philosophy in our age can still do for those who study it. (Russell, 1945, pp. xiii-xiv as quoted in Koch, 1981, pp. 262-263)

Russell's discussion of philosophy's functional role was in the context of what science can and cannot answer. Simple epistemological honesty tells that many meaningful questions are undecidable and that the ambiguity of the human condition resides over a broad range (Koch, 1981).

Alternative View Number Two: The Realist Approach

The realist alternative to understanding the nature of science should be viewed on two levels. The first, more general level identifies the realist view in terms of its insistence on the existence of an external independent reality that makes itself known to us. This view argues that reality has some message-laden pattern forced upon us through experiential contact, by which we are obligated to willingly submit to its claims (Torrance, 1981, pp. 67-68). It is this ontological realism to which a number of philosophers of science subscribe (Bhaskar, 1975, 1979; Harre, 1970; Polanyi, 1958). This general view will be discussed through the work of Michael Polanyi (1958, 1967).[2] The second, more specific level makes direct reference to the realist view of science promoted by Bhaskar (1975, 1979) and applied to psychology by Manicas and Secord (1983).

Ontological realism. A common erroneous reaction to Kuhn's work is the notion that his analysis has clearly debunked the objective claims of science (Thorsen, 1981). Such a claim must assume the mistaken ideal of objective knowledge held by the positivists whereby substance is entirely determined by observation of an external and independent (of our senses) reality. This mistaken ideal furthermore implies that any broader claim of objectivity, such as that posited by Polanyi (1958), really contains subjective elements. Yet as Polanyi points out, the difference between an event and knowledge of that event, is simply that the former is assumed to be part of an external reality while the latter is a representation of that reality within the framework of a personal judgment. Using Polanyi's own words. "... things are not labeled evidence in nature, but are evidence only to the extent to which they are accepted as such by us as observers" (p. 30). So knowledge cannot be understood or defined without first acknowledging the grid of personal judgments. As a result, in Polanyi's view there is no such thing as an abstract knowledge; even in science, knowledge by definition must be held by an individual through his/her belief system, and is to provide an encompassing framework by which the individual not only understands the world, but also relates to it and acts consistently with it (Thorsen, 1981).

But Polanyi goes even one step further. Not only does he recognize that knowledge is dependent on the observer because of the requirement of personal judgment, but is also dependent upon formal non-testable (in the empirical sense) commitments that guide and provide a motivation for the seeker of knowledge.[2] There is an external independent reality that makes itself known to us, the knowledge of which, however, is not complete until it has been filtered through our commitment framework. Polanyi correctly identifies a subjective element toward knowing defined as belief. But our beliefs must accept a subordinate place in our knowledge, secondary to the external pole that forces itself upon us (Torrance, 1981, p. 67). In other words, our beliefs (our commitment framework) should not, in good conscience, purposely deny or distort what independent reality is trying to tell us. There is therefore a freedom to express belief of the world (the subjective element) but it is a restricted freedom by obligation to the truth of independent reality.

Thus Polanyi's (1958) version of realist thought argues that there is an objective reality that forces itself upon us and that any claim of objective knowledge must not only recognize the existence of that reality but must become ontologically committed to an understanding of it.

Realism as a model for scientific activity. Bhaskar's (1975, 1979) model focuses primarily on the unique case of social science, as opposed to science in general. Though Bhaskar's clear anti-positivist stance carries over to the natural sciences, he differentiates the social sciences as requiring special philosophical consideration simply because the subject matter is *social*. Specifically, he contends that the social sciences differ from the natural sciences not in essence (i.e., both are scientific in the same *sense* of the word), but in method and objective. As Bhaskar himself puts it, "… the human sciences can be scientific in exactly the same sense, though not in exactly the same way, as the natural ones" (1979, p. 203). The realist theory thus rejects scientism or the unity of science model.

Key Features. In developing this perspective, certain essential features stand out. These features are nicely outlined by Manicas and Secord (11983) and will essentially, though with a different focus, be replicated here. First, the perspective can be identified as an ontological realism but an epistemological relativism (Bhaskar, 1979). That is, what is posited is the existence of a real world independent of human experience, and also a knowledge that can potentially correspond to this ultimate reality, though we can never be absolutely sure when this correspondence has been achieved. Indeed, the aim of science should be the construction of theories that represent the real world. But this is only a goal of science and the correspondence of theory to reality is supplied with error.

Now this fallibilist position assumes that knowledge is, in part, a social and historical product, similar to what Kuhn has proposed. However, it is the ontological realism that saves science from the irrational social tendencies implied in Kuhn's position. As Manicas and Secord (1983) put it: "… the practices of the sciences generate their own *rational* [emphasis theirs] criteria in terms of which theory is accepted or rejected. The crucial point is that it is possible for these criteria to be rational precisely because on realistic terms, there is a world that exists independently of cognizing experience" (p. 401).

Second, what is proposed in the realist view is an emergent view of social reality where the social world, and its representative theories in the social sciences, are stratified with more complex phenomena emerging from lower-level phenomena as distinctly different, and thus not accountable solely in terms of properties posited on the more fundamental level. Thus the natural science orientation of a research program insistently focused on the discovery of fundamental entities is futile in the social sciences (Margolis, 1986). The view here is that behavior is understood as an open systemic event involving a series of interactive levels including, in an increasingly complex order, the physical, biological, psychological, and sociological (Manicas and Secord, 1983). It is by virtue that these systems are open, that *invariant* empirical regularities cannot be identified. Or, from another angle, if invariant regularities are found in an experiment, then the phenomenon being studied is artificial. One cannot, in any legitimate way, experimentally close an open system, and expect a true test of a theory that aims to represent the world. It is primarily this problem of emergence as an ontological consideration that places limits on the possibility of naturalism, or the unity of science model (Bhaskar, 1979). The nature of the object determines the form of the possible science.

Third, the goal of the social sciences should entail explanation and not prediction, contrary to positivist philosophy. The realist holds that positivist tradition is correct in stressing causal laws, even in social reality. Where that tradition errs, however, is the insistence that these laws manifest empirical regularities. The problem again centers around the open-systemic nature of social events. That is, to demonstrate empirical regularity, one must incorrectly impose a closed system (e.g., the isolation of the independent variable so that it cannot be "contaminated" by other natural occurring events) on an event that by nature is not closed. The decisive test situation is artificial and thus, given the desired exactitude of science, becomes irrelevant. If this is the case, theories cannot be predictive, since a decisive test of predictability is unavailable, and science must therefore adopt an exclusively descriptive/explanatory framework (Bhaskar, 1979).

For example, the earthquake in Los Angeles in September, 1987 was the result of several different causal mechanisms operating in open systems. After the earthquake, geologists were able to explain this particular occurrence but were also quick to remind the public of their inability to predict when the "big one" will occur. The most that can be predicted is that, given our understanding of the geological causal mechanisms at work and the monitoring of actual conditions under which such mechanisms may be applied, at some point in time, when all of the causal mechanisms (including those currently unknown) in the open system converge, the "big one" should occur. If we are unable to predict an event such as an earthquake under relative closure compared to much social phenomena, then the predictive capacities of the social sciences should be seriously doubted and, indeed, even the goal of prediction questioned.

Fourth, the realist theory of science rejects a Humean theory of causation, defined as the concatenation of contingent events. Only the underlying structures, which are part of an open system are contingent relationships and therefore, causality can only be explained post-hoc and cannot be predicted. Empirical laws and causal laws are not synonymous. This distinction is crucial. The "risky shift" phenomenon (i.e., the tendency of the individual to take greater risks in decision making when a member of a group rather than when isolated) or apathetic bystander responses (i.e., the lessened tendency to help someone in need when others are present than when others are absent), even in a crowd, are not always found in real life settings. Whereas the standard account is that the empirically derived laws are not generalizable because of the existence of other variables, this alternative view questions the appropriateness and relevance of the law as representative of the social world, since the law was derived under an artificially closed system. This does opt deny the results of risky shift research, but simply questions whether such a lawlike principle has the predictive, or even explanatory, power expected of science.

Research model. Now that the primary features of the realist view have been outlined, the question of what this has to do with the activities of the scientist can now be addressed. Does the foregoing analysis suggest that the past efforts of empirical research are useless? This is not at all the case. The realist theory would suggest that even, for example, the endless number of 'prisoner's dilemma' experiments (a widely used social-psychological research game that demonstrates how easily people can become trapped in mutually destructive behavior in the bargaining and negotiation process), an extremely artificial model of real life negotiations

provide potentially useful information if viewed within their proper context. This context has been identified by Bhaskar (1979) as the "RRRE model of explanation in open systems" (p. 165).

Briefly, explanation, the proper goal of social science from the realist perspective can be accomplished through a four phase (**R**esolution, **R**edescription, **R**etrodiction, and **E**limination) process. First, a complex event must be *resolved* into its components. Realist theory recognizes that even the identification of a complex event will be influenced by the investigator's ultimate commitments or "tacit knowledge" (Polanyi, 1967). Vande Kemp's warnings against a narrow psychology resolution of an event into its components will require levelheaded philosophical and theoretical reasoning as to the basic nature of both the complex events and their component parts. Thus Vande Kemp's (1987) conclusion that "… research is meaningless without the prior affirmation of fundamentals" (p. 25) is in basic agreement with the realist position. Of course, this does not deny the important role of empirical research at this crucial first step, provided that it is undergirded with sound analytical arguments.

Bhaskar (1979) suggests that the causal components identified in the first stage be theoretically *redescribed*, the second stage. That is, an empirical regularity of stage one, based on a methodological individualism, will most likely require a modification once placed in a social context. One must again acknowledge reliance on other sources of knowledge (e.g., reason, intuition, etc.). The involvement of all of these sources of knowledge, from multiple levels of stratified reality, must then be incorporated into creative theory with the goals of description and explanation.

Necessarily involved in creative theory building is the third phase of explanation in open systems: namely *retrodiction* to (as opposed to prediction of) possible causes. Once a particular result occurs, the job of the scientist is to identify the underlying causal structures as well as the particular configuration of those structures that explain the phenomenon already observed. This will require knowledge of not only the causal properties, but also a historical grasp of the particular, and possibly changing configuration of those properties (Manicas & Secord, 1983). The only realistic goal of the scientist is, therefore, to explain the 1987 earthquake in Los Angeles by an analysis of the particular configurations, in this case, of the causal structures. Projecting the particular configurations of the yet-to-occur "big one" is beyond the ability of science. It is this process of retrodiction that the final of the four-phase process, *elimination* of alternative possible causes occurs. Again, on the basis of all sources of knowledge, some causal structures can be eliminated in a configuration, just as others are verified.

Now back to the question of the usefulness of empirical research. The realist theory recognizes the importance of empirical research particularly in step one, resolution, by combining its results with knowledge from other sources. But what is also suggested is that science involves far more than empirical research and that greater emphasis must be placed on those non-empirical activities in both our scientific conduct and in our research training programs than what a positivistic model allows for. If logistical constraints means that this must result in less research training of the empirical variety, then so be it.

Summary.

Several key elements of the realist alternative have been discussed.

1. Social behavior is an open-systemic event, far more open than many events observed in the natural sciences.

2. Because of its open-systemic nature, science cannot precisely predict a particular behavioral event. Thus, description and explanation of past events are favored as the proper goals of science rather than prediction and control, primary goals of the positivist tradition.

3. Description and causal explanation of open-systemic events require that stratified reality be recognized as such and that underlying causal structures from these multiple levels be identified. Each particular event can then, potentially, be explained by the specific configuration of these causal structures. A Humean analysis of causation, based on the observation of empirical regularity and accepted by the positivist view of science, is thus rejected.

4. The traditional experimental model requires that the open system of social behavior be artificially closed and, as a result, a decisive empirical test of a theory is unavailable.

5. The RRRE model of explanation in open systems is proposed.

Implications for Christian Thought

Van Leeuwen (1982) specifically addresses the shortcomings of empirical psychology in terms of its unwillingness to recognize the reflexive nature of being human, its inability to generalize research findings, and its tendency to allow areas of specialization to fragment human experience and behavior as an object of study. In addition, she questions the

morality of empirical research, particularly the use of deception and the infliction of psychological stress. She then proposes her alternative that psychology be a truly human science, which will place an appropriate emphasis on the significance of reflexivity in both the investigator and the person being studied, will stress the meaning behind human activity, and will focus its concern on the unity of human experience. Farnsworth (1985) echoes Van Leeuwen's contentions and proposes that the attitude and approach of phenomenological psychology (Giorgi, 1970), what he believes is currently the most developed human science orientation, be adopted. Farnsworth, like Van Leeuwen, sees the advantages of the human science alternative pretty much in black-and-white terms. "It [phenomenological psychology] is an attitude of respect for dignity and integrity of personal experience. It is also an approach or method for studying, without fear or favor, of the meaning of lived experience. The context for such study is collaboration and trust rather than manipulation and deception. The result of the phenomenological study is a qualitative description of the personal meaning of lived experience. This differs significantly in content as well as form from the results of natural science oriented research: quantitative analyses of impersonal measurements of observed behaviors" (p. 36).

Not everyone sees the advantages of the humanizer position in quite such absolutistic terms, if at all. Foster and Ledbetter (1987), for example, claim that Christian "anti-psychologists" such as Van Leeuwen, Farnsworth, and Kilpatrick (1983) devalue the knowledge gained through empirical research; that the methods used in traditional research including systematic observation, precise measurement, and experimentation yield data that, though not free of bias, should, if properly collected, minimize subjectivity. Just as Van Leeuwen pays lip-service to empirical research, Foster and Ledbetter identify other sources of knowledge such as authority, reason, and personal experience, but only in passing. It should be noted, in the spirit of fair play, that this lack of balance by both Van Leeuwen as well as Foster and Ledbetter may be due in part to the reactionary nature of their essays (Van Leeuwen reacting to the positivist tradition and Foster and Ledbetter reacting to anti-psychologists like Van Leeuwen). But it is also probable that each of these psychologists would reflect that imbalance in their own personal research agendas. It is not just reaction; it is also personal preference.

The fundamental problem that I see is the mistaken view of the nature of psychology as a science.

The positivist orientation of Foster and Ledbetter has been questioned throughout this article. Van Leeuwen and the other humanizers-of-science do not align themselves with any particular philosophy of the social sciences but in general with the number of philosophers (Kuhn, Polanyi, Toulmin, Hansen, Feyerabend) whose primary common thread is their anti-positivistic orientation. Of course, these revisionistic philosophers differ considerably from each other in terms of their own prescription for scientific activity. As a result, the humanizers, as anti-positivists, do a lot of griping but fail to provide a convincing alternative because they have not articulated a specific underlying philosophy of science. Indeed, Evans (1977) coined the term "humanizer-of-science" only as part of general taxonomy and never claimed this as a position with a well articulated epistemology. To say that a person is no longer a subject but is now a co-investigator sounds great. But does this approach work and on what basis do we decide whether it is a constructive alternative or not? A better articulated philosophical footing is necessary.

The realist theory of science can provide such a footing. By focusing on causal structures, rather than empirical behavior, as the proper subject matter of psychology, data from a variety of methodologies can be used to good effect. Once it is understood that the substantive domain of psychology is the underlying causal structure of behavior, and not empirical regularities, the importance of methodological pluralism takes on a new, brighter, light.

The first step of the RRRE model, resolution of a complex event into its components, will include not only traditional empirical methodology, but should be supplemented with data from other knowledge sources as well. This is more than mere verbal recognition of other sources of knowledge. It argues that other sources of knowledge are essential, not only in the first stage of resolution, but are inherent also within the subsequent stages of redescription, retrodiction, and elimination. The assumption that any single source of knowledge is the only required source or even inherently the best source, is therefore rejected and "dogmatic methodism" (Robinson, 1976) avoided. Thus many of the techniques of a "humanized" psychology are appreciated. Farnsworth's (1985) description of phenomenological psychology, including its unique methodology, can be embraced within a realist epistemology. The emphasis on co-investigation, the study of intentionality, the unique structure of each person's experience, the significance or value ("meaning") of the experience, and existential validation (in *addition* to statistical validation) are all potentially helpful in understanding underlying causal structures. And, of course, data from *multiple* levels of stratified experience including biology, sociology, and even theology, each with their own forms of methodological pluralism, will also increase our understanding.

But the realist theory also appreciates traditional empirical methods that yield important and valued data. I share Foster and Ledbetter's concern that value of such data may be underestimated by the humanizers, but for an entirely different reason. From the realist perspective, standard empirical research is essential, but not sufficient, for a complete understanding of reality. Both its necessity and insufficiency lies in the open systemic nature of social behavior. The empirical regularities found in the closed-system experiment may shed light, though incomplete, on the open-system phenomena of interest.

Earlier I suggested that psychology should heed the call of several revisionists and reconsider its desired independence from its philosophical heritage. Such a corrective would require that psychology broaden its methodology and thinking (Vande Kemp, 1987). The issue is not that an empirical approach is inherently problematic. (This author has conducted and expects to further conduct empirical research.) Rather, the issue becomes the overreliance on empirical techniques as the only valid means of gaining knowledge. Only when that overreliance is recognized can researchers experience liberation of thought. As Toulmin and Leary (1985), scholars who support the philosophizing of psychology, suggest, "… with reference to the residual dogmatic empiricism that is the legacy of the neobehaviorist era, we can hope and expect that an increased freedom of thought will typify future psychology. We are not thinking here of a lazy, undisciplined relativistic approach to psychological theory. Empiricism has its own legitimate role, as does the quest for universality. The search for empirically grounded theories of broad scope has characterized science in all its many forms. But there needs to be room for the creative play of the scientific imagination. History abounds with instances of important empirical observations that were made only after—and on account of—the formulation of significant theoretical insights" (p. 612).

It is suggested here that empiricism can be exceedingly useful to psychology as a scientific discipline, but only if kept in proper perspective. It is furthermore contended that the realist theory of science provides the needed corrective in conceptualizing the role of empirical research.

At the heart of all of this is the need for good theory. The four phase model of explanation in studying the configuration of causal structures requires theoretical ingenuity. Such ingenuity will include a view of human nature that is philosophically sophisticated, willing to consider (and reconsider) fundamental issues, empirically consistent, and for a Christian approach, theologically sound. This is a tall but not surprising order given the complexity of human nature.

The realist theory, especially in contrast to its positivistic counterpart, further opens the door to integrative research between psychological and Christian thought since empirical demonstration is no longer the acid test of valid data. If theological insight can help provide an understanding of causal structures, as it should, then our theoretical representations of the world should be even more complete.

Notes

1. Toulmin and Leary (1985) are quick to point out that though the confluence of behaviorism and logical positivism had a dominating impact on American psychology, to suggest that these two systems of thought provide a complete representation of psychology and philosophy is misleading. They are only a "slight caricature" (p. 603), but one with a lasting impression on contemporary psychology.

2. This "tacit knowledge" (Polanyi, 1967), or framework of ultimate commitments, is multidimensional and has been posited by at least one thinker heavily influenced by Polanyi's perspective (Joldersma, 1984 as cited in Niedhardt, 1984) in hierarchical fashion, whereby the broader ontological commitments guide the epistemological commitments which, in turn, determine the methodological techniques deserving of one's commitment. This commitment framework is not dependent upon systematic empirical evidence but rather exists prior to exploratory activity and that such activity is not necessarily limited to a single content domain (e.g., psychology, theology, etc.) nor a single epistemological approach, be it scientific, religious, rationalistic, artistic, etc (Niedhardt, 1984). What is further suggested in Polanyi's commitment framework is that the belief structure is maintained through feedback with reality in the reverse direction of the belief hierarchy discussed above (Joldersma, 1984, as cited in Niedhardt, 1984). That is, our methodological beliefs should confidently provide us *whole-person* experiences that reflect reality, which should further develop our epistemological and ultimately our ontological beliefs. If our beliefs about proper methodology do not correspond with our sense of reality, then our entire belief system (methodological, epistemological, and ontological) will require modification.

References

Bhaskar, R. (1975). *A realist theory of science.* Leeds, England: Leeds Books.

Bhaskar, R. (1979). *The possibility of naturalism. Brighton,* Great Britain: Harvester Press.

Evans, C. S. (1977). *Preserving the person: A look at the human sciences.* Grand Rapids, MI: Baker Books.

Farnsworth, K. (1985). *Whole-hearted integration: Harmonizing psychology and Christianity through word and deed.* Grand Rapids, MI: Baker Books.

Foster, J. D., & Ledbetter, M. F. (1987). Christian anti-psychology and the scientific method. *Journal of Psychology and Theology, 14,* 10-18.

Gergen, K. J. (1985). Social psychology and the phoenix of unreality. In S. Koch & D. E. Leary (Eds.). *A century of psychology as science* (pp. 528-557). New York: McGraw Hill.

Georgi, A. (1970). *Psychology as a human science.* New York: Harper & Row.

Hanson, N. R. (1958). *Patterns of discovery.* Cambridge, England: Cambridge University Press.

Harre, R. (1970). *The principles of scientific thinking.* Chicago: University of Chicago Press.

Harre, R., Horst, U. K., Metraux, A., Ockwell, A., & Wilkes, K. V. (1985). Antagonism and interaction. The relation of philosophy to psychology. In C. E. Buxton (Ed.). *Points of view in the modern history of psychology* (pp. 383-415). Orlando, FL: Academic Press.

Hull, C. L. (1943). *Principles of behavior.* New York: Appleton-Century-Crofts.

Joldersma, C. W. (1984). *Beliefs and the scientific enterprise: A framework model based on Kuhn's paradigms, Polanyi's commitment framework, and Radnitzky's internal steering fields.* Master's thesis. Institute for Christian Studies, University of Toronto.

Kilpatrick, W. (1983). *Psychological seduction. The failure of modern psychology.* Nashville, TN: Thomas Nelson.

Koch, S. (1959-1963). *Psychology: A study of a science* (6 vols.). New York: McGraw-Hill.

Koch, S. (1981). The nature and limits of psychological knowledge: Lessons of a century "qua science." *American Psychologist, 36,* 257-269.

Kuhn, T. S. (1970). *The structure of scientific revolutions* (2nd ed.). Chicago: University of Chicago Press.

Manicas, P. T., & Secord, P. F. (1983). Implications for psychology of the new philosophy of science. *American Psychologist, 38,* 399-413.

Margolis, J. (1986). Psychology and its methodological options. In J. Margolis, P. T. Manicas, R. Harre, & P. F. Secord. *Psychology: Designing the discipline* (pp. 12-51). Oxford, Great Britain: Basil Blackwell.

Niedhardt, W. J. (1984). Realistic faith seeking understanding: A structured model of human knowing. *Journal of the American Scientific Affiliation, 36,* 42-45.

Polanyi, M. (1958). *Personal knowledge.* London: Routledge and Kegan Paul.

Polanyi, M. (1967). *The tacit dimension.* New York: Doubleday.

Robinson, D. N. (1976). *An intellectual history of psychology.* New York: Macmillan.

Royce, J. R. (1982). Philosophic issues, Division 24, and the future. *American Psychologist 37,* 258-266.

Russell, B. (1945). A history of Western philosophy. New York: Simon & Schuster.

Rychlak, J. F. (1975). Psychological science as a humanist views it. In W. J. Arnold (Ed.). *Nebraska symposium on motivation*. Lincoln, NE: University of Nebraska Press.

Sampson, E. E. (1978). Scientific paradigms and social values: Wanted—a scientific revolution. *Journal of Personality and Social Psychology, 36*, 1332-1343.

Scriven, M. (1956). A possible distinction between traditional scientific disciplines and the study of human behavior. In H. Feigl & M. Scriven (Eds.). *Minnesota studies in the philosophy of science* (Vol. 1). Minneapolis, MN: University of Minnesota Press.

Thorsen, W. R. (1981). The biblical insights of Michael Polanyi. *Journal of the American Scientific Affiliation, 33*, 129-138.

Torrance, T. F. (1981). *Christian theology and scientific culture*. New York: Oxford University Press.

Toulmin, S. (1953). *The philosophy of science*. New York: Harper & Row.

Toulmin, S., & Leary, D. E. (1985). The cult of empiricism in psychology and beyond. In S. Koch & D. E. Leary (Eds.). *A century of psychology as science* (pp. 594-617). New York: McGraw-Hill.

Van Leeuwen, M. S. (1982). *The sorcerer's apprentice: A Christian looks at the changing face of psychology*. Downers Grove, IL: InterVarsity Press.

Van Leeuwen, M. S. (1985). *The person in psychology: A contemporary Christian appraisal*. Grand Rapids, MI: Eerdmans.

Vande Kemp, H. (1987). The sorcerer was a straw man—apologetics gone awry: A reaction to Foster and Ledbetter. *Journal of Psychology and Theology, 15*, 19-26.

Author Notes

An earlier version of this article was presented at the fourth annual conference of the Christian Association for psychological Studies—Eastern Region, Lancaster, PA, October, 1987.

The author thanks Hendrika Vande Kemp for her helpful comments on an earlier version of this manuscript.

13

A Constructive Relationship for Religion With the Science and Profession of Psychology: Perhaps the Boldest Model Yet

Stanton L. Jones
Wheaton College

This article goes beyond O'Donohue's (1989) "(even) bolder model" of the psychologist as metaphysician-scientist-practitioner to call for an explicit and constructive relationship between psychology and religion. Psychology's previously noninteractive stance toward religion was premised on an outmoded understanding of science and an overly narrow professionalism. Contemporary philosophy of science breaks down the radical demarcation between science and other forms of human knowing and action, including religion. Science and religion are different, but they cannot be categorically separated or viewed as mutually exclusive. A proposal is developed for how religion could participate as an active partner with psychology as a science and as an applied professional discipline.

Religion seems to play a minimal role in the lives of most psychologists in the United States. A 1984 survey of religious preferences of academicians found psychologists to be among the least religious, with fully 50% responding that they had no current religious preference, compared with only about 10% for the general population ("Politics," 1991). Bergin and Jensen (1990) summarized prior research on the religiosity of psychotherapists by saying, "Data from previous surveys indicated that therapists were less committed to traditional values, beliefs, and religious affiliations than the normal population at large" (p. 3). Their survey found clinical psychologists to be the least religious of the major psychotherapy provider groups. Perhaps their most striking finding was that only 33% of clinical psychologists described religious faith as the most important influence in their lives, as compared with 72% of the general population.

In spite of the prominent role that religion plays in many people's lives, religion and religious belief are basically neglected in psychology textbooks (Kirkpatrick & Spilka, 1989). Similarly, the religious issues and faith of clients are frequently not dealt with by nonreligious psychotherapists (Lovinger, 1984). Many psychologists, academic and applied, do not relate to religion as such; they maintain a stance of neutrality or silence toward it. For many, this is not a hostile stance at all, but rather is the most respectful position one can take toward that which one does not personally endorse or understand.

When a psychology as a discipline or profession has formally interacted with religion, it has typically been in one of three classic modalities. All three are unidirectional, with psychology being unaffected in any substantive way by the interaction. The first mode is the scientific study of religion by psychologists, referred to as the psychology of religion. The psychology of religion has a long and distinguished history, being one of the major areas of study in the field from the 1880s until the 1930s. Psychology of religion is alive and well today, as demonstrated by the resurgence in publication of psychology of religion textbooks (e.g., Meadows & Kahoe, 19184; Paloutzian, 1983; Spilka, Hood, & Gorsuch, 1985; Wulff, 1991), by the inclusion of a review of the area in the *Annual Review of Psychology* (Gorsuch, 1988), by the recent establishment of the successful *International Journal for the Psychology of Religion*, and by the establishment and growth of Division 36 (formerly Psychologists Interested in Religious Issues, now Psychology of Religion) within the American Psychological Association (APA).

The second major mode in which psychology has interacted with religion has been through supplying useful psychological information to guide the practice of pastoral care (what one might call the psychologizing of pastoral care). Holifield (1983) provided a historical analysis of this process. Beginning almost from the infancy of psychology in America at the end of the last century, clerics have looked to psychology and the related mental

© *American Psychologist,* March, 1994, *49,* 184-199. Used by permission.

health disciplines for insights to guide pastoral care, and psychologists have been unequivocally enthusiastic about providing these insights. Almost every trend and movement in the mental health field has been mirrored in pastoral psychology, as even the most cursory review of courses in pastoral care at seminaries or of pastoral care textbooks will show. Oden (1984), for example, has shown that pastoral care texts prior to 1920 were dominated by references to the historical and theological roots of the pastoral care tradition, whereas after 1920, pastoral care texts came to be dominated by references to the major psychotherapy theoreticians. Today, pastors are vigorously courted by psychologists as referral sources and mental health gatekeepers in almost every community.

The final type of interaction is the use of psychological findings or theories to revise, reinterpret, redefine, supplant, or dismiss established religious traditions. Each of the four major historic paradigms in psychology has been applied to this task. Such applications of psychoanalysis, behaviorism, and humanistic psychology are well known and have been documented by Rolston (1987) and others. An article by Sperry (1988) is a recent example of the current dominant paradigm, cognitivism, being used to redefine religious belief. Sperry essentially argued that the new mentalist paradigm, built on his concept of emergentist mind, provides the basis for a new understanding of religion, or more directly stated, a new religion. Religion should, according to Sperry, be based on biospheric ethics and the teleology of evolutionary cognitive emergentism. This religion, which he noted would easily merge with "antireligious ideologies such as communism or secular humanism" (p. 611), would "have to relinquish reliance on dualistic explanations" (p. 610) and thus be devoid of supernatural beliefs. He suggested that this should not "pose a major obstacle" (p. 610) to modern religion. In short, humanity should view itself as the highest known product of evolution and hence as our own ultimate concern (many theologians would call such a prioritization an attitude of worship). We should thus base our ethics on the promotion of our common good in order to enhance continued evolutionary progress. Sperry, like Freud and Skinner before him, called for his new understanding of religion after a brief period of cognitivist ascendancy (see also Sperry, 1993).

In each of the three modes discussed above, religion is treated as an object, either of study, for education and provision of services, or for reform. Each of these are, at least in some ways, legitimate facets of a relationship between psychology and religion, but as a group they are incomplete. In none of the three is religion a peer or a partner. This article constitutes a call for a different sort of relationship between psychology and religion, a relationship based on mutuality and respect.

In the first major section of this article, I argue for an understanding of science and religion that recognizes their differences but also understands the common ground they share. The fundamental thrust of this section is premised on an enlarged understanding of the nature of science and of psychology. A series of articles in the American Psychologist over the past decade have paved the way for this current proposal. None has more directly broken ground for this proposal than did O'Donohue's (1989) call for an "(even) bolder model" of understanding clinical psychologists, and indeed all psychologists, as not just practitioners, scientists, or scientist-practitioners, but as "metaphysician-scientist-practitioners" (p. 1460). Because there is no impassable chasm between science and religion, it is inevitable that religion and religious belief will and do relate to the scientific discipline of psychology, and some of the ways in which this is so are explored here. I then explore the way in which interaction occurs between religious belief and the application of psychology in the domain of clinical practice. In the second major section, I expand this analysis beyond the descriptive to the prescriptive by suggesting how religion ought to relate to and have an impact on psychology, both in its more distinctively scientific manifestations and in its professional applications.

The argument I advance is not unique or original, although it has previously not been fully developed for application to the entire discipline of psychology and its relationship with religion. Proposals for alternatives to the "naturalistic" approach to scientific psychology have advanced many of the core ideas in the critique of science that follows, but have not dealt with religion per se. Braybrooke (1987) classified the alternative approaches to disciplined study as falling into two groups. "Interpretative" approaches attempt through phenomenological and qualitative methods to understand the meaning of human action in the context of the meaning systems of the actors (and might include hermeneutic, structuralist, and existentialist approaches to the field). "Critical" approaches also use nontraditional methods of study to make meaning of the subjects of study, but do so from an explicitly value-committed framework (e.g., psychoanalytic, Marxist, or feminist approaches). Neither of these alternative approaches has given rise to a significant literature on its relationship with religion.

On the other hand, many facets of the views of science and religion expressed here have been worked out in more detail by such authors as Ian Barbour (1974, 1990), Holmes Rolston (1987), and Thomas Torrance (1980, 1984), although these authors have tended to be predominantly interested in the relationship of religion with the physical sciences. Furthermore, a diverse community of Christian psychologists have been conducting an isolated dialogue within their community for several decades on "the integration of psychology and theology," a dialogue of remarkable variability in scholarly quality. This dialogue has been encouraged and facilitated by the publication of several journals (e.g., the *Journal of Psychology and Theology* and the *Journal of Psychology and Christianity*) and by a number of books by such relatively prominent psychologists as Malcolm Jeeves (1976), Paul Meehl (Meehl, Klann, Schmieding, Breimeier, & Schroeder-Slomann, 1958), David Myers (1978; Myers & Jeeves, 1987), and Paul Vitz (1977) and by lesser-known authors (e.g., Carter & Narramore, 1979; Evans, 1982; Jones & Butman, 1991; Van Leeuwen, 1985). A similar dialogue is beginning to occur in the context of other traditional faith communities as well, as shown by the development of the *Journal of Psychology and Judaism*, by the publication of a few books (e.g., Rizvi, 1988), and by occasional paper presentations at APA conventions (e.g., Lax, 1993).

On the Supposed Incommmensurability"of Religion and Science

The classic formulation of the relationship of religion to science generally, and hence to psychology in particular, is that religion can have no integral relationship to science whatsoever, except perhaps as an object of study. This view has been expressed most tersely in recent times by the National Academy of Sciences in a resolution passed in 1981, which stated that "Religion and science are separate and mutually exclusive realms of human thought whose presentation in the same context leads to misunderstanding of both scientific theory and religious belief" (National Academy of Sciences, 1984, p. 6). The impetus for this resolution was a Louisiana trial regarding the teaching of creationism as science in public school classrooms.

The supposed separateness and exclusivity of religion and science seem to be derived from cherished notions of their incompatibility based on their respective essential natures. Barbour (1974) suggested that science and religion are often regarded as fundamentally incompatible because of the beliefs that (a) science rests on facts and religion on

faith, (b) scientific claims are verifiable or falsifiable whereas religious claims are not evaluated by objective experience, and (c) the criteria for choosing between scientific theories are clear and objective whereas the criteria for choosing between religions are ambiguous and subjective.

Some scientists conceive of religion as asking questions solely in the realms of significance, meaning, values, ultimacy, and ethics; these are regarded as making no factual claims on human reality. With this understanding of religion, how can it have any integral relationship with science? However, religion is a multifaceted entity that must be understood from a diversity of perspectives (Gorsuch, 1988). For the purpose of this article, I focus on the cognitive or declarative dimension of religious belief and doctrine. However defined or described, religion usually includes a declarative dimension, whether it is expressed explicitly in formal doctrine (at one extreme) or implicitly and tacitly through the rituals and practices prescribed by the religion (at the other extreme). Every religion asserts or presupposes views of the nature of the universe, the nature of some ultimate reality, the nature of human beings and other beings, the place of humanity in the ultimate scheme of things, and the nature of morality. I focus on that cognitive-declarative dimension of religion in analyzing the relationship of science and religion because it is the dimension of religion most relevant to science. I do not in the process claim that religion is only or even primarily a cognitive phenomenon. It is a presupposition of this article that there is no one entity of religion, but rather that there are religions, and that the present analysis may apply better to some religions than others. Nevertheless, the various religious faiths have enough in common to make a discussion of the relationship of science with religion (singular) meaningful.

Science, on the other hand, has often been viewed in the manner dictated by logical positivists (this has been especially true in the past among psychologists: Krasner & Hours, 1984; Mahoney, 1976; Toulmin & Leary, 1985. The essence of the positivistic view of science was summarized by Mahoney (p. 130) as asserting that scientific knowledge is grounded in empirical facts that are uninterpreted, indubitable, and fixed in meaning; that theories are derived from these facts by induction or deduction and are retained or rejected solely on the basis of their ability to survive experimental tests; and that science progresses by the gradual accumulation of facts. A growing consensus of scholars today, however, rejects the foregoing as an accurate understanding of science, as I discuss in the next major section. Furthermore, some scholars argue that psychology is not a unitary scientific discipline, but is rather a complex blend of natural and human sciences along with a culturally defined applied disciplinary arm (Koch & Leary, 1985). In short, many aspects of psychology and of science in general defy easy classification according to the logical positivist conceptions of science.

Postpositivistic Philosophy of Science

The traditional or positivistic view of science has been eroding since the late 1950s. Although preceded by a substantial amount of work in the philosophy and sociology of science (Laudan, 1984), the analyses of science promulgated by historian of science Thomas Kuhn (1970) were the first to really catch the attention of the scientific world, and especially the psychological world. Since that time, awareness of postpositivistic, postmodern, or "historicist" trends in the philosophy of science on the part of psychologists has increased (e.g., Bevan, 1991; Gergen, 1985; Gholson & Barker, 1984; Howard, 1985; Manicas & Secord, 1983; O'Donohue, 1989). These trends in understanding science might be summarized as follows.

First, postpositivistic philosophy of science has taught us that data are theory-laden. A simplistic empirical foundationalism or naive realism, the view that empirical data are unsullied and indubitable, is no longer tenable. Philosophers were the first to clearly see this. Results of contemporary perceptual and cognitive psychology clearly support the contention that data are sorted or processed from their first entry into the human organism's sensory equipment. For instance, expectancies have a profound impact on the perceiving process (e.g., the famous Postman studies cited by Kuhn), and these findings have made their way into the philosophy-of-science literature. It is commonly noted that all seeing is "seeing as."

The scientist, according to Toulmin (1962), "does not (and should not) approach Nature devoid of all prejudices and prior beliefs" (p. 45). Without preorienting conceptions of some sort, we cannot perceive data at all; the world would be a "bloomin' buzzin' confusion" (William James's term). We have data precisely because we sort our experience according to dimensions of relevance to our prescientific commitments and the demands of the ongoing scientific task. Koch (1981) said "We cannot discriminate a so-called variable ... without making strong presumptions of philosophical cast about the nature of our human subject matter" (p. 267; see also Tjeltveit, 1989). The nature of psychology,

given the complexity, irreducibility, and obscurity of its subject matter, is profoundly shaped by conceptual presuppositions we bring to our areas of study. This theory-ladenness (a term attributed to philosopher of science N. R. Hanson) of the data may be accentuated in the human or behavioral sciences, as I argue later. Recent attention to gender biases in social science might be cited as a case in point (Riger, 1992). So, in counterpoint to the notions that data are uninterpreted, indubitable, and fixed in meaning, contemporary views see data as interpreted (to a greater or lesser extent) and thus not necessarily fixed in meaning.

This assertion should not, however, be taken as an endorsement of relativism or the notion that expectations or theories create data. As Brown (1977) has noted, "we shape our percepts out of an already structured but still malleable material. This perceptual material, whatever it may be, will serve to limit the class of possible constructs without dictating a unique percept" (p. 93). In other words, although reality does not force one and only one structure on our perceptions, there are limits to the degree to which our preexisting conceptions can impose a structure on reality. It is expected that empirical evidence will "show [the scientist] how to trim and shape his ideas further" (Toulmin, 1962, p. 45), rather than theories or percepts leaping forth uncalled from the data (naive realism) or, alternatively, theories or percepts creating data (radical constructivism). This view has been called "critical realism" (Barbour, 1990; Brown, 1977).

Second, the new philosophy of science teaches that scientific theories are underdetermined by facts (Hesse, 1980; Laudan, 1984). Positivistic conceptions of science suggest or imply either that theories are built inductively on data alone and that ideally the data will unequivocally support the theory, or alternatively that we propose theories tentatively and then accept only those that survive critical tests. In either case, the data or facts are presumed to determine the theory. But these assertions have been strongly criticized. Induction is an inadequate description of the process of theory development, as Kuhn (1970) has shown. The data are rarely scrutinized exhaustively before we commit ourselves to a theory. After all, scientists usually believe in their theories before putting them to empirical test; what else would sustain the diligent effort necessary to ever put the theory to the test?

Furthermore, the process of theory "confirmation" is now recognized to be extremely complex and not predicated merely upon the objective data. The "facts" never "pick out one theory uniquely or unambiguously to the exclusion of all its contraries" (Laudan, 1984, p. 15). As a result, falsification of theories by critical tests is now seen as far more difficult than was previously realized. Theories consist of flexible webs of assertions, including major hypotheses, corollaries, and so forth, that can be shifted easily to rebut attempts at theory falsification. For instance, a disconfirming critical test of a personality theory can be dismissed as irrelevant by questioning the operationalization and measurement of the key concepts of the theory, the nature of the studied subject population, the external and internal validity of the experimental manipulations, and so forth. One can never test the central notions of a theory without presuming numerous other ancillary propositions, and thus theories are amazingly resilient to so-called crucial tests (Brown, 1977; Meehl, 1978; Wolterstorff, 1984).

Ultimately, the appraising of theories is a highly complex and sophisticated form of value judgment (Howard, 1985, p. 258). Our acceptance of any particular theory is never a result of mechanical methodological operations on the data; rather, empirical and extraempirical factors affect theory acceptance. The extraempirical influences that affect theory choices include what scientists value (e.g., 'epistemic values' such as predictive accuracy and internal coherence: Howard, 1985; Laudan, 1984), the hosts of nonepistemic values held by the scientist (e.g., feminism, naturalism, and rugged individualism; see Gergen, 1978, 1985), the beliefs of those whom we respect and are trying to emulate, and the contingencies of the scientific social network (e.g., what can get published; Mahoney, 1976). To the extent that this analysis is valid, making explicit the extraempirical determinants of decision making about scientific theories would enhance the honesty of the scientific community and possibly allow us to make more accurate judgments.

Third, numerous attempts have been made to reduce scientific method to a set of concrete, operationalized steps. although this approach has much to offer in understanding scientific activity, contemporary scholarship suggests that science itself is also a cultural and human phenomenon. As an example of this assertion, note that values—scientific and non-scientific—shape choice of objects of study (Laudan, 1984; O'Donohue, 1989; Sarason, 1984). It has been commonly noted that what is studied as a problem to conquer in modern American culture (e.g., authoritarianism) has been viewed positively in other settings (e.g., Germany in the 1930s). Frequently, our scientific formulations carry implicit within them a pressing value message by the labels

we give them and the way we conduct our research (see Gergen, 1978). In the words of Bevan (1991),

> Behind the worlds we construct, coloring both our logic and our rhetoric, are the ideologies that give our world views their dominant cast. Such ideologies are complex and not easily analyzed.... As forms of human thought, ideologies permeate virtually every aspect of our mental life, including our science. We ignore them at our intellectual, social, and personal peril. (p. 478)

The variety of extraempirical factors that shape the scientific process are not a chaotic collage of random beliefs, values, and the like. There is a certain cohesiveness to the fundamental commitments we bring to the tasks of life, leading some to characterize our starting points as "worldviews":

> Worldview (or vision of life) is a framework or set of fundamental beliefs through which we view the world and our calling and future in it.... It is the integrative and interpretive framework by which order and disorder are judged, the standard by which reality is managed or pursued. [It consists of] biophysical, emotional, rational, socio-economic, ethical, and "religious" elements. (Olthuis, 1985, p. 155)

In a very general and fundamental way, a worldview tells us what to expect and not expect to be the case in our world, and as such it forms the ground for all creative human thought and inquiry, for all of our ultimate answers about the nature of our existence. These foundational commitments, presuppositions, or "control beliefs" (Wolterstorff, 1984) are usually tacitly assumed on the basis of faith; they are rarely deliberately produced through rational or empirical inquiry.

How should these types of beliefs and commitments influence the process of doing science? Fletcher (1984) argued for a minimalist approach of only including those assumptions that were absolutely necessary for the conduct of the scientific enterprise and about which there was unanimous assent in the scientific community. In other words, we should only allow those assumptions without which a scientist would be paralyzed (e.g., that our sense experience is trustworthy, that there is a real world out there). Others argue for an explicit and intentionally expended role for worldview assumptions, including religious beliefs, in scholarly work. O'Donohue (1989), following Lakatos, suggested that "metaphysical sentences," those beliefs that are deeply imbedded in our web of belief and are affected by evidence but not directly testable against experience, "are internal to all the sciences in that they are contained in the hard core and the positive heuristic of a scientific research program. Therefore, there can be no rigid demarcation of science and metaphysics" (p. 1465).

Fourth, and finally, the new philosophy of science would teach us, as Kuhn (1970) most effectively pointed out, that science progresses not through the accumulation of bare facts, but through refinement of theories and theory-laden facts that are themselves imbedded in broader conceptual webs (paradigms, research programs, or research traditions; Gholson & Barker, 1985). Although the Kuhnian notion of science progressing by means of cataclysmic revolutions in which incommensurable paradigms supplant one another has been rather thoroughly refuted (Laudan, 19840, Kuhn's argument against the "slow accumulation of facts" understanding of scientific progress is well supported. Scientific progress is real, and change occurs even while fundamental conceptions of the subject matter are undergoing revision.

Commonalities and Distinctions Between Religion and Science

What commonalities do science and religion share? What distinguishes science from that which is not science? Viewing science from a postpositivist perspective reveals the human face of science. Science and the many non-scientific ways of knowing (including religion) are not identical, but "both are creations of the human mind" (Bevan, 1991, p. 476). Scientific knowing differs in degree and emphasis from other forms of human knowing. The work of the scientist is not easily comparable to the practice dimension of religious experience, be it the ecstatic worship of a Pentecostal Christian or the dispassionate meditations of a Zen Buddhist.

Nevertheless, contemporary philosophy of science does not support a radical or categorical separation of science from other forms of human knowing, including religious knowing or belief. The relative differences between them deserve to be carefully observed and maintained, but we cannot justify a failure to explore the interface of religion and science on the basis that religious belief is simply nonscientific. To the extent that science and religion are not "separate and mutually exclusive realms of human thought" (National Academy of Sciences, 1984) but are rather related and somewhat similar human activities, the supposed chasm between the two can begin to be seen in more realistic terms. A careful study of the human face of the postpositivist view of science reveals interesting parallels and similarities between science and the cognitive or declarative dimensions of religion. I would again reiterate that in using the term *religion* in this article, I am referring to the cognitive dimensions of religious belief.

Subject matter. First, we can note with Barbour (1974) and Rolston (1987) a difference in degree rather than a true dichotomy between the two activities with regard to subject matter, a difference that does not constitute an impassable crevasse between the two activities. Each grapples with real aspects of human experience. Science is more likely to deal with the more sensory, objective, public, quantifiable, and repeatable aspects of experience. Religion is more likely to deal with the more internal, subjective, qualitative, and unmeasurable aspects of human experience and with the nature of the transcendent through revelation, reason, and human experience. These distinctions, however, only hold to a certain point; iron-clad distinctions between the subject matters of two activities are harder to make than one might guess, especially in psychology. Science is not based on pure facts; rather, there is a certain degree of uncertainty and interpretation involved in all human knowing. Certainly, scientists grapple with the abstract, private, ephemeral, and subjective, especially in psychology.

Religion, on the other hand, is not based on blind faith that is insensitive to the contours of reality, but rather is sensitive to certain realities of the human experience. Religion does more than assert things about God; it structures our understanding of the ultimate context of our existence and asserts many things about the nature of human beings. Many assertions about God imply things about the human beings who are to relate to God. Religion commonly grapples with morality, and moral systems necessarily assert or imply things about humans who are supposed to adhere to the system (e.g., a moral system that recommends chastity implies things about the nature of human sexuality). Every religious system presumes to answer the question of the broadest purposes of human existence. Such teleological conceptions are the foundations for the conceptual analysis of human behavior, as the functionalists long ago posited. Finally, every religion attempts to understand the human dilemma, diagnosing our problems and offering an agenda for remediating our difficulties. In each of these cases, religion begins to make factual or quasi-factual assertions about human reality that have implications that can be checked against human experience. Thus, there is substantive overlap in the subject matter of religion and the science of psychology.

Perhaps when each is functioning in its stereotypical modality, as when religion is struggling intuitively or rationalistically with the nature of God and other ultimate realities, and when science is grappling with a narrow slice of the objective, material, impersonal universe (e.g., the behavior of particular acids under extreme conditions of temperature variation), there will be little interpenetration of the two forms of human knowing. But when the scientist begins to attempt to weave together discrete bits of empirical knowledge into a grand tapestry to explain and understand vast stretches of reality, she or he passes necessarily into domains of human thought that are also religious (i.e., these realms can be both religious and scientific, although not prototypically either). Prime examples are cosmology, sociobiology, and personality and clinical theory (Rolston, 1987). That the grand unifying theory is still an aspiration of psychological science is suggested by the work of Staats (1991; cf. Fowler, 1990) and others. Science has goals that transient the mundane description of discrete empirical reality, and religion often has aspirations of saying something about the empirical aspects of human reality.

Accountability to experience. A second area of concourse is that of accountability to rigorously examined human experience. Religion and science should and do each exhibit a certain epistemic humility and hold themselves open to correction and development, at the same time aiming toward verisimilitude—truth-likeness. Scientific theories are meant to have a rather direct and immediate accountability relationship to experience, but as we have seen, there are substantial complications and difficulties in that accountability. Barbour (1974) pointed out that falsifiability is not easy for either science or religion. The criteria for theory acceptance and rejection in science, as I have discussed in passing, are far from clear-cut. Thus, empirical theory testing is part, but not the total sum, of decision making between scientific theories. Furthermore, metaphysical assertions that are not immediately testable in experience are intrinsic to the scientific enterprise (O'Donohue, 1989); scientists normally understand their subject matter in the context of a web of belief, much of which is not directly testable, that they bring to their studies. So, as Kuhn (1970) pointed out clearly, scientists tend to cling to their broad paradigms and scientific revolutions tend to proceed by a new generation bypassing the older generation that fails to change.

Although scientific truth is less directly accountable to experiential testing than was previously imagined, religious truth is not as insulated from

experienced reality as its detractors might suggest. People sometimes put their religious beliefs to serious test against reality. Within the Christian tradition, Brunner (1939) said, "The decision about the truth or untruth of the Christian doctrine of man is made in experience" (p. 205). More broadly, Rolston (1987) stated that "religious experience provides a testing of dogmas, confirming or disconfirming them. The history of religion is strewn with abandoned beliefs, largely overcome by more commanding creeds or made implausible by new ranges of experience" (pp. 6-7). With some degree of similarity to the case of science, human experience is relevant to deciding between religions and to making decisions within religious systems. It seems that both religion and science stand in an accountability relationship with experience, although surely epistemic humility and experiential accountability take on a different flavor in the religious realm. "Neither science nor religion arrives at certainties. They at best predict probabilities, but religion is looser here than is science and often can predict only a range of possibilities" (Rolston, 1987, p. 28). One interesting area of empirical accountability to reality for religion is the moderate but demonstrable positive contributions of religious devotion to mental health and quality of life (Bergin, 1991; Larson et al., 1992).

Goals. A third commonality between religion and science is that of essential goals; science and religion are related human attempts to make sense out of a very complex existence (Barbour, 1974). A major goal of each is understanding, although the particular form of understanding for each differs (see Toulmin, 1962, for a discussion of understanding in science). Scientific explanations are distinguished by their emphasis on the development of what are commonly called universal mathematical covering laws—theories that attempt to explain by specifying the mathematical—quantitative relationships between naturalistic entities, with the specified relationships being assumed to hold universally when ever comparable conditions apply. Religious explanations typically resort to more poetic, dogmatic, metaphorical, or rationalistic explanatory mechanisms than do scientific explanations (Barbour, 1990). Despite their distinctive styles of explanation, both attempt to foster human understanding: "Religion does claim to be in some sense true as well as useful. Beliefs about the nature of reality are presupposed in all the other varied uses of religious language" (Barbour, 1974, p. 5).

Use of analogical models. Fourth, both religion and science use analogical models rooted in paradigms or worldviews to explain experience

(Barbour, 1974)). Many scientific psychologists are recognizing the constricting effects of traditional operationalism in science when they try overly rigorously to eliminate nonempirical conceptions from the human activity of science. There is an "as if" quality to much of science, especially at its frontiers. Certainly, however, scientific metaphors are held less tenaciously than their parallels in the religious realm. Even in religion, however, explanatory metaphors evolve.

Human enterprises. A fifth commonality between religion and science is that both are human communal and cultural enterprises subject to the same sorts of human influences that affect all of our activities. Because science and religion are both finely nuanced activities engaged in by human beings, the full scope of neither enterprise is readily reducible to a set of methodological rules or conceptual dogmas. We will never eliminate the human from either set of practices. Hence, a psychological and sociological analysis of the factors shaping each if appropriate. The distinction between shaping each of these activities and exhaustively determining them, however, must be maintained. The extreme conclusions of the "strong programme in the sociology of knowledge" (the view that reduces the determinants of science to social-cultural forces alone; Bloor, 1976; Livingstone, 1988) must be rejected, as should its counterpart in understanding religion (e.g., the reductionistic renderings of religion promulgated by Freud, Skinner, and others; Rolston, 1987).

Passionate devotion. Finally, as Mahoney (1976) noted, science can in fact elicit and inspire the same type of passionate devotion as religion can. Human beings seem to be drawn with religious reverence to some ultimate reality, and certainly science occupies that place in the life of many scientists. The scientific enterprise is sustained by the emotional commitment of its practitioners to both the grand aims of the pursuit of truth and the improvement of the human race, as well as by the more pedestrian dreams of personal advancement, prestige, and prosperity.

A bald assertion that there are no substantial differences between scientific and religious knowing would be ludicrous. The differences are perhaps too many and too obvious to bear mentioning. The objective of this section, however, is to highlight the similarities between the two as a vehicle for breaking down the supposed barriers preventing substantive intercourse between the two. Despite their many differences, scientific and religious attempts at understanding are both exercises of human rationality that

are shaped by our preorienting assumptions, are accountable to human experience, are influenced by the human communities of which we are a part, and are attempting to understand aspects of our experienced realities. They are different, but there is not an unbridgeable chasm between the two.

Interaction Between Religion and the Science of Psychology

In the foregoing section, I have argued that religion and science share common ground upon which interaction could take place. I now briefly examine the thesis that such interaction actually does take place on an ongoing basis. Thorough documentation of this thesis would require a separate monograph. Briefly, I would argue that interaction with religious and quasi-religious themes is most frequent and obvious in those arenas in which psychological scientists extend their reach to explain the broadest domains of human behavior and take on the prescriptive function of specifying what it means to be a "healthy" or "normal" or "mature" person. Because these aspects of psychology are generally coterminous with the grand personality theories that are the academic background for the practice of psychotherapy, I leave further discussion of this until the next section.

It may be helpful to explore briefly one concrete example of the intersection of religious concerns with scientific psychological inquiry. Herbert Simon (1990) proposed a new behavior genetics model of altruistic behavior (specifically, the choice to forgo or minimize progeny) that incorporated an explicit cognitive psychological or social learning element as its distinguishing characteristic. Simply put, he suggested that altruistic people are docile—that is, they are adept at social learning of useful skills and proper interpersonal behavior and highly motivated to do what others (society) deem to be good. Docility is made possible by *bounded rationality*, the failure to exercise rigorous rationality in independently evaluating all events for the benefits that those events will contribute to the person's potentialities for genetic propagation, to their personal "fitness." Simon then developed a probabilistic model justifying the continued survival of altruistic behavior in a species.

Simon's (1990) article illustrated the points of connection between the scientific and the religious. Most psychologists would view this article as scientific, on the basis of its publication in *Science* and its use of scientific concepts and mathematical formulae. However, Simon's subject matter clearly overlaps with the moral and the religious: He focused on people who choose to forgo progeny, referring to, among others, people who for moral reasons choose chastity as a life commitment or choose to restrain from procreative behavior prior to marriage. Simon clearly meant his hypothesis to be accountable to empirical data, but it is equally clear that it is accountable only in the broadest way imaginable. He invoked such difficult-to-quantify ideas as percentages of altruists in a population, the net cost of altruistic choices, and number of offspring in a population of nonaltruists that is attributable to their altruistic behavior. Clearly, a single critical test of this hypothesis is not likely, and disconfirming evidence could easily be attributed to inadequate measurement of key theoretical terms. His goal was the understanding of behavior that is counterintuitive from his paradigmatic assumptions (but that is easily comprehensible, even rational, from the perspective of certain specific religious traditions). Simon's broad explanatory matrix was explicitly identified as neo-Darwinism or sociobiology. He defined *fitness* as the "expected number of progeny" (p. 1665) one will eventually produce. Simon's model presumes an ultimate context for understanding human action: We are singularly material beings whose greatest advantage comes in maximizing the propagation of our genetic material into succeeding generations. It presumes an understanding of ultimate standards for judging the veracity of human rationality, with the ultimate standard being fitness. The explanatory analogy is that of an animal population in which certain inherited characteristics optimize survivability and in which gene propagation is the highest good. With this standard, clearly antirational behavior, such as the altruistic choice to constrain one's personal propagation, must be explained.

I am not here arguing that Simon's (1990) views were religious in a narrow sense. What I am suggesting, however, is that at the broadest levels many religious traditions would suggest an understanding of the ultimate meaning and context of human action that would be utterly at variance with that assumed by Simon. It is notable that Simon tried to gain understanding of behavior that is inexplicable from his orienting assumptions about meaning and purpose in human life (sexual abstinence), whereas such behavior is rational and quite explicable from other, more traditionally religious paradigm assumptions.

Other examples could be easily explored, including the way in which psychological study of moral development necessarily involves preconceptions (implicit or explicit) about what constitutes morality and moral action, how the study of social effectiveness or skill presupposes a pragmatic or utilitarian standard for the evaluation of human action, and

how the study of marital interaction in the paradigm of social exchange theory presupposes the ultimate contexts and motivations for human choice in the most intimate of human relationships. But the clearest examples of the manner in which psychological inquiry and practice intersect with religious understandings of the person come from the applied domains of psychology, to which I turn next.

Interaction Between Religion and the Professions of Clinical Psychology

Psychology is not just a scientific discipline, but a professional discipline as well: The "discipline of psychology includes both its science and its applications" (Fowler, 1990, p. 2). I examine the professional practice of psychotherapy as a case example of the relationship between religion and all of the professional application fields of psychology, both because it is the most common form of professional practice of psychology and because it is the domain in which the interrelationship of psychology and religion is most obvious.

London (1986) has made the most persuasive case from within the field of psychology that psychotherapy, in addition to its scientific dimensions, is a moralistic enterprise with substantial religious content. Psychotherapists are not neutral technicians; London characterized them as forming a "secular priesthood" (p. 148). By this, he meant that the mission of reform or healing that psychotherapists embrace is intrinsically a moralistic one. Building upon his analysis, I would argue that three types of factors make this inevitable: (a) factors intrinsic to psychotherapeutic relationships, (b) factors intrinsic to psychotherapeutic theories, and (c) factors intrinsic to the modern culture in which psychotherapeutic services are offered. In each of these areas, psychotherapists are treading on ground shared with both broadly and more narrowly defined religious understandings.

With regard to the factors intrinsic to psychotherapeutic relationships, I would suggest, following London (1986, pp. 10-11), that three relationship factors make psychotherapy an intrinsically moral enterprise. First, clients do not separate psychological and moral phenomena in the way that professionals often do, so that a question such as "Should I vent my anger at my wife?" is not just a question of psychological health. Clients, London argued, interpret therapist reactions to such commonplace choices as moral approbation or disapproval (cf. Meehl, 1959). Clients often do not separate the moral and the religious. Second, therapists are human beings whose values and morals must participate in their human relationship with the client, at the very least in the broad ways in which they evaluate the client as a person (cf. Kelly, 1990). An interesting empirical finding that supports this assertion came from the work of Kelly and Strupp (1992), who found that psychotherapy tends to change client values (although not consistently in the direction of similarity to the values of the therapist) and that therapists tend to rate as more successful those clients whose values regarding personal goals in life change most to match the goals of the therapist, even though other measures did not indicate that these clients did in fact improve more than other clients. Bergin (1991) has documented the undeniable participation of values, including religious values, in psychotherapy. Third, the various ethical codes of our professional bodies exert a normative influence on therapist behavior, impelling a direction to our efforts that a "neutral science" cannot instigate. Going beyond London's comments, I would add, fourth, that it seems that the concerns presented by clients often push the practitioners beyond the limits of what consensually validated scientific research has established. "Given that research supplies only a small fraction of the information needed to completely understand the psychotherapeutic process, we are often compelled to rely on our tacit, background metaphysical notions" (O'Donohue, 1989, p. 1467) for guidance in how to respond to a client. In so doing, we often pass into the moral or religious domain of action (Browning, 1987; London, 1986; Tjeltveit, 1989).

The second factor that makes it inevitable that psychotherapy will be a moral enterprise with substantial interrelationship with broad religious understandings is that what many regard to be religious presuppositions are intrinsic to the nature of psychotherapeutic and personality theory. O'Donohue (1989) pointed out the intractable presence of metaphysical presuppositions in all clinical theory. Psychotherapeutic theories embody value assumptions in that each includes explicit or implicit judgments about the nature of the human life that is "good" (healthy, whole, adaptive, realistic, rational, etc.) and "bad" (abnormal, pathological, immature, stunted, self-deceived, etc.). O'Donohue suggested that "therapy programs," or comprehensive views of the person that contain metaphysical assumptions and action principles for psychological or behavioral change,

> influence the problem statement and thereby ontic commitment. Whether a given problem is described in terms of medical/disease entities, behavioral excesses or deficits, unconscious con-

> flicts, or existential problems in living is determined by the therapy program.... that psychologists view a certain state of affairs as problematic is influenced by our metaphysical views concerning such issues as what constitutes the good life, human nature, and morality. (p. 1467; see also Tjeltveit, 1989)

Beyond the mere passive containment of metaphysical assumptions, psychotherapy theory systems are inherently prescriptive. London (1986) suggested that psychotherapy usually involves the retrospective repair of past damage and the prospective planning of how the client will live in the future; "Those that speak to the future are entangled with what, in short, are problems of salvation.... And the arguments which explain and justify those acts, taken together, total to a moral code" (p. 151). Browning (1987) argued that theories of psychotherapy necessarily go beyond the typical limits of scientific theories to answer questions of ultimate meaning and of human obligation. Any system, he argued, that is used as a guide to shape, heal, or reform human life cannot avoid metaphysics or ethics. In this way, psychological theories go beyond the basic scientific need for a metaphysical infrastructure to a much more extensive set of ethical and metaphysical commitments. Browning suggested that contemporary scientific models "are modern forms of religious thinking in so far as they attempt to answer our insecurities, give us generalized images of the world, and form the attitudes we should take toward the value of life, the nature of death, and the grounds for morality" (p. 120).

Behavior therapy is an excellent specific example of how moralistic and religious content is intrinsic to therapy theories, even though it seems the least moralistic and most neutral and scientific of all major approaches. Woolfolk and Richardson (1984) presented a sophisticated and sympathetic critique of behavior therapy, not as a psychotechnology, but as a socioculturally based system of belief with deep metaphysical and quasi-religious commitments. They started with a picture of behavior therapy's self-image, noting that

> virtually all have conceived of [behavior therapy] as a neutral structure, a body of "objective knowledge" verified by experimental test. Behavior therapy's self-image is that of an applied science, devoid of any inherent prescriptive thrust or implicit system of values, the

essence of which can be accounted for without reference to any cultural or historical context. (p. 777)

In contrast to this self-image, their conclusion at the broadest level was that behavior therapy is a worldview of sorts, one that is "closely linked with the values and patterns of thought characteristic of modernity" (Woolfolk & Richardson, 1984, p. 777) and is "implicitly predicated on modern epistemological and ethical assumptions" (p. 778). They suggested that behavior therapy contains "a prescriptive, ideological component: a favored mode of thinking and implicit criteria for making judgments that guide behavior therapists in their activities and also represent a vision of reality underlying those activities that justify and support them" (p. 777). Among the cherished assumptions of behavior therapy are technicism, rationality, amorality, and humanism. Behavior therapy, like all psychotherapy systems, is founded on subtle and often implicit assumptions that overlap with the domain of the moral and religious.

Third and finally, psychotherapy overlaps with the moral and religious because of factors in the contemporary cultural matrix within which psychotherapy is practiced. It seems that psychology is, in American society, filling the void created by the waning influence of religion in answering questions of ultimacy and providing moral guidance. The APA's commitment to promoting human welfare presumes morally laden visions of ultimate human well-being, as do the applied enterprises of the various psychotherapy models (London, 1986; Browning, 1987). The APA's involvement in social and juridical advocacy serves as one example of such a function in contemporary culture (e.g., Bersoff & Ogden, 1991). This perhaps helps to explain the potency of the mental health professions today: they have stepped in to fill the cultural niche vacated by the institutional church and have been in the business of answering questions of ultimacy with the powerful mantle of modern science cast about their shoulders. Kilbourne and Richardson (1984) have argued that therapy and religion each serve the function of establishing a "deep structure" for understanding life through the enactment of myths and ritual, which are given their power through the personal empathy and institutional settings in which they are administered. In addition, they both serve to elevate self-esteem and enhance social integration.

A complicating factor in occupying this cultural niche is the unquestionably high presence of nonreligious and antireligious sentiments among many practicing mental health professionals, as discussed in the opening paragraph of this article (see also Bergin, 1980; Braun, 1981; Richardson, 1991). Mental health professionals are an atypical subpopulation in America today, with lower levels of religious participation and higher levels of agnosticism, skepticism, and atheism than the general population. As Braun noted, this raises the possibility that applied psychologists especially may misunderstand or inappropriately evaluate client religiosity and the place of faith in their lives.

My argument in this section is that there is even more substantial overlap with the moral religious domain in the applied arena of professional therapeutic psychology. Browning (1987) has provided an apt summary of this point: "Traditional religion and modern [therapeutic] psychology stand in a special relation to one another because both of them provide concepts and technologies for the ordering of the interior life" (p. 2).

An Outline for a Constructive Relationship of a Religion With Psychology as a Science and as an Applied Discipline

I have argued that, to this point in its history, psychology has not interacted with religion as a peer. The premise that this noninteractive stance can be justified by the supposed incompatibility of science and religion has been examined and rejected. I have argued that science and religion (broadly speaking) are different, but they are not radically incompatible. Psychology is a prime academic discipline in which we could explore the interface between religion and science. Furthermore, psychology's substantial presence in the helping professions has shifted its institutional identity in the direction of a moral enterprise with considerable overlap with the domain of religious belief. Now I shift my analysis from the descriptive to the prescriptive, using the foregoing arguments as the background assumptions for the proposal. After discussing some foundations for a constructive relationship between psychology and religion or religious belief, I discuss several broad proposals for a constructive relationship between religious belief and scientific psychology, followed by a similar discussion with regard to applied psychology.

Foundations

If data are theory-laden, it follows that there must be sources for the expectations or thought forms we bring to the data. In the natural sciences, the sources for presuppositions about the data one sees in the lab, and about the shape one's theories will take, can come from advances in other scientific areas, from one's socialization history as a scientist in training, from the culture in general, and perhaps occasionally and tangentially from one's religion. It seems likely that psychological scientists carry more presupposed notions of religious origin into the study of persons than natural scientists bring to the study of material subjects (most people having been "lay personality theorists" since birth; see Wegner & Vallacter, 1977). This is descriptively true, but there is also a certain prescriptive validity to this, in that we would be paralyzed in our inquiries if we approached human reality devoid of expectations. We need to approach our subject matter with presuppositions and expectations and to be explicit and accountable in that process. In the human (behavioral, social) sciences, there is good reason to expect any understanding of human data to be profoundly affected by religious presuppositions, in addition to other factors, because religion has so much to say about the human condition.

The various sciences likely differ in terms of the pervasiveness and profundity of the influences that worldview (including religious) assumptions will have on them, with psychology being more permeable to or riddled with influential religious presuppositions than, say, physics, which may contain fewer and weaker extraempirical presuppositions. Is this because psychology is less of a science or a less mature science? Perhaps, but this might have less to do with the relative maturity or purity of the science than it does with the inherent complexity, irreducibility, and inaccessibility of the subject matter of interest. Meehl's (1978) list of 20 intractable difficulties intrinsic to psychological science gives a beginning idea of the difficulties faced in psychological science. For instance, Meehl discussed difficulties in response-class and situation-class taxonomies: How do we divide up the stream or organismic responding and stimulus environment into the most meaningful units? Chemistry has found meaningful joints of nature in molecules, atoms, and subatomic particles; the comparable elemental building blocks of our science are not readily apparent. When taxonomic boundaries are less readily obvious, it would seem that the influence of philosophic and religious presuppositions on the scientist's preconceptions would be more extensive. Does psychology's position as the "most philosophy-sensitive discipline in the entire gamut of disciplines that claim empirical status" (Koch, 1981, p. 267) mean that psychology is really less mature or rigorous as a science or, more radically, does it mean that psychology is necessarily a different type of science that cannot always be judged by adher-

ence to the path hewed out by physics and chemistry? Such issues are beyond the scope of this article, but I believe that the answer is probably yes to both halves of the question.

There is a rich tradition of reflection on the problems addressed by psychology in the field of philosophy (see Peters, 1962; Robinson, 1981) and in the field of theology (including practical theology; see Browning, 1987; McDonald, 1982). Alston (1985) has suggested that the philosopher can serve a role as a "concept analysis" consultant in interacting with the psychological scientist, bringing special analytic skills to bear at the beginning stages of problem formulation on the nature of the questions to be addressed empirically. Theology would serve a similar function, as I develop in the following section.

The explicit incorporation of values and worldviews into the scientific process will not necessarily result in a loss of objectivity or methodological rigor. What is new about this proposal is not the incorporation of assumptions into the process, but rather the proposal that psychological scientists and practitioners be more explicit about the interaction of religious belief and psychology. If scientists, especially psychologists, are operating out of worldview assumptions that include the religious, and if the influence of such factors is actually inevitable, then the advancement of the scientific enterprise would be facilitated by making those beliefs explicitly available for public inspection and discourse. Baumrind (1982) has argued a similar point, suggesting that the relative lack of credibility of the social sciences may be perpetuated in part by our tendency to obscure the values that shape our work. She suggested that social scientists must respond by making their values explicit and deliberately encouraging value pluralism among those active in the discipline. A commitment to explicitness and public accountability about such value matters would seem essential and compatible with the scientific spirit.

With these foundations, I now consider the outlines of how religion could and should interact with scientific and professional psychology.

Three Major Forms of Interaction Between Religion and the Science of Psychology

The first form of interaction is what might be called a *critical-evaluative* mode of functioning, whereby social scientific theories and paradigms are examined and evaluated by the individual scientist for their fit with his or her religious presuppositions. This is somewhat akin at an individual level to Kuhn's phase in scientific progress in which there is acute discontent with a prevailing paradigm and a search begins for new ways to conceptualize the subject. The core task of the psychologist is not to derive the substance of a discipline from divine revelation, religious tradition, or idiosyncratic religious faith, but neither is it to ignore religion in a vain attempt to be totally neutral in doing science.

Religious presuppositions properly operate at very broad and fundamental levels (Wolterstorff, 1984). However, these presuppositions are clear enough to lead us to be skeptical about some theories or paradigms and lean toward others. They are also broad and vague enough to allow a diversity of possible theories to be compatible with them. As a case example, a psychologist is within his or her "epistemic rights" (Plantinga, 1984) to be unconvinced by a radical operant behavioral view of the person because the fundamental behavioristic conception of the subject matter of humanity is so radically opposed to a given religious understanding of persons. Rejecting the paradigm, however, is not synonymous with rejecting the usefulness of the studies emerging from that paradigm, nor does it make one unable to appreciate some elements of the paradigm (after all, a paradigm is not really unintelligible to a person who does not accept it, as Kuhn seemed to have originally hypothesized).

One example of such an evaluative process is my work in evaluating behavior therapy (Jones, 1988). Although I suggested that there is much to commend about behavior therapy, the conclusion of that analysis was that, from the perspective of presuppositions about the person derived from Christian theism, (a) the presumption of determinism (both in radical behavioral and broadened social-cognitive views) is contrary to a Christian belief in limited human agency; (b) behavior therapy's radical atomism, its decomposition of the self into constituent habits, processes, and behaviors, undermines a reasonable understanding of selfhood; (c) the behavioral views of human motivation and the behavioral understandings and valuing of rationality do inadequate justice to what theists regard as humanity's higher potentialities; and (d) the amorality of the approach fails to reflect a coherent vision of human wholeness or maturity that could be compatible with Christian assumptions about the person. These findings represent challenges for the dialogue between religion and psychology, including possible fruitful areas of discourse that can advance both our religious and psychological understandings of the person.

The critical-evaluative mode for relating science and religion calls for the religious believer to evaluate scientific paradigms carefully in light of her or his most fundamental religious presuppositions, which are of relevance to the scientific paradigm. Such a critical-evaluative mode would also help major models and paradigms to be appropriately self-critical about the assumptions that undergird them. For instance, we are more likely to lapse into ethnocentrism when we are never confronted with ethnic diversity. Thus, the challenge of external evaluation from other perspectives might aid us in self-consciously and critically embracing the presuppositions intrinsic to a particular paradigm. As Browning (1987) has argued, "the clinical psychologies, especially, cannot avoid a metaphysical and ethical horizon and, for this reason, they should critically ground these features of their systems rather than unwittingly lapse into them" (p. xi).

Second, the *constructive* mode of relating religious presuppositions to science should occur when religious belief contributes positively to the progress of science by suggesting new modes of thought that transform an area of study by shaping new perceptions of the data and new theories. It is vital to point out that religiously influenced worldviews will not "actually contain [the scientist's] theories" (Wolterstorff, 1984, p. 77) and are not the source of the data by which we evaluate our theories, but our worldviews do influence what we see as the data and what form we expect a theory to take. An example of this is the contribution of Eastern forms of meditation to contemporary behavioral medicine, in which various forms of relaxation practices are among the most effective modes of intervention (Bernstein & Carlson, 1992; Carlson & Hoyle, 1993). Religious scientists will not function as scientists or scholars if they remain perpetually in a passive mode, passing judgment on scientific paradigms by the standards of their religious presuppositions. Rather, they must constructively contribute to the progress of human understanding by putting their suppositions to the test and seeing if they actually contribute to the progress of human knowing.

To the best of my knowledge, there are no clear examples of traditionally religious systems giving rise to major productive scientific paradigms within psychology, although there is a very long history of attempts to interrelate psychology with religion (Vande Kemp, 1984). Perhaps the closest we could get to the model would be the way the quasi-religious view of persons behind the Rogerian person-centered counseling model has produced a tremendous spate of empirical studies of therapist-client relationships, resulting in a deepened understanding of psychotherapy process. The nontraditionally religious foundations of existential psychology and of

Jungian analytic psychology seem indisputable, but these systems have had negligible scientific impact upon the field. Similarly, the transpersonal psychology movement has clear roots in the wave of experimentation with consciousness-altering techniques, largely derived from the eastern religions, that began in the 1960s (Goleman, 1980; Hutch, 1985; Tisdale, in press; Walsh & Vaughan, 1980). As I argued earlier, nontraditionally religious suppositions are fundamental to many positive scientific contributions in the field (e.g., the earlier discussion of Simon, 1990).

Philosopher Alvin Plantinga (1984; Plantinga & Wolterstorff, 1983) has argued that there is no compelling reason for individuals who believe in God not to include the existence of God among the fundamental worldview assumptions brought to the scholarly, scientific task. Plantinga (1984) asserted (and his suggestions for Christian philosophers were meant for all traditionally religious scholars):

> The Christian philosopher quite properly starts from the existence of God, presupposes it in philosophic work, whether or not he can show it to be probable or plausible with respect to premises accepted by all philosophers, or most philosophers, or most philosophers at the leading centers of philosophy. (p. 261)

Albert Ellis and B. F. Skinner, among others, have explicitly made naturalism (to the exclusion of belief in God and the transcendent) a part of the fundamental commitments they bring to the scientific task. If disbelief in the supernatural can suitably be among the control beliefs of some scientists, it would seem that belief in God and related beliefs about human persons could be allowable for others as a part of their control beliefs. "To insist on the objectivity of a science in terms of its separateness from the life experiences, intentions, values, and world views of the persons who create that science is to deny its fundamental character as a human activity" (Bevan, 1991, p. 477).

Although the truth value of the religion that is used to guide prescientific presuppositions will not itself be measured by its fruitfulness in inspiring scientific psychological studies, the truthfulness of the presuppositional conceptions derived from the religious beliefs will be partially tested by the empirical findings. For example, if a Christian understanding of persons suggested that a certain type of existential anxiety was an inevitable part of the human condition (perhaps following the tradition of Søren Kierkegaard; Evans, 1990), then perhaps a therapeutic program to understand, accept, and grow through that anxiety would increase the effectiveness of existing anxiety treatment programs. The failure of such a program to demonstrate empirical utility (assuming a definition of utility compatible with the conception of the phenomenon itself) would not seriously challenge the central truths of Christianity, but would challenge the alleged implications of this religion regarding human anxiety, leading to a productive interchange between science and religion regardless of the outcome of empirical findings.

This brings me to the third form of interaction. The relationship between science and religion must be dialogical and not unilateral. I opened this article by criticizing strongly the type of unilateral relationship that psychology has cultivated toward religion in the past. These roles should not be simply reversed, with religion dictating to the science of psychology (or any science). The relationship between the two must be dialogical (Barbour, 1990; Browning, 1987) or dialectical (Evans, 1982, p. 141). New findings in cosmology, sociobiology, philosophy, anthropology, sociology, and even psychology should infuse and affect the religious enterprise. Just as changing from a geocentric to a heliocentric vision of existence had a number of effects on religious belief, as have other scientific discoveries and revolutions, so also religion must be prepared to change as it engages in a constructive dialogue with psychology.

This commitment to a dialectical relationship between religion and science helps to address the two major concerns that some might raise regarding the dialogical relationship between religious worldview assumptions and the conduct and evaluation of science: (a) that such a move could lead to a "religious imperialism" of religion over science, or (b) that scientific progress could be impeded by the fragmentation of scientific psychology into competing religious camps. Does the present critique open the door to a religious psychology in which the dogmatic assertions of systematic theology replace the attempt to test our beliefs against reality, or in which science could degenerate into unproductive and endless squabbling about the relative merits of the assumptions of different religions as the starting point for psychological science? Although such an outcome may be possible, a commitment to modesty about the influence of control beliefs, to the value of pluralism for enhancing our understanding, and to the possibilities of testing our assertions against reality can prevent both of these undesirable outcomes from occurring. A willingness to establish such a dialogical relationship with religion will necessarily presume the willingness of scientists and professionals to become theologically and philosophically literate and for theologians and philosophers to become scientifically and professionally literate.

Three Major Implications for the Relationship Between the Profession of Psychology and Religion

What are the implications of the present argument for a respectful and productive interrelationship of religion or religious belief with the discipline of applied psychology, particularly with the profession of therapeutic psychology? First, there should be vastly more attention given in clinical training to the philosophical, ethical, and religious dimensions of human psychology and of professional practice. Bergin (1991), London (1986), and O'Donohue (1989) have paved the way for the present proposal by arguing, respectively, for enhanced efforts in clinical training directed at increasing the awareness of practitioners in training to the value, moral, and metaphysical dimensions of clinical theory and practice. I would echo their call for such enhancements and argue for the explicit extension of such efforts to expanded education in the religious domain.

As London (1986, p. xi)) noted, since the publication of the first edition of his book in 1964, hardly any movement has occurred in increasing the awareness and competence of psychotherapists in training with regard to matters ethical, philosophical, or religious. A recent survey reported that 85% of clinical psychologists describe themselves as having little or no training in psychology and religion (Shafranske & Malony, 1990). A substantial fraction of coursework in graduate programs in applied psychology should be devoted to religious traditions, religious and moral dimensions of professional practice, and the philosophical and theological parentage of contemporary systems of thought. Contemporary instruction in history and systems of psychology is a start, but only a start, toward this goal. Only with this sort of preparation can psychologists be aware of their inevitable interaction with the religious. As London (1986) has said, such concerns

> would be better handled if, to begin with, therapists became more vividly aware of their own moral investments and thought more about those of their clients. Students of therapy are too often encouraged to view their clients, themselves, and their work exclusively in terms of dynamics, drives, impulses, defenses, relationships, contingencies, and stimulus-response systems. Too little

attention has been paid to consonant and conflicting ideologies, philosophies, and moral codes which are important to therapists' and patients' lives. (pp. 11-12)

As suggested by Tan (1993), there is now a substantial and growing body of literature that can serve as a resource in the training of the next generation of applied psychologists (e.g., Lovinger, 1984, 1990; Malony, 1988; Miller & Martin, 1988; Propst, 1988; Stern, (1985; Tjeltveit, 1986; Worthington, 1988, 1989, 1991). These resources can be of use in expanding the competencies of psychologists already in practice as well, an enhancement urged by the recent American Psychological Association (1992) revision of its *Ethical Principles of Psychologists and Code of Conduct*, which in its new form mandates that psychologists should view religion as one facet of those human differences that require special attention, sensitivity, and training (Standard 1.08). Division 36 of the APA has for a number of years offered a continuing education workshop on working with religious issues in psychotherapy.

As a corollary to this first point, I would argue that the sectarian or religiously committed programs that require faculty or student compatibility with the religious stance of the institution or attempt to be sensitive to and serve the religious needs of their constituencies serve important functions in the field of professional psychology and in the entire discipline. Promotion of diversity (cf. Baumrind, 1982; Bergin, 1991; Tan, 1993) is served both by the creation of the heterogeneous environments of nonsectarian institutions and of the more focused environments of religiously committed schools, in much the same way that the advancement of women is served both by the complete integration of women into mainline academic programs and by the creation of special women's studies programs (Marsden, 1992; Riesman, 1993). Sectarian programs also raise the visibility of religious influences in applied psychological training, and they guarantee that a plurality of explicitly religious identities will be visible as professional subdisciplines develop. Baylor University (Baptist), Brigham Young University (Church of Jesus Christ of Latter Day Saints), Fuller Graduate School of Psychology (Christian Evangelical), and Rosemead Graduate School of Psychology (Christian Evangelical) are some of the schools that currently offer doctoral level APA-accredited professional training within an institutional context that requires, to greater or lesser degrees, at least some modicum of religious conformity to an explicit tradition. In other words, these institutions and others (perhaps explicitly embracing alternative religious paradigms or purposely representing religious pluralism) can serve as valuable resources for the whole of applied psychology.

Second, there should be greater honesty in public relations by practitioners about the value-ladenness of the mental health enterprise. If it is true (a) that psychotherapeutic practice is influenced by the religious, moral, metaphysical, and philosophical commitments of practitioners and theoreticians (Bergin, 1991; Tjeltveit, 1989); (b) that mental health practitioners are disproportionately nonreligious compared with the general public (Bergin & Jensen, 1990); and (c) that psychotherapy often involves changes in client values (including the moral and religious; Kelly, 1990), then a cultivated public image of psychotherapeutic practice as a value-neutral enterprise is a misrepresentation of reality. Practitioners who are explicit about their value and religious commitments often hear complaints from former clients of "secular" practitioners that the client presumed that religious and moral neutrality would be maintained by the practitioner, only to perceive later that a religious and moral agenda was being pressed by the therapist.

Two areas of contemporary empirical research are relevant to this point. First, despite the frequent claims about a supposedly negative relationship between mental health and religious belief and practice (e.g., Albee, 1991; Ellis, 1980), and despite the frequent negative stereotypes of religious belief and practice that are so much a part of the mental health subculture—such as those in the Diagnostic and Statistical Manual of Mental Disorders (3rd ed., rev.; American Psychiatric Association, 1987; Richardson, 1993)—the best contemporary research suggests a neutral to mildly positive relationship between the two variables (Bergin, 1991; Larson et al., 1992; also see Richardson, 1985, 1992, for reviews of research related specifically to new or "cult" religions).

Furthermore, there is beginning evidence that religious clients actually do respond better to therapy that is adapted to their religious values and concerns (Propst, Ostrom, Watkins, Dean, & Marshburn, 1992). Also, Kelly and Strupp (1992) found that "salvation," an explicitly religious value, was the only single client-therapist value that they studied on which therapists and clients significantly differed (due largely to the nonreligiosity of the therapists in the study) and found it to be the only variable on which patient-therapists similarity significantly predicted the outcome of therapy. Their tentative conclusion was an extremely provocative one: "This suggests that patient-therapist similarity on religious values may serve as a *matching variable*"

(p. 39), meaning that patient-therapist similarity on religious values may be one of the best predictors we have of successful outcome and thus a variable on which client and therapist ought to be matched. We might therefore be acting in the best interest of clients by directing them to therapists of similar religious commitments. The finding of Propst et al. (1992) that religious adaptation of the treatment approach was more important than the personal religious commitment of the therapist may soften the implications of Kelly and Strupp's finding.

Rather than recommitting ourselves to an impossible value neutrality, we should instead recognize that one cannot intervene in the fabric of human life without getting deeply involved in moral and religious matters. It thus seems incumbent on practitioners in our field to press for greater explicitness about this as we present our profession to the public. In addition, much more research in this area is needed.

Finally, greater thought should be put into the development of accountability relationships for individual practitioners, given the sensitivity of their work. At this time, supervisory and consultation relationships tend to focus on the technical aspects of applied practice; we need to join more explicitly in peer accountability in the moral-religious dimensions of our work. Psychologists whose background beliefs are identifiable with an established religious tradition should establish formal accountability relationships of some sort with that group in order to articulate that tradition more responsibly. Practitioners whose religious presuppositions are more idiosyncratic will need to develop more creative accountability linkages with like-minded individuals or persons who are of a compatible spirit so that practitioners with similar religious presuppositions can be helped to articulate that perspective responsibly while respecting the rights of their clients.

Conclusion

Psychological scientists and practitioners are human beings. As such, our activities and efforts as scientists and practitioners are connected to all dimensions of our personhood, including our religious beliefs and commitments, whether those beliefs and commitments are traditional and explicitly codified or nontraditional and implicit. Even in conducting scientific investigations, we act out of the entire web of our understandings of the world, others, and ourselves. Our religious beliefs (broadly understood) help to shape the contours of that web of belief.

My main objectives in this article have been (a) to demonstrate that no hard barrier separates the domain of religious thought and commitment from that domain of human activity that we call science, although at the same time I have argued that science and religion are quite different and should not be confused or overidentified; (b) to stimulate a greater awareness within the psychological community of the importance and pervasiveness of religious beliefs and commitments to the scientific and professional objectives of contemporary psychology; and (c) to encourage an increased awareness and unprecedented explicitness in discussing the part that religious beliefs (broadly defined) play in our scientific and professional activities, including specific proposals for relating religious belief with the science and profession of psychology. Psychology could be enriched by a more explicit exploration of the interface of religion with its scientific and applied activities.

McFall (1991) has recently called for a radical recommitment to advancing clinical psychology as an applied science, and he strongly rejected any compromise that would contaminate science with pseudoscience. His commitment to documented quality of care and of the protection of the public from speculative intervention methods is laudable. Is the present proposal opposed to his initiative? No. Rather I would argue that in the pursuit of empirical documentation of quality of care, we must not lose our understanding of how science and professional practice (derived from scientific and quasi-scientific models) are infused with metaphysical, moral, and religious beliefs. If psychological research and practice are going to be maximally effective in understanding and improving the human condition, psychologists would be well-advised to explicitly explore the connections of their work with the deepest levels of our human commitments. Even if we think about our religious beliefs as biases that we bring to psychological science and practice, we must come to realize first that such biases are intrinsic to our professional activities, in that it is our biases that allow us to perceive and understand anything at all, and second, that the most limiting and dangerous biases are those that are unexamined and hence exert their effect in an unreflective manner.

References

Albee, G. W. (1991)). Opposition to prevention and a new credal oath. *The Scientist Practitioner, 1,* 30-31.

Alston, W. (1985). Conceptual analysis and psychological theory. In S. Koch & D. Leary (Eds.), *A century of psychology as science* (pp. 594-617). New York: McGraw-Hill.

American Psychiatric Association. (1987). *Diagnostic and statistical manual of mental disorders* (3rd ed., rev.). Washington, DC: Author.

American Psychological Association (1992). Ethical principles of psychologists and code of conduct. *American Psychologist, 47,* 1597-1611.

Barbour, I. (1974). *Myths, models, and paradigms.* New York: Harper & Row.

Barbour. I. (1990). *Religion in an age of science: The Gifford lectures, 1989-91* (Vol. 1). New York: Harper Collins.

Baumrind, D. (1982). Adolescent sexuality: Comment of Williams's and Silka's comments on Baumrind. *American Psychologist, 37,* 1402-1403.

Bergin, A. (1980). Psychotherapy and religious values. *Journal of Consulting and Clinical Psychology, 48,* 95-105.

Bergin, A. (1991). Values and religious issues in psychotherapy and mental health. *American Psychologist, 46,* 394-403.

Bergin, A., & Jensen, J. (1990). Religiosity of psychotherapists: A national survey. *Psychotherapy, 27,* 3-7.

Bernstein, D. A., & Carlson, C. R. (1992). Progressive relaxation: Abbreviated methods. In P. M. Lehrer & R. Woolfolk (Eds.). *Principles and practices of stress management* (2nd ed., pp. 53-87). New York: Guilford.

Bersoff, D., & Ogden, D. (1991). APA amicus curiae briefs: Furthering lesbian and gay male civil rights. *American Psychologist, 46,* 950-956.

Bevan, W. (1991). Contemporary psychology: A tour inside the onion. *American Psychologist, 46,* 475-483.

Bloor, D. (1976). *Knowledge and social inquiry.* London: Routledge & Kegan Paul.

Braun, J. (1981). Ethical issues in the treatment of religious persons. In M. Rosenbaum (Ed.), *Ethics and values in psychotherapy* (pp. 131-162). New York: Free Press.

Braybrooke, D. (1987). *Philosophy of social science.* Englewood Cliffs, NJ: Prentice-Hall.

Brown, H. (1977). *Theory, perception, and commitment: The new philosophy of science.* Chicago: University of Chicago Press.

Browning, D. (1987). *Religious thought and the modern psychologies.* Philadelphia: Fortress.

Brunner, E. (1939). *Man in revolt.* (O. Wyon, Trans.). Philadelphia: Fortress.

Carlson, C. R., & Hoyle, R. H., (1993). Efficacy of abbreviated progressive muscle relaxation training: A quantitative review of behavioral medicine research. *Journal of Consulting and Clinical Psychology, 61,* 1059-1067.

Carter, J., & Narramore, B. (1979). *The integration of psychology and theology.* Grand Rapids, MI: Zondervan.

Ellis, A. (1980). Psychotherapy and atheistic values: A response to A. E. Bergin's "Psychotherapy and human values." *Journal of Consulting and Clinical Psychology, 48,* 635-639.

Evans, C. S. (1982). *Preserving the person: A look at the human sciences.* Grand Rapids, MI: Baker. (Original work published 1977)

Evans, C. S. (1990). *Søren Kierkegaard's Christian psychology.* Grand Rapids, MI: Zondervan.

Fletcher, G. (1984). Psychology and common sense. *American Psychologist, 39,* 203-213.

Fowler, R. D. (1990). Psychology: The core discipline. *American Psychologist, 45,* 1-6.

Gergen, K. (1978). Toward generative theory. *Journal of Personality and Social Psychology, 36,* 1344-1360.

Gergen, K. (1985). The social constructionist movement in modern psychology. *American Psychologist, 40*, 266-275.

Gholson, B., & Barker, P. (1985). Kuhn, Lakatos, and Laudan: Applications in the history of physics and psychology. *American Psychologist, 40*, 755-769.

Goleman, D. (1980). Perspectives on psychology, reality, and the study of consciousness. In R. N. Walsh & F. Vaughan (Eds.). *Beyond ego : Transpersonal dimensions in psychology* (pp. 29-35). Los Angeles: Tarcher.

Gorsuch, R. (1988). Psychology of religion. *Annual Review of Psychology, 39*, 201-221.

Hesse, M. (1980). *Revolutions and reconstructions in the philosophy of science*. Bloomington, IN: Indiana State University Press.

Holifield, E. B. (1983). *A history of pastoral care in America: From salvation to self-realization*. Nashville, TN: Abingdon.

Howard, G. (1985). The role of values in the science of psychology. *American Psychologist, 40*, 255-265.

Hutch, R. (1985). Who is it that we treat? The interface between religion and therapy. *Pastoral Psychology, 33*, 152-160.

Jeeves, M. (1976). *Psychology and Christianity: The view both ways*. Downers Grove, IL: InterVarsity.

Jones, S. (1988). A religious critique of behavior therapy. In W. Miller & J. Martin (Eds.). *Behavior therapy and religion: Integrating spiritual and behavioral approaches to change* (pp. 139-170). Newbury Park, CA: Sage.

Jones, S., & Butman, R. 1991). *Modern psychotherapies: A comprehensive Christian appraisal*. Downers Grove, IL: InterVarsity.

Kelly, T. (1990). The role of values in psychotherapy: A critical review of process and outcome effects. *Clinical Psychology Review, 10*, 171-186.

Kelly, T., & Strupp, H. (1992). Patient and therapist values in psychotherapy: Perceived changes, assimilation, similarity, and outcome. *Journal of Clinical and Consulting Psychology, 60*, 34-40.

Kilbourne, B., & Richardson, J. (1984). Psychotherapy and new religions in a pluralistic society. *American Psychologist, 39*, 237-251.

Kirkpatrick, I., & Spilka, B. (1989, August)). *Treatment of religion in psychology texts*. Paper presented at the 97th Annual Convention of the American Psychological Association, New Orleans.

Koch, S. (1981). The nature and limits of psychological knowledge. *American Psychologist, 36*, 257-269.

Koch, S., & Leary, D. (Eds.). (1985). *A century of psychology as science*. New York: McGraw Hill.

Krasner, L., & Houts, A. (1984). A study of the "value" systems of behavioral scientists. *American Psychologist, 39*, 840-850.

Kuhn, T. (1970). *The structure of scientific revolutions* (2nd ed.). Chicago: University of Chicago Press.

Larson, D. B., Sherill, K. A., Lyons, J. S., Craigie, F. C., Jr., Thielman, S. B., Greenwold, M. A., & Larson, S. S. (1992). Associations between dimensions of religious commitment and mental health reported in the *American Journal of Psychiatry and Archives of General Psychiatry*, 1978-1989. *American Journal of Psychiatry, 149*, 557-559.

Laudan, L. (1984). *Science and values: The aims of science and their role in scientific debate*. Berkeley: University of California Press.

Lax, W. E. (1993, August) *Narrative, deconstruction, and Buddhism: Shifting beyond dualism*. Paper presented at the 101st Annual Convention of the American Psychological Association. Toronto, Ontario, Canada.

Livingstone, D. (1988). Changing scientific concepts. *Christian Scholar's Review, 17*, 361-380.

London, P. (1986). *The modes and morals of psychotherapy* (2nd ed.). Washington, DC: Hemisphere.

Lovinger, R. (1984). *Working with religious issues in therapy*. New York: Jason Aronson.

Lovinger, R. J. (1990). *Religion and counseling: The psychological impact of religious belief*. New York: Continuum.

Mahoney, M. (1976)). *Scientist as subject*. Cambridge, MA: Ballinger.

Malony, H. N. (1988). The clinical assessment of optimal religious functioning. *Review of Religious Research, 30*, 3-17.

Manicas, P., & Secord, P. (1983). Implications for psychology of the new philosophy of science. *American Psychologist, 38*, 399-412.

Marsden, G. R. (1992). *The secularization of the academy*. New York: Oxford University Press.

McDonald, H. (1982). *The Christian view of man*. Westchester, IL: Crossway.

McFall, R. M. (1991). Manifesto for a science of clinical psychology. *The Clinical Psychologist, 44*, 75-88.

Meadows, M., & Kahoe, R. (1984). *Psychology of religion*. New York: Harper & Row.

Meehl, P. (1959). Some technical and axiological problems in the therapeutic handling of religious and valuational materials. *Journal of Counseling Psychology, 6*, 255-259.

Meehl, P. (1978). Theoretical risks and tabular asterisk: Sir Karl, Sir Ronald, and the slow progress of soft psychology. *Journal of Consulting and Clinical Psychology, 46*, 806-834.

Meehl, P., Klann, R., Schmieding, A., Breimeier, K., & Schroeder-Slomann, S. (1958). *What then, is man?: A Symposium of theology, psychology, and psychiatry*. St. Louis, MO: Concordia.

Miller, W. R., & Martin, J. (Eds.). (1988). *Behavior therapy and religion: Integrating spiritual and behavioral approaches to change*. Newbury Park, CA: Sage.

Myers, D. G. (1978). *The human puzzle: Psychological research and Christian belief*. New York: Harper & Row.

Myers, D. G., & Jeeves, M. A. (1987). *Psychology through the eyes of faith*. San Francisco: Harper Collins.

National Academy of Sciences (1984). *Science and creationism: A view from the National Academy of Sciences*. Washington, DC: Author.

Oden, T. C. (1984). *The care of souls in the classic tradition*. Philadelphia: Fortress.

O'Donohue, W. (1989). The (even) bolder model: The clinical psychologist as metaphysician-scientist-practitioner. *American Psychologist 44*, 1460-1468.

Olthuis, J. (1985). On worldviews. *Christian Scholar's Review, 14*, 153-164.

Paloutian, R. (1983). *Invitation to the psychology of reli-*

gion. New York: Scott, Foresman.

Peters, R. (Ed.). (1962). *Brett's history of psychology*. New York: Macmillan.

Plantinga, A. (1984). Advice to Christian philosophers. *Faith and Philosophy, 1,* 253-271.

Plantinga, A., & Wolterstorff, N. (Eds.). (1983). *Faith and rationality: Reason and belief in God*. Notre Dame, IN: University of Notre Dame Press.

Politics of the professoriate. (1991, July-August). *The Public Perspective*, pp. 63-87.

Propst, R. L. (1988). *Psychotherapy in a religious framework: Spirituality in the emotional healing process*. New York: Human Sciences Press.

Propst, L., Ostrom, R., Watkins, P., Dean, T., & Mashburn, D. (1992). Comparative efficacy of religious and nonreligious cognitive-behavioral therapy for the treatment of clinical depression in religious individuals. *Journal of Consulting and Clinical Psychology, 60,* 94-103.

Richardson, J. T. (1985). Psychological and psychiatric studies of new religions. In L. B. Brown (Ed.). *Advances in the Psychology of Religion* (pp. 209-223). New York: Pergamon Press.

Richardson, J. T. (1991). Cult/brainwashing cases and freedom of religion. *Journal of Church and State, 33,* 55-74.

Richardson, J. T. (1992). Mental health of cult consumers: Legal and scientific controversy. In J. Schumaker (Ed.), *Religion and Mental Health* (pp. 233-244). New York: Oxford University Press.

Richardson, J. T. (1993). Religiosity as deviance: Negative religious bias in and misuse of the *DSM-III*. *Deviant Behavior, 14,* 1-21.

Riesman, D. (1993). Quixotic ideas for educational reform. *Society, 30*(3). 17-24.

Riger, S. (1992). Epistemological debates, feminist voices: Science, social values, and the study of women. *American Psychologist, 47,* 730-740.

Rizvi, S. A. A. (1988). *Muslim tradition in psychotherapy and modern trends*. Lahore, Pakistan: Institute of Islamic Culture.

Robinson, D. (1981). *An intellectual history of psychology* (Rev. ed.). New York: MacMillan.

Rolston, H. (1987). *Science and religion: A critical survey*. Philadelphia: Temple University Press.

Sarason, S. (1984). If it can be studied or developed, should it be? *American Psychologist, 39,* 477-485.

Shafranske, E. P., & Malony, H. N. (1990). clinical psychologists' religious and spiritual orientations and their practice of psychotherapy. *Psychotherapy, 27,* 72-78.

Simon, H. (1990). A mechanism for social selection and successful altruism. *Science, 250,* 1665-1668.

Sperry, R. W. (1988). Psychology's mentalist paradigm and the religion/science tension. *American Psychologist, 43,* 607-613.

Sperry, R. W. (1993). The impact and promise of the cognitive revolution. *American Psychologist, 48,* 878-885.

Spilka, B., Hood, R., & Gorsuch, R. (1985). *The psychology of religion*. Englewood Cliffs, NJ: Prentice Hall.

Staats, A. (1991). Unified positivism and unification psychology: Fad or new field? *American Psychologist, 46,* 899-912.

Stern, M. E. (Ed.). (1985). *Psychotherapy and the religiously committed patient*. New York: Haworth Press.

Tan, S. Y. (1993, January). *Training in professional psychology: Diversity includes religion*. Paper presented at the midwinter conference of the National Council of Schools of Professional Psychology. La Jolla, CA.

Tisdale, J. R. (in press). Transpersonal psychology and Jesus' Kingdom of God. *Journal of Humanistic Psychology*.

Tjeltveit, A. C. (1986). The ethics of value conversion in psychotherapy: Appropriate and inappropriate therapist influence on client values. *Clinical Psychology Review, 6,* 515-537.

Tjeltveit, A. C. (1989). The ubiquity of models of human beings in psychotherapy; The need for rigorous reflection. *Psychotherapy, 26,* 1-10.

Torrance, T. F. (1980). *Christian theology and scientific culture*. Belfast, Northern Ireland: Christian Journals Limited.

Torrance, T. F. (1984). *Transformation and convergence in the frame of knowledge: Explorations in the interrelations of scientific and theological enterprise*. Belfast, Northern Ireland: Christian Journals Limited.

Toulmin, S. (1962). *Foresight and understanding*. San Francisco: Harper.

Toulmin, S., & Leary, D. (1985). The cult of empiricism in psychology and beyond. In S. Koch & D. Leary (Eds.), *A century of psychology as science* (pp. 594-617). New York: McGraw-Hill.

Vande Kemp, H. (1984). *Psychology and theology in Western thought (1672-1965): A historical and annotated bibliography*. Mill Wood, NY: Kraus.

Van Leeuwen, M. S. (1985). *The person in psychology: A contemporary Christian appraisal*. Grand Rapids, MI: Eerdmans.

Vitz, P. (1977). *Psychology as religion: The cult of self-worship*. Grand Rapids, MI: Eerdmans.

Walsh, R. N., & Vaughan, F. (Eds.). (1980). *Beyond ego: Transpersonal dimensions in psychology*. Los Angeles: Tarcher.

Wegner, D. M., & Vallacter, R. R. (1977). *Implicit psychology*. New York: Oxford University Press.

Wolterstorff, N. (1984). *Reason within the bounds of religion* (2nd ed.). Grand Rapids, MI: Eerdmans.

Woolfolk, R., & Richardson, F. (1984). Behavior therapy and the ideology of modernity. *American Psychologist, 39,* 777-786.

Worthington, E. L. (1988). Understanding the values of religious clients: A model and its application to counseling. *Journal of Counseling, 35,* 166-174.

Worthington, E. L. (1989). Religious faith across the life span: Implications for counseling and research. *The Counseling Psychologist, 17,* 555-612.

Worthington, E. L. (1991). Psychotherapy and religious values: An update. *Journal of Psychology and Christianity, 10,* 211-223.

Wulff, D. (1991). *Psychology of religion: Classic and contemporary views*. New York: Wiley.

Section III
Perspectives on Personhood

Conceptualizations of the nature and essence of humanness are of utmost importance for anyone seeking to understand or work with people. One's perspective on personhood sets the framework by which a person's strengths and weaknesses, capabilities and limitations, health and pathology are perceived. Our perspective on personhood lays the foundation for the modality that guides clinical intervention, structures our personal life and relationships, and even influences our affinities toward particular integration models.

Within psychology there are multiple perspectives on personhood. It makes a difference whether one looks at a person from the perspective of a behavioral, psychoanalytic, humanistic, cognitive, or a systemic practitioner. Each perspective approaches the human person with different assumptions, values, definitions, and prescriptions, and each has its own vision of humanity.

Multiple perspectives also share some commonalities. Each takes a naturalistic, scientific approach to knowledge. The behavioral and psychoanalytic approaches share a deterministic, reductionistic, and materialistic understanding of humanity. Although each is helpful, and at times useful in understanding our human tendencies, each is limited in grasping the whole of our humanity.

For psychologically minded Christians, a foundational understanding of the biblical perspective on humanity is essential. Although the Bible was not written to be a textbook on the human personality, it gives us God's perspective on human nature. Scripture tells us that God formed us from the dust of the earth (Genesis 2:7), that male and female were made in God's image (Genesis 1:27), that it is God who gives us life and breath (Acts 17:25), that we are crowned with glory and honor (Psalms 8:15), that we were made to love (Matthew 5:44-48; Matthew 22:36-40), and to be loved (Psalms 149:4a; Revelation 4:11).

A biblical view of humanity asserts that we were created as part of the natural order but were set apart from it by having been stamped with the image of God (Imago Dei). Scripture also tells us that we are creatures who did not remain as we were created. Although we are still bearers of God's image, our rejection of God in sin has damaged us at our core.

Like psychology, there are within Christianity multiple perspectives on personhood. It makes a difference whether one looks at a person from the perspective of a Reformed, Wesleyan, Anabaptist, Catholic, or Orthodox practitioner. Each perspective approaches humanity with different assumptions, values, and definitions than the other. Each has its own vision of humanity.

As with psychology, Christian approaches also share some commonalities. Each takes a supernatural, non-reductive approach to knowledge. Each recognizes human life as precious because it bears God's image, each finds essential human characteristics in the reflection of God's personal attributes, and for each, Christ is understood as the fullest expression of humanity. For each, it is therefore through redemption in Christ and the work of God in us that Christ-likeness can be realized and through it, our humanity redeemed.

The challenge and complexity of the topic of personhood is reflected in the limited articles in this section. The primary format for conveying a biblical anthropology is in extensive chapters or whole books from a particular theological perspective. For those interested in pursuing a more in depth study in this area, there are several excellent resources listed in the *Suggestions for Further Reading* section. Readers will also find there more extensive resources for the Christian in psychology. Several critique the assumptions and implications of differing psychological theories from a

Christian perspective on personhood and present what they believe are the key biblically-based aspects of humanity that must be addressed in the work of Christian therapists.

The two articles in this section represent works that challenge the Christian psychologist to confront and struggle with their perspective on personhood. In the first article, theologian H. D. McDonald (1986) summarizes a biblical and theological understanding of anthropology in his article, *Biblical Teaching on Personality.* Finding the scientific psychological understanding of personhood incomplete and misleading, McDonald suggests that only through a theistic view of creation can we begin to understand the meaning and purpose of humankind.

After reviewing the essential characteristics of our humanness in Scripture, he contrasts it with the assumptions and implications of the classic behavioral and Freudian perspectives. He challenges what he believes is the psychological propensity to see human beings as things and argues that it should be replaced with the more relational, biblically based I-Thou perspective. McDonald claims that we are spiritual beings who are responsible moral agents with limited freedom. McDonald ends his article by contrasting the opposing truths of the reality of our being: our inherent unity and duality, body and soul, and flesh and spirit. He concludes that the Christian scholar must judge every psychological theory in light of the biblical view of persons.

In the second article, *The Concept of the Self as the Key to Integration,* C. Stephen Evans (1984) argues that any Christian approach to understanding our humanness must be personalistic and that Christians in psychology must take seriously the concept of the self. Focusing on the doctrine of creation, Evans summarizes the Christian view of human persons who have been made in the image of God but formed out of the dust of the earth. Thus we possess both God-like and animal-like capacities.

He contrasts this with the naturalistic worldview found in psychology that, devoid of God in an impersonal universe, careens from reductionism to self-deification. He argues that we know we are more than bigger rats and slower computers, and that without a Christian worldview there is no way of escaping the one-sided naturalistic perspective.

Evans proposes that one solution to this dilemma is the concept of the embodied, responsible self who intends, desires, believes, and takes meaningful action. After raising four reasons people have objected to the concept of the self, Evans identifies the advantages of the concept of the self for understanding persons and the work of clinicians.

May these articles and the suggested readings lead you into a deeper awareness of your own perspective on personhood, and challenge you to ground your life and practice in a true Christian anthropological understanding.

Suggestions for Further Reading: Perspectives on Personhood

Anderson, R. S. (1982). *On being human: Essays on theological anthropology.* Grand Rapids, MI: Eerdmans.
    Explores the implications of a biblical understanding of personhood for understanding sexuality, family relationships, and the meaning of human life.
Balswick, J. O., King, P. E., & Reimer, K. S. (2005). The reciprocating self: Human development in theological perspective. Downers Grove, IL: InterVarsity Press.
    Presenting their model of reciprocal influence between the person and the external social structure in human development, the authors present an interdisciplinary exploration of what it means to be a relational being.
Beck, J. & Demarest, B. (2005). *The human person in theology and psychology: A biblical anthropology for the twenty-first century.* Grand Rapids: Kregel.
    A psychologist and a theologian address the fundamental integrative question of what it means to be human.
Beck, J. (1999). *Jesus and personality theory: Exploring the five-factor model.* Downers Grove, IL: InterVarsity.
    Author looks at prominent themes in Jesus' ministry and teaching, and how they relate to the highly researched Five-Factor Model of personality.

Brown, W. S., Murphy, N., & Malony, H.N. (1998). *Whatever happened to the soul?: Scientific and theological portraits of human nature.* Minneapolis, MN: Fortress.

This edited volume presents a collection of essays that relate cognitive neuroscience to conceptualizations of the human soul. It explores the implications of both dualistic and reductive materialistic approaches to the mind and brain, from psychological, theological and historical perspectives.

Browning, D.S., & Cooper, T.D. (2004). *Religious thought and the modern psychologies.* 2nd Ed., Minneapolis: Fortress Press.

Applies the hermeneutical approach to create a greater understanding of the ethical and quasi-religious assumptions that underlie modern psychological theories and to encourage the dialogue between psychology and religion.

Burk, T. J. (Ed.). (1987). *Man and mind: A Christian theory of personality.* Hillsdale MI: The Hillsdale College Press.

In this edited volume psychologists including Vitz, Vander Goot, and Van Leeuwen, as well as several reformed theologians explore personality theorizing.

Evans, C. S. (1977). *Preserving the person: A look at the human sciences.* Downers Grove. IL: InterVarsity Press.

In this classic work, Evans identifies the deficits in modern scientific thinking about the human person and in the writings of Comte, Freud, Watson and Skinner. He proposes ways in which scientists can integrate their Christian faith with their scientific understanding of the person.

Green, J. B. (Ed.). (2004). *What about the soul?: Neuroscience and Christian anthropology.* Nashville, TN: Abingdon.

This edited book containing essays from biblical scholars, Wesleyan theologians, psychologists and scientists addressing mind-body issues in light of modern neurobiology.

Hoekema, A. A. (1986). *Created in God's image.* Grand Rapids, MI: Eerdmans.

From a Reformed theological perspective Hoekema reviews the biblical understanding of humankind being made in the image of God but marred by sin.

Jeeves, M. A. (1997). *Human nature and the millennium.* Grand Rapids, MI: Baker.

Surveying past integration efforts, Jeeves challenges existing concepts of integration and encourages Christian psychologists to engage in a more scientific approach to research and practice in psychology and neuroscience

McDonald, H. D. (1981). *The Christian view of man.* Westchester, Illinois: Crossway.

McDonald reviews the Biblical and historical concepts of personhood.

Packer, J. I. (1978). *Knowing man.* Westchester, Illinois: Cornerstone Books.

In this classic and very readable work by the British theologian, he explores the nature and purose of humanness.

Packer, J. I. & Howard, T. (1985). *Christianity: The true humanism.* Waco, TX: Word.

Exploring the themes of freedom, hope, dignity, and virtue, the authors explore the meaning of humanness.

Speidell, T. H. (Ed.). (2002). *On being a person: A multidisciplinary approach to personality theories.* Eugene, OR: Wipf & Stock.

Twelve authors from varied disciplines wrote chapters focusing on the person and personhood.

Tournier, P. (1957). *The meanings of persons.* New York: Harper& Row, Publishers.

This classic work from one of the earliest integrationists explores in the writings of Freud, Jung and the Bible the meaning of personhood and applies it to counseling cases.

Tournier, P. (1964). *The whole person in a broken world.* New York: Harper & Row.

Through case studies explores the "ills" of modern humans and the role of the church in reconnecting humanity to their spiritual dimension.

Van Leeuwen, M. S. (1987). Personality theorizing within a Christian world view. In T.J. Burke (Ed.), *Man and mind: A Christian theory of personality* (pp. 171-198). Hillsdale, MI:

Using Maddi's approach to personality theorizing this article identifies core statements about personality from a biblical perspective.

Van Leeuwen, M. S. (1985). *The person in psychology: A contemporary Christian appraisal.* Grand Rapids, MI: Eerdmans.

    Addresses both theoretical and methodological issues in personhood and how it relates to the image of God as conceived in Christian theology.

Walsh, B. J., & Middleton, J. R. (1984). *The transforming vision: Shaping a Christian worldview.* Downers Grove, IL: InterVarsity Press.

    The chapter entitled, Based on Creation, is a thoughtful introduction to the concept of the *imago Dei.*

Watts, F. (2002). *Theology and psychology.* Hampshire, England: Ashgate.

    Fresh insights on the relationship between Christian belief and psychology are offered from a British perspective.

14

Biblical Teaching on Personality

H. D. McDonald
London Bible College

In the first chapter, it was pointed out that a significant number of Christians who work in the field of psychology see the primary task of integration as having our Christian commitment determine the fundamental presuppositions we bring to the social-scientific task. To accomplish this, we must know what the faith has to say about human nature. Every Christian in psychology, regardless of his or her views of integration, would agree that it is imperative for Christians to be informed about what the Bible and Christian theology have to say concerning the nature of human existence.

And yet it is very difficult to find a balanced, thoughtful presentation of what the Bible and Christian theology have to say about humanity. Many naive personality-theories have been proposed in religious books, each promoted as the Christian personality-theory. This chapter summarizes the essence of biblical and theological teachings about anthropology, the doctrine of humanity. The balanced and scholarly conclusions will challenge the reader to think deeply about the interface between Christian belief and psychological theory.

The question, "What is man?" is, according to Immanuel Kant, the last of the four basic issues which have to be faced in the pursuit of knowledge. And indeed, this question has been the last in the order of historical discussion. The immediate past and the present age have, in parallel with a growing interest in the conditions of the human person, witnessed the establishment of psychology as a creditable scientific methodology. Much of what we know today about man, about the psychological and sociological laws that govern his life, about his actions and his reactions, was unknown in past ages. Yet in spite of the abundance of material at the disposal of the modern researcher, the judgment of Martin Heidegger is essentially true: No age has known so much, and so many things about man, as does ours, and yet no age has known less than ours what man is.

The reason why this is so is not difficult to discern. We now live in what has come to be designated a post-Christian age, so that explanations of man's existence and nature are presently sought without reference to God. It is, in fact, characteristic of our times that the reality of a divine Creator and providential Ruler is either denied outright or politely ignored. The theistic view of the world is given short shrift by the makers of modern thought, with the result that accounts of man's presence and purpose in the world are elaborated solely in the context of the mundane and the natural. Earlier certainties about man, based on biblical data, are summarily dismissed as the antiquated notions of a prescientific age. And gone with them is that security man had in regarding himself as God's creature in God's world.

Yet in the final analysis it is the biblico-religious account of persons which accords best with our convictions about ourselves. We know that we carry deep within ourselves, as a property of our essential natures, a moral and spiritual sensitivity which gives us a special value and significance. In contrast with the many contemporary theories of personality, the dramatists and poets of former times better understood people for who and what they are because they more readily acknowledged the biblical view of persons which they saw validated in real life.

Taken as a methodology, a scientific psychological perspective on man may be authentic enough as far as it goes, or can go. But if taken as a final statement of all that belongs to human personhood, then its conclusions must be regarded as incomplete and misleading. The root meaning of the term *psychology* is "the science of the soul," but many psychological theorists deny to man the presence of soul. To regard psychology merely as the science of behavior is to leave unknown and unreached that existential selfhood behind and present in observable behavior patterns. For "however important the body may be, it can never be regarded as the whole self or even the most essential part of the self" (Stout, 1920, p. 661). The truth of the matter is that these realities about human beings—the person, the soul, the consciousness, and the self—are beyond the range of psychological probing and, indeed, of philosophical proving. As the ultimate constituents of personal human life they have their source and secret in the mystery of life itself.

The presence of life is an impenetrable mystery. Life just is; there is no scientific explanation of its source or its existence. Science can and does explain many things about *living*, but *life* itself it does not understand. It is not enough to say that life results from the activity of living phenomena, for living phenomena themselves presuppose life. In addition to the physical and the psychical or self-conscious, which are in their measure accessible to science, there is a life-principle which cannot be caught in any scientist's net, and which in union with or, better perhaps, in its action upon the physical and the psychical, gives an individual uniqueness and purpose as a person. Clearly, answers to the questions of the "whence?" and the "what?" of life are not to be sought within any actions or processes of the inorganic. Only by taking seriously the theistic view of creation can an entirely worthy and a completely acceptable explanation of the origin of life be laid bard. It is God, the living God, who "gives to all men life and breath and everything" (Acts 17:25, RSV). By means of the union of God's breath and dust from the ground, man became a living being (Gen. 2:7). Thus the life-principle which makes man man has its source in God.

Man as a Divine Creation

The world of inanimate things and animals was brought into being by God's declared word. "God said ... and it was so." God's *speech* was his creative act. Now God was more intimately involved in his creation of man than in his creation of the inanimate world and animals. At the same time he maintained a distance. Here there was the union of God's otherness from man—"the Lord God formed man of dust from the ground" (Gen 2:7, RSV)—and his likeness to man— "So God created man in his own image, in the image of God he created him" (Gen. 1:27, RSV). Thus man is at once of nature and of God, a combination of dust and deity. "As the Creator's creation, man reflects his Maker in mind and conscience and is both a part of nature yet distinct from it' (Henry, 1976, p. 248).

In creating man, the living God spoke and acted. And in his speech and acts there is man's life. By imparting breath to the man he formed, man lives (Gen. 2:7; cf. Rev. 11:11); and if God "should take back his spirit to himself, / and gather to himself his breath, / all flesh would perish together, / and man would return to dust" (Job 34:14-15, RSV; cf. Pss. 90:3; 104:29-30; Eccles. 12:7).

Such is man's dependence on the living God for his existence and his being that man's breath and spirit can be declared one with God's breath and spirit (Job 27:3; cf. 33:4; Gen. 6:3; Isa. 42:5). Man's life is maintained by everything that proceeds out of the mouth of the Lord (Matt. 4:4). Man's being is from God and his very life continues because of him. So throughout the Old testament revelation, God makes appeals to man on the grounds of being his Creator (e.g., Deut. 4:32; Isa. 40:28; 43:15). Furthermore, because of man's creation in the image and likeness of God, there is a kinship between the human spirit and the divine which constitutes the grounds for the appeal of the gospel.

Essential Characteristics of Human Beings

The Image of God

Human beings are unique. This fact is affirmed in their creation by a special resolve and distinct act of God; this sets them apart from the rest of the created order. Men and women are beings capable of fellowship with God himself, for they are created in his image.

The declaration of Genesis 1:27 is specific: "God created man in his own image, in the image of God he created him; male and female he created them" (RSV; cf. 5:2; 9:6). Man not only has his life from God, he has a fundamental likeness to God. Genesis declares both man and woman to be the bearers of the divine image; consequently, they are equally the objects of his concern and care. But what precisely is to be understood by the expression "the image of God"? This question has given rise to a large literature in which various answers have been given. These answers include assertions that the "image of God" refers to our bodily form, our existence as spirits, our lordship over nature, our existence as male and female, and our rational and moral personality (McDonald, 1981).

We suggest that all three views can be subsumed under the one concept of "sonship." Each of them is but one aspect of the deeper and more fundamental truth that we are all God's sons and daughters. All of the views we have mentioned coalesce in this idea. Herein lies the essence of the image in which man was created. Human beings were created for sonship; such was our original state before God. This does not mean that we may appeal to a natural and continuing kinship with God to assure every individual a ready acceptance with God, for the human race has rejected and sinned away this sonship. Nevertheless, the personal appeal of the gospel rests on the sonship which belongs to every person. The explanation of this fact is that the image of God itself, although defaced by sin, has not been totally destroyed. James Orr (1897) points out: "As made by God, and as standing in his normal relation to Him, man is without doubt a son.... The fact that the title "son of God" should belong to *any*, already implies a natural kinship between God and man, else the higher relationship would not be possible. If there were not already a God-related element in the human spirit, no subsequent act of grace could confer on man this spiritual dignity" (pp. 119-120; cf. Acts 17:28).

Sometimes in the history of Christian doctrine one aspect of the God-man relationship has been given exclusive emphasis to the denial of its opposite. In deism, God was so separated from man that the divine and human were thrown into absolute opposition. German speculative theology, on the other hand, under the influence of Georg Hegel, so accentuated the kinship between God and man as to present man as but an aspect of deity. Both these antitheses are false if taken by themselves. The truth is that there is between God and man an actual inner relationship, a connection between the divine spirit and the human spirit which makes man capable of receiving from God his living image.

The incarnation of God the Son is the supreme demonstration of this truth. For in the one person of the Word made flesh there is a union of the human and divine so close and intimate as to constitute Christ the perfect image of God (Col. 1:15; cf. Rom. 8:29; 2 Cor. 4:4; Col. 3:10). In this regard Christ is the personification of the biblical doctrine of man. To get a knowledge of the true essence of anything, as Aristotle has taught us, we should look at its best specimens, and not at its ruder and cruder forms. Christ is the best of humanity. For not only is he the organ of the divine revelation to humanity, he is our only example of what man was meant to be. All human beings are measured by this man. In him we have some idea of what kinship to God means. His eternal sonship in relation to the Father provided the pattern, the original image, in which man was created. All persons were created for sonship in the image of Christ's sonship. In this sense he was the archetypal man. By becoming man the uncreated Son revealed the ideal according to which human nature was originally planned. And having become man, he is now the head of a new humanity renewed to sonship "after the image of its creator" (Col. 3:10, RSV; cf. 1 Cor. 11:7; 2 Cor. 3:18).

Man's permanent dignity derives, then, from the reality of the *imago Dei* (the image of God) in which he was created. It is this relationship to God which gives him his unique worth in comparison to the rest of creation. Man was divinely fashioned for a high role in God's world. He was crowned with glory and honor (Ps. 8:5). A crown is a sign of a special status and standing. "As God's imagebearer, man was to hear God's word addressed to him and to respond in the joy of adoring obedience" (Henry, 1979, p. 215). Alas, however, for man as he now is, the crown has become somewhat tarnished, and slipped sideway on, if not altogether fallen off, his head. For no longer does the human race bear the image in its full splendor. No longer does man live before God as a son, and no longer does he act as a brother toward his fellows. How are the mighty fallen! Man soiled and spoiled his status with God. This is vividly evident in Genesis 5:3, for instead of reading that man was created in God's image (cf. Gen. 1:27), we are told that Adam "became the father of a son in his own likeness, after his image" (RSV).

Personhood

From the biblical declaration of man's creation in the image of God it follows that each member of the human family is to be regarded as a unique personhood. The Christian doctrine of God as personal carries with it this same certainty about man. The one conviction is indeed the guarantee of the other; both stand or fall together. Yet while Scripture uniformly presents both God and man as personal, it does not give any formal definition of the personhood of either party. Here, as is often the case, lack of exact definitions in the Bible results in our being unable to extract from it the precise nomenclature required by scientific psychology. Biblical revelation is less concerned with scientific psychology than with a presentation of man in terms of his relationship to God, to fellow man, and to natural phenomena. Throughout the biblical amount there is a constant awareness of the unique existence and personal identity of the individual, of a distinctive essence in each man by virtue of which he can be characterized as a selfhood. This requires that he speak as an "I" and be spoken to as a "you."

Person and personality. The term *personality* is generally held to be derived from the Latin *persona*, the mask worn by ancient actors. "Personality," then, literally refers to an individual's outward appearance or the role one plays. It may be viewed as the general impression a person makes. As a result of this impression, one individual may be described as having a pleasing disposition, another as being morose, and so forth. All such words are really adjectives which indicate the nature of an individual's behavior. Many psychologists, however, deliberately identify the two concepts, person and personality, and contend that a person is what his personality displays. There is, they say, nothing else behind the mask. Thus both terms are given the same definition: "person" and "personality" are defined as the sum of behavior traits bound together (or in the process of being bound together) into a particular unity to constitute a human selfhood. A variety of personality theories have been formulated in attempts to synthesize the manifold data of psychology into a coherent holistic view of human nature. But in the end, of course, each personality theory is built on assumptions about man and the essential characteristics of his being.

It is beyond our purposes to discuss the psychology of personality or to adjudicate between the hundreds of definitions of personality which are available. It is enough to observe here that two of the major personality theories are altogether conditioned by their initial approach. The classic behavioral view puts the emphasis on the external influences affecting the individual, the classic Freudian view on his internal structure. We will briefly explore these differing perspectives to highlight their implications for human personhood.

Behaviorism, as a body of psychological doctrine, had its birth in the wide acceptance of philosophical materialism, an understanding of the universe in terms of matter in motion. John B. Watson's (1913) article "Psychology as the Behaviorist Views It" provided the blueprint for this new psychological realism. Supported by experiments on animals which suggested that behavior results from reactions to stimuli, Watson set about establishing human psychology on an objective basis of external observable actions. Eliminating all conscious elements from psychological data, he sought to present a picture of the human organism as a sort of physical machine. Man is simply what he does. And so Watson states, "I believe we can write a psychology ... and ... never use the terms consciousness, mental states, mind, content, will, introspectively veritable imagery, and the like" (p. 167). Accordingly, the classical behaviorist presents man as a curious sort of empty shell without mind or soul. There is nothing in the individual beyond his overt bodily actions in response to stimuli. Classic behaviorism leaves no place for moral action. It makes a mockery of all ethical judgments based on anything other than physical phenomena, and so denies the existence of a divine moral absolute which calls for man's will response. The behaviorist denies the existence of "willed" events distinct from physical ones. By declaring all acts to be bodily functions, all man's behavior becomes, at least in theory, entirely predictable.

The consistent behaviorist must accept that if human actions are purely the result of irresistible universal laws (i.e., are mechanically determined),

then all life itself has no reason. And "if there is no rational grounds for anything, it is useless to ask the behaviorist why he writes books apparently aimed at inducing his reader on rational grounds to change his opinions" (Hodgson, 1930, p. 29). For if the basic behaviorist premise is correct, then the doctrines of behaviorism are nothing other than the physical activity of a number of like-bodied psychologists. Opposing theories could claim to be equally true, since they are also the reflexive reactions prevailing in the bodies of rival psychologists. Both philosophical materialism and its offspring psychological behaviorism suffer "from one great defect": they take "from man his significance in the cosmic scheme of things" and deny "reality to his mind" (MacMurray, 1957, p. 123). Because consciousness is denied, the person disappears from behavioristic psychology, a result which is unacceptable to the Christian. Classic behaviorism, then, though it may have its uses, cannot be judged to have an adequate view of the whole person.

Is classic Freudian psychology any more acceptable? According to J. C. Flugel (1945), Freud's "outstanding achievement" was "to have opened up a vast region (the unconscious psychic) which before him had been suspected to exist, but never entered by a scientist" (p. 293). It was on the basis of his hypothesized psychological structure of the human person that Freud developed his analytic method as a means to explore and explode man's inner stresses. This method led the way to the healing of psychological wounds and can be used by the Christian pastor as a helpful handmaid in applying the gospel to human needs. But we are concerned here with the propositions about religion and the nature of personhood which Freud believed to follow from his basic hypotheses and findings.

Freud regarded man as the product of his environment. In his efforts to relate to the environment, he develops a psychological neurosis. This fundamental neurosis, this unconscious reservoir of instinctual urges, is the cause of all man's woes. It gets its start from conflicts set up in early childhood and colors the person's outlook throughout life. From this perspective, Freud makes his theological pronouncements. Religion, he declares, "is comparable to a childhood neurosis" (1934. p. 92); and God is an illusion produced by the instinctual desire for protection, the outworking of the innate father--complex (1940, p. 237). Morality and conscience likewise have their origin in the conflict between the unconscious factors and the conscious in the developing individual.

Two implications of Freud's analysis of the structure of the human individual bring his view of man into conflict with that of Scripture. The first is *determinism*. Freud held that the origins and causes of all conscious action are to be found in the unconscious, which lies outside of the control of the individual. Conscious action is clearly a by-product of unconscious processes, and is thus determined by those processes. The conscience is also seen as a product of unconscious forces. The conscience, which Freud called the superego, is created by the incorporation into the self of the moral standards of society. Conscience, for Freud, is little more than society's way of imposing its collective demands on the individual. In the end, asserted Freud, all human action is determined by the interaction between the unconscious and the superego, neither of which is under the person's control.

It follows that the individual does not have responsibility for his or her deeds, a conclusion which undermines the traditional basis of general ethics (Smethurst, 1955). Such a fatalistic attitude regarding human nature affects moral conduct in two ways. First, there is a tendency (openly affirmed by many psychiatrists) to say that people cannot be blamed for their unethical ways since they are the victims of forces beyond their control. Second, Freud's thesis has weakened the desire to strive for right living in contemporary society, for it leads to the conclusion that one need not feel a sense of guilt for failure to do so.

The other implication which clashes with Scripture is that of *irrationality*. According to Freud, reason is the tool of the unconscious instincts. It is the instincts which determine and control the operations of the conscious mind. The sole function of reason is discovering means for the satisfaction of those instincts which employ it. For Freud the instincts are the real movers of human activity. "Reason, in other words, is a mechanism; it is the engine of the personality, and instinct is the steam that sets it going. And, since reason can operate only when driven by the impulsive force of instinct, it can proceed only along the path which instinct indicates to the goal which instinct dictates" (Joad, 1948, p. 263). This means that the reason is no longer to be regarded as free, and that all reasoning is but rationalization. But this is surely not a right view of the nature and function of reason in man, who was created for fellowship with God.

Maybe earlier ages gave to the reason too high a place in the catalogue of those properties which distinguish man from the rest of created beings. But to virtually denude man of reason altogether by declaring it the tool of the instincts is to make man no different from the animal kingdom and to deny him that otherness from the rest of creation on which the biblical account insists. Man's thoughts are not indeed God's thoughts, but man can have thoughts and can know truth. In fact, God would have man "reason together" with him (Isa. 1:181; cf. 1 Sam. 12:7; Job 13:3), and instructs him, "Be not like a horse or a mule, without understanding, which must be curbed with bit and bridle, else it will not keep with you" (Ps. 32:9, RSV). It is with rational beings God would have communion. Thus throughout Scripture we are called both to think and to understand.

In the Freudian view, people have neither true rationality nor true freedom. The effects on modern thought have been dramatic: the belief that we can know truth, the position that we are responsible moral beings, and our motivation to exercise moral restraint have all been undermined. Of course, psychoanalytic theory has also afforded many benefits. It has helped us to recognize that certain distresses and mental illnesses are beyond relief by mere physical antidotes. It has rightly contended that the area of conscious life is not of the same order as the physical. This is a profound insight with the potential for much good, for all mental disorders had previously been attributed to physical causes. But with the good has come the bad. Owing their allegiance to biological reductionism, the major spokespersons of psychoanalysis expended mechanical determinism from physical causation to all of the sequences of man's mental life. Psychoanalysts, anxious to secure for themselves the status of scientists, denied that the psychic in man can ever generate free action.

The truth is, however, that while our actions are in some respects predictable, we are nevertheless free beings. Thus, while "on the level of psychological analysis … freedom seems impossible … on the level of moral personality, freedom is essential" (Robinson, 1911, p. 292). The being of man cannot be absolutely determined. Man exists in the union of soul and body. The existence of human beings may "be thought of as material in so far as their behaviour is a passive functioning in accordance with forces acting on or through them, and spiritual in so far as it is the expression of their having made up their minds to do this or that. We use the word freedom to describe this ability of the spiritual being to act on purpose as contrasted with the inability of the material thing to do more than respond willy nilly to stimuli" (Hodgson, 1956, p. 171).

At the beginning of this section, reference was made to the distinction often drawn between person and personality. Personality, it was stated, is the role played by the person. It is with the personality that psychoanalysis is concerned. On the fundamental reality of personhood, the self, the soul, it has nothing to say, for into this ultimate citadel its techniques cannot penetrate. The psychoanalyst is, as it were, on the stage with the actor. He gives directions and makes corrections to assure that the mask is rightly adjusted so that the actor might better play his role in the community drama. Yet while the psychologist may make the mask easier for the actor to wear, he cannot get behind it; nor is he allowed into the actor's private dressing room where he may take off the mask to disclose his true selfhood. There the individual is with himself alone, beyond the reach of any probing intruder. Only the God who knows what is in us (John 2:25) can uncover what lies within the inner sanctuary of our soul. It is there the Spirit of God enters to bear witness with our human spirit that we are children of God.

Persons and things. By standing over against the world of natural phenomena, man becomes aware of his otherness. In relation to them he has a feeling of aliveness and a realization of selfhood. By confrontation with things, man knows that he is not a thing and so learns the use of "I" and "me." The reaction called for by the world of things is in marked contrast with that called for by the world of persons. Things are neutral in relation to human individuality. Things are there to be used by persons, not the other way around.

Martin Buber (1937), in his small but influential volume *I and Thou*, has made the fruitful distinction between our relations to the world of persons ("I-thou") and our relations to the world of things ("I-it"). His main contribution to our understanding of man is his deepening of our awareness of the other person, who is viewed not as an "it," but as a distinctive subject, "thou." Too often in the modern world of commerce, social science, and medicine, the person has been used as an "it" to increase production and advance knowledge. Humans have wrongly been reduced to mere means toward a specific end. From the Christian point of view, we also see the world transgressing the divine charge to love one's neighbor as oneself. It is essential to move in the world of persons and treat them as equals. For, as Paul Tournier (1957) has said, either "we move in the world of things, phenomena, personages, and God himself becomes just an abstract idea; or else we enter the world of persons; God becomes personal; we meet persons everywhere" (p. 190).

Most scientific disciplines study human beings as things. Anatomy and physiology study humans as somatic machines; psychology studies the mind as a brain mechanism; economics sees people as instruments of production and consumption; and to the sociologist, individuals are mere fractional elements in society. Each one of these disciplines has frequently presented its reductionist account of man as the full story about him. But not one of them has the full story; indeed, while each one of them has certainly laid hold of an aspect of what it is to be a man, all of them together fail to give the complete picture. In truth, they have all missed out on what is absolute about man, his fundamental personhood. Personhood, not "thinghood," is essential to being human.

Our interests turn readily to things; we seek in things satisfaction and fullness of life. But the more we become absorbed in things, the less truly personal we ourselves become. We become slaves of things, victims of their tyranny. "Everything with which we come in contact takes on the tone-quality of thing or of person, according as to whether we are ourselves a thing or a person, in respect to it" (Tournier, 1957, p. 183). In relating to others as persons, we reaffirm our own personhood.

The reality of personhood. To be a person is to be a self, a responsible moral agent with at least limited freedom. But it is presently questioned by psychologists and philosophers whether indeed man is a self in any sense which gives him the right to maintain that he has what in religious language is called a soul. Some dogmatic psychologists disregard the idea of soul; some empirical philosophers strongly deny the idea of self. Such repudiation of the ideas of soul and self is for the Christian believer a serious matter. Why?

First, if there is no soul, what then becomes of the possibility of life beyond the grave? For if all we are is a conglomeration of behavior patterns, their disintegration at death leaves nothing to endure beyond. But Christians are certain that there is in man a soul, a higher and inner nature which is related to, yet distinguished from, the body. Christians believe that the spiritual substance of the soul can live a life of its own after separation from the physical body, which is subject to corruption.

Second, if there is no self, that is, no seat of man's thinking, willing and doing, what then can be said about man's freedom and moral responsibility? They simply do not exist! But the reality of moral responsibility is recognized everywhere. This recognition requires a picture of man as the possessor "of a sort of inner man or self, who is essentially mysterious and unpredictable: the person's 'soul' or his 'will.' This inner man is inviolable, and not acted upon by causes" (Wilson, 1961, p. 20).

Many have attempted to repudiate these notions, but it is our conviction that the idea of self is given to us by and assured for us in our own self-awareness. We know ourselves to be our self, and that is, as Hywel Lewis (1961) contends, "as direct a way as any" (p. 210). The self is known intimately, personally, and existentially, in just being one's self. True, while we know that we are a selfhood, we do not fully understand the self that we are. For we "are just as mysterious to ourselves as we are familiar" (Trethowan, 154, p. 172). Yet we can most surely affirm that, from a psychological point of view self-consciousness of subsistent being constitutes man's uniqueness and subjectivity, just as does, from a theological point of view, his being created in the image of God. We begin with the "I am."

It may appear from the foregoing that the terms *self* and *soul* have been used synonymously. And from one point of view this is perfectly legitimate. If, however, differentiation is necessary, we will take the term *self* as the more general to specify the conscious subject of experience or, as stated by Leonard Hodgson (1930), "the spiritually alive subject of consciousness" (p. 10). The self is the experience of self-consciousness. To define what is meant by the soul is, however, more difficult. Soul cannot be identified with mind (for a man still possesses a soul, if he should lose his mind). Nor, of course, is the soul to be identified with the body. Later in this chapter we will see that soul is best defined as the inner aspect of a person's being.

Immortality

From the distinction affirmed here between the soul and the body, the spiritual and material elements of man's nature, there follows the idea of the person's immortality. There are powerful philosophical considerations which can be urged to corroborate the biblical presentation of the soul of man as fitted for eternity. There are also the facts of man's instinctive belief in his own continued existence and his persistent high estimate of his own value.

From his first appearance, man seems to have thought of himself as something special. He has felt himself to be distinct from the rest of the created order and to be other than a creature of passing time. He senses eternity in his heart (Eccles. 3:11), and he also believes that even death cannot finally annihilate his essential life. The idea that man possesses something immortal is one of humanity's strongest convictions. It is not a conclusion to which he has come as a result of hard thinking, but rather as a result of a strong feeling that his person possesses qualities which are imperishable, qualities which need eternal scope for their fulfillment. Unless we can be sure of immortality, energy and zest will necessarily be drained out of living. And that will mean loss of dignity, mockery of the self's hidden wealth, and negation of all things that are worthwhile.

While it must be allowed that the idea that immortality is an instinctive belief has its source in Platonic philosophy, the value of the human person as a premise for the everlastingness of the soul has a specific Christian origin. It is through Christ that the recognition that men and women have enduring value in their own right first found expression in human history. Christ gave his authority to the view that man possesses an immortal nature. Christ saw man as a spiritual being with a Godward inclination. For all his regard for man's body, Christ's supreme concern was for man's eternal welfare. He taught that true wealth is that of the soul. It profits nothing to gain the whole world and lose one's essential selfhood (Matt. 16:26), for life is more than food and the body than clothing (Matt. 6:25). In the pagan world of Christ's time, as in the pagan world since, however polluted or polished that world may be, the human person has always been regarded as having no lasting worth. Celsus, that early opponent of Christianity, even while proclaiming his disdain for the gospel, is a witness to one of its supreme blessings to human society. "The root of Christianity," he declares, "is its excessive valuation of the human soul, and the absurd idea that God takes an interest in man." The biblical view of man suggests that he is destined for some other port than any on these earthly shores. What man is in mind, heart, and spirit, in the range of his interests and the lift of his soul, can be explained only on the supposition that he is preparing, and being prepared, for another and vaster life hereafter.

Morality

It is the uniform teaching of Scripture that man in his very essence is a moral being. In a profound sense, to be human is to be morally capable and vice versa. To act according to moral principles is a human obligation. There must, then, be "something common to men in virtue of which they can be moral agents and can be treated as such" (Paton, 1955, p. 301). Paul tells us there is an inherent awareness in all men of the reality of a natural moral law to which they ought to subscribe (Rom. 2:14-15). So man is in himself a moral being with moral obligations and responsibilities. Moral neutrality in a being otherwise so evidently the possessor of rationality and freedom is impossible. Man "as created was like God in that he was good. He was not created morally neutral—indeed the whole notion of a morally neutral person is a monstrosity—but his nature was positively directed to right as opposed to wrong. Goodness was not something that came after he was created, but something that was stamped upon him from the beginning" (Machen, 1965, p. 147).

Consequently, the "good" deeds of a man need not be designated "virtuous sins." All of a man's acts are, indeed, the acts of a sinner; but not all his acts are sinful acts. A man decides to open his door and to go for a walk. It is certainly a sinner who goes through the activities, but these acts cannot, on that account, be designated "sinful." Similarly, a woman's decision to be generous to others in want, in spite of the many pressures to act otherwise, cannot be accounted "sinful," although, again, it is the act of a sinner.

Humans have an ability for morality and a capacity for religion. The key word of morality is "duty," and the key word of religion is "grace." As regards duty a person can act freely, while as regards grace he can but receive humbly. Thus morality is concerned with activities freely performed in which there is the possibility of doing otherwise and for which the agent is credited with either praise or blame. Religion, on the other hand, is a grace relationship with One whose mercy we desire and salvation we need. The presuppositions of each are consequently different. Responsibility is the essential note of morality, while responsiveness is the requisite attitude of religion.

The apostle Paul took the universality of conscience in man as attestation of his moral nature, and the universality of the sense of guilt arising out of its judgments as evidence of man's innate moral awareness (see Acts 23:1; Rom. 2:15; 9:1; 13:5). Paul taught that conscience is a natural property of man; it is not an addition to his being but a reality of his essential selfhood as rational and free. Conscience can stir man to nobler deeds as it can awaken in him a sense of need of God's forgiveness. Conscience, then, reveals man "to belong to the moral order" (Denney, 1918, p. 215).

The ideas of the soul's immortality and man's morality interrelate. It is, of course, true that a denial of man's immortality does not foreclose the possibility of a good life. There are those who, while believing that death ends existence, still find goodness to be good. They would do well to consider the question, But why be good? What is the good of goodness anyway?

The shortening of the soul's career to the span of this life alone necessarily brings about an impoverishment of our interests and a narrowing of our initiatives. It is the hope of life immortal that gives life its purpose and its poise. If there is, indeed, an eternal dimension to which our present experiences may be oriented, then a sense of worthwhileness is brought into the business of living. But if all come to the same end why bother to be good? Why should one follow, or be required to follow, the harder way of righteousness at cost and loss to oneself? If the good and bad alike consist only of dust, then the call to virtuous living is a hollow mockery, and the maxims of justice, patience, goodwill, brotherhood, and every other ethical virtue are so many empty words. Clearly, then, morality is intimately interrelated with immortality.

Man's Constituent Elements

The Bible is *not* a textbook of psychology, and thus it does not give us a precise scientific delineation of the elements of man's makeup. There are certain realities of our being, however, which Scripture presents as contrasting truths that yet interrelate in the structure of the human person. In seeking to relate these opposing truths we will gain a clearer view of what it is to be human; in clarifying these realities, we will begin to develop a more formal doctrinal statement of the Christian view of man.

Unity and Duality

Although the Genesis account specifies two constituents in the creation of man, the dust of the ground and the divine breath of life, the emphasis falls upon the resulting unity. Man becomes an animated being through the unity of these two diverse elements. It is the synthesis of these two factors which constitutes man as a person. It is therefore characteristic of the biblical presentation "to assert the solidarity of man's constitution—that human individuality is of one piece, and is not composed of separate or independent parts. This assertion is essential to the theology of the whole Bible—to its discovery of human sin and of divine salvation" (Laidlaw, 1895, p. 55).

Along with this stress on the unity of man's nature, there is also throughout Scripture the suggestion of a duality in the makeup of his being. But this duality does not leave man as a loose conjunction of conflicting opposites or antagonistic principles. There is certainly an antithesis of the physical and the spiritual, of the earthly and the heavenly, but these are *not* presented as two distinct and separable elements. There is the suggestion of a dualism of aspects, but as uniting in a single harmonious whole. It is this unity of two aspects which accounts for the imprecise use of terms, especially in the Old Testament. The terms *soul, heart,* and *spirit* are frequently used to designate our higher natures, sometimes used to designate the lower element, and at still other times used to designate the whole person. Occasionally two terms will be used in conjunction to point out that man's unity is a duality; for example, "flesh" and "life" (Job 13:14, RSV), "flesh" and "soul" (Job 14:22, KJV), "mind" and "flesh" (Prov. 14:30, RSV), "mind' and "body" (Eccles. 2:3; 10:11, RSV), "heart" and "flesh" (Ezek. 44:7, 9, RSV).

Body and Soul

In the Old Testament there is no sharp distinction between the body (Heb., g^ewiyah, etc.) and the contrasting terms *soul (nephesh)* and *spirit (ruah)*. The term *body* is thus occasionally used to designate the whole man. The New Testament word for body (Gr. *sōma*) follows closely the Old Testament usage and so lends no support to the Greek philosophical view which sharply distinguished between body and soul to make the former the source of sin and the soul's prison house. In harmony with the whole tenor of the Old Testament, the apostle Paul presents man as a unity, yet as seemingly dichotomous in nature. This unity of the two elements is so close as to make them mutually dependent. Johann Gerhard (*Loci Theologici 17*, p, 149) states: "For the soul does nothing whatever outside the body, nor does the body do anything independently of the soul." Although Paul sees the body as influenced by sin and subject to death, he does not regard sin and death as inherent in it. Neither sin nor death belongs to the body as such; they are aliens come to occupy a foreign territory. Distinctive of the fuller revelation of the New Testament is the concept of a resurrection body. In the resurrection the believer receives an incorruptible, or spiritual, body because of his new relationship with the living Christ (1 Cor. 15:442-43; 2 Cor. 5:1-5; cf. Rom. 8:11; Phil. 3:21; Col. 3:4).

The Hebrew word for soul (*nephesh*), which occurs more than seven hundred times in the Old Testament, has the general meaning "possessing life." In this connection it can be used of animals (e.g., Gen. 1:20). Most of its many uses in the Psalms carry the connotation of "life-principle." It has a distinctively physical reference in numerous passages (e.g., Job 33:20) and a psychological reference (moral action) in others (e.g., Job 7:15). It is sometimes used to specify the individual person (e.g., Lev. 7:21) or the self (e.g., Judg. 16:116; Ps. 120:6). The Greek word *psyche* has in the New Testament the same general meaning as *nephesh* in the Old. Its occurrences in the epistles of Paul are variously translated in the Revised Standard Version: "human being" (Rom. 2:9); "person" (Rom. 13:1); "living being" (1 Cor. 15:45); "self" (11 Thess. 2:8); "life" (Rom. 11:3; 16:4; Phil. 2:30); "mind" (Phil. 1:27); and "heart" (Eph. 6:6). This diversity of usage conditions its general meaning. As the vital principle of individual life, the "soul" may refer to the concrete individual (Rom 2:9) or to specific psychical elements which make up the person.

Although the terms *body* and *soul* can often overlap to indicate an individual as such, the fact that the person can be approached, now from the one perspective and now from the other, leaves the impression of a duality of elements. And this impression of a dichotomy leads us to characterize the body as the outer and the soul as the inner aspect of man's being (see 2 Cor. 1:23; 12:15). Other New Testament writers seem to give to *psychē* this heightened significance (see, e.g., Heb. 4:12; 3 John 2). The Epistle of James (1:21) and the Epistle to the Hebrews (10:39; cf. 1 Peter 1:9) speak of the Word of God and faith as the way of the soul's salvation.

Flesh and Spirit

The Hebrew word for flesh (*basar*) occurs over 250 times in the Old Testament. It can refer to human nature generally (e.g., Gen. 6:3; Job 34:15), to the substance of a living body (e.g., Gen. 2:21), or to the corporeal aspect of man (e.g., Job 19:26; Ps. 63:1). On some few occasions the term *basar* has the additional idea of man's frailty in relation to God (Pss. 56:4; 78:39). The parallel term in the New Testament (*sarx*) carries the same idea, but it has a deeper dimension with regard to the concept of human frailty in contrast with God's strength: because of our sin there is something more seriously wrong with the human condition than merely our physical weakness. Thus, what is in the Old Testament a relatively rare connotation of the word flesh becomes of first importance in the biblical gospel of salvation.

Of the more than ninety occurrences of the term *sarx* in the letters of Paul, the majority have merely a physical connotation (e.g., Rom. 11:3; 2:28; 4:1). In the rest of its New Testament usages, however, more is involved. References to the passions (Rom. 7:5), the filthiness (2 Cor. 7:1, KJV; cf. 1 Peter 3:21), the desires (Gal. 5:16; Eph. 2:3; 2 Peter 2:18), and the sins (Col. 2:11) of the flesh speak of man's whole personality as absorbed in earthly pursuits in organized opposition to what is good and of God. The mind set on the flesh is hostile to God and cannot please him (Rom. 8:6, 8). In the flesh there dwells no good thing (Rom. 7:18). A more precise understanding therefore of what Paul means by the term *flesh* in its religious significance relates it to human nature as affected by the fall. "Flesh" specifies man's fallen state inherited from the sinful race of which he is in essence and character an individual member. "What, indeed, does flesh mean," asks Karl Barth (1933), "but new man" (Eph. 4:24, KJV; cf. 2 Cor. 5:17; Gal. 6:15). The former terms characterize man in his state by nature, and the latter terms in his position by grace. Paul speaks also of the "outer nature" which abides and is daily being renewed in Christ (2 Cor: 4:16 RSV; cf. Eph. 3:16).

Although Paul contrasts body and soul, flesh and spirit, it is not his teaching that the source and cause of sin lies in the physical body or flesh as such. He does, indeed, speak of "the body of sin" (Rom. 6:6, KJV; cf, 8:10, 13), and of the evil "works of the flesh" (Gal. 5:16-21; cf. 2 Cor. 10:2-3;l Eph. 2:3). But the fact that the body can be sanctified to become a temple of the Holy Spirit and be presented to God in an act of spiritual worship (Rom. 6:13; 12:1; 1 Cor. 6:13-20; 2 Cor. 7:1) clearly argues against the heretical Gnostic view of the inherent evil of physical existence. Far from locating sin in the material of the body, Paul's introduction of a contrast between soul and spirit and his description of the "soulish" (*psychikos*) man as "unspiritual" (1 Cor. 2:14, NEB, RSV) or "natural" (KJV) indicate that man is a sinner in his total inwardness, and not just in his body. The "pneumatic" or "spiritual" man (*pneumatikos*), on the other hand, is the one with whom the Holy Spirit makes contact, bringing God's redemption through Christ to the whole person. The psychical or soulish man is then in Paul's account man as nature has constituted him and as sin has affected him. As such, his wisdom is "earthly, unspiritual, devilish" (James 3:15, RSV). He is "worldly..., devoid of the Spirit" (Jude 19). The pneumatic or spiritual man, by contrast, is man reconstituted by divine grace and indwelt by the spirit of God. In the process of his salvation his natural or psychical selfhood, which he shares with fallen humanity, is transformed and fashioned anew into the image of Jesus Christ, into God's "proper man," to borrow Luther's phrase. For as the first head of the race was made a living *psychē*, the second Adam is a life-giving *Pneuma* for as many as receive him (1 Cor. 15:44-47). By nature all people have their pedigree and their place in "the book of the generations of Adam" (Gen 5:1, KJV). By grace some also have a position in "the book of the generation of Jesus Christ" (Matt. 1:1, KJV).

In this concluding remark, we wish to affirm that there is no purely psychological theory of personality which can give effective account of the ethical and religious concerns of the human individual or of the sinful state of his natural life. Every proffered personality theory must be judged by the Christian scholar in the light of the biblical view of man, especially with regard to his dependence upon God and his relation to objective moral law. It is on these counts that the views of many psychological theorists fall short due to their necessarily naturalistic approach, even though they are in certain respects sensitive to man's religious needs. No personality theory, conditioned as it must be by its scientific approach, can give full and final account of personhood since there is that in man beyond its province and power to investigate.

This appraisal does not permit the decrying of the value and use of psychology as a method. Indeed, every personality theory has contributions to make as well as drawbacks. As E. Mansell Pattison (1973) reminds us, "all personality theories have scientific assets and liabilities with no necessary Christian or anti-Christian basis." He goes on to warn, however, that "it is fatuous to assume that we can emerge with some definitive 'spiritual psychology,' for personality theory must remain at the level of scientific hypothesis. As such, every personality theory is temporary, expedient, and subject to new experimental and clinical data. We should be alert to any theology that attempts to 'Christianize" a particular personality theory" (p. 502). For psychology is limited to man's psychical nature. Into the inner depths of that more fundamental reality of man, his substantial selfhood, scientific psychology cannot enter; for his more fundamental need it has no answer. In the innermost of man's being there is that sinful self which not even the best-equipped psychological oarsman can reach. Beyond the physical and the psychical, man, as Carl Jung (1936) says, "suffers in spirit" (p. 277). And into that sphere, that ultimate citadel of man's warped nature, only the Spirit of God can come to make the redemptive healing of the gospel of Christ effective for the whole person. Thus we must declare, with P. T. Forsyth (1909), that our supreme need "is not the education of our conscience, not the absorption of our sins, nor even our reconciliation alone, but our redemption. It is not cheer that we need but salvation, not help but rescue, not stimulus but a change, not tonics but life. Our one need of God is a moral need in the strictest, holiest sense. The best of nature can never meet it. It involves a new nature, a new world, a new creation. It is the moral need, not to be transformed, but to be saved" (p. 62).

References

Barth, K. (1933). *The Epistle to the Romans*. .E Hoskyns, (Trans.). London: Oxford University Press.

Buber, M. (1937). *I and thou*. Edinburgh: T. & T. Clark.

Denney, J. (1918). *The Christian doctrine of reconciliation*. New York: Doran.

Flugel, J. (1945). *A hundred years of psychology* (5th ed.). London: Duckworth.

Forsyth, P. T. (1909). *Positive preaching and the modern mind*. London: Hodder & Stoughton.

Freud, S. (1934). *The future of an illusion*. (W. Robson-Scott, Trans.). London: Hogarth.

Freud, S. (1940). *Totem and taboo*. (A. Brill, Trans.). London: Kegan Paul.

Henry, C. (1976). *God, revelation, and authority*, Vol. 2. Waco, TX: Word.

Henry, C. (1979). *God, revelation, and authority*, Vol. 4. Waco. TX: Word.

Hodgson, L. (1930). *Essays in Christian philosophy*. London: Longmans, Green.

Hodgson, L. (1956). *For faith and freedom*, Vol. 1. Oxford: Basil Blackwell.

Joad, C. (1948). *Guide to modern thought* (Rev. ed.). London: Faber and Faber.

Jung, C. (1936). *Modern man in search of a soul*. London: Kegan Paul.

Ladd, G. E. (1975). *A theology of the New Testament*. London: Lutterworth.

Laidlaw, J. (1895). *The Bible doctrine of man*. Edinburgh: T. and T. Clark.

Lewis, H. (1961). God and mystery. In I. Ramsey, (Ed.), *Prospect for metaphysics*. London: Allen and Unwin.

McDonald, H. D. (1981). *The Christian view of man*. Westchester, IL: Good News.

Machen, J. G. (1965). *The Christian view of man*. London: Banner of Truth.

MacMurray, J. (1957). *The self as agent*. London: Faber and Faber.

Orr, J. (1897). *The Christian view of God and the world* (3rd ed.). London: Morrison and Gibb.

Paton, H. (1955). *The modern predicament*. London: Allen and Unwin.

Pattison, E. M. (1973). Person and personality. In C. Henry, (Ed.). *Baker's dictionary of Christian ethics*. Grand Rapids, MI: Baker.

Robinson, H. W. (1911). *The Christian doctrine of man* (2nd ed.). Edinburgh: T. and T. Clark.

Smethurst, A. (1955). *Modern science and Christian beliefs*. London: Nisbet.

Stevens, G. (1941). *The theology of the New Testament* (5th ed.). Edinburgh: T. and T. Clark.

Stewart, J. (1941). *A man in Christ* (5th ed.). London: Hodder and Stoughton.

Stout, G. (1920). *Manual of psychology* (3rd ed.). London: W. B. Clive.

Tournier, P. (1957). *The meaning of persons*. London: SCM.

Trethowan, I. (1954). *An essay in Christian philosophy*. London: Longmans, Green.

Watson, J. B. (1913). Psychology as the behaviorist views it. *Psychological Review 20*, 158-177.

Wilson, J. (1961). *Philosophy of religion*. London: Oxford University Press.

Wingren, G. (1961). *Creation and law*. Edinburgh: Oliver and Boyd.

15

The Concept of the Self as the Key to Integration

C. Stephen Evans
Wheaton College

Although integration is not merely theoretical, theoretical integration is important. The context for theory for Christians must be a biblical worldview, which is fundamentally personalistic. Here the personal is ultimate and irreducible to the impersonal. This implies that a Christian psychology will be one which takes seriously such notions as that of self. Four reasons for avoiding a psychology of the self are analyzed and rejected. Positively the fruitfulness of the concept of self can be seen in both social learning theory and object-relations theory. The clinical value of the concept of self is also noted. The value of the concept of the self is that there is "common ground" for Christians and the discipline of psychology. Because of the connection between being a self and understanding self-hood the theoretical task of integration becomes also a practical one.

The Nature of Integration

Though it has become a by-word in christian education at all levels, integration of faith and learning is an ambiguous phrase: what two things are to be integrated, and what does it mean to integrate. At the widest and most basic level I understand the integration of faith and learning to be a personal task which is not mainly intellectual in character. Integrating faith and learning is one part of the general task of integrating faith with life or existence. It is trying to see that faith, one's basic trust and reliance upon God permeates every aspect of one's being. But if a person is a professional scholar, teacher, or therapist, that will include the integration of this life-faith with his or her being. One aspect of this will be the theoretical task of inter-relating the theories and beliefs of theology on the one hand and the various academic disciplines on the other. Integrating psychology and theology is an element in the personal task of integrating one's faith with one's scholarly life.

As I conceive this theoretical work of integrating psychology and theology, it can not really be done by a philosopher; it *must* be done by psychologists and theologians. One must not think of psychology and theology as two self-contained and distinct enterprises and then look around for some method or person who can somehow "integrate" them. To the extent that we think about integration in this way, we have failed to achieve true integration. True integration must be something that goes on inside the disciplines themselves. That is, theology must somehow make a difference to psychology and psychology must somehow make a difference to theology. I think that the difference christian theology must make to psychology lies primarily in this realm of theory. Christian theology affects psychological theory by providing a context for theorizing. Philosophers of science today have made us well aware that all theorizing is done in such a context. Theory is not devised purely from a set of theory-free facts; it is shaped in part by a person's broader beliefs, including metaphysical beliefs.

Between Reductionism and Self-Deification

The broader context in which christian psychologists must theorize is that of the great biblical drama of creation, fall, and redemption. In all three acts of this great drama, God is the central actor; he is the supreme person who created us in his image, who sorrowfully allowed us to reject him and break fellowship, and who sacrificially became one of us and suffered the effects of our rebellion so as to bring about a triumphant reconciliation.

I wish to focus briefly on the first act of this drama, the doctrine of creation, the view that human beings are made in God's image. There is a certain tension or paradox in the biblical view of human persons. Humans are on the one hand created in God's image: having a unique resemblance to God, not attributed to anything else in the created order. On the other hand, they are made from the dust of the earth: solidly part of the natural order of things. This means that human beings are in important respects unique and superior to other animals: in some important aspects similar to other animals. We have both god-like and animal-like capacities.

Contemporary psychology, from its beginnings influenced by a naturalistic world view, has trouble holding these contrasting themes together in a creative tension. What we see is a careening back and forth between *reductionism* and *self-deification*, an intellectual schizophrenia. The reductionist program is still going strong. Skinner assured us that "to man qua man we readily say good riddance" (Skinner 1971, p. 191). From his perspective a human is an animal who differs from other animals only in the complexity of behavior. The self-deifier sees humans as selves having the power to create meaning and value, still aspiring to the role offered by the tempter long ago as in Erich Fromm's, *Ye Shall Be as Gods*.

This schizophrenia is grounded in the loss of the christian center. Bereft of God in an impersonal universe, humans try to explain their own being and meaning in impersonal terms, but their own experience belies this reductionism. We know we are more than bigger rats or slower computers. Reacting against reductionism we posit ourselves as selves; regard ourselves as creators of our own uniqueness. Intellectually, however, the self-deifier's position cannot hold. Human beings are too obviously part of the natural order to see ourselves as possessing qualities foreign to that order. The attempt to lift ourselves by our boot-straps is a conjurer's trick which cannot survive the bracing intellectual air of genuine science which steadily increases our understanding of our dependence on the natural order. When that natural order is seen as impersonal, we are thrown back into reductionism, and the fruitless battle begins once more.

Christians have tended to respond to this schizophrenia in one of two ways. Those who find *reductionism* to be more appealing intellectually and therefore the most menacing threat, have tended to focus on the need to preserve the person (Evans, 1982). In this task the humanistic existential third-force type of psychology is often seen as a natural ally. Those, like Paul Vitz (1977) or David Myers (1978) who see the *self-deifier* as the greater evil have focused on "self-theory" and "selfism," seeing in such psychological theories the age-old attempt to pridefully put ourselves at the center of the universe. To such critics and reductionistic elements in a Skinner or a Freud are a bracing reminder of our finitude.

Christian psychologists must transcend these one-sided reactions. We must do more than react; we must positively and creatively develop a psychology which is authentically christian. We cannot do this in a vacuum or start from scratch. Our training and current state of the field must bear on the work, but once we have rejected the empiricist myth of a neutral scientific method which proceeds from purely objective data, the possibility of such an authentically christian psychology should glimmer before us luring us onwards towards a self-conscious recognition that our theorizing must be done in the context of a christian worldview. This means that the christian psychologist will do his theorizing in the context of a personalistic universe in which persons are not mere surface phenomena, late and accidental products of an essentially impersonal process. Ultimately for the Christian, the personal is ultimate, the impersonal is explained in terms of the personal. Since human persons are made in God's image the personal categories we employ to describe human beings have a kind of ultimacy and irreducibility. Even if human beings are the products of an impersonal evolutionary process, even if their current doings are made possible by impersonal, mechanistic processes, those impersonal processes were created by a person *in order* to make possible that level of personal functioning. The personal functioning is real, not an illusion, something which may or may not be explicable, but not to be explained away.

Here lies the key to transcending the swings between reductionism and self-deification. The Christian can affirm the continuity which holds between human persons and the natural order without fearing that the impersonal will reductionistically swallow up the personal. He can recognize the creatureliness of human persons and thereby deflate the pretensions of the self-deifiers which continuing to recognize the significance and reality of the personal.

The Need for the Self in Psychology

What does it mean to recognize the significance of the personal? In concrete terms, it means that humans must be regarded as embodied selves, responsible agents. Psychology, which is christian must be psychology which makes room for the concept of the *self*, and the related concepts which that central one presupposes, concepts such as belief, desire, meaningful action, responsibility, and intention. The christian psychologist will certainly be interested in the *ways* in which persons form their beliefs and carry out their actions; will recognize that the self is partially a product, and that the actions of human selves are made possible by various impersonal systems. In explaining how persons come to have the characteristics they have and carry out the activities they carry out, we do not show that persons are not really persons nor do we eliminate the need for personal descriptions and explanations.

The concept of the self is one which has been on the fringes of psychology for a long time. An attenuated self survives as the ego of Freudian psychology, but the ego does not look much like a self. The ego seems more like one aspect of a warring, three-part system, described from an essentially objective, third-person standpoint. Behavioristic theorists originally had little use for the concept of the self. Trait psychologists, while more hospitable to theoretical constructs, can hardly be said to have employed a true concept of self, with their tendency to reduce the person to a psychometrically observable set of tendencies.

Almost thirty years ago Gordon Allport dared to develop a concept of self in *Becoming* (1955). However, Allport's concept of the "proprium," while suggestive, was not a true concept of the self. Allport himself recognized this. While admitting that the concept of the self might be necessary for philosophical and theological purposes, he claimed that such a full-blooded concept was not necessary for psychology (pp. 55, 62). What I would like to suggest is that for a christian psychology such a concept is indeed necessary.

Objections to the Concept of Self

Why have psychologists, including Christians, avoided the concept of the self? There are four reasons, sometimes consciously formulated, at other times unconsciously felt. Nevertheless, their influence has been powerful.

First, there is the *homonculus problem*. The self has seemed to many psychologists to be an homonculus, a little man, a self inside the person, whose actions are supposed to explain the person's actions. It was this that prevented Allport from a concept of the self for psychology.

The homonculus objection sharpens our understanding of the nature and function of the self, but it is not a reason for rejecting concepts of the self. The self must be seen, not as an homonculus, but as the person conceived as a whole. The action of selves as responsible agents are accessible to psychological description and explanation, so long as we not insist that the explanations be impersonal. Viewing human beings as selves does not put them out of reach of psychological analysis, though it may keep open the possibility that aspects of persons are out of reach of psychological analysis.

The truth centered in homonculus theories is that there are times when the ultimate explanatory categories will be *personalistic categories* such as "choices" and "reasons." The Christian does not agree with Dennett's claim that a scientific psychology must ultimately "cash in" all personalistic concepts by giving impersonal mechanistic explanations of them (Dennett, 1981, pp. 12-13). The personal categories which are employed can be applied directly to the real person. He or she is a self. There is no need for a self inside the self.

Secondly, is the *freedom objective*. Admitting that human beings are selves, responsible agents, comes dangerously close to admitting that they are not simply machine-like products of a machine-like process. All psychologists learn at their mothers' knee that determinism is an essential assumption for scientific psychology!

The response to this objection is simply to point out that it is not an objection at all. If viewing persons as selves implies they are free and that determinism is false, from a christian perspective that is a point in favor of viewing humans as selves. Human beings must not be viewed by Christians solely as helpless products and victims, but as responsible agents who on some occasions have free choice.

Does admitting free choice spell the doom of scientific psychology? Hardly. It is erroneous that psychologists must assume the truth of universal determinism to carry on their business. Psychologists do not have to assume there are determining causes for all behavior in order to look for what determining causes there are. One does not need and cannot get a guarantee of success in order to try to do something. The rejection of determinism still leaves psychology free to investigate human behavior in any manner it wishes, to discover the actual degree to which human behavior is constrained.

Moreover, the regularities which psychologists discover are invariably probabilistic and statistical in character. The existence of such regularities neither presupposes or implies determinism. If human agents are sometimes rational in their behavior, their behavior might be regular and predictable to a high degree without being mechanistically determined. Such behavior may also be explainable in terms of the agent's beliefs and desires, even if we are not able to formulate any regularities.

Another objection to a psychology of the self is that to introduce a concept of the self is to embrace implicitly a *dualistic* theory of the self. The self sounds suspiciously like the soul of those days when psychology was a branch of philosophy and theology.

It is not obvious that a psychology of the self must be dualistic in its metaphysical view of the human person. Certainly a psychology of the self will reject any reductionistic form of materialism, but such a psychology may turn out to be compatible with some form of monism or holism, either a non-reductive form of materialism or some kind of neutral or double-aspect notion.

So a psychology of the self is not necessarily dualistic, but something must be said about the widespread retreat from dualism which has occurred among christian psychologists and theologians. Suppose that a psychology of the self did ultimately imply dualism. This is not reason to reject it. Many psychologists have accepted a simplified view of biblical anthropology. They have simplistically contrasted a supposedly monistic Hebraic view with dualistic Greek modes of thought. It must be said quite clearly that a reasonable case for dualism can be made from biblical source and that monism also has a philosophical ancestry. In fact, it is difficult to see how a Christian can avoid some form of dualism. Anyone who believes in an intermediate after-life between death and the resurrection certainly must accept some form of dualism. Even those who reject any intermediate state and hold only to a resurrected after-life may not be true monists. For such a person must still claim that I am not identical with my present body. Otherwise the death of my present body would be the end of myself; no sense could be made of the claim that I will live again in a new body. Christian psychologists must recognize that there are many forms of dualism—some biblical and some not, some compatible with contemporary scientific discoveries and some not. I am afraid that often the dualisms which are rejected are the most extreme caricatures of the position.

The final objection to a psychology of the self is the fear that a self-psychology will foster self*ism*. Some see attempts to recognize the dignity of the self as human pride, an incipient revolt against divine authority. Sometimes this leads to a denigration of the human self, a denial that there is anything unique about human beings as if God is somehow exalted by denigrating his creatures.

We cannot deny that humans are in revolt against the creator that in this condition of revolt they pridefully assert their selfhood, forgetting that every good quality they have is a gift and there is no basis for pride. However, we must not allow our regret over the way humans have utilized their God-given abilities to destroy our appreciation of those abilities nor should it dim our vision for the significance these abilities can have when used for their proper purposes in a redeemed race. The Christian knows that human selves are fundamentally relational and that the final goal of the self does not lie in becoming autonomous but in glorifying God through obedient service. Within a christian context self-fulfillment can

only be understood paradoxically within the framework of self-renunciation, but only a responsible agent, a true self, is capable of choosing to serve God and participating in meaningful personal relations. A community, as opposed to a herd or a colony, can only be formed from genuine selves.

Christians have been quick to respond to the Marxist charge that belief in God is humiliating to humans by pointing out that an exaltation of God is not equivalent to a debasing of mankind. Some Christians, however, have not learned that the converse is also true. Debasing human beings is not a way of exalting God.

So none of the four reasons for avoiding a concept of the self in psychology is substantive. A psychology of the self commits us to the irreducibility of the personal but does not commit us to an homonculus. A psychology of the self may commit us to belief in freedom but that is essential top christian belief, not detrimental to psychology as a scientific discipline. It is probably not true that a psychology of the self must be dualistic, but if it should turn out that such a psychology were dualistic, from a christian perspective that would be a point in its favor. Christians have theological reasons for favoring dualism. Nor does a psychology of the self commit us to selfism or individualism: a christian psychology can and must understand our nature as selves to be such that happiness and self-fulfillment is found only in self-sacrifice and devotion to God and our fellow human selves.

Theoretical Implications of a Psychology of the Self

There are no good reasons to avoid a psychology of the self, but are there good positive reasons for developing such a psychology? From a christian perspective, the best reason is surely that in viewing humans as selves we are preserving their personhood, recognizing their likeness to God, refusing to view the categories of personhood as derivative, surface phenomena. Christians see the universe itself as personal and human persons fit that universe rather nicely.

There are, however, other reasons for espousing a psychology of the self. Chief among these is the theoretical fruitfulness and even indispensability of the concept of the self. As evidence for this we may cite major trends in secular psychology itself. With its naturalistic bias, psychology has not been overly enamored of the concept of the self, as I noted earlier with respect to classical Freudian and behavioristic theory. However, in both of these traditions the self seems to be making a slow steady comeback. To me this is evidence that human persons *are* selves. It shows the pressure of God's reality on theories whose presuppositions were initially unfavorable to a christian view. Parenthetically, it also shows the limits of presuppositionalism; reality and experience are not infinitely elastic.

Within the behavioristic tradition, the "cognitivization" of psychology in the last 15 years has been remarkable. In place of the empty organism which only contains its learning history, Albert Bandura and Walter Mischel have developed social learning theories which recognize the importance of understanding the "self-system" in understanding behavior. This cognitivization of behaviorism has proceeded to such an extent that proponents of Albert Ellis' Rational-Emotive Therapy can claim with plausibility to be behavioral therapists.

However, this healthy movement stops short of the goal, as Allport did. Bandura (1978) does not have a true self, a responsible agent, but a "self-system" composed of environment, "person-variables" and behavior. Of these three it is hardest to understand the role of behavior. Who or what is it that engages in behavior for Bandura? Why is it that behavior is not simply a product of environmental variables and personal-variables? What gives behavior the power to interact with these variables on a more or less equal footing? The answer is that Bandura has implicitly given behavior the characteristic of the self as an agent, which he professes to avoid. Here is an opportunity for christian psychologists to show the power of the personalistic christian world-view as a context for psychology. A psychology of the self would allow for a genuine interaction between the individual's enduring capacities, environmental situation, and responsible *decisions*, just the kind of interaction Bandura wishes to maintain.

The self is not only making a comeback among behaviorists but among psychoanalysts as well. The history of the psychoanalytic movement is to a great extent the history of ego psychology. Freud himself began the process of seeing the ego as more than a product of the id, a process continued by Ann Freud, Jung, and Adler. Ego psychology still falls short of a true psychology of the self. The ego, no matter how important and strong, remains a part of a warring system, not a true subjective "I."

There is within the psychoanalytic movement, a development which looks like a true psychology of the self and that is the curiously named British school of "object-relations-theory" pioneered by Fairbairn and popularized by Harry Guntrip (1971). Object-relations theory is a psychology of the unconscious as is orthodox Freudian analysis. In a manner similar to Freud, object-relations theory postulates the exis-

tence of conflicting systems within the person. Contrary to an orthodox Freudian view, the object-relations theorists view the unconscious as *formed* or developed by the person. The person is not a bundle of instincts from which some quasi-personal elements emerge, but a conscious self which hides and disguises its own deepest longing and fears as it struggles to develop meaningful relations with others. As Guntrip puts it, the ego is seen not as a part of a system but as a true person. Such a development enriches psychoanalysis by giving it the power to incorporate the themes of the existential psychologists who recognize that a sense of meaninglessness and lack of purpose can be as damaging to the psyche as abnormal sexual development. It also squares with the biblical teaching that people are not transparent to themselves, the heart is not only desperately wicked, but deceitful, and yet humans are in some way responsible for the lack of self-understanding.

Hence, some psychologists in the behavioral tradition and in psychoanalysis, both originally inhospitable to the concept of the self, see the self as an important theoretical concept. The self is making a slow steady comeback. I have not taken my illustrations from humanistic or existential psychology because in those traditions there is a philosophical bias toward the self. The fact that something like a self has emerged in such diverse and inhospitable traditions, gives me hope that a psychology of the self will help christian psychology in yet another way. It will help us see the common ground which is clearly present.

Christian psychology, like psychology generally, is pluralistic today. There are christian therapists, for example, who are psychoanalytic therapists, behavior therapists, existentialist or phenomenological, some who practice cognitively in a manner somewhat akin to rational-emotive therapy,m and many who are eclectic, besides the great plurality among social psychologists, personality theorists, and experimentalists. No doubt this plurality at times tempts one to think that christian psychology is an illusory ideal and that being a Christian makes no difference to the way one practices psychology.

Christian psychology does not have to be monolithic. The current pluralistic state seems unhealthy to me, but some kind of commonality is necessary. Perhaps the theoretical concept of the person as a self, a true responsible agent can provide some of that commonality, can help christian psychologists of different theoretical orientations to see more clearly how their common christian commitment does impact on their psychological theorizing. Christians of all sorts must recognize that humans are embodied agents, responsible to their creator and their fellow humans.

The Importance of the Self for Clinical Psychology

The concept of the self is not merely important for psychological theory. It is equally significant for clinical practice. Good therapists know implicitly that human beings are responsible agents even if they are not always willing to admit this explicitly. This is true not just of Rogerian, humanistic, and existential therapists. It is equally true of Freudian and behavioral therapists. All therapists see the need to make the therapeutic relationship a genuinely human relation, for the therapist to regard the client with respect as a responsible human being. However many Freudians may claim that human behavior is mechanistically determined by unconscious forces, the goal of therapy is clearly to help the client become more of a self, a person who has a greater degree of freedom and autonomy. This requires the person to discover, own, and assume responsibility for his or her own desires and actions.

However much the behavioral therapist may claim that persons are determined products of their learning histories and environmental contingencies, in the therapeutic encounter the therapist finds himself exhorting and encouraging the client to *choose*, to *try harder*, to take responsibility for his behavior. The therapist can view that as a form of verbal reinforcement, justified by its success in eliciting the desired behavior, but such a standpoint in effect dehumanizes the client, regarding him or her as an object to be manipulated. It is incompatible with the trust and mutual respect, important in the therapeutic process.

Viewing human beings as responsible agents, selves, is therefore no radical departure for a clinician. It simply brings to an explicit theoretical level what is already implicitly presupposed by good clinical practice.

Conclusions

This article is focused on the concept of the self. However, Christians should not view persons merely as selves made in God's image, but as creaturely selves. One way of emphasizing this creatureliness is to employ the concept of an embodied self to describe persons. Doubtless disembodied selves exist, God himself and perhaps angelic power, but humans are not gods or angels. They are creatures. Hence it is completely consistent for a christian psychology of the self to recognize and explore the manifold ways human selves are shaped by forces within them and without. A psychology of the self does not need to be selfish or selfist; it does not need to lead to self-deification. Christian psychology will recognize human finitude. It can also come to terms with sin and the need for redemption. Ultimately, such a psychology is needed not just to make sense of the *imago dei*; it is also implicit in the notion of sin. Only a responsible agent could sin, and only a responsible agent is capable of being redeemed.

My concluding challenge to the christian psychological community is that as redeemed persons we energetically participate in the redemption of the scholarly world, especially the world of psychology. Let it start with me, with the christianizing of my own thinking. It is here that integration as a theoretical enterprise returns full circle and becomes a personal task. If I am right in urging that the concept of the self is the key to the integration of Christianity and psychology, this may have very personal implications indeed. For is it not plausible that to the extent that I have failed to *be* a self, I may have difficulty in understanding and applying this concept?

References

Allport, G. (1955). *Becoming*. New Haven, CT: Yale.

Bandura, A. (1978, April). The self-system in reciprocal determinism. *American Psychologist*, 344-358.

Dennett, D. (1981). *Brainstorms*. Cambridge, MA: MIT.

Evans, C. S. (1982). *Preserving the person*. Grand Rapids, MI: Baker.

Guntrip. H. (1971). *Psychoanalytic theory, therapy, and the self*. New York: Basic.

Myers, D. G. (1978). *The human puzzle*. New York: Harper.

Skinner, B. F. (1971). *Beyond freedom and dignity*. New York: Bantam.

Vitz, P. (1977). *Psychology as religion*. Grand Rapids, MI: Eerdmans.

Section IV
Levels and Types of Integration

It can be confusing to read about or discuss integration without first acknowledging what aspects are being discussed. The history of the literature reveals a confusing array of terms that are proposed to be integrated. Frequently, writers enumerate various terms that are supposed to be the focus: psychology and theology, psychology and Christianity, psychology and Scripture, psychology and religion, counseling and the Bible, faith and vocation, faith and learning, science and Christianity, and so forth. One of our authors in this section, Bouma-Prediger, proposes that we step back and have a "meta-integration" discussion so we know more precisely what we are integrating.

On the other hand, discussing levels and types typically implies acceptance of broader assumptions about integration as an ontological phenomenon. Speaking about *applied* integration as opposed to *theoretical* integration, for example, most likely means accepting the basic assumptions about the goodness and veracity of the broader term. This makes it an insider's discussion. Once we assent to the initial conception and are inside, we want to understand in a more fine-grained way. For example, we can discuss cancer and provide a general understanding of its nature, character, and typical course, but it is certainly more helpful to speak of lung, skin, pancreatic, or brain cancer. Knowing the type helps to visualize the issue more clearly, discuss symptoms, refine a treatment regimen, and make a more accurate prognosis. Knowing the type is fundamentally better than not knowing it.

So, as this line of thinking goes, we first subscribe to a particular integrative model, and then the nuances of that model unfold as we study, research, and practice its tenets. The ensuing discussion of levels or types promotes refinement, and therefore might be considered a "post-integration" or "post-models" category. One could argue, therefore, that the articles in this section belong *after* section five on broad integration models, in terms of proper flow and organization of thought.

While both perspectives have merit, it is the first perspective that we find most compelling. Quite obviously, we placed the "levels and types" category here as an advanced organizer for the models section to come. If the models made little sense to readers because of nagging feelings of confusion and doubt, it is prudent to convey this meta-integration set of articles first.

Robert Larzelere's (1980) article, *The Task Ahead: Six Levels of Integration of Christianity and Psychology*, addresses distinct levels of abstraction along a continuum up and down the hierarchy of general scientific theory-making and inquiry. There are particular integration tasks at each level that complement one another. Drawing from an earlier levels model from the interpersonal attraction literature, Larzelere adapts the scheme to apply it to his discipline. Specifically, the six levels from the more abstract to the concrete are worldview, general proposition, linkage, specific proposition, hypothesis, and data. He argues that no issue at one level can be adequately considered without dealing with the other levels.

Larzelere notes that there had been greater emphasis in earlier integrative works at the worldview level, and that there was a shortage of good empirical research from integrators. He pointed out the importance of interrelationships among worldviews, theoretical propositions, and empirical research. Attending to tasks isolated in one level only promotes a truncated view. We gain perspective on one level through allowing other levels to inform our views. As Larzelere warns, "All too often, a specific proposition or application is rejected as unbiblical by Christians because an associated general proposition contradicts Scripture. ..." We should reduce our tendency to "throw the baby out with the bathwater." As we attend to the six interrelated levels, a more adequate corrective of the big picture emerges.

In *The Task of Integration: A Modest Proposal*, Steve Bouma-Prediger (1990) distinguishes types or different kinds of integration, most all of which apply to Christian believers and nonbelievers. Applying the term levels does not work, for these are not necessarily aligned to form a neat continuum and hierarchy, but they demarcate moderately distinct kinds of integration.

This now-classic typology proposed integration that is interdisciplinary, intradisciplinary, faith-praxis, and experiential. Acknowledging that these four are not exhaustive, and are not perfect labels, Bouma-Prediger elaborates the nature of each type. The first two place a greater primacy on the theoretical, while the latter two are much more practical and atheoretical.

Interdisciplinary integration is *between* disciplines. Aspects of two or more disciplines—any disciplines—may be compared and contrasted with the hope of uniting and reconciling the assumptions, methods, and conclusions. This is a primarily cognitive-scholarly task at a theoretical level, and should be practiced by all scholars regardless of their theological commitments. The second type, intradisciplinary integration, occurs *within* a discipline, and promotes congruency of one's personal theory with one's professional practice. Although we might associate this most often with psychotherapists, it is also true of other professionals and persons who may or may not be believers: physicians, musicians, ministers, financial planners, attorneys, and many others. Our personal theory needs to be aligned with how we live out our professional roles. All academics and professionals ought to be doing this type of integration, for it stimulates "self-awareness" and "self-coherence," the result of rendering professional theory and practice consistent.

The third type of integration is faith-praxis, described as integrating faith commitment with one's way of life. In this type of integration we are called to be authentic, living out with integrity our faith commitment in our daily lives. It is broad and not confined to our professional lives. The congruence espoused by the intradisciplinary type (one's theory and one's professional practice) is more defined by the professional role, but here the praxis of daily living is what counts. Experiential integration, the last type, refers to integration within oneself and between self and God. The goal is an inner healing experience of wholeness and well-being. This type of integration is fundamental to all the rest. For the Christian, as Bouma-Prediger summarizes, "it involves a personal experience of divine grace in which alienation from God, self, and neighbor is replaced by the shalom and wholeness received in faith." The other forms of integration mean little, short of experiential integration, for this experience animates the tasks of the other types.

Finally, Siang-Yang Tan (2001) discusses areas of integration in his article *Integration and Beyond: Principled, Professional, and Personal*. Areas are more closely associated with types than levels and overlap more clearly with the Bouma-Prediger typology. Tan identifies three areas that encompass the integrator's life and which follow the alliteration of three Ps, borrowed from Newt Malony: principled (theoretical-conceptual and research), professional (clinical or practice), and personal (intrapersonal, including spirituality). The latter is the foundation of the others, for Tan believes that the mission will fall short without a profoundly personal experience of the Lordship of Christ. Character counts, and he emphasizes the ministry of the Holy Spirit and the spiritual disciplines in developing that character.

The "Beyond" term in the title is Tan's hedge against what we might call intellectual "integrationism," borrowing the "ism" from the twin extremes of either psychologism or theologism (i.e., the errors of accepting either psychological or theological procedures and theories as ultimate). "Beyond" represents keeping the perspective that there really is more to life than just the professional Christian psychologist's interest (and perhaps preoccupation) with intellectual integration per se.

The articles in this section are written across three decades. These meta-integration ways of thinking clarify how we may approach the integration dialog with increasingly fine-tuned understanding.

Suggestions for Further Reading: Levels and Types of Integration

Fleck, J. R., & Carter, J. D. (Eds.). (1981). *Psychology and Christianity: Integrative readings*. Nashville, TN: Abingdon.

> Thirty four diverse articles covering a wide array and types of integration, with an Introduction that outlines their three levels of integration.

McMinn, M. R., & Phillips, T. R. (Eds.). (2001). *Care for the soul: Exploring the intersection of psychology & theology*. Downers Grove, IL: InterVarsity.

> Articulating the four levels of integration proposed by Bouma-Prediger in 1990, the editors have collected papers from a particular Wheaton College conference on the soul that addresses these levels.

16

The Task Ahead: Six Levels of Integration of Christianity and Psychology

Robert E. Larzelere
University of New Hampshire

Notable strides have been made in recent years in the integration of Christianity and psychology. The growth of organizations such as the Christian Association for Psychological Studies indicates the increasing interest in this topic. Now books are appearing more frequently which integrate a Christian perspective with psychology in general (e.g., Collins, 1977; Myers, 1978) or with specific psychological topics (e.g., Dobson, 1974; Gorsuch & Malony, 1976; Meier, 1977; Narramore and Counts, 1974). Sufficient integration has been done to warrant categorization of various types of approaches to the integration task (Carter, 1978; Crabb, 1977; McLemore, 1976).

Progress has been somewhat uneven, however. The *Journal of Psychology and Theology* has seen a substantial increase in theoretical papers submitted but relatively little increase either in research papers or in clinical application papers that are relevant to integration.[1]

This article attempts to address the first of these shortcomings by developing a model designed to show the potential contribution of research to integration. This model also illustrates the interrelationships among a variety of integration tasks. Previous overviews of integration have generally clarified the distinctions among different types of approaches to integration. In contrast, this model attempts to suggest ways that different strategies could complement one another.

Briefly, the model specifies six levels of scientific inquiry, varying from a World View (presuppositional) level through theoretical levels to a Data level. A growing number of psychologists are becoming more aware of the interrelationships among world views, psychological theories, and psychological research. This seems to be largely due to a growth in the prestige of non-behavioristic perspectives, particularly in developmental psychology. Until the late 1960s behaviorism was clearly the dominant model in experimental psychology. Consequently, its presuppositions remained unex-

pressed and unquestioned and its propositions were largely unchallenged. After behaviorism competed with nonbehaviorist theorists such as Piaget for some time, it became obvious to some developmental psychologists that differences in world views and presuppositions were basic to many differences in theoretical propositions, data interpretations, and research questions (Overton and Reese, 1973; Reese and Overton, 1970). Other psychologists (e.g., Marx and Hillix, 1979) are also becoming aware of such issues, due largely to the influence of Kuhn's (1970) book on paradigms in science.

This is encouraging to Christian social scientists for several reasons. First, such discussions of world views make the area of major differences between Christianity and secular psychology more explicit. Previously, Christians were aware that some of their values and presuppositions conflicted with some conclusions made in the name of psychology. However, the general stance of psychologists was either to accept their own presuppositions uncritically or to deny the existence of any distinctive presuppositions of their own by claiming that their social science was value free. It can be argued that apparent differences between Christianity and secular psychology reflect a clash between world views similar to the clash between the behaviorist (or mechanistic) and organismic world views. This is not to say that the clash between mechanistic and organismic presuppositions is as basic as the differences between Christian and secular presuppositions.

Second, because of competing world views in experimental psychology, a Christian psychologist is often not alone in criticizing a position that is inconsistent with a Christian world view. For example, Collins (1977) uses mostly criticism from within secular psychology in discussing the shortcomings of each of the three major forces in contemporary psychology.

But another implication is of major importance for this article. Reese and Overton (1973), Kuhn (1970), and others emphasize the importance of the inter-

Table 1

Levels of Scientific Inquiry

Level	Description	Meaning of Repeated Disconfirmations
World View	Basic assumptions and values	Impossible, directly
General Proposition	General models and theories	Impossible, directly
Linkage	Induction and deduction	Need better linkages or unity of overall conceptual framework becomes questionable
Hypothesis	Deriving hypotheses and generalizing from data	Incorrect hypothesis
Data	Admissible elements of information	Original data not replicable or of limited generalizability

Adapted from Clore and Byrne (1974)

relationships among world views, theoretical propositions, and empirical research. This leads fairly directly to the model of six levels of scientific inquiry to be developed in this article. This model, in turn, can serve as a guide for the various integration tasks that need to be emphasized in coming years. An overview of the six-levels model will be presented first. Then each of the six levels will be discussed in turn, along with some potential tasks that could be done at that level to further the integration of Christianity and experimental psychology.

Six Levels of Scientific Inquiry

Table 1 outlines six levels of scientific inquiry, modified from Clore and Byrne (1974). Note that the levels vary from abstract (World View) to concrete (Data) and from theoretical to empirical. Movement down the table involves deduction; movement upward represents induction. As Clore and Byrne note, the meaning of confirmation or disconfirmation differs from level to level and confirmation or disconfirmation at one level affects neighboring levels the most and distant levels the least.

The World View level is in many ways the most basic and yet the most difficult to conceptualize. The central component of this level would be the world view adhered to. The major world views used in psychology today are mechanism (i.e., behaviorism) and organicism (e.g., Piaget, Kohlberg, Gestalt psychology). They are considered by many to be incompatible, with their incompatibilities reflected throughout all six levels (Collins, 1977; Overton, 1973; Overton and Reese, 1973; Pepper, 1942; Reese and Overton, 1970). A psychologist uses a particular world view, explicitly or implicitly, as a guide and

rationale for his or her theoretical and empirical work. World views determine the appropriateness of theoretical formulations, of types of questions, and of methods of gathering and analyzing data. Scientific procedures at each lower level must be consistent with the World View level. Consequently, the empirical evidence generated by psychologists generally supports the world view they adhere to (Overton, 1973; Overton and Reese, 1973).

The intermediate levels consist of two classifications of propositions (General and Specific) and two types of connections (Linkage and Hypothesis). Psychological theories and propositions cannot be neatly dichotomized into two categories. Instead, there is a continuum from general, inclusive propositions to specific, limited propositions. The dichotomy is useful, however, to simplify the discussion and yet highlight some important differences between general and specific psychological propositions.

Similarly, the connective levels are not neat dichotomies, but hypotheses can be generated more readily from specific propositions than general ones. Logical reasoning is usually the primary linkage between general and specific propositions, whether moving inductively (generalization) or deductively. Inductive generalization also links data to specific propositions, but hypotheses are the preferred way to linking those levels deductively.

No psychological issue at any level can be considered adequately without also dealing with related issues at other levels. All the levels are interdependent with each other. Clore and Byrne (1974) give examples of representative publications at each level pertinent to their research program on interpersonal attraction. At the Data level, they cite Byrne's (1961)

Table 2

Basic Presuppositions of Behaviorism and Christian Psychology

Behaviorism	Christian Psychology
empiricism	expanded empiricism
determinism	determinism and free will
relativism	biblical absolutism
reductionism	modified reductionism
naturalism	Christian supernaturalism

Adapted from Collins, 1977.

early finding that the more similar two strangers' attitudes are, the more attracted they tend to become toward each other. Byrne and Clore's (1970) statement of the reinforcement-affect model of attraction was cited as an example of related work at the General Proposition level. They noted, in turn, that this was related to assumptions of determinism, hedonism, and neobehaviorism (World View level).

Keeping in mind the interdependencies among the different levels of psychological inquiry, let us turn to a consideration of the tasks involved in integrating Christianity and experimental psychology at each of the six levels.

World View Level

The major task at this level is to clarify the presuppositions of world views used in secular psychology and to compare them with presuppositions appropriate for a Christian world view. Collins (1977) has done an excellent job of comparing Christian and behaviorist presuppositions which are summarized in Table 2.

For example, behaviorists assume that empirical data are the preferred if not the only sources of data. The expanded empiricism presupposition of Christian psychology indicates that the sources of data include the Bible, intuition, and logical thinking as well as empirical observation. This is the major presuppositional distinction affecting the task of integrating Christianity and psychology at the Data level. The major distinction between secular and Christian psychology at the Data level is that Christian psychology recognizes the Bible as data whereas secular psychology does not. As will be shown, this distinction affects the integration task at all the intermediate levels.

General Proposition Level

Most overt conflict between secular and Christian psychology occurs at this level. For example, the

apparent conflict over evolution is not basically over the special theory of evolution, but over the philosophical development of evolutionism and over the general theory of evolution (Bube, 1968). Also, the conflict over Skinner's behaviorism is not over the empirical findings of behaviorists, but over such generalizations as Skinner's (1971) *Beyond Freedom and Dignity.*

Most Christians have limited their responses to the General Proposition level, stating that such and such a position is wrong because it is inconsistent with the Bible. As noted in Table 1, however, it is virtually impossible to disconfirm any general proposition directly. Instead, an argument for modifying or rejecting some general psychological proposition must focus substantially on other levels of scientific inquiry.

Thus, one integration task at this level would be to clarify the assumptions (World View) behind the general proposition in question. Collins (1977) does a good job of this in regard to the often-accepted conclusion of secular clinicians "that religion is archaic, inhibiting, immature, and often harmful" (p. 100). He points out that such a conclusion is based on two assumptions: (1) that whatever cannot be observed satisfactorily by the scientific method does not exist, and (2) that the religious beliefs of the emotionally disturbed provide an accurate indication of religion itself.

As is evident from Table 1, such an argument cannot disconfirm a general proposition (e.g., that religion is harmful, etc.). It does make clear, however, that the proposition of interest is based substantially on some questionable assumptions and not on hard data alone.

It also opens the door to alternative general propositions which explain similar data but which are consistent with alternative presuppositions. Indeed, this is a second integration task at the General Proposition level: to develop alternative general propositions which are consistent with the other levels of Christian psychology. This will often involve reinterpretation of specific psychological propositions and data, which will be discussed at the appropriate levels.

A closely related third integration task is to integrate existing knowledge. This is one of the two major purposes of psychological theories (Koteskey, 1975). The other purpose, to predict new findings, is more directly relevant to the Specific Proposition and Hypothesis levels. Christian psychologists need to develop alternative general propositions that integrate existing psychological knowledge. For example, Koteskey (1975, 1978) has shown how Christian psychology could integrate behavioristic and humanistic propositions by recognizing that behaviorism is most relevant to the finite aspects of humans, and humanistic psychology is most pertinent for the personhood aspects.

Another integration task at this level is to reinterpret the importance of psychological propositions. World views often influence which propositions psychologists focus on. For example, Lewis and Spanier (1979) identify seventy-four specific propositions relating independent variables to marital quality and stability. By induction they derived thirteen more general propositions and three most general propositions. Each of the thirteen intermediate propositions summarized between two and eleven specific propositions. Yet four independent variables indicating religiosity and seven independent variables reflecting a common lifestyle of evangelical Christians were nowhere revealed in the thirteen intermediate propositions. Thus, religiosity and an evangelical lifestyle were regarded as of minor significance even though the actual data support their importance for marital adjustment at least as much as many of the intermediate propositions. (In contrast, Stephens, 1978, concludes that religiosity is one of the six most clearly supported predictors of marital adjustment.)

In sum, the integration tasks at the General Proposition level include clarifying the presuppositions of general psychological propositions, proposing alternate propositions if necessary, developing general propositions to integrate existing knowledge, and reinterpreting the importance of some propositions. Integration at this level must necessarily involve other levels as well, since disconfirmation or modification of general propositions is impossible directly. Therefore, let us turn our attention to other levels.

Linkage Level

This level involves connections between general propositions and specific ones, linkages that are crucial for the unity of an overall conceptual framework and are necessary for indirect evidences for or against general propositions. The opinion that a given general proposition is inconsistent with Scripture is only a starting place. Then, Christian psychologists need to identify relevant scriptural passages and relevant empirical data and develop generalizations for more theoretical levels from both kinds of data. At the Linkage level, this will involve generalizations from more specific propositions. It would be preferable, as Bannister and Wichern (1978) have suggested, to have Christian psychologists and theologians cooperate in such an endeavor. Better yet, if possible, is McQuilkin's (1977) recommendation to have both areas of expertise residing in the same person. The objective of either approach would be to achieve the proper balance between special and general revelation, in this particular case, in the task of making generalizations. Such generalizations should yield propositions that are more consistent than existing ones with Scripture and with empirical data. For example, Myers (1978) uses both psychological and theological data to support his holistic position on the mind-body problem.

Once some alternate general propositions are made, the Linkage level is again important for deducing specific propositions which can be tested empirically. With or without alternate general propositions, Christian psychologists could derive specific propositions from secular psychological propositions which seem questionable. If these, in turn, were not supported empirically, the general proposition in question would need to be modified.

Thus, at the Linkage level, the integration tasks include induction and deduction, both with the goals of developing alternative general propositions when necessary and of pointing out the limitations of accepted general propositions.

Specific Proposition Level

At this level, a Christian psychologist may find fewer apparent conflicts with secular psychology than at the General Proposition level. The major type of integration task at this level involves reinterpretation (Koteskey, 1975). We need to consider reinterpreting psychological conclusions if scriptural data sheds more light on it. Again several integration tasks are especially relevant at this level.

First, Christian psychologists may often need to reinterpret labels. While a research participant's responses to a questionnaire or to an experimental procedure may fit quite nicely into a Christian psychological perspective, the labels put on sets of those responses reflect the researcher's (or test designer's) presuppositions and biases. Consequently, a Christian psychologist should question whether the label actually describes the corresponding set of responses. For example, Glock and Stark (1966) concluded that American anti-Semitism was rooted in conservative Christian beliefs. One crucial link in their argument was the hostile attitude of Christians toward the contemporary Jewish religion. But this was indicated by agreement with such items as "The Jews can never be forgiven for what they did to Jesus until they accept him as the true Savior." If someone strongly disagreed because he believed that Jesus never existed or that the crucifixion never occurred, he would be given a score indicative of low anti-Semitism. Thus, Christian beliefs themselves were confounded with Glock and Stark's items.

This labeling problem is obvious in other areas of research as well. One study (Murrell & Stachowiak, 1967) predicted that authoritarianism would be lower in families with well-adjusted children than in families in which at least one child was seeking psychological counseling. When their findings indicated that the two groups differed in the opposite direction, they changed the label of authoritarianism to cooperation and effectiveness of leadership. Similarly Price (1973) had different explanations for the low proportion of individuals who changed their opinion after new relevant information was given. The group high in self-actualization was thought to have a realistic perspective and high awareness of the situation. In contrast, the group low in self-actualization was considered rigid and unwilling to assimilate new information. The data were quite similar for both groups (a middle group was much more flexible than either extreme), but widely contrasting labels were used depending on the level of self-actualization.

Christian psychologists need to be sensitive to the fact that labels reflect expectations and presuppositions as well as the actual data. Therefore, reinterpretation may involve searching for new labels which reflect the data fairly and also are consistent with a Christian world view.

Second, Christian psychologists need to reinterpret the importance of findings. Many psychologists seem to be expert at selectively attending to findings that support their own positions. Two examples relevant to Christians are the issues of the advisability of premarital sex and of spanking. In both cases, the general social scientific view is the opposite of the traditional Christian position. The data support the Christian stand on premarital sex and the social scientific position on spanking. Yet the data relating premarital sex to subsequent marital satisfaction are either ignored or pushed aside

as a minor finding full of methodological problems. In contrast, Sears, Maccoby, and Levin's (1957) finding that severity of punishment is associated with hostile aggressiveness in children is cited as a major basis for the elimination of corporal punishment (e.g., Steinmetz and Straus, 1974) with little or no mention of the size of the relationship ($r = .16$), methodological shortcomings, or the possibility that children's aggressiveness may influence parental discipline (Bell, 1968).

These examples also suggest a third related area of reinterpretation at the Specific Proposition level: the reinterpretation of the importance of methodological shortcomings. Psychologists are quick to search for methodological shortcomings of findings that do not fit their own viewpoint, but slow to criticize supportive findings. This situation is not necessarily bad as long as psychologists in different camps are subjecting each other's findings to the same amount of methodological scrutiny. The danger comes when the search for methodological shortcomings favors one group over another, as has been the case when so few Christian psychologists have asked such questions publicly.

Hypothesis Level

This brings us to the Hypothesis level, which links empirical data to specific propositions. One purpose of theoretical propositions is to predict new findings. Christians can find a wealth of ideas for new hypotheses as a byproduct of reinterpreting specific psychological propositions. Alternative labels, a broader picture of relevant research, and awareness of methodological shortcomings often lead quite naturally to research hypotheses. For example, it would be interesting to discover whether Glock and Stark's (1966) findings would be replicated if an alternative measure of hostility against the Jewish religion was used which was not confounded with basic Christian beliefs.

Such hypothesis testing is theoretically of crucial importance for increasing the prestige of a Christian psychology among non-Christian experimental psychologists. In reality, Bem (1979, p. 541) is probably right when he says that convenience of the vocabulary, current interests of psychologists, and relevance of a theory to those current interests affect the prestige of a theory more than do hypothesis tests. But that merely says once again that presuppositions and values influence how readily various theories will be accepted.

Although the name of this level emphasizes the deductive linkage between the Specific Theory level and the Data level, the inductive linkage (generalization) is just as important. The major integration task here, as at the Linkage level, is the appropriate interrelating of scriptural and empirical data.

Data Level

At this level there should be little problem with integrating psychological data into a Christian psychology. If all truth is God's truth, then reliable empirical data should fit into a Christian world view. However, two possible problems should be noted. The first is that the sample may be inadvertently biased by the researcher's presuppositions. This is a common criticism, for example, of Maslow's study of self-actualized persons (Koteskey, 1975). Another example is Leathers (1970), who eliminated a subject because he was a "religious fanatic." According to his research design, a confederate was to be supportive of his comments for the first half of a discussion period but then become very unsupportive for the second half. He was interested in discovering the effect of trust destruction on the communication process. Perhaps he discovered an important behavioral distinction of certain committed Christians, but, if so, it apparently did not fit his expectations or world view.

A second possible problem is that Christian psychologists may be much more familiar with empirical data than with biblical data in their areas of psychological expertise. A closer balance could be achieved by collaboration with theologians or by the development of biblical exegesis tools by psychologists.

Conclusions

These six levels of scientific inquiry provide an overview of the areas that need to be dealt with in integrating Christianity with secular psychology. Some specific integration tasks at each level have been suggested. Certainly the suggestions here can be refined and additional integration tasks can be added.

There seems to have been relatively little integration done at the intermediate levels. Most integration of Christianity and psychology has focused on broad issues, such as finding the proper balance between psychology and theology. More books are needed, such as Myers' (1978), which evidence good psychological scholarship as well as good understanding of relevant Scriptures. An apparent conflict between a psychological conclusion and a traditional Christian position could often be an excellent starting point for specialized integration work. One approach would be to identify the related integration tasks at each level of scientific inquiry. Then the integration tasks that seem to have the most potential fruitfulness could be worked on.

A secondary purpose of the six-levels model is to improve understanding among people interested in a Christian perspective of psychology. All too often, a specific proposition or application is rejected as unbiblical by Christians because an associated general proposition of presupposition contradicts Scripture (e.g., Vos, 1978). Hopefully, a better understanding of the interrelationships among world views, theories, and research findings will reduce this tendency to "throw out the baby with the bathwater."

Perhaps an analogous six levels could be developed for psychological applications in general, and psychological counseling in particular. The most obvious difference would be the substitution of practical application levels for specific research levels, yielding modified versions of the Hypothesis and Data levels. Some good initial attempts to relate presupposition and world views to counseling theory and practice are already available (Amundson & Willson, 1973; Collins, 1977).

The major thrust of the six-level model, however, involves research. Relatively little research has been done that relates directly to the integration of Christianity with secular psychology. Hopefully, the six levels clarify the place and importance of research for integration. If so, we should see a substantial increase in the quantity and quality of integration research and in the impact of Christian psychologists on our secular colleagues in the years to come.

Notes

1. J. R. Fleck, personal communication, April 3, 1979.

References

Amundson, N. E., & Willson, S. (1973). The effect of different reality perspectives on psychotherapy. *Journal of Psychology and Theology, 1*(3), 22-27.

Bannister, R. S., & Wichern, F. G. (1978). A theological research design towards a biblical psychology. *Christian Association for Psychological Studies Bulletin, 4*(1), 11-14.

Bell, R. Q. (1968). A reinterpretation of the direction of effects in studies of socialization. *Psychological Review, 75,* 81-95.

Bem, D. J. (1979). Social psychology. In E. R. Hilgard, R. L. Atkinson, & R. C. Atkinson (Eds.). *Introduction to psychology* (7th ed.). New York: Harcourt Brace Jovanovich.

Bube, R. H. (1968). Biblical revelation. In R. J. Bube (Ed.). *The encounter between Christianity and science.* Grand Rapids, MI: Eerdmans.

Byrne, D. (1961). Interpersonal attraction and attitude similarity. *Journal of Abnormal and Social Psychology, 62,* 713-715.

Byrne, D., & Clore, G. L. (1970). A reinforcement model of evaluative responses. *Personality: An International Journal, 1,* 103-128.

Carter, J. D. (1977). Secular and sacred models of psychology and religion. *Journal of Psychology and Theology, 5*(3) 197-208.

Clore, G. L., & Byrne, D. (1974). A reinforcement-affect model of evaluative responses. In T. L. Huston (Ed.). *Foundations of Interpersonal Attraction.* New York: Academic Press.

Collins, G. R. (1977). *The rebuilding of psychology.* Wheaton, IL: Tyndale House Publishers.

Crabb, L. J., Jr. (1977). *Effective biblical counseling.* Grand Rapids, MI: Zondervan Publishing House.

Dobson, J. (1974). *Hide or seek.* Old Tappan, NJ: Fleming H. Revell.

Glock. C. Y., & Stark. R. (1966). *Christian beliefs and anti-Semitism.* New York: Harper & Row.

Gorsuch, R. L., & Malony, H. N. (1976). *The nature of man: A social psychological perspective.* Springfield, IL: Charles C. Thomas.

Koteskey, R. L. (1975). Toward the development of a Christian psychology: Man. *Journal of Psychology and Theology, 3*(4), 298-306.

Koteskey, R. L. (1978). Toward the development of a Christian psychology: Learning and cognitive processes. *Journal of Psychology and Theology, 6*(4), 254-265.

Kuhn, T. S. (1970). *The structure of scientific revolutions* (2nd ed.). Chicago: University of Chicago Press.

Leathers, D. G. (1970). The process effects of trust-destroying behavior in the small group. *Speech Monographs, 37,* 180-187.

Lewis, R. A., & Spanier, G. B. (1979). Theorizing about the quality and success of marriage. In W. R. Burr, R. Gill, F. I. Nye, & I. L. Reiss (Eds.). *Contemporary theories about the family* (Vol. 1). New York: Free Press.

Marx, M. H., & Hillix, W. A. (1979). *Systems and theories in psychology* (3rd ed.). New York: McGraw-Hill Book Co.

McLemore, C. W. (1976). The nature of psychotheology: Varieties of conceptual integration. *Journal of Psychology and Theology, 4*(3), 217-220.

McQuilkin, J. R. (1977). The behavioral sciences under the authority of Scripture. *Journal of the Evangelical Theological Society, 20,* 31-43.

Meier, P. D. (1977). *Christian child rearing and personality development.* Grand Rapids, MI: Baker Book House.

Murrell, S. A., & Stachowiak, J. G. (1967). Consistency, rigidity, and power in the interaction patterns of clinic and non-clinic families. *Journal of Abnormal Psychology, 72,* 165-272

Myers, D. G. (1978). *The human puzzle.* New York: Harper & Row.

Narramore, B., & Counts, B. (1974). *Guilt and freedom.* Irvine, CA: Harvest House.

Overton, W. F. (1973). On the assumptive base of the nature-nurture controversy: Additive versus interactive conceptions. *Human Development, 16,* 74-89.

Overton, W. F., & Reese, H. W. (1973). Models of development: Methodological implications. In J. R. Nesselroade & H. W. Reese (Eds.). *Life-Span developmental psychology: Methodological Issues.* New York: Academic Press.

Pepper, S. C. (1942). *World hypothesis: A study in evidence.* Berkeley, CA: University of California Press.

Price, D. A. (1973). Relationship of decision styles and self-actualization. *Home Economics Research Journal, 2,* 12-20.

Reese, H. W., & Overton, W. F. (1970). Models of development and theories of development. In L R. Gouley & P. B. Baltes (Eds.). *Life-Span development psychology: Research and theory.* New York: Academic Press.

Sears, R. R., Maccoby, E. E., & Levin, H. (1957). *Patterns of child-rearing.* Evanston, IL: Row, Peterson.

Skinner, B. F. (1971) *Beyond freedom and dignity.* New York: Alfred A. Knopf.

Steinmetz, S. K., & Straus, M. A. (Eds.). (1974). *Violence in the family.* New York: Dodd, Mead.

Stephens, W. (1978). Predictors of marital adjustment. In T. F. Hoult, L. F. Henze, & J. W. Hudson (Eds.), *Courtship and marriage in America.* Boston: Little, Brown.

Vos, A. (1978). A response to God and behavior mod. *Journal of Psychology and Theology, 6*(3), 210-214.

17

The Task of Integration:
A Modest Proposal

Steve Bouma-Prediger
The University of Chicago

This article examines the issue of integration and proposes a typology of four different kinds of integration: interdisciplinary, intradisciplinary, faith-praxis, and experiential integration. The elaboration of the nature of each type of integration includes specific implications for Christians. The proposal is intended to clarify the integration discussion and stimulate dialogue on these important issues.

In recent years, the term integration has become something of a buzz word—often referred to, evoked, discussed—much like Thomas Kuhn's now famous word *paradigm*. In circles of Christian higher education, especially those involving the readers of this *Journal*, there has been much discussion of and debate about the integration of psychology and theology, psychology and Christianity, faith and learning, and the like. Indeed, this discussion/debate has produced a now considerable body of literature reflecting a concern on the part of Christian scholars to relate their faith to their respective disciplines and professions, particularly the discipline of psychology.

However, it has been my experience—and in talking with others their experience as well—that the discussion about integration is often a frustrating endeavor. It is frustrating because the literature is often unclear on what exactly integration is, and in personal conversations all too often the parties involved in a dialogue regarding integration proceed without clarifying just what it is they are talking about. Inevitably people talk past each other and inexorably misunderstanding occurs. Thus, the possibilities for authentic understanding, not to mention for agreement and disagreement, are hampered.

In reflecting on this state of affairs, it is obvious that greater clarity about the concept of integration, specifically the different types or kinds of integration, is necessary before fruitful discussion can be advanced. By types of integration here I do not mean substantive proposals for integration, for example, that one ought to adopt a particular position with respect to the task of integration. Rather, I wish to move the discussion back a step in order to gain greater clarity about the very terms of the discussion. Only with clarity about what is integrating with what and what the nature of that integrative relationship is can substantive proposals be clearly

presented and adequately assessed and genuine agreements and disagreements be ferreted out. In short, some type of meta-integration discussion—some exploration of what we mean when we talk about integration—is a necessary prerequisite to more fruitful dialogue and debate.

This article is one attempt to clarify the nature and task of integration. More specifically, this project proposes a framework, a typology of integration, designed to sort out the discussion of integration and to foster further reflection on the basic issues of integration. Before presenting the typology, I will first briefly survey some of the literature in order to gain a better sense of how the term integration is used and to validate the above claims regarding the need for such a proposal. Then I will delineate the typology, drawing attention to certain topics of special relevance and highlighting some implications for Christians. A short conclusion will bring this project to a close.

The Concept of Integration
in the Literature

The word integration is used in a variety of ways with a variety of objects. The following is merely a more or less random sample of that variety. According to Ellison (1977), integration has to do with "psychology and Christianity" (p. 424), while in the same volume Malony (1977) focused on "the problem of relating faith to vocation" (p. 408). Malony furthermore cited Clement, who listed five different ways that "faith can be expressed in the life of a psychologist." These included intrapersonal, professional, experimental, theoretical, and interpersonal types of integration (pp. 397ff).

In a different volume, Malony (1983) spoke of integration in terms of "wholeness and holiness" (p. 27), while Oden (1983) referred to "religionless psychotherapy" (pp. 214ff). In that same book, Parsons

(1983) spoke of relating "theology and therapy' (pp. 244ff) while Adams (1983) argued for "scriptural counseling" and advocated integrating the Bible with counseling (pp. 281ff). Myers (1978), on the other hand, variously referred to relating "Christian belief and human science," "psychology and religion," and "science and religion" (pp. 3, 5). He also spoke directly of integration when he advocated "the integration of theological and psychological perspectives on human nature" (p. 38).

Finch (1980) variously referred to "Christian psychology," "Christian existential therapy," "psychology and Christianity," and "psychology and theology" (pp. 182, 205, 286-287). He also spoke of the inseparability of "religious experience" and "psychological reality" (p. 282), and in his Finch Symposium lectures at Fuller Seminary he (1982) argued for the "integration of psychology and theology" in addition to pressing the need for "integrating psychology and the Christian faith" (p. 7, 13). Two of Finch's respondents, Rogers (1982) and Gilliland (1982) likewise talked of the integration of "psychology and theology," while a third, Smedes (1982), distinguished between three kinds of integration: inter-disciplinary, that is, between theology and psychology; intra-disciplinary, that is, between one's faith and one's psychology; and experiential, that is, the experience of grace in one's life whereby one becomes a more integrated and whole person.

Farnsworth (1985) referred to integration variously in terms of "psychology and Christianity," "psychology and religion," and "psychology and theology" (pp. 9-11, 16, 78). In addition, he spoke of integration between "thought and application" (p. 14) and contrasted "critical integration" with "embodied integration" (Chap. 3). Similarly, Collins (1981) referred to the objects of integration as "psychology and theology," "psychology and Christianity," and "psychology and religion." He also referred to the integration of "theory and practice" and "faith and lifestyle" (pp. 38, 83). Jeeves (1976) spoke of relating "psychology and religion," though his preferred usage had to do with the integration of "psychology and Christianity."

Like Myers, MacKay (1974) spoke of relating "science and Christianity," "science and biblical faith," and "science and religion." Carter and Narramore (1979), on the other hand, more like Farnsworth and Collins, referred to "the integration of psychology and theology" as well as to the relationship between "Christianity and psychology." They maintained, however, that their basic conception of integration involved "wrestling with the relationship between the findings of psychology and the revelation of the Bible" (pp. 16, 20).

In her Finch Symposium lectures, Van Leeuwen (1982) referred to "the ongoing challenge of integrating faith with learning" (p. 9). In the introduction of one of her more recent books, she spoke of "a Christian psychology of the person" and of "the relationship between a Christian worldview and the psychology of personhood" (1985, pp. xii, xiii). In that book she also referred to "the relationship between Christianity and psychology" and "the integration of faith and learning" (pp. 68, 257).

To conclude this whirlwind tour through a sample of the literature, Malony (1986) distinguished between three different kinds of integration: principle, professional, and personal integration. Finally, in his installation address as Dean of the Fuller School of Psychology, Hart (1985) spoke of "our commitment to the integration of psychology and theology" and of the need for the "reconstruction of psychology at the very core of its assumptions according to a Christian worldview" (pp. 1ff).

This survey illustrates the diversity of ways in which the term "integration" is used. From this plurality of usages, a number of important questions emerge. For example, what exactly is involved in integration? Does one integrate psychology with faith, or the Bible, or revelation, or theology, or a Christian worldview, or Christian belief, or Christianity, or religion? Does one integrate theology (or faith, Christianity, etc.) with psychology, or science, or therapy, or counseling? Does one integrate theory with practice, or faith with practice, or faith with learning, or faith with vocation, or religious experience with therapy? In other words, what precisely are the relata in the integrative relationship? And furthermore, what exactly does the term "integrate" mean? Does it mean merely to relate, or does it mean, more specifically, to combine, to harmonize, to unify, or some other possibility? As stated previously, the issue is: what integrates with what, and what is the precise character of that integrative relationship?

The plurality of expressions and usages cited above does not justify the conclusion that each author mentioned is suffering from conceptual fuzziness. There are many different meanings of the term integration, and that plurality is ineradicable. On the other hand, in some of the discussions one meaning slides into another or terms are used as if they are interchangeable, for example, the integration of psychology and theology is viewed as equivalent with the integration of psychology and Christianity or psychology and religion. What the above review of literature demonstrates is that there needs to be greater self-consciousness about the use of terms and greater effort given, in a particular discussion, to clarifying the usages and understandings operative in that discussion. In other words, before a proposal is set forth about the proper way to integrate psychology and theology, for example, it must be clear that in that discussion at least, it is psychology and theology that are being related and not faith and learning, or religion and science, or therapy and the Bible. All of these other relationships need explication too; however, understanding is not furthered if these different kinds of integration are conflated. In short, questions of meaning must, as far as possible, be addressed before questions of truth can be articulated without confusion.

A Typology of Integration

In an effort to sort out the different uses of the term integration, I propose a typology or classification schema in which there are four basic kinds of integration: interdisciplinary integration, intradisciplinary integration, faith-praxis integration, and experiential integration. While I am not entirely satisfied with these labels, they will suffice for now for the various concepts I have in mind. Also, while these labels and this typology bear a resemblance to Smedes' (1982) three models mentioned above, I have developed my typology independently of his, and only subsequently read of his similar approach. Finally, to conclude these prefatory remarks, this typology is by no means exhaustive. There are other kinds of integration in addition to the four described here. These four types are simply the ones that I have identified in trying to make sense out of the many different usages of the term integration.

Interdisciplinary Integration

The first type of integration I have called *interdisciplinary* integration because it is integration *between* disciplines. It is the attempt to unite or combine (integrate, from the Latin *integrare*, which means to unite or form into a whole) aspects of two different disciplines, for example, biblical studies and modern literary criticism, or philosophy and theology, or psychology and history, or psychology and theology. The aim is to compare and contrast and, if possible, reconcile and unite the assumptions, conclusions, methods, and so forth, of two distinct disciplines so as to combine them in some fruitful way.

This type of integration is primarily theoretical in nature and usually has to do with the examination of the foundational issues at the core of each discipline—the fundamental ontological, anthropological, and epistemological issues that lie at the heart of every discipline. Inasmuch, it is concerned with the basic assumptions, and ultimately the religious commitments that guide and shape those assumptions,

that inform the nature and scope of each discipline, the 'proper' methods, the relevant concepts and definitions, the accepted and acceptable canons of inquiry, the status of results, and so on. In other words, this type of integration is inescapably philosophical in nature and ultimately religious in character. By way of comparison, Malony's (1986) "principled integration," Smedes' (1982) "inter-disciplinary integration," and Clement's "theoretical integration" (Malony, 1977) all describe this kind of integration.

This type of integration should be practiced more regularly and diligently by *all* academics, Christian or secular, since it fosters two of the necessary prerequisites to informed scholarship, namely, a minimal understanding of the foundational issues and basic assumptions of one's discipline and a basic knowledge of the interconnections between one's discipline and other related disciplines. In addition, interdisciplinary integration encourages scholarly honesty and integrity. That is to say, to employ one of Gadamer's (1975) criteria of normative interpretation, it yields a greater awareness of one's own presuppositions—presuppositions in part inherited from one's disciplinary tradition.

The relevance of this kind of integration is enhanced when viewed in the context of the omnipresent contemporary temptation to overspecialization—a temptation found not just in psychology or theology but across the whole spectrum of the academic disciplines. Overspecialization is a danger because it often fosters an attitude of studied indifference to, and thus ignorance of, the theoretical "meta-issues" of the discipline in favor of concentration on a narrow range of topics within a subdiscipline. As John Maynard Keynes reportedly said: the person who eschews all theory is most likely in the grip of someone else's theory. Examples of overspecialization abound. A historian is not just a historian, or even a modern historian, but rather a historian of American religious history from 1870 to 1900. And a psychologist is not just a psychologist, or even a clinical psychologist, but a behaviorist specializing in the treatment of phobias.

Now I fully realize that with the knowledge explosion of this current century the days of the "renaissance man," if they ever existed, are long gone. And I also recognize that specialization does not necessarily preclude awareness of the larger "meta-issues." However, it seems clear that the tendency today is towards specialization to the exclusion of awareness of the larger or deeper picture. For example, to take cases close to home, far too many philosophers are oblivious to cross-cultural issues, too many biblical scholars are ignorant of contemporary hermeneutics, and too many psychologists are unaware of the historical and cultural factors that continually influence their theory and therapy. In so far as this reading of the present situation is correct, with its focus on connections with other fields, interdisciplinary integration could help rectify the apparent ignorance of or lack of attention to these larger concerns.

For the Christian scholar, interdisciplinary integration is especially crucial since it yields other important benefits in addition to preventing scholarship which is blind to its own roots or insulated from learning in other areas; for example, as one gains an increased awareness of the foundations of one's own discipline, the task of intradisciplinary integration, as elucidated below, is facilitated and hence the quest to bring one's faith commitment to bear upon one's discipline and profession is enhanced. That is to say, by examining the fundamental philosophical and religious assumptions of a discipline, interdisciplinary integration can help individuals to live out their Christian convictions in the practice of their profession. In addition, by exploring fundamental issues in other areas, interdisciplinary integration assists individuals in gaining a heightened sensitivity to the world view foundation of all scholarship and an increased appreciation of the role of religious commitment and secular ideology within the academy (Holmes, 1983, Olthuis, 1985).

In summary, interdisciplinary integration is the integration of two different disciplines. It is the attempt to combine in some fruitful way two distinct areas of study. To the degree that some awareness of the foundational assumptions of one's discipline is a necessary requirement of every scholar, this kind of integration is incumbent upon all scholars. And in so far as Christian scholars take seriously the call and the challenge to do their scholarship Christianly and apply their faith to their profession, interdisciplinary integration is a necessary dimension of and prolegomenon to the next type of integration, to which I now turn.

Intradisciplinary Integration

The second type of integration is named *intra*disciplinary integration since it is the integration of theory and practice *within* a given discipline or profession. It is the attempt to unite or bring into harmony theoretical perspective and professional practice, whether that be with regard to a historian writing history, a minister leading a worship service, or a psychologist doing therapy. To take an example in the last case, it would mean that a clinical psychologist was showing evidence of intradisciplinary integration of his or her psycho*therapy* was congruent with his or her psycho*theory*, for example, if his or her Freudian theoret-

ical orientation fit with his or her Freudian therapeutic practice. The goal here is internal self-consistency or coherence within a single discipline, profession, vocation, and so forth, rather than the unification of aspects of two distinct disciplines.

This type of integration is theoretical in nature in so far as it has to do with reflection on theory and the development of a practice within one's discipline or profession that flows from one's theoretical orientation. It is practical in so far as it involves the intentional application of theory to concrete life situations, for example, the implementation of psychological theory in a counseling setting. In either case, theory both guides and is guided by practice. To the extent that intradisciplinary integration is theoretical, like interdisciplinary integration, it involves the examination of the foundational issues of the discipline, since any well-formed and complete theoretical perspective, especially in psychology, must give explicit attention to ontological, anthropological, and epistemological questions. And consequently, as with the first type of integration, this type also involves reflections that are inevitably philosophical and religious in nature. By way of comparison, Malony's (1986) "professional integration," Smedes' (1982) "intradisciplinary integration," and Clement's "professional," "experimental," and "interprofessional integration" (Malony, 1977) all fit into this second category of integration.

As with the previous type of integration, intradisciplinary integration is also incumbent upon all academics and professionals, Christian or otherwise, since it fosters awareness of and honesty about one's presuppositions—necessary requirements for integrity in scholarship and/or professional practice. In other words, it nurtures the kind of hermeneutical consciousness that should more regularly characterize the scholarly and professional world. In short, intradisciplinary integration both promotes a minimum level of self-awareness about the assumptions one makes with respect to the foundations of one's discipline and encourages a reasonable degree of self-coherence between one's theoretical perspective and actual practice—characteristics of all sound scholarship and competent professional activity.

Of particular significance here is the growing consensus that the long-dominant Enlightenment ideal of "objective, neutral scholarship," based on a belief in universal, disinterested reason, can no longer be sustained. This ideal—this "prejudice against prejudice" to use Gadamer's words (1975, p. 240)—has in its various guises been systematically dismantled by an impressive host of contemporary thinkers (Bernstein, 1983; Bultmann, 1984; Cone, 1986; Dooyeweerd;

1979, 1980; Gadamer, 1975; Habermas, 1971; Heidegger, 1973; Kuhn, 1970; Kuyper, 1931; MacIntyre, 1988; Miranda, 1974; Planting & Wolterstorff, 1983; Polanyi, 1962; Ricoeur, 1974, 1980; Rorty, 1979; Ruether, 1983; Schussler-Fiorenza, 1983; Wolterstorff, 1976, 1983). The relevance to intradisciplinary integration of this move from a modern to a postmodern epistemology qua hermeneutics is that the imperative concerning hermeneutical consciousness has been greatly intensified. That is to say, the steady demise of the Enlightenment paradigm has meant the increasing recognition that all knowledge is guided by human interests and grounded in commitments of various kinds. And with this recognition, the intradisciplinary task of rendering theory and practice consistent, since it directly involves the discovery and acknowledgement of one's presuppositions or prejudices, has taken on added significance.

For the Christian scholar or professional, however, integration between theory and practice within one's discipline, while necessary, is not sufficient. If it is assumed that Christians should put into practice their basic religious convictions in all areas of life, then not only should they be aware of the basic assumptions and often unexamined commitments within their field, and not only should they exhibit a practice consonant with their own theoretical perspective, but as Christians they should also strive to guide their theorizing and thus their practice according to a world view that is shaped by their Christian faith commitment. For example, evangelical Christians in psychology should orient their practice within psychology not only in a manner consistent with their theoretical perspective, but in accord with a biblical sensitive and informed theoretical perspective. In other words, self-consistency or inner coherence, while necessary, is not sufficient, since it fails to address the *content* of one's perspective. It fails to address the possibility and necessity of a distinctively *Christian* practice.

It is at this point that the talk of integrating "faith and scholarship" is most germane, and that the connections between interdisciplinary and intradisciplinary integration are most evident. In brief, the challenge for Christians who are scholars and professionals consists of at least two parts. First, there is the challenge to engage in theory-practice integration that is informed by one's Christian faith. More specifically, this task is to allow one's Christian faith commitment and basic beliefs to inform one's world view in such a way that the world view will intelligently direct selection and responsibly guide practice (Holmes, 1983; Walsh & Middleton, 1987; Wolters, 1985; Wolterstorff, 1976, 1983). In this

regard, Wolterstorff spoke of "control beliefs" or a "controlling principle" as the basis upon which a Christian scholar accepts or rejects theories (1976, Chap. 11; 1983, Chap. 8). He rightly pointed to the neo-Calvinists Kuyper (1931) and Dooyeweerd (1979, 1980) as the thinkers who gave this concept its classic modern formulation.

Secondly, there is the challenge to engage in theory-practice integration which aims at changing the world. The concern here is not the adjudication of theories but the direction one's theorizing should take. Borrowing from the work of critical social theorists like Habermas (1971), who took a page from the notebook of Marx, Wolterstorff speaks of the need for Christian scholars, and in principle for all Christians, to allow their Christian beliefs to exercise a "governing interest" on their theorizing, that is, to shape "the *direction* in which scholars turn their inquiries" (1983, p. 166). Hence "praxis-oriented theory" that is directed toward obedient and responsible action in the world is needed in conjunction with "faith-based theory" which employs control beliefs to determine theory acceptance and rejection. Both of these tasks are included within intradisciplinary integrations.

In summary, intradisciplinary integration is the integration of theory and practice within a single discipline. It is the attempt to achieve inner consistency with respect to a particular dimension of one's life. In so far as hermeneutical awareness of one's guiding theoretical assumptions and congruence between those assumptions and current practice are legitimate requirements for professional life, this type of integration is incumbent upon all scholars and professionals. To the extent that Enlightenment epistemology is displaced by a hermeneutical epistemology that more accurately reflects the actual nature of human knowing, this kind of integration is doubly required of all scholars. And the the degree that Christians are called to spiritual integrity in their scholarly and/or professional life, allowing their faith to control theory choice as well as guide the direction of their research, intradisciplinary integration is an essential activity and in some ways a specific case of the next type of integration.

Faith-Praxis Integration

The third type of integration is called *faith-praxis* integration because it is the integration of faith commitment with praxis or way of life. It is the attempt to live out one's faith commitment as authentically as possible in everyday life, including one's vocation or professional life but usually going beyond that to include, for example, family relations, business decisions, educational endeavors, institutional religious involvement, ethical decision making, and so forth. The aim with this type of integration is internal harmony or consistency between faith commitment and way of life. In other words, the task is to live in accordance with one's faith commitment and world view.

This kind of integration is not primarily theoretical in nature but rather practical in character since its concern is neither the reconciliation of academic disciplines nor the achievement of congruence between theory and practice within a profession, but the integrity of faith and everyday life. Hence while it is similar to intradisciplinary integration in so far as it too strives for internal coherence, it is different in that faith commitment is related to praxis instead of theory related to practice. Since faith is the ultimate surrender of oneself to the ultimate—a universal human capacity or disposition by which a person finds meaning and certitude (Dooyeweerd, 1979, 1980; Gilkey, 1969; Smart, 1983; Smith, 1978, 1979; Tillich; 1957, Tracy, 1978)—and since praxis in this context refers to the dialectic of action/reflection (Bernstein, 1983; Freire, 1970; Gutierrez, 1973), neither faith nor praxis are theoretical categories. In other words, while faith gives rise to and ultimately grounds theory, it is not itself theoretical. And while praxis contains a theoretical dimension, it refers primarily to the continual process of "practice/reflection on practice/practice" or "reflective action" that characterizes everyday life, and as such is inclusive of but not limited to practice in the sense used with intradisciplinary integration.

Thus, unlike the first two types of integration, faith-praxis integration is not limited to scholars, professionals, and the like, nor limited exclusively to Christians. Rather, given the generally widespread assumption within faiths and traditions that a life of integrity is a necessary implication of religious commitment, faith-praxis integration is a task that all people engage in as they attempt to live their lives in accord with what they take to be of ultimate or final importance. As such it is typically viewed as incumbent upon all people. Even those who disavow any explicit religious commitment still feel compelled to order their lives around a cluster of values or a world view which has at its core a commitment to something as ultimate. For example, die-hard secularists show evidence of faith-praxis integration in living a secular lifestyle, just as Christians engage in faith-praxis integration when they intentionally order their lives according to their Christian commitment and world view.

The importance of this type of integration is increased when one realizes the effects of secularization on religious praxis. While the consequences of secularization are not all bad, for example, it contributed to the end of the kind of religious wars fought in the 17th century, and while the predictions from Comte on about the eventual disappearance of religion in general and Christianity in particular have not come true (Hammond, 1985; Lyon, 1985), nevertheless some of the effects of secularization—for example, the weakening of religious commitment and the marginalization or privatization of religious belief—have been both powerful and detrimental (Lyon, 1985). In so far as secularization has severed the connection between faith and praxis, the importance of faith-praxis integration is increased. And to the extent that secularization has relegated religion, against the intentions and deepest convictions of religion, to the private sphere and thus excluded it from the public sphere—thereby delimiting the scope of religious belief to certain restricted domains of life and rendering it culturally impotent and irrelevant—to that extent the significance and relevance of faith-praxis integration is also magnified.

In this context, faith-praxis integration takes on special significance for Christians since it is a valuable means by which the sacred/secular dichotomy, with its truncation of faith, may be overcome. In other words, given the fact that the call to spiritual integrity and the summons to extend the gospel to all areas of life are both widely acknowledged as verities of the Christian Scriptures and tradition, and that many of the people most revered within the Christian tradition, for example, the saints and heroes of the faith, are held in high esteem precisely because they lived exemplary Christian lives, faith-praxis integration gains in importance because of its ability to contribute to a recovery of spiritual integrity and an application of the Christian gospel to all dimensions of life, public as well as private. Taken seriously, it can increase the fit of faith with way of life and extend the scope of faith to all spheres of culture. In short, faith-praxis integration has been and continues to be an imperative for all Christians who seek to live out their Christian convictions.

In summary, faith-praxis integration is the integration of faith commitment and way of life. It is the attempt to direct one's everyday life according to one's faith-informed world view. To the extent that most people assume that consistency between religious commitment and life praxis is a virtue, this kind of integration is incumbent upon all people. In so far as the effects of secularization increase the privatization of religious belief and practice and render religion irrelevant to public and cultural concerns, this type of integration is also required of all.

And to the degree that a Christian takes seriously the challenge of both Scripture and tradition to live a life of spiritual integrity in all areas of life, faith-praxis integration is a necessary part of responsible and faithful discipleship.

Experiential Integration

The fourth type of integration I have somewhat reluctantly labeled *experiential* integration, since it refers to integration within oneself and/or between oneself and God resulting from personal experience. However, this kind of integration has to do with a particular type of experience, namely, a personal experience of healing, usually as a result of a religious encounter of some kind. The goal here is personal wholeness and spiritual well-being and may include, for example, the resolution of intrapersonal conflict, the healing of emotional scars or painful memories, the integration of feelings with faith, and reconciliation between the believing yet anxious soul and God. In other words, the task is to facilitate and engender the integration of broken lives and divided selves.

This type of integration is primarily if not exclusively atheoretical in nature, since it has to do with, as Smedes (1982) succinctly put it, "the healing of persons, not the refinement of ideas" (p. 101). Its focus is not on the combination of different disciplines or the consistency of theory and practice within one's discipline—both endeavors which involve a substantial concern with theory—but on the personal appropriation of wholeness. Like faith-praxis integration, experiential integration is both a practical and proxical matter. That is to say, it is characterized by concern for reflective action in concrete life situations. However, while similar, experiential integration is not identical with faith-praxis integration since the latter aims at consistency between faith and way of life while the former seeks to achieve personal wholeness. In this regard, Smedes (1982) rightly claims that this kind of integration "is the one that validates the others" (p. 106). In other words, since the authenticity of the other kinds of integration depends largely upon the possession of the requisite qualities, motives, virtues, and so forth—the possession of which can be gained only via certain experiences—experiential integration confirms and legitimizes interdisciplinary, intradisciplinary, and faith-praxis integration, and I suspect other types of integration as well. By way of comparison, this kind of integration corrresponds to Malony's (1986) "personal integration," Smedes' (1982) "the healing experience," and Clement's "intrapersonal integration" (Malony, 1977).

There are a variety of expressions that attempt to describe the religious nature of this experience, for example, an experience of the numinous (Otto, 1950), oneness with the ground of being (Tillich, 1951), reunion with the infinite (Pseudo-Dionysius, 1987), and contemplation and love of God (Bernard of Clairvaux, 1973). And this list does not include non-Christian examples like the Hindu concept of moksha or the Buddhist notion of nirvana. All of these different expressions point to the universal desire for personal wholeness and spiritual well-being and thus reflect the fact that experiential integration involves an inescapable religious quest. At the heart of experiential integration is the idea of a religious encounter in which a person is put in touch with or gains access to that which is ultimate, sacred, and holy, and thereby is made a more integrated and whole person.

For the Christian, and especially the Protestant Christian, experiential integration is usually expressed in terms of grace. That is to say, the personal experience of healing is spoken of in terms of the unmerited love and unconditional acceptance of the faithful God of the Scriptures. Grace and love characterize the very nature of the God who is not only Wholly Other, but also Immanuel—a God who is a tri-unity of three persons in relationship to each other and to all the cosmos. Furthermore, this grace is a gift, received only in faith, that liberates the self from sin, reconciles the believing soul with God, and frees the self for service to God and all creation. In short, for the Christian, experiential integration involves a personal experience of divine grace in which alienation from God, self, and neighbor is replaced by the shalom and wholeness received in faith.

In summary, experiential integration is integration within oneself and between oneself and God as a result of a personal religious experience. It is the attempt to foster and promote shalom with God and neighbor through the healing of brokenness. In so far as spiritual wholeness is a universal human need and desire, the search for this type of integration is characteristic of all people in all cultures. And to the degree that a Christian takes seriously the promise of divine grace that can heal the hurts of an aching heart—a promise fulfilled and incarnate in Jesus the Christ, experiential integration will be characteristic of the Christian search for shalom.

Summary

My typology consists of four distinct kinds of integration. Interdisciplinary integration is integration between different disciplines. In this type, foundational issues are examined with the aim of achieving some degree of unity between the two disciplines. Intradisciplinary integration is integration of theory and practice within a given discipline or profession. Here an effort is made to direct a specific practice according to a particular theoretical perspective. Faith-praxis integration is integration of faith commitment with way of life. In this case, life praxis is guided by religious commitment and world view. Finally, experiential integration is integration within the self and between the self and God. Here healing occurs as a result of a religious encounter—for the Christian, an experience of grace.

In conclusion, in this project I have sought to articulate a typology of kinds of integration that would help clarify the present discussion and thereby advance more fruitful debate. That is, I have attempted to sort out some of the various usages of the term integration in order to gain purchase on at least some of the different meanings of that plurivocal term. If this proposal stimulates further reflection and fosters dialogue on these important issues, then it will have succeeded in its modest intentions. Such reflection and dialogue are necessary if we as Christians are to take seriously the call to live authentic lives of Christian discipleship in today's challenging and ever-changing world.

References

Adams, J. (1983). Christian counseling is scriptural. In H. N. Malony (Ed.). *Wholeness and holiness* (pp. 281-291). Grand Rapids, MI: Baker.

Bernard of Clairvaux. (1973). *Treatises II: The steps of humility and pride and on loving God.* Kalamazoo, MI: Cistercian.

Bernstein, R. (1983). *Beyond objectivism and relativism.* Philadelphia: University of Pennsylvania Press.

Bultmann. R. (1984). *New Testament and mythology and other basic writings.* Philadelphia: Fortress.

Carter, J. D., & Narramore B. (1979). *The integration of psychology and theology.* Grand Rapids, MI: Zondervan.

Collins, G. (1981). *Psychology and theology.* Nashville, TN: Abingdon.

Cone, J. (1986). *A black theology of liberation.* Maryknoll, NY: Orbis.

Dooyeweerd, H. (1979). *Roots of Western culture.* Toronto: Wedge.

Ellison, C. (1977). Christianity and psychology—contradictory or complementary. In H. N. Malony (Ed.), *Current perspectives in the psychology of religion* (pp. 424-433). Grand Rapids, MI: Eerdmans.

Farnsworth, K. (1985). *Whole-hearted integration.* Grand Rapids, MI: Baker.

Finch, J. (1980). Toward a Christian psychology. In H. N. Malony (Ed.), *A Christian existential psychology* (pp. 175-188). Lanham, MD: University Press of America.

Finch, J. (1982). *Nishkamakarma.* Pasadena, CA: Integration.

Freire, P. (1970). *Pedagogy of the oppressed.* New York: Continuum.

Gadamer, H. G. (1975). *Truth and method.* New York: Continuum.

Gilkey, L. (1969). *Naming the whirlwind.* Indianapolis, IN: Bobbs-Merrill.

Gilliland, D. (1982). Integration: Integration is more than method. In J. Finch (Ed.),. *Nishkamakarma* (pp. 85-93). Pasadena, CA: Integration.

Gutierrez, G. (1973). *A theology of liberation.* Maryknoll, NY: Orbis.

Habermas, J. (1971). *Knowledge and human interests.* Boston, MA: Beacon.

Hammond, P. (Ed.). (1985). *The sacred in a secular age.* Berkeley, CA: University of California Press.

Hart, A. (1985). From the heart.... *Psychology News and Notes, 3*(1), 1-6.

Heidegger, M. (1973). *Being and time.* Oxford, England: Blackwell.

Holmes, A. (1983). *Contours of a world view.* Grand Rapids, MI: Eerdmans.

Jeeves. M. (1976). *Psychology and Christianity; The view both ways.* Downers Grove, IL: InterVarsity.

Kuhn, T. (1970). *The structure of scientific revolutions.* Chicago: University of Chicago Press.

Kuyper, A. (1931). *Lectures in Calvinism.* Grand Rapids, MI: Eerdmans.

Lyon, D. (1985). *The steeple's shadow.* Grand Rapids, MI: Eerdmans.

MacIntyre, A. (1988). *Whose justice, which rationality?* Notre Dame, IN: University of Notre Dame Press.

MacKay, D. (1974). *The clockwork image.* Downers Grove, IL: InterVarsity.

Malony, H. N. (Ed.). (1977). *Current perspectives in the psychology of religion.* Grand Rapids, MI: Eerdmans.

Malony, H. N. (Ed.). (1983). *Wholeness and holiness.* Grand Rapids, MI: Baker.

Malony, N. N. (1986). The three Ps of integration. In *Readings for Psychology* (p. 580). Pasadena, CA: Fuller Seminary.

Miranda, J. (1974). *Marx and the Bible.* Maryknoll, NY: Orbis.

Myers, D. (1978). *The human puzzle.* San Francisco: Harper & Row.

Oden, T. (1983). Theology and therapy. In H. N. Malony (Ed.), *Wholeness and holiness* (pp. 199-222). Grand Rapids, MI: Baker.

Olthuis, J. (1985). On worldviews. *Christian Scholars Review, 14,* 153-164.

Otto, R. (1950). *The idea of the holy.* London: Oxford University Press.

Parsons, H. L. (1983). Theology and therapy. In H. N. Malony (Ed.), *Wholeness and holiness* (pp. 244-253). Grand Rapids, MI: Baker.

Planting, A., & Wolterstorff, N. (1983). *Faith and rationality.* Notre Dame, IN: University of Notre Dame Press.

Polanyi, M. (1962). *Personal knowledge.* Chicago: University of Chicago Press.

Pseudo-Dionysius (1987). *The complete works*. New York: Paulist.

Ricoeur, P. (1974). *The conflict of interpretations*. Evanston, IL: Northwestern University Press.

Ricoeur, P. (1980). *Essays on biblical interpretation*. Philadelphia, PA: Fortress.

Rogers, J. (1982). Toward functional integration: Some prefatory notes. In J. Finch (Ed.), *Nishkamakarma* (pp. 69-82). Pasadena, CA: Integration.

Rorty, R. (1979). *Philosophy and the mirror of nature*. Princeton, NJ: Princeton University Press.

Ruether, R. (1983). *Sexism and God-talk*. Boston, MA: Beacon.

Schussler-Fiorenza, E. (1983). *In memory of her*. New York: Crossroad.

Smart, N. (1983). *Worldview*. New York: Scribners.

Smedes, L. (1982). Three models and one to call my own. In J. Finch (Ed.), *Nishkamakarma* (pp. 95-106). Pasadena, CA: Integration.

Smith, W. C. (1978). *The meaning and end of religion*. San Francisco: Harper and Row.

Smith, W. C. (1979). *Faith and belief*. Princeton, NJ: Princeton University Press.

Tillich, P. (1951). *Systematic theology* (Vol. 1). Chicago: University of Chicago Press.

Tillich, P. (1957). *Dynamics of faith*. New York: Harper & Row.

Tracy, D. (1978). *Blessed rage for order*. New York: Seabury.

Van Leeuwen, M. S. (1982). *The sorcerer's apprentice*. Downers Grove, IL: InterVarsity.

Walsh, B., & Middleton, R. (1984). *The transforming vision*. Downers Grove, IL: InterVarsity.

Wolters, A. (1985). *Creation regained*. Grand Rapids, MI: Eerdmans.

Wolterstorff, N. (1976). *Reason within the bounds of religion alone*. Grand Rapids, MI: Eerdmans.

Wolterstorff, N. (1983). *Until justice and peace embrace*. Grand Rapids, MI: Eerdmans.

18

Integration and Beyond:
Principled, Professional, and Personal

Siang-Yang Tan
Graduate School of Psychology
Fuller Theological Seminary

The integration of psychology and Christian faith is discussed in this article in three major areas (Malony, 1995): principled (theoretical-conceptual and research), professional (clinical or practice), and personal (intrapersonal, including spirituality). Personal or intrapersonal integration is viewed as the foundational category of integration without which integration in the principled and professional areas cannot be substantially achieved (Tan, 1987b). In particular, the crucial ministry of the Holy Spirit and the importance of spiritual disciplines are emphasized. Intentional integration covering both implicit and explicit integration in clinical practice is described, focusing on an approach that is Christ-centered, biblically-based, and Spirit-led. Going beyond integration per se, radical discipleship or apprenticeship under the Lordship of Christ is underscored as the ultimate in Kingdom living (Willard, 1998).

The integration of psychology and theology actually has a long history (Vande Kemp, 1996a) but distinctively evangelical attempts at such integration have been made more recently, especially in the last 25-30 years (Worthington, 1994). Carter and Narramore (1979) wrote the well-known basic introduction to the integration of psychology and theology. However, I prefer to use the term integration of psychology and Christian faith or Christianity, acknowledging that theology is crucial to our understanding and experience of Christian faith. Every scholarly discipline needs to be subjected to the Lordship of Christ (see Johnson, 1997) and hence it is more meaningful to speak of the integration of psychology and Christian faith or the integration of economics and Christian faith, and even the integration of theology and Christian faith! We need to think and reflect in biblical, Christian ways about every scholarly discipline we may be engaged in. The central idea behind integration has to do with the task of unifying or becoming united to form a complete whole (Eck, 1996; Hill & Kauffmann, 1996).

I have deliberately chosen as the title of my article, "Integration and Beyond." Let me briefly explain what I mean by "Beyond." There are two particular meanings with which I am using the term. First, there are times and situations when integration of psychology and our Christian faith is not possible—for example, when secular psychology, especially in the clinical or counseling areas, advocates values or methods that are contrary to clear biblical teaching. Whatever is immoral or unethical or unbiblical (i.e., anti-biblical) should not be integrated or accepted. Second, integration, while crucial, especially in a Christian Graduate School of Psychology, is not everything in life. We need to go beyond integration to the bigger picture or perspective on Kingdom living that God has called us to in Christ. Willard (1998) has recently written about such Kingdom living as "the Divine conspiracy" by the Triune God of leading us into radical discipleship or apprenticeship to Jesus Christ as our Lord so that we are transformed into greater Christlikeness.

Let us return then to the task of integration. Following Malony (1995), I will discuss integration of psychology and Christian faith in three major areas: principled (theoretical-conceptual and research), professional (clinical or practice), and personal (intrapersonal, including spirituality). Due to space constraints, I can only engage in somewhat brief reflections in these areas of integration.

Principled Integration

Space does not permit me to go into a detailed description of the many theoretical or conceptual approaches to integration that have been proposed over the years. Eck (1996) has written a helpful summary of 27 models of integration, organizing them into three major paradigms: the non-integrative paradigm, the manipulative paradigm, and the non-manipulative paradigm. In his own words:

> The *Non-Integrative Paradigm* does not seek integration of the data but rather builds its understanding of God's truth on one discipline alone. The *Manipulative Paradigm* seeks to integrate the data of

© *Journal of Psychology and Christianity*, 2001, *20*, 18-28. Used by permission.

both disciplines, but the data of one discipline must be altered before becoming acceptable to the other discipline. The final paradigm, the *Non-Manipulative Paradigm*, accepts the data from both disciplines directly into the integrative process.

Each paradigm contains certain processes that define the method for how the data of each discipline will be integrated. The Non-Integrative Paradigm contains only the *Rejects Process*; the Manipulative Paradigm contains both the *Reconstructs Process* and the *Transforms Process*; and the Non-Manipulative Paradigm utilizes the *Correlates Process* and the *Unifies Process*. (p. 103)

Carter (1996) recently emphasized again his view that there are four basic approaches academically to integration (see Carter & Narramore, 1979): Christianity Against Psychology (usually held by conservatives or biblically militant Christians), Christianity of Psychology (usually held by those of a liberal theological persuasion), the Parallels model (Christianity and Psychology are both seen as equally important but essentially separate fields), and Christianity Integrates Psychology.

A fundamental assumption made by almost all integrators is that all truth is God's truth, whether it is through special revelation in the Scriptures as God's inspired Word and in Jesus Christ, or through general revelation in nature and as a result of good research and scholarly reflection. Hence the Non-Manipulative Paradigm described by Eck (1996) that attempts to correlate or unify such special revelation and general revelation truth appeals to many. Vande Kemp (1996b) has emphasized the need to reject both psychologism and theologism. While I personally believe that ultimately all truth is God's truth, that is, in the unity of truth, it is also true that in a fallen world with fallen people, our interpretation of data is never perfect and, therefore, there are times when theological truth, based on the best exegesis and hermeneutics available of the biblical text, will conflict with psychological truth based on the latest research findings and theoretical conceptualizations. At such times, while we need to maintain an attitude of humility and receptivity to learning from both psychology and theology, I believe that we still need to give the Bible ultimate authority, as long as the interpretations of the particular texts being considered are relatively clear. Farnsworth (1996) recently made a similar point that clarifies his present position thus:

Psychology and theology are both vulnerable to error because of human fallibility. Therefore theology does not necessarily have functional authority over psychology (if the two are in conflict, but the theological inquiry was done poorly). Theology, however, is more dependable than psychology because of the object of its inquiry, the Bible. Therefore psychology never has functional authority over theology (if we have done poor theology, then we cannot proceed until we do it right). … Psychology addresses personal needs and developmental tendencies. Theology does also, but to a much more limited extent. Even so, when the two are in conflict, theological conclusions must prevail. Theology's primary domain is in the areas of ultimacy and moral obligation, where psychology has no legitimate say. (p. 132)

Crabb (1977, 1987) has made similar assertions about the ultimate authority of the Bible and how the Bible does deal with the major issues and problems in human living, in thematic and extended application contexts. It is comprehensive, even if it is not exhaustive (cf. Jones, 1996), regarding human beings and their functioning and dysfunctioning.

The danger of such a view, of course, is naïve biblicism and proof-texting with more eisegesis than proper exegesis! We must all be careful not to make the Bible say or mean more (or less) than what it actually says or means. However, it is my conviction that while there are naïve biblicists today who continue to propagate a narrow so-called "biblical" counseling approach as *the* only Christian approach to counseling, the greater danger in academic centers of Christian psychology is to swing to the other extreme and not take the Bible seriously enough. We do need to have more grace-filled dialogue and to build bridges with such "biblical" counselors (Monroe, 1997).

A recent special issue of the *Journal of Psychology and Christianity* (1997, 16[4], pp. 293-371) guest edited by James Beck dealt with the topic of "Sola Scriptura." The articles written by Welch and Powlison (1997a) who advocated the Scripture's constitutive role for counseling, and by Hurley and Berry (1997a) who argued for a more nuanced pro-integration position on the relation of Scripture and psychology in counseling are worth reading, and so are their respective responses (Hurley & Berry, 1997b; Welch & Powlison, 1997b). While I agree that both general revelation (and common grace) and special revelation should always be seen as part of God's truth, it is likely that the hard work of properly interpreting biblical truth systematically and then applying it appropriately to psychological issues and human problems in the clinical or professional area of psychology still remains a challenge to all of us. Collins (1993) recently attempted to apply basic Christian theology or doctrine (e.g., Bibliology: the doctrine of Scripture, Theology Proper: the doctrine of God the Father, Christology: the doctrine of God the Son, Pneumatology: the doctrine of God the Holy Spirit, Anthropology: the doctrine of human beings. Hamartiology: the doctrine of sin, Soteriology: the doctrine of salvation, Ecclesiology: the doctrine of the church, Angelology: the doctrine of angels, and Eschatology: the doctrine of the future) to the context of Christian counseling. He tried to provide the biblical basis of Christian counseling for people helpers. Although this is a helpful basic beginning (also see Collins, 1988), much more work needs to be done in this area by theologians and psychologists working together, or by theologically trained psychologists or psychologically trained theologians. We need to take the Bible much more seriously and truly believe that it is the inspired Word of God. We should study it and apply it much more deeply and systematically than we have so far in our attempts as Christian psychologists to do integration. A recent issue of the *Journal of Psychology and Theology* (1998, 26[1], 1-124) guest edited by Nancy Duvall did a good job in presenting biblically-based perspectives on the self/soul, a crucial area for integration.

I also wish to discuss briefly psychology-as-science. In the integration literature psychology is often used as a shorthand for psychotherapy or counseling, referring to psychology as clinical practice. We need to be clearer and cleaner with our terminology as Jeeves (1997) has repeatedly reminded us. Psychology is a far broader discipline than psychotherapy or counseling. It is indeed a scientific discipline with a solid foundation in empirical research. There are substantial areas of psychological knowledge such as neuropsychology, experimental psychology, and social psychology (see Myers, 1996), where empirical research methodology has significantly advanced the field. Even in the clinical practice area, empirically supported interventions are now becoming crucial or central. A recent issue of the *Journal of Consulting and Clinical Psychology* (1998, 66[1], pp. 3-167) had a special section on empirically supported psychological therapies, guest edited by Philip C. Kendall and Dianne L. Chambless. We should respect good science and empirical research as well as do good science and research.

However, I do take seriously the call of colleagues in the integration literature (e.g., Vande Kemp, 1996b) to go beyond a narrow empiricism that may end up being scientism or the worship of science and experimental methodology. We need to broaden our research methodology to include qualitative and phenomenological approaches, without negating the value of empirical research and experimental methods. However, ultimately, we must not end up being empirical pragmatists who will use whatever clinical interventions that have been found to work or to be effective—ultimately, we will only use empirically supported psychological therapies that do not contradict Scripture, especially morally and ethically (Tan, 1987a). For example, whatever leads to oppression, selfism or self-centered living, immorality and unethical consequences, even if effective, will not be utilized by Christian therapists.

When we speak about the integration of psychology and Christian faith, let us be clear therefore that we are referring to all of psychology as a scientific discipline and as a profession (Jones, 1994, 1996). If we really mean to speak more specifically about the clinical practice of psychology then we should refer to the integration of clinical or counseling psychology and Christian faith or even more specifically of psychotherapy or counseling and Christian faith. In this narrower area of psychotherapy or counseling, values become crucial and prominent and distinctively Christian perspectives and values need to be integrated. I therefore disagree with Jeeves (1997) who has asserted that any attempt to mix or integrate Christian beliefs with psychological accounts is sure to lead to confusion and to make nonsense of both domains or kinds of knowledge, at least in this narrower area of therapeutic practice. I do agree with him that we need to do good empirical research on the effectiveness of Christian approaches to psychotherapy.

I should also comment briefly on the psychology of religion (e.g., see Hood, Spilka, Hunsberger, & Gorsuch, 1996; Pargament, 1997; Wulff, 1997) as a special area of psychology as a discipline. While I believe that psychology of religion is an important area of scholarship and research basically using psychological research methods, especially empirical ones to study and investigate religious phenomena and experience, I do not view it as being synonymous with integration. There is a danger in contemporary psychology of religion of being reductionistic regarding religious issues.

Finally, I want to affirm once more my conviction that personal or intrapersonal integration including the spirituality of the integrator is the most fundamental and foundational category of integration, without which biblical integration of psychology and Christian faith in the principled (conceptual-theoretical and research categories) and professional (clinical or practice category) areas cannot be substantially achieved (Tan, 1987b; also see Carter & Narramore, 1979, p. 117). I have written elsewhere "that the most significant reason for the foundational importance of intrapersonal integration and the spirituality of the ... integrator, is a biblical one: It is the Holy Spirit who teaches us all things (Jn. 14:26) and guides us into all truth (Jn. 16:13), and hence the Christian psychologist or other mental health professional ... must first of all, and above all, be a Spirit-filled or spiritual person in order to more fully understand and appropriate truth, including 'psychotheological' truth" (Tan, 1987b, p. 35). I have more to say about the spirituality of the integrator later in this article when I deal with the area of Personal or Intrapersonal Integration.

Professional Integration

This area of integration refers to integration in clinical practice or what Hall and Hall (1997) recently called "integration in the therapy room." I have described two major models of implicit and explicit integration of religion or spirituality in clinical practice more generally as two ends of a continuum (Tan, 1996b):

> Implicit integration ... refers to a more covert approach that does not initiate the discussion of religious or spiritual issues and does not openly, directly or systematically use spiritual resources. ... Explicit integration ... refers to a more overt approach that directly and systematically deals with spiritual or religious issues in therapy, and uses spiritual resources like prayer, Scripture, or sacred texts, referrals to church or other religious groups or lay counselors, and other religious practices. (p. 368)

Whether a Christian therapist uses implicit or explicit integration or moves along the continuum in actual therapeutic practice depends on the client and his or her needs and problems, as well as the training and inclination of the therapist. *Intentional integration* is the key in professional practice: prayerfully depending on the Holy Spirit to lead and guide the therapeutic session, using implicit or explicit integration or both in a professionally competent, ethically responsible and clinically sensitive way for the benefit and growth of the client. This is

done with clear informed consent from the client, and hence without forcing the therapist's beliefs or spiritual practices on the client (Tan, 1994).

It should be noted that the integration of religion and clinical practice in general has recently become more accepted and respected in secular psychology, with several significant books published by both the American Psychological Association (Miller, 1999; Richards & Bergin, 1997, 2000; Shafranske, 1996), and the American Counseling Association (Kelly, 1995). Also published recently are books on spirituality in family therapy (Walsh, 1999), social work practice (Canda & Furman, 1999), and multicultural counseling (Fukuyama & Sevig, 1999).

The use of the spiritual disciplines such as meditation, prayer, fasting, study, simplicity, solitude, submission, service, confession, worship, guidance, and celebration (Foster, 1988) in clinical practice in the context of explicit integration can also be of benefit and help to some clients with particular types of presenting problems (Tan, 1996a). A specific spiritual intervention is the use of inner healing prayer for the healing of painful memories (Tan, 1996b).

Oden (1992) has emphasized in particular the historic pastoral care tradition as a unique resource for Christian psychologists. He has noted how the classical writers of this tradition anticipated therapeutic conditions such as warmth, empathy, and genuineness, as well as the complexity of therapeutic work and the subtlety of human character.

The Holy Spirit's ministry in effective Christian psychotherapy or counseling is crucial, based on the Spirit's power and spiritual gifts (e.g., exhortation or encouragement, knowledge, wisdom, healing, discerning of spirits, and mercy), truth, and fruit (Tan, 1992, 1999b; also see Gilbert & Brock, 1985, 1988; Ingram, 1996; Kunst & Tan, 1996; Vining, 1995a, 1995b, 1997; Vining & Decker, 1996). There has been a recent emphasis in the integration literature on the need to integrate psychology, theology, and spirituality, or psychological awareness, theological understanding, and spiritual formation (McMinn, 1996; McMinn & McRay, 1997), in line with my earlier call to focus more on spirituality (Tan, 1987b). While training is important, the spiritual gifting and personality characteristics of the Christian therapist may be of greater significance in producing therapeutic outcomes. A dissertation study completed by one of my Ph.D. advisees Ron De Vries (1994) showed that spiritual gifts, especially the gift of exhortation or encouragement and personality traits, especially 16PF Factor C, Emotionally Stable, were significantly related to measures of therapeutic competence (empathic understanding, respect, and genuineness).

Bufford (1997) recently suggested the following helpful distinctives of Christian counseling:

> Counseling is most truly Christian when the counselor has a deep faith; counsels with excellence; holds a Christian world view; is guided by Christian values in choosing the means, goals and motivations of counseling; actively seeks the presence and work of God; and actively utilizes spiritual interventions and resources within ethical guidelines. (p. 120)

The need to have a biblically based ethical approach to the practice and other business aspects of Christian psychotherapy or counseling has also been noted (Farnsworth, 1980, 1996; also see Dueck, 1995; Sanders, 1997; Tjeltveit, 1992). Under the Lordship of Christ, we need to conduct our professional practice in ways that are ethical and that include caring for the poor, oppressed, victimized, and disenfranchised. We also need to avoid elitism and arrogance or the dangers of "overprofessionalism."

A significant part of professional integration ironically is to acknowledge the effectiveness and crucial role of lay counselors or helpers, especially in the church and other ministry contexts (Tan, 1991). The professional psychologist or therapist can have the following roles in the development of lay counseling or paraprofessional helping: training and supervising paraprofessional helper or lay counselors; serving on boards of directors of lay helping organizations; educating groups about the positive contributions of psychological services; consulting with organizations interested in establishing lay helping services; serving as a referral source when professional therapy is needed; doing outcomes research and evaluation of lay helping; and educating psychologists and other mental health professionals about the significant role they can have in the development of lay counselors or paraprofessional helpers (Tan, 1997). While some encouraging results have been found supporting the effectiveness of lay Christian counseling (e.g., Toh & Tan, 1997; also see Worthington, Kurusu, McCullough, & Sandage, 1996), more controlled outcome research is needed in this area, as well as in the area of professional Christian psychotherapy and counseling.

Finally, the need to be sensitive to diversity issues, especially cross-cultural issues in Christian psychotherapy and counseling that is Christ-centered, biblically based, and Spirit-filled, should be pointed out (see Tan, 1999a; Tan & Dong, 2000).

Personal Integration

Personal or intrapersonal integration is the most foundational area of integration (Tan, 1987b; also see Carter & Narramore, 1979). Bufford (1997) recently emphasized that Christian counseling is primarily about character, including the personal godliness of the therapist or counselor. He pointed out that the person, life, and work of the counselor is therefore at the core of consecrated Christian counseling. Guy (1987) wrote a classic book over a decade ago on the personal life of the psychotherapist.

Intrapersonal or personal integration refers to a person's own appropriation of faith and integration of psychological and spiritual experience. As I have written elsewhere (Tan, 1987b):

> Carter and Narramore (1979) have suggested several essential attitudes and attributes relevant to intrapersonal or personal integration, which cover both psychological and spiritual aspects, including the following: humility and an awareness of finite limitations, tolerance for ambiguity, balanced expression of one's intellect and emotions, openness instead of defensiveness due to personal anxieties and insecurities, and an eternal perspective on our work as part of humanity's God-ordained task of reconciling human beings to God, themselves, and others. Crabb (1977) ... has emphasized the need for Christian psychologists to do the following: spend as much time in the regular and systematic study of the Bible as in the study of psychology; have both a general grasp of the structure and the overall content of Scripture as well as a working knowledge of Bible doctrine; and be involved in the fellowship of a Bible-believing church. (p. 35)

The crucial role of spiritual disciplines in Christian psychotherapy and counseling for both the therapist and the client, in facilitating personal and spiritual growth cannot be overemphasized (see Tan, 1998). Spiritual disciplines according to Dallas Willard (1996), "refer to an ancient tradition of activities which are means of grace, ways of approaching and relating richly to God ... activities in our power, things we can do, to meet God in such a way that we become able to do what we cannot do by direct effort" (p. 18). Willard (1988) has listed and described the *disciplines of abstinence* (solitude, silence, fasting, frugality, chastity, secrecy, and sacrifice) and the *disciplines of engagement* (study, worship, celebration, service, prayer, fellowship, confession, and submission). Foster's (1988) list of 12 major spiritual disciplines has already been mentioned earlier. They involve both individual and group life.

More recently, I wrote a book with Douglas Gregg on the disciplines of the Holy Spirit (Tan & Gregg, 1997). We focused on the following spiritual disciplines as power connectors to the presence and power of the Holy Spirit who enables us to grow spiritually in Christ: (a) Drawing near to God: Disciplines of Solitude (solitude and silence, listening and guidance, prayer and intercession, study and meditation); (b) Yielding to God: Disciplines of Surrender (repentance and confession, yielding and submission, fasting, and worship); (c) Reaching Out to Others: Disciplines of Service (fellowship, simplicity, service, and witness).

A recent book by Ortberg (1997) on spiritual disciplines for ordinary people may also be helpful, especially for use as a self-help book for clients (also see Tan & Gregg, 1997).

Concluding Comments

I have shared some brief reflections on integration and beyond in the areas of principled, professional, and personal integration. I would like to close by emphasizing again going beyond integration to the bigger picture or perspective of life, and the Christian life in particular: that of radical discipleship and apprenticeship to Jesus Christ in the context of a personal and loving relationship with Him that enables us, by the power of the Holy Spirit to live the eternal kind of life He came to give us *now*, and not just in the hereafter. Dallas Willard (1998) has recently written a profound and helpful book on this theme of Kingdom living now which he has called "the Divine conspiracy!"

Let me end with a quotation from Willard (1996) relevant to the narrower context of integration in psychotherapy and counseling:

Many counselors today are learning that for their own work, deep immersion in the disciplines is necessary, both for developing their own character, and beyond that, accessing special powers of grace for their work in counseling people. Many psychologists are learning how to use techniques of prayer and various kinds of ministry to have a much greater effect than they could have if all they had to go on were just the things they learned in their clinical training

programs. ... I think the most important and the most solid way is to begin to integrate prayer and spiritual teaching into the therapy process as it seems appropriate ... we can observe what the effects of prayer and spiritual understanding are, and advise clients as to how they can use Scripture, how they can worship, and so forth in a way most helpful to them. ... I think the key issue here lies deeper than even matters of integration as we commonly discuss it. It is a matter of our understanding of the gospel of Jesus Christ as one which breaks through the natural world and brings it into the spiritual world and invites us as individuals to learn to live an eternal kind of life now. (pp. 19-20)

References

Bufford, R. K. (1997). Consecrated counseling: Reflections on the distinctives of Christian counseling. *Journal of Psychology and Theology, 25*, 111-122.

Canda, E. R., & Furman, L. D. (1999). *Spiritual diversity in social work practice.* New York: The Free Press.

Carter, J. D. (1996). Success without finality: The continuing dialogue of faith and psychology. *Journal of Psychology and Christianity, 15*, 116-122.

Carter, J. D., & Narramore, S. B. (1979). *The integration of psychology and theology.* Grand Rapids, MI: Zondervan.

Collins, G. R. (1988). *Christian counseling: A comprehensive guide* (Rev. ed.). Dallas, TX: Word.

Collins, G. R. (1993). *The biblical basis of Christian counseling for people helpers.* Colorado Springs, CO: NavPress.

Crabb, L. J., Jr. (1977). *Effective biblical counseling.* Grand Rapids, MI: Zondervan.

Crabb, L. J., Jr. (1987). *Understanding people: Deep longings for relationship.* Grand Rapids, MI: Zondervan.

De Vries, R. J. (1994). *Is it a gift? The relationship between therapeutic competence and individual therapist characteristics of experience, personality, and spirituality.* Unpublished doctoral dissertation, Graduate School of Psychology, Fuller Theological Seminary, Pasadena, CA.

Dueck, A. C. (1995). *Between Jerusalem and Athens: Ethical perspectives on culture, religion, and psychotherapy.* Grand Rapids, MI: Baker.

Eck, B. E. (1996). Integrating the integrators: An organizing framework for a multifaceted process of integration. *Journal of Psychology and Christianity, 15*, 101-115.

Farnsworth, K. E. (1980). Christian psychotherapy and the culture of professionalism. *Journal of Psychology and Theology, 8*, 115-121.

Farnsworth, K. E. (1996). The devil sends errors in pairs. *Journal of Psychology and Christianity, 15*, 123-132.

Foster, R. (1988). Celebration of discipline (rev. ed.). San

Francisco: Harper & Row.

Fukuyama, M. A., & Sevig, T. D. (1999). *Integrating spirituality into multicultural counseling.* Thousand Oaks, CA: Sage.

Gilbert, M. G., & Brock, R. T. (Eds.). (1985). *The Holy Spirit and counseling: Vol. I. Theology and theory.* Peabody, MA: Hendrickson.

Gilbert, M. G., & Brock, R. T. (Eds.). (1988). *The Holy Spirit and counseling: Vol. II. Principles and practice.* Peabody, MA: Hendrickson.

Guy, J. D. (1987). *The personal life of the psychotherapist.* New York: Wiley.

Hall, M. E. L., & Hall, T. W. (1997). Integration in the therapy room: An overview of the literature. *Journal of Psychology and Theology, 25,* 86-101.

Hill, P. C., & Kauffmann, D. R. (1996). Psychology and theology: Toward the challenges. *Journal of Psychology and Christianity, 15,* 175-183.

Hood, R. W., Jr., Spilka, B., Hunsberger, B., & Gorsuch, R. L. (1996). *Psychology of religion: An empirical approach* (2nd ed.). New York: Guilford.

Hurley, J. B., & Berry, J. T. (1997a). The relation of scripture and psychology in counseling from a pro-integration position. *Journal of Psychology and Christianity, 16,* 323-345.

Hurley, J. B., & Berry, J. T. (1997b). Response to Welch and Powlison. *Journal of Psychology and Christianity, 16,* 350-362.

Ingram, J. A. (1996). Psychological aspects of the filling of the Holy Spirit: A preliminary model of post-redemptive personality functioning. *Journal of Psychology and Theology, 24,* 104-113.

Jeeves, M. A. (1997). *Human nature at the millennium: Reflections on the integration of psychology and Christianity.* Grand Rapids, MI: Baker.

Johnson, E. L. (1997). Christ, the Lord of psychology. *Journal of Psychology and Theology, 25,* 11-27.

Jones, S. L. (1994). A constructive relationship for religion with the science and profession of psychology: Perhaps the boldest model yet. *American Psychologist, 49,* 184-199.

Jones, S. L. (1996). Reflections on the nature and future of the Christian psychologies. *Journal of Psychology and Christianity, 15,* 133-142.

Kelly, E. W. (1995). *Religion and spirituality in counseling and psychotherapy.* Alexandria, VA: American Counseling Association.

Kunst, J., & Tan, S. -Y. (1996). Psychotherapy as "work in the Spirit": Thinking theologically about psychotherapy. *Journal of Psychology and Theology, 24,* 284-291.

Malony, H. N. (1995). *Integration musings: Thoughts on being a Christian professional* (2nd ed.). Pasadena, CA: Integration Press.

McMinn, M. R. (1996). *Psychology, theology, and spirituality in Christian counseling.* Wheaton, IL: Tyndale.

McMinn, M. R., & McRay, B. W. (1997). Spiritual disciplines and the practice of integration: Possibilities and challenges for Christian psychologists. *Journal of Psychology and Theology, 25,* 102-110.

Miller, W. R., (Ed). (1999). *Integrating spirituality into treatment.* Washington DC: American Psychological Association.

Monroe, P. G. (1997). Building bridges with biblical counselors. *Journal of Psychology and Theology, 25,* 28-37.

Myers, D. G. (1996). On professing psychological science and Christian faith. *Journal of Psychology and Christianity, 15,* 143-149.

Oden, T. C. (1992). The historic pastoral care tradition: A resource for Christian psychologists. *Journal of Psychology and Theology, 20,* 137-146.

Ortberg, J. (1997). The life you've always wanted: Spiritual disciplines for ordinary people. Grand Rapids, MI: Zondervan.

Pargament, K. I. (1997). *The psychology of religion and coping: Theory, research, practice.* New York: Guilford.

Richards, P. S., & Bergin, A. E. (1997). *A spiritual strategy for counseling and psychotherapy.* Washington, DC: American Psychological Association.

Richards, P. S., & Bergin, A. E., (Eds.). (2000). *Handbook of psychotherapy and religious diversity.* Washington, DC: American Psychological Association.

Sanders, R. K. (Ed.). (1997). *Christian counseling ethics: A handbook for therapists, pastors, & counselors.* Downers Grove, IL: InterVarsity Press.

Shafranske, E. P. (Ed.). (1996). *Religion and the clinical practice of psychology.* Washington, DC: American Psychological Association.

Tan, S.-Y. (1987a). Cognitive-behavior therapy: A biblical approach and critique. *Journal of Psychology and Theology, 15,* 103-112.

Tan, S.-Y. (1987b). Intrapersonal integration: The servant's spirituality. *Journal of Psychology and Christianity, 6*(1), 34-39.

Tan, S.-Y. (1991). *Lay counseling: Equipping Christians for a helping ministry.* Grand Rapids, MI: Zondervan.

Tan, S.-Y. (1992). The Holy Spirit and counseling ministries. *The Christian Journal of Psychology and Counseling, VII*(3), 8-11.

Tan, S.-Y. (1994). Ethical considerations in religious psychotherapy: Potential pitfalls and unique resources. *Journal of Psychology and Theology, 22,* 389-394.

Tan. S.-Y. (1996a). Practicing the presence of God: The work of Richard J. Foster and its applications to psychotherapeutic practice. *Journal of Psychology and Christianity, 15,* 17-28.

Tan, S.-Y. (1996b). Religion in clinical practice: Implicit and explicit integration. In E. P. Shafranske (Ed.), *Religion and the clinical practice of psychology* (pp. 365-387). Washington, DC: American Psychological Association.

Tan, S.-Y. (1997). The role of the psychologist in paraprofessional helping. *Professional Psychology: Research and Practice, 28,* 268-272.

Tan, S. -Y. (1998). The spiritual disciplines and counseling. *Christian Counseling Today, 6*(2), 8-9, 20-21.

Tan, S.-Y. (1999a). Cultural issues in Spirit-filled psychotherapy. *Journal of Psychology and Christianity, 18,* 164-176.

Tan, S.-Y. (1999b). Holy Spirit, role in counseling. In D. G. Benner & P. C. Hill (Eds.), *Baker encyclopedia of psychology and counseling* (2nd ed.), pp. 568-569. Grand Rapids, MI: Baker.

Tan, S,-Y., & Dong, N. J. (2000). Psychotherapy with members of Asian American churches and spirit traditions. In P. S. Richards and A. E. Bergin (Eds.), *Handbook of psychotherapy and religious diversity*. Washington, D. C.: American Psychological Association.

Tan, S.-Y., & Gregg, D. H. (1997). *Disciplines of the Holy Spirit*. Grand Rapids, MI: Zondervan.

Tjeltveit. A. C. (1992). The psychotherapist as Christian ethicist: Theology applied to practice. *Journal of Psychology and Theology, 20*, 89-98.

Toh, Y. M., & Tan, S.-Y. (1997). The effectiveness of church-based lay counselors: A controlled outcome study. *Journal of Psychology and Christianity, 16*, 260-267.

Vande Kemp, H. (1996a). Historical perspective: Religion and clinical psychology in America. In E. P. Shafranske (Ed.), *Religion and the clinical practice of psychology* (pp. 71-112). Washington, DC: American Psychological Association.

Vande Kemp, H. (1996b). Psychology and Christian spirituality: Explorations of the inner world. *Journal of Psychology and Christianity, 15*, 161-174.

Vining, J. K. (Ed.). (1995a). Pentecostal caregivers: Anointed to heal. East Rockaway, NY: Cummings and Hathaway.

Vining, J. K. (1995b). *Spirit-centered counseling: A pneumascriptive approach*. East Rockaway, NY: Cummings and Hathaway.

Vining, J. K. (Ed.). (1997). *The Spirit of the Lord is upon me: Essential papers on Spirit-filled caregiving. Theological foundations*. East Rockaway, NY: Cummings and Hathaway.

Vining, J. K., & Decker, E. E. (Eds.). (1996). *Soul care: A Pentecostal-Charismatic perspective*. East Rockaway, NY: Cummings and Hathaway.

Welch, E., & Powlison, D. (1997a). "Every common bush afire with God": The Scripture's constitutive role for counseling. *Journal of Psychology and Christianity, 16*, 303-322.

Welch, E., & Powlison, D. (1997b). Response to Hurley and Berry. *Journal of Psychology and Christianity, 16*, 346-349.

Willard, D. (1988). *The Spirit of the disciplines*. San Francisco: Harper & Row.

Willard, D. (1996). Spirituality: Going beyond the limits. *Christian Counseling Today, 4*(1), 16-20.

Willard, D. (1998). *The divine conspiracy: Rediscovering our hidden life in God*. San Francisco: Harper SanFrancisco.

Worthington, E. L., Jr. (1994). A blueprint for intradisciplinary integration. *Journal of Psychology and Theology, 22*, 79-86.

Worthington, E. L., Jr., Kurusu, T. A., McCullough, M. E., & Sandage, S. J. (1996). Empirical research on religion and psychotherapeutic processes and outcomes: A 10-year review and research prospectus. *Psychological Bulletin, 119*, 448-487.

Wulff, D. (1997). *Psychology of religion: Classic and contemporary* (2nd ed.). New York; Wiley.

Section V
Models of Integration

Relating the truths of psychology and Christianity is part of the larger issue of relating science and faith discussed in section II. This can occur when trying to relate outcomes from different perspectives on life (individualistic, communal, traditional, modern), on methods of investigation (natural science, religion), from independent disciplines (biology, sociology, philosophy), or from within a discipline (cognitive, behavioral, psychodynamic, systems). The more dissimilar the values, assumptions, methods, and organizing structures between the two perspectives, the harder it can be to relate them and the greater the challenge for the integrator. For instance, it is easier to relate cognitive and behavioral approaches than to relate behavioral and psychodynamic approaches.

Models for relating psychology and Christianity are helpful for guiding and clarifying the process. To be useful, these models must address several issues. They must determine the nature of the elements or disciplines they are seeking to relate. Each perspective, using its approved methods, goes through its own process of discovery and produces data from which it reaches conclusions. What findings, what data will one try to integrate? What content from the differing perspectives will be addressed?

A second issue is to determine the assumptions that guide the process by which this content will be related. Does one perspective take precedence over the other because its content, methods, or assumptions are viewed as more reliable? Are the two perspectives equal partners in the process with each making its unique contribution? Are there particular control beliefs such as Christian values and worldviews that guide the process? Is there a data source that trumps all other data sources, such as Scripture or empirical data?

A final issue addressed by an integrative model is the limitations of the model itself. A good model has heuristic value but all models fall short of reality. In using a particular model of integration, what are its limitations? What does the model not address? What biases does the model contain? Under what circumstances and conditions might a particular model best be used?

The three articles in this section represent classic and seminal works from the 1970s, 1980s, and 1990s that identify models for the integration of psychology and Christianity. Each establishes a unique framework of conceptual organization for their models of integration and with that, their unique language, definitions, and systematic conceptualizations.

John Carter's (1977) article is a classic in the history of integration writings. *Sacred and Secular Models of Psychology and Religion* was later expanded into a book co-authored with Bruce Narramore (see Carter & Narramore, 1979, under "Suggestions for Further Reading" below). Here Carter sets out the framework for his models of integration. Identifying developments in the psychology of religion and the growing interest of evangelical Christians in psychology, Carter identifies four secular models by which psychologists have attempted to relate psychology to religion, and four corresponding sacred models by which evangelical Christians have attempted to relate Scripture to psychology. Although these models mirror each other, Carter explains that there are specific differences in the terminology used within the sacred and secular versions of each model.

Using four of H. Richard Niebuhr's five models of interaction between Christ and culture, Carter identifies the assumptions and psychological representatives of the four secular models; Psychology *Against* Religion, Psychology *Of* Religion, Psychology *Parallels* Religion, and Psychology *Integrates* Religion.

The same four Niebuhrian models are used by Carter to identify the assumptions and Christian representatives of the four sacred models; Scripture *Against* Psychology, Scripture *Of* Psychology, Scripture *Parallels* Psychology, and Scripture *Integrates* Psychology. The article ends with an evaluation and critique of the use of these models and their perspectives on a range of issues. Believing that the integrates model is the only true model of integration, Carter challenges all Christians in psychology to become more aware of the model from which they operate.

Al Dueck's (1989) article, *On Living in Athens: Models of Relating Psychology, Church, and Culture*, wonderfully reframes for psychologists Tertullian's ancient question, "What has Jerusalem to do with Athens?" Dueck reinterprets Niebuhr's (1951) five models of interaction between Christ and culture as five strategies for relating psychology and Christianity. Responding to the church's tendency to reject either culture as pagan or to accept uncritically culture as a gift, Dueck offers his five models as a range of acceptable intermediate strategies.

Dueck presents an extended evaluation of the benefits and limitations of each model and identifies a Christian representative of each perspective. The Critique model challenges, rejects, and withdraws from psychology; the Analogy model assumes a continuity and comfort between psychology and Christianity; the Translation model views psychology and Christianity as distinctly separate systems; the Dialogue model takes a dialectical and constructivist approach to the relationship; and the Witness model seeks to transform and redeem psychology.

The article ends with four convictions regarding an approach to integration. He believes it needs to be pluralistic, discipleship focused, covenantal, and accepting of the priesthood of all believers. He argues that ultimately our Christian control beliefs should guide our research and lead to a more integrated psychology.

The last article in this section is by Brian Eck (1996). His work, *Integrating the Integrators: An Organizing Framework for a Multifaceted Process of Integration*, presents a meta-analysis of the 27 integration models that had been identified in the literature at that time and reorganizes them into three overarching paradigms, five integrative processes, and nine integration models.

The analysis begins by identifying three main areas of disagreement in the integration literature and recommends working toward agreement in the definition of the term, the data accepted for integration, and the processes by which integration is achieved.

For Eck, the overarching paradigms for the process of integration are defined by how they respond to the findings of psychology and theology. The Non-Integrative Paradigm refuses to integrate data from the other discipline, the Manipulative Integration Paradigm integrates only some, often altered, data from the other discipline, and the Non-manipulative Integration Paradigm accepts the data from each discipline directly into the integrative process.

From these three paradigms, Eck identifies five integrative processes; Rejects, Reconstructs, Transforms, Correlates, and Unifies. The nine models are defined by whether psychology or theology is using the integrative process.

Finally, Eck draws his analysis to a close with a critique of the legitimate use of each of these processes, depending on the nature and quality of the findings to be integrated.

These articles represent classic and seminal works on integration models. Additional models or alternative approaches to integration may be found in the list of resources identified below.

Suggestions for Further Reading: Models of Integration

Carter, J.D., & Narramore, S. B. (1979). *The integration of psychology and theology: An introduction*. Grand Rapids, MI: Zondervan.
  Perhaps the single most classic introduction to integration in the Reformed tradition by two pioneers in the field.
Collins, G. R. (1981). *Psychology & theology: Prospects for integration*. Nashville, TN: Abingdon.
  This book by one of the original integrationists proposes four models for integrating psychology and theology and lays out his approach for integration.

Entwistle, D. N. (2004) *Integrative approaches to psychology and Christianity: An introduction to worldview issues, philosophical foundations, and models of integration*. Eugene, OR: Wipf & Stock.
Develops further Carter and Narramore's models approach in the context of broader theological, philosophical, and historical insights.

Farnsworth, K. E. (1981). *Integrating psychology and theology: Elbows together but hearts apart*. Washington D.C.: University Press of America.
Sets out his models of integration, defines what embodied integration would look like and provides a helpful exploration of the nature of truth.

Farnsworth, K.E. (1982). The conduct of integration. *Journal of Psychology and Theology, 10* (4), 308-319.
This classic article presents a brief summary of how truth can be understood on several levels and concludes with the authors five models for integrating psychology and theology

Farnsworth, K. E. (1995). *Whole-hearted integration: Harmonizing psychology and Christianity through word and deed*. Grand Rapids, MI: Baker.
Emphasizes that integration must not be primarily cognitive (critical integration) but should be worked out in daily living, which he calls embodied integration.

Hathaway, W. L. (2002). Integration as interpretation: A hermeneutical-realist view. *Journal of Psychology and Christianity, 21*(3), 205-218.
Outlines a model for integration that attempts to do justice to the person's context and beliefs, while avoiding extreme relativism.

Johnson, E. L. & Jones. S. L. (Eds). (2000). *Psychology & Christianity: Four views*. Downers Grove, IL: InterVarsity.
Four eminent contributors provide differing perspectives, with critique by the others, and the editors' supply a wonderful historical introduction which is worth the price of the book.

Mathisen, K. (1980). Back to the basics: A broad conceptual model for the integration of psychology and theology. *Journal of Psychology and Theology, 8* (3), 222-229.
Applies Bube's levels of description for relating psychology and religion to the integration of psychology and theology.

Niebuhr, H. R. (1951). *Christ and culture*. NY: Harper and Row.
Classic work identifying five ways in which Christianity and culture can be related.

Roberts, R. C. & Talbot, M. R. (Eds.). (1997). *Limning the Psyche: Explorations in Christian psychology*. Grand Rapids, MI: Eerdmans.
Articulates the Christian Psychology perspective by Roberts, especially in the *Introduction: Christian Psychology?* and chapter 5, *Parameters of a Christian Psychology*.

19

Secular and Sacred Models of Psychology and Religion

John D. Carter
Rosemead Graduate School of Professional Psychology

Religion has been viewed with varying degrees of favor or disfavor by psychology. Early in psychology's history, Freud was critical of religion; many Christians reacted with equal disfavor to psychology. More recently, Christians have attempted to articulate the relationship between psychology and Christianity. These attempts have followed the same four approaches or models that psychologists traditionally have taken toward religion. The purpose of this article is to analyze and describe the secular and Christian versions of the four common models. The article describes these models and classifies psychologists such as Allport, Freud, Fromm, Frankl, Ellis, Jung, Mowrer, and Thorne as well as several Christians who have attempted to integrate psychology and Christianity.

For the last 15 to 20 years there has been a resurgence of interest in the psychology of religion as evidenced by such encyclopedic works as Strommen's *Research on Religious Development.* Psychology's interest in religion which was evident during the early decades of this century (James, Starbuck, etc.) appears to have virtually died out during the 1930s, 1940s, and early 1950s if the volume of publications is a criteria. Apparently, interest was rekindled at the 1959 APA convention symposium entitled: "The Role of the Concept of Sin in Psychotherapy." This renewed interest in psychology and religion by psychologists culminated two years ago in the APA's addition of Division 36—Psychologists Interested in Religious Issues.

A parallel interest in psychology's relationship to Christianity has developed in the evangelical Christian community. The growing number of books and articles and even evangelical psychological associations illustrates the evangelical psychologist's interest in psychology and Christianity (Collins, 1975). This interest seems to be part of what Bloesch (1973) has called the *Evangelical Renaissance.*

This article is an analysis of the four approaches or models by which psychologists have attempted to relate psychology to religion. It also analyzes a parallel version of these four models by which evangelical psychologists have attempted to relate to psychology and Christianity. These two analyses are called secular and sacred respectively; they constitute the bulk of this article. Since the parallel versions of the models have developed separately, there is some difference in terminology. Psychologists have been concerned with religious

phenomena and so explore religion while evangelical psychologists have been concerned with Christianity and so explore psychology and Christianity rather than religion in general. The difference in terminology will be reflected in each analysis. A section comparing the two analyses or versions of the four models including the issues and a summary will conclude this article. An outline of the four Secular and Sacred Models appears in Tables 1 and 2 respectively. These tables must be studied in conjunction with the explanation in the text in order to fully appreciate the coherent nature of each model.

Secular Models

The four approaches psychologists have taken to psychology and religion are described as four models. Each model has its own character and pattern which have also been described in more detail and summarized in Tables 1 and 2. These same four models also appear to parallel the four models that evangelical psychologists have used in their analysis of psychology and Christianity. Thus, it becomes apparent that sacred and secular versions of psychology and religion are two sides of the same model.

The first secular model is the Psychology *Against* religion model. This approach holds that religion has or had a detrimental effect on mankind and on society because it is unscientific and, therefore, perpetrates myths. Hence, religion is viewed as exploiting individuals by its institutional character, i.e., by its ability to control and inhibit free expression of humans in society, particularly in the area of sexual functioning. Thus, religion is viewed as being aligned with the oppressive forces in society.

© *Journal of Psychology and Theology*, 1977, *5*, 197-208. Used by permission.

Secondly, as an institution in the broader sense, religion is able to reach into the individual's family life and shape his conscience so that guilt is produced with all of its detrimental and pathological effects. Thus, religion is the creator of needless, personal, emotional pain. Third, religion is, at best, allowable for children and for primitive people who are not sophisticated enough to recognize its limiting function. At its worst, religion perpetuates immaturity in both a personal and intellectual sense: in the personal sense, religious views of personhood prevent autonomy and self-actualization in order to conform to the religious ideal; in an intellectual sense, religion perpetuates a view of the world and human nature which is intellectually and scientifically unacceptable. In summary, this model maintains that religion is essentially anti- or unscientific, i.e., mythological, while psychology (as defined by the holder's view) represents a scientifically acceptable view of man, his nature, and functioning. This model is thus based on naturalism and has an anti-supernaturalism stance. Freud (1957) and Ellis (1970) are examples of this approach.

The second model is the Psychology *Of* religion model. Holders of this view, like their counterpart in the Christian approach, tend to assume a mysticism, humanism, or parenthesism (and sometimes a naturalism) of the *Against* model. Thus, man is a spiritual-moral being whose being needs to be free of oppressive forces whether societal, technological, or religious. Second, religion is good in general, i.e., it is viewed as ally, at best, and as benign, at worst. Third, religious metaphors or concepts are accepted and integrated in a psychological manner. The pure religious nature or content of the religious concepts are excluded or overlooked (either explicitly or implicitly) and, in turn, the concepts are infused with or interpreted as having some psychological meaning derived from a particular psychological theory. The psychological benefits of religion and its functioning in healthy individuals are stressed, particularly in terms of the psychologized version of the religion(s). Jung (1967), Fromm (1966), Mowrer (1961) are the clearest examples of this model.

The third model—Psychology *Parallels* religion—is harder to define in its secular form than in its sacred form. Holders of this view do not write specifically on their view. Rather, they are active in both spheres and may have written in both. Since the psychological community generally is unaware of the religious one and vice versa, there is little need to communicate or articulate any intellectual or rational connection of the two spheres of functioning. The view appears to be that quality functioning and productivity in both areas of endeavor is desirable, but no interaction is necessary: Psychology is scientific and religion is personal (and perhaps social also). A major example provides the best articulation of this model.

Thorne (1950), for many years the editor of the *Journal of Clinical Psychology*, maintains that

> ... primary reliance should be placed on scientific methods when they are *validly* applicable, but that philosophy and religion also have their proper sphere of activities beyond the realm of science. (p. 471)

> A distinction should be made between religion-oriented *spiritual counseling* and scientifically-oriented *personality counseling*.... It must be recognized in the beginning, that the theoretical and philosophical foundations of spiritual and scientific approaches are basically different. (p. 481)

While Thorne goes on to discuss the place of religion in counseling, his position is clear. Counseling, as scientifically based and grounded, is separate and even at points in opposition to religiously oriented counseling, yet there is clearly a place for religion as part of knowledge and culture. Also, its influence on certain counselees must be recognized and addressed.

The Psychology *Integrates* religion model recognizes the healthy aspects of religion. It basically assumes that man needs a unifying philosophy of life and that religion, in its healthy expression, can provide an understanding of life both existentially and metaphysically which is broader than psychology. As a corollary, it assumes that religion can provide a personally integrating function in one's life, both intraspherically and interpersonally. The model also recognizes that the human condition is less than ideal and that personal and religious maturity does not automatically occur. Thus, there is unhealthy religion as well as individual and social pathology (i.e., hostility and defensiveness can occur inside as well as outside religion). Finally, a healthy religion is viewed as assisting or aiding in the transcendence of, or liberation from, pathology. Allport (1950) and Frankl (1975) are examples of this approach. Guntrip (1956, 1967) also appears to hold the Integrates' assumptions but articulation of these implications are not developed yet.

Sacred Models

Since the original presentation of the sacred models (Carter & Mohline, 1975), there have been

Table 1

Four Secular Models of Psychology and Religion

I. Psychology *Against* Religion
1. Science or scientific method is the only valid means to truth.
2. Truth claims other than science are destructive.
3. Religion (as myth) rather than truth is destructive.
4. Religion's destructiveness is its prohibitive or inhibitive effect on its members and society.
5. "Scientific" (valid) psychology is the solution to individual problems.

Examples: Ellis and Freud

II. Psychology *Of* Religion
1. Man is a spiritual-moral being (at least in a humanistic sense).
2. Religion, technology, science, or society which denies man's spirit, and thus his nature, creates pathology.
3. Most or all religions have recognized the spiritual-human quality of man and thus have the right approach.
4. The particular cultural-social-theological definition of man must be discarded in favor of a truly psychological definition of human functioning.
5. Good psychology translates the valid insights of religion into psychology and uses them for human good.

Examples: Fromm, Jung, and Mowrer

III. Psychology *Parallels* Religion
1. Religion and psychology are not related.
2. Each exists in its own sphere. One is scientific and the other is not.
3. Religion is a personal (and social) matter while psychology is intellectual and academic.
4. Both religion and psychology can be embraced. There is no conflict since they do not interact.

Examples: Thorne

IV. Psychology *Integrates* Religion
1. A unifying or integrating view of truth in religion and psychology is both possible and desirable.
2. The truth or insights from psychology or religion will have some correspondence with the other discipline.
3. The truth or valid principles of religion and psychology are in harmony and form a unity.
4. Religion as socially manifested may be pathological but its intrinsic nature is not.
5. Valid religion and religious experiences are helpful in transcending the pains of existence or in assisting in the maturing process of growth.

Examples: Allport, Frankl, and Guntrip

two other attempts to define the models used in integration psychology and Christianity (Crabb, 1975; Farnsworth, 1976). The former briefly outlines essentially the same four sacred models, but labels them differently and describes them in a confrontive (*Against*) rhetoric. The latter even more briefly outlines five models, three of which are directly equivalent to the *Against, Of,* and *Integrates* model and the other two appear to be versions of the *Parallels* model.

As indicated above, evangelicals have used the same four models that secular psychologists have used to describe and interpret relationship between Christianity

and psychology. It should be noted that though the structure of the models is the same, the content is different and was developed independently.

The first model is the Christianity *Against* Psychology approach. This model affirms that there is a radical difference between what the Bible says about man and what psychologists say. Holders of this view are either implicitly or explicitly committed to a presuppositionalism in which the unbelieving psychologists can discover no significant truths about the nature or functioning of man, especially Christian man. Second, they place a radical emphasis on the redemptive aspects of the Bible with a heavy stress on the difference between the believer and the unbeliever, between the old man and the new man. Thus, prayer, Bible reading, "trusting Christ," and "relying on the Holy Spirit" or a combination of these are pursued as scriptural means for coping with life and its problems.

Third, the discovery and application of God's laws from the Scriptures are stressed as solutions to all of life's problems. Thus, emotional problems or "nervous breakdowns" are a result of violation of divine laws. Therapy in this approach consists largely of telling or encouraging people to follow God's requirement. While salvation by grace alone is maintained by holders of this approach, solutions to emotional difficulties come from obedience to God's laws rather than accepting God's love and grace.

Psychologically, the approach of this school of thought can be summarized by the statement, "All emotional problems are really spiritual problems." It should be noted that with few exceptions those who hold this view have no graduate training in psychology. Many evangelical psychologists would maintain that Adams' (1973) counseling techniques are representative of this approach.

The Christianity *Of* Psychology model represents almost a direct antithesis of the first model discussed. This second approach also maintains that there is a difference between the Bible and the facts of science, experience, and reason, but in this case the latter is favored. The holders of this view tend to be committed to a naturalism, mysticism, or humanism rather than a supernaturalism. Also, they stress the universal aspects of the Bible rather than the redemptive aspects. The Christian is not viewed as essentially different from other men, but as all other men, he is in need of the therapeutic benefits which psychology offers.

A third characteristic of the Christianity *Of* Psychology model is its attempt to interpret the tenets of various "schools" of psychology as truly redemptive and Christian. They *selectively* translate or interpret various passages or concepts from the Bible into their particular psychology, i.e., aspects of the Bible are mapped into the writings of some "school" of psychology which a particular psychologist holds. The founder of the school, be he Freud, Jung, or Rogers, becomes elevated so that what is acceptable in the Bible is what fits into the particular theory. Thus, the view to be propagated and used as a therapeutic tool is the Christianized version of some psychological theorist. Only a slightly different version of this "Christianizing" process occurs when it is not a theory but some particular principle, process, or experience which becomes the criteria, e.g., group experiences or interpersonal relations, as stressed by some who take this approach. Various biblical passages are then used to give biblical sanction for the concept already accepted as true.

In its theological form, the Christianity *Of* Psychology approach has been the position of liberalism. However, there are some current evangelicals who tend to adopt this approach. These evangelicals become so involved with accepting the client and helping him to express his repressed emotions that they ignore or implicitly deny the existence of sinful actions and attitudes. To varying degrees they reject or ignore any passages of Scripture which speak of restraint, control, commitment, or mature *Christian* living. Other evangelicals so stress some experience, e.g., good interpersonal relations, that Christian experience tends to become synonymous with good interpersonal relations (Peterson & Board, 1977).

The *Against* and *Of* models just discussed represent extremes. Each has a cookie-cutter style. On to the dough of Scripture and psychology each presses its cookie cutter. The dough inside the cutter is retained as the truth and what is on the outside is rejected as false. Hence, the *Against* and *Of* models must be rejected as an inadequate approach to a Christian psychology. The remaining two approaches attempt to steer a middle course.

The third model—Christianity *Parallels* Psychology—emphasizes the importance of both the Scripture and psychology, but assumes either explicitly or implicitly that the two do not interact. There are two versions of this model. The first version can be called the *isolation* version. The holders of this version maintain that psychology and the Scripture or theology are separate and there is no overlap (Clement, 1974). That is, each is encapsulated, and there is no interaction because these methods and contents are different. However, since both are true, both must be affirmed but remain separate. The second version can be called the *correlation* version. Holders of this approach attempt to correlate, plug into, or line up certain psychological and scriptural concepts, e.g., superego is equivalent to the conscience, id is equivalent to original sin, and empathy is equivalent to love (agape). Holders of the correlation version often assume they are integrating when in actuality the are simply lining up concepts from different spheres. The basic difference between correlating and integrating (which will become clearer after the *Integrates* model is discussed) is that the correlating assumes there are two things which need to be lined up and thus ignores the system of configuration of concepts in each while the integrating assumes there is ultimately only one set (configuration) of concepts, laws, or principles which operates in two disciplines. It is the discovery of the one configuration which constitutes integration, not the lining up in concepts. Note that Farnsworth treats the correlation version as a separate model.

Correlating can be clearly seen in *What, Then, is Man?* Paul Meehl (1958), the general editor and author of several sections, outlines a solid theological view of salvation and then proceeds to discuss three psychological views of conversion and their implications for the orthodox biblical view he has just outlined. His theology never wavers, but it is as if his theology is on one side of a cliff and his psychology on the other and he is trying to build a bridge across but is not sure where to anchor the bridge on the psychological side.

Many Christian therapists either wittingly or unwittingly adopt this approach. Having been trained in the best institutions of the day, they practice the type of psychology they have learned. Being believers, they read their Bibles and attend church but there is little if any genuine meshing of their psychology and their Christianity. Bridge building is correlating not integrating.

The fourth model—Christianity *Integrates* psychology—basically assumes that God is the author of all truth, both the truth He has revealed in the Scripture and the truths discovered by psychology or any other scientific discipline. Hence, there is an expected congruence between Scripture and psychology because God has revealed himself in a special way in Scripture and in a general way in creation and also via His image in man (Genesis 1:26, 27). Man has fallen into sin and thus God's image in man has become marred, warped, or distorted. It is never lost, and it is being renewed through personal appropriation of salvation in Christ (Ephesians 4:24; Colossians 3:10). The holder of the Christianity *Integrates* psychology model never presumes that *all* the claims to discovered truths in psychology are genuine unless they are congruent and integratable with the Scripture, nor does he believe that certain traditional interpretations of Scripture are true either. God created psychology when he created man in His image. Man has become marred but yet he is redeemable, and thus psychology is congruent and integratable with the Christianity. This approach emphasizes both the Scripture and psychology *because they are allies.* Psychology used in this model has a small p, i.e., it is the psychology that existed before the word was discovered, while psychology as used by the other three models has a capital P and refers to systems or theories. This is a critical difference.

There are many psychologists and pastoral counselors who are seeking to promote both understanding and growth in individuals. Hence, there is a vast popular literature on psychology and the Scripture available. However, it is often very difficult to distinguish between the correlation version of the *Parallels* model and genuine integration in this popular literature because its goal is to promote practical Christian living rather than conceptual understanding. Much of the technical work exploring the nature and the content of the integration of psychology and the Scripture appears in two periodicals, *The Journal of the American Scientific Affiliation* and the *Journal of Psychology and Theology.* Many of the members of the Christian Association for Psychological Studies and Western Association of Christians for Psychological Studies hold to the *Integrates* model. Crabb (1975), Hulme (1967), van Kaam (1968), and Wagner (1974) are examples of this model.

Evaluation of the Four
Sacred or Christian Models

Since there is a plethora of literature currently being written on the integration of psychology and Christianity, a separate section is being given to the Christian or sacred models.

The four sacred or Christian models of psychology and Christianity just described, in reality, are only aspects of larger approaches to a Christian view of life which might be called Christianity and culture.

Space does not allow for the expansion of this idea but if the reader will substitute the word "culture" (in its anthropological sense) for "psychology" in each model, he will be able to see how the four models to psychology grow out of four approaches to a Christian view of life.

Specifically, the Christianity *Against* Psychology model assumes that there is no general revelation or common grace which God has revealed or given to man which can be discovered by a non-Christian psychologist. Besides running counter to systematic theology and Christian apologetics, this assumption is peculiar for two reasons. First, man was created in God's image (Genesis 1:26, 27), and though marred, it has not been destroyed by the Fall (Ephesians 4:24; Colossians 3:10). Second, the similar assumption does not seem to be held for medicine, economics, or physics, i.e., truth which applies to Christians may be discovered by nonbelievers in their fields. Why not in psychology?

Though largely implicit, the Christianity *Against* Psychology approach holds a surface view of sin and pathology. In practice, though not theologically, sin and pathology are reduced to symptoms.

The counselee is doing, saying, or thinking the wrong things, and he is not doing, saying, or thinking the right things. Thus, therapy essentially becomes telling the counselee what the Bible says and how he or she should respond regardless of how little or how much the counselor listens to the counselee. Therapy in this approach tends to become a symptoms removal or works sanctification depending upon whether it is viewed psychologically or theologically. At times, adherents to this approach sound remarkably similar to a parent lecturing an adolescent in their therapeutic techniques while the biblical emphasis on "out of the abundance of the heart the mouth speaks" (Matthew 12:34-35) or "truth in the inward parts" (Psalm 51:6) is bypassed in favor of behavioral compliance. Thus, the volume of scriptural quotation in "Christian" psychology books in no way guarantees its faithfulness to content or intent of Scripture. It is from this limited view of God's revelation in nature (man) and its limited view of sin and pathology that the Christianity *Against* Psychology practitioner criticizes the committed Christian professionals who accept one of the latter two approaches, presuming they are taking the *Of* model approach. The adherents of the Christianity *Against* Psychology approach appear to see only the scripturally invalid claims to psychological truth and thus essentially reject the integrity of Scripture.

However, since the propagators of the Christianity *Against* Psychology approach have had almost exclusively theological rather than psychological training, they do have many helpful insights into Scripture. Their works can be read with profit (if their oppressive rhetoric can be ignored) by those professionals whose training has been exclusively psychological in nature. Furthermore, since many problems have a behavioral symptom component, the Christianity *Against* Psychology approach helps to relive the pressure of symptoms for many persons.

Little needs to be said concerning the Christianity *Of* Psychology model. At best, in the opinion of those who hold this view, the Bible provides a convenient set of metaphors into which various psychological concepts can be translated. The evangelical, who operates from this approach, seems to be caught up with some psychological concepts or theoretical perspectives to such an extent that they are not able to see the larger implications of their approach. They tend to see only their favored concept or perspective in the Scripture. Thus, the totality of the biblical emphasis is limited. Ramm (1972) has described the weakness of such groups of evangelicals in a paper entitled "Is it safe to shift to 'interpersonal theology'?"

The greatest strength of the Christianity *Parallels* Psychology is also its greatest weakness. It avoids the pitfalls of the *Against* and *Of* models, but it offers no positive constructive alternatives. Many professionals who operate from this approach (especially the isolation version) have had little or no theological or biblical training but are competent psychologists. The militancy of the proponents of the *Against* model often has the effect of inhibiting many of this group who are searching from some biblical insight into psychology. The parallelists are aware of their own competency and the general psychological naivité of the *Against* proponent and, therefore, tend to be very wary of any claims regarding the discovery of "the" biblical psychology. Other parallelists seem to arrive at their position because they believe that the laws and methods of psychology are separate from the laws and methods of theology, or economics, or any discipline for that matter. However, all disciplines are integratable in a grand Christian philosophical scheme though this integration has little to do with their therapeutic practice.

Many evangelical psychologists who are only correlating believe they are integrating. This is confusing and unfortunate. As was indicated, genuine integration involves the discovery and articulation of the common underlying principles of both psychology and the Scripture, i.e., how general grace and special grace are related in reference to psychology. In addition, there are many evangelical counselors and therapists who "believe in" integration but whose therapy in no appreciable way differs from their secular colleagues except for an occasional reference to God or the Bible. It is difficult to know in what sense this kind of therapy can be called integrative or Christian, except that both therapist and client are Christians. This observation is not intended to be a pejorative comment but a descriptive categorization.

The strength and weakness of the Christian *Integrates* psychology model also rests on its basic assumption, and the burden of proof rests on the proponent of this mode. The practical proponents of this approach have proclaimed this assumption although they were not able singlehandedly to supply the details. The number of articles, not to mention books, appearing in the two scholarly journals mentioned, as well as in other periodicals, suggests that the more theoretically-oriented integrators are beginning to discover the details of integration. The process of integration takes time. The bulk of psychology as a discipline is less than 50 years old. Christians must study

Table 2
Four Models of the Scripture and Psychology

I. The Scripture *Against* Psychology
1. Basic epistemological assumption: Revelation is against reason, i.e., the Scripture is contradictory to human thought both rationally and empirically.
2. Soteriology and the Fall are stressed so as to eliminate and ignore creation and providence.
3. Basic psychological assumption: The Scripture contains all the precepts of mental health.
4. All emotional problems are spiritual problems because they result from disobedience.
5. All problems can be solved by obedience to Scripture if the individual is confronted with a relevant passage of Scripture.

Example: Adams

II. The Scripture *Of* Psychology
1. Basic epistemological assumption: Human reason is more fundamental, comprehensive (technical), and contemporary than revelation.
2. Creation and Providence are stressed so as to ignore or eliminate soteriology and the Fall.
3. Basic psychological assumption: Psychology has discovered the basic principles of emotional health, maturity, and good interpersonal functioning.
4. Emotional problems can be solved by consulting a therapist or applying the principles of emotional maturity and good interpersonal relations.

Examples: Relational theology

III. The Scriptural *Parallels* Psychology
1. Basic epistemological assumption: Revelation can never be reduced to reason nor can reason be reduced to revelation.
2. God requires obedience to both revelation and reason. Hence, there is an implicit tension existing in the approach.
3. Both Creation-Providence and soteriology are stressed but they belong to different spheres.
4. Spiritual problems should be dealt with by the pastor; emotional problems by a psychologist or psychiatrist.

Examples: Clement (Isolation), Meehl (Correlation)

IV. The Scripture *Integrates* Psychology
1. Basic epistemological assumption: God is the author of both revelation and reason because all truth (and truths) are God's truth and thus ultimately a part of a unified or integrated whole.
2. Creation-Providence is stressed equally with soteriology.
3. All problems are, in principle, a result of the Fall but not, in fact, the result of immediate conscious acts.
4. Since values are significant both for the Christian and for therapy, a genuine Christian therapy is necessary.
5. *Paraklesis* is the pattern for this type of therapy.

Examples: Crabb, Hulme, van Kaam, Wagner, Carter, & Mohline

---

psychology and then study the Scripture to discover its psychology. Little biblical psychology will be discovered if one does not know psychology.

The integrators tend to emphasize the inner or depth aspect of man, as the source of both problems and health, in keeping with the biblical emphasis on the heart as the motive source of actions (Matthew 15:18-19; Luke 6:45). Also, many integrators tend to approach therapy, however, implicitly from the biblical concept paraklesis, meaning support, comfort, consolation, or encouragement (exhortation). With its broad meaning, *paraklasis* could apply to any therapy from crisis intervention to long term analysis. *Paraklasis* is a gift given to the Church (Romans 12:8), and the integrator presumes Christian counseling is part of the larger ministry of the Church.

Thus, the *Integrates* model assumes a Christian view of man which includes God's special revelation in the Scripture and his general revelation in nature (Romans 1:20; Psalm 19:1) and man (Genesis 1:27).

Table 2 lists five therapists who are examples of those following the *Integrates* model. Each has a different theoretical orientation and is attempting to move from that base to an integrative one with the Scripture. Thus, the differences in style and vocabulary, hopefully, will not obscure the genuine integration in each.

Evaluation:
Christian and Secular Models

This section will begin with a comparison of the two versions of each model and conclude with a discussion of a broader base of the four models.

The four sacred and secular models of psychology and religion are clearly not equally similar. The greatest difference appears in the *Against* model. This difference occurs because either psychology or religion is rejected in the *Against* model but it is the opposite part in the sacred and secular versions. However, the difference in a content or orientation should not blind one to the striking equivalence in style and structure. However, the difference in content often leads the secular and sacred proponent of this model to dogmatic clashes. The difference in the *Of* models are much less noticeable. Both sacred and secular versions assume a humanistic-naturalistic or metaphysical view. The difference seems to be in the use of metaphors. The sacred approach predominately uses religious metaphors, but with understood psychological meaning, while the secular approach uses psychological metaphors in such a way as to incorporate religious meanings.

The sacred and secular *Parallels* model is perhaps the most similar, but it is also the least defined. It is most similar in that the central structures, religion and psychology, are separated in both versions. Because religion and/or Christianity and psychology are maintained separately, there is little definition to the model except the maintenance of the separate disciplines. However, the correlation version of the sacred *Parallels* model does attempt to line up the two disciplines.

There is a great deal of similarity between the secular and sacred *Integrates* model. There tends to be a broad philosophical or metaphysical orientation to this model. This seems to be a function of the nature of the *Integrates* model which calls for an awareness and integration of two distinct bodies of knowledge. The adherents of this model seem to

focus on the underlying issues in both psychology and religion without a loss of technical mastery of some area of the field of psychology. Also, the adherents' interest in a religious understanding and the integration of it with psychology is a result of personal belief, experience, and commitment.

As indicated, there have been only four approaches to the relationship between psychology and religion. Two versions of these models, sacred and secular, have been described and compared. Each version of each model (see Tables 1 and 2) is founded on a relatively coherent set of assumptions. In reading and discussing psychology and religion, it is important to bear in mind the model which is being assumed. Since individuals explicitly hold to one of these four models, misunderstanding often occurs when another individual holds to a different model. The misunderstandings often tend to degenerate into conflicts when the nature of implicit assumptions behind the models are not recognized. Also, there are psychologists who intellectually assume one model but who are affectively committed to another.

In conclusion, the four models may be viewed as a new interpretation of an old problem: relating the secular and the sacred. *Christ and Culture* (Niebuhr, 1951) describes five approaches Christians have taken in relating their religious faith to a secular world. The Christian, or religious version of the four models, represents an application or extension of four of these approaches to psychology. Thus, relating the Christian faith to psychology is really only part of the larger problem of relating the Christian faith to the world of life and thought.

Finally, the four models may be thought of as parallel to some of the proposed solutions to the mind-body problem. How can the mind and body, two different aspects of a person, be related in one individual? How can psychology, a scientific discipline, be related to religion or Christianity, a revealed and historic faith? While there have been a number of proposed solutions to the mind-body problem, Beloff (1962) maintains the mind-body problem may be reduced to four basic solutions. The four models presented in this article appear to parallel four of these solutions. The *Against* and *Of* models appear to parallel the materialism and idealism solution. Each model denies one aspect of the problem just as materialism and idealism deny one aspect of the mind-body problem. the *Parallels* model seems equivalent to psychophysical parallelism. The *Integrates* model appears to be similar to the double aspect solution of the mind-body problem. These mind-body problem parallels are not to be thought of as total or definitive, only suggestive. Any light this suggestion throws on the relationship between psychology and religion at this primitive stage of understanding will be helpful.

References

Adams, J. (1973). *The Christian counselors manual.* Grand Rapids, MI: Baker.

Allport, G. W. (1950). *The individual and his religion.* New York: Macmillan.

Beloff, J. (1962). *The existence of mind.* London: Macgibbon & Kee.

Bloesch, E. (1973). *The evangelical renaissance.* Grand Rapids, MI: Eerdmans.

Carter, J. D., & Mohline, R. J. (1975, April 12-14). *A model and modes for the integrative process.* A paper presented at the meeting of the Christian Association for Psychological Studies. Oklahoma City, OK.

Carter, J. D., & Mohline, R. J. (1976). The nature and scope of integration: A proposal. *Journal of Psychology and Theology, 4*(1), 3-14.

Clement, P. (1974, May 24-25). *Behavior modification of the spirit.* A paper presented at the Convention of the Western Association of Christians for Psychological Studies. Santa Barbara, CA.

Collins, G. (1975). The pulpit and the couch. *Christianity Today, 19,* 1087-1090.

Crabb, L. (1975). *Basic principles of biblical counseling.* Grand Rapids, MI: Zondervan.

Ellis, A. (1970). *Reason and emotion in psychotherapy.* New York: Lyle Stewart.

Farnsworth, K. (1976, June 25-29). *Integration of faith and learning utilizing a phenomenological/existential paradigm for psychology.* A paper presented at the Christian Association for Psychological Studies. Santa Barbara, CA.

Frankl, V. (1975). *The unconscious god.* New York: Simon & Schuster.

Freud, S. (1957). *The future of the illusion.* Garden City, NY: Doubleday.

Fromm, E. (1966). *You shall be as gods.* New York: Fawcett.

Guntrip, H. (1956). *Psychotherapy and religion.* New York: Harper & Row.

Guntrip, H. (1967). Religion in relationship to personal integration. *British Journal of Medical Psychology, 62,* 423-433.

Hulme, W. (1967). *Counseling and theology.* Philadelphia, PA: Fortress.

Jung, C. (1962). *Psychology and religion.* New Haven, CT: Yale University Press.

Meehl, P. (1958). *What, then, is man?* St. Louis, MO: Concordia.

Mowrer, O. H. (1961). *The crisis in psychiatry and religion.* Princeton, NJ: Van Nostrand.

Niebuhr, H. R. (1951). *Christ and culture.* New York: Harper.

Petersen, B., & Broad, S. (1977, July). Unmasking: An interview with Waldon Howard (including comments). *Eternity,* pp. 21-22.

Ramm, B. (1972). Is it safe to shift to an "interpersonal theology"? *Eternity,* pp. 21-22.

Thorne, F. (1950). Principles of personality counseling. Brandon, VT. *Journal of Clinical Psychology.*

van Kaam, A. (1968). *Religion and personality.* Garden City, NY: Doubleday.

Wagner, M. (1974). *Put it all together.* Grand Rapids, MI: Zondervan.

20

On Living in Athens: Models of Relating Psychology, Church, and Culture

Al Dueck
Mennonite Biblical Seminary

Using Niebuhr's (1951) five models of interaction between Christ and culture as heuristic, it is suggested that there are of necessity a variety of strategies between Christianity and psychology. Each proposed strategy for interaction is constructed to protect the integrity of the Church's vision while recognizing those aspects of culture which are useful and helpful to the Church. The five strategies proposed and discussed at length are critique, analogy, translation, dialogue, and witness.

What has Jerusalem to do with Athens, Christ with culture, Christianity with psychology? Like most Jewish-Christians, I am a resident alien in Athenian culture. While Jerusalem is psychologically home, it is here, in Athens, that my discipline of psychology is historically rooted.

On the road from Jerusalem to Athens, I discovered that some of my companions were eager to leave behind the restrictive provincialism of their religious heritage. They welcomed the cosmopolitan ethos of Athens. Occasionally, I encountered those, weary of schizoid existence as aliens in Athens, who returned to Jerusalem for the security of tradition, ritual, and kin.

Upon arrival in Athens, I found there were some who had simply capitulated to therapeutic Greek culture. There were others, however, who were clear about their story and recognized their pilgrim status. For them Yahweh existed as the God of both Jew and Gentile. Athens and its culture were seen from the perspective of Jerusalem where we first understood how God acted in history. The stories of Abraham, Sarah, Moses, Miriam, Jesus, Mary, and Paul interpreted our new cultural environment. The people who confess Jesus as Lord have become my primary community as I seek to remain faithful to my original story in a new culture.

It was Tertullian who first asked the question, "What has Jerusalem to do with Athens?" Jerusalem symbolizes all that is central to the vision and story of the Judeo-Christian tradition. Athens represents the alien cultures that Christianity has entered. Culture, in this essay, will refer not to culture as monolithic but as a composite of beliefs and practices.

Throughout the history of Christianity, the Church has responded in diverse ways to culture. The approach has sometimes been one of total rejection of culture as pagan while at other times it has been one of uncritical acceptance of culture as a gift. There is a range of acceptable intermediate strategies. Any strategy which leads to complete rejection of culture or complete identification with culture will be of limited usefulness to the Church in its interaction with contemporary mental health theories and practices.

Not only does the Church's response vary between absolute rejection or complete acceptance, the Church is also capable of freezing one specific response proper at one point in history as the approach appropriate for all cultures in all times. The Church's response to culture, I submit, is one of discernment rather than wooden positioning.

The thesis of this essay is that there are a variety of appropriate strategies for dialogue between Christianity and psychology and that a single strategy is of limited value. Whatever the strategy to be used, we will need to be sensitive to the specific psychological issue being addressed. Different responses are appropriate if we are relating scientific research, archetypal images or systems theory to the Christian story. I submit that a specific psychological issue needs, in part to influence our specific religions response. My intention at this point is to illustrate how a variety of approaches are legitimate and only indirectly to indicate how each strategy is acceptable.

This essay will explore five metaphors (Barbour, 1974) for dialogue between Church and culture, Christianity and psychology. These strategies will be briefly described here and developed in greater detail later in the essay. For each strategy, I will describe the approach and then illustrate its appropriateness in relation to the discipline of psychology.

© *Journal of Psychology and Christianity*, 1989, *8*(1), 5-18. Used by permission.

Strategies of Interaction: An Overview

In his classic treatment of the relationship of Christ and culture, Niebuhr (1951) delineated five strategies of interaction. The first type assumed a fundamental discontinuity between Christ and culture. All of culture is pagan and any interaction will result in compromise. Niebuhr rejected this strategy because cultural isolation and irrelevance were inevitable. The second strategy assumed an essential continuity between the ethic of Jesus and the highest ideals of human civilization. Niebuhr pointed out that a critique of culture is thereby rendered impossible. A third strategy assumed that culture makes a valid contribution but asserted that Christ is above culture. This position, in Niebuhr's estimation, too easily baptizes as Christian one aspect of culture and thus opens itself to the charge of provincialism. Another strategy assumed that Christ and culture are irreconcilable and that they must be held in tension. Such a strategy fails to provide a basis on which the Church has a unique contribution to make to society and hence tends too easily to support the *status quo*. A last position proposed that the relationship between Christ and culture is one of transformation. Culture can be converted and used to the glory of God. This appears to be Niebuhr's nomination for most appropriate strategy since he submitted no critique of it. In contrast to Niebuhr, my focus is not on culture as a coherent entity but as a composite of specific actions, beliefs, traditions and communities. It is not something which one either totally accepts, rejects, or transforms. Further, I will focus on the church's response to culture. It is the church as Jesus' symbolic presence and interpreter in the world that encounters the various dimensions of culture including the discipline of psychology (Yoder, 1964).

Using Niebuhr's five models of interaction between Christ and culture as heuristic, I will construct and briefly describe five models for the dialogue between Christianity and psychology. I seek to demonstrate that there are a diversity of strategies that are legitimate and useful in different settings. These strategies for interaction between faith and profession will be so constructed that on the one hand we protect the integrity of the Church's vision and on the other hand recognize those dimensions of culture which are good and useful in the work of the Church (Yoder, 1964).

(1) Critique. No profession can go unquestioned by a Christian who takes seriously the transcendence of God and the priority of the Reign of God. Uncritical incorporation of disciplinary insights is not an acceptable option. The difficult task is that of developing criteria and categories by which one judges the specific contributions.

(2) Analogy. The encounter of the Church with culture need not always result in withdrawal. There are some continuities between the two. These, I submit, can be seen as analogies rather than identical correspondences. Wherever we observe freedom, reconciliation and care consistent with the Reign of God, there we gratefully acknowledge God's presence in action. Though analogies are always partial, there are nevertheless similarities and they can be a point of affirmation.

(3) Translation. The vision of the Church and the content of psychology are both couched in language. There have been numerous attempts at translation. It is appropriate, then to determine the quality of the existing translations and to explore alternative ways the Christian message can be translated into the language of mental health professionals.

(4) Dialogue. If we recognize that God is at work in the world of both believer and unbeliever, then it is entirely appropriate for us to take the posture of listener in the dialogue of faith and culture. Moreover, both Christians and non-Christians face some of the same problems in Western culture (Palmer, 1988). Cannot the observations of those who do not confess the same Lord help us in our efforts to be faithful?

(5) Witness. There is a point where the Christian psychologist or psychotherapist has a distinct contribution to make to the conversation out of his or her unique story. It is not so much a response of imperialism as it is pointing to truth beyond ourselves. It assumes that there is Good News and that the human dilemma is in some way related to a rejection of it.

Critique

Throughout the history of the Church one legitimate response to culture has been that of critique. In this strategy one encounters both an emphasis on obedience to the commandment of Jesus Christ and also a rejection of the world. "Do not love the world or the things in the world. If any loves the world, love for the Father is not in him" (1 John 2:15). Jesus remains the absolute authority and this requires obedience to his commandments: love of enemy, prohibition of lust, hunger for justice, etc. In apocalyptic fashion, Christianity is seen as a way of life entirely separate from the host culture. Tertullian recommended that the Christian was to shun the pagan world with its idolatrous religion and to withdraw from occupations contrary to the spirit of Christ (e.g., public meetings, military service, business). For persons of this persuasion, there are no positive relationships between the faith of Christians and the philosophy of the Greeks. Whatever truth is to be found in culture one can derive from the Scriptures.

This is one legitimate response to culture. Thus it is appropriate for scholars or professionals to critically examine their discipline. However, what is needed is a more discerning response rather than a wholesale rejection of culture or profession. Which aspects of culture are to be rejected? The professions need not be rejected *en toto*, but we must reject the implicit autonomy that cultures and professions tend to claim for themselves. Theoretical systems that make a claim to universality, professional groups that claim our primary allegiance, or therapeutic approaches that presume exclusiveness of technique need the relativization that comes with a commitment to the priority of the Reign of God. When absolutized, theories, practices, and communities become the "principalities and powers" of our own age (Berkhof, 1962).

The strategy of critique assumes a point of departure other than the host culture. Culture as experienced is not given. For the Christian, the point of departure is the truth to which the Church witnesses. While we recognize that God's revelation occurs in history, it is our assumption that God in Jesus Christ both transcends history and tradition and chooses to be revealed in particular ways in human culture. Thus where aspects of culture presume transcendence, there should be conflict. When this is the case, challenge, rejection and withdrawal are proper responses.

A critique of the mental health and psychological professions is consistent with this historic response of the Church to culture. The following criticisms are intended to illustrate the appropriateness of this approach. For example, we should have spoken a resounding "No" when psychologists assisted in the A-bomb testing during the 1950s and wherever today our work directly or indirectly assists in the destruction of human life. A psychological theory of education or development which proposes, assumes or supports racism, sexism, ageism, or classism deserves critique. The individualism implicit in a wide array of contemporary psychological theories simply ignores our responsibility to live in accountability (Wallach & Wallach, 1983). A developmental psychology that implicitly takes the norms of prevailing culture as the goal of development desperately needs a critical appraisal of social realities (Peck, 1987). A behaviorism that cannot appreciate the elements of mystery in personality fails to recognize the limits of human understanding. Therapy that considers acceptance and nondirectiveness as primary may be antinomian and inimical to the development of tradition and culture (May, Rogers, & Maslow, 1986). A therapy which assumes that manipulation is essential to the therapeutic process may be simply an extension of a technological society (Ellul, 1964) which worships at the shrine of technique.

Virtually every psychological contribution is a mixture of data and theory, praxis and metaphysics, description and prescription. It seems to me that the discernment process involves a separation of the two (Barth, 1960). The objective description of behavior is presumed neutral and useful. Christianity does not propose an empirical description of modern physical and social realities. A comparison of the theoretical residue with the Christian story is then appropriate; both are at that point ideological. It is our task to discern what is consistent with the Christian story and what is inconsistent. When transcendence is sacrificed for immanence, rejection is appropriate (cf. Buss, 1979; Dueck, 1986).

The limitation of this strategy, when not complemented by other strategies developed below, is that the more systemic the critique the more easily the Christian professional lapses into cynicism and withdrawal. Critique is no justification for withdrawal from the culture of Athens, only for action more consistent with the convictions one has learned in Jerusalem.

Analogy

This strategy of relating Christ and culture assumes that there is more continuity than discontinuity. Whereas the first strategy says "No," this strategy says "Yes." The clearest Biblical example is the Wisdom literature in the Old Testament (Brueggeman, 1972). This literature assumes that proverbs have universal application and that their source is to be found in the larger human community. There is no sectarianism of the first strategy apparent here. Wisdom is collected from a variety of near eastern cultures and incorporated into the life of God's people. If the wisdom is consistent with the story of Yahweh's people, it is acceptable. If not, it is rejected.

This mode of conversation with culture is used by persons who consider themselves Jewish but who seek to maintain connection with the larger Athenian community. They feel equally at home in Church and in the world of culture. This position, in Niebuhr's estimation, has contributed to the extension of Christ's power over humanity. By finding likenesses between the teachings of Jesus and Socrates or the death of Christ and that of Gandhi, we make clear the presence of God in history. This position seeks to make apparent the universal meaning of the Gospel. Jesus is not simply the savior of a small band of followers but of the world (Palmer, 1988).

In my proposal this approach to the conversation with culture uses the strategy of analogy in order to protect the integrity of the unique confessional status of the church and society. Analogy assumes a correlation in the attributes of the objects or events compared. Thus any comparison will contain some points of similarity and some points of dissimilarity. It assumes a fundamental discontinuity and the possibility of continuity.

After two millenia of existence, there is a residual effect of Christianity even in what has been referred to as a post-Christian culture. The worlds of art, politics, welfare and mental health have all been affected in varying degrees by the Judeo-Christian heritage. Continuities can be affirmed when they are filtered through the vision of the Christian community. In the past this strategy tended to be an apologetic which made Christianity attractive and relevant. Rather, in this proposal it is an attempt to acknowledge in human culture that which is analogous to the story of the Church.

A presupposition of this strategy is that God is present in both the life of the Church and of the world, the believer and the unbeliever, among Jews and Gentiles. It is then entirely possible that one might find some similarities—in an analogous rather than identical way—between the word and acts of God's people and the words and acts of those who do not begin with a confession of Yahweh. This approach begins with God's self-disclosure and then moves by way of analogy from God's covenant to creation, from God's action to ours, from the Christ event to historical events. Human love then takes on meaning in the light of God's sacrificial love in Jesus Christ and our peacemaking in the light of God's acts of reconciliation. Where it is apparent that there is a clear, though partial, analogy between the message of Christianity and that of various voices of culture, our response can be one of grateful acknowledgment and acceptance.

Using the concept to "analogy of faith," Thomas Oden (1966) explored the implications for therapy. The following are some illustrations of this strategy from the field of therapy. The counselor who is immersed in the frame of reference of the troubled person, thereby obtaining an understanding of the person, reflects the fact that God in Jesus Christ understands who we are. In both cases there is an entry into the world of the other.

The therapist who participates in the estrangement of the client reflects God's participation in our estrangement in Jesus Christ. The therapist's identification with human plight images God's suffering in the death of Jesus Christ. The therapist faced with hostility, guilt, and anxiety and still remains faithful to the client mirrors God's covenant faithfulness to us.

The counselor who creates an environment in which a client can begin to exercise self-direction, models God's grace to us as we seek to grow in faithfulness. In both, healing is seen as a gift that emerges from beyond ourselves. If in the process of therapy an individual begins to move outward to others with genuine interest because of the love of the therapist, then that therapist's actions are analogous to those acts of love and care God shows toward us.

A therapist who facilitates movement toward reconciliation between alienated spouses parallels the reconciling work of God with humanity in the Christ event. The healer who exposes an individual's inconsistent, unacceptable, or unjust behavior reflects the God who calls us to obedience and faithfulness. The clinical psychologist who enables a client to develop covenant relationships imitates a covenant-keeping God (Friesen & Dueck, 1988).

The strategy of finding continuity is, like the others developed in this essay, limited and best used in conjunction with the others. Analogy is not total parity or disparity. To compare two objects or events is to assume that they are not entirely similar or entirely different. To use the notion of analogy in talking about the relationship of Christianity to aspects of culture is to assume that comparisons are neither univocal or equivocal.

However, the problem endemic to this strategy is the tendency toward equation of ideas or events compared. If one begins with a weak view of God's self-disclosure to us, the use of analogy degenerates into deriving conclusions about God's nature from natural processes and relationships. Though Oden (1966) made extensive use of Barth's (1960) development of the method of analogy, he also accepted the latter's caution that what we are dealing with is a similarity in spite of a greater dissimilarity. The therapist is clearly bound by cultural conditions, personal weaknesses and conflicts.

In addition to the problem of easy equation, there is the problem of bias in selecting analogies. Why are some actions of therapists seen as analogous to the actions of God while others are overlooked? In Oden's case, those actions of the therapist which are confrontational, directive or critical are neglected. Can they not be seen as analogous to God's call for just relationships? Why are only those analogies selected which focus on God's acceptance, forgiveness, understanding, and permissiveness?

The Christian community is the context in which analogies and correspondences are evaluated. They vary in their consistency with the story of the Church and hence discernment is necessary. Unless the Church expends the energy to reflect on the analogies between God's actions in history and our efforts to be therapeutic, the time will come when we will no longer remember the story of Jerusalem or we will assume that there is no appreciable difference between that story and the story of Athens.

Translation

Athens and Jerusalem speak different languages. To live in Athens, then, requires that we learn a new language. For Paul to assist in the establishment of Churches in Greece and Rome required translating the story of the Jerusalem Church into another culture. When the writer of the fourth Gospel compared Jesus to the logos, he was engaging in a process of translating familiar concepts into another universe of discourse. It was clear that the language of the early Church was the "mother tongue," but that it needed translation.

The role of the translator assumes the existence of two rather distinct, coherent language systems, each with its own unique vocabulary, rules of grammar and perspectives on reality. Faced with two different languages, confusion in communication, or the absence of good translations, a linguist sets about the task of immersion in language study, cultural analysis, and translation. The linguist is in the position of choosing those expressions which will best communicate ideas in the original language. It requires the translation of words, concepts, and nuances into another universe of discourse. Thus translation is another strategy, alongside critique and analogy, for the Christian psychologist as culture-broker.

The metaphor of "translation" assumes a clear point of departure. At issue is not the selection of a normative vision but choosing and testing the best language to communicate that vision. The process of translation is cognitive and empirical. The adequacy of a translation is tested both in terms of rational and linguistic consistency and in terms of its consequences or the life of the community.

In the modern world a variety of languages have been developed to describe the person. One can be descriptive at the biochemical level and define stress as excessive secretion of digestive hormones into the stomach with subsequent ulceration. One can use the language of neurology and interpret thinking in terms of brain processes. One can use the language of ethology and interpret learning using the vocabulary of conditioning, imprinting, reflexes, patterns of reinforcement and the learning environment. We can use the terminology of scientific psychology and employ the naturalistic concepts of cause and effect, regression analysis, controlled observation, manipulation of variables and opera-

tional definitions. Cognition can be examined using the lexicon of computer technology: input, storage, buffers, retrieval, networks, and organization. All of these languages have in common the fact that fundamentally natural metaphors are being used.

Historical metaphors are as common in psychological accounts and naturalistic ones. Some advocate that autobiography is the quintessential mode of understanding human nature. Others use historical change as the organizing motif; developmental or stage theories, age-related changes in behavior and dialectical development. Some use the language of decision: action, consequence, reflexiveness, responsibility, and change. One can use the language of the sociologist: roles, institutionalization, alienation, authority, tradition, class, rationalization, or status. One can also use the glossary of cultural anthropologists to examine human behavior in terms of mores, symbols, evolution, kinship, national character, adaption, taboos, sanctions, ritual, and acculturation.

Somewhere between the natural and the historical systems are the uniquely psychological metaphors. Structuralism focuses on consciousness, introspection, experience, attention, sensations, apperception, and chronometry. Functionalist language uses another vocabulary: adaption, adjustment, evolution, individual differences, drives, and problem solving. There is the dictionary provided by behaviorism: stimulus, response, reinforcement, conditioning, behavior, association, conditioned response, environmentalism, shaping, and spontaneous recovery. Phenomenology develops yet another set of terms: gestalt, context, qualities, holism, and closure. Even field-theory in physics and been employed to explain individual behavior: forces, topology, equilibrium, tension-systems, valence, life-space, locomotion, and permeable boundaries.

There are a number of appropriate responses by the Christian psychologist *qua* linguist to this plethora of languages. First, we can simply recognize the babel of tongues given the wide variety of languages available for describing human behavior. Second, one can guard against absolutizing any one language as the only or best language for mental health practice. Reductionism is a besetting sin of theoretical purists, a form of intellectual idolatry. Third, one can compare languages to determine the relative strengths and weaknesses of a particular symbol system. What aspect of human reality is slighted by a particular language? What is the fundamental metaphor that gives coherence to a particular universe of discourse? In what contexts are some languages more appropriate than others? While all languages listed above describe human reality, some focus on one aspect of that reality with greater intensity and provide greater differentiation. One theory may be more sensitive to the dimension of freedom, action, responsibility, and self-consciousness, while another may be more suitable to an analysis of committed relationships, friendship, tradition, and culture.

But in addition to the appropriateness of context and focus, are there any other ways of testing the usefulness of a particular language? If the Christian community is the context for the process of translation, one can ask about the consistency of any language with that of the Christian community and one must ask whether a particular language leads to greater community, faithfulness, and righteousness. Ultimately the test of adequacy of a language is its effect on the quality of life for an individual or the human community. A language system that inspires greater acts of justice, kindness, liberation, joy, and forgiveness is a useful language or theory. Note that the criteria are derived from a point other than the language itself. In Athens the usual test of a language is its correspondence to physical reality. When there is an acceptable level of correspondence, we say the theory is true. The Hebrews tended to test the truth of a statement by its ability to inspire truthful actions.

A number of attempts have been made by those who have theological concerns and psychological interests to translate the language of Christianity into a particular social science theory. Some have translated Christianity into the language of scientific psychology (Myers, 1978), existential psychology (Tweedie, 1961), transactional psychology (Malony, 1979), psychoanalysis (Tillich, 1964), Jungian psychology (Cox, 1959), and Rogerian nondirective therapy (Browning, 1996).

Thus one of the many strategies of the Christian psychologist in relationship to culture is to take a particular psychological theory and translate the terms as best one can. Oden (1966) for example, has translated theological language into that of nondirective therapy. Sin is translated as incongruence, introjected negative values, and conditional acceptance. Redemption is viewed as congruence, empathy, and unconditional positive regard. Growth in grace becomes openness to experience, congruence, and being able to function fully.

David Myers (1978) attempts to translate aspects of the Christian message into the language of scientific psychology. He justified this by stating that

> ... the historic Hebrew-Christian view sees God acting and revealing himself through all events of his creation. The spirit of God is understood as something greater than merely another force which

sometimes intervenes in nature. Christians can therefore see psychological research in Christian terms—as exploration of the natural revelation. (p. 267)

The Hebrew assumption that the person is a unity is translated into the scientific language of psychosomatic unity. The Jewish-Christian view of the relationship of thought and action is translated into research findings which demonstrate that "we are as likely to act ourselves into a way of thinking as to think ourselves into acting" (Myers, 1978, p. 268). The tension between divine sovereignty and human responsibility is translated into the language of environmental control and personal responsibility.

The most careful attempt to examine the relationship between the language of the Church as community and that of a particular model of mental health practice was developed by Myron Ebersole (1961). Ebersole focused on the conceptual model of the "therapeutic community." It provided "a theoretical basis for their interest in creating a primary group context of concern and trust in which clients could feel some confidence to reassume responsibility for their own attitudes and behavior" (Ebersole, 1961, p. 48). The approach assumed less hierarchical structure, less formalized patterns of communication, broader participation in decision-making and conscious use of the setting for treatment. Such an approach was consistent with a positive perspective on the nature of the Church and the importance of voluntary individual responsibility. The individual is seen in relational terms rather than individualistically. But Ebersole did not assume parity between Church and the notion of therapeutic community. The former is a community of devotion and has more permanent and holistic purposes. The latter has the more limited goal of finding resources to begin moving toward mental health. It is entirely possible that a patient might move on to participate in a community of devotion.

The strategy of translation has some clear implications. First, translation as a metaphor presumes that language systems have their own integrity and separateness. As such it is a safeguard against baptizing a specific language as Christian: Christian behaviorism, Christian phenomenology, Christian psychoanalysis, or Christian family systems therapy. Second, the language metaphor relatives all languages. This frees the Christian professional to use a variety of languages. It means that the language of contemporary Christianity is not absolutized either. The translation of Christianity and psychology is not well served by simply returning to the exclusive use of biblical language. Therapy is not simply spouting Bible verses.

No one language has a corner on reality. Third, one can use one language to counter the biases of other languages. Phenomenologically oriented psychological theories are a good counter for more empirically oriented approaches. Systems theories complement individualistic theories of human motivation.

This strategy has some besetting weaknesses. First, the language into which the Christian vision is translated tends to take on primacy and givenness. When this happens, the vision of Christianity is rewritten in the language of the prevailing culture. Second, it is easy for us to assume that a particular translation is permanent. New translations are needed as circumstances change. Reification of a translation too easily raises the translation to the level of dogma. Such an approach is too static. Third, languages are not entirely neutral. They do contain implicit assumptions about how relationships can be ordered, as feminists have pointed out for some time. Languages reflect the biases of a particular culture. They are not simply descriptive. Stripped of cultural biases, the variety of psychological languages referenced earlier are clearly useful to the Christian professional. Fourth, this strategy easily forgets that something always "falls between the cracks" in the process of translation. The test of the adequacy of the translation is the faithfulness to the praxis of the New Testament Church.

Critical to this strategy is the context of translation, since few translators work entirely alone and then submit their work as final. For the Christian in whatever occupation, the context of translation is the Church. Here the essential dimensions of the vision are hammered out and the translation tested for adequacy. Translation is a fundamentally communal process.

Dialogue

The relationship between Christ and culture, Jerusalem and Athens, in the strategy of dialogue is one of tension and paradox. We function simultaneously under law which condemns and grace which forgives. We recognize both revelation and reason; humankind is both sinful and justified. Niebuhr (1951) finds in Luther the best representative of this motif. For him there were two Kingdoms: the Kingdom of God and the Kingdom of this world. The former deals with the moral life and sets persons free to work in the world of culture. One develops the spirit of humanity, the other focuses on technique. Living in both worlds may require using strange instruments to achieve long-range goals. The relationship of Christ and culture for Luther is dynamic and dialectical.

The metaphor of dialogue as a way of describing the relationship of Christianity and culture is appropriate in view of the finiteness of our expressions of faith and the finiteness of cultural achievements. It recognizes that all theological constructions are human constructions bound to a greater or lesser extent by the social, historical, psychological, and economic conditions in which we live. The same can, of course, be said of the works of culture. This strategy then affirms the stance of partners in dialogue. It assumes the world of culture has a valid contribution to make to the work of the Reign of God.

In genuine dialogue, both partners in the conversation are changed as a result of the interaction. For such a dialogue to occur, it is appropriate for both members to bracket their preconceived notions, to listen empathetically to the other, and to set aside any demands one might have of the other. Most importantly, one must expect that the other also has something significant to contribute. The result may be a creative encounter in which the unexpected is a possibility, disagreement is accepted, and tension welcomed rather than avoided. It recognizes the uniqueness the other brings to the conversation as a result of a different history of experiences. Genuine dialogue requires the energy necessary to reconstruct the perspective of another. The farther apart the reference groups that have shaped our particular constellation of attitudes and our construction of reality, the greater the differences partners bring to the encounter. But "response-ability" implies responsibility to engage in dialogue.

In our dialogue with Freud we can learn that religion is sometimes projection, a satisfaction of individual wishes (Freud, 1961; Kueng, 1979). Freud said it in a less qualified way. Nonetheless, greater honesty about one's own motivation is appropriate. Also, Freud's sensitivity to the effects of an oppressive society (sexually or otherwise) on the individual needs to be heard. He detailed the havoc, the fragmentation, and the guilt produced by an oversocialized superego (Freud, 1976). Jung (1964) has reminded us of the importance of tradition and symbol in the life of the individual, even though Jung accepted the history of the West rather uncritically as the foundation of the individual self. Skinner (1971) was correct when he described human behavior as conditioned by the larger environment. We do well to examine the ways in which that occurs in American society. However, Skinner can be criticized for overstepping the bounds of objective research when he argues for the essential meaninglessness of concepts such as human freedom and dignity. Erikson (1953) described child development in Western societies in a helpful way. He demonstrated how a technological and capitalistic society has shaped the process of growth though he was less sensitive to the effects of sexism.

The danger endemic to the strategy of dialogue is compartmentalization. It assumes that each individual in the conversation is bound by roles. Clinical psychologists are to deal with the emotional issues while pastors are responsible for bringing religious insights to bear on healing. such a dichotomy will only serve to rationalize the *status quo*.

Witness

This strategy of interaction between Christ and culture begins with the text: "All things were created, in heaven and on earth, visible, and invisible, whether thrones or dominions, or principalities or authorities—all things were created through him and for him" (Col. 1:16). The focus is on the present transformation of all things cultural for the glory of God. It centers more on Christ the redeemer of culture than Christ the judge of culture. Sin in culture is seen as perversion rather than as inherent evil. Yet culture is under God's sovereign rule. There is in this strategy a hopeful attitude toward culture. Cultural work must be carried out in obedience to the Lord. The creative activity of God in Christ is a major theme. Niebuhr (1951) points out that "the problem of culture is therefore the problem of its conversion, not of its replacement by a new creation; though the conversion is so radical that it amounts to a kind of rebirth" (p. 194).

In Augustine we have a representative of this position in that he has the clear expectation of a universal regeneration of culture through Christ. He constructed a theory (theology) for the renewal of human cultural existence. Augustine illustrated in his own life the transformation of culture—one who was converted from being pagan to being a Christian. He employed language with a new brilliance. While he borrowed from the neo-Platonism of the time, it was given new depth and direction. The result was medieval Christendom. As a transformer of culture, Augustine redirected, reinvigorated, and regenerated human cultural achievements which were now perverted but were created good. Calvin followed the same motif in his call for the permeation of all of life with the Gospel.

When this strategy of the Church-culture relationship is applied to psychology, the focus will be on the distinctive contribution of the Church. By providing a different context for cultural achievements, something new is created that clearly reflects the Judeo-Christian heritage. It takes seriously the assumption that there is a uniquely Christian way of viewing some issues. It assumes that we begin with the fact of God's existence in our understanding of human nature, healing, and society. It views history as the arena of God's activity that began with the mighty deeds recorded by the Israelites and the New Testament Christians and that continues today. Our participation in that history, our work and purposes, are then understood and judged most clearly from the perspective of Yahweh. All of life is to be permeated with the Gospel. Christ is the redeemer of the world. The style of this strategy is a call for change in conformity with the fundamental vision of the Reign of God.

The following convictions emerge out of our heritage in Jerusalem and have implications for our approaches in mental health practice. They are beliefs that could be systematically and fruitfully explored. They are intended only as suggestive of some directions to be pursued.

(1) *Pluralism*. It is entirely inconsistent to engage in theological imperialism in therapy when historically there are Christians (the Anabaptists, for example) who died for religious pluralism. Religious liberty allows us to exercise and explore the implications of our faith commitments. That same freedom guarantees the freedom of the clients not to believe the way a therapist does and not to be rejected or turned away because of it. Religious pluralism grants integrity to the person who is not a Christian. However, that same freedom must also be respected when the therapist or mental health program points to an alternative way of life (Dueck, 1987a). Pluralism assumes that people are at different stages in their attitude toward the Reign of God. In what therapeutic ways can a therapist make explicit reference to faith dimensions without imperialism?

(2) *Discipleship*. Much of contemporary therapy has focused on the gospel to the exclusion of law (Friesen & Dueck, 1988). Such a separation is problematic in theology and in therapy. It results in acceptance without confrontation, individual actualization without sacrifice, and freedom without structure (cf. Browning, 1976). Discipleship assumes that the model set by Christ is what it means to be human. Here there is no dichotomy between gospel and law. Whether the client is a Christian or not, to the extent that one's life is patterned on this model, new life is a possibility. This suggests that there is not one ethic for Christians and another for those who choose not to be. For the therapist there is only one ethic, though different individuals bring different resources to the encounter. How would a model

of therapy be structured which took seriously the biblical notion of law?

(3) *Covenant.* Life is not lived alone nor is life understood only from an individual perspective. God's covenant with the human race remains unbroken and hence human life can be understood only in the light of that covenant (Brueggeman, 1979). But covenant language applies also to human relationships. In what ways would we restructure therapy if our goal were the restoration of covenant both with God and humanity?

(4) *Priesthood of all believers.* Before God we are all priests. No distinction is made between clergy and laity (Dueck, 1987b, 1987c). All are called to minister to the needs of brother, sister, and neighbor. The Church would then be a significant context for healing. It is unfortunate that we have not explored the Christian community as a resource for healing the broken. At least part of the problem is that the present nature and structure of the Church precludes it. One can effect little change when "church" means meeting Sunday morning and Wednesday night. But in the context of small covenant groups that take seriously the other's welfare, healing is possible. Would this have implications for the way a Christian therapist then functions in conjunction with the Christian community?

Conclusion

Wolterstorff (1976) cogently argues that the beliefs of the Christian ought to affect the process of our research. He states:

> The Christian scholar ought to allow the belief content of his authentic Christian commitment to function as a control within his devising and weighing of theories. For he like everyone else ought to seek consistency, wholeness, and integrity in the body of beliefs and commitments. Since his fundamental commitment to following Christ ought to be decisively ultimate in his life, the rest of his life ought to function both negatively and positively. Negatively, the Christian scholar ought to reject certain theories on the ground that they conflict or do not comport well with the belief-content of his authentic commitment. And positively he ought to devise theories which comport as well as possible with, or at least consistent with, the belief-content of his authentic commitment. (p. 73)

Control beliefs serve, for Wolterstorff, to govern one's actual research. The control beliefs emerge from one's commitment as a Christ-follower and a member of the Christian community. The Scriptures function authoritatively in that community. Control beliefs are consistent with that authority. Control beliefs are not theories in themselves, but heuristic pointers. The Christian scholar must use the same creative capacities of imagination that scholars in general use. The data for a theory come by careful observation and reflection on the world around us. This essay is an attempt to take Wolterstorff's proposal seriously.

The Church is caught between the temptations of assimilation and isolation. In terms of the strategies listed above, assimilation occurs most easily when we are defensive about a critique, focus on continuity, assume the identity of languages, underestimate the differences between the partners in dialogue and minimize the uniqueness of the Christian contribution. On the other hand, isolation is a consequence of exclusive critique, rejection of all continuity reifying the differences between languages, compartmentalizing the partners in the dialogue and proclaiming imperialistically the Church's distinctiveness.

Neither of these modes of response is acceptable.

References

Barbour, I. G. (1974). *Myths, models, and paradigms.* New York: Harper and Row.

Barth, K. (1960). *Church dogmatics Vol. III. The Doctrine of Creation,* Part 2 (The Creature). London: T. & T. Clark.

Berkhof, H. (1962). *Christ and the powers.* (John Howard Yoder, Trans.) Scottdale: Herald Press.

Browning, D. (1966). *Atonement and psychotherapy,* Philadelphia: The Westminster Press.

Browning, D. (1976). *The moral context of pastoral care.* Philadelphia: The Westminster Press.

Brueggeman, W. (1972). *In man we trust.* Nashville, TN: Knox.

Brueggeman, W. (1979). Covenanting as human vocation. *Interpretation, 33,* 115-129.

Buss. A. R. (Ed.). (1979). *Psychology in social context.* New York: Irvington Pub. Inc.

Cox, D. (1959). *Jung and Saint Paul.* New York: Association Press.

Dueck, A. (1985). North American psychology: Gospel of modernity. *Conrad Grebel Review, 3,* 165-178.

Dueck, A. (1987a). Ethical contexts of healing: Peoplehood and righteousness. *Pastoral Psychology, 35,* 239-253.

Dueck, A. (1987b). Ethical contexts of healing: Ecclesia and praxis. *Pastoral Psychology, 36,* 49-60.

Dueck, A. (1987c). Ethical contexts of healing: Character and ritual. *Pastoral Psychology, 36,* 69-83.

Ebersole, A. (1961). *A critical comparison of the Anabaptist view of the church and the therapeutic community in contemporary psychiatric practice.* Unpublished master's thesis, University of Chicago.

Ellul, J. (1964). *The technological society.* New York: Vintage Books.

Erikson, E. (1953). *Childhood and society.* New York: W. W. Norton & Co.

Friesen, W., & Dueck, A. (1988). Whatever happened to law? *Journal of Psychology and Christianity, 7,* 13-22.

Freud, S. (1961). *Civilization and its discontents.* New York: W. W. Norton.

Freud, S. (1976). *The future of an illusion.* (W. D. Robson-Scott, Trans.). Garden City, NJ: Doubleday.

Kueng, H. (1979). *Freud and the problem of God.* (E. Quinn, Trans.). New Haven: Yale University Press.

Malony, N. (1979). Transactional analysis and Christian counseling. In G. Collins (Ed.), *Ways of Christian counseling.* Irvine, CA: Vision House.

May, R., Rogers, C., & Maslow, A. (1986). *Politics and innocence: A humanistic debate.* Dallas, TX: Saybrook.

Myers, D. G. (1978). *The human puzzle: Psychological research and Christian belief.* New York: Harper and Row.

Niebuhr, H. R. (1951). *Christ and culture.* New York: Harper and Row.

Oden, T. (1966). *Kerygma and counseling.* New York: Harper and Row.

Palmer, P. (1988). *The company of strangers: Christians and the renewal of America's public life.* New York: Crossroads.

Peck. S. (1987). *The different drum: Community making and peace.* New York: Simon and Schuster.

Skinner, B. F. (1971). *Beyond freedom and dignity.* New York: Knopf.

Tillich, P. (1964). The theological significance of existentialism and psychoanalysis. In *Theology of culture* (pp. 112-126). New York: Oxford University Press.

Tweedie, D. (1961). *Logotherapy and the Christian faith.* Grand Rapids, MI: Baker.

Wallach, M. A., & Wallach, L. (1983). *Psychology's sanction for selfishness: The error of egoism in theory and therapy.* San Francisco: W. H. Freeman.

Wolterstorff, N. (1976). *Reason within the bounds of religion.* Grand Rapids, MI: William B. Eerdmans Pub. Co.

Yoder, J. H. (1964). *Richard Niebuhr—Christ and culture: Analysis and critique.* Mennonite Student Services Summer Seminar, Elkhart, IN.

21

Integrating the Integrators:
An Organizing Framework for a
Multifaceted Process of Integration

Brian E. Eck
Azusa Pacific University

Over the last quarter century, several models for the integration of psychology and theology have been proposed. Each of these models holds underlying assumptions about the admissibility of data to the integration process and has identified specific methods by which that data may be integrated across disciplines. The present article reviews and organizes these models according to their underlying assumptions and processes for integration and identifies the three data assumption paradigms, five integration processes and nine meta-models that underlie the field of integration. To advance integrative efforts, the need for agreement on the definition of integration, admissibility of data, and use of integration models is proposed and a multiperspectival application of the meta-models is suggested.

Christians in the field of psychology have spent the last quarter of a century writing about the integration of Christian beliefs with their practice of the discipline. Worthington (1994) summarizes these efforts by describing an unsystematic and rudimentary early period prior to 1975; a vigorous and sophisticated model building middle period from 1975-1982; and a stagnant period from 1982 to the present. He suggests that this dormancy results from a lack of guidelines for how to do integration at a practical level.

Others (Bouma-Prediger, 1990; Clinton, 1990a, 1990b; Foster & Bolsinger, 1990; Foster, Horn & Watson, 1988; Ingram, 1995) have also expressed dissatisfaction with the disjointed direction that integrative efforts have taken. They call for a shift away from theorizing about integration models, and instead, to begin looking for those consistent themes or facts that can serve as the basis for building a truly integrated psychology. If such a psychology could be created there is a need to establish agreement on at least three areas of the integrative process.

Three Areas in Need of Agreement

Definition of Integration

First, there is a need to develop a consistent definition of what integration means. To the present, other than to say that the basis of integration rests on the proposition that all truth is God's truth (Carter & Narramore, 1979; Clinton, 1990b; Collins, 1977, 1981; Crabb, 1977; Evans, 1977, 1982; Farnsworth, 1981, 1985; Foster & Bolsinger, 1990), authors of new books or articles have found it necessary to define in new terminology the type of integration about which they are writing. Even then, the definition of integration is usually stated in such generalized terms as the "interaction" or "interface" of psychology and theology, or as the "discovery and articulation of the common underlying principles" of these two fields. The key to creating a uniform definition of integration lies in defining the ultimate goal that the *processes* of integration are attempting to achieve.

I would argue that the goal of integration is to come to a greater, more holistic and unified understanding of human persons and their social/ecosystemic worlds than is possible through any unitary disciplinary window alone. Integration does not detract from the truths of psychology, theology or any other discipline, but rather deepens those truths through a greater cross-disciplinary application and unification of their truths. This more unified perspective enables us not only to celebrate the truths of Scripture, but to marvel at how "fearfully and wonderfully" we are made (Ps. 139:4, NIV). Although this article limits itself to the integration of psychology and theology, the most complete form of integration would go beyond a psychology-theology duality and fully integrate the truths from all disciplines (Carter, 1983; Ingram, 1995).

Admissible Data

The second area requiring agreement is the type of data that is admissible to the integrative process. This involves first defining a response to the different types of truth (the data of psychology and theology), and second to the different means of knowing those truths (the methods of study in each discipline). In spite of the generally accepted belief among Christians that all truth is God's truth, many Christians make distinctions that attribute different levels of acceptance to the data from general (natural universe based) versus special (biblically based) revelation (Carter & Narramore, 1979; Collins, 1977, 1981; Crabb, 1977; Johnson, 1992). They also differentiate between scientific/academic and personal truths. (For an excellent elaboration on types of truth see Farnsworth, 1981).

No matter the source of the data for the integrative process, scientific/academic truth cannot be divorced from the means by which it is obtained (Evans, 1977, 1982; Farnsworth, 1981, 1985; Johnson, 1992; Van Leeuwen, 1982). Truths come through a particular academic or personal means of knowing. Academically, these means are the accepted methods of study in each discipline. In theology, the data are shaped by the methods used to translate, exegete, and interpret the truths of Scripture (Cranmer & Eck, 1994). In psychology, the data are shaped by the scientific method and although the modernist methods with their positivistic, materialistic, and reductionistic assumptions may be gradually changing in the postmodern world (Ingram, 1995), it still remains the primary means for discovering truth in psychology (Foster & Bolsinger, 1990).

The goal of a fully integrated understanding of human persons and their social/ecosystemic worlds is constrained by the limitations inherent in the methods of study in both psychology and theology. Multidisciplinary integration may thus require different models using different processes to overcome the existing limitations of method and data in growing areas of knowledge.

Personal truth reflects the need for integrated truth to be personally relevant and practically applicable (Farnsworth, 1981). For integration to be complete, the truths of the integration process must move beyond the theoretical (Worthington, 1994) and become "embodied" (Farnsworth, 1981) in the individual's own unique existential experience.

The issue of admissibility of a discipline's data reflects one's belief in the accuracy, appropriateness, usefulness and reliability of that data. There seems to be extensive agreement among Evangelicals on the supremacy of the truth of Scripture (Carter & Narramore, 1979; Clinton 1990b; Collins, 1977, 1981; Crabb, 1977; Evans, 1977, 1982; Farnsworth, 1981, 1985; Foster & Bolsinger, 1990; Johnson, 1992), but

very little agreement on how to use that truth in the integrative process.

What Processes for Integration

A final area for agreement would be on the *process* or *processes* by which truth is integrated. A number of authors (e.g., Carter & Narramore, 1979; Collins, 1977, 1981; Crabb, 1977; Evans, 1977, 1982; Farnsworth, 1981, 1985) have between them provided 27 separate models for the integrative process.

Integrating the Integrators

The 27 models mentioned above can be organized into three integrative **paradigms** that define the admissibility of the data from each discipline, five basic integration **processes** that define a method for relating the data of each discipline, and nine specific **meta-models of integration** (see Figures 1 and 2). The processes and models identified here could be used in the integration of any group of disciplines.

The integrators can be organized into three broad paradigms that are defined by the assumptions they make regarding the data from the disciplines of psychology and theology. The *Non-Integrative Paradigm* does not seek integration of the data but rather builds its understanding of God's truth on one discipline alone. The *Manipulative Paradigm* seeks to integrate the data of both disciplines, but the data of one discipline must be altered before becoming acceptable to the other discipline. The final paradigm, the *Non-Manipulative Paradigm*, accepts the data from both disciplines directly into the integrative process.

Each paradigm contains certain processes that define the method for how the data of each discipline will be integrated. The *Non-Integrative Paradigm* contains only the *Rejects Process*; the *Manipulative Paradigm* contains both the *Reconstructs Process* and the *Transforms Process*; and the *Non-Manipulative Paradigm* utilizes the *Correlates Process* and the *Unifies Process*.

As each discipline utilizes a particular integrative process, it produces a unique meta-model for the integration of psychology and theology. Except for the Unifies and Correlates processes in which there is a mutual coming together, the discipline listed first controls the integrative process.

Non-Integrative Paradigm

The Non-Integrative Paradigm does not seek to integrate multiple sources of truth, but rather attempts to keep the pure truth of one discipline unsoiled by the fallen (unacceptable) untruth of the other. Because acceptable data are believed to come from only one discipline, each discipline must reject the other as a source for truth. The *REJECTS* process is the only process within this category and it contains two meta-models.

Rejects Integration Process
Psychology Rejects Theology Model.

In the first Rejects model, PSYCHOLOGY REJECTS THEOLOGY, scientific knowledge is the only recognized source for truth while theology is generally reduced to the status of superstition and myth. The data from theology are thus perceived as inadmissible for integration. This position is perhaps best represented by Freud's (1961) conception of religion as an "illusion" that needs to be replaced by reason, or by Skinner's (1971) conception of religion as "prescientific thinking" that needs to be replaced by scientific explanation. Another representative of this model would be secular psychologist Albert Ellis (1980). Among the integrators, this view is only represented by Carter and Narramore's (1979) SECULAR AGAINST model in which the only reliable means of finding truth is through the scientific method and its use of rationalism and empiricism.

Theology Rejects Psychology Model.

In the second Rejects model, THEOLOGY REJECTS PSYCHOLOGY, biblical revelation becomes the only admissible data because it is perceived as the one pure source for truth and the knowledge of how to live in God's created world. Weaver (1986) points out that Christian counselors from this perspective view psychology with "outright suspicion and rejection" (p. 205). An excellent proclamation of this model is Richard Ganz's (1976) statement that, "It takes an unpolluted spring to form an unpolluted pond. Likewise, the only way to have a nonpolluted system of counseling is to fill it from an unpolluted source. That source is the Scriptures" (p. 196). Other representatives of this model would include Adams (1970), Martin and Diedre Bobgan (1978, 1985, 1987), and Kilpatrick (1983).

Among the integrators, this position is found in Carter and Narramore's (1979) SACRED AGAINST model in which biblical revelation is the only reliable means of finding the truth; Crabb's (1977) NOTHING-BUTTERY MODEL in which psychology is altogether disregarded; and Evans' (1977) the LIMITER OF SCIENCE, TERRITORIALIST model, which accepts physiology as a science of the human body, but rejects the notion of a science that ignores the soul.

Manipulative Integration Paradigm

The second paradigm, the Manipulative Integration Paradigm, accepts that some truth exists in each discipline but does not believe that the truth from the other discipline is directly admissible into the integration process. In this paradigm, data from the other discipline must be altered to become acceptable as data for the process of integration. This paradigm contains two integrative processes, each of which contains two meta-models.

Reconstructs Integration Process

The RECONSTRUCTS Integration Process is characterized by taking the truth from one discipline and subsuming it within the truth of the other. Although there is a beginning acceptance that some admissible truth resides in both disciplines, the data of one discipline are reconstructed in such a way that the outcome is similar to the rejects models in that it yields only one acceptable body of knowledge.

Psychology Reconstructs Theology Model

In the first Reconstructs model, PSYCHOLOGY RECONSTRUCTS THEOLOGY, the truths of theology must be brought into their proper psychological context. The most frequent reconstruction is the elimination of the supernatural. This model reconstructs theological truth into a theologically informed system of psychology.

Examples of this model include Jung's (1961) statement that among his patients in the second half of their lives, there was not one whose problem did not require "finding a religious outlook on life" (p. 69). He does not here mean a supernatural, theologically religious outlook on life. This becomes clear, when in another work he states,

> It would be a regrettable mistake if anybody should understand my observations to be some kind of proof of the existence of God. They prove only the existence of an archetypal image of the Deity, which to my mind is the most we can assert psychologically about God (Jung, 1938, p. 73).

Other representatives of this model include Fromm (1950), May (1969), and most recently, Sperry (1988) who, writing in the *American Psychologist,* called for a rapprochement between psychology and religion, but without religion's supernaturalism.

Among the integrationists, this approach is first found in Carter and Narramore's (1979) SECULAR OF and SACRED OF models which minimize the purely religious nature or content of religious concepts, reject supernaturalism, place science above the authority of Scripture, and interpret Scripture as an expression of psychological truth. Collins (1981) also identifies a reconstructive approach that he calls nothing BUT-ERY in his review of Crabb's models.

Figure 1

Eck (1996)		Integration Models	Conceptual Relationship	Representatives
Non-Integrative Paradigm				
REJECTS PROCESS	Ψ ⊗	Ψ rejects Θ	**Theology rejected** as a source for truth. No Integration possible.	Albert Ellis Sigmund Freud B.F. Skinner John B. Watson
	⊗ Θ	Θ rejects Ψ	**Psychology rejected** as a source for truth. No Integration possible.	Jay E. Adams David Hunt W.K. Kilpatrick M. & D. Bobgan
Manipulative Integration Paradigm				
RECONSTRUCTS PROCESS	Ψ (Θ)	Ψ reconstructs Θ	**Eliminate the Supernatural.** Integration produces a Theologically informed Psychological System	Carl Jung Erich Fromm Rollo May R.W. Sperry
	Θ (Ψ)	Θ reconstructs Ψ	**Eliminate the Natural Scientific.** Integration produces a Psychologically informed Theological System.	Alcoholics Anonymous Morton Kelsey Leanne Payne J. & P. Sanford
TRANSFORMS PROCESS	Ψ ← Θ	Ψ transforms Θ	**Both Legitimate.** Integration involves first filtering or altering the world view of Theological data.	William Sargent Gordon Allport Bernard Spika
	Ψ → Θ	Θ transforms Ψ	**Both Legitimate.** Integration involves first filtering or altering the world view of Psychological data.	Filter Larry Crabb Minirth & Meier - - - - - - - - - - - World View Gary Collins Mark Cosgrove
Non-Manipulative Integration Paradigm				
CORRELATES PROCESS	Θ ▨ Ψ ▤	Ψ correlates with (levels) Θ	**Both Legitimate.** Integration involves deepening one's awareness through multilevel analysis of the data.	David Meyers Malcolm Jeeves Bob Larzallere Donald MacKay John Ingram natural scientists
	Ψ═Θ Ψ═Θ Ψ═Θ	Ψ correlates with (linkages) Θ	**Both Legitimate.** Integration involves creating linkages between related data from each field.	Carter & Mohline Thomas Oden
UNIFIES PROCESS	Ψ◆Θ	Ψ unifies with Θ	**Both Legitimate.** Integration involves seeking unified concepts and living them out in the world.	

Figure 2

Carter & Narramore (1979)	Collins (1981)	Crabb (1977	Evans (1977)	Farnsworth (1981, 1985)	Foster et al. (1988)	
				Non-Integrative Paradigm		
Secular Against (pp. 76-7)	——	——	——	——	——	REJECTS
Sacred Against (pp. 76-7)	——	Nothing Buttery p. 40	Limiters of Science (Territorialists) p. 89	——	.	REJECTS
				Manipulative Integration Paradigm		
Secular Of Sacred Of p. 82, 85	Nothing But-ery p. 31	——	Reinterperter (Capitulators) p. 88	Convertibility B p. 100	0%	RECONSTRUCTS
——	Nothing But-ery p. 31	——	——	——	——	RECONSTRUCTS
Filter ——	——	——	——	Convertibility A p. 99	0%	TRANSFORMS
World View ——	——	——	——	——	26%	TRANSFORMS
Filter ——	Spoiling the Egyptians p. 32	Spoiling the Egyptians p. 47	Humanizers of Science (Particularists) p. 97	Credibility p. 97	8%	TRANSFORMS
World View ——	Rebuilding pp. 33-36	——	Humanizers of Science (Generalists) p. 97	Conformability p. 101	36%	TRANSFORMS
				Non-Manipulative Integration Paradigm		
Parallels (Isolation) p. 91	Levels of Analysis p. 26	Separate But Equal p. 33	Limiters of Science (Perspectivalists) p. 89	Complementarity (Levels) p. 104	0%	CORRELATES
Parallels (Isolation) p. 92	Railroad Tracks p. 22 (unzipped zipper)	——	Reinterpreter (Compatibilist) p. 88	Compatibility A p. 102	30%	CORRELATES
Integrates p. 104	Zipper p. 30	Tossed Salad p. 35	——	Compatibility B (zipped) 1981, p. 6	0%	UNIFIES

Here the psychologist, according to Collins, "redefines all theology in psychological terms" (p. 31). This is not, however, Crabb's NOTHING-BUTTERY. Crabb (1977) defines his nothing buttery as a Rejects process in which psychology is "altogether disregarded" (p. 40). What Collins is describing is instead closer to Jeeves' (1976) NOTHING-BUTTERY concept, in which all aspects of the human person are reduced to being "nothing but a complex animal, a complex machine, or the result of environmental forces" (p. 83).

A third integrator, Evans (1977), describes this reconstructive model as the REINTERPRETER, CAPITULATOR who assents to the truth of the scientific and reinterprets theological data to make it consistent with a scientific view. Farnsworth (1985) is a final integrator who identifies a reconstructive process that he calls the "CONVERTIBILITY" model. This model of integration, which I have identified as CONVERTIBILITY B, involves either "demythologizing" or "psychologizing" the theological findings (p. 100). Revelation is rearranged so that interpretations of data leave no room for the spiritual side of human nature.

In all of these models theological truth is acknowledged but is not independently accepted. Integration becomes possible only if theological truth can be manipulated into a scientific framework by losing its supernatural context. Because only the scientific remains, this model produces a theologically informed, psychological system.

Theology Reconstructs Psychology Model

In the second Reconstructs model, THEOLOGY RECONSTRUCTS PSYCHOLOGY, the truths of psychology must be brought into their proper theological context. The most frequent reconstruction is to eliminate the natural scientific basis of psychological truth. This model reconstructs psychology into a psychologically informed, theological system.

Examples of this model would include Shostrom and Montgomery's (1978) description of healthy psychological and spiritual growth in the core, or innermost being of the person. They state that the core is not the raw, chaotic power of Freud's unconscious, but rather it is "an innate guidance system energized by the power of God's love" (p. 128). Another example is Payne (1981), who counsels her clients that dreams are an intuitive way of knowing and serve as important vehicles for the revelation of the heart of God to our hearts and heads. Her process of dream interpretation removes the scientific while highlighting the spiritual. She states that in the company of others that are Spirit led, "The most important factor in dream interpretation of the unconscious, is a complete dependence upon the Holy Spirit and the Word of God" (p. 178).

When representatives of this model have finished their integrative process, one is struck by the lack of the scientific and the strong presence of a theological system at the core of their approach. Other representatives of this model would include Kelsey (1986), Sanford and Sandford (1982), and the approach of Alcoholics Anonymous. Among the integrationists, this model is only found in Collins' (1981) NOTHING BUT-ERY, where the theologian reduces all psychology to theology.

Transforms Integration Process

The second process within the manipulative integration paradigm is the transforms integration process. This is the first approach that truly accepts the legitimacy of the data from both disciplines. It remains a manipulative approach, however, because the data from one discipline must be altered before becoming admissible to the integrative process. In general, the data from the other discipline must either pass through a set of control beliefs or be reworked into a more acceptable worldview framework.

Psychology Transforms Theology Model

In the first Transforms model, PSYCHOLOGY TRANSFORMS THEOLOGY, theological truths must either pass through a particular psychological filter, usually empirical methodology, or be altered to fit into a particular psychological worldview. Examples of this approach would include psychologists who empirically study religion, such as Spilka, Hood, and Gorsuch (1985). For them the use of "empirical" frameworks and "the utilization of the scientific method" are crucial for understanding religious phenomena and for conveying the excitement and fascination of the nature and place of religion in people's lives. After passing through this empirical filter, something of the other discipline is screened out and, in this case, it is the supernatural that is removed. This model is illustrated by Spilka et al.'s (1985) statement that, "it is not the place of psychologists to challenge religious institutions and their theologies. God is not our domain; neither is the world vision of churches" (p. 3). In other words, admissible data for the study of religion or religious experience must first pass through an empirical filter. Other representatives of this model include Allport (1950) and Sargent (1957).

Among the integrationists, this perspective is represented by Farnsworth's (1985) CONVERTIBILITY model, which I have identified as CONVERTIBILITY A. This model revises theological findings by filtering them through the psychological.

Theology Transforms Psychology Model

In the second Transforms model, THEOLOGY TRANSFORMS PSYCHOLOGY, psychological truth must either pass through a particular theological filter (which is usually Scripture), the FILTER TRANSFORMER SUBTYPE, or is altered to stay in keeping with a particular theological worldview, the WORLDVIEW TRANSFORMER SUBTYPE.

Filter transformer subtype.
An example of a filtering transformer subtype is Crabb (1977), who states that the most important job of the integrationist is to "screen secular concepts through the filter of Scripture." The integrationist should then align those concepts which pass through with appropriate theological matter and attempt to assimilate them into a comprehensive whole. Crabb goes on to state that anyone who wants to work toward a truly evangelical integration of Christianity and psychology should "agree that psychology must come under the authority of Scripture" and that "regardless of its support from empirical research, any idea that conflicts with Scripture will not be accepted as truth" (p. 49). Other representatives of this model would include Minirth and Meier (1982).

Among the integrators, the filter transformer model is represented by Crabb's (1977) SPOILING THE EGYPTIANS model and Collins' (1981) restatement of Crabb's SPOILING THE EGYPTIANS model. The filter transformer is also found in Evans' (1982) HUMANIZERS OF SCIENCE, PARTICULARISTS model. Jones (1986) redefines this model of Evans as the Humanizers or Christianizers of Science. For them, the Christian psychologist who is committed to integration uses "Christian control-beliefs to radically depart from the methods and conclusions of their nonbelieving colleagues" (p. 23). A final representative is Farnsworth's (1985) credibility model, in which psychological concepts are seen as secular concepts, and therefore must be "screened through the filter of scripture to give them credibility" (p. 97).

Worldview transformer subtype.
The goal of the worldview transformer is to produce a Christianized science of psychology. Examples of the worldview transformer subtype include Cosgrove (1979), who feels that psychology had gone awry because of errors in its underlying belief systems. He seeks to replace the current psychological worldview with Christian theism because it "offers the most defensible worldview available to psychology" (p. 149). He believes that such a transformed worldview best fits our data and experience, is broad enough to explain all the data on humanity, and is detailed enough to be tested.

Collins (1981) is another representative of this model. He seeks to rebuild psychology from the ground up by changing its foundational presuppositions to be more consistent with a Christian worldview. "I believe that the whole science of individual human behavior could be changed if it were to be built on such a biblically oriented base. This is integration at the foundational presuppositional level" (p. 36). A final representative of this model is Koteskey (1980).

Among the integrators, the worldview transformer subtype is found in Gary Collins' (1981) REBUILDING APPROACH. It is also found in Evans' (1977) HUMANIZER OF SCIENCE, GENERALIST model, which opposes the positivist view of science as a whole and attempts to build psychological science on explicitly Christian presuppositions (Jones, 1986). A final worldview transformer is found in Farnsworth's (1985) conformability model, labeled CONFORMABILITY A by Foster et al. (1988), where psychological findings must conform to a Christian worldview before being admitted into the integration process.

Non-Manipulative Integration Paradigm

The final paradigm is the Non-Manipulative Integration Paradigm. This paradigm accepts the legitimacy of the truth from both disciplines, but unlike the Manipulative Paradigm, this perspective admits the data from each discipline directly into the integrative process. This paradigm contains two integration processes and three meta-models.

Correlates Integration Process

In the first process within the non-manipulative paradigm, the CORRELATES process, the truth to be integrated from each discipline is left within the discipline from which it was derived. This approach maintains that because each discipline has its own worldviews, methods, and focus, the integrity of the data requires that it be kept in its original context. The integrative process involves forming relationships between the separated truths that are contained in each discipline.

Psychology Correlates With Theology Model

In the first model, PSYCHOLOGY CORRELATES WITH THEOLOGY, there are two subtypes. The first subtype, CORRELATES-LEVELS, involves assigning psychological and theological truth to different but often related levels of explanation.

Correlates-levels subtype. This model is perhaps the most popular among those working as natural scientists. Bube's (1971) second thesis for relating science and religion illustrates the separation of the data from each discipline when he states that "there are many levels at which a given situation can be described. An exhaustive description on one level does not preclude meaningful descriptions on other levels" (p. 28).

Within psychology an example of correlating levels would be David Myers (1986), who believes that God has written two books, nature and the Bible. For him, professional scientists and biblical scholars are needed to help us discern these two revelations and, while remaining open to the insights from either nature or Scripture (remembering that no single interpretation of nature or Scripture is final truth), one should be skeptical of any attempts to "subject theology to science or science to theology" (p. 218). Myers fears that confusion results when any one of these disciplinary levels is asserted to be primary. This is because "a given event can very often be described by simultaneous, correlated explanations at various levels, it makes no sense to say that one level is causing the other" (p. 13). Other representatives of this model would include MacKay (1974), Jeeves (1976), Larzalere (1981) and Ingram (1995).

Among the integrators this position is first represented in Carter and Narramore's (1979) PARALLELS (ISOLATION) MODEL, where each discipline is carefully relegated to the confines of its own methodology, language, and perspective. The CORRELATES-LEVELS model is also found in Collins' (1981) LEVELS OF ANALYSIS APPROACH, in which the universe can be viewed from a variety of equally valid levels. Larry Crabb (1977) describes a CORRELATES-LEVELS model called SEPARATE BUT EQUAL, in which the two disciplines deal with different problem areas.

Evans (1982), using Jeeves (1976) and MacKay (1974) as examples, lists a LIMITERS OF SCIENCE, PERSPECTIVALISTS model that emphasizes the observation of unitary reality from different viewpoints so that multiple aspects will appear. A final CORRELATES-LEVELS model is found in Farnsworth's (1985) COMPLEMENTARITY, LEVELS model in which the findings from two equally valid but different views of the same phenomenon are correlated.

Correlates-linkages subtype. In the second correlates model, PSYCHOLOGY CORRELATES WITH THEOLOGY-LINKAGES, the truth of each discipline is to remain separate and contextualized within the discipline from which it came. Rather than assigning the data from each discipline to different levels, this approach gives more equivalent acceptability to the data from each discipline and integration involves establishing linkages between each discipline's truths. This model takes a middle position between the CORRELATES-LEVELS model, and the Non-manipula-

tive paradigm's UNIFIES model. An example of this approach would be Pecheur (1978) who, in relating cognitive therapy and sanctification, writes "the processes in these two spheres are seen as the same, but the contents are seen as different. Cognitive therapy appears to make explicit the process of growth indicated in Scripture" (p. 239). Other representatives of this perspective are Oden (1966) and some of Carter and Mohline (1981).

Among the integrators, this model is first found in Carter and Narramore's (1979) PARALLELS, CORRELATION VERSION, which attempts to correlate or align certain psychological and scriptural concepts. Collins (1981) calls this approach the RAILROAD TRACK APPROACH, in which psychology and theology are "like two railroad tracks—going in the same direction, linked together with common ties, but meeting each other only on the distant horizon, and then, only in the mind of the beholder" (p. 22).

Evans (1977) calls this approach the REINTERPRETER, COMPATIBILIST who tries to "have it both ways." They would, for example, accept the traditional view of the person as free and responsible, while also accepting that one's behavior is driven by deterministic mechanisms and Divine sovereignty. Finally, Farnsworth's (1985) compatibility model relates psychological and theological findings by correlating the data from each discipline that clearly seem to be saying the same thing.

Unifies Integration Process

In the final process of the non-manipulative paradigm, the UNIFIES process, the truth to be integrated from each discipline is brought together to create a unified set of truths that mirror the wholeness and unity of God's created and revealed truths. This process seeks to use the data gathered through the best methods each discipline has to offer while recognizing that we are "looking through a glass darkly" (I Cor. 13:12, NIV). This approach recognizes the limitations of human understanding that impact our ability to know and understand the truth from *both* disciplines, yet seeks to live out a unified set of truths in one's life and practice of psychology.

Psychology Unifies With Theology Model

The only model in this process is PSYCHOLOGY UNIFIES WITH THEOLOGY. The basis for this approach is usually found in the incarnation of Christ. As Christ was both fully human and fully Divine, so too our approach as Christian psychologists should represent a unity of God's world and God's word. The goal of this approach and its one model is to seek the underlying truths of God's world in psychology and God's word in theology, and unite them by incarnationally living them out in one's life.

An example of the first half of this model would be found in Ellens' (1980) affirmation that wherever truth is disclosed it is always God's truth. "Whether it is found in General Revelation or Special Revelation, it is truth which has equal warrant with all other truth. Some truth may have a greater weight than other truth in a specific situation, but there is no difference in its warrant as truth" (p. 3). The second half of this model would be found in Farnsworth's concept of EMBODIED INTEGRATION. For Farnsworth (1985), wholehearted integration is incarnational, that is "God's truth lives through us as we live as Jesus lived" (p. 108). This unifying process of integration occurs in a lifelong, never ending process of living out integrated truths in our lives. This, for Farnsworth, is the practical application of integration that others have called for (Bouma-Prediger, 1990; Clinton, 1990a, 1990b; Foster & Bolsinger, 1990; Foster, Horn & Watson, 1988; Ingram, 1995). It involves taking what we intellectually understand to be God's truth and using it as the framework for interpreting our experience and as guidelines for making responsible choices.

Among the integrators, this model is first found in Carter and Narramore's (1979) INTEGRATES model, where psychological and theological understandings are not seen as distinct and unrelatable fields of study, but rather assume that there is ultimately only one set of explanatory hypotheses. This model looks for "unifying concepts" that broaden the understanding that comes from either psychology or theology in isolation (p. 104).

Collins (1981) relabels the INTEGRATES model of Carter and Narramore as the ZIPPER APPROACH. He feels that Carter and Narramore's model forces psychology "into a procrustean bed of theological doctrines, and that the two disciplines have been lined up and zippered together" (p. 30). Farnsworth (1981) echoes this sentiment in what I have termed the compatibility B model. Here one lines up the psychological findings on one side and theological findings on the other and "Where they seem on the surface to be saying the same thing, point for point, (you) zip 'em up" (p. 6). Finally, Crabb (1977) refers to this model as the TOSSED SALAD APPROACH. In comparing this form of integration to a cooking technique, Crabb feels that this model "mixes several ingredients together into a single bowl to create a tasty blend" (p. 36). He feels this approach aligns the two disciplines by finding where the subject matter overlaps and then blending the insights of both disciplines together.

Conclusion and Application

The nine models presented here identify and integrate the underlying data assumptions and five basic processes for relating the data from psychology and theology that have been described in the integration literature. A truly integrated psychology requires agreement on the definition of integration, what data are admissible to the integration process, and which processes can be used to produce integrated truth. When seen from God's perspective, the truths of God's revealed Word and created world are a unified whole regardless of their data source. The vastness of God's unified truth goes far beyond the scope of any one human discipline and the use of only one integration model is unlikely to achieve the full incarnation of God's truth. This use of different models, depending on the nature of the data or context, is consistent with the growing trend toward a post-modern research paradigm and its acceptance of multiperspectival analysis and procedures, the use of smaller scale rather than universal models, and a more holistic orientation (Ingram, 1995).

One application of this multiperspectival approach to integration would be to implement a particular process, depending upon the nature of the data provided by each discipline. Given the unity of God's truth, the UNIFIES model would be preferred in areas of knowledge where the data from each discipline have substantial corroboration and acceptance, can be conceptually related, and can be incarnationally lived out. In areas of knowledge where the data from each discipline have substantial corroboration, can be conceptually related, but cannot at the present time be unified, the CORRELATES models may be most appropriate. The TRANSFORMS or RECONSTRUCTS models may be the most helpful where the data from one discipline have only minimal corroboration, can be only superficially related, and cannot be incarnationally lived out. Finally, in areas where the data from one discipline are not corroborated, it may be inappropriate to conceptually relate those data to the corroborated truth in the other discipline until further study. In this case the REJECTS model might actually be helpful in keeping the unwarranted, unsupported data from one discipline from being integrated with the corroborated data of the other discipline. Future research should seek to identify which model, and its assumptions about data, is going to be most helpful for integration in specific areas of study in each discipline.

Another application of a multiperspectival approach is to see the varied usefulness, depending on the work setting of the integrator, of the different integration processes. For those with training in both disciplines, but whose work occurs primarily within the rigid methodological framework of only one discipline, the CORRELATES MODELS are an easier starting place. For those whose training, work, and professional identity are primarily in only one discipline, the TRANSFORMS or RECONSTRUCTS models are perhaps the best beginning places for understanding and communicating in an integrated way. In fact, the lack of representation of the THEOLOGY RECONSTRUCTS PSYCHOLOGY model among the integrators suggests that they have ignored the contributions of the more charismatically oriented integrative efforts. For those Christian psychologists working in secular settings and in dialogue with their secular colleagues, the PSYCHOLOGY TRANSFORMS or PSYCHOLOGY RECONSTRUCTS models may provide the most appropriate starting points to bridge the gap between science and religion.

The stagnation in the field of integration described by Worthington (1994) may be due to an inappropriately narrow understanding of integration. Foster et al. (1988) found that over a five-year period 60% of the articles published on integration used only one model (See Figure 2). Contemporary efforts at integration would be broadened by reassessing the five processes and adopting a more multiperspectival approach. That is not to say that all models are equally helpful to the ultimate goal of understanding the unity of God's truth. Each model has its own limits and disadvantages. But, by having an awareness of those limits and the potential problems contained in each model, we can come to appreciate the particular window which that model uniquely provides into a corner of God's truth.

References

Adams, J. (1970). *Competent to counsel.* Grand Rapids, MI: Baker.

Allport, G. W. (1950). *The individual and his religion.* New York: Macmillan.

Bobgan, M., & Bobgan, D. (1978). *The psychological way/The spiritual way.* Minneapolis: Bethany.

Bobgan, M., & Bobgan, D. (1985). *How to counsel from scripture.* Chicago: Moody.

Bobgan, M., & Bobgan, D. (1987). *Psychoheresy: The psychological seduction of Christianity.* Santa Barbara, CA: Eastgate.

Bouma-Prediger, S. (1990). The task of integration: A modest proposal. *Journal of Psychology and Theology, 18,* 21-31.

Bube, R. H. (1971). *The human quest: A new look at science and Christian faith.* Waco, TX: Word.

Carter, J. D. (1983). *To integration and back again.* Paper presented at the annual meeting of the Christian Association for Psychological Studies, Chicago.

Carter, J. D., & Mohline, R. J. (1981). The nature and scope of integration: A proposal. In J. R. Fleck, & J. D. Carter (Eds.), *Psychology and Christianity: Integrative readings.* (pp. 97-111). Nashville, TN: Abingdon.

Carter, J. D., & Narramore, B. (1979). *The integration of psychology and theology.* Grand Rapids, MI: Zondervan.

Clinton, S. M. (1990a). A critique of integration models. *Journal of Psychology and Theology, 18,* 13-20.

Clinton, S. M. (1990b). The foundational integration model. *Journal of Psychology and Theology, 18,* 115-122.

Collins, G. R. (1977). *The rebuilding of psychology: An integration of psychology and Christianity.* Wheaton, IL: Tyndale.

Collins, G. R. (1981). *Psychology and theology: Prospects for integration.* Nashville, TN: Abingdon.

Cosgrove, M. (1979). *Psychology gone awry.* Grand Rapids, MI: Zondervan.

Crabb, L. J. (1977). *Effective biblical counseling: A model for helping caring Christians become capable counselors.* Grand Rapids, MI: Zondervan.

Cranmer, D., & Eck, B. E. (1994). God said it: Psychology and biblical interpretation, how text and reader interact through the glass darkly. *Journal of Psychology and Theology, 22,* 207-214.

Ellens, J. H. (1980). Biblical themes in psychological theory and practice. *The Bulletin: Publication of the Christian Association for Psychological Studies, 6* (2), 2-6.

Ellis, A. (1980). Psychotherapy and atheistic values: A response to A. E. Bergin's "psychotherapy and religious values." *Journal of Consulting and Clinical Psychology, 48,* 635-639.

Evans, C. S. (1977). *Preserving the person: A look at the human sciences.* Downers Grove, IL: InterVarsity.

Evans, C. S. (1982). *Preserving the person.* Grand Rapids, MI: Baker.

Farnsworth, K. E. (1981). *Integrating psychology and theology: Elbows together but hearts apart.* Washington, DC: University Press.

Farnsworth, K. E. (1985). *Whole-hearted integration: Harmonizing psychology and Christianity through word and deed.* Grand Rapids, MI: Baker.

Foster, J. D., & Bolsinger, S. A. (1990). Prominent themes in evangelical integration literature. *Journal of Psychology and Theology, 18,* 3-12.

Foster, J. D., Horn, D. A., & Watson, S. (1988). The popularity of integration models, 1980-1985. *Journal of Psychology and Theology, 16,* 3-14.

Freud, S. (1961). *The future of an illusion.* New York: W. W. Norton.

Fromm, E. (1950). *Psychoanalysis and religion.* New York: Bantam.

Ganz, R. (1976). Nouthetic counseling defended. *Journal of Psychology and Theology, 4,* 193-205.

The Holy Bible: New International Version. (1984). Grand Rapids, MI: Zondervan.

Ingram, J. A. (1995). Contemporary issues and Christian models of integration: Into the modern/postmodern age. *Journal of Psychology and Theology, 23,* 3-14.

Jeeves, M. (1976). *Psychology and Christianity: The view both ways.* Downers Grove, IL: InterVarsity.

Johnson, E. L. (1992). A place for the Bible within psychological science. *Journal of Psychology and Theology, 20,* 346-355.

Jones. S. L. (1986). Relating the Christian faith to psychology. In S. L. Jones (Ed.), *Psychology and the Christian faith: An introductory reader.* (pp. 15-33). Grand Rapids, MI: Baker.

Jung, C. G. (1938). *Psychology and religion.* New Haven: Yale.

Jung, C. G. (1961). *Memories, dreams, reflections.* New York: Random House.

Kelsey, M. (1986). *Christianity as psychology: The healing power of the Christian message.* Minneapolis, MN: Augsburg.

Koteskey, R. L. (1980). *Psychology from a Christian perspective.* Nashville, TN: Abingdon.

Kilpatrick, W. K. (1983). *Psychological seduction: The failure of modern psychology.* Nashville, TN: Thomas Nelson.

Larzalere, R. (1981). The task ahead: Six levels of integration of psychology and Christianity. In J. R. Fleck & J. D. Carter, (Eds.), *Psychology and Christianity: Integrative readings.* (pp. 54-65). Nashville, TN: Abingdon.

May, R. (1969). *Love and will.* New York: W. W. Norton.

MacKay, D. M. (1974). *The clockwork image.* Downers Grove, IL: InterVarsity.

Minirth, F. B., & Meier, P. D. (1982). *Counseling and the nature of man.* Grand Rapids, MI: Baker.

Myers, D. G. (1978). *The human puzzle: Psychological research and Christian belief.* New York: Harper & Row.

Myers, D. G. (1986). Social psychology. In S. L. Jones (Ed.), *Psychology and the Christian faith: An introductory reader.* (pp. 217-239). Grand Rapids, MI: Baker.

Oden, T. (1966). *Kerygma and counseling.* Philadelphia: Westminster.

Payne, L. (1981). *The broken image: Restoring personal wholeness through healing prayer.* Westchester, IL: Crossway.

Pecheur, D. (1978). Cognitive theory/therapy and sanctification: A study in integration. *Journal of Psychology and Theology, 6*, 239-253.

Sandford, J., & Sandford, P. (1982). *The transformation of the inner man.* South Plainfield, NJ: Bridge.

Sargent, W. (1957). *Battle for the mind.* London: Pan.

Shostrom, E. L., & Montgomery, D. (1978). *Healing love: How God works within the personality.* Nashville, TN: Abingdon.

Skinner, B. F. (1971). *Beyond freedom and dignity.* New York: Knopf.

Sperry, R. W. (1988). Psychology's mentalistic paradigm and the religion/science tension. *American Psychologist, 43*, 607-613.

Spilka, B., Hood, Jr., R. W., & Gorsuch, R. L. (1985). *The psychology of religion: An empirical approach.* Englewood Cliffs, NJ: Prentice-Hall.

Van Leeuwen, M. S. (1982). *The sorcerer's apprentice: A Christian looks at the changing face of psychology.* Downers Grove, IL: InterVarsity.

Weaver, G. (1986). Psychology of religion. In S. L. Jones (Ed.), *Psychology and the Christian faith: An introductory reader.* (pp. 196-216). Grand Rapids, MI: Baker.

Worthington, E. L. (1994). A blueprint for intradisciplinary integration. *Journal of Psychology and Theology, 22*, 79-86.

Section VI
Applied Integration

The articles in the previous sections have looked primarily at the issues and processes for integrating psychology with Christianity primarily from the "balcony" perspective, as mentioned in the Preface. They have provided meta-analytical or grand theoretical perspectives that address the overarching issues, values, perspectives, and processes that one must consider in doing integration.

The questions raised in this section ask, *what difference does integration make in what one does?* How might integrating one's faith with one's practice affect the values that are reflected in the goals of therapy, the interventions one chooses to use, how one listens to a client's life story, and how religious issues are addressed in therapy? In other words, how do integrated practitioners care for and respond to the needs of their clients?

Applied integration often leads to the greatest levels of challenge and conflict. To begin talking about how one does therapy requires identifying the presuppositions, values, and worldview perspectives upon which each modality is based. For the Christian therapist, these arguments go beyond the standard *intra*-disciplinary arguments between behaviorists and psychoanalysts, to the *inter*-disciplinary discussions between a theological position and a psychological one. This, for instance, leads those who practice therapy from an anti-psychology, biblical counseling perspective to reject all attempts at integration with a psychological modality. For those seeking to integrate their theology with their therapeutic modality, there are a range of challenges. As Jones and Butman (1991) and others have summarized, every modality used for therapy from within a scientific psychological framework falls short of a full model of biblical anthropology. Although they may fall short of this complete truth, each modality reflects, in part, some aspect of God's truth and as such, have been found useful by Christian therapists. Christian therapists have written integrative works from the perspective of all of the therapeutic modalities in psychology, and these are often helpful in allowing the clinician to address these issues in their own clinical practice. Several of these works can be found in the *Suggestions for Further Reading section* below.

The challenge in applied integration is to avoid either a simplistic acceptance or rejection of a therapeutic modality or technique and instead to work through how one might address and resolve the integrative issues in one's own practice of therapy.

One of the key issues in therapy is the role of the therapist. Within different modalities a therapist may be active or passive, reflective or educative. In each modality, therapists bring themselves to the relationship. David Benner's (1983) article, *The Incarnation as a Metaphor for Psychotherapy*, leads this section with a reflection on how the therapeutic relationship reflects something of God's relationship with us. Beginning with a review of the curative factors in psychotherapy found by Frank, Rogers, Ferenczi, and Oden, he concludes that therapist factors such as empathy, respect, genuiness, and congruence lead to the non-specific, curative expectations of the client in therapy of faith, hope, and love. Benner reviews how God has provided for humanity an intimately personal and costly solution to our problems through the incarnation of Christ and His atoning death. Through the incarnation, Christ remained separate and fully Himself as God. He came close enough to us to identify with our humanity while also allowing us to identify with Him. Benner finds this intimate, relational dynamic expressed through the relational dimension of the *Imago Dei*, which he translates into object relations therapy terms. He concludes ultimately that the primary curative factor in psychotherapy may be a relationship of incarnational involvement between the therapist and client that allows for the absorption of suffering and the sharing of strength.

Another way to look at the role of the therapist is found in the conclusion of Rodger Bufford's (1997) article, *Consecrated Counseling: Reflections on the Distinctives of Christian Counseling*. Seeking to identify what makes Christian counseling Christian, Bufford conducted an extensive review of the literature. Beginning with a definition of counseling and a clarification of the differences between spiritual counseling and mental health counseling he provides a helpful review of the history of counseling, which includes Christian counseling. Bufford then seeks to identify from the literature what makes Christian counseling distinctive. Reviewing the writings of Adams, Crabb, Collins, Benner, Worthington, Powlison, and himself, Bufford concludes that there is widespread disagreement between the authors, with the one exception of the personal character and motivations of the counselor. His literature review found that distinctively Christian counseling is defined by seven elements, six of which primarily involve the worldview, commitment, and character of the counselor. Thus for Bufford, the core of Christian counseling is the person, life, and work of the counselor.

Another key issue for psychotherapy is identifying the goals for treatment. Treatment goals should define the focus of psychological therapy, determine the interventions made by the therapist, and help the therapist and client know when treatment has been successful.

Ev Worthington (1994), in his article *A Blueprint for Intradisciplinary Iintegration*, seeks to provide a template that can be used by therapists to build their own practical integration. Beginning with a review of Bouma-Prediger's models of psychological/theological integration and what he feels have been the three distinct periods in the history of integration, Worthington reviews the literature and identifies the most frequently used types of *inter*-disciplinary and *intra*-disciplinary integration. From this review, Worthington concludes that in the history of integration, practice-focused articles have been scarce to non-existent. With the caveat that the practical integrationist must know both their psychology and theology, Worthington poses integrative questions that challenge the therapist to think through their beliefs. Using the analogy of building a house, Worthington identifies four areas for the practical integrationist to address. These include their foundation, in Jesus Christ; the weight bearing pillars, of their Christian beliefs; their frame, of therapeutic goals and methods; and the covering of their clinical content. In walking the therapist through the issues of building an integrated model for clinical practice, Worthington provides clinicians with a framework from which they can build their own personal integrated approach to therapy.

Focusing on one of the areas identified by Worthington, Alan Tjeltveit (1992) challenges therapists in his article, *The Psychotherapist as Christian Ethicist: Theology Applied to Practice*, to recognize the ethical aspects of their clinical practice. As Tjeltveit states, "To transform, to be transformed, is to be immersed in matters ethical." He argues that the answers to such questions as what changes are right, best, good, or virtuous can only be answered within an ethical framework. The question is not *if* therapeutic goals are framed by ethics, but rather by *which* ethics they are framed. After rejecting the modern and ambiguous use of the term values, and asserting that the facts of science can never produce knowledge of what is good and right, Tjeltveit finds that a grounding in ethics is essential for the practicing therapist. After describing three motifs (deliberate, prescriptive, and relational) for how ethical standards are set in Christian ethics and describing an additional three motifs for implementing ethical decisions (institutional, operational, and intentional), Tjeltveit guides the clinician through the application of these motifs to psychotherapy. He ends his article with a discussion of the implications for educating and training Christian psychotherapists to do applied ethics well.

A final key area addressed in this section is the integration of therapeutic technique and interventions with Christian faith and practice. For each psychotherapist, this area of applied integration is the most specific and narrowly defined.

The article, *Integration in the Therapy Room: An Overview of the Literature* by M. Elizabeth Lewis Hall and Todd W. Hall, provides an excellent and helpful summary of 25 years of the literature on clinical integration. They begin by identifying the key research that has laid the foundation for clinical integration over the years. They then explore the spectrum of clinical integration including client and therapist values and beliefs, the impact those values and beliefs have on the therapeutic process, the issues involved in the inclusion of spiritual issues in therapy, and the process for considering spiritually oriented goals and techniques as part of the therapeutic process. Hall and Hall conclude with a discussion of some of the ethical issues faced by therapists when attempting to employ clinical integration.

Coming from a philosophical perspective in which Kierkegaard can be considered a "psychologist," Robert Roberts takes a very different approach to applied integration in his article, *Psychotherapeutic Virtues and the Grammar of Faith*. Roberts takes a "virtues approach" for integrating secular psychotherapies into Christian practice where virtues, which are found in both psychology and Christianity, provide the picture of the ideal person. He explains how the concept of virtue can be used to critique the similarities and conflicts between "Christian theory" and secular models of psychotherapy. For him, integration occurs when the "acceptable" elements from a secular psychology become part of the practice of a Christian therapist. After explaining the functions of virtues, he compares the virtues found in REBT with their Christian counterparts. Focusing on the virtues of equanimity, self-acceptance, and sense of humor, Roberts concludes that the Christian therapist must be aware of potential conflicts of virtue when using some of the techniques of REBT.

Next, Bruce Narramore (1994) addresses one of the central tasks for success in psychotherapy and provides guidance for dealing with resistances when they are reinforced by the client's religious experience, worldview, or biblical interpretation. In *Dealing with Religious Resistance in Psychotherapy*, he explores some of the early developmental fears behind therapeutic resistance from a psychodynamic perspective and the potential countertransferential issues religious resistance might raise in the therapist. Narramore reviews the process for handling resistance in therapy in general and the special issues to be considered when working with religious resistances. Finally, he concludes with a clinical case example and provides examples of therapeutic responses to what he believes are five commonly used scriptural defenses.

The final article in this section, *An Exploration of the Therapeutic Use of Spiritual Disciplines in Clinical Practice*, by Brian Eck (2002), provides an overarching look at the use of spiritual interventions in therapy. After reviewing the ethical, cultural, and clinical contexts for psychotherapy, Eck addresses the general practice issues for working with spiritual issues and the therapeutic use of spiritual interventions. After setting the context for the use of spiritual interventions, he reviews the historical understanding of the spiritual disciplines and provides and organizing structure for their use. Eck identifies 39 traditional spiritual disciplines and practices within the Christian tradition, summarizes the literature on their clinical use by Christian therapists, and then organizes them into three categories. In his analysis, he finds that some of the disciplines are cognitively oriented, some behaviorally oriented, and others interpersonally oriented. The article ends with suggestions for further research and presents ideas for the future direction of using spiritual interventions in psychotherapy.

Suggestions for Further Reading: Applied Integration

Benner, D. G. (1998). *Care of souls: Revisioning Christian nurture and counsel.* Grand Rapids, MI: Baker.
    Integrates spirituality and psychotherapy in theory and practice by reviewing the history of Christian soul care, a wholistic understanding of persons, and interventions that address the psychological and spiritual.

Benner, D. G. (1988). *Psychotherapy and the spiritual quest.* Grand Rapids, MI: Baker.
    Reviews the understanding of spirituality in select psychologies and Christian traditions and propos-
    es a psychospiritual approach to human care.
Benner, D. G. (Ed.). (1987). *Christian counseling and psychotherapy.* Grand Rapids, MI: Baker.
    Emphasizes particular techniques (chapters 7 through 12) and then a series of 19 case studies allow-
    ing readers to see what happens in therapy and showing the many ways to be a Christian psy-
    chotherapist.
Bufford, R. K. (1977). God and behavior mod: Some thoughts concerning the relationships between biblical
    principles and behavior modification. *Journal of Psychology and Theology, 5* (14), 13-22.
    An exploration of God's use of contingencies in the lives of people presented in scripture.
Collins, G. R. (Ed.). (1980). *Helping people grow: practical approaches to Christian counseling.* Ventura, CA:
    Vision House.
    This edited volume contains 16 different approaches to Christian counseling and explores the dis-
    tinctives of Christian counseling.
Dueck, A. C. (1995). *Between Jerusalem and Athens: Ethical perspectives on culture, religion, and psychother-
    apy.* Grand Rapids, MI: Baker
    Proposes that Christian ethics should provide the context for therapy, the church serve as healing
    community, and the importance of the character of the therapist.
Gaultiere, W. J. (1990). The Christian psychotherapist as a transitional object to God. *Journal of Psychology
    and Theology, 18* (2), 131-140.
    Integrating object relations therapy with Christianity, the therapeutic relationship is presented as a
    means for helping clients develop a more loving image of being in relationship with God.
Jones, S. L. & Butman, R. E. (1991). *Modern psychotherapies: A comprehensive Christian appraisal.* Downers
    Grove, IL: InterVarsity Press.
    Provides some of the most comprehensive and balanced coverage of therapeutic psychology from
    a Christian perspective; a new edition coming out shortly.
McMinn, M. R. (1996). *Psychology, theology, and spirituality in Christian counseling.* Wheaton, IL: Tyndale
    House Publishers, Inc.
    Reviews the role of dealing with religious issues in therapy and integrating prayer, Scripture, con-
    fession, forgiveness, and redemption in clinical practice.
Narramore, S. B. (1984). *No condemnation: Rethinking guild motivation in counseling, preaching, and par-
    enting.* Grand Rapids, MI: Zondervan Publishing House.
    A classic exploration of guilt and the differences between the objective condition of guilt before God
    versus the subjective feeling of guilt and the treatment of this in therapy.
Olthuis, J. H. (2001). *The beautiful risk: A new psychology of loving and being loved.* Grand Rapids, MI:
    Zondervan.
    Encourages therapists to move beyond theory and technique and to connecting, caring and suffer-
    ing with those with whom they work.
Olthuis, J. H. (1999). Dancing together in the wild spaces of love: Postmodernism, psychotherapy, and the
    spirit of God. *Journal of Psychology and Christianity, 18,* 140-152.
    From a postmodern perspective this article explores psychotherapy as care, not cure; as art, not sci-
    ence; as adventure, not treatment; and as spiritual process, not secular psychology plus prayer.
Olthuis, J. H. (1994). Being-with: Toward a relational psychotherapy. *Journal of Psychology and Christianity,
    13* (3), 217-231.
    This article presents a holistic, biblically attuned relational psychotherapy addressing gift/call, alien-
    ation/evil, personal agency, embodiment, inter-subjectivity, genser, and formation/development.
Olthuis, J. H. (1994). God with-us: Towards a relational psychotherapeutic model. *Journal of Psychology and
    Christianity, 13* (1), 37-49.
    This article continues a presentation of a holistic, biblically attuned relational psychotherapy focus-
    ing on empathy, re-story-ing, and transformation through letting-in, letting-go, letting-out, and let-
    ting-transformation.

Shults, F. L., & Sandage, S. J. (2003) *The faces of forgiveness: Searching for wholeness and salvation*. Grand Rapids, MI: Baker Academic.

    Winner of the Narramore Award as an outstanding book on integration, this book treats the topic of forgiveness from an explicitly integrative perspective by focusing on relational patterns of human knowing and being.

Shults, F. L. & Sandage, S. J. (2006). *Transforming spirituality: Integrating theology and psychology*. Grand Rapids, MI: Baker Academic.

    This book, written by a theologian and a psychologist, develops and explores a relational model of spirituality integrated around the theme of transformation.

Thoresen, C., Worthington, E.L., Jr., Swyers, J. P., Larson, D. B., McCullough, M. E., & Miller, W. R. (1998). Religious interventions. In D. B. Larson, J. P. Swyers, & M. E. McCullough (Eds.), *Scientific research on spirituality and health: A consensus report* (pp. 104-128). Rockville, MD: National Institute for Healthcare Research.

    The whole report is a significant advance in the literature by a blue-ribbon panel.

Yarhouse, M. A., Butman, R. E., & McRay, B. W. (2005). *Modern psychopathologies: A comprehensive Christian appraisal*. Downers Grove, IL: InterVarsity.

    Designed as a companion volume to Jones & Butman's (1991) *Modern Psychotherapies*, it examines psychopathology in the light of Christianity and offers a vision for Christian health professionals and the church.

Richards, P. S., & Bergin, A. E. (2005). *A spiritual strategy for counseling and psychotherapy* (2nd ed.) Washington, DC: APA.

    The first edition was the first APA book by single authors showing the field had reached the mainstream.

Willard, D. (1998). Spiritual disciplines, spiritual formation, and the restoration of the soul. *Journal of Psychology and Theology, 26* (1), 101-109.

    Presents this modern theologian's spiritual and psychological insight on the relationship of the soul to the person and the role of the spiritual disciplines for producing wholeness and soul reformation.

Worthington, E. L., Jr. (2006). *Forgiveness and reconciliation; Theory and application*. New York: Routledge.

    Written by a renowned researcher on forgiveness, the focus here is on individual experiences with forgiveness, aiming to create a theory of what forgiveness is and connect it to clinical efforts to promote forgiveness in clients.

Worthington, Jr., E. L., Dupont, P. D., Berry, J. T., & Duncan, L. A. (1988). Christian therapists' and clients' perceptions of religious psychotherapy in private agency settings. *Journal of Psychology and Theology, 16* (3), 282-293.

    Presents the results of a clinical study regarding the use of spiritual interventions and identifies both common clinical practices and what client's prefer.

22

The Incarnation as a Metaphor for Psychotherapy

David G. Benner
Wheaton Graduate School

The incarnation of Christ is considered as a metaphor for the role of the psychotherapist. The tendency of children to attempt to purge parental badness by taking it upon themselves, as noted by object relations theorists, is considered as a reflection of the *imago Dei*. Ways in which a similar process may occur in psychotherapy are then considered. It is concluded that the incarnational element of psychotherapy may be one of the basic curative factors present in any successful therapy.

The question of how therapy works has largely been obscured by the more primary questions of whether it works. As more and more consensus develops that at least under some circumstances psychotherapy can produce significant changes, Garfield (1983) has argued that it is now time to turn our attention to the question of how these changes occur. Yalom's (1970) list of the curative factors operative in group psychotherapy seems to have been well received by practitioners of many different styles of group therapy. No such list, however, exists for individual therapy. In fact it appears that although we have an abundance of theories of psychotherapy, we seem to possess very little understanding of the way in which talking with someone about personal problems produces change.

The Search for Curative Factors

One reason for the uncertainty as to how therapy works relates to the difference between what therapists say they do in therapy and what they actually do. It has become clear that labels of theoretical orientation do very little to describe actual therapeutic operations. Thus, one might describe himself or herself as analyzing and working through a transference reaction, getting the patient in touch with his or her body, or restructuring dysfunctional cognitions. However, these theory-laden descriptions tell us much more about the therapists' conceptualizations than about their interventions. When the actual interventions are observed from a more theoretically neutral vantage point, they often turn out to be very similar to those used by therapists working with supposedly very different treatment approaches. These similarities in actual therapist behavior increase as therapy effectiveness increases, with the most effective therapists showing more similarities among themselves than differences (Bergin & Lambert, 1978).

Another reason for our limited understanding of how therapy works is that attempts to identify and label the curative factors have usually been within the framework of one of the competing theoretical models. Thus, psychoanalysts have tended to rely on the concept of insight, behaviorists on the concept of learning, and cognitive therapists on the concept of cognitive restructuring as they attempt to explain therapeutic gains. The general difficulty in demonstrating differential effectiveness of one type of therapy over another has, however, been discouraging for those arguing for such concepts. One would expect that if one of these were *the* major curative factor in psychotherapy, then a treatment approach based specifically on this factor should maximize its role in treatment and, therefore, be demonstrably superior in effectiveness. However, in general, this has not proven to be the case. Rather, we find most therapies studied to be approximately equal in effectiveness, the exceptions being rare and with specific disorders.

This difficulty in demonstrating differential effectiveness of various types of therapy has, however, also made a positive contribution to the search for the illusive curative factors. Frank (1961) is one who has called our attention to the on-specific factors in therapy such as faith, hope, and other expectation variables. Such factors, sometimes referred to as placebo factors, are general to all therapies and may therefore be the common active ingredient. Frank's demonstration of the role of such factors in both formal and informal helping relationships in Western and non-Western societies make his argument powerful.

Rogers' (1957) position is in some ways quite similar. Identifying the necessary and sufficient conditions for therapeutic effectiveness as empathy, respect, and congruence, Rogers argued that other ingredients contribute to effectiveness only in as much as they communicate these essential relationship factors. Qualities of the therapist's personality and style of relating thus become primary and techniques secondary.

While research has not been consistently supportive of Rogers' assumption of the necessary and sufficient conditions of therapy, it would appear that there is still considerable promise in expecting that the active curative factors in therapy may not be as closely related to the skillful application of one or another technique as we might want to think. When I have asked parents at the end of a successful course of therapy to reflect back on the things that were helpful, I have yet to have someone tell me that the big breakthrough came the day we penetrated to the core of the repressed Oedipal conflict, completed the aversive conditioning, or identified the faulty cognitions behind their self-defeating behavior. Usually they have had trouble precisely identifying any one specific factor. However, when they have, they have frequently pointed to some process occurring between the two of us rather than to something I did to them. They then talk about feeling loved or accepted by me, or describe themselves as experiencing healing or growth through the manner in which we related to each other.

Considering love as the essential dynamic in the therapeutic process is not new. From the early psychoanalyst Ferenczi (1952) to the more recent work of Erich Fromm (1956) love has often been suggested as the major curative ingredient in therapy. From a Christian perspective, Calabrese and Proctor (1977) have described the intensive therapy experience as healing through love. But what is love and how does it heal? Rogers' answer has been translated into more theological language by Oden (1966) who sees therapy as the mediation of divine grace through the therapist's unconditional acceptance of the patient. Oden also suggests that the therapy relationship reflects something of God's relationship to us. It seems relevant therefore to examine God's way of relating to us in our problems and determine whether this can assist us in understanding psychotherapeutic healing.

God's Solution to Humanity's Problem

Orthodox Christian theology has always affirmed that sin is ultimately behind all of humanity's problems. However, to reduce this to specific personal sin lying behind any particular problem is to misunderstand this doctrine. It is also to fail to accept Jesus' explicit teaching that some problems are not the result of personal sin but rather are allowed by God for his glory (John 9:1-3). However, in an ultimate sense, sin in the world and in the lives and relationships of individuals results in all the manifestations of brokenness and pain which all experience.

As a God of love and mercy, He chose to act to remedy humanity's sin problem. He could have destroyed his creation and started again, perhaps taking some precautions to insure against another fall. Or perhaps his solution could have been purely judicial, clinical, or in some other way impersonal and safe. But God's solution to the problem of human nature was none of these. It was an intimately personal and immensely costly process. God's solution was the incarnation (John 1:14; Philippians 2:6-8, Hebrews 9:11-14)—Christ's coming "in the flesh" so that He could die in our place. He became a person, making himself like us so that he could substitute for us by carrying our suffering in himself. He did not solve our sin problem at arm's length but took us into himself and purged our sin from us. Our sin, taken upon him, was overcome by his grace. Where sin did abound, there grace did much more abound (Romans 5:20).

But there is another equally important aspect of the incarnation: God became human but did not cease to be God. In the incarnation he came close enough to identify with humanity and allow humanity to identify with him. However, he never lost his separate identity. Nor does humanity. Rather, in new relationship to him, persons *find* their identity and their unique selves. Paul teaches that Christians are crucified with Christ but that paradoxically they continue to live, only now it is his power and presence living in and through them (Galatians 2:20). Individuals do not merge with God in a fusion experience where they become him and he becomes them. Rather, both retain separate identities.

In a partial and imperfect way this truth is also reflected in the biblical image of the shepherd and his sheep, an image frequently used to picture God's relationship to Christians. The shepherd is with the sheep but is not a sheep. Even though the shepherd suffers the long cold nights on the hillside with the sheep, suffering not only with them but for them, the shepherd remains separate.

The gospel is, in essence, the good news that God came to provide for healing by taking humanity's suffering upon himself. But what has this to do with psychotherapy? How far can we take such divine activity as a model for the human helping relationship? Before considering this question more directly, it seems important to first consider some basic aspects of human nature which may more clearly reveal God as a model, and humankind as the image of God.

The *Imago Dei* and Object Relations

What does it mean to speak of humans as created in the image of God? Traditionally the answer to this question has been to identify attributes of human personality such as reason, morality, volition, and creativity which are said to correspond to attributes of God. This is undoubtedly a helpful beginning, but Barth (1962), Brunner (1947) and others have suggested that such a list misses a much more basic attribute which we share with God, namely, our social nature. So humanity, reflecting this quality of God, is also intrinsically relational or social.

The need for relationship is fundamental to human nature, perhaps *the* most fundamental need. People are created for intimate communion with God as well as others; apart from both relationships, they remain incomplete. Berkhouwer (1962) states that to look at people apart from their intended relationship to God is to fail to understand them. This is an inherent limitation of any psychology which refuses to admit spiritual realities within its field of vision.

Humanity's basic relational need, not just for God but also for others, has often been overlooked or de-emphasized in psychology. Freud pointed us in the wrong direction by identifying gratification of biological drives as the most basic need. Although contemporary behavioral theorists are not likely to talk about basic needs, implicit in operant learning theory seems to be an assumption not too dissimilar from Freud's pleasure principle. It appears that people avoid pain and seek out pleasure, and this simple awareness provides basic guidance in the behavior therapist's selection of reinforcers to change behavior.

Interpersonal psychologists, following in the tradition of Harry Stack Sullivan (1953), have been much more aware of the basic relational needs. They have made the examination of a person's relationships the primary source of data for diagnosis or personality assessment. They have done much to make clear that individuals are their relationships and that their need for relationships is basic. However, the tradition which has given us the clearest understanding of the dynamics of this relational need within personality may be object relations theory, a recent hybrid of psychoanalysis.

Object relations theory has given particular emphasis to early relationships between infant and parents or caretakers. The use of the term "object"

reflects the mechanistic influence of classical psychoanalysis as well as the earlier tendency to view people's struggles from the outside rather than empathically. It is used to refer to both animate and inanimate objects since the infant relates to both in similar ways, that is, by developing internal representations of them. American object relations theorists (such as Kernberg, 1980) have developed this approach within what remains a basically classical psychoanalytic framework. British theorists, most particularly Fairbairn (1954), have been more radical, abandoning much of Freud's metapsychology and replacing it with an equally complex structural developmental theory. It is in the work of Fairbairn that we find the most complete understanding of humanity's intrinsic relational nature.

For Fairbairn (1954), people do not seek discharge of biological drives, but rather they seek relationships. This object-seeking quality of humans describes their most basic drive. Pleasurable tension discharge is an accompaniment of relationships. Similarly, aggression is not a basic drive but rather a reaction to frustration in object-relationships. However, people do not just seek relationships, they seek good relationships. Fairbairn describes individuals as longing for a perfect father and perfect mother. The Christian understands this longing as reflective of our intended relationship to God. All long for a perfect father-mother and yet all experience imperfect, limited parents. The frustration produced by encountering good parents who also have bad or frustrating qualities sets in motion a complex intrapsychic process wherein people try to make relationships that more closely approximate the ideal for which they long.

To describe in detail the process by which this occurs would lead too far from the present focus (see Fairbairn, 1954). The major step in the process is hypothesized to be the development of internal object representations of external objects, particularly of bad or frustrating objects. Fairbairn explains the child's paradoxical action of internalizing, rather than rejecting, the frustrating object by suggesting that the child cannot afford to reject the parent who is still needed: Better a bad parent than no parent at all. Furthermore, Fairbairn suggests that the internalization of the object is both an attempt to control the parent and an attempt to purge the parent's badness through taking this badness into oneself. The child, according to Fairbairn (1954), would "rather be bad himself than have bad objects…. One of his motives in becoming bad is to make his objects good" (p. 65).

This purgative process is only one possible response to predominately frustrating parents. It is, however, a major way in which the infant attempts to cope with less than perfect objects in the search for the good and ideal object.

Stepping back from this highly speculative metapsychology, it is necessary to determine if it corresponds to anything observable. One frequently made observation which is made intelligible by object relations theory is the fact that children do not simply or even primarily feel angry when their parents fail them in serious ways. Instead they feel shame. The child who was placed for adoption by a young single mother who was unable to meet the parenting responsibilities will, in later life, probably feel deep shame associated with thoughts such as "I must have been an awful child for my mother to have to give me up." Rather than feel anger and experience the pain of imperfect parents, the child through identification purges the parent of badness, takes this upon self and feels shame and lessened self-worth. It is also interesting to note how the parent is viewed: Typically the parent is idealized and seen as the longed-for perfect parent. This is also seen in children who are removed from a child-abusing home. Once again the badness of the parent is internalized and the parent, now purged of this, is idealized. The pattern frequently involves the child wanting to return to the home, denying the problems. They are registered, however, on the intrapsychic structure of the child where the internalized and split object representations devalue self-worth and produce shame.

It appears that woven deep within the basic fabric of personality may be a tendency to take the badness of significant others upon oneself in order to purge them of their evil. Perhaps this is part of the image of God—part of the way in which humans, like him, tend to relate to others. Obviously the internalization of someone else's badness does not produce any objective purging or atonement for them. It is here that the divine incarnation breaks down as an analogy for any human activity. There is nothing that individuals can do to atone for their own sins or for those of anyone else. However, perhaps this tendency to attempt to purge others of their evil reflects something of the *imago Dei*.

For the child, Fairbairn (1954) suggests that this tendency reveals the longing for a perfect parent. In the mature adult where needs are reasonably well met in relationships, might it represent a more altruistic desire to help the other? This question becomes significant then in considering the implications of this concept for the therapy process.

Incarnation in Psychotherapy

Star Trek fans will remember the television episode where Captain Kirk encountered an alien woman, called an Empath, who was able to absorb his physical afflictions and thereby provide him with healing. Furthermore, while her absorption of the sickness caused her real pain, she was eventually able to overcome it, and she avoided the permanent injury which should have been associated with the affliction.

This woman did more than respond with empathy, respect, and congruence; she also did more than accept the suffering individual. She entered into the life and experience of the sufferer, took the suffering upon herself, and then overcame it. The result was the healing of the suffering one. This is the metaphor for psychotherapy which is seen also in the incarnation.

Saretsky (1981) has described the psychotherapist as a container for the sickness of the patient. He views the patient as dumping all his toxic internal garbage into the therapist. The therapist absorbs these toxic materials but is not destroyed by them: Some are absorbed, and others are temporarily contained, eventually detoxified, then being available for reabsorption by the patient.

In more concrete terms this is seen when the therapist accepts the projections and transferences of the patient and bears them patiently. Sometimes the anger received in such encounters causes pain. However, out of a position of strength, the pain is absorbed without retaliation or defensiveness and eventually the patient stops projecting and can begin to own the projected material. At other times what the therapist accepts is more benign. However, through empathic involvement the therapist enters into the suffering, miserable, confused world of the patient and offers strength. The suffering and confusion is absorbed by the therapist for the ultimate healing of the patient.

Kenneth Leech, in his book *Soul Friend* (1977), describes the role of the spiritual director or guide (a "soul friend") in similar terms. Although Leech recognizes differences between one giving spiritual direction and the psychotherapist, he sees important similarities. In discussing the origins of the contemporary concept of spiritual guide he identifies the Russian *startsy* as one of the earliest role models. The *startsy* were qualified for service as spiritual guides by virtue of three qualities: Insight, love, and the capacity to make the sufferings of others their own. Dostoyevsky, who frequently visited the famous *startsy* Amvrosy (1812-1891), described the spiritual director in *The Brothers Karamazov* as one who takes "your soul and your will into his soul and his will" (Leech, 1977, p. 49). Leech suggests that such vicarious participation of one in the life of another is the living symbol of the good shepherd, this being the task of the soul friend.

Leech also recognizes the importance of the soul friend not allowing too much dependence to develop. This reflects the other side of the incarnation metaphor, the separateness of the helper. Just as God did not stop being God as he came into humanity, so too the therapist does not get lost in incarnation to the patient. The therapist remains the therapist and does not become the patient. Even in the presence of intense involvement and shared experience, there must remain a separateness of identity.

An understanding of the difference between empathy and sympathy illustrates this point. In empathy, one enters into another's experience and shares it without losing sight of the fact that it is truly the other person's experience. If this distinction is lost the autonomy of the other is likewise lost and the resulting relationship is more likely to be characterized by sympathy. Sympathy, thus understood, is seen to be a way of responding to one's own pain by attempting to cover it over with reassurance to the other.

In English translations of Freud, his use of the German word *teilnahmsvoll* has usually been rendered "sympathy." However, a more accurate translation of this frequently used word is "to feel along with" or "to suffer along with." Either of these expressions show the richer meaning of the original term and reflect the participation in the experience of another which he intended to communicate as an essential quality of the therapist.

How does the therapist's entering into the suffering of the patient in such a way produce change? Answers have been varied and at present are incomplete. Loewald (1960) has focused on the therapeutic effect of the patient internalizing the positive interaction of the therapy situation. This is reminiscent of Alexander's (1948) concept of the "corrective emotional experience." Bion (1968) and Winnicott (1965) have both emphasized the integrating function which occurs within the patient when the therapist emotionally and cognitively absorbs the patient's inner chaos. They view this as relieving pressure on and in the patient, thus allowing a new degree of integration of personality.

Saretsky (1981) places more emphasis on the healing of splits in the internal self-representations (corresponding to the different ways of experiencing self). This is made possible by the projections put onto the therapist being gradually re-owned and reabsorbed. Saretsky sees this as the "natural outgrowth of the rich tapestry of healthy interchange" (p. 93) between the therapist and the patient and not primarily as a result of correct technical interventions.

But perhaps it is more parsimonious to view the curative factor in this basic process as love. Love involves giving of oneself to another, making oneself available to bear someone else's burdens and to share in their struggles. This is not "sloppy sentimentalism" but rather tough, disciplined, and personally costly love. Its mode of communication is involvement. Its effect is healing.

Such love can be communicated in a great many different ways. This is precisely why it may be seen to be present in each of the approaches to therapy. Well-conducted behavior therapy, gestalt therapy, existential therapy, and psychoanalysis all involve the therapist entering the patient's world and becoming available to the patient. In one way or another all these (and other) modalities then encourage the patient to put inner confusion and chaos onto the therapist who then attempts to render it less chaotic and frightening, more intelligible and benign. This assumption and transformation of the patient's inner world constitutes the incarnational element of psychotherapy.

Perhaps it also represents one of the basic curative factors in psychotherapy. Obviously it is not the only one and taken alone it de-emphasizes the role and responsibility of the patient. It also is not the only way in which the therapist relates to the patient; thus, if this mode could be viewed as corresponding to Christ's priestly role, other aspects of the therapist's modes of relating could be tied correspondingly to Christ's prophetic and pastoral roles (Carlson, 1976). However, behind these various roles lies the relationship of the patient and therapist which is basic to all else that is done. Involvement by the therapist which allows for absorption of suffering and sharing of strength may well be the essence of this relationship.

Obviously it is possible for psychotherapists to avoid this sort of incarnational involvement. Those who fear such engagement often hide behind professionalism and technical rules. Both of these have an important role in disciplining our involvement to ensure that it is not primarily meeting our needs but rather those of our patients. Professionalism also serves to maintain the necessary degree of separateness. However, Rogers (1961) was probably correct when he argued that professionalism in psychotherapy has done more to protect therapists from their fears of involvement than it has done to aid thera-peutic practice (p. 52).

Implications

The Apostle Paul calls all Christians to the chal-lenge of bearing each other's burdens. This is what Christ did and continues to do for humankind, and it is this which we do in psy-chotherapy. But who is capable of bearing not only one's own burdens but also those of others? What enables the therapist to share personal health and absorb the illness and suffering of another without personal hazard? The answer is that therapists must have their own health contin-uously ensured by ongoing relationships where their needs are met and burdens shared.

It is important to emphasize that the sharing of strength and health does deplete the therapist's resources and that they must, therefore, be contin-uously renewed. In Luke 8:45-46, Jesus reported an experience quite similar, even if not identical, to that experienced by the psychotherapist. Jesus was touched by a woman who was suffering from a hemorrhage which had afflicted her for 12 years. As soon as she touched Jesus she was healed, but immediately he perceived strength issuing out of him. It is much the same in therapy. However, it is possible for the therapist to receive renewed strength. In personal relationship to Christ, believ-ers find and renew their strength. Today Christ is incarnate in the Church, his new body. Ultimately, therefore, it is only in the context of the Church that the Christian therapist finds the strength neces-sary for "incarnational therapy." Here the Christian therapist receives strength from God who, in the words of Paul, "comforts us in all our troubles so that we can comfort those in any trouble with the comfort we ourselves have received from God" (2 Corinthians 2:4).

References

Alexander, F. (1948). *Fundamentals of psychoanalysis.* New York: Norton.

Barth, K. (1962). [*Church dogmatics: A selection*]. (G. W. Bromiley, Ed. and Trans.). New York: Harper and Row.

Bergin, A. E., & Lambert, M. M. (1978). The evaluation of therapeutic outcomes. In S. Garfield & A. Bergin (Eds.), *Handbook of psychotherapy and behavior change: An empirical analysis* (2nd Ed.). New York: John Wiley & Sons.

Berkhouwer, G. C. (1962). *Man: The image of God.* Grand Rapids, MI: Eerdmans.

Bion, W. R. (1968). *Second thoughts: Selected papers of psy-choanalysis.* New York: Basic Books.

Brunner, E. (1947). *Man in revolt.* Philadelphia: Westminster.

Calabrese, A., & Proctor, W. (1977). *Rx: The Christian love treatment.* Boston: G. K. Hall.

Carlson, D. E. (1976). Jesus' style of relating: The search for a biblical view of counseling. *Journal of Psychology and Theology, 4,* 181-192.

Fairbairn, W. R. D. (1954). *An object-relations theory of the personality.* New York: Basic Books.

Ferenczi, S. (1952). *Further contributions to the theory and technique of psychoanalysis.* New York: Basic Books.

Frank, J. D. (1961). *Persuasion and healing.* Baltimore: Johns Hopkins.

Fromm, E. (1956). *The art of loving.* New york: Harper and Row.

Garfield, S. L. (1983). Effectiveness of psychotherapy: The perennial question. *Professional Psychology: Research and Practice, 14,* 35-43.

Kernberg, O. (1980). *Internal world and external reality: Object relations theory applied.* New York: Jason Aronson.

Leech, K. (1977). *Soul friend.* San Francisco: Harper & Row.

Loewald, H. W. (1960). On the therapeutic action of psy-choanalysis. *International Journal of Psycho-Analysis, 41,* 16-33.

Oden, T. C. (1966). *Kerygma and counseling.* Philadelphia: Westminster.

Rogers, C. R. (1957). The necessary and sufficient condi-tions of therapeutic personality change. *Journal of Consulting Psychology, 21,* 95-103.

Rogers, C. R. (1961). *On becoming a person.* Boston: Houghton Mifflin.

Saretsky, T. (1981). *Resolving treatment impasses.* New York: Human Sciences Press.

Sullivan, H. S. (1953). *The interpersonal theory of psychia-try.* New York: Norton.

Winnicott, D. W. (1965). *The maturational process and the facilitating environment.* New York: International Universities Press.

Yalom, I. D. (1970). *The theory and practice of group psy-chotherapy.* New York: Basic Books.

23

Consecrated Counseling: Reflections on the Distinctives of Christian Counseling

Rodger K. Bufford
Graduate School of Clinical Psychology
George Fox University

Authors seeking to clarify the distinctives of Christian counseling have chiefly emphasized (a) the context of counseling—church and parachurch settings, (b) the context or intervention techniques and the topics addressed in counseling, (c) the motivations or goals of counseling—conversion, discipleship, and service, and (d) counselor characteristics—assumptions/world view, personal relationship with God, and ecclesiastical role (e.g., pastoral). Viewed superficially there seems little agreement. Considering factors that are implied, but not emphasized, significantly increases agreement among authors. Clear identification of the distinctives of Christian counseling has been complicated by the failure to distinguish between spiritual counseling and mental health counseling. Christian counseling (a) requires a deep personal faith, (b) is done with excellence, (c) reflects a Christian world view, (d) is guided by Christian values, (e) actively seeks God's presence and work, and (f) uses spiritual resources and interventions within ethical guidelines. Such consecrated counseling is primarily concerned with the person of the therapist, is consistent with many theoretical models and techniques, and can be adapted to the great variety of human needs.

The question of relationship of psychology and Christian beliefs is one which has a long history and contemporary significance. Vande Kemp (1996) stated the following:

> efforts to reintegrate psychology and theology constituted an immediate response to the alleged emancipation of psychology from theology and philosophy in the mid-to-late 19th century.... At the end of the 20th century, it is clear that these integrative efforts have coalesced into a distinct psychological and interdisciplinary specialty. (pp. 76-77)

While psychology is much broader than counseling, much of the integrative effort has concentrated on counseling, often implying that counseling is the main (or entire) concern of psychology.

The material which follows will briefly define counseling, summarize the history of Christian counseling, examine distinct emphases which various Christian authors have identified, outline a wide range of common ground, explore factors held in common with non-Christian approaches, and offer some conclusions regarding how tensions among the various approaches proposed by Christian authors may be resolved. It is postulated that Christian counseling is primarily distinguished by the personal qualities of the counselor. These personal qualities often subtly change the counseling process, but may dramatically transform it at times.

Nature of Counseling

According to Egan (1994), counseling "includes a series of activities in which helpers and clients engage ... [that] lead to valued outcomes in clients' lives. Helping is about *constructive change* [italics original]" (p. 6). Egan continued, "helping clients review their problems and the options they have for dealing with them is ... a central part of the helping process" (p. 7). Counselors help their clients accomplish two things: "talk about their problem situations and unused opportunities in terms of action, what they do and don't do; and initiate problem-managing action" (p. 71).

Clearly, counseling is a general term which covers a wide array of activities. Attorneys provide legal counsel; teachers provide academic and vocational counseling; accountants provide financial and tax counseling; stockbrokers provide investment counseling; pastors provide spiritual counseling; business consultants provide counseling in the management of businesses. Thus to talk about Christian counseling without further clarification is to be silent about a very important distinction: What kind of counseling do we have in mind?

This silence about the type of counseling is unfortunate, and may not be entirely accidental. It contributes to a major confusion. When Christian

© *Journal of Psychology and Theology*, 1997, *25*, 111-122. Used by permission.

counseling is discussed, two distinct kinds of counseling seem most often to be involved. The first is spiritual counseling, which is directed toward encouraging a person to enter into the spiritual life, to resolve spiritual problems, or to grow and mature spiritually. This has traditionally been the role of the church. The second is not so clearly or consistently labeled, but can be called mental health counseling. Mental health counseling is primarily concerned with the kinds of psychological, emotional, and relational distresses described in the *Diagnostic and Statistical Manual of Mental Disorders* (4th ed.), often referred to as DSM-IV (American Psychiatric Association, 1994). Prior to the mid 19th century, to the extent it was provided at all, mental health counseling was also largely the province of the church. Today, however, while some churches offer mental health counseling, more commonly mental health counseling is provided in professional settings linked with medicine, psychology, and social work.

The boundaries between spiritual counseling and mental health counseling cannot be drawn easily or clearly. As Bufford (in press) notes, a major complication of DSM-IV is that it encompasses a wide variety of conditions that stem from various causes. Any comprehensive model of mental functioning must include the following components: (a) biological factors, including diseases, and endocrinological, anatomical, biochemical, and genetic causes; (b) psychological factors, including personal, developmental, and family history, and relationships with others; (c) social factors such as societal and cultural norms and standards; (d) spiritual factors, including personal sin, ethical and moral responsibilities, relationship to God, and spiritual growth and development. It is doubtful that any existing model fully encompasses the diversity of conditions included in DSM-IV, and DSM-IV is deficient in that it only minimally acknowledges spiritual factors.

While the distinction is important, the frontier between spiritual counseling and mental health counseling cannot be clearly drawn. Powlison's (1992) view that "integrationists imported secular visions into Christianity" (p. 206) in part reflects this confusion. Mental health counselors and spiritual counselors at times deal with common issues. This acknowledged, however, the distinction remains. While the work at times overlaps, there are significant differences. These include the problem initially presented by the client, the goals of the client, the counselor's goals, counselor's professional identity, specific intervention strategies—or at least their relative emphases, counseling settings, and many other factors typically distinguish spiritual counseling and mental health counseling. Perhaps most important is that mental health counseling and spiritual counseling have different goals: Mental health counseling seeks to alleviate conditions which make intervention medically necessary—typically as reflected by DSM-IV diagnoses; spiritual counseling is centrally concerned with evangelism and discipleship. The failure in the Christian community to distinguish mental health counseling from spiritual counseling is one of the most significant obstacles that has hampered the work of both Christian mental health counselors and Christian spiritual counselors.

History

The rise of modern psychology is commonly dated to the 1870s and the founding of Wilhelm Wundt's laboratory in Leipzig, Germany (Koch, 1985). The emergence of logical positivism and the development of radical behaviorism in psychology roughly paralleled the liberal/fundamentalist split in American theology in the 1920s and following. Liberal groups supported science and psychology, and the clinical pastoral education movement emerged in liberal denominations during this period (Beit-Hallahmi, 1974; Gorsuch, 1988; Sexton, 1978). In contrast, fundamentalist groups turned away from science and showed little interest in psychology until the 1960s. The year 1970, with the publication of Adams' (1970) book, *Competent to Counsel,* marked a major transition in the rise of interest in "Christian counseling" as it is now widely known, although the roots of this development trace back to the 1960s (e.g., Narramore, 1960) or earlier (e.g., Tournier, 1957). The 25 years since the publication of Adams' book have been marked by a dramatic growth of interest in counseling among more conservative Christian groups. It is largely in this context that the term "integration" has been used and that interest in "Christian counseling" arises. In the ensuing years several major developments have occurred, including adoption of the term "integration," formation of professional societies, development of courses and degree programs, publication of journals and specialized texts, establishment of research laboratories and programs, and development of distinctive approaches to clinical practice (Vande Kemp, 1996). Table 1 briefly summarizes this history.

The Emergence of Christian Counseling

In the late 1960s and early 1970s two major themes could readily be detected in the Christian community's interest in psychology. The first involved efforts to address the theoretical and con-

Table 1

Selected History of Christian Counseling

Date	Event
1952	Christian Association for Psychological Studies (CAPS) was founded.
1957	Paul Tournier's book *The Meaning of Persons* was published.
1965	Fuller Theological Seminary's Graduate School of Psychology was founded.
1969	Rosemead Graduate School of Psychology was founded.
1970	Jay Adams' book *Competent to Counsel* was published.
1976	APA Division 36, for Psychologists Interested in Religious Issues, was founded.
1973	*Journal of Psychology and Theology* was founded.
1975	CAPS Bulletin (now *Journal of Psychology and Christianity*) was founded.
1988	First International Congress on Christian Counseling.
1990	Rech Conference on Graduate Training in Christian Counseling.

Adapted from Bufford (1991, 1992).

ceptual issues that arise when examining the relationship between psychology—or more commonly, clinical and counseling psychology—and Christian faith. The second, closely related, involved the development of Christian counseling approaches. This enterprise quickly came to be known as integration although the term is both awkward and unsatisfactory. Awkward because the term integration suggests that knowledge is fragmented, although many theorists emphasize the unity of truth (e.g., Carter & Narramore, 1979). Unsatisfactory in the sense the the term integration is used in many other contexts with different meanings. For example, "integrative models" of psychotherapy are those which emphasize more than one major domain of human functioning (affective, behavioral, biological, cognitive, and personal) and are influenced by more than one of the major therapeutic models (behavioral, biological, cognitive, experiential, psychodynamic), each of which originally tended to emphasize one major domain (Craighead, Craighead, Kazdin, & Mahoney, 1994; Mahoney, 1988).

With the passage of time, the field of Christian counseling has broadened and become more diverse. By 1992, 10 distinctive themes could be identified in the Christian counseling movement: (a) Christian anti-psychology; (b) biblical counseling; (c) Christian lay counseling; (d) pastoral counseling/psychology; (e) missionary psychology; (f) psychological measurement of Christian constructs; Christian marriage and family education/counseling; (h) the Christian recovery movement; (i) professional psychotherapy/counseling guided by Christian values. While there is conceptual and practical overlap among some of these areas, others are largely independent (Bufford, 1992).

Distinctives of Christian Counseling

A survey of the literature reveals that Christian counseling has been distinguished in a variety of ways. These include the role of the counselor, the goal of counseling, the setting for counseling, and the content of counseling. Early discussions tended to focus on one distinctive, while later commentators tend to summarize early distinctives and at times add new ones as well. The following examples illustrate this diversity.

Adams (1970) defines Christian counseling as nouthetic confrontation. He suggests that the Christian pastor is the ideal counselor: "nouthetic activity particularly characterizes the work of the ministry" (p. 42); "a good seminary education ... is the most fitting background for a counselor" (p. 61). Adams explicitly rejects psychiatry and clinical or counseling psychology, claiming to draw his techniques from the Bible (Benner, 1985). Adams appears to make a false dichotomy, however. Many of his counseling techniques are basic behavioral techniques.

Like Adams, Bobgan and Bobgan (1979) and Powlison (1992) suggest there is no place for clinical or counseling psychology in Christian counseling. According to Powlison, "the interpretive categories that psychologists use are highly distorted.... They inevitably end up feeding covert or overt idolatries" (Powlison, 1992, p. 211). While Powlison conceded that "psychologists make acute observations and have valid concerns" (p. 210), he proposes that they and integrationists need a complete paradigm shift.

Crabb (1977, 1981) emphasized the goal of discipleship: "the goal of biblical counseling is to promote Christian maturity ... worship ... and service" (1977, p. 29). Kirwan (1984) states a similar three-fold goal: "imparting a sense of belonging ('you are a part of God's family'), edification, and service, (which are) the major tasks of the church" (pp. 119-120).

Strong (1976) proposed three distinctives for Christian counseling. Christian counseling views persons as fallen but justified and worthy of grace. It emphasizes individual responsibility rather than personal rights. Finally, it proposes that both willpower and grace are required for effective change.

At the opposite extreme, some have argued that the notion of Christian counseling is ridiculous, making no more sense than Christian plumbing. For example, Vanderploeg (1981) argued that "there is no difference between Christian and non-Christian therapy. The goals are the same ... the means are the same.... The difference lies not within therapy, but within the therapists themselves. One group is Christian and the other is not" (p. 303, cited in Benner, 1985). Collins (1988) quotes a chaplain from a seminar which he led: "There is no uniquely Christian form of surgery, Christian auto mechanics, or Christian cooking, and neither is there Christian counseling" (p. 17).

Initially, little agreement is apparent among writers on Christian counseling. Beginning some more unifying reflection, Benner (1985) reported that Christians who hold that Christian counseling is unique do so on the basis of "uniqueness in theory or uniqueness in role and/or task" (p. 160). Benner concluded, however, that no commonly accepted Christian theory of personality had been developed. Benner said that the major themes which define a biblical view of persons are "the unity of personality, creation in the image of God, and the reality of sin" (p. 160). With regard to role and/or task of the counselor, Benner (after Klausner, 1964) identified four task/role combinations; reductionist, dualist, alternativist, and specialist. Material reductionists (such as Albert Ellis and B. F. Skinner, signers of the *Humanist Manifesto II*) view human emotional/psychological problems in scientific terms, allowing no place for spiritual approaches. Conversely, such authors as Adams, the Bobgans, and Powlison view human problems as primarily spiritual and propose spiritual approaches to counseling (though they allow for rare organically-based problems which may be treated medically, disallowing a role for counselors not involved in Christian ministry). Dualists recognize both psychological and spiritual problems, but believe both can be addressed by

one person. Alternativists, conversely, hold there is only one kind of problem which can be approached in two equally legitimate ways. Finally, specialists hold that there are two tasks and two roles; this view requires both spiritual and psychological specialists, each of whom works in the appropriate sphere.

Those who profess to be Christian counselors represent all four approaches. Benner (1985) concluded that

> Christian therapy ... is an approach to therapy offered by a Christian who bases his or her understanding of persons on the Bible and allows this understanding to shape all aspects of theory and practice ... the Christian therapist ... views himself in God's service in and through his profession and ... sees his primary allegiance and accountability to his God, and only secondarily to his profession or discipline. (p. 164)

Bufford (1992) proposed a motivational explanation: Counseling is Christian when counselors consciously set themselves apart for service to God and their fellow humans. Such "consecrated counseling" may include evangelism and discipleship, but it is much broader, and may be aimed at alleviation and prevention of human suffering in situations where evangelism or discipleship is not an immediate goal.

Collins (1988) identified four distinctive features of Christian counseling: (a) unique assumptions, (b) unique goals, (c) unique methods, and (d) unique counselor characteristics. Collins suggests that each of these is an aspect of what it means for counseling to be Christian. Among the assumptions are those of a Christian world view, which implies that the therapist himself or herself is a Christian.

Worthington (1986) suggests that Christian counseling is defined in terms of context and content. With regard to context, counseling is Christian when it occurs in Christian and religious settings—churches, parachurch organizations, and the like. Worthington, Dupont, Berry, and Duncan (1988) suggest that another distinctive feature of some approaches to Christian counseling is that they emphasize the goal of counseling as conversion and discipleship or spiritual growth. Worthington et al. (1988) identified two distinguishing content emphases: first, techniques derived from Scripture and the spiritual guidance literature; second, focus on Christian topics or issues as an emphasis of therapy or counseling.

The commentaries of Benner (1985), Collins (1988, 1993), and Worthington (1986) summarize previously proposed Christian distinctives, but offered little evaluative reflection. The conceptualization offered by Benner of sociopsychophysical (or biopsychosocial) and spiritual unity is consistent with recent views on psychotherapy such as those of Mahoney (1988). Within the unity approach, one dimension or another may be emphasized, but the dimensions are thought ultimately to be inseparable. Recent reports of spiritual benefits of psychotherapy are consistent with the unity model (Bufford & Renfroe, 1994; Bufford, Renfroe, & Howard, 1995; Richards, Owen, & Stein, 1993; Toh & Tan, 1997; Toh, Tan, Osburn, & Faber, 1994).

Table 2 summarizes this review of the distinctive features of Christian counseling proposed by various authors. While several themes emerged, considerable disagreement exists among Christian authors regarding what makes counseling Christian. No clear way of resolving the disagreement has been proposed.

Before leaving the topic of Christian distinctives, one additional observation is needed. Careful examination reveals that most of the authors imply or support other distinctives in addition to those that they emphasize. Although Adams (1970) for example, emphasizes the role of the counselor, a careful examination of his writing reveals that he also presumes that counseling should be done from a Christian world view and that the counselor should have Christian faith and values, have a personal calling to ministry, and engage in discipleship and evangelism. Adams advocates the use of prayer, and perhaps other distinctively Christian approaches, and addresses topics of special interest to Christians. Similar conclusions may be drawn about many of the other theorists as well. When these implicit views are considered there is much greater agreement among Christian writers than appears at first reading. Table 3 shows this additional information. Role and setting are seldom deemed important. Excellence is rarely emphasized, but probably considered important by all. Most authors are concerned that the counselor have a Christian world view and values, which stem from a personal faith and calling. Emphasis on Christian techniques and topics has emerged since the mid 1980s, but was implicitly present in much of the earlier writings as well.

Writers are about equally divided between those who emphasize evangelism and discipleship as a goal and those who emphasize the goal of Christian service. This division likely stems at least in part from the lack of clarity about the distinction between spiritual counseling and mental health counseling. Those who favor a spiritual counseling model emphasize evangelism and discipleship, while those who advocate a mental health model emphasize service. It appears that there is a need and a place for both approaches. However, at the present time proponents of both perspectives tend to be critical, even disparaging, of those who hold the alternative model.

Factors Shared with Non-Christian Approaches

The examination of distinctives of Christian counseling might suggest that Christian counseling has little in common with non-Christian approaches. However, the extent of common elements is quite broad—so much that some theorists claim, as noted above, that there is little about counseling which is uniquely Christian. What are these common elements? First, the problems that are addressed in Christian counseling are often the same problems addressed by other counselors: depression, anxiety, relationship conflicts, addictions, and so on. Explicit treatment of spiritual factors was for a time unique; however, there is a growing interest in spirituality among counselors who are not explicitly Christian (e.g., Kelly, 1995; Lovinger, 1984; Shafranske, 1996).

Second, almost all theories of Christian counseling have been adopted or adapted from existing counseling theories. Even those which are generally considered most distinctive, such as Adams' nouthetic counseling (1970, 1979) and Crabb's biblical counseling (1977) bear striking resemblances to behavioral (Carter, 1975) and rational emotive (Wilson, 1985) theories, respectively.

Third, intervention strategies and techniques are largely common among Christian and non-Christian approaches. These include emphasis on the importance of the counseling relationship, providing support and confrontation, making cognitive and behavioral interventions, and so on—almost all the traditional counseling or psychotherapy interventions are used by at least some Christian counselors. Interventions based on spiritual disciplines, as proposed by Moon and his colleagues (Moon, Bailey, Kwasny, & Willis, 1991; Moon, Willis, Bailey, & Kwasny, 1992) and others (e.g., Ball & Goodyear, 1991; Jones, Watson, & Wolfram, 1992) include a number of techniques which may be seldom used by non-Christians. But some of these, such as forgiveness, journal keeping, meditation, celebration, and rest, are commonly used by non-Christian counselors, although the emphasis may be different in Christian approaches. An example of wider use of a "Christian" approach is the reported use of forgiveness among American Association of Marriage

Table 2

Christian Counseling Distinctives Explicitly Proposed by Various Authors

Study	Excellence	Setting	Counselor Qualities					Goal		Interventions	
			Role	World view	Values	Faith	Call	Evangelism/ Discipleship	Service	Techniques	Topics
Adams, 1970			X								
Crabb, 1975, 1977								X			
Vanderploeg, 1981	X										
Benner, 1985				X				X	X		
Worthington, 1986		X								X	X
Worthington, et al., 1988				X				X		X	X
Collins, 1988, 1993				X	X	X	X			X	X
Bufford, 1992				X		X	X				
Powlison, 1992								X	X		
Bufford, 1995	X			X	X	X	X		X	X	X

Note: X denotes explicit emphasis.

Table 3

Christian Counseling Distinctives Explicitly Proposed by Various Authors

Study	Excellence	Setting	Counselor Qualities					Goal		Interventions	
			Role	World view	Values	Faith	Call	Evangelism/ Discipleship	Service	Techniques	Topics
Adams, 1970			X								
Crabb, 1975, 1977								X			
Vanderploeg, 1981	X										
Benner, 1985				X				X	X		
Worthington, 1986		X									
Worthington, et al., 1988				X				X		X	X
Collins, 1988, 1993				X	X	X	X			X	X
Bufford, 1992				X	X	X	X				
Powlison, 1992								X	X		
Bufford, 1995	X			X	X	X	X		X	X	X

Note: X denotes emphasis; shading identifies implied importance.

and Family Therapist (AAMFT) members (DiBlasio & Benda, 1991).

Finally, while goals such as discipleship and spiritual maturity clearly are distinctive, many of the more immediate goals, such as alleviation of depressive symptoms, reduction of anxiety, management of anger, self-discipline, or control over addictions, are common in both Christian and non-Christian approaches despite the underlying differences in world view and values.

Perhaps the broad similarity among Christian and non-Christian approaches is one reason many Christians claim to have been helped by non-Christian counselors. Likely, objective evaluations of their case histories would often bear out such claims. Such similarity of goals may also account for the reported mental health benefits when spiritual factors are intentionally incorporated into a cognitive-behavioral counseling approach (Propst, 1980) even when conducted by persons who are not themselves overtly Christian (Propst, Ostrom, Watkins, Dean, & Mashburn, 1992), and for reported spiritual benefits of mental health counseling (Bufford & Renfroe, 1994; Bufford, Renfroe, & Howard, 1995; Richards, Owen, & Stein, 1993; Toh & Tan, 1997; Toh, Tan, Osburn, & Faber, 1994). An alternative explanation for these findings is that people function as whole persons; thus benefits in any given area of functioning tend to be reflected throughout the client's life.

Putting it Together: Consecrated Counseling

Several key themes emerge. First, Christian counseling commonly refers to two forms of counseling, spiritual counseling and mental health counseling, without clearly distinguishing them. Second, the different Christian approaches are, nonetheless, much more alike than they might initially seem. Third, Christian approaches have much in common with non-Christian approaches. Finally, while some differences in techniques and topics are likely to be found, the major factor which distinguishes Christian and non-Christian approaches to mental health counseling involves the personal character and motivations of the counselor. Chiefly these involve the personal Christian faith, calling, world view, and values of the counselor.

Collins (1988) pointed in the right direction when he implied that Christian counseling involved several major elements; Benner (1985) and Worthington (Worthington, 1986; Worthington et al., 1988) have suggested similar views. Here I will amplify that notion, describing the basic elements of consecrated counseling.

1. *Pursuit of excellence*: Surely counseling is less than Christian unless it involves careful, quality work. Doing counseling well—as unto the Lord—is an important dimension of Christian counseling. But that by itself is not enough.

2. *Christian world view*: For counseling to be Christian the counselor must be committed to a Christian world view. It would be a mockery to call counseling Christian which is conducted from a non-Christian (or, more aptly, anti-Christian) world view. In this vein, Powlison (1984) advocates a biblical view of persons.

3. *Christian values*: Similarly, to be Christian, the values of the particular approach to counseling must be guided by Christian theology; means, ends, and motives must be examined against the backdrop of our best understanding of Scripture (Bufford, 1985; Collins, 1988, 1993).

4. *Personal faith of the counselor*: While it seems conceivable that a counselor could hold a Christian world view and Christian values without a personal relationship with God, such would not normally be the case. For counseling to be Christian, the counselor must have a personal faith, a personal relationship with the God of Christian theology—the creating, sustaining God who is always there. Wahking (1984) proposes that Christian counselors must "be warm and lively Christians who read the Bible and attend church" (p. 58).

5. *Personal calling of the counselor*: Wahking (1984) states "counselors must have … an intuitive sense of calling to be Christian counselors (p. 58). In a similar vein, Bufford (1992) proposes that counselors be set apart or consecrated for Christian counseling. Farnsworth (1980) also proposes "accountability to the Christian community" (p. 115).

6. *Person and work of God*: Christian counseling must acknowledge, invite, and involve the presence and work of God in the counseling process. Christian counseling is not merely a human enterprise. God is involved through the guiding and empowering work of the Holy Spirit, the forgiveness and reconciliation of Jesus Christ, and the justice and mercy of God the Father.

7. *Spiritual interventions and resources*: Christian counseling does not limit itself to the tools of non-Christian approaches; it gratefully includes those resources which are derived from Christian traditions, including giving and receiving forgiveness, prayer (by, with, and for clients). Scripture, solitude, and a host of other resources included under spiritual disciplines (Foster, 1988; Willard, 1988), as has been suggested by a number of theorists (Adams, 1994; Bufford, 1994; Moon et al., 1991,

1992; Stratton, 1993). Finally, Christian counseling does not limit itself to the use of the resources available within the counseling setting. It also avails itself of all the resources of the Christian community, including referral to pastors and other spiritual leaders, encouraging involvement in the Christian community through worship, fellowship, sacraments, and service (Bufford & Johnston, 1981; Bufford & Buckler, 1987; Kirwan, 1984; Uomoto, 1982; Vander Goot, 1983; Visser, 1983).

Tan (1991) incorporates several of these themes. He argues that religious values are central to Christian counseling and proposes that what makes counseling distinctively Christian includes the explicit use of Christian interventions such as prayer and Scripture, and reliance on spiritual gifts and the power of the Holy Spirit. Similarly, Johnson and Ridley (1992) suggest four factors commonly assumed to make Christian counseling effective, including adoption of Christian values, instilling spiritual hope, offering guidelines for wholeness based on spiritual truths, and the role of divine agency. Ideally, all approaches which profess to be Christian should be united in these respects.

Certain elements are missing from this list, however. As Adams has pointed out (e.g., Adams, 1970), the role and ministry of the Godhead, the use of spiritual resources, and the use of spiritual interventions are all limited when the counselee is not Christian. Furthermore, the effectiveness of Christian interventions will differ dramatically depending on where the client is in his or her spiritual development and openness to exploring these concerns. While the counseling relationship is clearly not the place for coercive manipulation, within the ethical constraints of informed consent there is room for exploring the client's openness to investigate Christian faith or try various Christian interventions as possible means for finding the wholeness and health which the client seeks.

Second, some have suggested that to be fully Christian, the counseling must be conducted in a Christian setting such as a church. However, such settings are not vital to Christian counseling. While it is difficult to conceive of Christian counseling being conducted in some settings (e.g., in a bar), any form of counseling is doubtful in such circumstances. Whatever the setting, the other factors identified above seem far more important in determining whether counseling is Christian.

In fact, diversity of counseling context and the spiritual status of the client, as well as diversity in the contents, intervention strategies, and even the goals of counseling, seems desirable. Such diversity is consistent with the diversity which exists (and has existed since the early days of the Christian church) among Christian groups and denominations. It acknowledges that no single person or approach can meet the diversity of human needs. Such diversity is also consistent with the variety of Christian counseling emphases today, as manifested at the Second International Congress on Christian Counseling (Bufford, 1992). Diversity should be welcomed and encouraged.

In reviewing the elements of consecrated counseling, it is noteworthy that six of the seven elements—pursuit of excellence, Christian world view, Christian values, personal faith of the counselor, personal calling of the counselor, and the counselor inviting the presence and work of God in the counseling process—primarily involve the world view, commitment, and character of the counselor. In a recent publication, McMinn (1996) also voices this view: "throughout my years of professional work, I have become increasingly convinced that the value of counseling interventions is found less in one's technical training and theoretical orientation than in one's character" (p. xi). He added: "redemptive Christian counselors ... see character ... the character that God is producing and renewing in their lives—as the greatest tool they offer in counseling" (p. 257).

The final element of spiritual interventions and resources requires the informed consent of the client and necessitates active client involvement as well. Tan (1996) provides a thoughtful discussion of the informed consent issues involved in the explicit address of religious issues in the practice of clinical or counseling psychology addressed by the ethics code for psychologists (American Psychological Association, 1992, 1993). The role of the client in Christian counseling cannot be underestimated. The client chooses the setting and seeks out, or agrees to work with, the Christian counselor. The client, too, quite likely is responding to the working of God through the Holy Spirit in his or her life.

Christian counseling is primarily about character—about the personal godliness of the counselor. Thus, the core of consecrated counseling is the person, life, and work of the counselor. Inevitably such consecration shapes the counseling in myriad subtle ways; at times it will shape counseling profoundly. However, apart from the explicit involvement of spiritual interventions and resources, most of the techniques and intervention strategies the counselor employs, and even many of the goals, will look familiar to counselors who operate from other world views. Finally, the professional role, the setting or context, and the clientele served are inevitably intertwined, and together will likely play a major role in determining the extent to which religious topics and religious techniques or strategies will be used. Yet setting or context are least essential to the essence of Christian—or consecrated—counseling. Counseling is most truly Christian when the counselor has a deep personal faith; counsels with excellence; holds a Christian world view; is guided by Christian values in choosing the means, goals, and motivations of counseling; actively seeks the presence and work of God; and actively utilizes spiritual interventions and resources within ethical guidelines. The client by his or her choices can enhance or minimize the extent to which these goals are implemented in any given counseling relationship.

References

Adams, J. E. (1970). *Competent to Counsel.* Grand Rapids, MI: Baker.

Adams, J. E. (1979). *Lectures in counseling.* Nutley, NJ: Presbyterian and Reformed.

Adams., S. A. (1994). *Spiritual well-being, religiosity and demographic variables as predictors of the use of Christian counseling techniques among members of CAPS, U.S.A.* Ann Arbor, MI: UMI Dissertation Services, 93-16275.

American Psychiatric Association. (1994). *Diagnostic and statistical manual of mental disorders* (4th ed.). Washington, DC: Author.

American Psychological Association (1992). Ethical principles of psychologists and code of conduct. *American Psychologist, 47,* 1-5.

American Psychological Association (1993). Guidelines for providers of psychological services to ethnic, linguistic, and culturally diverse populations. *American Psychologist, 48,* 45-47.

Ball, R. A., & Goodyear, R. K. (1991). Self-reported practices of Christian psychotherapists. *Journal of Psychology and Christianity, 10,* 144-153.

Beit-Hallahmi, B. (1974). Psychology of religion 1880-1930: The rise and fall of a psychological movement. *Journal of the History of the Behavioral Sciences, 10,* 84-90.

Benner, D. G. (1985). Christian counseling and psychotherapy. In D. G. Benner (Ed.), *Baker encyclopedia of psychology* (pp. 158-164). Grand Rapids, MI: Baker.

Bobgan, M., & Bobgan, D. (1979). *The psychological way/the spiritual way.* Minneapolis, MN: Bethany Fellowship.

Bufford, R. K. (1985). Behavioral psychology. In D. G. Benner (Ed.), *Baker encyclopedia of psychology* (pp. 158-164). Grand Rapids, MI: Baker.

Bufford, R. K. (1991, June). *Integration: State of the art for the 90s.* Presented at the annual meeting of the Christian Association for Psychological Studies, Anaheim, CA.

Bufford, R. K. (1992, Fall). *Reflections on Christian counseling.* CAPS West Newsletter, 3-5.

Bufford, R. K. (1994, August). *Christian techniques in psychotherapy: What, who, and ethical questions.* Paper presented at the annual meetings of the American Psychological Association, Los Angeles, CA.

Bufford, R. K. (1995, June). *What makes counseling Christian?* Presented at the Christian Association for Psychological Studies Western Region Annual Convention, Fresno, CA.

Bufford, R. K. (in press). Models of mental illness. In D. G. Benner & P. Hill (Eds.), *Baker encyclopedia of psychology* (2nd ed.). Grand Rapids, MI: Baker.

Bufford, R. K., & Buckler, R. E. (1987). Counseling in the church: A proposed strategy for ministering to mental health needs in the church. *Journal of Psychology and Christianity, 6,* 21-29.

Bufford, R. K., & Johnston, T. B. (1981). The church and community mental health: Unrealized potential. *Journal of Psychology and Theology, 10,* 355-362.

Bufford, R. K., & Renfroe, T. W. (1994, June). *Spiritual well-being and depression in psychotherapy outpatients.* Presented at the Christian Association for Psychological Studies Western Region Annual Meeting, Del Mar, CA.

Bufford, R. K., Renfroe, T. W., & Howard, G. (1995, August). *Spiritual changes as psychotherapy outcomes.* A Division 36 Hospitality Suite presentation at the annual meeting of the American Psychological Association, New York.

Carter, J. D. (1975). Adams' theory of nouthetic counseling. *Journal of Psychology and Theology, 3,* 143-155.

Carter, J. D., & Narramore, B. (1979). *The integration of psychology and theology.* Grand Rapids, MI: Zondervan.

Collins G. R. (1988). *Christian counseling: A comprehensive guide* (rev. ed.). Dallas, TX: Word.

Collins, G. R. (1993). *The biblical basis of Christian counseling for people helpers.* Colorado Springs, CO: NavPress.

Crabb, L. J., Jr. (1975). *Basic principles of biblical counseling.* Grand Rapids, MI: Zondervan.

Crabb, L. J., Jr. (1977). *Effective biblical counseling.* Grand Rapids, MI: Zondervan.

Crabb, L. J., Jr. (1981). Biblical authority and Christian psychology. *Journal of Psychology and Theology, 9,* 305-311.

Craighead, L. W., Craighead, W. E., Kazdin, A. E., & Mahoney, M. K. (1994). *Cognitive and behavioral interventions: An empirical approach to mental health problems.* Boston: Allyn and Bacon.

DiBlasio, F. A., & Benda, B. B. (1991). Practitioners, religion, and the use of forgiveness in the clinical setting. *Journal of Psychology and Christianity, 10,* 166-172.

Egan, G. (1994). *The skilled helper: A problem-management approach to helping* (5th ed.). Pacific Grove, CA: Brooks/Cole.

Farnsworth, K. E. (1980). Christian psychotherapy and the culture of professionalism. *Journal of Psychology and Theology, 8,* 115-121.

Foster, R. J. (1988). *Celebration of discipline* (2nd ed.). San Francisco: Harper San Francisco.

Gorsuch, R. L. (1988). Psychology of religion. *Annual Review of Psychology, 39,* 201-221.

Johnson, W. B., & Ridley, W. B. (1992). Sources of gain in Christian counseling and psychotherapy. *The Counseling Psychologist, 20,* 159-175.

Jones, S. L., Watson, E., & Wolfram, T. (1992). Results of the Rech conference survey on religious faith and professional psychology. *Journal of Psychology and Theology, 20,* 47-158.

Kelly, E. W., Jr. (1995). *Spirituality and religion in counseling and psychotherapy.* Alexandria, VA: American Counseling Association.

Kirwan, W. T. (1984). *Biblical concepts for Christian counseling: A case for integrating psychology and theology.* Grand Rapids, MI: Baker.

Klausner, S. Z. (1964). *Psychiatry and religion.* New York: Free Press.

Koch, S. (1985). Foreword: Wundt's creature at age zero and as centenarian. In S. Koch & D. E. Leary (Eds.), *A century of psychology as a science.* New York: McGraw-Hill.

Lovinger, R. (1984). *Working with religious issues in therapy.* Northvale, NJ: Jason Aronson.

Mahoney, M. J. (1988). The cognitive sciences and psychotherapy: Patterns in a developing relationship. In K. S. Dobson (Ed.), *Handbook of cognitive-behavioral therapies.* New York: Guilford.

McMinn, M. (1996). *Psychology, theology, and spirituality in Christian counseling.* Wheaton, IL: Tyndale.

Moon, G. W., Bailey, J. C., Kwasny, J. C., & Willis, D. E. (1991). Training in the use of Christian disciplines as counseling techniques within explicitly Christian graduate training programs. *Journal of Psychology and Christianity, 10,* 154-165.

Moon, G. W., Willis, D. E., Bailey, J. C., & Kwasny, J. C. (1992). Self-reported use of Christian spiritual guidance techniques by Christian psychotherapists, pastoral counselors, and spiritual directors. *Journal of Psychology and Christianity, 12,* 24-37.

Narramore, C. (1960). *The psychology of counseling.* Grand Rapids, MI: Zondervan.

Powlison, D. (1984). Which presuppositions? Secular psychology and the categories of biblical thought. *Journal of Psychology and Theology, 12,* 270-278.

Powlison, D. (1992). Integration or inundation? In M. S. Horton (Ed.), *Power religion: The selling out of the evangelical church?* Chicago: Moody Press.

Propst, R. L. (1980). The comparative efficacy of religious and non-religious imagery for the treatment of mild depression in religious individuals. *Cognitive Therapy and Research, 4,* 167-178.

Propst, R. L., Ostrom, R., Watkins, P., Dean, T., & Mashburn, D. (1992). Comparative efficacy of religious cognitive-behavioral therapy for the treatment of clinical depression in religious individuals. *Journal of Consulting and Clinical Psychology, 60,* 94-103.

Richards, P. S., Owen, L., & Stein, S. (1993). A religiously oriented group counseling intervention for self-defeating perfectionism: A pilot study. *Counseling and Values, 37,* 96-104.

Sexton, V. S. (1978). American psychology and philosophy, 1876-1976: Alienation and reconciliation. *The Journal of General Psychology, 99,* 3-18.

Shafranske, E. P. (Ed.). (1996). *Religion and the clinical practice of psychology.* Washington, DC: American Psychological Association.

Stratton, S. W. (1993). *Effects of graduate education and counselor setting on professional practices among members of the Christian Association for Psychological Studies.* Ann Arbor, MI: UMI Dissertation Information Service, 93-11582.

Strong, S. R. (1976). Christian counseling. *Counseling and Values, 20,* 151-160.

Tan, S.-Y. (1991). Religious values and interventions in lay Christian counseling. *Journal of Psychology and Christianity, 10,* 173-182.

Tan, S.-Y. (1996). Religion in clinical practice: Implicit and explicit integration. In E. P. Shafranske (Ed.), *Religion and the clinical practice of psychology.* Washington, DC: American Psychological Association.

Toh, Y.-M., & Tan, S.-Y. (1997). The effectiveness of church-based lay counselors: A controlled outcome study. *Journal of Psychology and Christianity,* in press..

Toh, Y.-M., Tan, S.-Y., Osburn, C. D., & Faber, D. E. (1994). The evaluation of a church-based lay counseling program: Some preliminary data. *Journal of Psychology and Christianity, 13,* 270-275.

Tournier, P. (1957). *The meaning of persons.* New York: Harper and Row.

Uomoto, J. M. (1982). Prevention intervention: A convergence of the church and community mental health. *Journal of Psychology and Christianity, 1,* 12-22.

Vande Kemp, H. (1996). Historical perspective: Religion and clinical psychology in America. In E. P. Shafranske (Ed.), *Religion and the Clinical Practice of Psychology.* Washington, DC: American Psychological Association.

Vander Goot, M. (1983). The shingle and the manse: Should pastors be counselors? *The Reformed Journal, 33,* 15-18.

Vanderploeg, R. D. (1981). Imago Dei as foundational to psychotherapy. *Journal of Psychology and Theology, 9,* 299-304.

Visser, D. A. (1983, April). *Should pastors be counselors?* Paper presented at the annual meeting of the Christian Association for Psychological Studies, Chicago, IL.

Wahking, H. (1984). A church-related professional counseling service. *Journal of Psychology and Christianity, 3,* 58-64.

Willard, D. (1988). *The spirit of the disciplines.* New York: Harper and Row.

Wilson, R. (1985). Biblical counseling. In D. G. Benner (Ed.), *Baker encyclopedia of psychology* (pp. 116-117). Grand Rapids, MI: Baker.

Worthington, E. L., Jr. (1986). Religious counseling: A review of the empirical research. *Journal of Counseling and Development, 64,* 421-431.

Worthington, E. L., Jr., Dupont, P. D., Berry, J. T., & Duncan, L. A. (1988). Christian therapists' and clients' perceptions of religious psychotherapy in private and agency settings. *Journal of Psychology and Theology, 16,* 282-293.

24

A Blueprint for Intradisciplinary Integration

Everett L. Worthington, Jr.
Virginia Commonwealth University

Although much has been written about interdisciplinary integration—integrating the two broad disciplines of psychology and theology—little has been written about exactly how to do intradisciplinary integration, which is how to construct a Christian theory of psychological counseling that integrates one's personal faith and personal practice of counseling. The present article poses questions, using an organizing metaphor of constructing a building, to help trainees and other interested professionals articulate their own Christian theory of counseling. Questions are grouped within four areas: foundation (Jesus Christ), weight-bearing pillars (fundamental Christian beliefs), frame (goals and methods), and covering (content of counseling). Theory construction is seen as recursive, requiring correction from experience, Scripture, and clients.

Bouma-Prediger (1990) has suggested that four types of integration of psychology and theology occur. *Interdisciplinary integration* seeks to articulate the relationships between psychology and theology or more broadly among all the academic disciplines. *Intradisciplinary integration* examines what occurs within psychology (or more narrowly) within psychotherapy. It asks: How do I integrate my faith with my theory and practice of psychology (or psychotherapy)? *Faith praxis integration* seeks answers to the question: How do I live in a secular world as a Christian? Finally, *Experiential integration* seeks answers to the question: How do I integrate and reorganize my life because of a healing, saving encounter with the living God?

Writings about the interdisciplinary integration of psychology and theology have occurred in three distinct waves. In the early years, prior to 1975, the writings were unsystematic and rudimentary (Bube, 1971; Collins, 1973; Meehl, 1958; Tournier, 1964).

The founding of the *Journal of Psychology and Theology* inspired a new generation of theorists, who addressed the integration of psychology and theology with vigor. During the period from 1975 through 1982, models of the integration of psychology and theology proliferated (Carter, 1977; Carter & Mohline, 1976; Carter & Narramore, 1979; Collins, 1977, 1981; Crabb, 1977, 1981; Farnsworth, 1982; Fleck & Carter, 1981; Guy, 1980, 1982; Larzalere, 1980; Malony, 1981).

Since 1982, model development has slowed to a trickle (cf. Clinton, 1990a, 1990b), suggesting that the field is in a third phase. Recently, psychologists have apparently settled down actually to do the task of integration—that is, intradisciplinary integra-tion—proposing a variety of ways to integrate Christian values, beliefs, and assumptions and various theories of therapy.

In addition, the study of interdisciplinary integration per se has been more empirical. For example, Foster, Horn, and Watson (1988) used Farnsworth's (1982) five types of interdisciplinary integration to classify articles published in the *Journal of Psychology and Theology* during the six years from 1980 through 1985. Foster et al. (1988) found that there was a de facto consensus about the models used in articles published in the *Journal*. About two-thirds used a "conformability" model, in which psychological facts were reinterpreted in light of Scripture or vice versa. The remaining articles used a "compatibility" model, in which secular and theological concepts and facts were given equal weight, or less often a "credibility" model in which the Bible was used to filter ideas and concepts. In 1990, Foster and Bolsinger examined the literature on integration within the *Journal* and determined that a substantial consensus existed about seven themes: (a) modeling and imitation are effective ways to learn; (b) there is no one form of Christian counseling; (c) imagery is an effective counseling tool; (d) people can be mentally ill without being demon possessed or sinful; (e) homosexuality is not normal, healthy behavior; (f) the scientific method is here to stay and is not un-Christian; and (g) all truth is God's truth.

Generally, intradisciplinary integration has been performed in four primary ways. First, conducting an analytic critique of secular theories and concepts from a Christian perspective is one way of doing intradisciplinary integration. Although there have been many examples of this, one of the best recent examples is Jones and Butman's (1991) analysis of secular theories of counseling and psychotherapy from a Christian perspective. This analysis criticizes the assumptions and premises of each approach, pointing out challenges to Christian presuppositions and identifying ways that each theory contributes to or is compatible with an evangelical Christian worldview.

A second type of intradisciplinary integration is synthetic. It proposes problem-focused Christian perspectives on such topics as self-esteem (e.g., Ryan, 1983), guilt (Narramore, 1984), and parenting (Stehouwer & Stehouwer, 1983)—to name but a few.

A third type of intradisciplinary integration is also synthetic. It proposes Christian-oriented versions of secular theories of psychotherapy. For example, Crabb (1977) articulated a Christian cognitive therapy, Malony (1980) described a Christian version of Transactional Analysis, Wright (1981) and Worthington (1990) each proposed a cognitive, behavioral, and biblical version of marital therapy. Recently, Smith (1990) has articulated a systematic integrative therapy that is oriented toward Christians. As with problem-focused intradisciplinary integration, theory-focused efforts are legion and only a few are mentioned.

A fourth important type of intradisciplinary integration has been largely neglected within the professional literature. These synthetic efforts aim at helping new professionals build their own integrated theory of Christian counseling. One of the legitimate functions of a professional journal is to train students, new professionals, and more experienced professionals who are changing their specializations. This requires a practical emphasis. Collins (1983) has noted that the major emphasis in the *Journal* appears to be theoretical. He said that

> Even if most practical ideas were to be published elsewhere, in one applied area the *Journal* must take leadership. We must give more attention to the previously mentioned issue of integration methodology. How do we do integration? What skills and methods are involved? ... [H]ow we approach the integrative task could be a major emphasis of this Journal in the coming decade. (p. 5)

In the near decade since Collins' (1983) article, his prediction has not come true. While some efforts at intradisciplinary integration have appeared, an emphasis on the practical has not been realized. Practice-focused, training-oriented articles have been scarce to non-existent. This has recently been recognized as a pressing need. At the Rech conference on Christian graduate training, two sessions considered the paucity of practical integration of faith in counseling. For example, Jones (1992) said, "At the most basic level, we are trying to encourage integration of psychology and *Christian faith*, not psychology and theology (as an academic discipline)" (p. 81).

While this scarcity of practice-focused integrative articles has not deterred established professionals from articulating their integrative theories (e.g., Smith, 1990), the neophyte Christian counselor often struggles. In some training programs, there are explicit courses in integration of psychology and theology. Yet, Foster, Horn, and Watson (1988) showed that at least half of the recent writers about integration had secular training in psychology but no theological training. Such professionals need a brief reference source for beginning their journey toward creating their own integrated theories of Christian counseling.

Many books and papers deal with how to integrate psychology and theology. Most are useful, but very theoretical, often prompting criticism by concerned Christians looking to integrate Christianity and counseling in a practical way. For example, Collins reprinted a reaction to his 1978 Finch Lectures at Fuller Seminary. It began:

> Psychologists! Tired of being pushed around by psychoanalysts and Sunday school teachers? ... Now there is an amazing new product for you: iopat (Integration of Psychology and Theology);... Over the years I've ordered many of these, in various sizes and models ... [but] I've never even gotten a blueprint so I could build one myself.... I'm beginning to suspect, however, that I might not know how to recognize an "integration" if I saw one. (Doran, cited in Collins, 1981, pp. 126-127)

The present article develops a blueprint that can be used to build one's own practical integration of Christian faith and therapy.

Precondition: Bi-lingual Skills

As a precondition to building a working integrated theory of therapy and theology, the Christian counselor should strive to become bi-lingual in theology and therapy (or more broadly, psychology) to some extent. This is not easy. In fact, Hunter (1989) compiled the papers from a symposium at the Society for the Scientific Study of Religion on the case for theological literacy in the psychology of religion. The issues addressed by those scholars were many and varied, but the main theme was that our understanding of the psychology of religion is greatly enriched by bi-lingual competency in theology and psychology. Further, just as there are many traditions in psychology, there are also many traditions within theology, or even (more narrowly) within Christianity. For those who train or who practice counseling or psychotherapy, building both theological and psychological literacy requires hard work, creative study, and patience in learning.

Once counselors are moderately bi-lingual, they may inform their attempts at therapy with the language of the true Christian faith. It is not necessary to use religious language with clients, forcing them often into a language system with which they are frankly uncomfortable. However, Christian therapists should at least keep in mind universal Christian principles. The story of Christianity is one of God's grace, human rebellion, human fall, and God's mercy, repeated endlessly. That story permeates the life of Christians and should be a framework within which counselors see their clients' problems. People often come to counseling at steps two and three of this cycle—human rebellion or human fall. People have lost hope because of the pain in their circumstances. Thus, one thing counselors do throughout counseling is to help restore their clients' hope in God's redemptive powers.

A Blueprint for Building an Integrated Personal Theory of Christian Counseling

Purpose

Being aware of the necessity to continually improve their bi-lingual competencies, Christian counselors may begin to develop a blueprint for integrating therapy and faith. Building a house is used as a metaphor for building an integrated personal theory of one's Christian therapy. Each house has a general purpose—safety and security—and purposes unique to the owner. Similarly, each personal theory of Christian counseling has a general purpose—to provide a guide for Christ-honoring, effective counseling or psychotherapy—and other purposes unique to the personality, style, clientele, community, and counseling setting of the Christian counselor.

The following blueprint is not the building. Rather, it is a list of issues that each Christian counselor must resolve to create a personal theory of Christian counseling. My assumption is that a personal theory of Christian therapy will be more consistent and effective if one addresses issues explicitly rather than leaving them implicit.

Foundation

Like any lasting structure, a Christian theory of counseling must be built on a firm foundation. This foundation is Christ, the rock, the son of God, who has been revealed to us by the Holy Spirit most reliably through the Scriptures but also through personal encounters with the living God. The foundation, which is the person of Christ, is solid and is broad enough to accommodate a variety of structures— theologically liberal, moderate, and conservative. In most neighborhoods, there are different kinds of houses built on the same basic foundation. Without that foundation, though, the environment of modern life erodes support from the structure, which may eventually collapse.

This foundation of Jesus Christ simultaneously provides a personal view of God (because Jesus is the incarnation of God) and a Christian anthropology (because Jesus is the ideal person). Jesus is truly the cornerstone of Christian theory that integrates faith and practice.

Weight-bearing Pillars

Growing out of the broad but solid foundation are weight-bearing pillars. Weight-bearing pillars will support the structure as it is built upward from the rock foundation, allowing the structure to function as it is designed to function.

These weight-bearing pillars are the fundamental beliefs of Christianity. C. S. Lewis (1946) called these "mere Christianity." Whatever therapeutic combination of theological and therapeutic beliefs the counselor later arrives at depends on his or her canon of mere Christianity. Individuals consider a varying number of denominational doctrines to be essential. Creating a strong personal theory of Christian counseling is facilitated by explicitly stating one's fundamental theological beliefs.

In the construction of buildings, weight-bearing columns are often made of reinforced concrete. Reinforced concrete has steel rods placed under tension inside of concrete. The tension in the rods strengthens the concrete.

There are many tensions within the weight-bearing columns of mere Christianity. For example, there is tension between the authority of Scripture and the authority of general revelation. While some believe that Scripture is a sufficient counseling manual (Adams, 1970; Bobgan & Bobgan, 1985), others do not. In fact, Malony (1981) described an index system that categorized models of interdisciplinary integration along a continuum of synthetical through antithetical positions. For example, he classified I as Integrative attitudes (i.e., Carter & Mohline, 1976), as most synthetical. These were followed in turn by N,

Nullification attitudes (i.e., denial, Tournier, 1964; levels of analysis, Bube, 1971); D, Dialogical attitudes (i.e., railroad track, Meehl, 1958); E, Eristical (prone to argue; i.e., Collins, 1977; Crabb, 1977); and X, Xenophobic (fear of strangers; i.e., Adams, 1970).

This tension between Scripture and general revelation is a practical tension that bears on each counselor's decision about when, how, and how often the counselor uses Scripture or principles of Scripture directly in counseling, and on how much he or she looks to Scripture to determine ways of counseling versus how often he or she looks to psychology for such information.

The background and current experiences of each counselor will help determine how he or she resolves this tension. For example, a Christian psychologist is likely to find that empirical sources more strongly influence his or her therapy behavior than do traditional ecclesiastical or pastoral practices. Psychological training enculturates a psychologist to value systematic scientific observation. On the other hand, a pastor whose primary responsibility is to preach will likely look to Scripture to deduce methods for counseling. Pastors who primarily preach have been enculturated into a world view that extracts truth from the Scripture. More theological sensitivity of psychologists and more counseling and pastoral care responsibilities of pastors usually mitigate extreme positions.

A second tension involves what part Scripture plays in counseling. For the Evangelical Christian, Scripture necessarily plays a role as a weight-bearing pillar of one's personal theory. Yet the level at which Scripture is used in counseling must be decided. Does the counselor exhort the client to adhere to specific biblical commands? Does the counselor help the client identify more general scriptural principles? Does the counselor stress the general message of Christianity? While most counselors use each level at different times, most counselors stress one level more than others. Making this decision consciously is preferable to being governed by implicit decisions.

A third tension concerns the nature and activity of God versus the nature and activity of humans. How often does God directly affect people's lives? Does God primarily work through other helpers? How determined are humans' behaviors? How much free will do people really have? Answers to these questions influence behavior and expectations in counseling. For example, consider two people. Person 1 believes that God actively changes people's lives through God's direct intervention. As a counselor, she prays with clients for their healing and is less concerned about preparing for a counseling session by getting a

clear conceptualization of the problem and designing a strong psychological intervention than about searching for Scriptures to support her suggestion that God can and wants to heal the person miraculously.

Person 2 is also a committed Christian, but she thinks that although God can and does at times heal miraculously and directly, God generally heals through his body—that is, through the ministry of people to each other. She may pray for God's help, but she also carefully conceptualizes her clients from a psychological perspective and plans her interventions carefully.

Both counselors believe God heals counselees. Both counsel by faith working through love. Neither is more Christian than the other nor more therapeutic than the other. Rather, different assumptions about God's and humans' activities may translate into different counseling behavior for these two therapists. To develop an integrated therapy, the counselor must be aware of his or her positions on these issues because they support much of the weight of the structure of the person's Christian counseling.

Frame

The frame of a structure gives it shape. The frames of a wigwam, ranch style house, and skyscraper are quite different. The frame, along with its covering, determines the function of the structure.

The frame of an integrated approach to Christian counseling involves questions about goals and methods of counseling. Decisions about goals and methods will be influenced by one's answers to previous questions. In fact, each level influences all other levels. This of course is not unique to building an integrated theory of Christian counseling. The person who builds a building does not construct the foundation without knowing what the frame and covering will be like. One must answer all the questions before one can answer any of the questions.

In a sense, the builder (or more accurately the architect) conceptualizes the building in its entirety. Then the architect performs thought experiments to test the initial conception: Is it aesthetically pleasing? Can it handle internal stresses? Finally, a physical model is constructed and tested. By observing effects of the tests on the model, the architect gradually refines his or her design and builds the building.

Similarly, the Christian counselor, armed with tentative answers to all of the questions posed in the present article, constructs a mental model of an integrated faith-practice. Thought experiments are performed: Will it withstand criticism from the environment outside of Christianity? Is it an elegant system? Will it meet criticisms from within Christianity? Finally, the model is overtly articulated—tentatively practiced (at best while being supervised by an experienced supervisor). As results from counseling accumulate, modifications are made and a working integration is available for use.

Goals. In one sense, the ultimate goals of therapy present a stark contrast. Therapies tend to be either growth therapies or problem solving therapies (Haley, 1987). Growth therapies help people perform above the normal levels, while problem solving therapies help people solve problems that prevent them from functioning normally. If goals of Christian counseling include evangelism, sanctification, holiness, or discipleship, then those are growth therapy goals. On the other hand, if the counselor strives to help people solve problems in living, he or she is adopting problem solving goals. One discussion of appropriate goals for counseling occurs within the *Journal's* "Integrative Inquiry" section (Jones, Sabom, and Worthington, 1991), where a variety of positions are discussed.

In that Integrative Inquiry section, I suggested that which goal is emphasized, if either, is usually determined by the context of the counseling. If the client is coming to a private Christian counselor because of serious problems and is paying (or having insurance pay) for therapy, then problem solving is likely to be emphasized—at least as a precondition to growth therapy. If the person seeks counsel and has a good social support network and good coping skills, then growth therapy goals may be more appropriate. If a person seeks help in an explicitly Christian setting, generally the person will be more open to the counselor addressing Christian growth rather than limiting the focus to problem solving. In fact, such a person might be dissatisfied if Christian growth were *not* emphasized.

The professional Christian psychotherapist interacts with a client in only one setting—clearly demarcated counseling aimed at solving problems or helping change personality patterns. The bounded interaction actually makes the choice among goals simpler and more uniform than for pastors and lay counselors. Pastoral counseling is only one of many ways that the pastor may relate to the parishioner. Further, pastors have different relationships with different parishioners. Their choice of goals for counseling is thus dependent on more pre-established roles, norms, and expectations than is a professional psychotherapist's choices. Like a pastor, a lay Christian helper may also relate to a person in many different roles. As a representative of the church, an elder may be expected to emphasize spiritual growth more than problem solving. However, the elder may also be a friend who interacts with the parishioner at other less

formal occasions. On those occasions, the expectation for explicitly Christian counsel may be less than the expectation for simple support or specific advice about matters not directly related to Christianity.

These three examples are over-simplified for discussion. In reality, the choice of goals is considerably more complicated. There are several levels of goals, including ultimate goals, mediating goals, and tactical (moment-by-moment) goals (Gurman, 1978). Each may be subject to different constraints.

Methods. Like goals, counseling methods are influenced by several factors: context, counselor, community, and clients (Strupp, Hadley, & Gomez-Schwartz, 1977; Worthington, 1991). Many goals are actually negotiated informally and unconsciously. Only occasionally is the negotiation explicit.

The client chooses the context. Most of the time a particular type of counseling is chosen for non-theoretical reasons, such as there being no fee, insurance companies having a certain provider on their list, a friend or relative recommending a therapist, or the office of a certain therapist being accessible.

Most counselors like to believe that counseling methods are under their direct control, and indeed much control over methods is exercised by the therapist. One can hardly imagine Freud refusing to treat a patient by psychoanalysis, in preference for behavior therapy. In reality, though, most therapists use a variety of counseling methods, which they tailor to the client. If a client is verbal and insightful, therapists—even those wedded to a particular theory—usually try to promote more insight. If the client is action-oriented, therapists may use more active methods. Counselors accommodate their methods to the client.

The client, then, by virtue of the style that he or she presents to the counselor, will influence the counselor's methods. The values of the client often also influence counselor style, too. For example, lower socio-economic status clients usually value different things than do higher socio-economic status clients (for a summary see Ernst, 1990). Low SES clients tend to value such things as obedient children, reliable job performance, and cleanliness. High and middle SE clients tend to value such things as intimacy, sharing, communication, equality, education, and insight. Counselors want to communicate with clients in ways that the client can understand, so counselors usually tailor their methods to their clients.

The client's community also often influences counseling methods. The influence may be direct, as when a parent states goals for the children who are being seen by the counselor or when the employer (who is paying for counseling through an employee assistance program) demands client improvement in terms of job performance. Or the influence may be less direct. Indirect influence occurs because of what the counselor and client believe to be the standards of behavior expected by the community. For example, in a theologically conservative community, many counselors dare not recommend to a couple that they divorce, except under dire circumstances.

To integrate one's psychology and theology, then, one must understand one's context, clientele, community, and self. Then one must answer other questions about counseling methods. For example, here are a few.

1. Am I more active or passive during counseling?
2. Which do I favor, a reactive style of counseling, or a proactive, planful style?
3. Am I more of an expert who has answers that I think will help the client learn, or a facilitator who helps the client learn his or her own answers?
4. Do I work from a standard theory of counseling, or am I more eclectic?
5. Do I have an explicitly stated theory about my counseling, or is my counseling implicit and perhaps poorly articulated even in my own mind?
6. Do I have a general plan for the conduct of a counseling session, or are sessions generally different?

Answering such questions will help identify a method and goals in helping.

Covering

Conceivably, the structure of the tropical school house, Mexican hacienda, and space station could be similar in foundation, supporting columns, and frame. Yet, the structures would never be mistaken for each other because the covering differs widely.

In the same way, answers to all prior questions will not determine the content of your counseling. What is dealt with in counseling again depends on context, client, counselor, and community, as did the goals and methods. Christian counselors may discuss forgiveness, salvation, faith, sin, back-sliding, repentance, and redemption. They may anoint with oil (though few do), pray for their clients, or explain Scripture. Or Christian counselors may do none of those, and still be Christian counselors (see Ball & Goodyear, 1991; DiBlasio & Benda, 1991; Jones, Watson, & Wolfram, 1992; Moon et al., 1991; Worthington, Dupont, Berry, & Duncan, 1988 for empirical examinations of techniques used in religious counseling).

In a study of practicing Christian professionals, Worthington, Dupont, Berry, and Duncan (1988) investigated seven therapists and their use of explicitly Christian counseling techniques. They found such divergence that they concluded that it was probably misleading to talk of Christian counseling

as if it were something as clear as Rational Emotive Therapy or behavior therapy. There is wide variation in what is actually talked about in professional counseling with Christians. That knowledge should free the Christian counselor to design a Christian counseling approach that is based on the negotiation among the counselor, client, community, and context. At the same time, it makes the task of integrating theology and therapy more daunting, because there are no agreed upon norms to guide the counselor about what to talk about.

Even with the firm foundation of Jesus Christ, the weight-bearing pillars of mere Christianity, the frame of goals aimed at problem solving or growth and methods informed by context, counselor, community, and clients, the covering of content will give individual character to counseling and will make intradisciplinary integration individually shaped.

To briefly diverge to a different metaphor, the structure of one's Christian counseling is prescribed like the basic style of a traditional suit. But suits can be individually tailored to fit the person more accurately. Similarly, choices you make in constructing your integration of your faith and practice move from very basic—reliance on Jesus as foundation—to the tailoring of the content of your counseling.

Summary

The present article has summarized steps for integrating theology and therapy. It is not intended as a guide to assemble some prefabricated theory. Integrating theology and therapy is a labor that spirals repeatedly. It is a recursive or iterative process. Experience, Scripture, and clients correct approximations at integration. Every time the practicing Christian therapist writes his or her integration of theology and therapy, he or she rewrites it. It is hoped, though, that this present article provides a starting place for students and new professionals for articulating their integration of theology and psychotherapy.

References

Adams, J. E. (1970). *Competent to counsel.* Nutley, NJ: Presbyterian and Reformed Publishing.

Ball, R. A., & Goodyear, R. K. (1991). Self-reported practices of Christian psychotherapists. *Journal of Psychology and Christianity, 10,* 144-153.

Bobgan, M., & Bobgan, D. (1985). *How to counsel from Scripture.* Chicago: Moody.

Bouma-Prediger, S. (1990). The task of integration: A modest proposal. *Journal of Psychology and Theology, 18,* 21-31.

Bube, R. J. (1971). *The human quest: A new look at science and the Christian faith.* Waco, TX: Word.

Carter, J. D. (1977). Secular and sacred models of psychology and religion. *Journal of Psychology and Theology, 5,* 197-208.

Carter, J. D., & Mohline, R. J. (1976). The nature and scope of integration: A proposal. *Journal of Psychology and Theology, 4,* 3-14.

Carter, J. D., & Narramore, B. (1979). *The integration of psychology and theology: An introduction.* Grand Rapids, MI: Zondervan.

Clinton, S. M. (1990a). A critique of integration models. *Journal of Psychology and Theology, 13,* 13-20.

Clinton, S. M. (1990b). The foundational integration model. *Journal of Psychology and Theology, 18,* 115-122.

Collins, G. R. (1973). Psychology on a new foundation: A proposal for the future. *Journal of Psychology and Theology, 1,* 19-27.

Collins, G. R. (1977). *The rebuilding of psychology: An integration of psychology and Christianity.* Wheaton, IL: Tyndale.

Collins, G. R. (1981). *Psychology & theology: Prospects for integration.* Nashville: Abingdon.

Collins, G. R. (1983). Moving through the jungle: A decade of integration. *Journal of Psychology and Theology, 11,* 2-7.

Crabb, L. J., Jr. (1977). *Effective biblical counseling.* Grand Rapids, MI: Zondervan.

Crabb, L. J., Jr. (1981). Biblical authority and Christian psychology. *Journal of Psychology and Theology, 9,* 305-311.

DiBlasio, F. A., & Benda, B. B. (1991). Practitioners, religion, and the use of forgiveness in the clinical setting. *Journal of Psychology and Christianity, 10,* 166-172.

Ernst, L. (1990). Value differences in families of differing socioeconomic status: Implications for family education. *Family Perspective, 24,* 401-410.

Farnsworth, K. E. (1982). The conduct of integration. *Journal of Psychology and Theology, 10,* 308-319.

Fleck, J. R., & Carter, J. D. (Eds.). (1981). *Psychology and theology: Integrative readings.* Nashville: Abingdon.

Foster, J. D., & Bolsinger, S. A. (1990). Prominent themes in Evangelical integration literature. *Journal of Psychology and Theology, 18,* 3-12.

Foster, J. D., Horn, D. A., & Watson, S. (1988). The popularity of integration models, 1980-1985. *Journal of Psychology and Theology, 16,* 3-14.

Gurman, A. S. (1978). Contemporary marital therapies: A critique and comparative analysis of psychoanalytic, behavioral and systems theory approaches. In T. J. Paolino and B. S. McCraty, (Eds.), *Marriage and marital therapy* (pp. 445-566). New York: Brunner/Mazel.

Guy, J. D., Jr. (1980). The search for truth in the task of integration. *Journal of Psychology and Theology, 8,* 27-32.

Guy, J. D., Jr. (1982). Affirming diversity in the task of integration: A response to "Biblical authority and Christian psychology." *Journal of Psychology and Theology, 10,* 35-39.

Haley, J. (1987). Problem solving therapy (2nd ed.). San Francisco: Jossey-Bass.

Hunter, W. F. (Ed.). (1989). Theme issue: The case for theological literacy in the psychology of religion. *Journal of Psychology and Theology, 17,* 327-393.

Jones, S. L. (1992). Overview of the Rech conference on graduate training in psychology and introduction to the collected papers. *Journal of Psychology and Theology, 20,* 77-88.

Jones, S. L., & Butman, R. E. (1991). *Modern psychotherapies: A comprehensive Christian appraisal.* Downers Grove, IL: InterVarsity Press.

Jones, S. L., Watson, E. J., & Wolfram, T. J. (1992). Results of the Rech conference survey on religious faith and professional psychology. *Journal of Psychology and Theology, 20,* 147-158.

Larzalere, R. E. (1980). The task ahead: Six levels of integration of Christianity and psychology. *Journal of Psychology and Theology, 8,* 3-11.

Lewis, C. S. (1946). *Mere Christianity.* New York: Macmillan.

Malony, H. N. (1980). Transactional analysis. In G. R. Collins (Ed.), *Helping people grow: Practical approaches to Christian counseling* (pp. 99-112). Santa Ana, CA: Vision House.

Malony, H. N. (1981). Integration: The adjoinders. In G. R. Collins (H. N. Malony, Ed.), *Psychology & theology: Prospects for integration* (pp. 885-123). Nashville: Abingdon.

Meehl, P. (1958). *What, then, is man?* St. Louis: Concordia.

Moon, G. W., Bailey, J. W., Kwasny, J. C., & Willis, D. E. (1991). Training in the use of Christian disciplines as counseling techniques within explicitly Christian graduate training programs. *Journal of Psychology and Christianity, 10,* 154-165.

Narramore, S. B. (1984). *No condemnation.* Grand Rapids: Zondervan.

Ryan, D. S. (1983). Self-esteem: An operational definition and ethical analysis. *Journal of Psychology and Theology, 11,* 295-302.

Smith, D. (1990). *Integrative therapy: A comprehensive approach to methods and principles of counseling and psychotherapy.* Grand Rapids, MI: Baker Book House.

Stehouwer, N. d. V., & Stehouwer, R. S. (1983). A Christian approach to authority and discipline in the family: Theological-theoretical issues and research findings. *Journal of Psychology and Theology, 11,* 341-348.

Strupp, H. J., Hadley, S. W., & Gomez-Schwartz, B. (1977). *Psychotherapy for better or worse.* New York: Jason Aronson.

Tournier, P. (1964). *To resist or surrender.* Richmond: John Knox Press.

Worthington, E. L., Jr. (1990). Marriage counseling: A Christian approach to counseling couples. *Counseling and Values, 35,* 3-15.

Worthington, E. L., Jr. (1991). Psychotherapy and religious values: An update. *Journal of Psychology and Christianity, 10,* 211-223.

Worthington, E. L., Jr., Dupont, P. A., Berry, J. T., & Duncan, L. A. (1988). Therapists' and clients' perceptions of religious psychotherapy in private and agency settings. *Journal of Psychology and Theology, 16,* 282-293.

Wright, H. N. (1981). *Marital counseling: A biblical, behavioral, cognitive approach.* New York: Harper and Row.

25

The Psychotherapist as Christian Ethicist: Theology Applied to Practice

Alan C. Tjeltveit
Muhlenberg College

The ethical nature of human transformation in general and psychotherapy in particular means that therapists function as applied ethicists. Efforts to relate or integrate theology and therapy must therefore address ethical issues. Disciplines that might provide a basis for ethical positions—science and ethics (including Christian ethics)—are reviewed, along with the adequacy of the scientist-practitioner model to inform the ethical aspects of practice. The specific contributions of Christian ethics to the dialogue needed between ethicists, theologians, and psychotherapy theorists and practitioners are discussed. Implications for training and continuing professional development are considered.

To transform, to be transformed, is to be immersed in matters ethical. Which directions, which ways of changing, are good? Which are best? Which behaviors are right? Which decisions are right? Which personal characteristics are virtuous? Which are not?

Christian faith and psychotherapy both cause personal transformation. They have to do with issues and questions of goodness, rightness, and virtue. Therapists can avoid these ethical questions or attempt neutrality. Doing so, however, will likely mean, not value-free therapy, but the captivity of therapists to the ethical claims of contemporary culture.

This will not concern Christians who think that modern (or "post modern") culture, including psychology and psychotherapy, warrants no critique or who ascribe to the position that Niebuhr (1951) termed "the Christ of Culture." However, other Christians see society as problematic. They hold that the proper relationship of Christ and culture is best expressed in one of Niebuhr's other options: (a) Christians should reject "the world," (b) the goodness of culture needs the addition of Christ and the Christian virtues, (c) culture—though in some sense appropriately authoritative—is in continual paradoxical tension with Christ, or (d) culture is in need of transformation. For these persons, conformity to culture is scarcely a desirable state.

Christian therapists holding one of those four views need to be intimately acquainted with, indeed shaped by, Christian ethics. This is because psychotherapy theorists and theologians sometimes give conflicting answers to the ethical questions involved in human transformation. Accordingly, few issues are of more importance to Christian therapists striving to provide therapy consistent with Christian faith or attempting to integrate psychology and theology.

In this article, I will first clarify how therapy is value-laden and how therapists function as ethicists. The sources of the ethical convictions to which therapy is inextricably tied will then be discussed, along with the claim that science alone is an adequate basis for therapy. Some ways in which Christian ethical traditions and the realities about which they speak might address and influence therapeutic transformations will then be discussed. Finally, implications for training and ongoing professional development will be considered.

Value-laden Therapy: The Therapist as Applied Ethicist

Although therapy was once widely considered to be value-free, it is no longer (London, 1986; Strupp, 1980). Values appear to be inescapably involved in theories of pathology and personality, the goals of therapy, the selection of method, and the evaluation of therapeutic outcome (Bergin, 1985, 1991). Further, the values in therapy may (and often do) pertain to religious and spiritual issues (Bergin, 1980, 1991; Bergin & Payne, 1991; Worthington, 1988, 1991). Models of human beings, which underlie and have an impact on therapy, contain normative or prescriptive elements, ideas about what human beings should be. These ideas influence the divisions between disciplines and professions, disciplinary methodology, codes of professional ethics, and therapist behavior (Tjeltveit, 1989b).

The ethical assertions (which is what I mean by "values" in this section) that are inherent in therapeutic goals are of particular importance. The values in some goals, such as reducing unnecessary suffering, are not controversial, but others, especially those in positive images of ideal human functioning, are. Suppose a client is exhausted and depressed, in part because of her frustrating work on her congregation's evangelism committee. All therapists would want to see her less depressed and able to deal with stress more effectively. What would be *best* for her, however? What would be ideal? What should she be free *for*? Some therapists, sharing the common view of American intellectuals that evangelism is intrinsically bad because it falsely claims that one religious position is superior to others, would be happy to see her devoting her time and energy to pursuits other than evangelism. Christian evangelism would hold no place in such therapists' visions, or range of visions, of optimal human functioning, an opinion that the client would undoubtedly detect; evangelism, in and of itself, would not be seen as *good*. Other therapists would be more neutral in their evaluations of evangelism. Still others would view it positively. Evangelism would be included in such therapists' range of visions of optimal human functioning; it would be seen as intrinsically good. All three sets of therapists would want to eliminate her depression; beyond that, differences, *ethical* differences, appear.

Given that values, ideas about ethical matters, are involved in therapy, therapists function as applied ethicists. That is, therapists reflect on, have convictions about, and/or attempt to influence others about the ethical aspects of practical situations.

I do not mean that the therapist is only an ethicist, or primarily an ethicist, but only that ethical tasks are one aspect of what a therapist does. No matter how he or she is intervening, a therapist has ideas about what is good, right, and virtuous and exercises some (greater or lesser) influence on clients concerning those ideas.

The influence of those ideas has been established in a line of research initiated by Rosenthal (1955). He found that in successful therapy, clients' values, including moral values, moved in the direction of therapists' values. Although the use of a wide variety of definitions of values in this line of research makes interpretation difficult (Kelly, 1990), some conclusions can be drawn. Beutler, in his (1981) review of the empirical research spawned by Rosenthal's study, concluded that therapists do, in fact, often influence client values. This value conversion raises questions, not only about the appropriateness of this influence, but also about the values with which therapy *should* be laden and how knowledge about values can be obtained.

The Intellectual Basis for Holding Particular Values or Ethical Positions

When therapists strive to deal with values in therapy in an appropriate way or when psychologists seek to understand the ethical aspects of psychotherapy, many turn to the literature on values and therapy. However, anyone attempting an intellectual understanding of values faces a profound difficulty: the plethora of definitions of values, too often unstated or contradictory (Kelly, 1990). This conceptual confusion makes clear thinking about the ethical aspects of psychotherapy extremely difficult—if, that is, the term *values* is used without being carefully and explicitly defined. Accordingly, before turning to a discussion of the intellectual basis for holding particular ethical positions, I will first spell out some of the varied (and often confused and conflated) contemporary definitions of values, doing so by reviewing some of the term's history. This discussion is intended both to document my assertion that a variety of definitions of values is extant and to contribute to the critical analysis of the literature on values and therapy by differentiating some of the various definitions used.

Borrowed from economics, the term *values* was, according to Tillich (1959), first applied to the ethical realm in the 19th century by the philosopher Lotze. Lotze's intent was to protect human dignity against the onslaught of a mechanistic, naturalistic, reductionistic philosophy associated with science. By *value*, he meant "what ought to be." Furthermore, about at least some aspects of value, he asserted that neither ontological nor scientific assertions could be made.

However, the concept of values, brought to the United States by Harvard's second psychologist, Hugo Munsterberg (Munsterberg, 1909; Rescher, 1969; Tillich, 1959; Werkmeister, 1970, 1973), was soon redefined to mean *beliefs* or *feelings* about what ought to be. A new generation of psychologists subjected these redefined values to scientific scrutiny.

Values can thus either refer (a) to what is good, right, or virtuous, what ought to be (with or without Lotze's metaphysical assumptions) or (b) to what is *believed* or *felt* to be good, right, or virtuous (Frankena, 1967). The first definition gets at the central, classical issues of ethics (my concern in this paper); the second type of definition (variants of which are usually used in psychology) does not.

Other important historical developments resulted in additional definitions of values. Logical positivists (e.g., Ayer, 1950) argued that it is impossible to make meaningful cognitive assertions about what is good, right, or virtuous. Existentialists denied that there is a human nature that might ground convictions about what is good, right, or virtuous, insisting instead that individual choice is of paramount importance (e.g., Sarte, 1943/1958, 1947). These forces and others combined to form a third common meaning of values: arbitrary choices for which no intellectually respectable reasons can be offered. Bellah, Madsen, Sullivan, Swidler, and Tipton (1985) found that Americans frequently use the term *values* in this sense, meaning "the incomprehensible, rationally indefensible thing that the individual chooses when he or she has thrown off the last vestige of external influence and reached pure, contentless freedom" (pp. 79-80). Those who use the term values in this set of senses would regard as nonsense the assumption implicit in this section's heading: that one can articulate an intellectual basis for values or ethical assertions.

In part as a reaction to these trends, some conservative Christians have loudly trumpeted the need to return to "American" or "Christian" or "family" values. Unfortunately, their approach—often rigid and moralistic—has led to a fourth connotation of *values*: the dogmatic imposition of authoritarianism. This has alienated them from many who share at least some convictions with them.

The use of four (or more) conflicting definitions of the term *values* in the literature on values and psychotherapy—often without clarity about which is intended—produces confusion and ambiguity. Although some uses of the term *values* may help illumine the ethical aspects of psychotherapy, I will instead generally use the term *ethical*. I do so to emphasize the fact that psychotherapy involves issues—such as what is good or bad, right or wrong, and virtuous or blameworthy—that are by their very nature ethical.

This question must then be faced: On what intellectual grounds can we make *ethical* assertions?

Science as the Source for Ethical Positions

When a question is posed, many turn first to science. But can scientific experiments, in and of themselves, produce knowledge about what is good, right, or virtuous? In a word, no. Ethical assertions cannot be derived logically from strictly factual assertions. (One ethical theory, *ethical naturalism*, for which some claim scientific status, is, in fact, a melange of science and philosophy. That is, it is an ethical theory not based solely on science.) Science can, of course, produce knowledge that is very pertinent to ethical judgments, including those made in therapy. One often needs to know what is the case to determine what *ought* to be the case (Frankena, 1973). If, for instance, we assume that a

decrease in the symptoms of mental illness is a good outcome, science can help us know if, or in what ways, psychotherapy produces that good outcome. Science cannot tell us, however, which outcomes are properly labeled "good."

This inability of science to provide the ethical positions involved in therapy presents a serious problem for the conscientious psychologist. The dominant training model in clinical psychology (and to varying degrees in other mental health professions) holds that the psychotherapist is, or ought to be, a scientist-practitioner. According to some interpretations of that model, and some ideas about applied psychology in general, clinical practice should stem from science. However, science cannot produce knowledge about the ethical issues that therapy involves. Therapists are thus saddled with an impossible task: They are to receive something from science that it cannot give them.

One proposed solution to this problem is to focus on consensus among mental health professionals. Bergin (1985), Strupp (1980), and Strupp & Hadley (1977) proposed sets of values believed to be consensual. Jensen and Bergin (1988) documented a broad consensus in therapist values. Consensual values, though important, are insufficient —for three reasons: (a) It is unclear why we ought to give any weight to consensus—the crowd may, after all, be wrong; (b) if there is no consensus among therapists regarding values related to religion of even a fairly general sort (Jensen & Bergin), even less agreement is likely about beliefs as specific as, "It is good to worship God" (understood in terms of the doctrine of the Trinity); and (c) Christian theology stands in reasoned dissent to some consensual values, for example, to mental health professionals rating salvation the lowest of eighteen terminal values (Cross & Khan, 1983). Is there warrant for belief in the goodness of worshiping God and of salvation? If yes, then a consensus against it ought not be determinative for the Christian. Indeed, some assert that discussions of worship and salvation under the heading of "values" reflect a profoundly impoverished understanding of the nature of transcendent spiritual reality.

O'Donohue (1989) recently suggested a promising alternative to deriving ethical positions from science or consensus: "The (even) bolder model: The clinical psychologist as metaphysician-scientist-practitioner" (p. 1460). His stress on the clinician as metaphysician (anticipated by Vande Kemp, 1976) underscored Browning's (1987) contention that science alone is inadequate to ground clinical practice. Fortunately, there is another discipline—ethics—

that, when joined with science, permits the development of a more adequate intellectual basis for holding the ethical positions with which therapy is laden.

Ethics as the Source for Ethical Positions

Ethical issues have long been addressed by the discipline of ethics. I believe that it is to this venerable scholarly tradition that therapists—all therapists—need to turn to address well the ethical questions involved in therapy. In fact, the ethical principles of the American Psychological Association (Ethics Committee of the American Psychological Association, 1990) hold that psychologists recognize the limitations of their competence. If called upon to address matters beyond those limitations, therapists are to refer, obtain consultation, or obtain pertinent training. If therapists trained only as scientists function ineluctably as ethicists, training in ethics (in general, not simply professional ethics) and metaphysics seems indicated. Christian theology and ethics address metaphysical and ethical issues. They can thus be one source of types of knowledge that therapists need but that science cannot provide.

What is the appropriate relationship between science, psychotherapeutic theories, ethics in general, and Christian ethics in providing a basis for therapeutic practice? I am convinced that if Christian therapists wish public recognition as professionals and want the best possible answers to ethical questions, the relationship must be dialogical, with the questions and explanations of each of the four taken seriously. Dialogue will not, of course, resolve all these issues. This is in part because the various explanations will sometimes conflict, so choices will need to be made. Optimal solutions will only emerge from such dialogue, however.

What I will stress in the remainder of this paper is but one part of that dialogue: the contributions of Christian ethics to the role of therapist as applied ethicist. Christians need to articulate such contributions thoughtfully and not yield to those claiming "scientific" status for the ethical convictions implicit in their therapeutic theories.

The Relevance of Christian Ethics to the Christian Therapist

Christian Ethics

How do Christian ethicists approach ethical issues? In his overview of Christian ethics, Long (1967, 1982) focused on two basic issues: setting ethical standards and implementing ethical decisions. Therapists, of course, set goals (which involve ethical positions) and seek, in cooperation with clients, to implement those goals.

Three motifs express how ethical standards are set in Christian ethics (Long, 1967). The *deliberative* motif emphasizes reason, seen as the major or sole source of such standards or as that which provides the categories within which specifically Christian themes are articulated. In the second motif, the *prescriptive*, particular ethical injunctions or prescriptions, such as loving one's neighbor, are stressed. These are seen to stem from God's will—expressed in authoritative Scripture, through Christian community, or both (cf. Mouw, 1990). Advocates of the third motif, the *relational*, argue that in the gracious relationship between God and human beings, human beings are transformed. From that transformation come behavior and personal characteristics later seen to be ethical in nature.

Recently, Christian ethicists (e.g., Hauerwas, 1975, 1981; Meilaender, 1984) have stressed the ways in which community shapes personal character. Character and community have to do with the sort of persons we are and thus how we approach ethical issues and answer ethical questions.

When Long (1967) reviewed Christian ethicists' discussions of *implementing* ethical decisions, he again found three motifs. The *institutional* motif stresses the authority of institutions; orders of creation; or offices, spheres, or structures within society (such as the family, government, or church). These are believed to foster ideals such as justice more effectively than alternatives. Persons occupying roles in such God-given structures therefore ought to command respect.

Similarly, some argue that therapists occupy a divinely established "office" or "order of creation." This means that a competent therapist who provides excellent "secular" therapy in a "secular" setting—that is, whose actions are in accord with the office of the therapist in contemporary society—is fully doing the work of God. This office also means that therapists refrain from certain behaviors with clients, for instance, espousal of ethical, political, or religious positions, even though it would be appropriate for non-therapists to engage in such behaviors. By limiting their behaviors to those appropriate to the office of therapist, therapists optimally implement the ideals of therapy as set forth in society.

The *operational* motif stresses the importance of power and influence in ensuring justice and societal well-being. Similarly, some psychologists have stressed the role of persuasion or social influence in producing change in therapy (Brehm & Smith, 1986; Strong & Claiborn, 1982), such as change stemming from implementing therapist goals, values, or ethical positions.

The *intentional* motif involves the creation of "special communities of dedication and renewal" (Long, 1967, p. 168). This may mean monasticism; sectarian removal from the world (e.g., the Amish); and small groups to develop religious zeal, moral improvement, or both. Those small groups may be a part of (e.g., those of the early Wesley) or apart from (e.g., InterVarsity) organized church structures. Their commonality is "a heroic ethic, a demanding morality, and the satisfaction attending the performance of special duties" (Long, p. 252).

Long (1967) concluded by suggesting the complementarity of the sets of motifs and arguing that all the motifs be used in concert, with the strengths of one correcting the weaknesses of another.

Application to Psychotherapy

What contributions can Christian ethics make to a distinctively Christian therapy? It should go without saying that I reject one meaning of "distinctively Christian." To say, for instance, that the ideal of loving one's neighbor is distinctively Christian does *not* mean that Christians alone love their neighbors or believe that they should. It means that an emphasis on love *distinguishes* a Christian ethical approach from at least one other approach to ethics, for example, Nietzsche's.

What role, then, should Christian ethics play in the therapy provided by the Christian therapist? Christian ethics can help therapists set ethical ideals and determine ideal ways of implementing those ideals.

Setting ethical ideals. The deliberative motif in Christian ethics can acquaint a therapist with the history of ethical reflection in the Church and foster clear thinking about ethical issues. Of central importance is clear thinking about the relationship between the ethical positions of therapists and those of Christian ethicists. Browning (1987) illustrated this. He discussed Freud's radical criticism of the idea of loving one's neighbor in relationship to Niebuhr's theological understanding of agape. The result? A rejection of Freud's position on neighbor love along with an appreciation for some of his analysis. Similarly, from an explicitly Christian perspective, Jones has critiqued behavior therapy (1988) and rational-emotive therapy (1989), and Jones and Butman (1991) critically analyzed other therapeutic approaches.

The prescriptive motif calls the Christian to take seriously the Bible as the source of ethical standards. The relational motif stresses the importance of taking seriously the role of relationship with God and Christian community in shaping ethical charac-

ter. The relational motif and the recent emphasis on community and character also serve to counteract what is sometimes an overly rational approach by ethicists. Christian action and character are seen to develop, not primarily from intellectual reflection, but through one's history of transformation in relationship with God and Christian community.

Critical interaction is essential, critical interaction between Christian ethics and the ethical positions in psychotherapeutic theorists' ideas about mental health and ideal human functioning. Christians ought not ignore those ideas or the value consensus among therapists. This is not necessarily because of the *full* adequacy of those ideas or that consensus, but because there is some empirical support behind them and undoubtedly some wisdom. This is true even when the extra-scientific, ethical aspects of such ideas go unrecognized by their adherents.

However, it is clear that there are several ways in which Christian views of ideal human functioning will diverge from the value consensus of therapists (Tjeltveit, 1991). To the extent that there is distinctiveness to the Christian worldview and to Christian ethical perspectives, there will be distinctively Christian ethical positions about optimal ethical ideals in therapy. For instance, if worshiping God and loving one's neighbor (even when requiring personal sacrifice) are good and valuable, then a Christian therapist's vision of human wholeness should include them, even though a consensus about those ideals is not present among therapists.

It is also the case that Christian ethics places ideals about mental health within a broader context, the context of what is ultimately worthwhile. This means that Christian ethics may well produce a different ordering of various goods. For instance, the Christian therapist may *not* consider the goodness of complete freedom from anxiety to be of ultimate importance, as other therapists might. Rather, the (genuine) goodness of freedom from anxiety may be considered less important than the goodness of salvation or the goodness of insuring justice for the oppressed.

Implementing ethical ideals. Well-socialized therapists are surely by now asking: But isn't it dangerous for therapists to bring their theological and ethical convictions to bear on therapy they provide? Shouldn't therapy be value-free?

The phrasing of those questions is, of course, problematic. Therapists—Christian or not—inevitably bring their values and theological and ethical convictions to bear on the therapy that they provide. However, those questions do point to an important ethical issue: the *manner* in which therapist values impact psychotherapy, that is, how therapists *implement* ethical ideals.

Such ethical questions should be addressed both in an interpersonal dialogue (between psychotherapy professionals and Christian ethicists) and in an intrapersonal dialogue (a dialogue within the Christian therapist between ideas derived from the psychotherapeutic professions and ideas derived from Christian ethics). We need to clarify the relationship between (a) the codes and principles of professional ethics and (b) Christian ideas about how ethical decisions should be implemented. If one has an ethical ideal, there are better and worse ways of bringing about the desired end. There are less than optimal, unethical, and even dangerous ways of implementing ideals. For instance, there is a decided difference between an atheistic therapist manipulatively coercing a Christian client into conversion to atheism and that therapist simply raising questions about a client's faith in a way which preserves the client's freedom.

As I discussed above, Christian ethicists have used several motifs to address how ethical ideals should be implemented. Reconciling these motifs with each other and with professional codes of ethics can, at times, be very difficult. In the remainder of this section, I will first review how the three motifs suggest that therapists should implement ethical positions in therapy. I will then sketch out my own, decidedly paradoxical position, which combines professional ethics and all six of the motifs of Christian ethics in a way that embraces each of them yet also makes clear how they can, in at least some instances, conflict with each other.

The first of Long's (1967) motifs, the institutional, suggests that such institutions as the family and the church play a crucial role in helping a person move in the direction of ideal (psychological/ethical/spiritual) human functioning. Given the individualistic tendencies of contemporary society and psychology (Bellah et al., 1985; Sampson, 1977; Vitz, 1977; Wallach & Wallach, 1983), this motif may be of particular contemporary importance.

This motif may also suggest that the office or institution of therapist is God-given and ought to function autonomously, according to its own norms and rules. As government, instituted by God, ought to be followed, so ought contemporary schools of therapy. This implies that, regarding mental health issues, Christian ethics is essentially coterminous with professional ethics. The "good Christian therapist" is the professionally responsible therapist —nothing more, nothing less. As government officials appropriately keep their religious convictions separate from their official duties, therapists appropriately keep their religious convictions (including associated ethical positions) separate from their work with clients.

Other ethical motifs would stress the importance of power and influence and the role of special, intentional communities in implementing ethical decisions. These motifs hold that society, including the role of therapy in it, may need to be challenged and that some sort of differentiation from society may be crucially important in helping people reach an ethical ideal, a spiritual ideal, or both. These motifs may thus lead Christians to criticize therapists' deemphasis on family and church, challenge the sufficiency of therapeutic procedures isolated from Christian community, or argue for the importance, not of involvement with "the world," but of some sort of conscious distinction from it. In other words, the ethical convictions of Christian psychotherapists should be part of, not "separate from," their work with clients.

How do these motifs of Christian ethics connect with the codes and standards of professional ethics? I have elsewhere (1986, 1989a) discussed the professional ethical issues raised by therapists' influence on clients' values, including moral values and religiously grounded values. Therapists appropriately clarify values, correct cognitive mistakes in clients' ethical positions, and convert clients to mental health values as distinguished from moral or religious values. (Although it is now more clear to me how inextricably ethical and religious issues are tied to mental health values, and thus how difficult it is to draw a distinction between mental health values and moral or religious values, I still defend a form of the distinction.) I pointed out the ethical problems of eliminating or reducing clients' freedom to choose their own values, of violating the therapeutic contract, of failing to provide clients with adequate information about psychotherapy (including its possible impact on values), and of therapists venturing beyond their competence. I discussed proposals to address those problems, including, "therapist training, therapist-client matching, referral, informed consent, and changing roles" (1986, p. 515). While acknowledging the inevitability of values being present in therapy, I urged therapists to be very cautious in actively addressing client values, especially client moral, religious, and political values.

How can that be reconciled with my (scarcely cautious) position in this article that theology should be applied to therapy? Does my (1986) call for caution stem from my (perhaps excessive) reliance on the institutional motif (consistent with my Lutheranism), which holds that God generally works well through "secular" structures in society, especially when those in such structures stay within their appropriate limits and uphold pertinent standards of professional conduct? Not entirely.

I believe that there is a more or less explicit contract between therapists and society as a whole (including third party reimbursers) concerning psychotherapy. According to this contract, the primary focus of therapy is to be psychological disorder; client moral and religious values are not to be influenced. Therapists therefore ought to minimize their influence on those values; to do otherwise is to violate the contract. (Alternately—to use more explicitly theological language, language that is perhaps reflective of a more adequate theological grounding for the professional role of the therapist—therapists who unduly influence clients' values violate the covenant between therapist and client [cf. Bouma, Diekema, Langerak, Rottman, & Verhey, 1989; and Ramsey, 1970]). Bergin's (1980) critique of therapist insensitivity to religious values is exactly on the mark here.

Isn't value influence inevitable, though? Yes, it is. Therefore, Christian therapists working in the public arena ought to think as carefully as possible about ideals for human functioning so that their inevitable (and appropriate) value influence will be as consistent with Christian ethics as possible.

However, might not a focus only on eliminating mental disorders or on consensual mental health values (generally agreed upon therapy goals in the typical therapy contract) lead to a truncated, impoverished, or perhaps even fundamentally misguided view of optimal human functioning? Again, yes. Christians ought not to see the elimination of mental illness (the central goal of the office of the psychotherapist) as the highest human good. Consensual values do not express what is most important in the Christian vision of human fulfillment.

However, both professional and Christian ethics suggest that Christian therapists need to be very careful when striving to bring about full-orbed (that is, psychological, ethical, *and* spiritual) behavior change and personal growth. Change agents (therapists, counselors, or pastors) need to have the requisite training in *all* areas addressed, third party reimbursement ought *not* be sought where the primary focus of the relationship is on ethical or spiritual problems, clients need to be given adequate information about the nature of the relationship (including its deviation from "typical" psychotherapy), clients must give informed consent, and client freedom needs to be protected (Tjeltveit, 1986).

When these (far too often ignored) crucial differences between ordinary psychotherapy and explicitly Christian therapy are acknowledged and taken into account, psychotherapy that is informed by Christian ethics can reach, and reach appropriately, its full and very substantial potential.

Implications for Education and Professional Development

How can therapists be trained to do applied ethics well? How can Christians learn to apply Christian ethics to clinical practice? These are difficult questions, involving issues of moral education beyond the scope of this paper. Some brief comments are in order, however.

To develop ethical acumen, therapists need to interact with others about ethical matters. This should include persons whom Meehl (1981) called "ERDERVE-qualified," those who have, concerning ethical issues, engaged in "Extended Rational Discussion [based on] Extensive Real [and] Vicarious Experience" (p. 7). Learning Christian ethics well, of course, also requires both the development of wisdom (as discussed by Evans, 1992) and being rooted in Christian community.

Which training model should be used? The scientist-practitioner model clearly needs to be expanded to the metaphysician-scientist-ethicist-practitioner model (cf. O'Donohue, 1989). To train psychotherapists in these ways is obviously no easy matter, but neither is psychotherapy.

Where fidelity with Christian faith is sought, the ethical component of training requires pursuit of five educational goals: (a) knowledge of the content of the Christian ethical traditions; (b) skill in ethical reflection, including application of ethical principles and ideals to particular cases; (c) ability to critically analyze the ethical positions implicit in therapeutic theories and practices and in client statements and behaviors; (d) ability to critically relate Christian ethics and the ethical positions of therapists and clients, affirming what is good and challenging what is not; and (e) ability to integrate Christian ethical positions into the practice of psychotherapy.

Two aspects of the content of the Christian ethical tradition are important. The emphasis in much recent ethical reflection on ethical dilemmas and on obligation needs to be joined with clear thinking about ethical *ideals*—moral health, mental health, and spiritual health. At issue here is not only which decisions are right but also which ways of living are good and best. How does one order the various goods in life? For instance, where a choice must be made, which is of more importance—the good of personal fulfillment or the good of commitment to spouse and family?

Secondly, we need to return regularly to the broader context of ethical reflection, the context of relationship with God and Christian community. For the Christian, it is not sufficient merely to be an ethicist. Indeed, it is most dangerous to assert that particular values (even in the sense of ethical assertions) are *the* distinguishing mark of the Christian therapist, for that reduces faith to ethics. This danger is illustrated by a student of Lotze, the originator of a modern usage of *values*. According to Tillich (1959), that student, Albrecht Ritschl, brought the term *values* to theology and reduced theology to value judgments, judgments unconnected to ontology. A focus on the broader theological context of ethics and therapy can help therapists avoid repeating Ritschl's mistake. That context is essential, lest the ethics that informs therapy cease to be *Christian* ethics.

The broader context of the relationship of persons with God and Christian community also pertains to the challenge of the fifth educational goal. According to many psychological theorists and many Christian ethicists, translating ethics into action is not simply, and perhaps not even primarily, a rational process. Rather, it involves some sort of personal transformation. This may involve emotional issues, resolving issues from childhood, and relearning. For the Christian, however, it also involves Christian community, sin, spirituality, and grace. A therapist untransformed is unlikely to transform clients optimally.

Conclusion

Psychotherapy cannot be based on science alone, in part because therapy is inextricably ethical in nature. Therapists therefore function as ethicists. Christians seeking to provide therapy consistent with Christian faith need immersion in the traditions of Christian ethics. When applied to therapy with openness, clear thinking, humility, and conviction, Christian ethics can help assure that the transformations of psychotherapy are transformations consonant with Christian faith, that they are ethical transformations of grace.

References

Ayer, A. J. (1950). *Language, truth, and logic.* New York: Dover.

Bellah, R. N., Madsen, R., Sullivan, W. M., Swidler, A., & Tipton, S. M. (1985). *Habits of the heart: Individualism and commitment in American life.* New York: Harper & Row.

Bergin, A. E. (1980). Psychotherapy and religious values. *Journal of Consulting and Clinical Psychology, 48,* 170-184.

Bergin, A. E. (1985). Proposed values for guiding and evaluating counseling and psychotherapy. *Counseling and Values, 29,* 99-116.

Bergin, A. E. (1991). Values and religious issues in psychotherapy and mental health. *American Psychologist, 46,* 394-403.

Bergin, A. E., & Payne, I. R. (1991). Proposed agenda for a spiritual strategy in personality and psychotherapy. *Journal of Psychology and Christianity, 10,* 197-210.

Beutler, L. E. (1981). Convergence in counseling and psychotherapy: A current look. *Clinical Psychology Review, 1,* 79-101.

Bouma, H., III, Diekema, D., Langerak, E., Rottman, T., & Verhey, A. (1989). *Christian faith, health, and medical practice.* Grand Rapids: Eerdmans.

Brehm, S. S., & Smith, T. W. (1986). Social psychological approaches to psychotherapy and behavior change. In S. L. Garfield & A. E. Bergin (Eds.), *Handbook of psychotherapy and behavior change* (pp. 69-115). New York: Wiley.

Browning, D. S. (1987). *Religious thought and the modern psychologies: A critical conversation in the theology of culture.* Philadelphia: Fortress.

Cross, D. G., & Khan, J. A. (1983). The values of three practitioner groups: Religious and moral aspects. *Counseling and Values, 28,* 13-19.

Ethics Committee of the American Psychological Association. (1990). Ethical principles of psychologists (Amended June 2, 1989). *American Psychologist, 45,* 390-395.

Evans, C. S. (1992). Developing wisdom in Christian psychologists. *Journal of Psychology and Theology, 20,* 110-118.

Frankena, W. K. (1967). Value and valuation. In P. Edwards (Ed.), *Encyclopedia of philosophy* (Vol. 8, pp. 229-232). New York: Macmillan.

Frankena, W. K. (1973). *Ethics* (2nd ed.). Englewood Cliffs, NJ: Prentice-Hall.

Hauerwas, S. (1975). *Character and the Christian life: A study in theological ethics.* San Antonio, TX: Trinity University Press.

Hauerwas, S. (1981). *A community of character: Toward a constructive Christian social ethic.* Notre Dame: University of Notre Dame Press.

Jensen, J. P., & Bergin, A. E. (1988). Mental health values of professional therapists: A national interdisciplinary survey. *Professional Psychology: Research and Practice, 19,* 290-297.

Jones, S. L. (1988). A religious critique of behavior therapy. In W. R. Miller & J. E. Martin (Eds.), *Behavior therapy and religion: Integrating spiritual and behavioral approaches to change* (pp. 139-170). Newbury Park, CA: Sage.

Jones, S. L. (1989). Rational-emotive therapy in Christian perspective. *Journal of Psychology and Theology, 17,* 110-120.

Jones, S. L., & Butman, R. (1991). *Modern psychotherapies: A comprehensive Christian appraisal.* Downers Grove, IL: InterVarsity.

Kelly, T. (1990). The role of values in psychotherapy: A critical review of process and outcome effects. *Clinical Psychology Review, 10*, 171-186.

London, P. (1986). *The modes and morals of psychotherapy* (2nd ed.). Washington: Hemisphere.

Long, E. L., Jr. (1967). *A survey of Christian ethics*. New York: Oxford University Press.

Long, E. L., Jr. (1982). *A recent survey of Christian ethics*. New York: Oxford University Press.

Meehl, P. E. (1981). Ethical criticism in value clarification: Correcting cognitive errors within the client's—not the therapist's—framework. *Rational Living, 16*, 3-9.

Meilaender, G. C. (1984). *The theory and practice of virtue*. Notre Dame: University of Notre Dame Press.

Mouw, R. J. (1990). *The God who commands: A study in divine command ethics*. Notre Dame: University of Notre Dame Press.

Munsterberg, H. (1909). *The eternal values*. New York: Houghton Mifflin.

Niebuhr, H. R. (1951). *Christ and culture*. New York: Harper & Row.

O'Donohue, W. (1989). The (even) bolder model: The clinical psychologist as metaphysician-scientist-practitioner. *American Psychologist, 44*, 1460-1468.

Perry, R. B. (1954). *Realms of value: A critique of human civilization*. Cambridge: Harvard University Press.

Ramsey, P. (1970). *The patient as person*. New Haven: Yale University Press.

Rescher, N. (1969). *Introduction to value theory*. Englewood Cliffs, NJ: Prentice. Hall.

Rosenthal, D. (1955). Changes in some moral values following psychotherapy. *Journal of Consulting Psychology, 19*, 431-436.

Sampson, E. E. (1977). Psychology and the American ideal. *Journal of Personality and Social Psychology, 35*, 767-782.

Sarte, J. (1947). *Existentialism* (B. Frechtman, Trans.). New York: Philosophical Library.

Sarte, J. (1958). *Being and nothingness: An essay on phenomenology ontology* (H.E. Barnes, Trans.). London: Methuen. (Original work published 1943)

Strong, S. R., & Claiborn, C. D. (1982). *Change through interaction: Social psychological processes of counseling and psychotherapy*. New York: Wiley.

Strupp, H. H. (1980). Humanism and psychotherapy: A personal statement of the therapist's essential values. *Psychotherapy: Theory, Research and Practice, 17*, 396-400.

Strupp, H. H., & Hadley, S. W. (1977). A tripartite model of mental health and therapeutic outcomes with special reference to negative effects in psychotherapy. *American Psychologist, 32*, 187-196.

Tillich, P. (1959). Is a science of human values possible? In A. Maslow (Ed.), *New knowledge inhuman values* (pp. 189-196). New York: Harpers.

Tjeltveit, A. C. (1986). The ethics of value conversion in psychotherapy: Appropriate and inappropriate therapist influence on client values. *Clinical Psychology Review, 6*, 515-537.

Tjeltveit, A. C. (1989a). Dealing with value dilemmas in therapy. In P. A. Keller & S. R. Heyman (Eds.), *Innovations in clinical practice: A source book* (Vol. 8, pp. 405-415). Sarasota, FL: Professional Resource Exchange.

Tjeltveit, A. C. (1989b). The ubiquity of models of human beings in psychotherapy: The need for rigorous reflection. *Psychotherapy, 26*, 1-10.

Tjeltveit, A. C. (1991). Christian ethics and psychological explanations of "religious values" in therapy: Critical connections. *Journal of Psychology and Christianity, 10*, 101-112.

Vande Kemp, H. (1976, March). *The therapist as metaphysician*. Paper presented at the convention of the Kansas Psychological Association, Topeka.

Vitz, P. C. (1977). *Psychology as religion: The cult of self-worship*. Grand Rapids: Eerdmans.

Wallach, M. A., & Wallach, L. (1983). *Psychology's sanction for selfishness: The error of egoism in theory and therapy*. San Francisco: Freeman.

Werkmeister, W. H. (1970). *Historical spectrum of value theories, Vol. 1: The German group*. Lincoln, NE: Johnsen.

Werkmeister, W. H. (1973). *Historical spectrum of value theories, Vol. 2: The Anglo-American Group*. Lincoln, NE: Johnsen.

Worthington, E. L., Jr. (1988). Understanding the values of religious clients: A model and its application to counseling. *Journal of Counseling Psychology, 35*, 166-174.

Worthington, E. L., Jr. (1991). Psychotherapy and religious values: An update. *Journal of Psychology and Christianity, 10*, 211-223.

26

Integration in the Therapy Room:
An Overview of the Literature

M. Elizabeth Lewis Hall
Family Life Counseling and Educational Center
Todd W. Hall
Raymond W. Bliss Army Community Hospital

Clinical integration refers to the incorporation of religious or spiritual beliefs, values, and methods into the process of psychotherapy that results in a different way of being as a therapist, understanding the client, and/or doing therapy. Two goals are pursued in this article: (a) to provide an overview of what has been done in clinical integration over the past 25 years; and (b) to point the reader to resources in each of the areas addressed in this article. First, the foundations for clinical integration that have been laid over the years are outlined. These include pragmatic, ethical, empirical, and personal reasons for engaging in clinical integration. Following this, an overview of the spectrum of clinical integration is described. The incorporation of religious values and beliefs, religious content in traditional psychological frameworks, and spiritually-derived goals and techniques are discussed. Finally, some ethical considerations in pursuing clinical integration are outlined.

In this article, the term clinical integration, broadly defined, refers to the incorporation of religious or spiritual beliefs, values, and methods into the process of psychotherapy that results in a different way of being a therapist, understanding the client, or doing therapy. Over the past 25 years a large and varied body of literature has emerged that addresses the task of clinical integration. This literature has taken the form of books and articles that demonstrate clinical integration through case studies or address theoretical issues and prescribe clinical interventions based on theory. Over time the impetus for clinical integration has gained momentum as therapists from a range of backgrounds, religious and nonreligious, have recognized the importance of taking religious beliefs and values into account in the therapy process.

Some leading proponents of psychotherapy have argued that clinical integration is the next logical step in attempting to make psychotherapy more effective by incorporating all aspects of individuals in the psychotherapy process. Bergin (1980, 1988; Bergin & Payne, 1991), for example, suggests that religion should be incorporated more systematically into psychotherapy in order to be more effective. He describes how a spiritual approach can be integrated into psychotherapy in three ways that enhance therapy's ability to produce change. In the first place, it contributes to one's understanding of human nature by acknowledging that there is a spiritual reality and that spiritual experiences make a difference in human behavior. This perspective can lead to an exploration of the laws or principles that guide this spiritual "system," which can then guide interventions. Second, a spiritual perspective anchors values in universal terms, which help to determine the goals of treatment, the selection of techniques, and the evaluation of outcomes. Finally, a spiritual perspective allows the therapist to draw on a broad range of techniques, including intrapsychic methods such as prayer, rituals, and Scripture study, as well as community resources such as communal spiritual experiences.

The growing awareness of clinical integration is evident in several milestones in the recent past: (a) the inclusion of religion as an element of human diversity in the American Psychological Association's (APA) (1992) code of ethics; (b) the inclusion of spiritual problems as a V-code in the DSM-IV (American Psychiatric Association, 1994); and, most recently, (c) a number of important publications dedicated to religious therapy (see Worthington, Kurusu, McCullough, & Sandage, 1996, for a review), including APA's Religion and the Clinical Practice of Psychology (Shafranske, 1996), a comprehensive book on clinical integration. Two goals are pursued in this article: (a) to provide an overview of what has been done in clinical integration over the past 25 years; and (b) to point the reader to resources in each of the areas addressed in the article.

© *Journal of Psychology and Theology*, 1997, *25*, 86-101. Used by permission.

Several caveats are in order. Space limitations preclude this article from being comprehensive; rather, the purpose is to provide a general overview. Nor will it provide in-depth coverage of each area. Readers are encouraged to use the cited references as starting points for further inquiry into different areas. In addition, it is beyond the scope of this article to evaluate or endorse approaches to clinical integration, since use of a particular model should be decided by each clinician on the basis of his or her religiosity, comfort level, training, and the needs of each clinician's clientele. This article will primarily address clinical integration within a Judeo-Christian tradition. Much of the available literature is descriptive, in the form of case studies and prescriptions for clinical interventions, but the available empirical literature will also be summarized. For a more detailed account of research in clinical integration, see Worthington et al. (1996).

In the following paragraphs, three broad areas of clinical integration will be addressed. First, the foundations for clinical integration that have been laid over the years are outlined. Following this, an overview of the spectrum of clinical integration is provided. Finally, some ethical considerations in doing clinical integration are discussed.

Foundations for Clinical Integration

The development of clinical integration by psychotherapy practitioners has been in response to the needs of their clientele. With time, a solid foundation for the practice of clinical integration has been laid, in the form of a strong apologetic for its existence. In the following paragraphs the pragmatic, ethical, empirical, and personal reasons for practicing clinical integration will be briefly outlined.

Two pragmatic reasons exist for the role of integrative psychotherapy: a significant proportion of the population seem to prefer religiously-sensitive psychotherapy, and religious material may be unavoidable in therapy. Quackenbos, Privette, and Klentz (1985) found that 35 percent of people in a random sample preferred religious counseling, while 79 percent felt that religious values should be discussed in therapy. Numerous studies have shown that highly religious clients of several religious orientations were reluctant to seek conventional psychological help (Dougherty & Worthington, 1982; Gass, 1984; King, 1978; Richards & Davison, 1989; Wyatt & Johnson, 1990). After reviewing a number of studies, Worthington (1986) noted that highly religious clients appear to fear having their values changed and being misunderstood or misdiagnosed, and that the former, though not the latter, fear was

well-founded. After a comprehensive review of the pertinent literature, Worthington et al. (1996) concluded that highly religious people may prefer religious counselors and explicitly religious counseling, and that this type of therapy may facilitate the exploration of intimate topics.

A second pragmatic reason for addressing religious values in therapy is that religious material may be unavoidable. The persistence and pervasiveness of religious concerns and moral values is an indication that this is an important area for most people. In addition, psychotherapy and religion overlap in their scope of concern with regard to the meaning of life and moral values.

Second, ethical reasons exist for integrating religious values into the psychotherapy process. Religion is an important variable in human diversity, and, as with all factors of diversity, it should be respected and taken into account in therapy. Religious beliefs and values are an important motivational force in many religiously-committed clients. Worthington et al. (1996) have noted that multiculturalism is a "fourth force" in psychology, and consequently the needs of religious clients are becoming a more prominent and acceptable focus of research and treatment.

It has long been recognized that psychotherapy is not a value-neutral process, and that therapist values tend to influence both the goals and the process of therapy (Bergin, 1980). In addition, a substantial body of research suggests that successful therapeutic outcome involves the client taking on the therapist's values, a phenomenon known as value convergence (see Worthington, 1991; Worthington et al., 1996 for reviews). Research shows that value changes tend to occur more with personal and mental health values than with religious values, which appear to be quite resistant to change (Kelly & Strupp, 1992). Although recent findings have questioned the pervasiveness of value convergence (Kelly & Strupp, 1992), it is clear that therapy is a value-laden enterprise, and that values play an important role in what transpires between client and therapist.

When the therapist's perspectives on religion and spirituality diverge widely from those of the client, the therapist is in danger of acting unethically by imposing his or her values without the client's consent. If this imposition occurs, it shows a lack of respect both for the client's value system and for the social system represented by the value system (McMinn, 1984). In order to avoid unethical behavior, the therapist should be careful to obtain informed consent from the client, which may involve revealing the therapist's values, goals, and therapeutic procedures (Bergin, Payne, & Richards, 1996; Humphries, 1982; Lewis & Epperson, 1991). This information allows clients to exercise freedom and take responsibility for the choice to participate in a potentially value-changing experience. Another alternative is to match the client and therapist on religious values. In either case the clinician should be sensitive to how religious issues and values impact the therapeutic process.

A third reason for the existence of clinical integration is that this type of therapy may be more effective than traditional psychotherapy for religiously committed clients. Two lines of research suggest this: (a) client-therapist matching on religious variables in relationship to outcome; and (b) effectiveness of religiously-oriented psychotherapy approaches.

Similarity in client-therapist values has been found to relate to outcome. Kelly and Strupp (1992), echoing early research (e.g., Cook, 1966), found the best match to be between therapists and clients whose values were neither too similar nor too different. This may be because dyads that are too similar could potentially fail to recognize and explore important values because of a lack of cognitive dissonance. In contrast, a wide disparity in values could hinder the building of a therapeutic alliance and lead to premature terminations.

Although research in client-therapist matching in the general population has not led to conclusive results regarding its importance, in a highly religious population, the research does seem to suggest that client-therapist similarity is beneficial (Worthington, 1991), influencing expectations about therapy and the quality of the therapeutic relationship (see Worthington, 1988, for a review). Kelly and Strupp (1992), for example, found only one value on which client-therapist matching correlated positively with outcome: "salvation." Worthington (1988, 1991) suggested that three religious variables seem to be important to highly religious clients in evaluating therapy: (a) the authority of Scripture; (b) the authority of ecclesiastical leaders; and (c) the degree to which the person identifies with the norms of his or her religious group.

A second empirical reason for clinical integration is that some research indicates that it may be more effective with religiously committed clients than secular therapy. Johnson (1993), in a review of the literature found only five studies that compared religious interventions to similar secular interventions. Two of these showed better treatment outcomes for religious therapy (Propst, 1980; Propst, Ostrom, Watkins, Dean, & Mashburn, 1992). This conclusion should be held tentatively, as other research did not

yield significant results (Johnson & Ridley, 1992; Pecheur & Edwards, 1984). Since Johnson's review, Azhar & Varma (1995a, 1995b; Azhar, Varma, & Dharap, 1994) have shown religious psychotherapy to achieve therapeutic results more quickly than secular therapy in a sample of Islamic patients. The results of these studies suggest that religious therapy may indeed be more effective than secular therapy with highly religious clients, although, as Johnson noted, further research with good methodologies is needed.

A fourth reason for doing clinical integration is that it may be more congruent for the religiously-oriented clinician. Worthington (1994) has provided a helpful outline for integrating personal faith with the practice of therapy. Religious clinicians may feel it is important to incorporate their world view and values into their work for the sake of personal integrity (e.g., Bergin, 1980). For example, a Christian world view might suggest that certain procedures or goals in therapy are preferable to others. Tjeltveit (1991) argues that Christian ethics are relevant to therapy in that they provide a basis for determining good and right outcomes and processes, a framework of the ultimate context of life, and the meaning of moral and religious aspects of therapy.

The Spectrum of Clinical Integration

Tan (1996) makes a useful distinction between implicit and explicit integration. He states that "implicit integration of religion in clinical integration refers to a more covert approach that does not initiate the discussion of religious or spiritual issues and does not openly, directly, or systematically use spiritual resources like prayer and Scripture or other sacred texts, in therapy" (p. 368). This form of integration consists of practicing therapy in a way that is consistent with the therapists' own values, for example, praying for a client, respecting a client's religious values, and dealing with religious and spiritual issues when they are brought up by the client. Explicit integration, in contrast, refers to "a more overt approach that directly and systematically deals with spiritual or religious issues in therapy, and uses spiritual resources like prayer, Scripture or sacred texts, referrals to church or other religious groups or lay counselors, and other religious practices" (p. 368). He suggests that implicit and explicit integration can be conceptualized as two ends of a continuum of integration.

Attempts to take an individual's religiosity or spirituality into account in therapy can take place at two levels: understanding the client in a different way, and doing therapy in a different way. A different understanding of the client occurs when the therapist is aware of how the client's religious beliefs and values impact the therapeutic process, as well as how the therapist's beliefs and values come to bear in this task. A different way of doing therapy may involve different goals and techniques. Spiritually-sensitive techniques take two forms: (a) techniques originating from a psychological theory, but with spiritually-oriented content; and (b) techniques that originate from a spiritual tradition and are used within the context of the therapy in order to achieve a therapeutic outcome (Bergin & Payne, 1992; cf. Worthington, Dupont, Berry, & Duncan, 1988).

In the following paragraphs, the different approaches to clinical integration will be explored. The integration of religious beliefs and values, spiritual content, and spiritual goals and techniques will each be reviewed, although it should be noted that there is some overlap between these categories. These three areas can be considered a rough spectrum of clinical integration, ranging from an acknowledgment of religious beliefs and values, to a more intentional effort to include spiritual issues in the framework of traditional psychotherapy, and, finally, to an integration, not only of spiritual issues, but also of spiritual goals and techniques. This spectrum corresponds to Tan's (1996) description of a continuum between implicit and explicit integration.

Values and Beliefs in Clinical Integration

Clinical integration in its most minimal form involves the therapist's knowledge of basic religious belief systems, awareness of the impact of religious beliefs and values on the therapeutic process, and self-awareness of religious values. The competencies provide the framework for an integrative listening perspective or attitude in the therapy room. Each of these areas will be discussed in the following paragraphs.

Knowledge areas. The therapist should, at a minimum, be familiar with the basic beliefs of different religious traditions in order to take into account this important area of client diversity (Greenberg & Witztum, 1991; Spero, 1981). This knowledge will also help the clinician to recognize when the client uses religious values or practices in a distorted way (e.g., Greenberg & Witztum, 1991; Pruyser, 1971). Several authors have outlined the beliefs of specific groups (e.g., the Amish, Wittmer & Moser, 1974; evangelical Christianity, DiBlasio, 1988; fundamentalist Christianity, Moyers, 1990, Whipple, 1988; Mormonism, Koltko, 1990; Orthodox Judaism, Strean, 1994). Others have reviewed the relationship between different kinds of religiosity and mental

health variables (e.g., Gartner, 1996; Gartner, Larson, & Allen, 1991).

Impact of beliefs on the therapeutic process. An awareness of how religious beliefs and values impact the client's perception of the problem and the therapeutic process can help the clinician in understanding how to enlist the client's beliefs in the service of therapeutic progress. The client's belief system can impact how he or she conceptualizes a problem, for example, seeing a compulsion as a sin. Religious beliefs and values can have a negative impact on the therapeutic process through the use of religious resistances to the therapeutic process or change (Kehoe & Gutheil, 1984). Narramore (1994) notes that religious defenses are fundamentally psychological mechanisms that are framed in religious language, have religious content, or are tied in with the client's religious experience. He suggests that the therapist affirm the healthy aspects of the religious experience that is used as the defense, use biblical language in confrontations, then work with the resistance as the therapist would with any other (cf. Lovinger, 1984). On the converse side, religious beliefs and values can have a positive impact through religious sources of community support, through inhibition of destructive behavior, by acting as a socializing agent, and by providing meaning and a sense of control to the client (see also Brink, 1985; Cooper-Lewter, 1988).

Self-awareness of values. A large discrepancy between the religious beliefs of mental health professionals and the general population has been well documented (Bergin, 1980), although this gap may have diminished somewhat in recent years (Shafranske & Malony, 1990). Whether clients and therapists share the same valued or are diametrically opposed, self-awareness of one's values as a therapist and their impact on therapy are necessary in order to practice in the most ethical and effective manner, as mandated by APA's (1992) ethical code. The failure to be self-aware of values can lead to a number of therapeutic difficulties, including countertransference issues, acting out of therapist value conflicts, and value clashes with clients.

Shafranske and Malony (1990), in a study of APA members, found that psychologists' religious and spiritual beliefs, rather than clinical training, determined how they approached therapeutic interventions with religious clients. This study highlights the impact of therapists' values on the therapeutic process, whether these values be congruent or discordant with those of religious clients. Kochems (1993) stated that there are two basic countertransference positions: to react against, or to support the client's spirituality. Both types can undermine the therapist's attempts to understand the client's experiences of his or her religion. Moshe and Mester (1988) suggest that at times negative countertransference may result from the therapist's envy of the client's religious experience. Negative countertransference can lead to attempts to correct a client's position through extended philosophical discussions with no specific therapeutic value, or may lead to evaluations of the client as resistant. Religious material may be insufficiently explored because the therapist prematurely judges and labels it. Therapists should seek to overcome these potential problems through self-examination of prejudices, and through acquiring knowledge of the client's belief system (Greenberg & Witztum, 1991).

Positive countertransference arises from the neurotic use of religion by both therapist and client (Spero, 1981) and can lead to its own problems. Shared religious ideals may be held as sacred and left unexamined (Giglio, 1993), the therapist and client may collude to avoid certain painful areas (Narramore, 1994), overidentification with the client can lead to therapeutic errors (Peteet, 1996), or shared dysfunctional religious communities can lead to blurring of boundaries and dual relationships (Carbo & Gartner, 1994). Several suggestions have been given as to how to avoid these problems (Giglio, 1993; Spero, 1981): the therapist should be aware of possible neurotic uses of religion in both the client and the therapist; shared belief systems should be questioned in order to better understand the client's experience of it; and the therapist should be aware that the choice of therapist may have been partially motivated by the desire to avoid certain topics (e.g., "sinful" sexual thoughts and feelings) (Kehoe & Gutheil, 1993; Narramore, 1994).

A conflict may exist between a therapist's religious values and the values of his or her profession or theoretical orientation (Grimm, 1994; Spero, 1981). For example, a therapist might have a professional commitment to nondirectiveness, while feeling tension because of the perception of neutrality as a sanctioning of religious impropriety (Kahn, 1996). Or religious values of loving others and sacrificing self might conflict with therapeutic values of maintaining boundaries and setting limits (Kehoe & Gutheil, 1993). The internal conflict generated by this tension could lead to avoidance of religious issues in therapy, or, alternatively, to pursuing these in order to meet the needs of the therapist rather than the client. It is the obligation of the therapist to recognize when personal issues may be impairing professional judgment and effectiveness (APA, 1992).

Discrepancies between the beliefs of client and therapist can also lead to value clashes that limit the effectiveness of therapy or lead to unethical imposition of values (McMinn, 1984). Miller (1992) suggests that awareness of the type of religiosity of both the client and the clinician are important in identifying possible areas of conflict. Using Batson and Ventis' (cited in Miller, 1992) model of Quest, End, and Means religiosity, and Spilka's (cited in Miller, 1992) four uses of religion as secondary control (predictive, vicarious illusory, and interpretive), Miller illustrates how large differences in the way the client and the therapist use religion can result in therapeutic mismatches. She suggests that when severe discrepancies exist, the therapist should refer the client to other therapists or church leaders.

Spiritually-Oriented Content

Including spiritual issues in therapy is labeled explicit integration by Tan (1996), although it is not the most explicit form of clinical integration (see below). This type of integrative therapy involves openly discussing spiritual issues that come up in therapy, taking a religious history and assessing the client's spiritual functioning, dealing with certain issues on the boundary between psychology and religion in a way that explicitly incorporates their spiritual aspects, as well as dealing with spiritual issues overtly within the framework of specific therapeutic modalities (cf. Worthington, 1986).

There are a number of spiritual issues that may arise in psychotherapy. For example, clients may wish to discuss broad issues such as value clarification, spiritual dryness, meaning and direction in life, and trust and dependence on authority (Peteet, 1981; Tan, 1996). More specific issues such as patterns of sin behavior, spiritual doubt, experience of relationship with God, difficulty feeling close to God, anger and bitterness toward God, discerning God's will, and conflicts regarding specific religious beliefs and practices (e.g., the role of women) may be of concern to clients as well. Clinical sensitivity is paramount in dealing with such issues. The therapist must seek a balance between avoiding spiritual issues when he or she does not want to do so. Tan (1996) notes that the therapist should be sensitive to the client's pace and respect his or her responsibility in making personal decisions (see also Lovinger, 1984, 1990, 1996; and McMinn, 1996, for helpful discussions of working with religious issues in therapy).

In order to work effectively with religious issues in therapy, it is critical to take a religious history during intake procedures. Healey (1993), Kelly (1995a), Rizzuto (1996), and Tan (1996) give helpful suggestions for initiating the gathering of a religious history. This is particularly important in working with highly religious clients who wish to deal with spiritual issues in therapy, and for whom the most effective treatment may involve working with spiritual issues. Gaining an understanding of clients' religious affiliation, degree of religious commitment (Kelly, 1995a), image of God (see Brokaw & Edwards, 1994; Hall & Brokaw, 1995; Hall, Brokaw, Edwards, & Pike, 1996; McDargh, 1986; Rizzuto, 1979, 1993, 1996; Tisdale, Brokaw, Edwards, & Key, 1993), religious beliefs and practices, and familial religious beliefs, practices, and attitudes can provide valuable information on their religious development and perceptions of self and significant others. It can also clarify the relationship between clients' religiosity and their presenting problems (Kelly, 1995a). The therapist should also assess the client's spiritual functioning or maturity (cf. Hall, Tisdale, & Brokaw, 1994; Lovinger, 1996; Malony, 1993). Malony's (1988) Religious Status Interview provides a helpful clinical interview for assessing religious functioning. Hall and Edwards' (1996) Spiritual Assessment Inventory is an objective instrument that may be useful in assessing clients' spiritual functioning.

There are certain topics about which both psychology and religion have much to say. This form of explicit integrative therapy deals openly with such spiritual issues in a way that is informed by the therapist's modality as well as the client's and therapist's theological understanding of such issues. Examples of these clinical issues are anger (see Cerling, 1974; Gaultiere, 1989; Mowbray, 1986), forgiveness (see Beck, 1995; Benson, 1992; Cunningham, 1985; DiBlasio, 1992; DiBlasio & Benda, 1991; Gartner, 1988; Gassin & Enright, 1995; Hope, 1987; Kaufman, 1984; McCullough & Worthington, 1994; McMinn, 1996; Pingleton, 1989; Strong, 1977; Veenstra, 1992; Worthington & DiBlasio, 1990), guilt (see Narramore, 1974a, 1974b, 1974c, 1974d, 1984) and shame (see Thurston, 1994).

Spiritual issues are often explicitly addressed within the framework of a traditional therapeutic modality utilizing traditional techniques. This approach is advocated by Benner (1988) who provides a helpful discussion of the role of spirituality in psychotherapy. Benner argues that spiritual issues have an appropriate place in psychotherapy, but they should be approached just like any other issue. In other words, the psychological meaning and experience of the spiritual issues should be addressed.

A number of authors have discussed dealing with spiritual issues from a particular therapeutic modality. The majority of these articles are theoretical in nature and address cognitive-behavioral and psychodynamic modalities, although some literature is available on marriage and family therapy and existential therapy. It is beyond the scope of this article to go beyond highlighting some of the literature available on these topics. Propst (1988, 1996) has provided the most systematic integration of religious content with cognitive-behavioral therapy (CBT). Tan (1987) has also offered suggestions for a biblical approach to CBT. Craigie and Tan (1989) discuss approaches to changing resistant assumptions and incorporating Christian beliefs. McMinn and Lebold (1989) advocate collaborative techniques for working with religious concerns in a CBT context. Parsons and Wicks (1986) discuss the use of a theology of God's love in cognitive restructuring. Lawrence (1987) discusses dealing with a client's religious belief system from a rational-emotive perspective. Miller and Martin (1988) edited a book that addresses the role of spiritual techniques and issues in behavior therapy and CBT.

Regarding psychodynamic therapy, Healey argues for a different listening perspective, rather than different interventions. Finn and Gartner (1992), Randour (1993), and Spero (1996)) have edited books that deal with a wide range of issues related to dealing with spiritual content in psychodynamic therapy. Fleischman (1989) illustrates how psychodynamic issues are reflected in religious concerns through a series of case studies, and demonstrates how different religious traditions address these dynamic concerns. Jones (1991) discusses the impact of the more recent emphasis on relationships within contemporary psychoanalysis on religious issues in psychoanalytically-oriented therapy (see also Jones, 1997). Rizzuto (1996) and Spero (1992) both address dealing with clients' God images from an object relations perspective (see also McDargh, 1986; Spero, 1990). Several helpful works are available on spiritual issues in existential therapy (e.g., Mahrer, 1996) and marriage and family therapy (e.g., Anderson, 1987; Roberts, 1991; Sperry & Giblin, 1996; Watson, 1997; Worthington, 1990). Burton (1992) edited a book that contains several practical chapters on integrating spirituality within a systems perspective. Vande Kemp (1991) also has an edited book that provides examples of systemic clinical integration.

Spiritually-Oriented Goals and Techniques

Some authors (e.g., Farnsworth, 1996), argue that counseling that is truly Christian or integrative must be somehow unique in its procedures. This last category of clinical integration is the most unique in terms of what the therapist actually does in the therapy room. This most explicit form of clinical integration involves different overall goals for the client. In addition to psychological growth, spiritual growth is an explicit goal of the therapy. Moreover, techniques originating from a spiritual tradition (e.g., spiritual guidance techniques) are used within the therapy context. These techniques include the use of Scripture, prayer, confession, worship, forgiveness, fasting, deliverance, and solitude (see Moon, Bailey, Willis, & Kwasny, 1993, for a list of 20 spiritual guidance techniques). As with therapy that includes spiritual issues (described above), it is necessary to gather a religious history as part of the intake procedures. At times, the boundaries between psychotherapy, pastoral counseling, and spiritual direction are blurred in this form of clinical integration. Schneider (1989) asserts that it represents the birth of a new discipline which Moon et al. (1993) call *clinical theology.*

Let us first consider the area of therapeutic goals. In implicit integrative therapy, the goals defined for a particular client are generally psychological in nature. Likewise, when spiritually-oriented content is incorporated within traditional therapy techniques, the goals typically remain within the traditional psychological framework. Depending on one's therapeutic modality, insight, more mature relatedness, integration of the personality, clarification of family roles and boundaries, more accurate cognitions, or more adaptive behaviors may be the primary goal of therapy even though spiritual issues are discussed.

Some authors (e.g., Benner, 1988), however, argue that the ultimate goal of Christian therapy is to promote spiritual welfare and growth. While this type of explicit integration often includes traditional psychological goals, spiritual goals are an explicit part of the therapy. Problems of living and the promotion of mental health are addressed to a large extent in the spiritual domain. For example, Finney and Malony (1985b) point out that religiously-oriented persons view positive mental health not just as the absence of illness, but also as the continual development of a relationship with the supernatural.

The results of Moon et al.'s (1993) investigation of the use of spiritual guidance techniques suggest that Christian psychotherapists do address spiritual goals to some degree since they engage in spiritual guidance techniques with up to 25 percent or more of their clients. Further evidence of this is Worthington and Scott's (1983) findings that counselors in Christian settings tend to define problems in spiritual terms and to set spiritual goals for religious clients more often than counselors in secular settings.

Several studies attest to the fact that Christian psychotherapists make significant use of spiritually-ori-

ented techniques. Worthington et al. (1988) found that spiritual guidance techniques were used by Christian mental health professionals in many of the sessions. The five techniques reported to be used most by therapists (ranging from 32-46 percent of the sessions) were assigning religious homework, quoting Scripture, interpreting Scripture, discussing the client's faith, and praying during the session. Therapists used spiritual guidance techniques more frequently when they perceived the religious intensity of the client to be high (although not extremely high). Encouraging forgiveness of others and assigning religious homework were perceived by clients as the most helpful techniques. Ball and Goodyear (1991) similarly found that prayer, teaching religious concepts, use of Scripture and forgiveness were the most frequently used spiritual guidance techniques among Christian counselors. Jones, Watson, and Wolfram (1992) surveyed alumni of explicitly Christian graduate psychology programs and Hales, Sorenson, Jones, and Coe (1995) surveyed Christian alumni of secular psychology doctoral programs. Again, both studies found that implicit teaching of biblical concepts, prayer for clients outside of the session, and instruction in forgiveness were the most frequently used spiritual techniques.

Moon et al. (1993) examined the self-reported use of 20 Christian spiritual guidance techniques by Christian psychotherapists, pastoral counselors, and spiritual directors. The percentage of Christian psychotherapists who had used each of the spiritually-oriented techniques ranged from 24.1 percent to 93.3 percent. The most commonly used techniques for Christian psychotherapists were forgiveness, intercessory prayer, pro-active use of Scripture by the counselor, and confession. Doctoral-level counselors were less likely to use spiritually-oriented techniques than master's level practitioners which corroborated Winger and Hunsberger's (1988) finding that level of graduate education was negatively correlated with the use of religious techniques. These studies clearly indicate that various spiritually-oriented techniques are being used regularly by Christian psychotherapists.

Shafranske and Malony (1990) investigated the use of religious interventions by a random sample of members of the American Psychological Association Division 12 (clinical psychology), providing valuable information regarding the use of spiritually-oriented techniques among the general population of psychologists. They found that approximately one third of their sample felt competent in dealing with religious/spiritual issues in therapy. Their results indicated that as interventions became more explicitly religious and participatory in nature, they were used less frequently. Shafranske and Malony, and Shafranske (cited in Shafranske, 1996) found that the majority of the subjects were aware of their clients' religious backgrounds and used religious language or concepts. Clinicians' personal experience of religion was significantly correlated with engaging in spiritually-oriented interventions. Participation in organized religion and positive religious experiences were associated with increased use of religious interventions. Jones et al.'s (1992) findings of a modest relationship between the religiosity of the therapist and the use of spiritually-oriented techniques corroborate these results.

In addition to empirical studies on the relative use of various spiritual techniques, numerous authors have addressed the use of specific spiritual techniques within therapy such as prayer/meditation, use of Scripture, and referral to religious groups.

Prayer. Prayer can be broadly defined as any kind of communion or conversation with God, including focusing attention on God and an experiential awareness of God (Finney & Malony, 1985a; Tan, 1996). Tan (1996) notes that prayer can be used by a therapist at various times such as before, during, or after a therapy session. Saussy (1986) suggests spending time in silence before God before seeing a client. Prayer can also be used in different ways in therapy. The therapist can pray silently for a client, or aloud with a client about specific or general issues. Other forms of prayer that can be used in therapy or as an adjunct to therapy are contemplative prayer and inner healing prayer.

Finney and Malony (1985b) discuss the use of contemplative prayer as an adjunct to psychotherapy. They define it as "a particular form of Christian prayer in which one gives one's full attention to relating to God in a passive, nondefensive, nondemanding, open way" (p. 173). These authors highlight three key psychological processes that contribute to its effects: (a) hypnotic suggestion; (b) a nondirective trance; and (c) decreased physiological arousal. They cite research suggesting that mystical experience and meditation are associated with increased psychological well-being as support for the notion that contemplative prayer may have potential therapeutic benefits. In an empirical study of its effectiveness as an adjunct to psychotherapy, Finney and Malony found a significant decrease in distress on target complaints. However, evidence shows a positive relationship between contemplative prayer and spiritual development.

While contemplative prayer may be a helpful adjunct to psychotherapy, Finney and Malony (1985b) emphasize several important caveats for using it in psychotherapy. Therapists using it must keep in mind its fundamental nature as prayer. It is not merely a meditation technique; it is also a means of relating to God. Therefore, it should be used in a way that is consistent with its religious meaning. It should not be used solely to bring repressed material into consciousness or to decrease physiological arousal. This would be inconsistent with the Christian understanding of prayer as self-dedication rather than self-seeking. Finally, since it is essentially a technique for spiritual development, it should be used only with religiously-committed clients for whom spiritual development is a specific therapy goal.

Another type of prayer that is used in psychotherapy is inner healing prayer, which is used for the healing of memories. Inner healing prayer is particularly appropriate with clients who have suffered childhood traumas (such as sexual and physical abuse, rejection, and abandonment) that remain unresolved and emotionally painful (Tan, 1996). Several authors such as Seamands (1985) and Propst (1988) have emphasized guided imagery as an essential part of inner healing prayer. The therapist uses guided imagery of Jesus, who is invited to be present, heal and comfort the client as he or she walks back into the past and re-experiences a traumatic event through imagery. However, Tan points out that there is a danger in the therapist imposing imagery onto a client because he or she may not feel comfortable with certain imagery. Tan suggests an approach to inner healing that places the emphasis more on prayer and waiting on God than on guided imagery. While inner healing prayer can be a helpful spiritual technique, the therapist must use it with much sensitivity to the client's therapeutic goals, personality, and comfort level.

For a therapist and client who share the same religious tradition and spiritual heritage, prayer can be vital in promoting a more holistic, psychospiritual development (see Edwards, 1976). Prayer, however, can be counterproductive in the therapeutic process at certain times, with certain clients, and if used in certain ways. Prayer may be used by a client in a defensive manner to avoid dealing with the interpersonal process with the therapist, or to avoid probing a painful issue in more depth (cf. Johnson, 1987; Kelly, 1995b; Tan, 1996). Religiously committed clients may not want to pray at times due to unresolved anger toward God. Moreover, if prayer is used by the therapist in a superficial manner, ignoring the complexity of a client's problem, it can be damaging (see Alsdurf & Malony, 1980; Malony, 1987; Tan, 1996). The therapist should be sensitive to the client's presenting problem, developmental history, and the interpersonal dynamics between him or her and the client when using prayer in psychotherapy.

Use of the Bible and other sacred texts. Scripture use is one of the most frequently used spiritually-oriented techniques (e.g., Moon et al., 1993; Worthington et al., 1988). There are numerous resources that are helpful in using Scripture or sacred texts in a therapeutic way. Meyer (1974) discusses the use of the Psalms' symbolic structure as a method of facilitating expressing the inner life, identifying with others who have experienced similar dilemmas, and relating to God on an experiential level. Edwards (1977) highlights the role of scriptural truth in the change process. Backus (1985) articulates the use of Scripture in cognitive restructuring or "misbelief therapy." Several other authors discuss the use of the Bible in cognitive restructuring (e.g., Backus & Chapian, 1980; Crabb, 1977; Craigie & Tan, 1989; McMinn, 1991; Propst, 1988; Tan, 1987; Tan & Ortberg, 1995a, 1995b; Thurman, 1989; Wright, 19186). Cloud and Townsend (1995) coauthored a Christian psychology book for the general public that uses Scripture to correct common distorted beliefs. Collins (1988, 1993) has also written two helpful books dealing with the use of Scripture in therapy.

As is the case with prayer, Scripture or sacred texts can be used in a counterproductive manner in therapy (Johnson, 1987). Tan (1996) gives as an example of this the therapist using specific biblical passages in an authoritarian way so as to coerce the client to repent from maladaptive behaviors. Differing interpretations of Scripture must also be dealt with in a sensitive manner by the therapist. Benner (1988) states that psychotherapy is not an appropriate place to engage in intellectual discussion about God, theology, or biblical interpretation. Rather, Scripture should be used in the service of dealing with the client's experience of God and the meaning and experience of other facets of his or her spiritual life, or to explore blocks to spiritual growth. As Edwards (1976) points out, the use of Scripture in therapy requires creativity and sensitivity on the part of the therapist, and must take into account the client's presenting problem, developmental history, and belief system.

Referral to religious groups and clergy. A client's religion and religious community can have a positive therapeutic impact (Brink, 1985; Cooper-Lewter, 1988; Sacks, 1985). Consequently, an explicit spiritual resource that can be used as an adjunct to psychotherapy is a referral to a pastor or priest, or to a church, parachurch, or other religious group. There are times when dealing with specific spiritual issues may be beyond the competence level of the therapist and may require a referral to a priest, pastor, pastoral counselor, or other religious authority. Such individuals often have a different perspective, as well as different skills, which may be needed to deal with certain faith issues. Various religiously oriented groups such as Bible study groups, fellowship groups, prayer groups, discipleship groups, recovery groups, or religiously-oriented 12-step groups can provide much needed support and help clients cope with difficulties.

Clinical Considerations in Implicit Versus Explicit Integration

The determination of where along the integration spectrum a therapist should practice will depend on several factors: (a) the Client's needs and preferences; (b) the therapist's training; (c) the therapist's religious beliefs and comfort with religious techniques; and (d) therapeutic modality. The client's needs and preferences should be discussed during intake, and the client's comfort with spiritual techniques assessed. Some research has suggested that addressing religious issues is important with highly religious people, but may be less important or even irrelevant with nominally religious or nonreligious populations (Worthington, 1991). In any case, professional ethics dictate that religious approaches should only be taken with the informed consent of the client. As with all areas of psychotherapy, therapists not trained or supervised in explicit integration should refer to other clinicians when this type of integrative psychotherapy is requested by a client. Although both secular and religious therapists can incorporate religious beliefs to some extent into their counseling (Propst et al., 1992; Tan, 1996), it may be that religiously committed therapists are more comfortable in doing so, or more motivated to do so. More explicit approaches to clinical integration may be easily incorporated into certain modalities (e.g., cognitive-behavioral therapy), and may not be as appropriate to other modalities (e.g., classical psychoanalysis). The therapist's theoretical orientation may be as important a factor in whether or not clinical integration occurs as the therapist's religious beliefs (Worthington et al., 1996).

Ethics in Clinical Integration

With the increased interest in clinical integration has come a growing awareness of potential ethical pitfalls and attempts to safeguard against them. Although work remains to be done in clarifying the ethics of clinical integration, several authors have addressed this issue (e.g., Tan, 1994, 1996; Tjeltveit, 1986, 1991, 1992), and at least two codes of ethics have been proposed: the ethical guidelines for the Christian Association for Psychological Studies (CAPS) (1992), and a code of ethics for Christian counselors (Beck & Matthews, 1986). Four of the general principles of APA's (1992) code of ethics are particularly relevant in addressing integration: Principle A, Competence; Principle B, Integrity; Principle D, Respect for People's Rights and Dignity; and Principle E, Concern for Others' Welfare (cf. American Psychiatric Association, 1990). These principles express concern with professional competence, respect for the beliefs and values of therapy. The three ethical concerns found in these principles will be used as a framework for summarizing some prominent ethical issues in clinical integration.

Competence

Psychologists are urged to recognize the limits of their competence and provide services or use techniques for which they are qualified by education, training, or experience (Principle A, Standard 1.04). With the exception of graduate programs that specialize in integration (e.g., Graduate School of Psychology at Fuller Theological Seminary; George Fox University; Rosemead School of Psychology at Biola University; Wheaton College), little training in the implicit or explicit acknowledgment of religion and use of religious techniques is available. Therapists interested in practicing clinical integration should seek appropriate training (Standard 1.08; Payne, Bergin, & Loftus, 1992; Tan, 1994). When training is not readily available, competence must be established through seeking appropriate resources regarding religious matters, for example, consulting with a religious professional (Presley, 1992; Standard 1.20). The therapist should also be aware of the limitations or boundaries of therapy, and should avoid the role of priest or religious professional (see Benner, 1988; Payne, Bergin, & Loftus, 1992; Tan, 1996). Blurring of boundaries can violate the therapeutic relationship, impairing the effectiveness of therapy (Tan, 1994).

Respect for Beliefs and Values

Psychologists should be aware of and respectful of individual differences due to religion (Principle D; Standard 1.09). Likewise, awareness of their own belief systems and values and the effect of these on their work need to be maintained (Principle B). Potential pitfalls include imposing beliefs or values on the client, and failing to provide sufficient infor-

mation regarding therapy to the client (Tan, 1994). The implication for clinical integration is that a therapist should not impose his or her value system on the client and, consequently, should use techniques that are consistent with the client's value system (Bergin & Payne, 1991; Payne, Bergin, & Loftus, 1992; Tan, 1994). Nelson and Wilson (1984) proposed that clinical integration is ethical: (a) when done with appropriate clients (e.g., not with psychotic clients who might be harmed) and at the appropriate time (e.g., not in a crisis situation, after evaluating the client's level of psychological and spiritual maturity); (b) when working within the client's ethical belief system; and (c) when informed consent has included the use of religious or spiritual interventions. McMinn (1984) suggests that in order to ethically avoid imposing values on the client, therapists should: (a) recognize and assess religious value issues during intake; (b) communicate their own religious values to those clients whose therapy may be affected by value issues and the potential effects of conflicting religious values; and (c) discuss with the client his or her choice to continue or discontinue therapy. Informed consent is a key component in assuring respect for the clients' values and an awareness of the therapist's values (Standard 4.02; Bergin, 1980; Grimm, 1994; Hawkins & Bullock, 1994; McMinn, 1984; Presley, 1992).

Effectiveness of Therapy

In the areas of clinical psychology in which recognized professional standards do not yet exist, psychologists should exercise judgment and take precautions to protect the welfare of clients (Principles A and E) and avoid harm (Standard 1.14). Just as religiosity can vary in its degree of health, clinical integration, when performed poorly, can be harmful to clients. Clinicians should avoid practicing clinical integration in a haphazard, atheoretical manner. Tan (1994) notes additional pitfalls that may stand in the way of effectiveness: arguing over doctrinal issues rather than clarifying them, misusing or abusing spiritual resources in order to avoid painful issues in therapy (e.g., praying or using Scripture in a defensive manner), and applying only religious interventions to problems which may require medication or other medical and/or psychological treatments.

In concluding this discussion of ethical concerns, it should be noted that failure to take into account a client's religious beliefs and values and to provide integrative treatment that is required by a client, may also be unethical (Nelson & Wilson, 1984). Bergin (1980) suggests that therapists will not be fully effective until they take into account the theistic belief system held by a large segment of the population.

For some, religion is almost as basic as family structures and relationships (Albany, 1984) and, consequently, is a powerful motivator of behavior.

Summary

An attempt has been made to provide an overview of the scope of clinical integration, and to detail some of the more important advances in its conceptualization and application. The theoretical and empirical foundations for clinical integration have been outlined, and it was concluded that a need exists for the integration of religious values and beliefs with psychotherapy. The spectrum of clinical integration was described, and existing integrative efforts detailed, ranging from an implicit acknowledgment of religious values and beliefs, to the incorporation of explicitly religious content, goals, and techniques into the psychotherapy process. Finally, the ethics of clinical integration were briefly reviewed. Although a rich body of theoretical material and some empirical studies exist, further work needs to be done to better articulate theologically and psychologically sound methods and processes of integrative therapy that also demonstrate empirical effectiveness.

References

Albany, A. P. (1984). Clinical implications of religious loyalties: A contextual view. *Counseling and Values, 28,* 128-133.

Alsdurf, J. M., & Malony, H. N. (1980). A critique of Ruth Carter Stapleton's ministry of "inner healing." *Journal of Psychology and Theology, 8,* 173-184.

American Psychiatric Association. (1990). Guidelines regarding possible conflict between psychiatrists' religious commitments and psychiatric practice (official actions). *American Journal of Psychiatry, 147,* 542.

American Psychiatric Association. (1994). *Diagnostic and statistical manual of mental disorders* (4th ed.). Washington, DC: Author.

American Psychological Association (1992). Ethical principles of psychologists and code of conduct. *American Psychologist, 47,* 1597-1611.

Anderson, D. A. (1987). Spirituality and systems therapy: Partners in clinical practice. *Journal of Pastoral Psychotherapy, 1,* 19-32.

Azhar, M. Z., & Varma, S. L. (1995a). Religious psychotherapy as management of bereavement. *Acta Psychiatrica Scandinavica, 91,* 233-235.

Azhar, M. Z., & Varma, S. L. (1995b). Religious psychotherapy in depressive patients. *Psychotherapy and Psychosomatics, 63,* 165-173.

Azhar, M. Z., Varma, S. L., & Dharap, A. (1994). Religious psychotherapy in anxiety disorder patients. *Acta Psychiatrica Scandinavica 90,* 1-3.

Backus, W., & Chapian, M. (1980). *Telling yourself the truth.* Minneapolis, MN: Bethany House.

Ball, R. A., & Goodyear, R. K. (1991). Self-reported professional practices of Christian psychotherapists. *Journal of Psychology and Christianity, 10,* 144-153.

Beck, J. R. (1995). When to forgive. *Journal of Psychology and Christianity, 14,* 269-273.

Beck, J. R., & Matthews, R. K. (1986). A code of ethics for Christian counselors. *Journal of Psychology and Christianity, 5,* 78-84.

Benner, D. G. (1988). *Psychotherapy and the spiritual quest.* Grand Rapids, :MI: Baker.

Benson, C. K. (1992). Forgiveness and the psychotherapeutic process. *Journal of Psychology and Christianity, 11,* 76-81.

Bergin, A. E. (1980). Psychotherapy and religious values. *Journal of Consulting and Clinical Psychology, 48,* 95-105.

Bergin, A. E. (1988). Three contributions of a spiritual perspective to counseling. *Counseling and Values, 33,* 21-31.

Bergin, A. E., & Payne, I. R. (1991). Proposed agenda for a spiritual strategy in personality and psychotherapy. *Journal of Psychology and Christianity, 10,* 197-210.

Bergin, A. E., Payne, I. R., & Richards, P. S. (1996). Values in psychotherapy. In E. P. Shafranske (Ed.), *Religion and the clinical practice of psychology* (pp. 297-325). Washington, DC: American Psychological Association.

Brink, T. L. (1985). The role of religion in later life: A case of consolation and forgiveness. *Journal of Psychology and Christianity, 4,* 22-25.

Brokaw, B. F., & Edwards, K. J. (1994). The relationship of God image to level of object relations development. *Journal of Psychology and Theology, 22,* 352-371.

Burton, L. A. (Ed.). (1992). Religion and the family; When God helps. New York; Haworth Pastoral Press.

Carbo, R. A., & Gartner, J. (1994). Can religious communities become dysfunctional families? Sources of countertransference for the religiously committed psychotherapist. *Journal of Psychology and Theology, 22,* 264-271.

Cerling, C. E. (1974). Anger: Musings of a theologian/psychologist. *Journal of Psychology and Theology, 2,* 12-17.

Christian Association for Psychological Studies. (1992). *Ethical guidelines for the Christian Association for Psychological Studies.* Temecula, CA: Author.

Cloud, H., & Townsend, J. (1995). *Twelve "Christian" beliefs that can drive you crazy.* Grand Rapids, MI: Zondervan.

Collins, G. R. (1988). *Christian counseling; A comprehensive guide* (rev. ed.). Dallas, TX: Word.

Collins, G. R. (1993). *The biblical basis of Christian counseling for people helpers.* Colorado Springs, CO: NavPress.

Cook, T. E. (1966). The influence of client-counselor similarity of values on change in meaning during brief psychotherapy. *Journal of Counseling Psychology, 18,* 123-131.

Cooper-Lewter, N. C. (1988). Do counselors have the right to deny counselees' God? *Medical Hypnoanalysis Journal, 3,* 63-67.

Crabb, L. (1977). *Effective biblical counseling.* Grand Rapids, MI: Zondervan.

Craigie, F. C., Jr., & Tan, S.-Y. (1989). Changing resistant assumptions in Christian cognitive-behavioral therapy. *Journal of Psychology and Theology, 17,* 93-100.

Cunningham, B. B. (1985). The will to forgive: A pastoral theological view of forgiving. *Journal of Pastoral Care, 39,* 141-149.

DiBlasio, F. A. (1988). Integrative strategies for family therapy with evangelical Christians. *Journal of Psychology and Theology,16,* 127-134.

DiBlasio, F. A. (1991). Forgiveness in psychotherapy: Comparison of older and younger therapists. *Journal of Psychology and Christianity, 11,* 181-187.

DiBlasio, F. A., & Benda, B. B. (1991). Practitioners, religion and the use of forgiveness in the clinical setting. *Journal of Psychology and Christianity, 10,* 155-172.

Dougherty, S. G., & Worthington, E. L., Jr. (1982). Preferences of conservative and moderate Christians for four Christian counselors' treatment plans. *Journal of Psychology and Theology, 10,* 346-354.

Edwards, K. J. (1976). Effective counseling and psychotherapy: An integrative review of research. *Journal of Psychology and Theology, 4,* 94-107.

Farnsworth, K. E. (1996). The devil sends errors in pairs. *Journal of Psychology and Christianity, 15,* 123-132.

Finn, M., & Gartner, J. (Eds.). (1992). *Object relations theory and religion: Clinical applications.* Westport, CT: Praeger.

Finney, J. R., & Malony, H. N. (1985a). An empirical study of contemplative prayer as an adjunct to psychotherapy. *Journal of Psychology and Theology, 13,* 284-290.

Finney, J. R., & Malony, N. N. (1985b). Contemplative prayer and its use in psychotherapy: A theoretical model. *Journal of Psychology and Theology, 13,* 172-181.

Fleischman, P. R. (1989). *The healing spirit: Explorations in religion and psychotherapy.* New York: Paragon House.

Gartner, J. (1988). The capacity to forgive: An object relations perspective. *Journal of Religion and Health, 27,* 313-320.

Gartner, J. (1996). Religious commitment, mental health, and prosocial behavior: A review of the empirical literature. In E. P. Shafranske (Ed.), *Religion and the clinical practice of psychology* (pp. 187-214). Washington,DC: American Psychological Association.

Gartner, J., Larson, D. B., & Allen, G. D. (1991). Religious commitment and mental health: A review of the empirical literature. *Journal of Psychology and Theology, 19,* 6-25.

Gass, C. S. (1984), Orthodox Christian values related to psychotherapy and mental health. *Journal of Psychology and Theology, 12,* 230-237.

Gassin, E. A., & Enright, R. D. (1995). The will to meaning in the process of forgiveness. *Journal of Psychology and Christianity, 14,* 38-49.

Gaultiere, W. J. 1989). A biblical perspective on therapeutic treatment of client anger at God. *Journal of Psychology and Christianity, 8*(3), 38-46.

Giglio, J. (1993). The impact of patients' and therapists' religious values on psychotherapy. *Hospital and Community Psychiatry, 44,* 768-771.

Greenberg, D., & Witztum, E. (1991). Problems in the treatment of religious patients. *American Journal of Psychotherapy, 45,* 554-565.

Grimm, D. W. (1994). Therapist spiritual and religious values in psychotherapy. *Counseling and Values, 38,* 154-164.

Hales, S. W., Sorenson, R. L., Jones, J., & Coe, J. (1995). *Psychotherapists and the religious disciplines: Personal beliefs and professional practice.* Paper presented at the 1995 National Conference of The Christian Association for Psychological Studies, Virginia Beach, VA.

Hall, T. W., & Brokaw, B. F. (1995). The relationship of spiritual maturity to level of object relations development and God image. *Pastoral Psychology, 43,* 373-391.

Hall, T. W., Brokaw, B. F., Edwards, K. J., & Pike, P. L. (1996). *The relationship of spiritual maturity to level of object relations development and God image and the impact of spiritual direction on these variables.* Unpublished manuscript, Rosemead School of Psychology, Biola University, La Mirada, CA.

Hall, T. W., & Edwards, K. J. (1996). The initial development and factor analysis of the Spiritual Assessment Inventory. *Journal of Psychology and Theology, 24,* 233-246.

Hall, T. W., Tisdale, T. C., & Brokaw, B. F. (1994). Assessment of religious dimensions in Christian clients: A review of selected instruments for research and clinical use. *Journal of Psychology and Theology, 22,* 395-421.

Hawkins, I. L., & Bullock, S. L. (1994, April). *Informed consent and religious values: A neglected area of diversity.* Paper presented at the California Psychological Association Annual Convention, San Francisco, CA.

Healey, B. J. (1993). Psychotherapy and religious experience: Integrating psychoanalytic psychotherapy with Christian religious experience. In G. Stricker and J. R. Gold (Eds.). *Comprehensive handbook of psychotherapy integration* (pp. 267-275.). New York: Plenum Press.

Hope, D. (1987). The healing paradox of forgiveness. *Psychotherapy: Theory, Research, and Practice, 24,* 240-244.

Humphries, R. H. (1982). Therapeutic neutrality reconsidered. *Journal of Religion and Health, 21,* 124-131.

Johnson, C. B. (1987). Religious resources in psychotherapy. In D. G. Benner (Ed.), *Psychotherapy in Christian perspective* (pp. 31-36). Grand Rapids, MI: Baker.

Johnson, W. B. (1993). Outcome research and religious psychotherapies: Where are we and where are we going? *Journal of Psychology and Theology, 21,* 297-308.

Johnson, W. B., & Ridley, C. R. (1992). Brief Christian and nonChristian rational-emotive therapy with depressed Christian clients: An exploratory study. *Counseling and Values, 36,* 220-229.

Jones, J. W. (1991). *Contemporary psychoanalysis and religion: Transference and transcendence.* New Haven, CT: Yale University Press.

Jones, J. W. (1997). Looking forward: Future directions for the encounter of relational psychoanalysis and religion. *Journal of Psychology and Theology, 25,* 136-142.

Jones, S. L., Watson, E., & Wolfram, T. (1992). Results of the Rech Conference Survey on religious faith and professional psychology. *Journal of Psychology and Theology, 20,* 147-158.

Kahn, P. (1996). Religious values and the therapeutic alliance, or "help me, psychologist; I hate you, rabbi!" In M. H. Spero (Ed.), *Psychotherapy of the religious patient* (pp. 85-95). Northvale, NJ: Jason Aronson.

Kaufman, M. E. (1984). The courage to forgive. Israeli *Journal of Psychiatry and Related Sciences, 21,* 177-187.

Kehoe, N. C., & Gutheil, T. G. (1984). Shared religious belief as resistance in psychotherapy. *American Journal of Psychotherapy, 38,* 579-585.

Kehoe, N. C., & Gutheil, T. G. (1993). Ministry or therapy: The role of transference and countertransference in a religious therapist. In M. L. Randour (Ed.), *Exploring sacred landscapes: Religious and spiritual experiences in psychotherapy* (pp. 55-80). New York; Columbia University Press.

Kelly, E. W. (1995a). Assessing the spiritual/religious dimension in counseling. In E. W. Kelly, *Spirituality and religion in counseling and psychotherapy* (pp. 131-188). Alexandria, VA: American Counseling Association.

Kelly, E. W. (1995b). Counseling approaches and techniques: Treatment intervention and the spiritual/religious dimension. In E. W. Kelly, *Spirituality and religion in counseling and psychotherapy* (pp. 189-240). Alexandria, VA: American Counseling Association.

Kelly, T. A., & Strupp, H. H. (1992),. Patient and therapist values in psychotherapy: Perceived changes, assimilation, similarity, and outcome. *Journal of Consulting and Clinical Psychology, 60,* 34-48.

King, R. R. (1978). Evangelical Christians and professional counseling: A conflict of values. *Journal of Psychology and Theology, 6,* 276-281.

Kochems, T. (1993). Countertransference and transference aspects of religious material in psychotherapy: The isolation or integration of religious material. In M. L. Randour (Ed.), *Exploring sacred landscapes: Religious and spiritual experiences in psychotherapy* (pp. 34-54). New York: Columbia University Press.

Koltko, M. E. (1990). How religious beliefs affect psychotherapy: The example of Mormonism. *Psychotherapy: Theory, Research, and Practice, 27,* 132-141.

Lawrence, C. (1987). Rational-emotive therapy and the religious client. *Journal of Rational Emotive Therapy 5,* 13-21.

Lewis, K. N., & Epperson, D. L. (1991). Values, pretherapy information, and informed consent in Christian counseling. *Journal of Psychology and Christianity, 10,* 113-131.

Lovinger, R. J. (1979). Therapeutic strategies with "religious" resistances. *Psychotherapy: Theory, Research, and Practice, 16,* 419-427.

Lovinger, R. J. (1984). *Working with religious issues in therapy.* Northvale, NJ: Jason Aronson.

Lovinger, R. J. (1990). *Religion and counseling: The psychological impact of religious belief.* New York: Continuum.

Lovinger, R. J. (1996). Considering the religious dimension in assessment and treatment. In E. P. Shafranske (Ed.), *Religion and the clinical practice of psychology* (pp. 327-364). Washington, DC: American Psychological Association.

Mahrer, A. R. (1996)). Existential-humanistic psychotherapy and the religious person. In E. P. Shafranske (Ed.), *Religion and the clinical practice of psychology* (pp. 433-460). Washington, DC: American Psychological Association.

Malony, H. N. (1987). Inner healing. In D. G. Benner (Ed.), *Psychotherapy in Christian perspective* (pp. 171-179). Grand Rapids, MI: Baker.

Malony, H. N. (1988). The clinical assessment of optimal religious functioning. *Review of Religious Research, 30,* 2-17.

Malony, H. N. (1993). The relevance of "religious diagnosis" for counseling. In E. L. Worthington, Jr., (Ed.), *Psychotherapy and religious values* (pp. 105-122). Grand Rapids, MI: Baker.

McCullough, M. E., & Worthington, E. L., Jr. (1994). Encouraging clients to forgive people who have hurt them: Review, critique, and research prospectus. *Journal of Psychology and Theology, 22,* 3-20.

McDargh, J. (1986). God, mother, and me: An object relational perspective on religious material. *Pastoral Psychology, 34,* 251-263.

McMinn, M. R. (1984). Religious values and client-therapist matching in psychotherapy. *Journal of Psychology and Theology, 12,* 24-33.

McMinn, M. R. (1991). *Cognitive therapy techniques in Christian counseling.* Wheaton, IL: Tyndale.

McMinn, M. R. (1996). *Psychology, theology, and spirituality in Christian counseling.* Wheaton, IL: Tyndale.

McMinn M. R., & Lebold, C. J. (1989). Collaborative efforts in cognitive therapy with religious clients. *Journal of Psychology and Theology, 17,* 101-109.

Meyer, S. G. (1974). The Psalms and personal counseling. *Journal of Psychology and Theology, 22,* 26-30.

Miller, G. A. (1992). Integrating religion and psychology in therapy: Issues and recommendations. *Counseling and Values, 36,* 112-122.

Miller, W. R., & Martin, J. E. (1988). *Behavior therapy and religion: Integrating spiritual and behavioral approaches to change.* Newbury Park, CA: Sage.

Moon, G. W., Willis, D. E., Bailey, J. W., & Kwasny, J. C. (1993). Self-reported use of Christian spiritual guidance techniques by Christian psychotherapists, pastoral counselors, and spiritual directors. *Journal of Psychology and Christianity, 12,* 12-37.

Mowbray, T. L. (1986). The function of psalms dealing with anger: The angry psalmist. *Journal of Counseling, 21,* 34-39.

Moyers, J. C. (1990). Religious issues in the psychotherapy of former fundamentalists. *Psychotherapy: Theory, Research, and Practice. 27,* 42-45.

Narramore, S. B. (1974a). Guilt: Christian motivation or neurotic masochism? *Journal of Psychology and Theology, 2,* 182-189.

Narramore, S. B. (1974b). Guilt: Its universal hidden presence. *Journal of Psychology and Theology, 2,* 104-115.

Narramore, S. B. (1974c). Guilt: Three models of therapy. *Journal of Psychology and Theology, 2,* 260-265.

Narramore, S. B. (1974d). Guilt: Where theology and psychology meet. *Journal of Psychology and Theology, 2,* 13-25.

Narramore, S. B. (1984). *No condemnation*. Ann Arbor, MI: Zondervan.

Narramore, S. B. (1994). Dealing with religious resistances in psychotherapy. *Journal of Psychology and Theology, 22*, 249-258.

Nelson, A. A., & Wilson, W. P. (1984). The ethics of sharing religious faith in psychotherapy. *Journal of Psychology and Theology, 12*, 15-23.

Parsons, R. D., & Wicks, R. J. (1986). Cognitive pastoral psychotherapy with religious persons experiencing loneliness. *Psychotherapy Patient, 2*(3), 47-59.

Payne, I. R., Bergin, A. E., & Loftus, P. E. (1992). A review of attempts to integrate spiritual and standard psychotherapy techniques. *Journal of Psychotherapy Integration, 2*(3), 171-192.

Pecheur, E., & Edwards, K. J. (1984). A comparison of secular and religious versions of cognitive therapy with depressed Christian college students. *Journal of Psychology and Theology, 12*, 45-54.

Peteet, J. R. (1981). Issues in the treatment of religious patients. *American Journal of Psychotherapy, 35*, 559-564.

Peteet, J. R. (1996). Clinical intersections between the religion of the psychiatrist and his patients. In m. H. Spero (Ed.), *Psychotherapy of the religious patient* (pp. 63-84). Northvale, NJ: Jason Aronson.

Pingleton, J. P. (1989). The role and function of forgiveness in the psychotherapeutic process. *Journal of Psychology and Theology, 17*, 27-35.

Presley, D. B. (1992). Three approaches to religious issues in counseling. *Journal of Psychology and Theology, 20*, 39-46.

Propst, L. R. (1980). The comparative efficacy of religious and non-religious imagery for the treatment of mild depression in religious individuals. *Cognitive Therapy and Research, 44*, 167-178.

Propst, L. R. (1988). *Psychotherapy in a religious framework: Spirituality in the emotional healing process*. New York; Human Sciences Press.

Propst, L. R. (1996). Cognitive-behavioral therapy and the religious person. In E. P. Shafranske (Ed.), *Religion and the clinical practice of psychology* (pp. 391-408). Washington, DC: American Psychological Association.

Propst, L. R., Ostrom, R., Watkins, P., Dean, T., & Mashburn, D. (1992). Comparative efficacy of religious and nonreligious cognitive-behavioral therapy for the treatment of clinical depression in religious individuals. *Journal of Consulting and Clinical Psychology, 60*, 94-103.

Pruyser, P. (1971). Assessment of the patient's religious attitudes in the psychiatric case study. *Bulletin of the Menninger Clinic, 35*, 272-291.

Quackenbos, S., Privette, G., & Klentz, B. (1985). Psychotherapy: Sacred or secular. *Journal of Counseling and Development, 63*, 290-293.

Randour, M. L. (1993). *Exploring sacred landscapes: Religious and spiritual experiences in psychotherapy*. New York: Columbia University Press.

Richards, P. S., & Davison, M. L. (1989). The effects of theistic and atheistic counselor values on client trust: A multidimensional scaling analysis. *Counseling and Values, 33*, 109-120.

Rizzuto, A. M. (1979). *The birth of the living God*. Chicago: University of Chicago Press.

Rizzuto, A. M. (19930. Exploring sacred landscapes. In M. L. Randour (Ed.), *Exploring sacred landscapes* (pp. 16-33). New York: Columbia University Press.

Rizzuto, A. M. (1996). Psychoanalytic treatment and the religious person. In E. P. Shafranske (Ed.), *Religion and the clinical practice of psychology* (pp. 409-431). Washington, DC: American Psychological Association.

Roberts, R. C. (1991). Mental health and the virtues of community: Christian reflection on contextual therapy. *Journal of Psychology and Theology, 19*, 319-333.

Sacks, J. M. (1985). Religious issues in psychotherapy. *Journal of Religion and Health, 24*, 26-30.

Saussy, C. (1986). How do you integrate your theology into your clinical work? *Pastoral Psychology, 35*, 56-60.

Schneider, S. (1989). Spirituality in the academy. *Theological Studies, 50*, 676-679.

Seamands, D. (1985). *Healing of memories*. Wheaton, IL: Victor Books.

Shafranske, E. P. (Ed.). (1996). *Religion and the clinical practice of psychology*. Washington, DC: American Psychological Association.

Shafranske, E. P. (1996). Religious beliefs, affiliations, and practices of clinical psychologists. In E. P. Shafranske (Ed.), *Religion and the clinical practice of psychology* (pp. 149-162). Washington, DC: American Psychological Association.

Shafranske, E. P., & Malony, H. N. (1990). Clinical psychologists' religious and spiritual orientations and their practice of psychotherapy. *Psychotherapy: Theory, Research, and Practice, 27*, 72-78.

Spero, M. H. (1981). Countertransference in religious therapists of religious patients. *American Journal of Psychotherapy, 35*, 565-575.

Spero, M. H. (1990). Parallel dimensions of experience in psychoanalytic psychotherapy of the religious patient. *Psychotherapy: Theory, Research, and Practice, 27*, 53-71.

Spero, M. H., (1992). *Religious objects as psychological structures*. Chicago: University of Chicago Press.

Spero, M. H. (Ed.). (1996). *Psychotherapy of the religious patient*. Northvale, NJ: Jason Aronson.

Spero, M. H., & Mester, R. (1988). Countertransference envy toward the religious patient. *American Journal of Psychoanalysis, 48*, 43-55.

Sperry, L. L., & Giblin, P. (19996). Marital and family therapy with religious persons. In E. P. Shafranske (Ed.), *Religion and the clinical practice of psychology* (pp. 511-532). Washington, DC: American Psychological Association.

Strean, H. S. (1994). *Psychotherapy with the Orthodox Jew*. Northvale, NJ: Jason Aronson.

Strong, S. R. (1977). Christian counseling in action. *Counseling and Values, 27*, 89-128.

Tan, S.-Y. (1987). Cognitive-behavior therapy: A biblical approach and critique, *Journal of Psychology and Theology, 15*, 103-112.

Tan, S.-Y. (1994). Ethical considerations in religious psychotherapy: Potential pitfalls and unique resources. *Journal of Psychology and Theology, 22*, 389-394.

Tan, S.-Y. (1996). Religion in clinical practice: Implicit and explicit integration. In E. P. Shafranske (Ed.), *Religion and the clinical practice of psychology* (pp. 365-387). Washington, DC: American Psychological Association.

Tan, S.-Y., & Ortberg, J., Jr. (1995a). *Coping with depression.* Grand Rapids, MI: Baker.

Tan, S.-Y., & Ortberg, J., Jr. (1995b). *Understanding depression.* Grand Rapids, MI: Baker.

Thurman, C. (1989). *The lies we believe.* Nashville, TN: Thomas Nelson.

Thurston, N. S. (1994). When "perfect fear casts out all love": Christian perspectives on the assessment and treatment of shame. *Journal of Psychology and Christianity, 13,* 69-75.

Tisdale, T. C., Brokaw, B. F., Edwards, K. J., Key, T. L. (1993). *Impact of psychotherapy treatment on level of object relations development, God image, and self-esteem.* Paper presented at the American Psychological Association, Toronto, Canada.

Tjeltveit, A. C. (1986). The ethics of value conversion in psychotherapy: Appropriate and inappropriate therapist influence on client values. *Clinical Psychology Review, 6,* 515-537.

Tjeltveit, A. C. (1991). Christian ethics and psychological explanations of "religious values" in therapy: Critical connections. *Journal of Psychology and Christianity, 10,* 101-112.

Vande Kemp, H. (Ed.). (1991). *Family therapy: Christian perspectives.* Grand Rapids, MI: Baker.

Veenstra, G. (1992). Psychological concepts of forgiveness. *Journal of Psychology and Christianity, 11,* 160-169.

Watson, W. H. (1997). Soul and system: The integrative possibilities of family therapy. *Journal of Psychology and Theology, 25,* 123-135.

Whipple, V. (1988). Counseling battered women from fundamentalist Christian backgrounds. *Counseling and Values, 32,* 140-143.

Winger, D., & Hunsberger, B. (1988). Clergy counseling practices: Christian orthodoxy and problem solving styles. *Journal of Psychology and Theology, 16,* 41-48.

Wittmer, J., & Moser, A. (1974). Counseling the Old Order Amish child. *Elementary School Guidance and Counseling, 8,* 263-271.

Worthington, E. L., Jr. (1986). Religious counseling: A review of published empirical research. *Journal of Counseling and Development, 64,* 421-431.

Worthington, E. L., Jr. (1988). Understanding the values of religious clients: A model and its application to counseling. *Journal of Counseling Psychology, 35,* 166-174.

Worthington, E. L., Jr. (1990). Marriage counseling: A Christian approach to counseling couples. *Counseling and Values, 35,* 3-15.

Worthington, E. L., Jr. (1991). Psychotherapy and religious values: An update. *Journal of Psychology and Christianity, 10,* 211-223.

Worthington, E. L., Jr. (1994). A blueprint for intradisciplinary integration. *Journal of Psychology and Theology, 22,* 79-86.

Worthington, E. L., Jr., & DiBlasio, F. A. (1990). Promoting mutual forgiveness within the fractured relationship. *Psychotherapy: Theory, Research, and Practice, 27,* 219-223.

Worthington, E. L., Jr., Dupont, P. D., Berry, J. T., & Duncan, L. A. (1988). Christian therapists' and clients' perceptions of religious psychotherapy in private and agency settings. *Journal of Psychology and Theology, 13,* 29-41.

Worthington, E. L., Jr., Kurusu, T. A., McCullough, M. E., & Sandage, S. J. (1996). Empirical research on religion and psychotherapeutic processes and outcomes. A 10-year-review and research prospectus. *Psychological Bulletin, 119,* 448-487.

Worthington, E. L., Jr., & Scott, G. G. (1983). Goal selection for counseling with potentially religious clients by professional and student counselors in explicitly Christian or secular settings. *Journal of Psychology and Theology, 11,* 318-329.

Wright, H. N. (1986). *Self-talk, imagery, and prayer in counseling.* Waco, TX: Word.

Wyatt, S. D., & Johnson, R. W. (1990). The influence of counselors' values on clients' perceptions of the counselor. *Journal of Psychology and Theology, 18,* 158-163.

27

Psychotherapeutic Virtues and the Grammar of Faith

Robert C. Roberts
Wheaton College

A new method for integrating secular psychotherapies into Christian practice, "the virtues approach," is present-ed, which promises more fine-grained assessment of continuities and discontinuities between Christian theory and practice and secular theory and practice, and more hope of a richly and distinctively Christian psychotherapy. Albert Ellis' therapy is examined as a test case. Three Rational-Emotive Therapy (RET) virtues—equanimity, self-acceptance, and a sense of humor—are compared grammatically (structurally) with their Christian counterparts, and suggestions are made about consequences for Christian RET.

Efforts at integrating therapies into Christian thought and practice have tended to suffer two-con-nected defects. First, they have been prone to trade on continuities, and not to be clear enough about subtle discontinuities, between a psychological can-didate for integration and the tradition and life into which it is proposed to be integrated. Second, the psychological views of "integrators" have sometimes been thin in distinctly *Christian* psychological con-tent. I propose an approach which may get deeper "inside" a therapy and afford a clearer view of its structural details, while at the same time offering an entré into the riches of "personality theory" implicit in the New Testament and Christian tradition.

The Virtues Approach to Integration

In an earlier article (Roberts, 1985) I sought to use the idea of a virtue as a bridge-concept in assessing Carl Rogers' theory and practice. In the present one I am more explicit about the use of virtue-concepts, and use Albert Ellis' version of RET as a test case for the method.

A virtue, classically considered, is a characteristic, the possession of which contributes to a person's being fulfilled as a human: realized, actualized, whole, healthy, fully functioning, happy, mature, and well adjusted (Aristotle, 1985). Although the word "virtue" rings archaic in the ears of most psy-chologists, therapists work with some package of concepts such as congruence, openness, being in touch with one's feelings, autonomy, positive self-regard, integration, assertiveness, responsibility, self-acceptance, self-understanding, adaptivity, and "rationality." Most therapies have a picture of ideal personhood, and this picture of the actualized human is determined by and reflected in the theo-ry and techniques. Thus the list of traits composing a theorist's picture of the fully functioning person is really a list of virtues.

On the Christian side, too, a package of virtues forms the picture of a fully functioning person: patience, kindness, joy, stewardliness, humility, hospitality, obedience, confidence, self-control, peace, compassion, contentment, patience, trust, forgiveness, gratitude, hope, generosity, peaceable-ness, perseverance, and several others. Corresponding to these traits are a set of disciplines for nurturing persons in them: meditation, prayer, ministry, fellowship, exhortation, liturgical acts, scripture reading, spiritual guidance, and catechism. Thus, not only is there a list of virtues implicit in a psychotherapy; there is a body of practice in the Christian tradition that corresponds to the "interven-tions" of a psychotherapy.

The virtues approach trades on these analogies between therapies and Christianity. After the Christian integrator has become familiar with a ther-apy—preferably through clinical experience as well as reading and conversation with therapists—he or she draws up a small list of the central virtues pro-jected by the therapy in question, and then looks for the Christian counterpart of each of these psy-chotherapeutic virtues. What, for example, is the Christian virtue most closely analogous to Rogerian congruence, or RET rationality? In many cases the integrator will not be able to find a virtue *named* in the New Testament that corresponds to the thera-peutic virtue. But there will, presumably, be some trait in the Christian repertoire that will more or less correspond. (If none can be found, this too will provoke integrative reflection.) In the discussion of Albert Ellis below I discuss an RET virtue which I call "equanimity' (not explicitly named so by Ellis) which is the opposite of catastrophizing. I call the Christian counterpart "Christian equanimity."

Once the integrator has lists of counterpart virtues on both sides of the integration process, he or she is ready to think critically and creatively about their relationships. In what ways are the two traits similar, and in what ways different? How, for example, does Christian "integrity" differ from, and how is it similar to, the Rogerian virtue of "congruence"? (see Roberts, 1985, pp. 269-270). How does Christian "thoughtfulness" ("think about these things" Phil 4:8) differ from, and how is it similar to, the RET virtue of "rationality"? In pursuing such questions, the integrator primarily pursues a "grammatical" investigation, which enables him or her to go below the surface similarities and differences to structural ones. This pursuit will both presuppose and foster a critical understanding of the relationships that exist between the *goals* of therapy/sanctification (i.e, the virtues) and the *means* by which those goals are achieved (therapy procedures, Christian disciplines).

When the integrator has a perspicuous view of the relationships, at the level of detail, between Christianity and a psychotherapy, the real process of integration can begin. Integration occurs when certain Christianly acceptable elements from a secular psychotherapy become part of the actual practice of a Christian therapist. Integration in this sense is beyond what a theoretician such as I can do, being exemplified not just in therapists' beliefs, nor even in their powers of diagnostic inference and prescriptive skill, but in their perceptual and emotional dispositions, their ways of "seeing the world." Psychotherapy and Christian faith come together here in the integral *person* of the therapist. In the virtues approach, integration starts out as a theoretical and reflective activity, but eventuates in wisdom—something almost "intuitive." Indeed, it materializes in the Christian and therapeutic virtues of the therapist.

In a recent revival of an ancient Greek and Christian tradition, a philosophical literature is rapidly growing on the nature of virtues (and vices). This literature addresses, among other things, questions about how virtues relate to beliefs about the nature of reality and to ethical beliefs, as well as to other "cognitive" states; about the relationship between virtues and such mental states as desires, emotions, impulses, and other motivations; about the formation of virtues through modeling; about the relation between virtues, habits, and skills; about which traits qualify as virtues and which do not; about elusive differences between traits that may go by the same name; about the systematic interconnection between different virtues in the structure of a personality, and between different *kinds* of virtues; and about the relationship between virtues and the fulfillment of human life. (For examples of this literature, see Anscombe, 1958; Dykstra, 1981; Foot, 1978; Geach, 1977, Hauerwas, 1981; Holmer, 1978; MacIntyre, 1984; and Meilaender, 1984; for a large recent bibliography, see Kruschwitz & Roberts, 1986).

Kierkegaard also belongs to the tradition of reflecting about the virtues. In the history of philosophy and psychology, he is among the most penetrating thinkers about the development of personality and the determination of traits by features of individuals' "views" of themselves and their world. He is especially interesting to the integrator because, being a Christian thinker about personality, his thought is already an "integration of psychology and Christianity."

The virtues-approach is not so much a formula for integration (indeed, it will teach a person to distrust formulae, or simple "methods" of integration), nor a concrete proposal about the details of integrating one or another therapeutic system with Christianity. It is a way of focusing the issues of integration, and of refining one's critical skills as they apply to personality theory. It aims to be an enhancement of psychological common sense and wisdom.

Virtues Have a "Grammar"

An essential step in the virtues-approach is that of comparing psychotherapeutic virtues with their Christian counterparts. In making this critical comparison the integrator looks at the structure of the virtues on each side of the comparison. This "structure" is a function of rules governing the use of a virtue name within such contexts as a psychotherapy on the one hand, or Christian thought and life on the other. The rules for the use of the virtue *name* are in their turn determined by the *concept* of the virtue in question—which is to say, what the virtue is like, what it includes and excludes, what it is connected with, and so forth. To say that Christian gratitude or Aristotelian pride or Rogerian congruence each have a "grammar" is just to say that the concepts of these virtues differ in determinate ways which can be expressed in rule-like formulae specifying the connections and disconnections of these virtues with other virtues, beliefs, experiences, emotions, motives, actions, and so forth. (I borrow the term "grammar" from Wittgenstein, 1953). To know the grammar of a virtue is to have a schematic notion of the kind of "life" lived by someone who possesses the virtue in question.

To speak of a grammar is to call to mind the rules which govern how, in a given language, words or forms of words go together. Thus "I goes to school" is bad grammar because it violates the rule for which form of the verb "go" goes with "I." One could formulate this rule variously, with varying degrees of specificity, and to do so is to say what goes with what. English has a grammatical "structure" in virtue of the rule-based usage of its words, and because of this any word in English makes certain demands with regard to what goes with it. To know what goes with what is to possess grammatical knowledge. But neither the knowledge of the grammar nor the existence of the rule depends on there being a *formulation* of it; mostly we have this knowledge without being able to produce any felicitous formulations of the rules in question. Most of us just say things like, "'I' doesn't go with 'goes,'" and let it go at that.

To say a virtue has grammar is to say that it does not exist in isolation from other parts of the moral/spiritual/psychological existence of its possessor, any more than "goes" exists in isolation from other English words; just as "I" in English demands a certain form of the verb, the virtue of Aristotelian pride has *implications* for how its possessor behaves and experiences the world, for what he or she believes, and for what other traits can be virtues within the Aristotelian framework. Let me illustrate.

In Book IV of *Nicomachean Ethics*, Aristotle (1986) discussed the virtue of magnanimity—being "great-souled." To be magnanimous in Aristotle's sense is to have all the virtues—courage, temperance, justice, generosity, practical wisdom, and so forth—and thus to be in all respects an excellent specimen of humanity. But beyond being excellent, magnanimous individuals also *know* they are excellent and superior to other people and set great store by this fact. They have unbounded high self-regard and demand that others have it for them too. Aristotle remarks:

> He is the sort of person who does good but is ashamed when he receives it; for doing good is proper to the superior person, and receiving it to the inferior. He returns more good than he has received; for in this way the original giver will be repaid, and will also have incurred a new debt to him, and will be the beneficiary.
>
> Magnanimous people seem to remember the good they do, but not what they receive, since the recipient is inferior to

the giver, and the magnanimous person wishes to be superior. And they seem to find pleasure in hearing of the good they do, and none in hearing what they receive. (p. 1124b)

Aristotle's picture of excellence here is one to which independence from others and superiority to them are very central. Since being indebted is a form of dependency and inferiority, magnanimous persons seek not to be indebted to others, but to keep others indebted to themselves. Thus one Christian virtue is ruled out by Aristotelian magnanimity, namely *gratitude*—if we mean by gratitude a glad willingness to be indebted, perhaps even permanently indebted, to others. A package of virtues that includes Aristotelian magnanimity cannot also include Christian gratitude. This, then, is a grammatical remark about these two virtues.

But we can go further into the grammar of these virtues by asking what Christian beliefs make gratitude an aspect of human flourishing, and what Aristotelian beliefs make magnanimity an aspect of human flourishing. One answer is that in the Christian framework dependency and indebtedness are not bad things, indeed they can be very good things–because they reflect the way things are. We are creatures, and thus by nature fundamentally indebted to God. Beyond that we are redeemed sinners, dependent for our righteousness and hope on God's grace. It is thus an expression of our nature and most fundamental situation, and a matter of joy to acknowledge our indebtedness. And this willingness spills into our human relationships. The mature Christian does not mind being in another's debt, and does not connect all indebtedness, as Aristotle does, with being substandard. Thus when we go deeper into the grammar of Christian gratitude, we see a "doctrinal" background. Magnanimity will have a corresponding background, some set of beliefs about the nature of persons and their place in the cosmic order: the negative one of not acknowledging that we are creatures of a personal God, and the belief that some people are by nature superior to others, in such a way as not ever to be in a position of deep indebtedness to them.

In describing a person's character it is not enough, except for the roughest purposes, to give the *name* of some traits he or she may have. Nor, in comparing the character of two persons, is their having traits that go by the same name enough to indicate that they have the same trait. The Aristotelian virtue I have just discussed is sometimes called "pride." But Robert Schuller (1982), speaking as a Christian, also recommends pride as a virtue, and certainly does not mean to rule out gratitude and humility. This can be confusing, and we might long for a vocabulary in which one and only one virtue is named by each term. No such vocabulary is available, so where we must keep our concepts straight to avoid confusion, as in integration, we must attend to the grammar of the virtues.

Thus, we might say of two people that they both have the virtue of equanimity, meaning that they are quite unflappable in the face of the slings and arrows of fortune. Neither of them "catastrophizes" when they lose their job or a third of their net financial value, nor do they come down with a case of "can't-stand-it-itis" (Ellis, 1977a, p. 11) at the prospect of such an event. That they both have this trait is evidenced by their behavior in testing circumstances. But if this were the whole story about traits, then traits would have only a "surface-grammar": they would be dispositions to certain kinds of behavior (or non-behavior) in certain circumstances. However, we can see from the magnanimity/gratitude example that traits have semantic connections that determine their character fully as much as behavioral consequences do. A trait is embedded in, and shaped by, its possessor's view of things or philosophy of life. At a level below that of the surface-grammar, the identity of a trait is determined by these *semantic connections* or "depth-grammar." Thus, it is likely that a person who has equanimity as a result of Ellis' version of Rational-Emotive Therapy has a different virtue than somebody whose equanimity results from nurturance in Christian faith. Since their behavioral response to circumstances may be quite similar, the person who lacks an eye for the depth-grammar of virtues may not notice that different, and even incompatible, traits are being exemplified in the two cases. Another way to make the same point would be to say that, "spiritually," the two people may be poles apart—behaviorally similar, spiritually dissimilar.

Here one recognizes that virtues have their peculiar "shape" within systems of concepts, and in systematic connection with other virtues. Just as grammatical rules are always indexed to a particular language, so comments (rule-formulations of a sort) about the grammar of a virtue are always indexed to some tradition or system of thought. One asks questions like the following: What does congruence amount to (i.e., imply and exclude) within Rogerian therapy, and what does its Christian analog amount to in the Christian context? What does pride amount to in Aristotle's thought? What does adaptivity amount to within the thinking of RET, and what does its Christian analog amount to in the Christian context? What are the doctrinal connections of rationality in the RET context? (For an extended illustration of the grammatical analysis of the virtue of forgiveness, see Roberts, 1986.)

Bearing these general comments in mind, let us apply the virtues approach to the integration of RET into Christianity. I realize that there are different versions of RET, including some Christian ones. On the principles I have just laid out, there is no such thing as the grammar of RET virtues in general. Our remarks must therefore be indexed to a fairly definite context. Since Albert Ellis has a privileged position with respect to RET, I shall have his version of it in mind in what follows. For simplicity, however, I shall refer to the virtues implied by Ellis' therapy as "the RET virtues."

The RET Virtues

The central RET virtues are rationality, self-transparency, mutuality in relationships, responsibility, self-acceptance, equanimity, and a sense of humor. Together these pretty much constitute the RET picture of the flourishing human person (compare Ellis, 1971b, pp. 159-160). Rationality is a disposition to believe only propositions that can be backed up empirically, not to commit logical fallacies such as overgeneralization when deriving beliefs from evidence, and generally to seek to have beliefs that promote in oneself such other virtues as mutuality, self-acceptance, and equanimity. Ellis' ideal person is roughly a consistent logical empiricist and a pragmatist of an enlightened hedonist variety (see Ellis, 1962, chap. 6). Self-transparency is a general awareness of the influence that beliefs, particularly those that are negative, have on one's emotions and behavior (Ellis, 1971b, chap. 2). Thus it is the capacity to "troubleshoot" psychotherapeutically for oneself, and is basic for responsibility. Responsibility, as an RET virtue, is the disposition to take responsibility for your emotions, behavior, and beliefs, and thus to undertake strategies for self-improvement (Ellis, 1971b, p. 159). Mutuality is the ability to maximize your satisfactions insofar as they depend on other people's attitudes and behavior, through maximizing the satisfactions that others experience in relation to yourself (Ellis, 1971a, cap. 8; Ellis & Harper, 1961, chap. 19). Self-acceptance is the disposition not to rate yourself globally, nor to generalize ratings of your particular performances, attitudes, and traits to ratings of your "self" (Ellis, 1962, chap. 8. Equanimity is the ability to remain relatively undisturbed and emotionally level in a wide variety of potentially upsetting circumstances (Ellis, 1977a). A sense of humor is the ability to see and appreciate, from the perspective of RET rationality, the comical character of one's own irrational beliefs (Ellis, 1977c).

It is not difficult to see, even from these brief remarks, that the RET virtues form an interconnected "package," with the sort of structural and semantic dependency-relations among them that I have called their "depth grammar." They differ markedly in "grammar" from other traits, lodged in other systems of thought, which may go by the same or similar names.

The rest of this article will be devoted to a grammatical examination of three of these virtues: equanimity, self-acceptance, and a sense of humor. I select these three somewhat arbitrarily because there is not space to discuss the whole range of RET virtues. Hopefully the grammar of these three will connect them with several of the other virtues in the RET package, thus giving a glimpse of the total picture. A complete assessment of RET would require a close look at the full range of RET virtues and their Christian counterparts.

"Musturbation" and Equanimity

Much of emotional disturbance, according to Ellis (1977a), is a consequence of making unreasonable demands on oneself, one's associates, and one's environment: "What we normally call 'emotional disturbance,' 'neurosis,' or 'mental illness,' then largely consists of demandingness—or what I now refer to as *musturbation*" (p. 27). Thus if I believe that I *must* succeed at love-making, or *must* get the job I'm interviewing for, or *must* not make a fool of myself in the seminar, I set myself up for experiencing failure as horrible, awful, terrible, catastrophic, and unbearable. I make myself anxious about the prospect of love-making, interviewing, and seminar participation, thus increasing my chances of failure. Then when I do fail I experience despair and loss of self-esteem. It would be much healthier, says Ellis, to believe that while it would be nice to succeed in these areas, it is certainly not required; and while it is no doubt *disappointing* to fail, it is hardly catastrophic. Ellis (1977a) advises that we adopt a generally non-musturbating view of ourselves and the world:

> *All* awfulness or awfulizing, as far as I can see, makes ... nonsense—because it goes *beyond* empirical reality and invents a *surplus* badness or greater-than-badness to add to the obnoxious element in human living that, because of our choice of basic values (again, surviving and remaining reasonably happy while surviving), actually exist [sic]. (p. 25)

If we can learn to see *all* our goals as attractive and even important but not required—then we will have the RET virtue of equanimity. We will be emotionally flexible and adaptable, relatively content regardless of what happens. (Since I want to focus on the RET virtues I give this trait a name—something that Ellis does not do. He usually refers only to the vices, such as musturbation, to which this virtue corresponds.)

Another virtue that can be called equanimity is evident in the writings of the Apostle Paul. It, too, is an adaptability to varied and potentially distressing circumstances. "Give thanks in all circumstances" (1 Thess. 5:18), he says, and, "I have learned, in whatever state I am, to be content. I know how to be abased, and I know how to abound; in any and all circumstances I have learned the secret of facing plenty and hunger, abundance and want" (Phil. 4:11-12). "We are afflicted in every way, but not crushed; perplexed, but not driven to despair; persecuted, but not forsaken; struck down, but not destroyed" (2 Cor. 4:8-9). "So we do not lose heart. Though our outer nature is wasting away, our inner nature is being renewed every day. For this slight momentary affliction is preparing for us an eternal weight of glory beyond all comparison, because we look not to the things that are seen but to the things that are unseen" (2 Cor. 4:16-18). "So we are always of good courage ..." (2 Cor. 5:6). One can detect in these utterances a trait contrary to what Ellis calls "can't-stand-it-itis." Paul has, in his psychological repertoire, the capacity to "stand" a lot of adversities, sufferings, setbacks, and failures, without losing his "cool"—indeed, without losing his joy! And an element of this is a kind of non-musturbation—he does not *demand* that things go his way.

Undoubtedly, demandingness is both a source of unpleasant emotions and, for the Christian, in many cases highly inappropriate spiritually. Christians ought not to ascribe ultimate significance to such things as sexual performance, succeeding in a job interview, and making a good impression in a seminar. If highly upset over failure in such areas, they betray spiritual immaturity; were they mature, their Christian equanimity would prevent these circumstances from upsetting them. They ought to be able to treat these goals with a light touch, out of respect for a more appropriate order of priorities. And it seems that a Christian can even parallel the rational-emotive therapist in explaining *how* such attitudes are distortions. The Christian can agree that it is just silly to be ultimately concerned over success in a seminar. If you think critically about the rationale for giving the seminar this degree of significance, it becomes obvious in both the Christian and the RET conceptual schemes that it just doesn't *have* this much significance.

So the Christian and the rational-emotive therapist can agree that musturbating in this context is irrational. But their reason is only partly the same. Ellis' (1977a) rationale is that catastrophes don't' exist; that nothing is ultimately appalling:

> The very worst thing that could happen to me or any other person would presumably consist of our getting tortured to death very slowly. But even that would not be 100% badness, for we could always get tortured to death *even slower!* ... No matter what you desire, even the moon, you can always conclude in the end, "Well, I just don't seem to get what I want, and maybe I'll never get it. Too bad! I'll just have to live without it, for now and probably forever." (pp. 23, 26)

By contrast, the Christian's main rationale for not musturbating is that something else is of such great importance that success in a seminar pales to insignificance by comparison—not that nothing is of ultimate value, but that something is so much more wonderful and important than seminars and orgasms, that the latter get decisively "put in their place." For one with the eternal destiny of a child of God, to catastrophize over a job interview is to get things out of perspective, to say the least. For somebody who stands in the noble line of apostles, prophets, saints and martyrs, awfulizing over failure to get an erection is more embarrassing than the failure itself. For one who seeks first the kingdom of heaven—who has only one master whom he loves with all his heart—musturbating over a seminar looks downright comical!

Kierkegaard (1980) has expressed the point about Christian equanimity in this way:

> What the natural man catalogs as appalling—after he has recounted everything and has nothing more to mention—this to the Christian is like a jest. Such is the relation between the natural man and the Christian; it is like the relation between a child and an adult: what makes the child shudder and shrink, the adult regards as nothing. The child does not know what the horrifying is; the adult knows and shrinks from it. The child's imperfection is, first, not to recognize the horrifying, and then, implicit in this, to shrink from what is not horrifying. (p. 8)

In other words, the mature Christian has gained equanimity in little things like job interviews by getting them into perspective where, by comparison with what is truly momentous, they are seen as relatively unmomentous. This momentous Christian project Kierkegaard (1980) calls becoming a "self": "It is Christian heroism—a rarity, to be sure—to venture wholly to become oneself, an individual human being, this specific individual human being, alone before God, alone in this prodigious strenuousness and this prodigious responsibility" (p. 5).

Christianity raises the stakes by conceiving life as an arena where a person's acceptability before God is at issue; life is a matter of life and death. Such a view of life is, as Kierkegaard remarks, "strenuous," with the potential for producing or heightening disturbing emotions like anxiety and despair as well as the happy passion of faith. Ellis proposes that we avoid anxiety and despair by lowering the stakes, by adopting a less strenuous view of life, by making our highest goal not heaven and the love of God and neighbor, but "surviving and remaining reasonably happy while surviving" (1977a, p. 25), or leading "a longer, pain-avoiding, and satisfaction-filled life" (Ellis, 1977b, p. 110).

RET equanimity is thus very different from Christian equanimity. Although both virtues are dispositions not to be "disturbed" by a certain range of things, the goals or ultimate values projected in them are mutually inconsistent, and in consequence the attitudes themselves have a different semantic structure. Christian equanimity has its background in a Christian "heroism," a passionate pursuit of "the prize of the upward call of God in Christ Jesus" (Phil. 3:14), a transcendent valuing of human life. RET contentment is achieved precisely by *eschewing* all prizes of upward calls and reducing one's life-goals to manageable, obviously attainable ones—by telling oneself that nothing is of ultimate value. The Christian who is clear about the grammar of RET equanimity will judge that to possess this "virtue" is not triumph and health, but a spiritual defeat. Lacking anything that corresponds to the passionate response to an "upward call," the RET virtue of contentment seems to belong to what Kierkegaard (1980) calls "the philistine-bourgeois mentality," which

> lacks every qualification of spirit and is completely wrapped up in probability.... Bereft of imagination, as the philistine-bourgeois always is, whether alehouse keeper or prime minister, he lives within a certain trivial compendium of experience as to how things go, what is possible, what usually happens. In this

way the philistine-bourgeois has lost his self and God. (p. 41)

Self Acceptance

Another main source of upset, according to Ellis, is self-evaluation and self-justification. This he sharply distinguishes from rating one's *performances*, which is a legitimate activity (Ellis, 1962, p. 147), necessary to leading a "rational" life. People strongly tend to let their evaluation of their performances stain their evaluation of their selves. (Indeed, Ellis [1976] believes this tendency has a biological basis.) Thus, if I perform an awkward act, I tend to think myself an awkward person; if I do a culpable act, I tend to rate myself as a guilty person, thus feeling generally guilty and depressed. People don't become emotionally disturbed as a result of believing they have performed badly, but only as a result of the further belief, leaving their "selves" a complete evaluative blank, we will eradicate a lot of anxiety and depression.

(In another paper [Roberts, 1987] I have investigated the difficult question of what Ellis' rationale is, finally, for thinking it fallacious to ascribe value [negative *or* positive] to selves. My conclusion is that though he offers three rationales, none of these is, by his own standards, rational. I also note that while he often tells people, for practical therapeutic effect, that they have positive value just because they exist [Ellis, 1971b, p. 157], this policy is inconsistent with his theory, and he himself repeatedly notes that existence is no reason for thinking that a self has value [Ellis, 1962, p. 148; Ellis, 1971a, p. 131; Ellis, 1971b, pp. 19-20].)

Ellis (1977b) draws a strong contrast between self-acceptance and self-esteem:

> Self--acceptance means that the individual fully and unconditionally accepts himself whether or not he behaves intelligently, correctly, or competently and whether or not other people approve, respect, or love him. Whereas, therefore, only well-behaving (not to mention perfectly behaving) individuals can merit and feel self-esteem, virtually all humans are capable of feeling self-acceptance. (pp. 101-102)

Here Ellis needs help understanding his own position. He refers to the "feeling" of self-acceptance as though it is something positive, not just an evaluational blankness about oneself. And if I read his therapy right, he does want people to feel good about themselves. It would not really be human

flourishing to feel nothing one way or the other about ourselves, but only to have feelings about our performances.

A feeling, in Ellis' view, is a function of a belief or self-statement. But Ellis has instructed us not to believe anything, one way or the other, about the value of our "selves." So how can one have a feeling of self-acceptance. If Ellis wants to retain his implicit and common sense view that self-acceptance is a positive feeling, and still deny that it is based on any belief about our selves, he must give up two things: his blanket rejection of self-esteem, and his belief that feelings are all grounded in beliefs.

One kind of feeling of self-esteem is a function of the belief that one is performing well or has good traits, and Ellis is right that persons with this kind of self-esteem risk hating themselves if the conditions of their self-regard cease to be fulfilled. But there is another kind which he should not reject., This is a precognitive "sense of identity" or "feeling of personal security' which derives not from anything one *believes* about oneself, but instead from experiences of being unconditionally regarded by significant others, such as parents (largely long ago in forgotten childhood) and friends. One strongly *construes* oneself as having worth, but without a basis in any beliefs about oneself. So there is a self-acceptance which is a positive feeling of worth, but is not based on any fallacious (or valid) inference from beliefs about one's performances. I speculate that Ellis has this concept, though he is not disposed to admit it because of his view that all feelings are based in beliefs. The "self-acceptance" he officially countenances, which is the erasure of all evaluative beliefs from one's self-concept, is parasitic upon this precognitive self-esteem. It is only because a person already has some precognitive self-esteem that the process of abandoning self-evaluative beliefs can bring about the feeling of self-acceptance that he mentions in the above quote.

What, then, is the RET virtue of self-acceptance? It would seem to be *a precognitive self-esteem protected against the overlay of cognitive self-rejection or self-condemnation by a systematic abstinence from all propositions of global self-assessment.*

Let us turn now to integration. The first step is to find a counterpart, a Christian virtue as similar as possible to RET self-acceptance. I have already noted that in looking for counterparts we must not limit ourselves to virtues *named* in the New Testament. It is permissible to pick virtues that are not named, but are only exemplified there. But when we turn to the New Testament for a virtue resembling self-acceptance, we find nothing named, and perhaps nothing exemplified. The modern preoccupation with issues of self-love/hate, self-acceptance/rejection, self-esteem/downing seems strangely absent. The New Testament thought-world is not a world without selves, exactly, but it is short on self-preoccupation. In an address to the American Psychological Association in 1961, biblical scholar Krister Stendahl argued that, contrary to the standard western interpretation since Augustine, the Apostle Paul did not struggle with a guilty conscience, nor did he think of the gospel as an answer to any such "subjective" or "psychological" problem as self-rejection, self-hatred, or self-condemnation (Stendahl, 1963). In the Gospels we find some examples of self-condemnation, but it is this rather than a subsequent self-acceptance that is commended (see Luke 7:36-50 and 18:9-14). It appears that the point of recommending self-condemnation in these cases is not as a stage in the process towards fully liking or accepting oneself, but as a recognition of sin for what it is and thus a certain clarity about what the kingdom of God is and what acceptance or forgiveness by God is. Indeed, we find a great deal in the New Testament about God's acceptance of sinners, at the same time that we find nothing about their acceptance of themselves.

It would be hopeless for us, as 20th century Christians, to be so rigidly biblicist as to reject any virtue in the family of self-acceptance, just because the New Testament has none. Whether the concern is biblical or not, self-esteem issues are inescapable for us, and in the light of the gospel it is incredible to think that self-condemnation, for which there is such abundant biblical warrant, should be the last word. Besides this, the New Testament contains conceptual materials, such as forgiveness, reconciliation, the love of God, being a child of God, and others, that have a clear bearing on Christian self-acceptance. So it seems right to *construct* a virtue-concept on these lines.

If we do not eschew self-esteem as a virtue, what are we to make of the fact that the Apostle never applied the gospel to self-esteem issues, and that the New Testament in general never directly applies concepts like God's love and being a child of God to them? I think these facts should caution us against giving self-esteem a *central* place in our picture of maturity and mental health. It would be injudicious to make self-esteem foundational in Christian psychology if the Bible does not address it.

The conceptual materials I just referred to will be beliefs and images concerning who believers are. Distinctive about the Christian virtue of self-acceptance are the *terms* in which the person accepts himself. These beliefs will be evaluative ones such as

that I am a sinner, that I have rebelled against God and am helpless apart from grace, that he has adopted me along with these others to be his child, that God loves me and nothing can separate me from his love, and that I am destined for an eternal weight of glory.

Implicit in the New Testament are two different modes of self-evaluation which we might call the imputation mode and the responsibility mode. In the imputation mode, a person is evaluated, apart from his or her performances, by relationship to someone—either to Adam, in which case the individual is a sinner (a member of a race of sinners), or to Christ, as one justified by his blood and saved by him from the wrath of God (Rom. 5). In the responsibility mode, a person is evaluated on the basis of his or her performances. Because the individual has scorned some of God's children, refused them succor in time of need, and committed other identifiable sins, he or she is a sinner (Matt. 25). The more deeply self-condemning persons come to construe themselves, in these same terms, and at the same time to rejoice in the positive self-evaluation (forgiven, accepted, adopted as son or daughter), the more Christianly self-accepting they are.

Thus we see a stark grammatical difference between Christian self-acceptance and RET self-acceptance. To accept oneself in the RET model is to avoid all terms of self-evaluation, so that the only feeling of self-acceptance left is whatever precognitive self-esteem one possesses; in the Christian model it is to adopt some definite *terms* of self-evaluation, and consequently to feel a variety of "rejoicing" emotions such as gratitude, hope, and peace, now focused in a way somewhat different from New Testament examples, on *oneself*. A therapist who succeeded in Ellis' strategy of getting the client to forswear all global self-evaluations would also have precluded the client's development of Christian self-acceptance.

This is a significant point at which Ellis' psychotherapy resists Christian integration. Christian therapy, in contradiction with RET, necessarily encourages global self-evaluations. However, much of the actual practice of RET disputation of self-evaluations might be compatible with Christian therapy. If clients insist on deprecating themselves because they make insignificant social mistakes, the Christian therapist too might find it useful to point out that such mistakes hardly make them overall failures. A lot of the therapy with some clients might turn out to be correcting these sorts of mistakes. The difference will be that in addition to this ground-clearing the Christian therapists will have some global self-conceptualizations to promote, and that these will be central to the formation of self-acceptance in the client.

A Sense of Humor

I now explore another parallel between RET and Christianity, a virtue which is also a resource for fostering equanimity, self-acceptance, and other RET virtues and their Christian counterparts.

To see something in a comic *light*—to enjoy the humor in it–implies a certain detachment from it. To be amused by, for example, an eastern Kentucky accent is to take this version of the language as *not* being the unqualified standard for spoken English. Persons who laugh at Archie Bunker's bigotry cannot be wedded with qualification to Archie's views on ethnic relations. Even if only for the moment of the laugh, they have glimpsed the world from another standpoint.

I shall restrict the present discussion to cases of humor in which what is perceived comically is an action or trait of a person—something that requires the comical person to have a "viewpoint." "Can't-stand-it-itis," as Ellis is so keenly aware, requires a particular outlook. If others' can't-stand-it-itis appears comical to me, this will be because their outlook is manifested in things they say and do and feel. But further, I, as a person to whom their can't-stand-it-itis appears in a comic light, must also have a "viewpoint," and this viewpoint must be incompatible with that of the sufferers. (There are, of course, many cases of humor in which this interplay of contrasting viewpoints is not ingredient. When a fancily dressed gentleman falls into a mud puddle, the comic apprehension doesn't require much awareness of the gentleman's outlook on life.)

Because of the detachment involved in the experience of comic perception, if my *own* behavior, beliefs, actions, or traits come to seem funny to me, then a wedge has been driven between me and my world view and an opportunity for transformation has occurred. For example, let us say I insist on doing certain things perfectly, and refuse to do them at all if not perfectly. If I can be brought to see the humor in this, then I have to some extent and at least momentarily dissociated myself from my trait. If this perception then becomes more than momentary—if I dwell on it, and learn to dwell *in* it—then a personal development away from the comically apprehended viewpoint, and toward the new viewpoint, has begun.

Two characteristics give humor this transforming power. First, the standpoint of the humorous apprehension is always felt as *superior* to that taken by the person perceived as comical. The reason is that to grasp the humor in a situation is always to perceive some incongruity in it (Kierkegaard, 1941; Morreall, 1983), an incongruity which does not characterize the orienting standpoint. This explains the dissociation of the amused person from the comically-apprehended viewpoint. (To say that the standpoint of the humorous apprehension is felt as superior is not to say that the pleasure of humor is that of feeling superior to somebody.) Second, humor is *pleasant*, and thus has a natural power to "seduce" people into adopting the orienting standpoint and dissociating themselves from the comic one. This pleasure is often increased manyfold by the presence of other persons laughing "with" oneself and enjoying the fun. This helps to explain the power of humor to draw us into a viewpoint which at first may be alien to us.

Together, these two points explain the liberating power of humor, what is sometimes called "comic relief"—for example, the power of Erma Bombeck's humorous portrayal of oppressive housewife situations to relieve the sense of oppression by enabling her reader to dissociate herself, in this heartily pleasant way, from the oppressive situation (cf. Bombeck, 1985).

Ellis' humor is sometimes little more than playfulness, as when he puns or pokes fun at psychoanalysis. Even this has the therapeutic effect of causing people to relax. But the more essentially therapeutic employment of humor consists in getting his clients to see *themselves* (strictly speaking, their behavior, beliefs, and emotions)) in a comic light, from the RET perspective. Thus, he drives a little wedge between them and their world view, viscerally recommending to them, by the pleasure of humor, his own "rational" world view as a replacement for their "irrational" one.

Perhaps the simplest way that Ellis (1977a) does this is through a comic RET vocabulary in which he describes the client's beliefs and self-talk; this belief is a case of "musturbating"; that one is "awfulizing" or "horribilizing" or "catastrophizing"; and that attitude we call "can't-stand-it-itis." The comedy in these words makes clients more willing to be drawn into the RET view of themselves, and thus to abandon the viewpoint which they now more or less laugh at as a case of musturbating or horribilizing. Where clients are perhaps expecting the therapist to tell them they are suffering from an involutional psychotic reaction or a mildly oncoming case of presbyophrenia, Ellis tells them their problem is their "nutty ideas" (Ellis, 19177c, p. 263). This comic simplicity has a liberating effect, that of bringing the problem within the arena of things about which clients can do something. Insofar as they are tickled by the humor, seeing their ideas as nutty and their problems as stemming from them, they are in the process of beginning to accept responsibility for their problems (another RET virtue).

Ellis (1977c) uses comic exaggeration to reflect back to clients their low self-esteem, and to underline the "irrationality" of it: "But if I keep referring to their slobhood, their wormhood ... they not only realize how they keep rating themselves but also laugh at their own self-downing and tend to help themselves give it up" (p. 266). He also uses irony. To promote self-acceptance by dispelling perfectionism, Ellis (1977c) says to a member of his therapy group:

> You mean you only repeated that idiotic act five times this week? I don't see how we can let you remain in a crummy group like this one. Now don't you think you'd better go out next week and do it at least ten times more, so that you can remain a worthy member of this group? (p. 265)

The irony of rejecting this member of the group because, having only goofed up five times this week, she was becoming too good for them, has the effect of saying to her, "your belief that you need to be perfect is one of your nutty ideas." It also has the effect of saying unsentimentally, "We accept you with your warts." If she enjoys the humor, she will to some extent have been drawn over into Ellis' ideological (and thus emotional) camp. Perceiving the humor in her perfectionism, she sees herself from the perspective of Ellis' beliefs about what is valuable, appropriate, and rational, and thus affectively dissociates herself from her perfectionism. And she is on the way to becoming emancipated from its emotional and behavioral consequences.

Kierkegaard's writings are peppered with examples of a Christian therapeutic use of humor, and with reflections on the Christian significance of humor. He calls Christianity "the most humorous view of life in world-history" (Kierkegaard, 1970, p. 1681). "Humorist" seems to be for him a special calling and role—that of seeing human behavior in the comic dimension that it reveals to a Christian perspective and of devising ways to make this comic perception available to others. His humorist is a very serious comedian in the services of Christianity and is, as such, a therapist and liberator to an age which locked itself into unhealthy and un-Christian patterns of self-assessment and world-assessment.

Kierkegaard (1970) describes the comic power of the new view of things brought about by the advent of the Christian gospel.

> Everything which hitherto had asserted itself in the world and continued to do so was placed in relation to the presumably single truth of the Christians, and therefore to the Christians the kings and the princes, enemies and persecutors, etc., appeared to be nothing and to be laughable because of their opinions of their own greatness. (p. 1674)

As long as there was no higher viewpoint from which to see the pretentions of kings and princes, poets, and philosophers, there was nothing humorous in their claims to greatness. If this is not greatness, what is? But in the light of an eternal God, infinitely greater than any king, the pretensions of these mortals to deific grandeur begins to look a bit incongruous. The incongruity is heightened immeasurably by the fact that this eternal ruler of the universe humbled himself, became a man, ministered largely to the poor and outcast, and then died the ignominious death of criminal execution, for the sins of people like kings and philosophers. This leaves the kings and philosophers looking a little silly if they strut about as though they are something great. Also, pretentiousness among Christians becomes laughable, along with a worldly ordering of values such as sometimes occurs in Christians. And when this worldly ordering gets focused in a comic light (probably only with the help of a skilled humorist), it tends to dissolve; thus humor becomes "therapeutic" in the Christian context as well—it becomes a confederate of conversion first, and then of sanctification.

It is not difficult to imagine a Christian art of therapeutic humor in which, taking as viewpoint the fact that God has entered history and died for sinners, the humorist-therapist skillfully casts in a comic light the musturbating, catastrophizing, horribilizing, and self-downing—as well as the rejoicing, the pride-taking, the hoping, and the equanimity—of those who are oriented in these attitudes by the "secular world view." Just as Ellis' humor is a device for "converting" clients from one set of beliefs about themselves and the world and what matters, to *his* set of beliefs, and thus nurturing them in the RET virtues of equanimity, self-acceptance, responsibility, rationality, and mutuality, so the Christian therapist might use humor as a device for "converting" people from their set of character-shaping beliefs to the Christian set, thus nurturing them in the Christian virtues.

My point in this section has been that humor, as a therapeutic expedient for engendering equanimity and self-acceptance, works by moving people from one "viewpoint" to another "viewpoint" inconsistent with the first. But just as there is no such thing as equanimity or self-acceptance *as such*, but only equanimity or self-acceptance as hanging in one or another ideological web, so also this therapeutic expedient is inevitably a matter of moving the client from one set of "ideas" to another quite particular set of ideas. If a sense of humor is a human virtue, then we must say that "sense of humor," too, is not a univocal term: It does not denote a single virtue, but a family of virtues which will differ in their ideological backgrounds and thus in their grammars. There is a Christian sense of humor, founded upon the Christian viewpoint, and there are secular counterparts to this virtue, such as the RET sense of humor which is founded upon Ellis' viewpoint. Christian therapists must beware, in using some of the techniques of RET, with its very different basic beliefs, of slackening their hold on those particular beliefs which lie behind the Christian virtues of equanimity, self-acceptance, and humor.

Concluding Remarks

I have proposed a new method of integration and tested it by applying it to a small but significant portion of one's psychotherapy. The virtues approach holds out some hope of mapping an avenue through secular psychology to a therapy and theory of personality which is both distinctively Christian and solidly informed by the mainstream. The present article has only been a trial run. If this approach is deemed a fruitful avenue, then the ambitious task just mentioned will involve an application of it to the whole range of current psychotherapies. Studies of the relative grammars of the virtues projected by dynamic therapies, by the Rogerian, gestalt and reality therapies, by Jungian therapy, behavioral therapies, and the various forms of family therapy, will need to be conducted by Christian psychological thinkers.

References

Anscombe, G. E. M. (1958). Modern moral philosophy. *Philosophy, 33*, 1-19.

Aristotle. (1985), *Nicomachean ethics* (T. Irwin, Trans.). Indianapolis: Hackett.

Bombeck, E. (1985). *Four of a kind*. New York; McGraw-Hill.

Dykstra, C. (1981). *Vision and character*. New York: Paulist.

Ellis, A. (1962). *Reason and emotion in psychotherapy*. Secaucus, NJ: The Citadel.

Ellis, A. (1971a). *Growth through reason*. North Hollywood, CA: Wilshire.

Ellis, A. (1971b). *Humanistic psychotherapy*. New York; McGraw-Hill.

Ellis, A. (1976). The biological basis of human irrationality. *Journal of Individual Psychology, 32*, 145-168.

Ellis, A. (1977a). The basic clinical theory of rational-emotive therapy. In A. Ellis & R. Grieger (Eds.), *Handbook of rational-emotive therapy* (pp. 3-34). New York: Springer.

Ellis, A. (1977b). Psychotherapy and the value of a human being. In A. Ellis & R. Grieger (Eds.), *Handbook of rational-emotive therapy* (pp. 99-112). New York: Springer.

Ellis, A. (1977c). Fun as psychotherapy. in A. Ellis & R. Grieger (Eds.). *Handbook of rational-emotive therapy* (pp. 262-270). New York: Springer.

Ellis, A., & Harper, R. (1961). *A guide to successful marriage*. North Hollywood, CA: Wilshire.

Foot, P. R. (1978). *Virtues and vices*. Berkeley, CA: University of California Press.

Geach, P. T. (1977). *The virtues*. Cambridge, MA: Cambridge University Press.

Hauerwas, S. (1981). *Community of character*. Notre Dame, IN: University of Notre Dame Press.

Holmer, P. (1978). *The grammar of faith*. San Francisco: Harper and Row.

Kierkegaard, S. (1941). *Concluding unscientific postscript*. (D. Swenson & W. Lowrie, Trans.). Princeton, NJ: Princeton University Press.

Kierkegaard, S. (1980). *The sickness unto death*. (H. Hong & E. Hong, Trans.). Princeton, NJ: Princeton University Press.

Kierkegaard, S. (1970). *Søren Kierkegaard's journals and papers,* Vol. 2. (H. Hong & E. Hong, Trans.). Bloomington, IN: Indiana University Press.

Kruschwitz, R. B., & Roberts, R. C. (1986). *The virtues: Contemporary essays on moral character*. Belmont, CA: Wadsworth.

Lazarus, A. (1977). Toward an egoless state of being. In A. Ellis & R. Grieger (Eds.). *Handbook of rational-emotive therapy* (pp. 113-118). New York; Springer.

MacIntyre, A. (1984). *After virtue* (2nd ed.). Notre Dame, IN: University of Notre Dame Press.

Meilaender, G. D. (1984). *The theory and practice of virtue*. Notre Dame, IN: University of Notre Dame Press.

Morreall, J. (1983). *Taking laughter seriously*. Albany, NY: State University of New York Press.

Roberts, R. C. (1985). Carl Rogers and the Christian virtues. *Journal of Psychology and Theology, 13*, 263-273.

Roberts, R. C. (1986). Forgiveness as therapy. *The Reformed Journal, 36*, 7, 19-23.

Roberts, R. C. (1987). *Albert Ellis on evaluating selves*. Manuscript submitted for publication.

Schuller, R. (1982). *Self-esteem: The new reformation*. Waco, TX: Word.

Stendahl, K. (1963). The apostle Paul and the introspective conscience of the west. *Harvard Theological Review, 56*, 199-215.

Wittgenstein, L. (1953). *Philosophical investigations*. (G. E. M. Anscombe, Trans.). New York: Macmillan.

28

Dealing with Religious Resistances in Psychotherapy

Bruce Narramore
Rosemead School of Psychology
Biola University

Managing resistance to insight and change is one of the central tasks in psychotherapy. When working with religious patients, therapists face the added task of dealing with resistances which may be supported by the patient's religious belief system. When this happens, therapists may be tempted to either avoid confronting the resistances for fear of undermining (or being accused of undermining) the patient's faith or to interpret the resistances in ways that do either undermine the patient's faith, or at least imply that faith is irrelevant to the patient's emotional health. This article deals with the management of resistances with Christian patients who are using their religious faith to reinforce their defensive structure in the psychotherapeutic process.

In spite of the burgeoning interest in the integration of psychology and theology and Christian approaches to counseling and psychotherapy, there is a paucity of scholarly publications that address specific ways in which a Christian understanding can impact the interventions of professional psychotherapists. A number of books and articles have discussed basic models of integration (Carter & Narramore, 1979; Farnsworth, 1981), introductory issues (Jones, 1986; Evans, 1989) and pastoral or lay approaches to counseling (Adams, 1970; Tan, 1991). Several excellent works relating psychoanalytic object relations theory to God concepts and the religious experience of patients in psychotherapy (Meissner, 1984; Rizzuto, 1979; Spero, 1992) have also been published. But relatively little has been written about the specifics of how the professional psychotherapist's religious understanding and commitment (let alone a specifically Christian understanding and commitment) impacts the actual interventions of the professional psychotherapist—especially within an insight oriented, in-depth approach to psychotherapy (Lovinger, 1984; Peteet, 1981).

This article is written to further our understanding of ways in which traditional depth psychotherapeutic interventions may be modified or applied in ways that incorporate attention to the patient's spiritual life and add an explicitly Christian dimension to the therapeutic work. Specifically, this article deals with one aspect of the psychotherapy process—dealing with resistances that are reinforced by the patient's religious experience, worldview, or biblical interpretation. It suggests a way of dealing with these resistances that incorporates the psychotherapist's biblical understanding and Christian commitment within a traditional understanding of the dynamics of resistances and technical procedures for dealing with them.

One of the paradoxes of psychotherapy is that no matter how strongly patients want to overcome their problems and no matter how much time and money they invest in therapy, they also persistently engage in efforts to fight the treatment, to avoid facing their pain, to resist growth, and to hang on to their maladaptive patterns. Sometimes these efforts, known as resistances, are obvious, as in the case of patients who routinely fill the hour with a stream of intellectual sounding analysis of their plight but who never allow themselves to experience or feel their plight. Other times resistance is more subtle, as in the case of dependent patients who are outwardly cooperative and who work hard to please their therapists and to be good patients but who fail to grow out of their dependency because they never face the hurt and anger beneath it.

But whether obvious or subtle, resistances play such a key and ongoing role in psychotherapy that Freud (1912) described them as accompanying "the treatment step by step" (p. 103). Menninger (1961) spoke of the "never ending duel between the analyst and the patient's resistance" (p. 102). And all dynamically oriented therapists agree that the success of therapy is to a significant degree determined by the success of overcoming resistances.

Although theorists have debated the precise nature and meaning of resistance, for the purpose of this article I will simply define resistance as the manifestation of defensive processes within the psychotherapeutic

© *Journal of Psychology and Theology*, 1994, *22*, 249-258. Used by permission.

situation. Seen in this light, resistances refer to any effort on the part of patients, whether conscious or unconscious, to avoid gaining awareness of their hidden psychological conflicts and painful or upsetting thoughts, feelings, and experiences. Resistances are always motivated by the belief that no matter how painful or frustrating the current state of affairs may be, it is in some ways preferable to what the patient would experience if he or she should give up the resistance and face the hidden need, feeling, thought, memory, or conflict beneath it. From the patient's perspective, resistance is the only way he knows of coping. This creates the fundamental dilemma patients face. At one level they know their current state of affairs is undesirable and unacceptable. But at another, they are terrified by the alternative so they rigidly cling to the old and familiar.

Although resistances can be manifested in unlimited ways (silence, obsessive talking, missing sessions, lateness, speaking in generalities, intellectualizing, avoiding topics, idealizing or devaluing the therapist, flight into health, acting out, etc.) and while most resistances are overdetermined, there are a limited number of early developmental fears that consistently trigger these resistances. From a psychodynamic developmental perspective, these include:

1. The fear of loss of boundaries and regression into psychosis
2. The fear of destroying the therapist, and consequently all hope for help
3. The fear of abandonment
4. The fear of attack by the therapist or others
5. The fear of being unloved (later developmentally than abandonment)
6. The fear of bodily damage or punishment
7. The fear of loss of self esteem through the punishment of guilt

Since just about anything can be used in the service of resistance, it should come as no surprise that our patient's religious experiences and understandings may also be used for defensive purposes. And since experiences and concepts like union with God, alienation, justice, love, guilt, and forgiveness are at the heart of Christianity, it is natural that Christians attempt to cope with their deepest fears within the context of their faith. But since deep fears distort our perceptions and since all of our earthly relational fears are likely to be transferred or projected onto God, it is natural that Christian patients will at times misuse their faith to try to avoid their fears and pain instead of use their faith to help them confront their deepest anxieties.

Although I will occasionally use the term "religious resistance" that term is not technically accurate. The better way of framing this is "religiously reinforced resistance." There is no such thing as a unique defense mechanism that is strictly religious. Religious patients use all of the standard defense mechanisms and no new ones. Any or all of the standard defenses, however, may be cloaked in religious language and meaning. Patients who rely excessively on intellectualization will naturally attempt to use their faith to reinforce or justify their intellectualizing by appealing to scriptures that discuss thinking or cognitive processes. Patients who rely on reaction formation to maintain a precarious psychic balance are likely to be drawn to scriptures that seem to suggest that we can become suddenly and completely loving, kind, or holy instead of verses that talk about pain, relationships and the process of growth. And patients who utilize projection will be prone to appeal to scripture to justify their projections. Since the Bible has a lot to say about God and Satan, these patients are likely to grab onto isolated biblical teachings to support their projections of warded off parts of themselves into an external object. What better place could they find to locate the unacceptable parts of themselves than Satan and his demons and what better place to locate their healthy, loving thoughts and feelings than God?

Because of the power of religious symbols, language, and experiences, resistances that involve religion may at times seem stronger and more difficult to manage, but they are fundamentally no different from any other resistance. When we discuss religious resistances, we are merely discussing psychological mechanisms that have a religious content, or that are framed in religious language, or that are tied in with our patient's religious experience. The actual psychological dynamics are no different.

The Christian Therapist's Dilemma

For the religious therapist, the patient's attempt to utilize faith in the service of resistance raises several important questions and therapeutic issues centering around the therapist's own countertransference feelings about the use and misuse of faith, technical procedures for dealing with religiously reinforced resistances, and the ethics of working in ways that are intended to impact a patient's values and belief system. Although it is impossible to comprehensively address the problem of religiously framed resistances apart from an understanding of the therapist's countertransference, that is beyond the scope of this article and has also been dealt with elsewhere (Kehoe & Getheil, 1984; Spero, 1981).

This article is written from the assumption that there can be significant therapeutic advantages to a general matching of patient and therapist values and beliefs, including religious faith. Although this matching can erect barriers to effective psychotherapy if the therapist is unaware of the potential transference and countertransference elements of her relationship with her patients (Spero, 1990) it can also provide a level of understanding and appropriate safety that is a significant asset to the therapeutic process. In fact, the interpretation of resistances is one of the areas where the religiously oriented practitioner can be especially sensitive to the needs, fears, and conflicts of her patients and intervene in ways that are consistent with the patient's religious world view, therefore avoiding unnecessarily heightening the resistances. Other things being equal, religiously oriented therapists should also be in a better position to discriminate between healthy and unhealthy uses of faith.

For the purposes of this article I have limited myself to discussing the work of a Christian therapist with a Christian patient in order to have time to focus on some technical procedures which can be used by therapists to address religiously reinforced resistances of their Christian patients. Given a shared Christian commitment between the therapist and patient and an implicit shared assumption that the therapist will not attempt to undermine the patient's religious faith, we can frame the Christian therapist's dilemma in dealing with religiously reinforced resistances this way: If we believe that our patients will not be able to grow unless they modify and give up some of their defenses, and if some of those defenses are strongly tied up with their Christian faith, how can we help our patients see the defensive, maladaptive way they are using faith without undermining that faith?

For example, if a patient wants us to read the Bible with him and we believe he is desiring this in order to control us or keep the therapy on a cognitive level in order to avoid experiencing upsetting emotions or warded off thoughts, feelings or desires, and we choose not to read the Bible, are we suggesting to him that the Bible is irrelevant to his problems? Or if he wants to pray and we choose not to, are we implying that prayer is irrelevant? Worse yet, if we point out that he is using these spiritual disciplines defensively, are we telling him that prayer and Bible reading are not only irrelevant intrusions into his therapy, but negative experiences which he uses to avoid reality? I think if we are honest with ourselves we must admit that some patients of Christian therapists have reached precisely these conclusions even though their therapists may not have held these beliefs at all.

On the other hand, if we unthinkingly engage in these activities with our patients, may we not be reinforcing their defensive, or even pathological use of faith? And what about less direct interactions when we are not asked to do something, but a patient merely describes his involvement in some religious activity? Let us say a patient tells us he prays about his sessions or about some problem in his life. Do we affirm that as a positive step? Do we interpret any defensive or connective motives that may be involved in his prayers? Or do we simply ignore his discussion of prayer and move on to the *real* work of therapy—the emotional/relational—and in so doing appear to assume that prayer is irrelevant? What about the patient who tells us he has had some kind of special experience with God which we suspect may be more a reflection of early, primitive mental processes like omnipotent thinking or fusion than it is a real experience with God? Or what about the patient who we know is approaching some very scary memories, desires, or feelings and who suddenly tells us someone prayed for him and he is fine now so he does not need to continue with therapy? Do we dare interpret the potentially resistive component of these experiences to our patients? And if so, how do we do that? In the remainder of this article I will spell out one way of working with resistance that I believe can help deal with these dilemmas.

Techniques for Handling Resistances

Before offering some suggestions on handling the specifically religious aspects of resistance I would like to set out a basic approach to dealing with any kind of resistance. Although theorists like Freud (1912) and Greenson (1967) have variously labeled the steps in the process of dealing with resistances, for our present purposes we can sum them up in four technical procedures: pointing out (demonstrating or confronting) the resistance, clarifying the resistance, interpreting the resistance, and working through.

Patients are in no position to modify their resistances until they become consciously aware of them. The first step in the process, then, is to help the patient begin to observe his resistance. This can be done by simply saying something that calls attention to the resistance. We might say, "I notice that each time you begin to feel sad, you rather quickly change the subject," or "I notice that each time you begin to feel upset with your mother, you quickly say, 'But she was doing the best she could.'"

Once patients begin to see their resistance, we need to help them clarify how it works. We need to help them see what painful feelings they are avoiding and how they do it. Sometimes I try to stir up my patient's curiosity about their defenses by following up a confrontation like those above with a reflective question like, "I wonder why?" If a patient is more resistant and continues changing the subject or avoiding the affect, I may say, "You don't seem very curious as to why you change the subject. And if they say "No, I guess I'm not," I will ask, "Do you have any thoughts about why?" or comment, "I get the feeling it's pretty important to you that you not be very curious." The goal of this step is to help the patient become more fully aware that he is running from something frightening, and to help him see what seems to trigger the cycle and the price he pays for his excessive reliance on defenses.

The third step in the process is to interpret the resistance. Like the first two stages, this is an ongoing process. It involves gradually exploring any thoughts, memories and fantasies which the patient has in connection with the frightening affect. There are many ways of doing this. One is to simply listen to the patient's undirected associations and see where they lead. We can also direct their thoughts by saying, "You seem so frightened by your angry (or whatever) feelings. What comes to mind that might happen if you allow yourself to feel them?" Or we can say, "What thoughts and feelings do you have when you think of being angry with me?" or, "What other times come to mind when you feel (or have felt) this way? This last question begins to trace the history and original purposes of the defense. This is another important step in interpreting a resistance, as long as it follows a re-experiencing of the affect in the present instead of being a substitute for that essential process.

The final step is working through. This simply means that we go through the first three steps of pointing out, clarifying and interpreting the resistances many times until the patient starts feeling less afraid, more confident and safe, and more open to his inner experience—both positive and negative. It also involves finding alternative, healthy ways of dealing with pain and conflict. In this process of regaining access to previously warded off parts of the self, our patients become emotionally stronger, and less anxious, angry, and depressed.

Special Considerations
for Religious Resistances

With this background into a general way of working with resistances, let's turn to the unique aspects of dealing with resistances that have a religious component. I would like to sum up my understanding in four basic propositions: First, like all resistances, religiously tinged resistances must be interpreted. Second, the methods and techniques for dealing with religious resistances are in most ways identical to techniques for dealing with all resistances. Third, because of both the temporal and eternal consequences of dealing with religious resistances, we need to take special care when confronting, clarifying and interpreting them. Fourth, since Christian patients often twist scriptural interpretations in order to support their resistances, there are times when the judicial use of alternative interpretations or corrective biblical passages can be a very helpful part of the therapeutic process. Lovinger (1979) refers to this as finding "alternative translations or connotations in the text."

When therapist and client both share a Christian commitment, these last two assumptions can be fleshed out in several ways. It is often possible, for example, to affirm the healthy aspects of the religious experience in question before interpreting the defensive aspects. To a patient who is trying to avoid a meaningful relationship with us by saying the Bible is all he or she should need, we might say something like, "Yes, God certainly wants us to study the Bible," before we go on to say, "but I notice that sometimes you especially read the Bible when you are afraid to talk with another person." Although it is neither necessary nor helpful to preface all interpretations of religious resistances this way, for certain patients, especially in the early phases of therapy or at certain critical junctures, this step reduces their conscious fear that we are trying to undercut their faith, thus strengthening the therapeutic alliance and making it easier for them to hear. It also lets them know that we too believe that faith and the exercise of spiritual disciplines is an important part of their life which is naturally related to their emotional and relational adjustment. The technical procedure here is not fundamentally different than one we take in interpreting almost any kind of resistance. We look for the adaptive ingredient of our patient's defenses, affirm the healthy aspects of that, and then move sensitively into the more maladaptive part of the resistance. In the case of religiously reinforced resistances we are simply doing the same thing with the patient's religious experience.

Once patients know that we are not questioning the validity and significance of all of their spiritual experience, but only a selected, maladaptive portion, we can sometimes confront the resistance with a very brief scripture passage that challenges their distorted perception or defensive use of faith. For example, when a patient says, "But I shouldn't need anyone but God," we might respond, "Yes, our relationship with God is absolutely crucial but you know, when God saw that Adam was alone, He didn't tell Adam, 'What's the matter with you Adam? You have me. That should be enough.' He created Eve. God apparently made us so that we need each other."

We have to be careful not to be drawn into a theological argument here, but this technique can be very helpful if it is used judiciously. By offering an alternative biblical perspective we are telling our patient, "The issue is not between a Christian perspective (held by a patient) and a threatening non-Christian perspective (held by the therapist). Instead the issue is a conflict between a perspective previously assumed to be biblical (by the patient) and an alternative way of looking at things that may be equally or more biblical. This enables the patient to consciously perceive the therapist as a potential ally of his faith—at least the healthy components of it—rather than as a potential threat. This can be especially helpful in the initial phase of therapy, before patients understand how extensive their tendency to deny, distort or avoid aspects of their internal emotional life may be and how that can lead to distortions and misuse of faith.

Framing some confrontations of our patients' resistances in biblical language also helps minimize a potentially negative result of some psychotherapy with Christians—the tendency for patients to segregate their spiritual life and relationship with God from the emotional growth they experience in therapy. When the psychotherapist, especially a Christian psychotherapist, does not incorporate biblical insights or perspectives directly into her work, it is easy for the patient to conclude, "The Bible and my faith are not relevant to my emotional adjustment. The resolution for my problems is strictly a psychological one."

This kind of isolation of the spiritual from the emotional deprives the patient of the opportunity to experience the rich provisions for growth, insight and change that can come from a personal relationship with God and reinforces, if not actually helps create, an artificial dichotomy between the spiritual and the emotional. That topic, however, is large enough to deserve separate consideration. For now, I simply want to observe that if we therapists do not in some way affirm our patients' spiritual commitment or address their problems and needs within the context of their faith, we may unknowingly be contributing to this unfortunate separation and to an undermining of the patients' holistic and impactful understanding of their faith. By interpreting religiously reinforced resistances within the context of our patient's faith we minimize this potential problem.

Before leaving this step, one other potential dynamic deserves discussion. At the same time that working from within the context of a patient's faith can be a major asset to the therapeutic process, we also need to remember that patients seek out therapists with similar values for a variety of reasons, not all of which are healthy. For example, some Christian patients choose Christian therapists precisely because they assume a Christian therapist will play along with their spiritualized defenses. They know at some level that a good therapist is likely to help them get in touch with very painful and upsetting thoughts and feelings so they select a Christian therapist whom they assume will share their commitment to avoidance. When that is the case, we need to be aware of that dynamic and prepared to work with the feelings of anger, betrayal or fear that our use of scripture to frame a confrontation of a resistance may bring.

After confronting a patient's resistance once with a potentially corrective biblical quotation, I continue to interpret the religiously reinforced resistance like I would any other. I look for the anxiety that is motivating the defense and attempt to help my patients recognize the pain, fear or guilt beneath it. I would rarely offer more than one biblical corrective because that can shift the focus of the therapeutic work from the current affective relationship between the therapist and patient to an intellectualized, cognition discussion.

If the patient succeeds in engaging the therapist in an intellectualized debate about faith, the resistances are only reinforced and the work of therapy cannot proceed. This is one of the potential countertransference issues of which the Christian therapist must be aware. In working within the context of the patient's faith, and especially in utilizing scripture, we must be sure that our goal is to help the patient come into a fuller awareness of his internal experience, not to work out our own unresolved feelings about our faith or to insure our patient's "correct" interpretation of scripture. Hidden motives like this actually move patients further away from their warded off thoughts, feelings and wishes, or collude with them in dealing with them in an intellectualized, defensive fashion. As our patients become less defensive and more open they will naturally be less likely to distort their scriptural understandings.

Clinical Example

This article was initially presented orally to a group of psychological practitioners and graduate students. The participants indicated that they found several brief clinical vignettes helpful in fleshing out the ideas of the article. Consequently I am including a few typical therapeutic interactions with patients who are utilizing their faith in support of their resistances. I will present one excerpt that communicates something of the give and take involved in interpreting resistances during the therapeutic hour. Then I will briefly discuss several of the most common scripture passages or religious beliefs that are used to reinforce resistances in therapy and offer a biblical corrective that I have sometimes found helpful in working with Christian patients.

As I put these vignettes on paper, I realized how much is lost in selecting isolated interactions from the therapeutic hour and presenting them without the context, affect and relationship that forms the foundation for our therapeutic work. Without the ability to communicate an affective sensitivity to my patient's struggles, some of these interventions fail to convey the empathic understanding and connection that is absolutely essential if patients are going to hear and respond to our interpretations. Consequently I remind the reader that the most crucial variables that enable patients to gradually face and give up their resistances are not cognitive. They are the relationship between the therapist and patient, the sensitivity of the therapist, and the timing of the intervention. To place these interventions in the context of my own therapeutic work, I generally only engage in this type of highly active therapeutic interaction after rather lengthy periods of empathic listening to my patient's struggles and I frequently follow this type of interaction with similar periods of active, receptive, but often silent listening. Each of the following vignettes will be best understood when they are placed within this broader context of the ongoing therapeutic relationship and not seen as reflecting the majority (or even a substantial amount) of the intervention during any one therapeutic hour.

During the intake interview a patient who specifically sought out a Christian therapist tells me, "I shouldn't need therapy. I should just trust God." We have many options here, with the ultimate goal being to help the patient realize that in addition to the positive side of trusting God, he may be using his faith to avoid self disclosure and close emotional involvement with other human beings, including his therapist.

Therapist: So you are feeling uncomfortable about coming to me for counseling. (I first attempt to help the patient become aware of the anxiety he is feeling about meeting with me.)

Patient: I just think I ought to take my problems to God. (The patient doesn't connect with either his anxiety or my effort to hear his fear. Instead, the patient repeats that he should take his problems to God.)

Therapist: Sometimes it's uncomfortable to try a new way of working on our problems. (I again try to connect with the patient's anxiety.)

Patient: Yes, but I'm not just uncomfortable. I think it's wrong. (The patient again rejects my efforts to focus on his anxiety and continues to present the problem as a theological one. At this point I have two choices at least!). I can continue pursuing the patient's anxiety and discomfort (which doesn't look like it is going to be productive) or I can present a brief biblical/educative and challenging statement (like the following).

Therapist: It just doesn't seem right to talk with anyone about your problems.

Patient: No. It doesn't. I'm a Christian and I should take my problems to God.

Therapist: That's true. But you know, God also tells us to bear each other's burdens and to confess our faults to each other. (I attempt to use the patient's own biblical commitment to challenge his defensive posture.)

Patient: I know, but I'm not much for that. (Patient gives the first indication that he has some awareness that his hesitancy to see a therapist may reflect more than just a theological issue.)

Therapist: You aren't used to talking much about your problems and your feelings. (I continue to pursue the patient's discomfort and schizoid relational style that interferes with his desire to seek help.)

Patient: No. I'm not. (Patient is again able to acknowledge that his reason for not wanting to open up to another person is not necessarily a theological issue.)

Therapist: Sometimes it's really scary to talk with another person. (I continue to attempt to connect with the patient's anxiety.)

Patient: Well, I do feel nervous. (At this point I have apparently been successful in reducing the patient's anxiety and challenging his defense with other scripture sufficiently that he now acknowledges his anxiety without having to attribute it to a theological concern.)

This interaction helped the patient move from his religiously phrased and reinforced resistance, "I shouldn't need therapy. I should just trust God" to a very slight, initial awareness that his hesitancy to engage in a meaningful relationship with me was not strictly a theological or cognitive issue, but rather a question of his own fear. I did that by focusing on the patient's anxiety while also using my understanding of his faith to confront his initial resistance in a way that would maximize the likelihood that he could receive my confrontation and minimize the likelihood he would believe that I might not understand or appreciate his faith.

In the remainder of the article I will discuss several of the most common religiously phrased resistances that Christian patients use and the scriptural passages they cite in support of them. Then I will suggest ways of challenging those resistances that incorporate alternative biblical interpretations or passages.

Commonly Used "Scriptural" Defenses

1. *"The Bible says we should forget the past."* (Phil. 3:13-14)

I imagine that every Christian psychotherapist has heard this one: "I don't think we ought to dredge up the past. The Bible says we are supposed to 'forget the things that are behind us.'" The primary dynamic here is almost certainly a desire to avoid facing and reexperiencing a painful past and the fundamental therapeutic technique should be to help the patient recognize his fear and gain courage to confront the hidden pain. At the same time, however, there may be a justifiable reason for consciously believing the Bible encourages us to forget the past. The Bible does say, "Forgetting what lies behind and reaching forward to what lies ahead, I press on toward the goal for the prize of the upward call of God in Christ Jesus" (Phil. 3:13-14, NASB). And some pastors and religious leaders do teach that this means we shouldn't explore or think about anything in our past, especially painful things. Consequently, it is natural that a Christian patient who has heard that teaching will reinforce his unconscious resistance with this bit of conscious data.

When I see a patient using this passage in that way, I sometimes say, "You know, that is an interesting verse you bring up and some people do think it means we should avoid facing anything painful in our past. But if you read it in context, Paul has just listed off all of the great things he had done in the past. He was circumcised the right day, born into the right tribe, been a good Pharisee and been very zealous. Then he says "forgetting what

lies behind ..." Paul really isn't saying we shouldn't look at some painful, difficult experiences. He is simply saying we shouldn't be proud of our past accomplishments and that the central issue in life is knowing Christ."

This, of course, will not immediately make a radical change in a strongly held resistance. But it does challenge the distortion within the conscious context of the patient's faith. It also helps avoid the appearance of attacking or attempting to undermine the patient's faith and presents the work of psychotherapy, including the facing of resistances, within the context of faith. Essentially it tells the patient, "I share your commitment to God and the Bible but the Bible does not encourage us to avoid our problems." Once this framework is established, the next time the patient uses a similar defense we can confront the anxiety directly with less likelihood that we will be misunderstood to be minimizing or undermining his faith.

2. *"The Bible says we should think on things that are lovely and pure. I don't think we should be trying to think about these upsetting things."* (Phil. 4:8)

This is another scripture that Christians may resort to when they are afraid that therapy is going to uncover upsetting thoughts and feelings. I occasionally respond to this resistance by saying something like, "It's interesting that you quote Paul's statement about thinking on things that are lovely and pure. Do you remember what Paul says in the first part of that verse?" If the patient says, "No, not exactly," I remind him that the verse begins with, "Whatever is true ..." (Phil. 4:8). Then I say, "I know it would seem nice if we could only talk about the positive, but Paul starts off by telling us that we should think about whatever is true. Some true things are very painful and not very lovely and it is scary to think about them." With other patients I say, "It's interesting that you focus on the part of Paul's comments that encourage us to think about positive things but you pass over his comment in the same verse that tells us to think about whatever is true. I guess you feel much more comfortably trying to focus on nice things than on painful things that are also true."

3. *"I'm supposed to be submissive."* (Eph. 5:22)

A university student sought me out to talk about her relationship with her boyfriend. According to her report, he was quite verbally abusive, demanding, and controlling. When I reflected this back to her, the following dialogue ensued:

Patient: Yes, but I'm supposed to learn to be submissive. God calls us to perfect love and I think he wants me to learn that so that I can be a good wife.

Therapist: Yes, God actually calls us to submit to each other (Eph. 5:21). And he also calls husbands to love their wives like Christ loves the church. But you seem to choose men who want to dominate you and hurt you instead of men who want to be like Christ.

Patient: But sometimes he is really nice.

Therapist: Yes, and sometimes he is really not nice.

After exploring more of the patient's feelings and dynamics, and her pattern of getting close to her boyfriend, being hurt, withdrawing, and then returning, I suggested:

Therapist: So each time you leave him you feel better and stronger for awhile. But after you are on your own you begin to feel lost and isolated and almost unreal. That is so unbearable that you would rather take a chance on being abused than being alone.

Again, the bulk of this particular work is no different than that which an effective non-Christian therapist would do. It focuses on the patient's fear of being abandoned or losing her sense of reality. But the Christian therapist is in a position to understand and challenge the patient's scriptural distortions from within the context of faith. In doing this, we also lay a foundation to help her clarify a major misconception she has about God and the entire Christian life. We can begin to help her see that perhaps God is not a sadistic, controlling person who wants women to lose their personhood at the expense of abusive males.

4. *"The devil made me do it."*

Other Christian patients try to cope with disturbing thoughts or feelings by attributing them to either God or Satan. Like the church soloist who, when complimented on her contribution to the service, replied, "It wasn't me. It was God that did it," they can neither accept a positive affirmation nor a negative thought or affect. Everything good is attributed to God and everything negative to the devil because they are unable to contain their own emotions or let conflicting emotions co-exist. This Christianizing of the defenses of splitting and projection can be very difficult to deal with. I have found comments like the following, however, when offered in a timely fashion, to sometimes be helpful.

Therapist: It's true that ultimately everything good comes from God and all evil comes from Satan. But I notice that each time you do something positive you so quickly attribute it to God and

each time you do something less well than you would like you quickly attribute it to Satan. You don't seem to give yourself any space to exist. There is no room for you to have any thoughts or feelings. They all belong to God or Satan. (By beginning by agreeing that ultimately all good comes from God and all evil from Satan, we find common ground with our patient. Then we move on to challenge the pathological portion of his biblical understanding and, consequently, his defensive structure.)

After further dialogue I might say,

Therapist: I think there is a real way in which you wished you didn't have any feelings, positive or negative—almost like you wished you didn't even exist as a separate thinking, feeling, alive person.

Having spoken once to the limitations of his split Christian worldview, we attempt to speak directly to his (at least partially unconscious) desire to have absolutely no feelings, or even to his wish that he were not emotionally alive. Again, the framing of our initial confrontation within the context of the patient's Christian world view will not by itself make a major dent in such a rigid defensive system. It can, however, help the patient feel slightly less defensive so that we can then move closer to his emotional reasons for separating his world so rigidly into the good, the bad, the (non) self, and the other.

5. *"Christians shouldn't be angry."* (Eph. 4:26)

Every time a sexually abused patient allowed herself to experience her hatred of her father she quickly repressed it again and became suicidal. At one point she spewed out, "I hate him. I wish he'd die and go to hell." Then she quickly used her faith to reinforce and justify her repression and self hatred by saying, "This is awful. I'm a Christian and I shouldn't feel this way."

On previous instances I had handled her resistance by pointing out how, when she allowed herself to feel her hatred, she became utterly terrified that she would drive her father away and lose the little love she did receive from him. Although her depression and suicidal wishes were terrible, she felt more comfortable wanting to end it all than she did tolerating the thought of confronting her father and experiencing his absolute rejection. Her fear of her father's absolute abandonment was compounded by the fact that her mother had already emotionally abandoned her, leaving her father as her last hope for any familial attachment. Because her depression, self hate, and tendency to avoid angry and aggressive feelings were so rigidly tied in with her religious belief system, I decided to challenge her belief that anger was so evil directly and very strongly. I responded to her statement about wishing her father would die and go to hell and her subsequent self hatred by saying,

> *Therapist*: You feel so terrible for wishing your father would die and go to hell but that's exactly where God sends a lot of people. In fact, Christ saved some of his strongest language for anyone who abused or misled little children. As terrible as you feel when you want to die, I don't think it's because your anger is so bad and so un-Godlike. I think you would rather die than face your hatred of your father and chance his absolute rejection.

By bringing God's justice and righteous anger into the picture I was able to help my patient give herself a little room for her own angry feelings. The bulk of our work on this particular dynamic still centered around her fear of abandonment and her fear of identifying with her hateful mother who she was petrified she would be like if she too felt her hatred of her father. But challenging her conscious claim that her homicidal wishes toward her father were so bad that she deserved to die by pointing out that God had similar feelings helped her be a bit more open and to give herself a little more space to accept her hatred and to explore her desire to avoid the horrible pain of absolute rejection from her father.

Conclusion

Like all patients, Christian patients frame their resistances within the context of their worldviews. When patients utilize biblical passages or Christian concepts to reinforce their resistances, therapists need to find ways of interpreting those resistances without undermining or challenging the healthy aspects of the patients' faith and without unnecessarily heightening their resistances by appearing to set our psychological interpretations against their theological beliefs. This can be done by affirming the healthy aspects of a patient's faith while offering balancing biblical passages or alternative scriptural interpretations that challenge the defensive use of scripture.

Like any other confrontation or educative clarification, this must be done in a manner that preserves or heightens the patient's affective awareness and contact with the therapist rather than in a way that leads to a defensive, intellectualized discussion. When done in this manner, the use of scripture to confront religiously reinforced resistances can lessen our patient's anxiety concerning whether we may not understand or appreciate their faith at the same time that it helps them sort out the healthy from the unhealthy aspects of faith. This can also model an approach to life that does not separate faith and biblical understanding from the resolution of pathology in therapy. Our modeling shows patients how their relationship with God and an understanding of the Bible can be a resource toward growth and increasing self awareness which leads to increased personal health and freedom rather than a source of external control, repression, and avoidance of pain.

References

Adams, J. (1970). *Competent to counsel*. Grand Rapids: Baker.

Carter, J., & Narramore, B. (1979). *The integration of psychology and theology*. Grand Rapids: Zondervan.

Evans, S. (1989). Wisdom and humanness in psychology. Grand Rapids: Baker.

Farnsworth, K. (1981). Models for the integration of psychology and theology. *Journal of the American Scientific Affiliation, 30*, 6-9.

Freud, S. (1912). The dynamics of transference. In J. Strachey (Ed.), *Standard edition of the complete works of Sigmund Freud* (Vol. 12, pp. 97-108). London: Hogarth.

Greenson, R. (1967). *The technique and practice of psychoanalysis*. New York: International Universities Press.

The Holy Bible: New American Standard Bible. (1963). Anaheim, CA: Lockman Foundation.

Jones, S. (Ed.). (1986). *Psychology and the Christian faith*. Grand Rapids: Baker Books.

Kehoe, N., & Getheil, T. (1984). Shared religious belief as resistance in psychotherapy. *American Journal of Psychotherapy, 38*, 579-585.

Lovinger, R. (1979). Therapeutic strategies with "religious" resistances. *Psychotherapy: Theory, Research and Practice, 16*, 419-427.

Lovinger, R. (1984). *Working with religious issues in therapy*. New York: Jason Aronson.

Menninger, K. (1961). *Theory of psychoanalytic technique*. New York: Basic Books.

Meissner, W. (1984). *Psychoanalysis and religious experience*. New Haven: Yale University Press.

Peteet, J. (1981). Issues in the treatment of religious patients. *American Journal of Psychotherapy, 35*, 559-563.

Rizzuto, A. M. (1979). *The birth of the living God*. Chicago: University of Chicago Press.

Spero, M. (1981). Countertransference in religious therapists of religious patients. *American Journal of Psychotherapy, 35*, 565-575.

Spero, M. (1990). Parallel dimensions of experience in psychoanalytic psychotherapy of the religious patient. *Psychotherapy, 27*, 53-71.

Spero, M. (1992). *Religious objects as psychological structures*. Chicago: University of Chicago Press.

Tan. S.-Y. (1991). *Lay counseling: Equipping Christians for a helping ministry*. Grand Rapids: Zondervan.

29

An Exploration of the Therapeutic Use of Spiritual Disciplines in Clinical Practice

Brian E. Eck
Azusa Pacific University

This article explores the use of spiritual interventions in psychotherapy by identifying the ethical, cultural, and professional practice contexts for their use. Issues related to the client, therapist, clinical setting, and professional practice that effect the use of spiritual interventions are identified. A framework to assess for the appropriateness of these interventions is provided. A review of the literature on spiritual disciplines and practices is provided and it is suggested that these spiritual interventions address disordered cognitions, behaviors, and relationships. Beginning points are offered for the therapist seeking to integrate these interventions into their work with religious clients. Research related to the clinical use of spiritual interventions is reviewed and future directions are discussed.

Over the past several years, there has been an explosion in the literature on integrating religion and spirituality into clinical practice. Bergin (1988, 1991), Lovinger (1984, 1990), Miller (1988, 1999), Propst (1988, 1996), Shafranske (1996) and others (Fleischman, 1990, Koenig, 1998; Shafranske & Malony, 1996) argue for the inclusion of religion and spirituality into treatment. Within the Christian psychological community there has been a shift from a theoretical, conceptual integration to a practice oriented, applied integration (Brokaw, 1997; Bufford, 1997; Hall & Hall, 1997; McCullough & Sandage, 1996; McMinn, 1996; McMinn & McRay, 1997; Moon, 1997; Moon, Bailey, Kwasny, & Willis, 1991; Worthington, 1986; Worthington, Kurusu, McCullough & Sandage, 1996). Research in the larger secular psychological community has contributed to a growing recognition that psychotherapy that includes religion and spirituality may lead to better clinical outcomes (Payne, Bergin, Bielema, & Jenkins, 1991; Propst, 1980).

There has also been an increasing recognition that the values and practices of religious clients, their ethno-religiosity, deserve the same level of respect and sensitivity as any other ethno-cultural aspect of a client's life (Bergin, 1980; Bergin, Payne, & Richards, 1996; Fukuyama & Sevig, 1999; Payne, Bergin, & Loftus, 1992). The concept that religion and spirituality are relevant to clinical practice and are as much a part of a person's orientation to life as their ethnicity, gender, and culture is becoming a standard within the therapeutic community. Even managed care companies now let their clients identify if they wish to work with a therapist of their own faith.

Unfortunately this emerging standard of care does not seem to have become incorporated into the education, training, and practice of psychotherapists, even for those within the Christian community (Jones, Watson, & Wolfram, 1992; Moon, Willis, Bailey, & Kwasny, 1993).

This article will explore the use of spiritual interventions in psychotherapy by identifying the ethical, cultural, and professional practice contexts for their use and suggesting starting points for more fully integrating spiritual disciplines and practices into clinical treatment with religious clients.

Ethical, Cultural, and Clinical Contexts

Use of spiritual disciplines in clinical practice takes place in the broader ethical and cultural context of psychotherapy. Each of these contexts help to define the parameters of appropriate therapeutic care.

Ethical Context

The first context for the use of spiritual disciplines in psychotherapy is ethical clinical practice. Contemporary ethical practice has shifted from exclusion of religion in psychotherapy to requiring that therapists respect religion as an orienting framework in the client's life. The American Psychological Association's (APA's) Ethical Principles, Principle D (1992), says in part, "Psychologists are aware of cultural, individual, and role differences, including those due to age, gender, race, national origin, *religion* [italics added], sexual orientation, disability, language, and socioeconomic status" (p. 1599). This principle challenges the therapist to properly assess, become aware of, and respect the spiritual and religious dimensions of a client's life.

© *Journal of Psychology and Christianity*, 2002, *21*, 266–280. Used by permission.

Second, the APA's Ethical Principles for psychologists and Code of Conduct, Section 1.08 (1992) states that, "Where differences of age, gender, race, ethnicity, national origin, *religion* [italics added], sexual orientation, disability, language, or socioeconomic status significantly affect psychologists' work concerning particular individuals or groups, psychologists obtain the training, experience, consultation, or supervision necessary to ensure the competence of their services, or they make appropriate referrals" (p. 1601).

This standard challenges every practicing therapist to obtain the training necessary to demonstrate competence in understanding the role of spirituality and religion in their clients' lives. Just as one must take coursework on cultural, ethnic, racial, and gender diversity, therapists should also obtain training in religious and spiritual diversity.

A final professional ethical statement of relevance is the APA's Guidelines for Providers of Psychological Services to Ethnic, Linguistic, and Culturally Diverse Populations (1993). This states in part that, "Psychologists respect clients' *religious and or spiritual beliefs and values, including attributions and taboos* [italics added] since they affect worldview, psychosocial functions and expressions of distress" (p. 461). Ethical practice as a psychologist recognizes the central role religion plays in a client's life and requires that the therapist demonstrate an awareness, sensitivity, and respect for the client's religious beliefs, values, and practices.

To summarize, APA ethical codes require a therapist to assess, understand, and respect the religious and spiritual beliefs, values, and practices of their clients, and to obtain the training and experience necessary to sensitively and appropriately address this aspect of a client's life in their clinical practice.

The standard of care in psychology is to be culturally competent in responding to a client's life context. Just as there is a need to be sensitive to cultural, racial, ethnic, and gender aspects of a client's life, there is a corresponding need to be sensitive to the religious aspects of the client's life when making therapeutic interventions. Clinicians need to be culturally and religiously competent. In support of this, the American Psychological Association has in recent years published several major books on integrating spirituality into treatment. Shafranske's (1996) *Religion and the clinical practice of psychology*, Richards and Bergin's (1997) *A spiritual strategy for counseling and psychotherapy*, Miller's (1999) *Integrating spirituality into treatment*, and Richards and Bergin's (2000) *Handbook of psychotherapy and religious diversity* are essential resources for the clinician seeking to develop ethno-religious competen-

cy. There have also been an increasing number of articles published in recent years to increase clinician understanding of the effects of spiritual and religious issues in specific areas of therapy including coping (Ashby & Lenhart, 1994; Baugh, 1988; Bickel, Ciarrocchi, Sheers, Estadt, Powell, & Pargament, 1998; Gartner, Larson, & Allen, 1991; Hathaway & Pargament, 1990; Pargament, 1996; Pargament, Smith, Koenig, & Perez, 1998; Wong-McDonald & Gorsuch, 2000), forgiveness (DiBlasio, 1992; DiBlasio & Benda, 1991; McCullough & Worthington, 1994; Worthington & DiBlasio, 1990), and health (Bearon & Koenig, 1990; Chamberlain & Hall, 2000; Hill & Butter, 1995; Koenig, 1997; Larson, 1994; Larson, Swyers & McCullough, 1997; Martin & Carlson, 1988; McIntosh & Spilka, 1990; Propst, 1980).

Cultural Context

Given that religion and spirituality are being more widely recognized as part of a person's orientation to life, what might a therapist expect to see walk through the clinic doors? How frequently might one encounter a religious client?

Religious practice is actually quite pervasive in the United States. From a number of studies (Gallup, 1994; Greeley, 1989; Hoge, 1996), 95% of Americans report that they believe in God, 93% identify with a religious group, 88% report they pray and 87% report that God answers prayers, (apparently one percent pray, but do not believe that God answers prayers). Of relevance to clinicians, 84% try to live according to their religious beliefs, 82% report they pray for health or success, 80% report that religion is very or fairly important in their lives, or that they consider themselves to be a spiritual or religious person. This research would seem to indicate that eight or nine out of every ten clients who show up in the waiting room would report that religion is important to them. At the lowest level of reported religious practice, 58% feel the need to experience spiritual growth. What this research would seem to indicate is that somewhere between fifty and ninety percent of the clients that are seen in therapy have a spiritual or religious orientation that is important to them. One would think that such a significant part of a client's orientation to life should be a part of the growth therapy is trying to facilitate.

Clinical Context

If eighty to ninety percent of Americans identify religion and spirituality as important to them, how many of them would like this area to be included in their psychotherapy? Research seems to indicate that clients prefer therapy that includes their belief systems with Quackenbos, Privette and Klentz

(1985) reporting that 78% of clients feel that religious values should be discussed in counseling. Clients who identify themselves as religious, report the preference for the use of prayer, scripture, and explicitly religious themes in their counseling (Worthington, Dupont, Berry, & Duncan, 1988).

If clients prefer that therapists include their religious and spiritual values in treatment, why don't more clients bring them up in therapy? It may be difficult for clients to initiate talking about their religion for a number of reasons. First, religion has in large part been removed from the public square. Clients don't necessarily expect it to be part of their public lives. American Christians often seem to separate sacred from secular and thus may talk to a priest or member of the clergy about spiritual concerns and a therapist if they perceived it to be a psychological problem. This kind of intrapersonal splitting prevents a more holistic, integrated approach to treatment. Therapists routinely encourage clients to talk about their ethnic and cultural background, personal and family backgrounds, history of substance use, and past history of sexual, physical, or emotional abuse. Why not also invite them to incorporate their spiritual life in therapy? This silence on the therapist's part may be due to therapist-client collusion in which clients don't talk about their spirituality or religion and therapists don't ask them about it (the therapeutic equivalent of don't ask, don't tell). If religion is uncomfortable or irrelevant to the therapists they may be resistant to engage it as a clinical concern. As clinicians are trained to deal with collusion in other aspects of therapy perhaps clinician training should include the collusion of silence in the area of spirituality and religion.

It may also be difficult for clients to bring up religious issues due to fear of religious coercion. Religion was removed from the public square in part due to concerns that religion can become coercive. Research reports that most clients want to talk about their spirituality, not hear about the therapist's religion (Worthington et al., 1988). Therapists should respect, honor, and be sensitive to the boundaries that make religion a safe topic in therapy.

Given these client and cultural contexts, why hasn't spirituality and religion become better incorporated within our clinical models, training, practice, and protocols? A final issue related to religious silence in psychotherapy may be due to bias in our own profession (Gibson & Herron, 1990). In contrast to the eighty to ninety percent of the general population who identify religion as important to them, only forty-eight to sixty-five percent of psychologists identify religion as very or fairly important (Bergin & Jensen, 1990; Shafranske, 1996; Shafranske & Malony, 1990).

Therapists need training in the area of religion and spirituality so that they can competently engage the 80% to 90% of their clients for whom this is an important area of their lives. Appropriate education and training would ensure that therapists practice within the scope of their training and experience and provide them with the skills necessary for engaging a client's ethno-religiosity as easily as any other issues in a client's life.

General Practice Issues for Spiritual Intervention

A second context for the use of spiritual disciplines in clinical practice involves the standards of professional practice. These would include issues of therapeutic appropriateness related to the client, therapist, and clinical setting.

Client Issues

Before introducing spiritual interventions into clinical practice, the therapist should assess whether such interventions would promote the overall welfare of the client. A thorough assessment of the client's life situation, developmental history, and spiritual or religious involvement help to insure that interventions are congruent with and respectful of the client's beliefs, values, and religious practices.

Therapeutic interventions should be consistent with a client's goals and desires. If the client does not want therapy to engage their religious or spiritual life, the therapist may probe and interpret the exclusion of this area from therapy as they would the exclusion of any other area of the client's life, but the use of spiritual interventions should be based on client assent and informed consent (Lewis & Epperson, 1991). It is essential that the client explicitly understands and consents to the use of each spiritual intervention. This helps to ensure that the client does not experience the use of spiritual interventions as either religious manipulation or coercion.

A final client issue would be an assessment of the fit between a spiritual intervention and the client's diagnosis. Clients with certain disorders such as schizophrenia or a personality disorder may contraindicate the use of certain forms of treatment including spiritual interventions. The therapist needs to assess whether the use of a spiritual intervention would foster increased defensiveness, manipulation, dependency, emotional repression, or increased pathology. If uncertain about the use of any intervention, including a spiritual intervention, the therapist should consult with experienced colleagues.

Therapist Issues

The therapist is responsible for facilitating client growth and maintaining ethical practice. The therapist should be sensitive to any conflicts that might occur between a client's spiritual and religious practices and their own (Bergin, 1991; Bergin, Payne, & Richards, 1996). If a conflict exists, the therapist should discuss it with the client and if necessary make a referral. This does not mean that a therapist cannot explore, interpret, or confront client behavior, but it does mean that it is the therapist's responsibility to sensitively talk about these issues as they arise.

The therapist is also responsible for using interventions, including spiritual interventions, that are within the scope of their training and experience. Before utilizing spiritual interventions in treatment, one must obtain the necessary education, training, and supervised experience. For spiritual interventions, this may require the therapist to get supervision or consultation from a qualified peer, clergy member, or priest.

A final issue for the therapist is that spiritual interventions must be properly documented and that arrangement for reimbursement for the use of a spiritual intervention is clarified before it is used. Spiritual interventions may or may not meet the parameters for reimbursement by third parties, and as such, part of a client's informed consent relates to fee arrangements for any non-reimbursable interventions (Chappelle, 2000).

Working with Spiritual Issues in Psychotherapy

How then does one begin working with spiritual issues in psychotherapy? A starting point is the realization that for the majority of clients, religion and spirituality are important to them and that they would like to be able to talk about this area of their lives in therapy. Therapists should facilitate this by creating a setting of openness, trust, and respect for client spiritual expression. Therapists should invite clients to share their spiritual or religious concerns, issues, and values in the same way they share any other area of their life.

Beyond the creation of an environment accepting of the client's religion and spirituality, there are several suggested guidelines for using spiritual interventions in therapy (Chappelle, 2000; Miller, 1999; Richards & Bergin, 1997; Richards, Rector, & Tjeltveit, 1999; Tan, 1994). As a general overview, it includes a thorough assessment of the client's spiritual and religious life, an evaluation of the therapist's ability to appropriately utilize spiritual inter-

ventions, and an awareness of the limits set by the therapeutic setting and treatment modality.

Client Assessment

Assessment of the client permits the therapist to understand the client's belief system, values, and religious practices. Without this knowledge, the therapist cannot engage the client in a way that is ethno-religiously congruent and that does not potentially violate their religious tradition and practices. There are many models for assessing religion and spirituality in clinical practice (Conners, Tonigan, & Miller, 1996; Hall, Tisdale, & Brokaw, 1994, Lovinger, 1996; Miller, 1999; Richards & Bergin, 1997; Tan, 1996a), and what follows provides a basic outline of an assessment protocol.

Assessment of the client's religion and spirituality begins with the initial intake assessment. In addition to a good developmental and family history, the intake form or interview can include a number of open-ended questions about a person's spirituality and religion. These would inquire about current concerns such as what gives the client's life meaning and purpose, whether they consider themselves to be a spiritual or religious person, and whether they participate in any religious practices or organizations. The therapist should also inquire about the personal and family history of religious experience and if the client's religious practices have changed, it would be important to assess what has led to those changes.

An additional aspect of this initial assessment could include the use of standardized measures of spirituality or religion. These could include Richards and Bergin's (1997) Religious-Spiritual Assessment Questionnaire, measures of intrinsic/extrinsic religiosity, measures of spiritual well being or maturity, measures of God image, measures of spiritual/religious practices and beliefs, or measures of spiritual or religious values or lifestyle.

If in the first assessment the client identifies that religion or spirituality is important to them, this should lead to more specific questions about the nature of their religious life. Spilka, Hood, and Gorsuch (1985) have identified multiple approaches for conceptualizing the religious dimension, but Glock's (1962) five dimensions of religious experience can perhaps best serve the clinician as a framework for this assessment. These dimensions include (1) ritualistic practices and behaviors, (2) ideological or formative doctrines and beliefs, (3) personal-experiential components, (4) cognitive based intellectual knowledge and teachings, and (5) consequential-relational including ethical living and community life.

This second level of client assessment should include questions concerning the client's religious or spiritual rituals, beliefs, or practices, their participation in a religious community, their level of religious knowledge, any supportive connections to priests or clergy, and their guiding values and ethical positions.

As part of this second level of client assessment the therapist should look for areas of strength or dysfunction within the client's religious or spiritual life and how, if at all, the client believes that their religion or spirituality is involved in their current life circumstances. It should also include a general assessment of whether the client's spiritual development is age appropriate and consistent with other areas of development, and if there is congruence between the client's religious beliefs and lifestyle. The nature of the client's image of God, religious motives, and ways of incorporating religion and spirituality into their coping or problem solving behaviors should be explored. These assessments could include information from one of the standardized instruments and/or a clinical interview.

The purpose of this client assessment is for the clinician to become aware of how religion and spirituality function in the life of the client and whether it serves a healthy and constructive or dysfunctional and destructive role. Spiritual interventions would be contra-indicated or used with caution with clients who present with a dysfunctional or poorly formed religion or spirituality, have been wounded by past religious abuse, or for whom spiritual interventions would exacerbate existing pathology.

Therapist Assessment

In addition to an assessment of the client, the therapist must perform a self-assessment to determine if spiritual interventions are appropriate and compatible with their role and scope of practice. Depending on the nature of the therapeutic relationship, their therapeutic modality, and the therapeutic contract, the therapist should decide whether to use implicit or explicit spiritual interventions (Tan, 1996a). Implicit spiritual interventions are not brought overtly into the clinical setting and can include such things as the therapist praying for the client outside of the session. Explicit interventions bring religion and spirituality directly into the therapeutic process. To do this, the therapist must determine that the spiritual interventions are compatible with the therapeutic setting, treatment modality, and are in the best interests of the client. Explicit interventions that arise out of the therapeutic alliance are least likely to violate the client's values and most likely to facilitate client growth.

Part of a therapist self-assessment should also be to determine whether a spiritual intervention is within the scope of his or her training and experience. As with any therapeutic technique, the therapist must be properly trained, supervised in its use, and able to practice the technique safely. The therapist should also be self-aware enough that their own personal values, beliefs, conflicts, and biases do not hinder their service to the client or impose practices that violate the client's own beliefs and values. Spiritual interventions outside the scope of one's own religious experience or for which one has not had the education, training, or supervision should not be utilized until such training and experience have been obtained.

Clinical Setting Assessment

A final professional practice context is assessing the clinical setting itself. Spiritual interventions should be congruent with the rules and protocols governing the clinical setting. Therapists in public funded agencies and clinics or those in research and training settings must carefully assess the appropriateness of the use of spiritual interventions in their work settings (Richards & Bergin, 1997). Therapists who are reimbursed by third parties must also work within the parameters of their contracts and any required conditions such as medical necessity. Spiritual interventions may therefore not be appropriate with some settings or therapeutic contracts. Agency approval, written informed consent and prior client agreement to any spiritual interventions may help to address some of these concerns.

Utilizing Spiritual Intervention in Therapy

After assessing the client's spirituality or religion and determining that it is consistent with the use of spiritual interventions, after obtaining client consent for the use of each spiritual intervention, and after determining that the use of spiritual interventions takes place within ethical practice guidelines, the therapist should seek to identify which spiritual interventions might best meet the client's needs. Interventions should be appropriate for the client's spiritual or religious tradition, diagnosis, level of spiritual development, treatment modality, and clinical setting without fostering defensiveness, inappropriate dependency, increased manipulation of the therapeutic setting, or increased pathology.

Spiritual or religious interventions should be congruent with and address the client's needs related to their cognitions (beliefs and knowledge), behaviors (practices and lifestyle), or interpersonal relationships (social support, belongingness, and attachment). All of the major religious traditions have developed rituals, disciplines, and practices to address the ills of humanity. Within the Christian tradition there has been a resurgence of interest in reclaiming the disciplines and practices of the faith as means for facilitating change and transforming the human condition (Bass, 1997; Foster, 1988; Mangis, 2000; Ortberg, 1995, 1997; Tan, 1996b; Tan & Gregg, 1996; Willard, 1988).

Nature of the spiritual Disciplines

Spiritual disciplines and practices have been utilized over the centuries as a means to help people of faith reorder their lives. Their purpose is to address disorder, dysfunction, and disconnection by reorienting how one thinks, behaves, and relates to God and one's community. Willard (1998) says that sin is a "psychological reality" where, "The inner resources of a person are weakened or dead, and the factors of human life do not interrelate as they were intended by their nature and function to do" (p. 104). He goes on to state, "In this condition the mind is confused, ignorant, and misguided. The emotions are simultaneously dominant of personality and conflicting. The body and the social environment are filled with regular patterns of wrongdoing and are constantly inclined toward doing what is wrong" (p. 105).

These sound like a client's presenting problems. Their thinking, feeling, behavior, or relationships are, "defective and connected wrongly with reference to life as a whole" (Willard, 1998, p. 105).

In utilizing the spiritual disciplines to address this condition Willard writes that, "The disciplines are activities of mind and body purposefully undertaken, to bring our personality and total being into effective cooperation with the divine order" (1988, p. 68). In a later article he writes that, "a discipline is an activity within our power—something we can do—which brings us to a point where we can do what we at present cannot do by direct effort" (1998, p. 106).

Among other key figures writing on this topic, Ortberg states that, "a disciplined person is someone who can do the right thing at the right time" (1997, p. 54). Foster states that "the spiritual disciplines are intended for our good. They are meant to bring the abundance of God into our lives" (1988, p. 9). Bass writes that Christian practices, "… have practical purposes: to heal, to shape communities, to discern," and that one incorporates Christian practices, "… not just because it works, but because it is good" (Bass, 1997, p. 7).

At their heart spiritual disciplines and practices are activities that help one to live the life God intended rather than a life of brokenness, sin, and disconnection. Spiritual disciplines are activities that allow the person to do what they presently cannot do for

themselves. Willard says that the aim of the spiritual disciplines is, "the renewal of the whole person from the inside, involving differences in thought, feeling, and character" (1998, p. 107). Spiritual disciplines, in other words, work toward the same goals as the therapeutic process, change in human functioning.

Use of spiritual disciplines and practices must also take place in a context which recognizes that, "true character transformation begins and is continually assisted by the pure grace of God" (Willard, 2000, p. 20). Spiritual disciplines are not barometers of spirituality or a way to earn God's merit, forgiveness, and goodwill. They are not to be used as soul killing legalistic practices performed from guilt and coercion (Ortberg, 1997, Tan & Gregg, 1997). They exist for humanity's sake, not God's. They work to mold and shape the embodied human person through activities that open one to more of God's life and power (Foster, & Yanni. 1992; Tan & Gregg, 1997; Willard, 1988). The use of the spiritual disciplines and practices in the clinical setting must remain true to this grace filled, God empowered focus as a means of grace and mercy and not as a legalistic or coercive process.

Guidelines for Using Spiritual Disciplines and Practices.

There are three key issues that need to be addressed in the use of spiritual disciplines in clinical practice. First, the disciplines should be used in a way that is consistent with and shows respect for their religious intention. Even though research has demonstrated that non-religious therapists can have better outcomes when they incorporate religion and spirituality into therapy (Propst, Ostrom, Watkins, Dean, & Mashburn, 1992), the specific use of a spiritual discipline or practice should not be ripped from its spiritual heritage. Therapists need to respect the religious tradition and intention of the discipline, the context in which it was developed and the context in which it has historically been used.

For a therapist of faith, a second issue involves the role of the Holy Spirit in the therapeutic process. There have been several discussions of this in the literature (Decker, 2002; Dodds, 1999; Ingram, 1996; Kunst & Tan, 1996). The therapist of faith should be sensitive to and aware of the Holy Spirit's guidance in themselves and the client, using spiritual interventions only in concert with the leading and guiding of the Holy Spirit.

Third, there needs to be a better integration of spiritual disciplines and practices into our treatment models, theories, and clinical practice. This would require the development of a more systematic way of thinking about how spirituality and the use of spiritual disciplines can become part of each clinical modality.

There also needs to be more ongoing research identifying the best practices for integrating spiritual disciplines and practices into treatment. This would include research identifying which spiritual interventions are most efficacious with which disorders or client populations. An excellent example of this kind of research is McCullough and Larson's (1999) review of the literature on prayer in which they report that in chronic pain patients petitionary prayer decreases level of functioning while the use of a more contemplative prayer style improves coping.

Spiritual disciplines and practices should become incorporated into standard clinical practice in an ethical, appropriate, and effective fashion congruent with the overall goals and modalities of therapy. In recapturing this rich spiritual heritage, psychotherapy with a client of faith can be more integrated and effective in addressing the needs of the whole person as body, mind, and spirit.

Therapeutic Use of Spiritual Disciplines in Clinical Practice

How would one integrate spiritual disciplines and practices into the therapy hour? A beginning point, as with all therapy, is with the goal of treatment. When choosing a spiritual discipline to practice, Ortberg (1997) recommends beginning with understanding the goal of a Christian life and identifying the barriers that keep one from living the life desired. The choice of which spiritual discipline to use is, as in therapy, determined by the problem definition and need of the person. The choice of a discipline should respect the freedom of the Holy Spirit, the uniqueness of the client, and the barriers they want to overcome (Ortberg, 1997; Tan & Gregg, 1997). Every client is a unique person in various stages of spiritual development for whom one or more of the disciplines can be critical in helping them to grow.

Each of the spiritual disciplines address particular deficits, distortions, or dysfunctions in the human condition and, as Willard says, assists one to do what cannot presently be done on one's own. Although each of the spiritual disciplines and practices may address multiple areas of a person's life, each seems to address in a primary way a particular type of dysfunction.

Key authors in this literature have identified thirty-nine different spiritual disciplines or practices (see Figure 1). In the chart of spiritual disciplines and practices, each author identifies specific disciplines and assigns them to particular categories. Foster (1988) identifies nine disciplines that he divides into

inward, outward, and corporate. Willard (1988, 1998, 2000) identifies 15 disciplines divided into engagement and abstinence, while Tan and Greg (1997) identify 17 disciplines that are divided into solitude, service, and surrender. Ortberg (1997) talks about 18 disciplines divided into guidance, core, slowing, servanthood, and confession, and finally Bass (1997) identifies 13 practices of the Christian faith.

As a starting point for clinicians interested in integrating spiritual disciplines into clinical practice, it is suggested that one begin by targeting the dysfunction in the client. Willard's (1998) identification that the disciplines target the disordered mind, body and relationships due to sin suggests that some of the disciplines and practices address disordered thinking, disordered behaviors, or disordered relationships. Although client concerns may include multiple issues, by incorporating spiritual disciplines into the cognitive, behavioral, and interpersonal/psychodynamic modalities in clinical practice, it seems that clinicians targeting disordered thoughts or employing cognitive interventions could integrate those disciplines which target disordered thinking. Clinicians working with disordered behavior and lifestyle patterns could utilize those disciplines targeting excessive or deficient behaviors while those targeting disordered relationships or utilizing interpersonal interventions could use the more relationally oriented disciplines.

Cognitive Oriented Disciplines

Those disciplines and practices which most seem to address a disordered thought life would include meditation, listening, scripture, study, prayer, and discernment. Research has already investigated the clinical use of meditation (Carlson, Bacaseta, & Simanton, 1988), and prayer (Abramowitz, 1993; Byrd, 1988; Dossey, 1993, Duckro & Magaletta, 1994; Finney & Malony, 1985; Magaletta, 1998; McCullough, 1995). Research (see Figure 1) also indicates that almost all of the disciplines is this group are already being used by Christian therapists (Ball & Goodyear, 1991; Jones, et al., 1992; Moon, et al., 1991; Moon, et al., 1993; Worthington, et al., 1988). Therapists working with the destructive self-talk evidenced in depression or the anxiety disorders, clients impaired by excessively negative or grandiose self-appraisal, or any destructive pattern of thought may seek to incorporate with their religious clients the disciplines that address disordered thinking.

Behaviorally Oriented Disciplines

The second group of disciplines and practices is the largest group. They address either excessive or inadequate behavioral patterns and lifestyles practiced in everyday living. Bass's 1997 concept of the

		Richard Foster Disciplines (1988)	Dallas Willard Disciplines (1988)	Tan & Gregg Disciplines (1997)	John Ortberg Disciplines (1997)	Bass, et al. Practices (1997)	Worthington et al. (1988)	Ball & Goodyear (1991)	Moon et al. (1991 1993)	Jones et al. (1992)	Richards & Bergin (1997)
Cognitive	1. Meditation	Inward		Solitude	Guidance		1		2	1	2
	2. Listening			Solitude	Guidance						
	3. Scripture				Core		4	1	2	2	2
	4. Study	Inward	Engagement	Solitude	Guidance		1	1			1
	5. Prayer	Inward	Engagement	Solitude	Guidance		2	1	4	2	3
	6. Discernment					Practice			1		
Behavioral	1. Simplicity	Outward		Service					1		
	2. Frugality		Abstinence			Practice					
	3. Fasting		Abstinence	Surrender	Celebration				1		1
	4. Chastity		Abstinence								1
	5. Body Care					Practice					
	6. Saying no/yes					Practice					
	7. Slowing				Core						
	8. Sabbath				Celebration	Practice					
	9. Solitude	Outward	Abstinence	Solitude	Slowing				1		
	10. Silence		Abstinence	Solitude					1		
	11. Secrecy		Abstinence		Core						
	12. Service	Outward	Engagement	Service							1
	13. Servanthood				Core						
	14. Sacrifice		Abstinence								
	15. Suffering				Core						
	16. Dying well					Practice					
Interpersonal	1. Confession	Corporate	Engagement	Surrender	Core		2		1		1
	2. Repentance			Surrender					1		1
	3. Forgiveness					Practice	3	1	1		1
	4. Submission		Engagement	Surrender							
	5. Humility				Servanthood						
	6. Worship	Corporate	Engagement	Surrender	Guidance				1		1
	7. Eucarist					Practice					1
	8. Singing					Practice					1
	9. Celebration	Corporate	Engagement		Core						
	10. Fellowship		Engagement	Service							1
	11. Community					Practice					
	12. Hospitality					Practice					
	13. Healing				Confession	Practice	1	1	1	1	
	14. Witnessing			Service							
	15. Testimony					Practice					1
	16. Intercession			Solitude			1	1	1		
	17. Guidance			Solitude	Core						

The numbers indicate the number of sub-categories for a spiritual discipline that was identified by a researcher. A blank indicates that the discipline was not incorporated in the study.

Figure 1.
Thirty-nine Spiritual Disciplines and Practices

discipline of saying yes and saying no is already well explored in the literature on boundaries (Cloud & Townsend, 1992, 1999). Many of the disciplines listed in this section would support a client's development of appropriate boundaries and limits for a healthier life. The research would seem to indicate that these are the least frequently used by Christian therapists (see Figure 1).

Disciplines that address excessive behaviors would include simplicity, frugality, fasting, chastity, body care, and saying yes and no. These disciplines address behavior that is out of control and lifestyle excesses such as materialism, gluttony, and promiscuity. Therapists frequently work with clients struggling with addictions and lack of self-control while those involved in life coaching and case management help their clients budget, manage money and practice better self-care. Integrating spirituality into treatment has already proven helpful in several of these areas (Johnson, 1993), and the use of spiritual disciplines to support self-limiting practices should be encouraged.

Other disciplines in this group relate to managing stress, controlling an excessive pace of life and assisting clients caught up in pursuing material success. Disciplines such as slowing, Sabbath, solitude, silence, and secrecy, help clients find balance and meaning in life outside of compulsive activity, or the pursuit of money and power. These disciplines help to re-center the person and remind them that they are more important than what they do or can achieve. Solitude and silence have received some coverage in the literature (Van Meter, McMinn, Bissell, Kaur, & Pressley, 2001) and one article reported how a Jewish couple was assigned the homework of keeping Sabbath by their marriage counselor. They reported that by taking a day away from computers, yard work, and shopping, in order to be together as a couple, they were able to rebuild and deepen the depth of communication and the spiritual foundation of their marriage (Chase, 1997).

A final set of disciplines in this group target self-absorption or an inadequate understanding of the struggles of life. Disciplines such as service, servanthood, sacrifice, and suffering help one transcend a worldview of narrow self-interest or one that does not appreciate the relationship between struggle and growth. These disciplines address distortions of the self and facilitate greater generativity and personal growth. Within this group of disciplines there is a significant amount of literature on religion and coping (Baugh, 1988, Hathaway & Pargament, 1990; Pargament, 1996, 1997; Pargament, Ensing, Falgout, Olsen, Reily, Van Haitsma, & Warren, 1990). There is

more limited literature on obedience (Wong-McDonald & Gorsuch, 2000), acceptance and hope, (Brody & Semel, 1993; Farran, Herth, & Popovich, 1995; Snyder, 1994) and suffering (Allender, 1999). Therapists should be encouraged to help their clients transcend their life circumstances by incorporating the spiritual disciplines that assist them to find life's meaning in something greater than themselves.

Interpersonally Oriented Disciplines

The final group of disciplines identified in Figure 1 address relational problems. These disciplines focus on repairing damaged relationships, creating interpersonal connections, healing spiritual disconnection, and facilitating mentoring relationships. About half of these disciplines and practices are reportedly being used by Christian counselors (see Figure 1).

The disciplines of confession, repentance, forgiveness, submission, and humility focus on repairing relationships. Therapeutic use of these disciplines would assist those clients of faith, seeking to rebuild broken relationships to restore both the interpersonal and spiritual dimensions of the relationship. Research on these has focused primarily on the use of forgiveness in therapy (DiBlasio & Benda, 1991; DiBlasio & Proctor, 1993; McCullough & Worthington, 1994; Worthington & DiBlasio, 1990). Trust and faith in one's partner are essentials for openness and vulnerability in relationships and reestablishing these inherent spiritual attributes are essential for healing relational brokenness.

The disciplines of worship, eucharist, singing, celebration, fellowship, community, hospitality, and guidance focus on the horizontal and vertical connections of a client's life. These are the means for overcoming an isolated and lonely existence by connecting one to community. Of all of the spiritual disciplines, it seems strange that these are virtually unexplored in the clinical research literature and are not widely used by Christian counselors (see Figure 1). One of the most basic issues humans face is disconnection and isolation. Helping people find community in a loving supportive church may provide the client with the extra support necessary for pursuing personal growth and change. Clients may also be helped through the development of mentoring relationships that provide them the experience of caring, connection, and guidance necessary to take the risks required for growth.

The disciplines of healing, witnessing, testimony, and intercession address areas of spiritual concern or brokenness. When the problem the client is facing is at its core a spiritual problem and the client is seeking spiritual renewal as part of their personal growth, these disciplines most directly address these concerns. Healing and intercession are reportedly used by Christian counselors (see Figure 1), however there is little in the clinical literature on their use in treatment. Because of their foundational spiritual focus, these disciplines might best be incorporated into treatment by pastoral counselors or by referring the client to their own priest or minister.

Current Status and Future Directions

Research on the actual use of spiritual interventions indicates that some therapists have begun to incorporate spiritual interventions into therapy (Ball & Goodyear, 1991; Jones, et al., 1992; Moon, et al., 1991; Worthington, et al., 1988). This research indicates that the use of spiritual disciplines in treatment varies greatly with Jones, et al. (1992) reporting that 23.2% to 30.6% of Christian counselors self-report the use of spiritually oriented techniques with their clients. Use also appears to have an inverse relationship to the therapist's level of education and their affiliation with professional clinical associations like the APA (Moon, et al., 1993). Doctoral prepared therapists who are members of their national professional association are the least likely to use spiritual interventions.

The spiritual interventions therapists report using most frequently in these studies are implicit techniques like praying for clients outside of session and the implicit teaching of biblical concepts. Among the more explicit techniques therapists report using are discussing the client's faith, praying with the client in session, instruction in repentance and forgiveness, explicit quoting or interpreting of scripture, assigning religious homework, using guided religious imagery, teaching religious meditation, and confronting the client over sinful life patterns (Jones, et al., 1992; Moon, et al., 1993). Worthington, et al. (1988) found that the techniques which clients report were the most helpful in treatment were encouraging them to forgive others, forgive God, and to have been assigned religious homework.

Future Directions

This article has identified some beginning places for therapists who wish to integrate spiritual disciplines into clinical practice. A future direction for the use of these disciplines and practices would be the establishment of research protocols that identify which disciplines and practices are most effective in the treatment of specific disorders. Even as research has begun to identify the differential effects of petitionary versus contemplative prayer in chronic pain patients (McCullough & Larson, 1999), further research is needed to better understand and validate the efficacious effects of all of the identified spiritual disciplines and practices. By revisiting the historical guidelines for the use of spiritual disciplines and practices throughout the history of the faith and by empirically validating the conditions under which they can best be used in the contemporary therapeutic setting, these interventions can become part of the standards of care for religious clients. Any widespread integration of spiritual interventions into standard clinical practice with religious clients will need to be guided by future research in this area.

A second direction for the future is the development of a set of "best practice" treatment models that integrate spiritual disciplines and practices into the major treatment modalities. Although existing literature most frequently integrates spiritual interventions into directive treatment approaches (Hawkins, Tan, & Turk, 1999; Johnson & Ridley, 1992; Miller & Martin, 1988), there is a growing openness to integrating spiritual perspectives with the non-directive therapies (Finn, & Gartner, 1992). The goals of psychotherapy and those of the spiritual interventions are the same—change in human functioning. More work needs to be done to develop integrated theoretical models for treatment intervention so that spiritual interventions for religious clients become fully integrated into every therapeutic change modality.

A final future direction is to increase the education and training therapists receive on spiritual interventions with religious clients. The fact that even Christian therapists are reluctant to engage the religion and spirituality of their clients reflects deficiencies in their education and training. As with all other areas of cultural diversity, an educational and training curriculum needs to be developed that clearly identifies the role of religion in our society, the orienting framework it provides in the client's life, its proper clinical assessment, and "best practice" models for making spiritual interventions a standard part of treatment.

By clearly identifying the primary spiritual disciplines and practices and suggesting beginning places for the therapist interested in integrating these spiritual interventions into their clinical practice, it is hoped that a greater number of therapists will utilize them when working with religious clients. More needs to be done with regard to clinical research and theoretical model building; however, if each therapist is challenged to at least assess for religion and spirituality in the life of their client and is trained in how to incorporate this essential area of their religious client's life into treatment, psychotherapy could begin to address the whole person, body, mind, and spirit. It is hoped that this wold lead to not only a more holistic therapy but also to better treatment outcomes.

References

Abramowitz, L. (1993). Prayer as therapy among the frail Jewish elderly. *Journal of Gerontological Social Work, 19,* 69-95.

Allender, D. B. (1999). *The healing path: How the hurts in your past can lead to a more abundant life.* Colorado Springs, CO: Waterbrook.

American Psychological Association. (1992). Ethical principles of psychologists and code of conduct. *American Psychologist, 47,* 1597-1611.

American Psychological Association. (1993). Guidelines for providers of psychological services to ethnic, linguistic, and culturally diverse populations. *American Psychologist, 48,* 45-47.

Ashby, J. S., & Lenhart, R. S. (1994). Prayer as a coping strategy for chronic pain patients. *Rehabilitation Psychology, 39,* 205-209.

Ball, R. A., & Goodyear, R. K. (1991). Self-reported professional practices of Christian psychotherapists. *Journal of Psychology and Christianity, 10,* 144-153.

Bass, D. C. (Ed.). (1997). *Practicing our faith: A way of life for a searching people.* San Francisco: Jossey-Bass.

Baugh, J. (1988). Gaining control by giving up control: Strategies for coping with powerlessness. In W. L. Miller & J. E. Martin (Eds.), *Behavior therapy and religion: Integrating spiritual and behavioral approaches to change* (pp. 125-138). Newbury Park, CA: Sage.

Bearon, L. B., & Koenig, H. G. (1990). Religious cognitions and use of prayer in health and illness. *The Gerontologist, 30,* 249-253.

Bergin, A. E. (1980). Psychotherapy and religious values. *Journal of Consulting and Clinical Psychology, 48,* 95-105.

Bergin, A. E. (1988). Three contributions of a spiritual perspective to counseling, psychotherapy, and behavior change. *Counseling and Values, 32,* 21-31.

Bergin, A. E. (1991). Values and religious issues in psychotherapy and mental health. *American Psychologist, 46,* 394-403.

Bergin, A. E., & Jensen, J. P. (1990). Religiosity of psychotherapists: A national survey. *Psychotherapy, 27,* 3-7.

Bergin, A. E., Payne, J. R., & Richards, P. S. (1996). Values in psychotherapy. In E. P. Shafranske (Ed.), *Religion and the clinical practice of psychology* (pp. 297-325). Washington, DC: American Psychological Association.

Bickel, C. O., Ciarrocchi, J. W., Sheers, N. J., Estadt, B. K., Powell, D. A., & Pargament, K. I. (1998). Perceived stress, religious coping styles, and depressive affect. *Journal of Psychology and Christianity, 17,* 33-42.

Brody, C. M., & Semel, V. G. (1993). *Strategies for therapy with the elderly: Living with hope and meaning.* New York: Springer.

Brokaw, B. F. (1997). Applying theory in clinical practice: Clinical integration of psychology and theology. *Journal of Psychology and Theology, 25,* 81-85.

Bufford, R. K. (1997). Consecrated counseling: Reflections on the distinctives of Christian counseling. *Journal of Psychology and Theology, 25,* 111-122.

Byrd, R. C. (1988). Positive therapeutic effects of intercessory prayer in a coronary care unit. *Southern Medical Journal, 81,* 826-829.

Carlson, C., Bacaseta, P., & Simanton, D. (1988). A controlled evaluation of devotional meditation and progressive relaxation. *Journal of Psychology and Theology, 16,* 362-368.

Chamberlain, T. J., & Hall, C. A. (2000). *Realized religion: Research on the relationship between religion and health.* Philadelphia: Templeton Foundation Press.

Chappelle, W. (2000). A series of legal and ethical decision-making steps for using Christian spiritual interventions in psychotherapy. *Journal of Psychology and Theology, 28,* 43-53.

Chase, N. (1997). Ancient wisdom. *Hemispheres,* July, 118-119.

Cloud, H., & Townsend, J. (1992). *Boundaries.* Grand Rapids, MI: Zondervan.

Cloud, H., & Townsend, J. (1999). *Boundaries in marriage.* Grand Rapids, MI: Zondervan.

Connors, G. J., Tonigan, J. S., & Miller, W. R. (1996). A measure of religious background and behavior for use in behavior change research. *Psychology of Addictive Behavior, 10,* 90-96.

Decker, E. E. (2002). The Holy Spirit in counseling. A review of Christian counseling journal articles (1985-1999). *Journal of Psychology and Christianity, 21,* 21-28.

DiBlasio, F. A. (1992). Forgiveness in psychotherapy. Comparison of older and younger therapists. *Journal of Psychology and Christianity, 11,* 181-187.

DiBlasio, F. A., & Benda, B. B. (1991). Practitioners, religion and the use of forgiveness in the clinical setting. *Journal of Psychology and Christianity, 10,* 166-172.

DiBlasio, F. A., & Proctor, J. H. (1993). Therapists and the clinical use of forgiveness. *American Journal of Family Therapy, 21,* 175-1814.

Dodds, L. A. (1999). The role of the Holy Spirit in personality growth and change. *Journal of Psychology and Christianity. 18,* 129-139.

Dossey, L. (1993). *Healing words: The power of prayer and the practice of medicine.* San Francisco: HarperCollins.

Duckro, P. N., & Magaletta, P. R. (1994). The effect of prayer on physical health: Experimental evidence. *Journal of Religion and Health, 33,* 211-219.

Farran, C. J., Herth, K. A., & Popovich, J. M. (1995). *Hope and hopelessness: Critical clinical constructs.* London: Sage.

Finn, M., & Gartner, J. (Eds.). (1992). *Object relations theory and religion: Clinical applications.* Westport, CT: Praeger.

Finney, J. R., & Malony, H. N. (1985). An empirical study of contemplative prayer as an adjunct to psychotherapy. *Journal of Psychology and Theology, 13,* 284-290.

Fleischman, P. R. (1990). *The healing spirit: Explorations in psychotherapy and spirituality.* New York: Paragon Press.

Foster, R. J. (1988). *Celebration of discipline.* San Francisco; Harper & Row.

Foster, R. J., & Yanni, K. A. (1992). *Celebrating the disciplines.* San Francisco: Harper.

Fukuyama, M. A., & Sevig, T. D. (1999). *Integrating spirituality into multicultural counseling*. Thousand Oaks, CA: Sage.

Gallup, G., Jr. (1994). *The Gallup Poll: Public Opinion 1993*. Wilmington, DE: Scholarly Resources.

Gartner, J., Larson, D. B., & Allen, G. D. (1991). Religious commitment and mental health: A review of the empirical literature. *Journal of Psychology and Theology, 19*, 6-25.

Gibson, W. C., & Herron, W. G. (1990). Psychotherapists' religious beliefs and their perception of the psychotherapy process. *Psychological Reports, 66*, 3-19.

Glock, C. Y. (1962). On the study of religious commitment. *Religious Education, Research Supplement, 57*(4), 98-110.

Greeley, A. W. (1989). *Religious change in America*. Cambridge, MA: Harvard University.

Hall, M. E., & Hall, T. W. (1997). Integration in the therapy room: An overview of the literature. *Journal of Psychology and Theology, 25*, 86-101.

Hall, T. W., Tisdale, T. C., & Brokaw, B. F. (1994). Assessment of religious dimensions in Christian clients: A review of selected instruments for research and clinical use. *Journal of Psychology and Theology, 22*, 395-421.

Hathaway, W., & Pargament, K. (1990). Intrinsic religiousness, religious coping, and psychosocial competence: A covariance structure analysis. *Journal for the Scientific Study of Religion, 29*, 423-441.

Hawkins, R. S., Tan, S.-Y. , & Turk, A. A. (1999). Secular versus Christian inpatient cognitive-behavioral therapy programs: Impact on depression and spiritual well-being. *Journal of Psychology and Theology, 27*, 309-318.

Hill, P. C., & Butter, E. M. (1995). The role of religion in promoting physical health. *Journal of Psychology and Christianity, 14*, 141-155.

Hoge, D. R. (1996). Religion in America: The demographics of belief and affiliation. In E. P. Shafranske (Ed.), *Religion and the clinical practice of psychology* (pp. 21-41). Washington, DC: American Psychological Association.

Ingram, J. A. (1996). Psychological aspects of the filling of the Holy Spirit: A preliminary model of post-redemptive personality functioning. *Journal of Psychology and Theology, 24*, 104-113.

Johnson, W. B., & Ridley, C. R. (1992). Brief Christian and non-Christian rational-emotive therapy with depressed Christian clients: An exploratory study. *Counseling and Values, 36*, 220-229.

Jones, S. L., Watson, E. J., & Wolfram, T. J. (1992). Results of the Rech conference survey on religious faith and professional psychology. *Journal of Psychology and Theology, 20*, 147-158.

Koenig, H. G. (1997). *Is religion good for your health? The effects of religion on physical and mental health*. New York: Haworth Press.

Koenig, H. G. (Ed.). (1998). *Handbook of religion and mental health*. New York: Academic Press.

Kunst, J., & Tan, S.-Y. (1996). Psychotherapy as "work in the Spirit": Thinking theologically about psychotherapy. *Journal of Psychology and Theology, 24*, 284-291.

Larson, D. B. (1994). *The faith factor: An annotated bibliography of systematic reviews and clinical research on spiritual objects (Vol. 1)*. Rockville, MD: National Institute of Healthcare Research.

Larson, D. B., Swyers, J. P., & McCullough, M. E. (Eds.). (1997). *Scientific research on spirituality and health: A consensus report*. Rockville, MD: National Institute for Healthcare Research.

Lewis, K. N., & Epperson, D. L. (1991). Values, pretherapy information, and informed consent in Christian counseling. *Journal of Psychology and Christianity, 10*, 113-131.

Lovinger, R. J. (1984). *Working with religious issues in therapy*. Northwale, NJ: Jason Aronson.

Lovinger, R. J. (1990). *Religion and counseling: The psychological impact of religious belief*. New York: Continuum.

Lovinger, R. J. (1996). Considering the religious dimension in assessment and treatment. In E. P. Shafranske (Ed.), *Religion and the clinical practice of psychology* (pp. 327-364). Washington, DC: American Psychological Association.

Magaletta, P. R. (1998). Prayer in psychotherapy: A model for its use, ethical considerations, and guidelines for practice. *Journal of Psychology and Theology, 26*, 322-330.

Mangis, M. W. (2000). Spiritual formation and Christian psychology: A response and application of Willard's perspective. *Journal of Psychology and Theology, 28*, 254-258.

Martin, J. E., & Carlson, C. R. (1988). Spiritual dimensions of health psychology. In W. Miller & J. E. Martin (Eds.), *Behavior therapy and religion: Integrating spiritual and behavioral approaches to change* (pp. 57-110). Newbury Park, CA: Sage.

McCullough, M. E. (1995). Prayer and health: Conceptual issues, research review, and research agenda. *Journal of Psychology and Theology, 23*, 15-29.

McCullough, M. E., & Larson, D. B. (1999). Prayer. In W. R. Miller (Ed.), *Integrating spirituality into treatment* (pp. 85-110). Washington, DC: American Psychological Association.

McCullough, M. E., & Worthington, E. L., Jr. (1994). Encouraging clients to forgive people who have hurt them: Review, critique, and research prospectus. *Journal of Psychology and Theology, 22*, 3-20.

McIntosh, D., & Spilka, B. (1990). Religion and physical health: The role of personal faith and control. In M. Lynn & D. Moberg (Eds.), *Research in the social scientific study of religion* (Vol. 2, pp. 167-194). Greenwich, CT: JAI Press.

McMinn, M. R. (1996). *Psychology, theology, and spirituality in Christian counseling*. Wheaton, IL: Tyndale.

McMinn, M. R., & McRay, B. W. (1997). Spiritual disciplines and the practice of integration: Possibilities and challenges for Christian psychologists. *Journal of Psychology and Theology, 25*, 102-110.

Miller, W. R. (1988). Including clients' spiritual perspectives in cognitive behavior therapy. In W. R. Miller, & J. E. Martin (Eds.), *Behavior therapy and religion: Integrating spiritual and behavioral approaches to change* (pp. 43-55). Newbury Park, CA: Sage.

Miller, W. R., (Ed.). (1999). *Integrating spirituality into treatment*. Washington, DC: American Psychological Association.

Miller, W. R., & Martin, J. E. (Eds.). (1988). *Behavior therapy and religion: Integrating spiritual and behavioral approaches to change*. Newbury Park, CA; Sage.

Moon, G. W. (1997). Training tomorrow's integrators into today's busy intersection: Better look four ways before crossing. *Journal of Psychology and Theology, 25,* 284-293.

Moon, G. W., Bailey, J. W., Kwasny, J. C., & Willis, D. E. (1991). Training in the use of Christian disciplines as counseling techniques by Christian psychotherapists, pastoral counselors, and spiritual directors. *Journal of Psychology and Christianity, 12,* 24-37.

Moon, G. W., Willis, D. E., Bailey, J. W., & Kwasny, J. C. (1993). Self-reported use of Christian spiritual guidance techniques by Christian psychotherapists, pastoral counselors, and spiritual directors. *Journal of Psychology and Christianity, 12,* 24-37.

Ortberg, J. (1995). Rethinking the kingdom of God: The work of Dallas Willard and some applications to psychotherapeutic practice. *Journal of Psychology and Christianity, 14,* 306-317.

Ortberg, J. (1997). *The life you've always wanted.* Grand Rapids, MI: Zondervan.

Pargament, K. I. (1996). Religious methods of coping: Resources for the conservation and transformation of meaning. In E. P. Shafranske (Ed.), *Religion and the clinical practice of psychology* (pp. 215-239). Washington, DC: American Psychological Association.

Pargament, K. I. (1997). *The psychology of religion and coping: Theory, research, practice.* New York: Guilford.

Pargament, K. I., Ensing, D. S., Falgout, K., Olsen, H., Reily, B., Van Haitsma, K., & Warren, R. (1990). God help me: Religious coping efforts as predictors of the outcomes to significant life events. *American Journal of Community Psychology, 18,* 793-824.

Pargament, K. I., Smith, B. W., Koenig, H. G., & Perez, L. (1998). Patterns of positive and negative religious coping with major life stressors. *Journal for the Scientific Study of Religion, 37,* 711-725.

Payne, I. R., Bergin, A. E., Bielema, K. A., & Jenkins, P. H. (1991). Review of religion and mental health: Prevention and the enhancement of psychosocial functioning. *Prevention in Human Services, 9,* 11-40.

Payne, I. R., Bergin, A. E., & Loftus, P. E. (1992). A review of attempts to integrate spiritual and standard psychotherapy techniques. *Journal of Psychotherapy Integration, 2,* 171-192.

Propst, L. R. (1980). The comparative efficacy of religious and nonreligious imagery for the treatment of mild depression in religious individuals. *Cognitive Therapy and Research, 4,* 167-178.

Propst, L. R. (1988). *Psychotherapy within a religious framework: Spirituality in the emotional healing process.* New York: Human Sciences Press.

Propst, L. R. (1996). Cognitive-behavioral therapy and the religious person. In E. P. Shafranske (Ed.), *Religion and the clinical practice of psychology* (pp. 391-407). Washington, DC: American Psychological Association.

Propst, L. R., Ostrom, R., Watkins, P., Dean, T., & Mashburn, D. (1992). Comparative efficacy of religious and nonreligious cognitive-behavioral therapy for the treatment of clinical depression in religious individuals. *Journal of Consulting and Clinical Psychology, 60,* 94-103.

Quackenbos, S., Privette, G., & Klentz, B. (1985). Psychotherapy and religion: Rapprochement or antithesis? *Journal of Counseling and Development, 65,* 82-85.

Richards, P. S., & Bergin, A. E. (Eds.). (1997). *A spiritual strategy for counseling and psychotherapy.* Washington, DC: American Psychological Association.

Richards, P. S., & Bergin, A. E. (2000). *Handbook of psychotherapy and religious diversity.* Washington, DC: American Psychological Association.

Richards, P. W., Rector, J. M., & Tjeltveit, A. C. (1999). Values, spirituality, and psychotherapy. In W. R. Miller (Ed.), *Integrating spirituality into treatment.* Washington, DC: American Psychological Association.

Shafranske, E. P. (Ed.). (1996). *Religion and the clinical practice of psychology.* Washington, DC: American Psychological Association.

Shafranske, E. P., & Malony, H. N. (1990). Clinical psychologists' religious and spiritual orientations and their practice of psychotherapy. *Psychotherapy, 27,* 72-78.

Shafranske, E. P., & Malony, H. N. (1996). Religion and the clinical practice of psychology: A case for inclusion. In E. P. Shafranske (Ed.), *Religion and the clinical practice of psychology* (pp. 561-586). Washington, DC: American Psychological Association.

Snyder, C. R. (1994). *The psychology of hope.* New York: Free Press.

Spilka, B., Hood, R. W., & Gorsuch, R. L. (1985). *The psychology of religion: An empirical approach.* Englewood Cliffs, NJ: Prentice Hall.

Tan, S.-Y. (1994). Ethical considerations in religious psychotherapy: Potential pitfalls and unique resources. *Journal of Psychology and Theology, 22,* 389-394.

Tan, S.-Y. (1996a). Religion in clinical practice: Implicit and explicit integration. In E. P. Shafranske (Ed.), *Religion and the clinical practice of psychology* (pp. 365-390). Washington, DC: American Psychological Association.

Tan, S.-Y. (1996b). Practicing the presence of God: The work of Richard J. Foster and its applications to psychotherapeutic practice. *Journal of Psychology and Christianity, 15,* 17-28.

Tan, S.-Y., & Gregg, D. H. (1997). *Disciplines of the Holy Spirit.* Grand Rapids, MI: Zondervan.

Van Meter, J. B., McMinn, M. R., Bissell, L. D., Kaur, M., & Pressley, J. D. (2001). Solitude, silence, and the training of psychotherapists: A preliminary study. *Journal of Psychology and Theology, 29,* 22-28.

Willard, D. (1988). *The spirit of the disciplines.* San Francisco: Harper & Row.

Willard, D. (1998). Spiritual disciplines, spiritual formation, and the restoration of the soul. *Journal of Psychology and Theology, 26,* 101-109.

Willard, D. (2000). Spiritual formation in Christ: A perspective on what it is and how it might be done. *Journal of Psychology and Theology, 28,* 254-258.

Wong-McDonald, A., & Gorsuch, R. L. (2000). Surrender to God: An additional coping style? *Journal of Psychology and Theology, 28,* 149-161.

Worthington, E. L., Jr. (1986). Religious counseling: A review of the published empirical research. *Journal of Counseling and Development, 64,* 421-431.

Worthington, E. L., Jr., Dupont, P. D., Berry, J. T., & Duncan, L. A. (1988). Christian therapists' and clients' perceptions of religious psychotherapy in private and agency settings. *Journal of Psychology and Theology, 16,* 282-293.

Worthington, E. L., Jr., Kurusu, T. A., McCullough, M. E., & Sandage, S. J. (1996). Empirical research on religion and psychotherapeutic processed and outcomes: A 10-year review and research prospectus. *Psychological Bulletin, 119,* 448-487.

Worthington, E. L., Jr., & DiBlasio, F. A. (1990). Promoting mutual forgiveness within the fractured relationship. *Psychotherapy, 27,* 219-223.

Worthington, E. L., Jr., & Scott, G. G. (1983). Goal selection for counseling with potentially religious clients by professional and student counselors in explicitly Christian or secular settings. *Journal of Psychology and Theology, 11,* 318-319.

Section VII
Integrative Research

In this final section of articles of this celebratory volume, we remind readers of the privileged position granted to empirical research within the discipline of psychology. The extent to which Christian psychologists hold to (or should hold to) empiricism as a philosophical position has been discussed at length in the integration literature, with a representation of that literature reprinted here, primarily in section II. Now is not the time, nor is this the place, to deal substantively with that question; however, one need not adopt a strict positivistic empiricism to acknowledge and appreciate what the empirical tradition brings to psychology as a whole and to the integration effort, specifically. Indeed, empirical research has and will continue to be useful to the science of psychology and will likely remain in a privileged position for the foreseeable future as long as it continues to serve as a necessary, though perhaps insufficient, test of new theoretical ideas, and thereby identify empirical regularities of the human psyche in the process. And so, it is within this vein that the following four research articles represent what we believe are among the best of integrative research within the empirical tradition.

The first of these reprints is a little-known article to psychologists published in the *Journal of the American Scientific Affiliation*, the academic face of one of CAPS' sister organizations consisting mostly of Christian theologians, philosophers, and scientists whose primary focus is the interface of the Christian faith with the biological and physical sciences. The 1982 article, *Lying in the Laboratory: Deception in Human Research from Psychological, Philosophical, and Theological Perspectives*, is an interdisciplinary collaboration (something that, regrettably, we discovered to be underutilized in the integration literature) in that it was written by a psychologist (Rod Bassett), a philosopher (David Basinger), and a theologian (Paul Livermore). This team focused on deception, a tool sometimes used in empirical research, and considered the extent to which research deception can be justified from an integrative perspective. Thus, though the authors in this particular article did not directly conduct empirical research, they analyzed an issue often facing researchers and did so within an interdisciplinary format. Each contributor analyzed deception from within his own area of specialty from which the team pulled together a corporate analysis of what is indeed a complex issue. After discussing many important qualifications and considerations, the authors concluded that deception in research may be an acceptable methodology under certain conditions.

The article by Sorenson, Derflinger, Bufford, and McMinn (2004), entitled *National Collaborative Research on how Students Learn Integration: Final Report*, is included as a representative of good integrative research on a number of criteria: 1) it represents not a single study, but a systematic program of research over a ten year period; 2) it involves some of the latest and most sophisticated statistical methodology available, yet makes such results accessible to persons not familiar with that level of statistical sophistication; 3) it involves a collaborative effort among colleagues at several leading integration programs; 4) it identifies and seriously grapples with the complexity of integration, recognizing it as a process; and 5) it focuses on a topic of great interest and central importance to both the academic and practitioner integrationist. Specifically, the issue that drew their interest was, how do students best learn fundamental principles of integration during their graduate level training? Perhaps, most importantly, though, the five-part series of studies empirically supports and confirms what many integrationists have suspected all along. Integration, like spirituality, is not foremost an abstract cognitive concept to be learned by a set of conceptual rules, but rather it is a vibrant, embodied phenomenon implicitly caught as much, or more than, explicitly taught. In summarizing this impressive and important research program, Sorenson et al. in the final paragraph state:

> Our research indicates that what is transformative for students is not reducible to Christian belief, not creedal orthodoxy, and not even professorial piety.... Instead, our research shows that what is crucial to students' integration is a dynamic, ongoing process that a mentor is modeling before the students' eyes in way in which students feel they have real access personally, perhaps even as collaborators in the project together.

It is a fitting tribute to include this *Final Report* in this commemorative volume for it was published in late December, 2004, just weeks before Sorenson's unexpected and untimely death at the age of 51.

A topic of considerable interest among psychologists beginning in the 1990s and showing no signs of abatement early in the 21st Century is forgiveness. It is hardly an insight to claim forgiveness as a topic with substantial integration fertility and, indeed, many of its leading researchers, some with international reputations, are Christians who approach this topic from an integrative perspective. Therefore, if our specific goal was to identify a research article on forgiveness (which it was not), we could have approached any number of sources. To maintain fidelity with the purpose of this volume, instead we scoured the integration literature for outstanding research examples and found in our own backyard an important article on this very topic of such strong interest to many. A team of researchers at Hope College (Witvliet, Ludwig, & Bauer, 2002), investigated the effect of transgressors' forgiveness imagery both in terms of seeking forgiveness and their victim's possible response to the (actual) offense on self-reported emotions and physiological indicators. Their research report, *Please Forgive Me: Transgressor's Emotions and Physiology during Imagery of Seeking Forgiveness and Victim Responses*, conceptualized forgiveness through the eyes of faith, and was also faithful to recent theoretical and empirical advances in the psychological literature. These researchers found that imagery of merciful responses from victims evoked more positive and less negative emotions, including "moral" emotions (e.g., guilt, gratitude), and that these self report findings were corroborated by some (but only some) physiological indicators.

We conclude this research section by reprinting an article on yet another relevant, and for some highly-charged, topic: attitudes toward homosexual persons and homosexual behavior. Again, however, the topic, though important, was a less important criterion in our decision to include this article as much as the quality of the research process. Led by Rod Bassett et al. (2005), the team of researchers at Roberts Wesleyan College developed an innovative intervention program, consisting of both psychological and spiritual components, designed to foster more positive attitudes toward homosexual persons by Christian college students. Their report, *Being a Good Neighbor: Can Students Come to Value Homosexual Persons?* provides results of a within-subjects pretest-posttest (both immediate and one-month later) design. The results suggest that the intervention had some of the intended effects, though how it worked depended upon the initial attitudes of the students and the type of object (homosexual person or homosexual behavior) toward which the student expressed his or her opinion.

It is not surprising and perhaps even encouraging that the three empirical articles in this section were all published after the year 2000 and in the fifth decade of the integration work celebrated by this volume. Also, the research reported by both Witvliet et al. and Bassett et al. consisted of manipulated intervention designs that, when combined with random assignment to conditions, represent the gold standard of empirical research. Though these two studies represent research that is often encumbered by lack of random assignment and sampling limitations (affecting internal and external validity, respectively), they do suggest that the field of integration is becoming sufficiently mature to test many ideas and claims empirically.

Suggestions for Further Reading: Integrative Research

Emmons, R. A. (1999). *The psychology of ultimate concerns: Motivation and spirituality in personality*. New York: The Guilford Press.

This secular book with a research component is loaded with Christian insight into the nature of personality.

Hill, P. C. (1999). Giving religion away: What the study of religion offers psychology. *The International Journal for the Psychology of Religion, 9*, 229-249.

The author shows how religious insight can provide fresh new ideas for psychological research with three case studies.

Hill, P. C., & Hood, R. W., Jr. (Eds.). (1999). *Measures of religiosity*. Birmingham, AL: Religious Education Press.

A compendium of 125 measures in the psychology of religion, this book reviews a number of measures useful to the integration researcher.

Myers, D. G. (1978). *The human puzzle: Psychological research and Christian belief*. San Francisco: Harper & Row.

Though now dated, this little gem masterfully weaves psychological research findings with Christian belief and practice.

Paloutzian, R. F., & Park, C. L. (Eds.) (2005). *Handbook of the psychology of religion and spirituality*. New York: The Guilford Press.

This definitive handbook for recent research in the psychology of religion has many implications for research on integration topics.

Ripley, J. S., Worthington, E. L., Jr., & Berry, J. W. (2001). The effects of religiosity on preference and expectations for marital therapy among married Christians. *American Journal of Family Therapy, 29*, 39-58.

This survey study documents preferences among highly religious Christians for therapists who are Christians and who use Christian practices.

Watts, F., Nye, R., & Savage, S. (2002). *Psychology for Christian ministry*. London: Routledge.

Published in the UK, this book applies many insights from psychological research to Christian ministry.

Worthington, E. L., Jr. (1986). Religious counseling: A review of published empirical research. *Journal for Counseling and Development, 64*, 421-431.

This review of research was the first in a mainstream journal.

30

Lying in the Laboratory: Deception in Human Research from Psychological, Philosophical, and Theological Perspectives

Rodney L. Bassett
David Basinger
Paul Livermore[1]
Roberts Wesleyan College

Deception, as a research tool, is "objectively" considered from three perspectives. The major arguments found in psychology are summarized and the possibility of substituting role playing for deception is discussed. The article also reviews the major philosophical positions and what they imply for the use of deception. A scriptural approach to lying suggests that, although generally unacceptable, lying may be justified in the specific case of trying to gain understanding. Finally, approaching deception "subjectively" the authors conclude that under certain limiting conditions deception may be an acceptable methodology for Christian researchers.

Browsing through the evening newspaper you find an ad soliciting subjects for a psychology experiment. The prospect of participating seems intriguing and the pay is good so you call for an appointment. As a result, several days later you report to a scientist (at least he's wearing a lab coat and glasses) at a laboratory on the campus of a prestigious local university. Since the other subject, a friendly man in his mid-fifties, has already arrived, the experiment begins. The scientist explains he will be studying the effects of punishment upon learning. Your task will be to help the other subject learn lists of paired associate words by administering electric shock whenever he makes a mistake. All of you then go to an adjacent room where the other subject is strapped into a chair with electrodes attached to his arm. You then return to the original room with the scientist, and sit in front of an impressive-looking shock generator. The face of the machine has a series of switches with the last one marked "Danger: Severe Shock." In the learning task that follows, you find yourself administering increasingly higher levels of shock to the other subject. Very soon the subject begins to complain, then begins to groan in agony, and eventually refuses to even attempt the task. Of course, you feel uncomfortable and unsure. You press the switches as lightly as possible and even repeatedly ask the scientist to discontinue the experiment. But the scientist, accepting personal responsibility, orders you to continue. Finally, after what seems hours, you press the last switch marked "Danger: Severe Shock," and the experiment is over.

You've just been deceived. The other subject, an accomplice of the experimenter, never received any shock. And the experimenter was not studying the effectiveness of punishment but rather your willingness to obey hurtful commands. You participated in what's become known as the Milgram obedience paradigm.

Not too surprisingly, Stanley Milgram's methods and results (in the original study Milgram [1963] found unexpectedly high levels of obedience) have aroused considerable controversy.[2] It would be erroneous to assume, however, that the use of deception in psychological research has been limited to a few, highly publicized experiments. In the applied areas we find placebos, misattribution therapy, and control groups which provide a baseline comparison for the effectiveness of therapeutic techniques. In the basic branch of the family tree some areas of research rely almost exclusively upon deception (e.g., conformity and attitude change). This is not to say that all or even most psychologists use deception. But it is a technique provisionally allowed by the American Psychological Association's guidelines for research with humans (APA, 1973), it does appear in the method sections of many psychological journals (Menges, 1973), and it has been recommended as a therapeutic technique (Goldstein, Heller, & Sechrest, 1966).

The purpose of this article is to analyze critically the general practice of intentional lying within the domain of laboratory research (with a particular emphasis upon psychology). We first attempt to identify and discuss the relevant issues from the perspective of three disciplines: philosophy, theology, and, of course, psychology. Fortunately, each of us makes a living in one of these three fields. We then attempt to integrate our perspectives and outline what we consider to be an acceptable Christian position on this topic.

A Psychological Perspective

Psychologists have developed reasonable arguments for and against the use of deception. This section of the article presents some of the major arguments and briefly summarizes the relevant empirical literature. Finally, the potential for role playing as a substitute for deception is discussed.

Most psychologists concede that the use of deception is ethically problematic, but for methodological reasons some argue that deception is a necessary research tool. Four reasons for using deception are commonly cited.

Arguments for Deception

1. Deception allows the experimenter to increase the impact of a laboratory setting (Aronson & Carlsmith, 1965; Cooper, 1976). Presumably as the experimental situation becomes more realistic and involving, the independent variables are more likely to have the impact (but not necessarily the results) intended by the experimenter. Campbell (1957) calls this internal validity, a necessary condition for generalizing from the laboratory to the outside world.

As an extreme example of increasing internal validity consider a study by Berkun, et al. (1962) which assessed the effects of panic upon performance. In this study military personnel were led to believe they were in immediate danger of losing their life because of misdirected incoming artillery shells. The only means of escape was to repair a faulty radio transmitter and contact someone outside the area. Of course, the personnel were never really in danger. But it seems safe to conclude that the study did provide an accurate view of performance under emergency conditions.

2. Some significant areas of human life simply cannot be explored ethically using the experimental method. By using deception, however, the experimenter can sometimes sidestep this ethical dilemma by creating a facsimile of the area of interest.

Darley and Latané's (1970) work with bystander intervention provides a good example. Typically, these researchers staged emergencies (someone experiencing a seizure, breaking a leg, etc.), manipulated other situational factors, and then determined the impact of these factors upon bystanders' willingness to help. This research produced valuable information about how people respond to such situations without having to create an actual emergency. Certainly, an alternative methodology would have been us use a more descriptive approach, but then, the causal relationships might not have been so clear.

3. Using deception may protect the experimenter from certain "subject problems." This argument is based on the assumption that a subject's motives can profoundly affect how he or she responds to the experimental situation. It has been argued that some motives place subjects in roles that threaten the validity of research results. Three such problem roles have been extensively discussed.

The negativistic subject (Cook, Bean, Calder, Frey, Krovetz, & Reisman, 1970; Masling, 1966) wants to disconfirm the experimenter's hypothesis. Such an expression of hostility may result from the inconvenience of participating in the study or perhaps may be a reaction to the experimenter's temporary control over the subject. But, regardless of the reason, the subject now wants to invalidate the experimenter's study.

The good subject (Orne, 1962) is motivated in a more positive, but still misguided, direction. This subject wants to benefit science and/or the experimenter. However, the subject attempts to "help" by conscientiously confirming the experimenter's hypothesis. This kind of help can lead the experimenter to conclude falsely that the validity of his or her hypotheses has been verified.

The apprehensive subject (Rosenberg, 1965) wants to "look good" in the eyes of the experimenter. Most everyone is at times concerned about the image he or she presents to others. The presence of an expert in psychological health (the experimenter as viewed through some subjects' eyes) probably amplifies such a concern. Thus, in an experiment, a subject might not respond honestly when such a response could make him look like a psychological pygmy.

Weber and Cook (1972) review the research assessing the impact of subject roles upon experimental results. They conclude the apprehensive subject role has the strongest empirical base. However, given the right situation, it seems likely that all three roles could profoundly affect how subjects respond.

4. Psychologists favoring deception typically assume any potential negative effects resulting from deception (e.g., disruption of the subject-experimenter relationship, hurtful self-revelations, or dismay at being deceived) can be removed through debriefing. This technique essentially involves removing any false information (dehoaxing) or negative feelings (desensitizing) resulting from deception. As a rule most researchers attempt to guarantee that subjects will finish an experiment in as good or better psychological shape than they began.

The empirical evidence supporting the effectiveness of debriefing is mixed. In a well-known study, Berscheid, Abrahams and Aronson (1967), after using deception to manipulate social skills feedback, found dehoaxing immediately ineffective for all subjects and ineffective for an even longer period of time with certain personality types. But, after weighing all the available empirical evidence, Holmes (1976a, 1976b) concluded that dehoaxing and desensitizing were actually effective.

Arguments Against Deception

Those opposing the use of deception take exception to some of the ideas presented above and advance arguments of their own. The following paragraphs summarize some of the more common arguments against deception.

1. Some psychologists argue that deception promotes an unfortunate role for subjects in research (e.g., Kelman, 1967). They argue that too often subjects assume roles that are second-rate and powerless compared to the experimenter. The eventual result may be a negativistic reaction by subjects (withdrawal, hostility, etc.) which can lead to a subversion of the ultimate goal of research, understanding.

Deception may contribute to such a situation in at least two ways. First, to the extent that knowledge produces power, deception (at least initially) reduces the subject's power. And secondly, the use of deception means the subject is no longer free to choose intelligently what conditions he or she will be exposed to. Such a loss of freedom again results in a reduction of relative power. Probably the most famous example is the Milgram (1963) experiment, referred to earlier, where some subjects displayed their willingness to obey destructive commands. Such information may have given the subjects a broader understanding of themselves, but obtaining it was not part of the original agreement when they decided to participate.

The most commonly proposed remedy for this state of affairs is participatory research (Kelman, 1967). Such an approach views research as a joint effort with the subject and experimenter collaborat-ing toward the goal of gaining understanding. Unlike deception, the experimenter attempts to increase the subject's sophistication. Ideally, this approach enhances the interest of the subject and, thus, produces behavior that is honest and natural. A good example of participatory research is role playing, a technique discussed in more detail later.

2. Interwoven with the above position is the notion that deception implies an unfortunate view of the nature of man. Essentially, deception implies that man must be deceived under certain conditions because he cannot be trusted. Opponents of deception argue that mankind deserves the benefit of the doubt (Jourard, 1971; Kelman, 1967). They suggest that treating people as if they are honest and trustworthy promotes the same.

3. Deception is poor public relations for psychology. Presumably, the average citizen believes that people who lie are bad. Thus, some psychologists fear that as it becomes common knowledge that psychologists use deception, psychology's public image will receive a "black eye." Such a state of affairs could produce at least two unpleasant consequences. First, a reputation for lying might make it more difficult for a psychologist to establish a trusting relationship in therapy. And secondly, a negative public image might lead to overly restrictive legislation controlling the research process.

Looking at the available empirical evidence provides at least some assurance for the psychologist. First, it seems that when applying an ethical ruler to research, psychologists are more conservative than potential student subjects (Sullivan and Deiker, 1973). This graciousness on the part of students may reflect a general feeling in our society of the importance of science and a desire to allow science freedom to grow. Second, in the public mind, deception by itself seems to be a secondary consideration that becomes significant only when used in a particularly stressful way (Mannucci, 1977; Rugg, 1975).

4. Using deception may eventually prove to be self-defeating. Successful deception produces an unsuspecting group of subjects. But as word of the use of deception spreads, the eventual result may be a generally suspicious subject population. Certainly one solution to such a problem would be to seek out new subject populations (i.e., look beyond the college sophomore), but such a solution seems short-sighted at best.

Empirically, consideration of the suspicion issue has focused primarily on three issues: 1) Do deceived subjects talk about their experiences to other potential subjects? 2) Does suspicion affect experimental results? and 3) Is it possible to assess suspicion independently?

The issue of subjects' willingness to discuss experimental procedures is significant since it is related to the general level of suspicion in a subject population. At least two studies provide mixed results. Wuebben (1967) found that most subjects talked even though they promised not to. Interestingly, he found this tendency to talk was more pronounced for later-borns than first-borns or only children. But Aronson (1966) found no evidence for inter-subject communication. Comparing the two studies, it becomes apparent that Aronson took greater care than Wuebben in convincing subjects of the importance of not discussing the experiment and generally encouraged a higher level of subject involvement in the debriefing process. This suggests that if an experimenter is willing to debrief subjects extensively and carefully, they will reciprocate by complying with requests not to discuss procedures.

When looking at the impact of suspicion upon research results, again the evidence is mixed. Some studies have found that suspicion affects how subjects respond to an experimental situation (Adair, 1972; Cook, Bean, Calder, Frey, Krovetz, & Reisman, 1970; Rubin & Moore, 1971; Holmes & Appelbaum, 1970; Silverman, Shulman, & Wiesenthal, 1970; Stricker, Measick, & Jackson, 1967) while others have found little or no effect of suspicion (Allen, 1966; Brock & Becker, 1966; Fillenbaum, 1966). It is, therefore, impossible to draw general conclusions. Rather, the effect of suspicion probably depends upon such factors as previous research experience, the role adopted by a subject, the level of suspicion, the personality of the subject, and the specific situation (those eliciting special concern about self presentation are probably most vulnerable).

Since the above discussion suggests that under certain conditions suspicion can affect performance, the issue of detecting suspicion becomes significant. At this time the strongest statement that can be made is that often the task of assessment can be difficult and the specific methods used may profoundly affect the outcome (Golding & Lichtenstein, 1970; Levy, 1967; Rubin & Moore, 1971).

Role Playing as an Alternative

A lot of energy, time, and thought has gone into the deception controversy. And even now the conflict continues. Perhaps the ideal solution would be to introduce a new methodology as effective as deception but without the ethical baggage associated with deception. Such a proposal has been made

before (Kelman, 1967). Currently, the leading candidate as a replacement for deception is role playing.

Role playing is a global term covering a large number of variations along a basic theme. Essentially this theme involves providing the subject with more information than is typical with a deception paradigm. The polar extremes of this theme are what Horowitz and Rothschild (1970) call forewarning and prebriefing. Forewarned subjects are simply told before a study begins that deception may be involved and at this point have the opportunity of freely choosing to place themselves in a situation where they may be misled. Prebriefed subjects are given a detailed explanation of all the deceptions which will be part of a study (essentially the same information as would be contained in a debriefing) and then are asked to participate in the study as if they had not been informed.

The key question, of course, is can role playing produce the same results as deception?[3] Empirically, the evidence for prebriefing has been mixed (for example, see: Gallo, Smith, & Mumford, 1973; Greenberg, 1967; Holmes & Bennett, 1974; Willis & Willis, 1970). The effectiveness of prebriefing is probably a function of various factors: the extent to which the subjects play an active or passive role, whether subjects role play themselves or the role of another, the staging of the experimental situation, the inherent acting ability of the subject, and the type of dependent variable (behavioral vs. self-report). Interestingly, so far the results for forewarning have been less ambiguous. To our knowledge, every empirical test of forewarning has found no difference between the results produced by it and deceptions (Gallo, Smith, & Mumford, 1973; Horowitz & Rothschild, 1970; Holmes & Bennett, 1974). Thus, the validity of role playing seems to depend upon the type of role playing, the nature of the experimental situation, and the subject. Therefore, it does seem premature to conclude summarily that role playing is a methodologically acceptable substitute for deception.

Summary

This section has attempted to summarize current psychological thought concerning deception. One danger of such an approach is oversimplification leading to a "good guy vs. bad guy" mentality. Clearly, from a psychological perspective, both a pro- and anti-deception position can be defended intelligently and with integrity.

A Philosophical Perspective

It is the function of the social scientist to identify needed areas of study, design relevant experiments to generate the necessary data, and then analyze and utilize the results. But the social scientist *qua* scientist cannot tell us which areas of human experience, if any, ought not be studied, which methodologies, if any, ought not to be used, or how the anticipated or accrued results ought or ought not to be utilized. These are ethical judgments that should be based on one's fundamental philosophical beliefs about the nature of reality, especially one's beliefs concerning personhood and knowledge and the proper relationship between them. Accordingly, it is the social scientist (or other interested observer), *qua* philosopher or theologian, who must make such decisions.

There are three popular philosophical approaches to ethical questions.

1. ***Relativism***. The relativist's fundamental ethical belief is that no moral absolutes exist. What is right is what an individual (a subjectivist) or group (a cultural relativist) thinks is right. Given this perspective, the question of deception in experimentation obviously poses no major ethical problems. If an individual scientist, or group of scientists, believes such deception is justifiable in a given situation, it is.

This does not mean, though, that such deception could never generate a moral dilemma for the relativist. He or she might, for example, feel it is wrong to use deception in a specific experiment but believe it is important to gain and use the information such deception would supply. Such a dilemma, however, would be primarily psychological, not logical, since for the relativist no objective standard exists against which the moral consistency of his or her ultimate decision can be judged.

It is, of course, questionable whether anyone is (or can be) totally relativistic in practice. But many individuals are "selective" relativists, and it may be that some social scientists (rightly or wrongly) feel justified in affirming a relativistic position with respect to the issue at hand.

2. ***Consequentialism (Teleological theories)***. For the consequentialist there are, in principle, no intrinsically right or wrong actions. An action is (or becomes) right if it has good consequences. There are two popular consequentialist theories.

a) *Utilitarianism*. The utilitarian maintains that the right action is that which generates the greatest amount of happiness (or pleasure) for the greatest number of people. More specifically, the "act utilitarian" is concerned with the amount of happiness actually generated for those directly involved in a given activity, while the "rule utilitarian" is concerned with the potential for happiness inherent in the repeated and widespread performance of a given type of activity.

If a social scientist were an act utilitarian, accordingly, he or she would be interested in assessing the amount of happiness or unhappiness generated in each specific experiment utilizing deception. Will the deceived individuals experience a lessening of self-worth when they later assess their actions? Will they lose trust in the experimenter when they learn of the deception? Is the use of deception the best way to achieve the desired results in this case? Could the desired results significantly benefit certain individuals? Will the experimenter feel a sense of shame? If, after considering these and related questions, the social scientist felt that a greater amount of happiness for those directly involved (e.g., subjects, experimenter, beneficiaries) would be achieved by using deception in a given experiment, it would be justifiable. The key point to keep in mind is that, under act utilitarianism, the ethical propriety of each experiment involving deception would have to be judged individually.

On the other hand, if our social scientist were a rule utilitarian, he or she would be concerned, not with any specific instance of deception, but with the practice in general. Will the general practice of deception in experimentation tend to make subjects suspicious and thus induce "artificial" responses? Will the general use of deception lead to a general disregard for the rights of individuals, and thus lead to a general disregard for personhood? Are other, equally satisfactory methodologies available? If, after considering these and related questions, it was felt that the general practice should have negative consequences (i.e., generate a net increase in unhappiness or pain) for society as a whole, it would be wrong for any social scientist to use deception in experimentation, even if a given scientist felt strongly that the practice would have positive consequences in his or her own situation.

b) *Ethical egoism*. The ethical egoist believes that an individual ought to act in his or her own self-interest—i.e., equate good consequences with self-fulfillment. Egoism, it should be noted, is distinct from relativism. The relativist denies that an objective methodology exists by which to make ethical decisions; the egoist affirms this claim. Relativism, accordingly, allows for greater ethical variation. The relativist can, if he or she desires, act in his or her own self-interest, or in the interest of others, or on the basis of no rational considerations at all. The ethical egoist does or should always act in an openly self-indulgent manner. The egoist, for example, might appear altruistic. Egoism requires only that the primary reason for any form of ostensive behavior ultimately be self-interest.

When considering the question of deception, therefore, the egoistic social scientist must decide whether such a practice will benefit him or her personally. Such a decision would, of course, be relative to the perceived "interests" of each scientist utilizing this ethical methodology. Moreover, such a social scientist could well find himself or herself facing a moral dilemma. For example, an egoist scientist might desire the professional fame he or she believes could result from an experiment utilizing an especially creative, but quite embarrassing, form of deception, but not desire the anticipated loss of respect by the subjects involved. In such cases, the egoist would need to develop a priority rating for the given "interests" involved and make a decision accordingly.

We see then that consequentialism allows for a wide variety of answers to the question at hand. But each social scientist who espouses this methodology faces a similar problem: the difficult task of attempting to predict future consequences.

3. *Nonconsequentialism (Deontological theories)*. For the nonconsequentialist, an action is right if performed in accordance with accepted moral laws. The anticipated consequences are not relevant. Under non-consequentialism, accordingly, actions have intrinsic moral value.

Nonconsequential theories fall into three basic categories. The "intuitionist" believes that the right rule or specific action is known intuitively (self-evidently) by the morally mature individual. Not surprisingly, almost all "intuitionists" consider lying to be wrong. The "rationalist' believes that the right rule or specific action can be identified by the use of reason. Kant, for example, believed that an action was moral only if it could become a universal law without generating a contradiction. Moreover, he felt that under this principle lying is an immoral activity. For if everyone gave false promises (lied), he argued, the concept of "telling the truth" would become meaningless and thus lying, itself, would become impossible (self-contradictory). Most other "rationalistic" nonconsequentialists agree that lying is wrong. Finally, the "revelationist' believes that the right rule or specific action in any situation is that which is (or has been) dictated by God in some form of written or "mystical" communication. Almost all "revelationists" believe lying to be intrinsically wrong.

It might appear that the social scientist who espouses a nonconsequentialist theory could not under any condition condone the use of deception in experimentation, but such is not necessarily the case. In addition to believing that lying is wrong, many (if not most) nonconsequentialists also

believe that the acquisition of human knowledge, the alleviation of human pain and suffering, and the improvement of the quality of human life are morally proper activities. Hence, for such social scientists, the use of deception in experimentation generates a *prima facie* conflict. The experiments themselves, when viewed as a means to the acquisition of knowledge—knowledge which is generally seen as potentially beneficial for humanity—must be considered good. But since such experiments necessitate the willful use of deception, they must also be viewed as morally unacceptable. Such a social scientist, accordingly, will be forced to violate an accepted moral norm. However, it must be emphasized that in making the decision to act in accordance with one moral principle at the expense of another, the social scientist would not be saying that an intrinsically unacceptable action can become intrinsically acceptable in some situations. He or she would simply be saying that circumstances sometimes dictate that an intrinsically unacceptable action must be performed in order to avoid the performance of an even less acceptable action. Such dilemmas, moreover, point out a fundamental difficulty facing the nonconsequentialist: the prioritizing of intrinsically good moral principles. Unfortunately, there seems to be no standard method for accomplishing this task.

We see then that there is no single philosophical response to the question of human deception in experimentation. One's response depends not only on one's basic ethical stance but on how one resolves the potential conflicts between various intrinsic or consequential "goods" which are inherent in each.[4]

A Theological Perspective

The question whether a Christian ought to deceive under any circumstance at first seems out of order. In Colossians 3 lying is viewed as a reflection of the old nature, and thus, Paul encourages Christians to avoid it (Col. 3: 9-10; cf. Eph. 4:25; Ex. 20:16; Deut. 5:20). But, in stark contrast to Paul's admonition, other passages of Scripture not only allow for deception but approve it. The writer to the Hebrews characterized Rahab's concealment of the Israelite spies from the citizens of Jericho as an act of faith (Heb. 11:31; cf. Josh. 2:1-21; 6:17, 22-25). We cannot claim then that there are no circumstances under which the Judaeo-Christian tradition allows one to conceal the whole truth. But is one of those cases that of research into behavior by a Christian psychologist? That is the question we want to deal with. In order to answer it we need to inquire: are there clear, biblical and theological principles that apply to the issue of using deception in psychological research? We proceed primarily by examining relevant scriptural evidence. Then we summarize how these results apply to our inquiry.

Scriptural and Theological Principles that Prohibit Deception

God is truth, he does not lie, and in his dealings with us he is reliable (cf. Ps. 36:5-7; Rom. 3:1-7; 11:30; Titus 1:2). God's integrity, in fact, provides a basis for the structure of our relationships with him and with one another. God has entered into covenants with humans and the stability of these depends upon his truthfulness. Thus, Scripture calls him faithful (he keeps his word, Deut. 7:9; Ps. 89:1-4; 1 Thess. 5:24) and righteous (his action conforms to his covenant commitment, Ps. 85:10-13; 96:13; Jer. 12:1; Rom., 1:17; 3:21-26). The dependability of God is so certain that we can confidently live in the face of obstacles and know that the future will be as he promised (Ps. 31:5; 57:1-3; 91:1-6). His purpose is not to deceive or lead us astray but to conduct us on the way of truth (Ps. 25:8-10).

From this affirmation about God we move to the corresponding one concerning the world he created. We can generalize by saying that he established truth as a principle woven into the fabric of the cosmos (Ps. 89:1-18; 96:10-13; Prov. 10:9). It is among the principles or laws by which this world (whether physical or social) operates. When the principles are ignored or violated, disorder and chaos break out (Prov. 11:4-6). God will in some way and at some time bring the liar into judgment and punishment for his deed (Ps. 12; 59:6-13; 63:11; 101:3-5; Prov. 17:20; 19:5, 9; Isa. 29:18-21; 59:1-4, 12-15; Jer. 5:12-17). When we adhere to them there is stability—a natural, forward movement in which life prospers and is good (Ps. 34:11-14).

Thus, when the Bible describes an instance of deceit it also observes the results (compare Gen. 24:5-30 with 32:3-32, where Jacob has to face up to the results of his deceit). It is not as if a simple lie had been told and that was the end of the matter. Rather, deceit sets in motion a chain of events. Things can happen to make the chain move into different directions, but in no instance is the chain reversed as if nothing ever happened. The relation of deed and consequence is unbreakable. Thus, as a fallout of telling a falsehood, innocent people may suffer injustice (Prov. 10:15; 11:3; Prov. 12:13; 20:17; Prov. 14:11, 25; 15:27; 28:16). Poverty and its tragic results may dog one because he has depended on deceit (Prov. 12:19; 21:6). Lying causes a breakdown in social stability (Prov. 29:12; 19:28). What if a wife cannot be certain of the word of her husband, a child of his parent, one neighbor of another (Prov. 25:18; 26:18b), a master of a servant, or a citizen of his king (Prov. 16:13; 17:7)? Second-guessing and cautiousness inevitably result when naive trust is betrayed. Oaths and securities are taken to guarantee a promise that will not stand alone (Matt. 5:33-37. Cf. Gen. 29-31—the entire cycle of the Laban and Jacob stories where the two are constantly trying to outmaneuver one another). And beyond all this there is the internal personal chaos that breaks out. The man who deceives, no matter what others think, knows what he has done and hence, is. He has eroded his own self-respect that results from integrity, skill, and diligence. He plays the game of concealing the truth not only from others but also from himself. This requires enormous psychic energy. The human exhausts himself juggling the data to hide the truth (Ps. 32:3-4).

A dependence upon deceit indicates a flaw in character, a defect in spirit (Ps. 36:1-3). The person does not live as God made and intended, and he cannot reach his potential of character development and moral achievement (Prov. 19:22; 20:6). He has taken a short-cut to success and there is an inevitable loss in personhood. The use of deception reveals and aggravates this loss. One, for example, resorts to deception to conceal an evil action or thought rather than deal with it (Ex. 32:22-24). Consequently, the evil persists and the new problem of deception makes it worse. Or people may deceive hoping to satisfy greed (Prov. 20:14). By lying they may succeed in overcharging for a product and get more for themselves (Prov. 21:6; Prov. 20:10). On the other hand, people sometimes lie because they hate or have contempt for another (Prov. 10:18; 26:28). They might rationalize that the other human being does not deserve an honest comment. What he is or who he is, is not their personal responsibility, and any thought or action that one can make to another's disadvantage because he is deceived is of no concern to him. Thus, the person who deceives believes that he can control others by deceit and that he has a right to do so (Ps. 62:3-4; Ps. 119:69).

There are many cases in which biblical heroes are the subjects who deceive but in which the intentions are wrong and the actions are not approved, even when the long range objectives were identical with God's will. For example, both Abraham (Gen. 12:10-20; 20:1-18) and Isaac (Gen. 26:6-11) deceived monarchs about their wives so that the kings, seeing and desiring the beautiful women, would not kill the husbands and place the women in their harems. In these instances, God's will, the preservation of Abraham's family, was not set aside by the sin of his servants. But it is also clear that God did not approve of the deceit and the patriarchs were publicly rebuked for it.

In the biblical view, then, something is wrong with the person who lies as a matter of course. He believes that it is his prerogative to manipulate others through deception and he, therefore, has an inadequate view of personhood. The use of lying breaks Scripture's basic principle of human relationship—love (Lev. 19:18; Deut. 6:4-5; Mk. 12:28-34; Mt. 22:34-40; Lk. 10:25-28; Rom. 13:8-10; Gal. 5:14; 1 John 2:7-11; James 2:8). Whatever specific action we choose in a particular situation, it must arise from a love of the individual. This is not merely an emotion of sympathy or tenderness, but a motive toward positive, respecting and redeeming action. The dignity of the other human cannot be sacrificed for any reason or at any cost.

Scriptural or Theological Principles that Might Require Deception

The case against the use of deception might seem so strong that it excludes any exceptions. There are instances, however, of its use in Scripture which make such a generalization impossible. We need to examine these now to see how they make our inquiry more precise. There are three instances that we consider.

First, deceit receives divine approval, or at least tacit approval, when it is necessary to preserve life or the integrity of life (1 Sam. 19:9-17). In these cases there is a ranking of values. One tells the truth as a general policy, but in an instance in which telling the truth would forfeit someone else's life, one does what he can to protect it. Here there is not a choosing between a good and an evil but between the lesser of two evils.

Second, there are cases where God is the subject of the deceit, or at least initiates it. Exodus 3:16-20 reports how God intended to deceive Pharaoh in order to liberate Israel from slavery. He instructed Moses to ask Pharaoh's permission for Israel to go three days' journey into the wilderness and worship him there. Would they return afterward? This is not said although it is implied in the request. But obviously at that time God had in mind the eventual destination of the Promised Land rather than a three-day detour in the desert. One of the reasons for this high level of manipulation is clear. Pharaoh was of such a mind, arrogating to himself the role of a god, and was so given to injustice that there could be no appeal to his religious or humane motives. He would respond only to what he thought was to his best advantage; thus, he was deceived into furthering, not hindering, God's will.

Third, we consider another use of deceit that appears to have divine approval: deception to obtain understanding. An example of this is found in the Joseph story (Gen. 37:39-50). Long after Joseph's brothers had sold him into slavery, he rose to second place in Egypt's court, and during the seven years of famine was responsible for the distribution of the stored grain. When Joseph's brothers came to Egypt to buy grain, Joseph did not reveal himself to them for a good while. In fact, the things which he did before he finally disclosed his identity are very interesting. On their first trip to Egypt he accused them of being spies (Gen. 42:7), claimed that they lied to him (Gen. 42:15), threatened to put them all in prison (Gen. 42:16), finally did keep Simeon (Gen. 42:24), and then demanded that the next time they came they had to bring the younger brother (Gen. 42:20). He also returned their money secretly (Gen. 42:25). On their second trip his actions were even more complex. He assured them that the returned money was put there by their God (Gen. 43:23), gave a benediction over Benjamin, (Gen. 43:29), ate with them seating them in order of age, (Gen. 43:33), returned their money again, (Gen. 44:1), and had his silver cup put into Benjamin's sack (Gen. 44:2). But then he had them overtaken and threatened the man who took the cup (Gen. 44:4, 17). Finally, after Judah's offer of himself in Benjamin's place, Joseph revealed himself (Gen. 45:3).

Why did Joseph conceal the whole truth for such a long time? Biblical scholarship is always suspicious of attempts to psychologize the motives of biblical characters. There can be several reasons for a certain action; unless a story gives us a good clue, we must guard against projecting our own tendencies into the account. Perhaps there was some revenge in Joseph's mind. But the story also implies, especially because of the tacit approval, something like this: through his questions, demands, and actions, Joseph was able to determine the true character of his brothers, and he discovered that they had changed a great deal. Whereas previously they had been jealous and selfish, they were now repentant and willing to sacrifice themselves. Joseph would have been unable to discover this, at least to its depths, without the testing. Here is a case in which concealment of truth was the means by which character and behavior traits were discovered.

In another case, the Bible reports how a prophet through deception revealed the enormity of a monarch's unacknowledged crime. David had committed adultery with Bathsheba (2 Sam. 11:2-5), and then, to protect his legal innocence, had schemed for Uriah, her husband, to be slain in battle (2 Sam. 11:6-25). Here was someone in a powerful position who was not about to accept the truth of his own behavior. Nathan, the prophet, however, deceived

David into revealing that his actions did not conform to his own values (2 Sam. 12:1-10). He told the king the parable of the poor man and his one little ewe lamb. After hearing how the rich man had mercilessly stolen the lamb, the king with righteous indignation pronounced the verdict against the powerful rich man. Then the prophet shattered the complacent, arrogant king with the charge, "You are the man." In this case, deception was necessary in order to compel a powerful and rationalizing person to admit the truth about himself.

Conclusion

There are at least three types of cases, then, in which a form of deceit is approved within Scripture and Christian theology: (1) Deception may be necessary to protect life or the integrity of life. (2) God may deceive a person who had determined to go contrary to the divine will in order to further his plan of salvation. (3) Deception may be used to test or reveal the truth about character and behavior. This third type comes closest to our inquiry about the use of deception in psychological research. Deception is necessary here because human nature tends to conceal the truth when its revelation would prove embarrassing or costly. By deception one can be brought to see the truth, even against one's will.

In the three cases where Scripture allows deception, it does so because of the human predicament in sin. One may have to lie in order to save a life from violence by another. God may use the rebellious person to further his plan of salvation by deceiving him. Or by deception, the truth about character or behavior may be shown where it would otherwise go unrevealed. This is not a perfect but a fallen world, and on occasion Scripture endorses deception to expose its fallenness or to protect the innocent. Therefore, with respect to our inquiry we can say the Bible and Christian theology allow for deception when it appears necessary to expose the truth about character and behavior.

On the other hand, Scripture by no means gives unqualified approval of its use. In general, deception contradicts the established principle of human relationships, arises from a defect in character, and inevitably introduces instability and distrust. The suspicion that sometimes surrounds psychologies conforms to this pattern.

Discussion

We now face the task of integrating these three perspectives. We acknowledge that there is room for honest differences of opinion on this issue. But, given our understanding of all the data at hand, it is our belief that under certain conditions, deception may be a justifiable technique for the Christian psychologist.

1. As nonconsequentialists, we consider deception to be intrinsically wrong. Therefore, even if it were decided that some greater good could be brought about by the use of deception, it must first be demonstrated that there is no other morally preferable methodology such as role playing that would be essentially as effective.

We are especially attracted to the use of forewarning as an alternative to straight deception. From an ethical perspective, even limited informed consent seems an improvement over straight deception in that the former shows greater respect for the subject's freedom of choice than does the latter. Unfortunately, not many studies directly testing the validity of forewarning as a research technique have yet been conducted, but the evidence to date suggests that forewarning and straight deception produce the same results. This may be the case because many subject populations are already aware of the psychologist's use of deception and are, thus, in this sense already "forewarned." Moreover, when a subject freely chooses to risk deception, we suspect that from a psychological perspective debriefing would be simpler and the relationship between subject and experimenter less vulnerable. It also seems that by at least partially taking the subject into his or her confidence, the experimenter takes a significant step toward removing the inequity between the roles of subject and experimenter.

However, we acknowledge that forewarning may not always be as effective as deception. There are some situations where advertising the possibility of deception may bias the results (especially under those conditions where the possibility of deception may not already be salient for the subject). This seems especially true when the research paradigm is moderately transparent. Our reasoning is that with a clearly transparent paradigm the subject needs no clues to discover that deception is being used, while with a barely transparent paradigm no amount of prompting is going to allow the subject to penetrate the deception. Yet it should be noted that even if forewarning does allow the subject to discover the true purpose of the study, being at least partially brought into the experimenter's confidence may motivate the subject to put aside his hypothesis awareness and behave as naturally as possible. Of course, these speculations are subject to empirical test.

2. We do not subscribe to the popular scientific maxim that the pursuit of knowledge (no matter how potentially beneficial its application) is justifiable under any circumstances. More specifically, it is our contention that no amount of potentially beneficial

information which an experimenter might gather by deceiving his or her subjects can justify the use of such deception if there exists the real possibility that the deceived individuals will permanently and/or severely be psychologically or physically harmed.

3. We realize that experimentation is at times undertaken primarily for the benefit of the researcher. However, while a desire for "personal gain" may not necessarily be wrong in all contexts, it is in our estimation never justifiable to use or manipulate another for personal advantage (monetary profit, prestige, or power). For to do so is to treat the individual in question as an object, someone we stand over-against in moral and personal superiority. We are equals in the challenges and responsibilities of life; and our duty is to respect, love, and serve, even when professional expertise gives us an advantage. Accordingly, a necessary condition for the use of deception, we believe, is that the experimentation be undertaken primarily because of its potential for benefiting mankind.

Perhaps this and the preceding qualifications can be stated most succinctly by saying that a Christian researcher's motives should always reflect a love for God and a love for man. In this context, if deception reflects a love for God, the researcher will examine his motives to determine if they are as pure as possible. If deception reflects a love for man, the researcher will be concerned about the relationship between himself and the subject, avoiding potential harm to the subject, and making sure the research has a potential for benefiting mankind.

4. Finally, we do not feel that the individual researcher is always the best judge of the value of, or motive(s) for, his or her research. Thus, when weighing the potential value of, or motive(s) for, research—especially research involving deception—it may well be helpful for the investigator to consult with colleagues and perhaps even a sample of the potential subject pool.

Our discussion to this point has, of course, been based on the assumption that deception can provide a path toward understanding. Christian psychologist Ronald Kotesky (1979) seems to find this assumption unacceptable. He argues that "the end of any process is inexorably embedded in the means used to reach it, so that a process which uses deceptive means cannot lead to truth. Thus, deception is not only not a legitimate means to truth, but not a means to truth at all." If we substitute "false" for "deceptive" in Kotesky's argument, there is a sense in which he is correct. A true conclusion cannot be deduced validly from false premises. But if Kotesky means that the experimenter who uses deception cannot arrive at empirically valid results (or results that are more

empirically valid than those which would have been produced by non-deceptive means), his argument is dubious. First, deception is often used to duplicate a situation in the real world. And it seems reasonable to conclude that the closer an experimental situation is to its "real world" counterpart, the more likely that paradigm is to reveal truth about how people typically respond. Second, as a result of the Fall, people are not always honest (especially when such honesty provides an unpleasant view of the self). Sometimes an effective cover story may help a subject to be more honest (at least in terms of the research question). This does not rule out the possibility that honesty can elicit honesty, but it does recognize that as a result of the Fall there are certain limits to man's ability to be truthful. And since self-report often provides the primary dependent variable in an experiment, such a limitation is a significant concern.[6]

Conclusion

We have in our discussion attempted to articulate and defend one general perspective on the question of deception in experimentation. We, of course, realize that many thoughtful Christians may object strongly to our conclusions but find the prospect of such critical reaction encouraging. For it is our hope that this article will stimulate further thought on the specific issue of deception as well as the more general issue of doing research within a Christian worldview.

Notes

1. All three authors contributed significantly to this project, and thus, we all accept equally the credit or the blame for its contents. In addition, we are indebted to Harold Hurley for responding to an earlier version of this article and Ben Whitsel for contributing to the review of the psychology literature.

2. For an extended discussion of the ethical issues involved with the Milgram obedience studies, see Baumrind (1964) and Milgram (1964).

3. Some authors have turned this question around and suggested the true criterion of validity should be role playing (Forward, Canter, and Kirsch, 1976).

4. For a well-organized, readable discussion of the various ethical theories I have mentioned, see Jacques Theroux, Ethics: Theory and Practice (Encino, CA: Glencoe Press, 1977).

5. The citations of scriptural references are by no means exhaustive. We have merely drawn on representative passages.

6. For another response to Kotesky, see Johnson (1979).

References

Adair, J. G. (1972). Demand characteristics of conformity: Suspiciousness of deception and experimenter bias in conformity research. *Canadian Journal of Behavioural Science, 4,* 238-248.

Allen, V. L. (1966). Effect of knowledge of deception on conformity. *Journal of Social Psychology, 69,* 101-106.

American Psychological Association, Inc. (1973). *Ethical Principles in the Conduct of Research with Human Participants.* Washington DC: American Psychological Association.

Aronson, E., (1966). Avoidance of intersubject communication. *Psychological Reports, 19,* 238.

Aronson, E., & Carlsmith, J. M. (1968). Experimentation in social psychology. In G. Lindzey & E. Aronson (Eds.). *The Handbook of Social Psychology* (Vol. 2). Reading, MA: Addison-Wesley Publishing Co.

Baumrind, D. (1964). Some thoughts on ethics of research: After reading Milgram's "Behavioral Study of Obedience." *American Psychologist, 19,* 421-423.

Berkun, M. M., Bialek, H. M., Kern, R. P., & Yagi, K. (1962). Experimental studies of psychological stress in man. *Psychological Monographs, 76,* (15, Whole No. 534).

Berscheid, E., Abrahams, D., & Aronson, V. (1967). Effectiveness of debriefing following deception experiments. *Journal of Personality and Social Psychology, 6,* 371-380.

Brock, T. C., & Becker, L. A. (1966). "Debriefing" and susceptibility to subsequent experimental manipulations. *Journal of Experimental Social Psychology, 2,* 314-323.

Campbell, D. T. (1957). Factors relevant to the validity of experiments in social settings. *Psychological Bulletin, 54,* 297-312.

Cook, T. D., Bean, J. R., Calder, B. J., Frey, R., Krovetz, M. L., & Reisman, S. R. (1970). Demand characteristics and three conceptions of the frequently deceived subject. *Journal of Personality and Social Psychology, 14,* 185-194.

Cooper, J. (1976). Deception and role playing: On telling the good guys from the bad guys. *American Psychologist, 31,* 605-610.

Darley, J. M., & Latané, B. (1970). *The unresponsive bystander: Why doesn't he help?* Englewood Cliffs, NJ: Prentice-Hall.

Fillenbaum, S. (1966). Prior deception and subsequent experimental performance: The "faithful" subject. *Journal of Personality and Social Psychology, 4,* 532-537.

Forward, J., Canter, R., & Kirsch, N. (1976). Role-enactment and deception methodologies. *American Psychologist, 31,* 595-604.

Gallo, P. S., Smith, S., & Mumford, S. (1973). Effects of deceiving subjects upon experimental results. *Journal of Social Psychology, 89,* 99-107.

Golding, S. L., & Lichtenstein, E. (1970). Confession of awareness and prior knowledge of deception as a function of interview set and approval motivation. *Journal of Personality and Social Psychology, 14,* 213-223.

Goldstein, A. P., Heller, K., & Sechrest, L. B. (1966). *Psychotherapy and the psychology of behavior change.* New York: John Wiley & Sons, Inc.

Greenberg, M. S. (1967). Role playing: An alternative to deception. *Journal of Personality and Social Psychology, 7,* 152-157.

Holmes, D. S. (1976a). Debriefing after psychological experiments: Effectiveness of postdeception dehoaxing. *American Psychologist, 31,* 858-867.

Holmes, D. S. (1976b). Debriefing after psychological experiments: II. Effectiveness of postexperimental desensitizing. *American Psychologist, 31,* 868-875.

Holmes, D. S., & Appelbaum, A. S. (1970). Nature of prior experimental experience as a determinant of performance in a subsequent experiment. Journal of *Personality and Social Psychology, 14,* 195-202.

Holmes, D. S., & Bennett, D. H. (1974). Experiments to answer questions raised by the use of deception in psychological research: I. Role playing as an alternative to deception: II. Effectiveness of debriefing after deception: III. Effect of informed consent on deception. *Journal of Personality and Social Psychology, 29,* 385-367.

Horowitz, I. A., & Rothschild, B. H. (1970). Conformity as a function of deception and role playing. *Journal of Personality and Social Psychology, 14,* 224-226.

Johnson, D. E. (1979). Deception in social psychological research: A reply to Kotesky. *Journal of the American Scientific Affiliation, 31,* 174-175.

Jourard, S. M. (1971). *The transparent self.* New York: Van Nostrand.

Kelman, H. C. (1967). Human use of human subjects: The problem of deception in social psychological experiments. *Psychological Bulletin, 67,* 1-11.

Kotesky, R. L. (1979). Deception and the Christian psychologist. *Journal of the American Scientific Affiliation, 31,* 58-59.

Levy, L. H. (1967). Awareness, learning, and the beneficent subject as expert witness. *Journal of Personality and Social Psychology, 6,* 365-370.

Mannucci, E. G. (1978). Potential subjects view psychology experiments: An ethical inquiry. *Dissertation Abstracts International, 38,* 3958B-3959B. (University Microfilms No. 78732059)

Masling, J. (1966). Role-related behavior of the subject and psychologist and its effects upon psychological data. *Nebraska Symposium on Motivation, 14,* 67-103.

Menges, R. J. (1973). Openness and honesty versus coercion and deception in psychological research. *American Psychologist, 28,* 1030-1034.

Milgram, S. (1963). Behavioral study of obedience. *Journal of Abnormal Social Psychology, 67,* 371-378.

Milgram, S. (1964). Issues in the study of obedience: A reply to Baumrind. *American Psychologist, 19,* 848-852.

Orne, M. T. (1962). On the social psychology of the psychological experiment: With particular reference to demand characteristics and their implications. *American Psychologist, 17,* 776-783.

Rosenberg, M. J. (1965). When dissonance fails: On eliminating evaluation apprehension from attitude measurement. *Journal of Personality and Social Psychology, 1,* 28-42.

Rubin, Z., & Moore, J. C. (1971). Assessment of subjects' suspicions. *Journal of Personality and Social Psychology, 17,* 163-170.

Rugg, E. A. (1975). Ethical judgments of social research involving experimental deception. *Dissertation Abstracts, International, 36,* 1976B. (University Microfilms No. 75-22, 288).

Silverman, I., Hulman, A. D., & Wiesenthal, D. L. (1970). Effects of deceiving and debriefing psychological subjects on performance in later experiments. *Journal of Personality and Social Psychology, 14,* 203-212.

Stricker, L. J., Messick, S., & Jackson, D. N. (1967). Suspicion of deception: Implications for conformity research. *Journal of Personality and Social Psychology, 5,* 379-389.

Sullivan, D. S., & Deiker, T. E. Subject-experimenter perceptions of ethical issues in human research. *American Psychologist, 28,* 587-591.

Theroux, J. (1977). *Ethics: Theory and Practice.* Encino, CA: Glencoe Press.

Weber, S. J., & Cook, T. D. (1972). Subject effects in laboratory research: An examination of subject roles, demand characteristics, and valid inference. *Psychological Bulletin, 77,* 273-295.

Willis, R. H., & Willis, Y. A. (1970). Role playing versus deception: An experimental comparison. *Journal of Personality and Social Psychology, 16,* 472-477.

Wuebben, P. L. (1967). Honesty of subjects and birth order. *Journal of Personality and Social Psychology, 5,* 350-352.

31

National Collaborative Research on How Students Learn Integration: Final Report

Randall Lehmann Sorenson
Rosemead School of Psychology

Kimberly R. Derflinger
Private Practice

Rodger K. Bufford
George Fox University

Mark R. McMinn
Wheaton College

A relational attachment model of how students learn integration at Rosemead and Fuller was replicated with clinical psychology doctoral students at George Fox University and Wheaton College (Illinois). Structural equation modeling of multitrait-multimethod matrices tested how well faculty members could recognize what students readily identify in professors as most useful to students' integration, and Latent Semantic Analysis interpreted what students found most important.

This is the fifth in a series of five articles on how students learn integration. In scope, focus, and approach, this programmatic research on integration is groundbreaking. Its scope is national collaborative research spanning 10 years and more than 5,000 data points drawn from student perceptions of over 80 faculty members at the four evangelical schools with the longest-standing accreditation by the American Psychological Association (APA). Its focus is a relational model for integration that emphasizes process as much as content, in contrast to more typical integrative models that tend to focus almost exclusively on content. And its approach is something that has never been done before: research that starts from the students' experience and builds inductively from there, using quantitative measures that recognize students as consumers of integrative training.

The Swiss physician and Christian counselor Paul Tournier once remarked that we avoid listening to others because if we do, even briefly, people speak up so immediately and honestly that we find what they have to say disturbing. In short, we don't listen as a defense so that we won't hear anything upsetting. The present program of research is based on an attempt to listen to integrative clinical psychology doctoral students and to try and hear from them about how they say they actually learn integration.

If anything is at all disturbing about what they have to tell us, it is that how they say they learn integration and how we think to teach it are often not the same, and are sometimes even inimical. This is because our various substantive models of integration—whether these involve the relationship between Christ and culture, psychology and theology, philosophical hermeneutics and postmodernism, brain physiology and the existence of the soul, and so forth—offer nothing by themselves to assure us that students exposed to these models will encounter the relational process that students say is necessary for integration to occur.

Our program of research investigated what this relational process is, how it works, and how well we as faculty are able to identify it in our colleagues and ourselves. To introduce our final report we summarize the four studies that preceded it, to which we now turn.

The First Four Studies

The pilot project for what eventually became our national collaborative research began with an unintended observation. An instructor noticed that it seemed possible to match student essays on: (1) how students worked with issues of faith with their own clients; (2) the student's experience of parents, faith, and God from the student's family of origin; and (3) how the student's own therapist worked with the student in his or her personal therapy (Sorenson, 1994b). Matching student essays on these topics did not seem to be based simply on a particular typeface or style of prose, and seemed instead to be more about what the students had to say, as well as an appreciation of the students as people. The study hypothesized, for example, that "if persons had a representation of God as a distant and cold figure, they seemed to be much less comfortable hearing about religious issues from their clients." Likewise, if faith was "avoided when they were the patient, these same people as therapists seemed to avoid it with their clients" (Sorenson, 1994b, p. 328).

To test these impressions empirically, 12 faculty members from Fuller Graduate School of Psychology (Fuller) or Rosemead School of Psychology (Rosemead) were presented with anonymous, laminated 8 1/2 x 11" cards that excerpted students' written comments about these issues. Each card was formatted with the same type font and line spacing, and analyses of variance indicated no significant differences between the protocols on a wide variety of lexical criteria (i.e., lines of text, words per sentence, letters per word, syllables per 100 words, percent of sentences in the passive voice, and level of reading difficulty; $p > .05$ for all).

The most striking finding of the first study was that, in the eyes of professors at Fuller and Rosemead, the student's personal therapist had a greater impact on the student's integration than did even the student's parents from the student's family of origin. Professors at the two schools concurred that integration is as much about a who as a what; affectively engaged relationships seemed to shape how students learn integration, with current mentoring relationships (in this case, the student's therapist) eclipsing earlier ones, including the student's childhood experience of parents and faith.

This result was replicated in a second study with a sample five times larger, using structural equation modeling (SEM) to test explicitly the judgments that Fuller and Rosemead professors in the first study said had been implicit (Sorenson, 1997c, pp. 166-199; revised and updated in Sorenson, 2004, pp. 73-103). The second study found that how students worked with others integratively had to do with how their own therapist worked with them on these issues, but their therapist's behavior was uncorrelated with students' faith prior to therapy, including students' accounts of their developmental experience in childhood. This outcome is not what a wide array of clinical theories predicts. Most clinical theories—whether cognitive-behavioral, psychoanalytic, family systems, and others—emphasize the enduring significance of

early learning and early life experience, so much so that contemporary interactions (including contemporary interactions with a psychotherapist) are presumably filtered through old patterns of perception that resist modification, thereby constraining or confining how any therapist can intervene when it comes to integrative issues. That, however, was not what the second study found. Instead, it found that an affectively engaged relationship with a significant person in a student's current life became personally formative for that student's integration of psychology and faith in ways that are difficult to overstate and were impossible to predict based on the client's past. That is, a student could enter therapy with a warm and inviting God representation arising from childhood, and then exit therapy with a punitive or deistic God representation, or vice versa. Similarly, a student could exit therapy with a God representation unchanged from what it was before therapy, whether the God representation was wrathful or gracious. Everything hinged on what the therapist did.

Specifically, the second study identified six therapist behaviors that were crucial in the current relationship and had a differential impact (favorably or detrimentally) on the student's subsequent integrative development. Favorable outcomes were associated with therapists who: (1) made interventions that treated the student's relationship with God as real, as opposed to a psychological projection only; (2) approached integrative issues in an open and nondefensive manner, as opposed to an approach that was more conflicted and inhibited; (3) made connections between the student's experience of his or her parents, the therapist, and God, and did so at the therapist's own initiative, as opposed to remaining passively open to the topic that was the student's responsibility to broach, and otherwise viewing integrative inquiry as fraught with special peril; (4) saw the student's relationship with God as something at least partially positive and a potential resource for healing, as opposed to emphasizing the exclusively pathological elements in faith; (5) expected that integrative issues would come up in therapy and belonged there as appropriate topics of investigation, as opposed to thinking that they had no legitimate place in psychotherapy; and (6) showed a personal openness to mystery and an orientation to the transcendent that the student admired and wanted to emulate personally.

The results of the first two studies were consistent with a finding of the Rech Conference published several years earlier (Jones, Watson, & Wolfram, 1992). After surveying nearly 1,500 alumni from integrative graduate programs, the Rech study found that when graduates reflected on their integrative training, they said their personal psychotherapy had a greater impact on their faith than did anything else, including their integrative courses on psychology and theology (p. 153).

From this, several questions naturally arise. What about integrative coursework? How does it relate to the integration that students learn? If the upshot of the first two studies was that how students learn to work with integrative issues clinically depends on current figures with whom students have close personal attachments, what about integrative teachers in the classroom? Might not students have similar attachments with professors? A faculty colleague who had seen these early studies on the impact of students' personal therapists once teased that it's also possible students may actually learn something from us in classes. To this, Sorenson (1994a) responded:

> I hope so. Whatever they learn from us, I also hope it's something students will deem positive. I know that theological education, for example, with all its good intentions, often robs graduating students of a personal sense of transcendence. I hope our work can train critical thinkers, but also develop gentle and courageous souls, persons who are as reluctant to foreclose experience of the numinous as they are the experience of its opposite, the dark night of the soul (p. 350).

Arising from this concern, the third study in our programmatic research was the first to explicitly investigate how students say they learn integration from professors who teach at APA-accredited clinical psychology doctoral programs with evangelical Christian affiliations. This shift from therapists to teachers was politically risky. What if, apropos Tournier's earlier quip about listening, what students had to say about their teachers was disturbing? If student perceptions of faculty proved damaging to the school's reputation for how well it was fulfilling its expressed mission to integrate psychology and faith, not to mention how the school compared with rival programs, what then? And what if students said that some professors were more helpful than others? Wouldn't this fuel intra-staff rivalry and bruise academic egos?

In light of these fears, and in order to limit others' exposure to potential fall-out or embarrassment due to the political risks involved, the third study was once more solo-authored (Sorenson, 1997a) and conducted on the author's own institution

(Rosemead). Forty-eight doctoral students sorted 19 Rosemead faculty members according to how much they seemed to be similar to each other, and the resulting dissimilarity matrix was submitted to multidimensional scaling (MDS). Traditional multivariate techniques like factor analysis work well in domains whose substantive content is well established, but for research in areas previously unexplored there is a limitation: factor analysis only works on the items the researcher includes in the study. If important items are omitted, the resulting factor structure omits important variance. MDS offers an advantage for exploratory research because it builds a model of the latent dimensions by which students are evaluating faculty without requiring either the researcher or the student to define in advance the criteria employed to make these judgments. In short, MDS is akin to factor analysis without items, or, more accurately, a factor analysis whose items are tacit and inexplicit.

Results showed that Rosemead students were evaluating faculty across three latent dimensions, one of which correlated with how exemplary and helpful the professor was to students' integration ($r = .729$, $p < .01$). Canonical correlation showed that this dimension loaded on the professor's Evidence of an Ongoing Process in a Personal Relationship with God (.847), Emotional Transparency (.827), and Sense of Humor (.736). Individual differences scaling (INDSCAL) revealed that this dimension was crucial to all students, but women put a greater priority on it than did men, and women toward the end of their doctoral training placed an even higher value on this dimension than did those in the initial years.

These findings were replicated in a fourth study (Staton, Sorenson, & Vande Kemp, 1998), which found that clinical psychology doctoral students at Fuller learn integration the same way Rosemead students do. Not only were Fuller students evaluating Fuller faculty along three latent dimensions, but the dimension that correlated most highly with students' integration ($r = .40$, $p < .01$) loaded on a canonical variate involving the same variable that loaded the most highly in the Rosemead data: the professor's Evidence of an Ongoing Process in a Personal Relationship with God (.967). Even more compelling, SEM of the multivariate model from the Rosemead data fit the Fuller data (Comparative Fit Index = .992, average off-diagonal absolute standardized residuals = .0130, $N = 585$). While this relational dimension to learning integration was valued by all Fuller students, for the nearly three out of four students who chose to attend Fuller primarily because of its specialization in integration, they placed an even higher value on this dimension than did the remaining students for whom integration was a penultimate concern or less.

Staton, Sorenson, and Vande Kemp (1998) concluded: "From the students' point of view, the most salient dimension to contribute to their own integration was how well they could determine that a given professor had an authentic, lively, and growing relationship with God, coupled with the professor's nondefensive, emotionally unguarded, and even vulnerable relationship with students" (p. 348). This conclusion fit another summary of the previous studies:

> Too often we think that teaching students our integrative models is what they need in order to learn integration. Often what they want, however, is not our models but ourselves—or perhaps more accurately, they want us to model our own integration, and to give them access to our own relationship before God in an open and nondefensive manner. It is as though when they have access to us as not just professors but persons, and to our ongoing life before God—doubts and all, our joys and terrors—students are well served in finding their own integrative pilgrimage. (Sorenson, 1997b, p. 257)

It should be stressed that students were evaluating something other than mere professorial piety. Professors could be estranged from God, angry with God, confused by God—and still be of great use to students' integration. What mattered were not the contours of the professor's relationship with God per se, so much as students being able to tell what those contours were. And according to students, not all professors were equally accessible in this regard; those who were less so were of less use to students' integration.

This Final Report

This fifth and final report expands the decade-long programmatic research in three areas. First, the results from Rosemead and Fuller were tested for replication at the next two clinical psychology integrative doctoral programs with the longest-standing APA accreditation after Fuller and Rosemead, George Fox University (GFU), and Wheaton College (Illinois), using exploratory MDS and confirmatory SEM. Second, a whole new round of student perceptions of faculty at Rosemead—using all-new students and many new faculty members five years after the Sorenson (1997a) data—was submitted to SEM analysis of multitrait-multimethod matrices. By this it is

possible to compare how well faculty members are able to recognize in themselves and in their faculty peers what students see. Third, in order to flesh out what students mean by the most salient feature of this research—a faculty member's ongoing process in a personal relationship with God—excerpts of student qualitative interviews on this topic were subjected to Latent Semantic Analysis, as detailed in the following Method section.

Method

First, we sampled 48 upper-division students (27 male, 21 female) from the Graduate School of Clinical Psychology at GFU who voluntarily participated in card-sorting and questionnaire data on 18 GFU faculty members, replicating the research protocol detailed in Sorenson (1997a) and Staton, Sorenson, and Vande Kemp (1998).[1] This protocol instructs students to sort faculty members' names on note cards into stacks according to how the student thinks the professors seem to be similar to each other, using as many different stacks as the student wishes, but no fewer than two stacks and at least two faculty names in each stack. After this, students rate faculty on criterion variables presented on five-point, paper-and-pencil Likert scales. How many times each professor is not paired with another professor generates a dissimilarity matrix, which is then submitted to multidimensional scaling. The resulting dimension scores are correlated with a pooled Integration variable of how exemplary and helpful the professor was to students.

Because MDS only generates dimensions that are orthogonal and never oblique, a particularly elegant solution for empirical interpretation of the resulting dimensions is to regress criterion variables on dimension scores via canonical correlation because this provides an omnibus solution of multiple, multiple regressions orthogonally. We did this using the Evidence, Transparency, and Humor criterion variables from the Rosemead and Fuller studies, along with new variables that included Approaches Career as a Spiritual Vocation (abbreviated hereafter as Calling), Emotionally Secure, Self-Confident and Non-Threatened, and Socially Conscious and Respectful of Others. Replication, ad infinitum, using exploratory MDS on other integrative doctoral programs in the United States offers limited utility, however, because exploratory studies capitalize on chance associations in a particular data set and offer no means by which to compare results between studies with explicit levels of statistical probability. Accordingly, after exploratory MDS on the GFU data, we also employed confirmatory SEM to test if the relational model of integration derived from the Rosemead and Fuller data fit the GFU data. Next, we performed a second, revised SEM analysis on a large data set that combined all the GFU data with 23 Wheaton College clinical psychology doctoral students' perceptions of 16 professors in Wheaton's program, plus new data from Rosemead students, described below.

Up to this point, all the studies in our national collaborative research had measured how students learn integration from the students' point of view as consumers of integrative training, an approach that is consistent with outcomes-based educational trends in the training of psychologists (APA, 2000). The accumulating evidence from MDS and SEM that students demonstrate high concordance in their assessment of what they find helpful in faculty members for integration raises an important question: How accurately are faculty members able to assess this relational dimension in each other and themselves that students so readily identify? The empirical approach for answering this question is known as multitrait-multimethod matrices (MTMM). Originally presented by Campbell and Fiske (1959), this approach parses variance into trait factors about which different raters concur, and method factors that are a function of who's making the rating.

Although MTMM make intuitive sense, their limitation has been that there was no good way to determine the presence of method or trait factors objectively. In the 1950s, all Campbell and Fiske could recommend was to look at the correlation matrices and to use ambiguous and subjective criteria to determine if trait and method factors were present. As exploratory factor analysis arose in prominence in the 1960s and 1970s, two-step factor-analytic procedures were proposed as a more objective alternative to the Campbell and Fiske criteria. In this procedure, traits were subjected to orthogonal rotation prior to assessing method factors (Golding & Seidman, 1974; Jackson, 1975), but this strategy also suffered from conceptual and statistical liabilities (Golding, 1977; Jackson, 1977) and it still offered no way to compare method and trait factors according to explicit probability levels. By the 1980s and 1990s, however, SEM surfaced as the treatment of choice for handling MTMM because nested models of traits and methods can be objectively compared using difference Chi-square tests (Widaman, 1985; see also Byrne, 1994), thereby finally affording adjudication of trait and method factors at quantifiable levels of probability (such as $p < .05$).

For the next portion of our research we therefore used SEM and nested models to measure MTMM. Eighteen Rosemead students rated 19 Rosemead faculty members on the criterion variables that were used in the pooled SEM analysis of the GFU and Wheaton data mentioned earlier in the present study. Following this, the Rosemead faculty members rated themselves and their faculty peers on how they thought students rated them on the same criterion variables. Because the challenge to faculty was to see how well they could recognize what students knew about them, it is important to note that faculty members made their ratings based not on how *they* rated themselves or their peers, but on how they thought their *students* rated the professor and his or her peers.

Our programmatic research indicates that the single most important variable in how students learn integration is that the professor "gives evidence of an ongoing process in a personal relationship with God." Until now, however, we had not scrutinized what students meant by this phrase in any detail. So for the last part of our final report we took excerpts from transcribed interviews with 12 fourth-year integrative doctoral students who had been participants in a qualitative dissertation on integration (Graham, 2002), and submitted these excerpts to Latent Semantic Analysis (LSA). LSA is a theory and method for extracting and representing the semantic meaning of words (Landauer, Foltz, & Laham, 1998), and its capacities are remarkably sophisticated. For example, the grades that LSA assigned college students' essays agreed with the grades marked by professional readers at Educational Testing Service (Landauer, Laham, Rehder, & Schreiner, 1997). As Foltz, Kintsch, and Landauer (1998) explain, "Unlike methods which rely on counting literal word overlap between units of text, LSA's comparisons are based on a derived semantic relatedness measure which reflects semantic similarity among synonyms, antonyms, hyponyms, compounds, and other words that tend to be used in similar contexts" (p. 4). LSA uses singular value decomposition to generate a similarity matrix, which can be input into MDS for interpretation. At one point in the two-hour interviews, Graham asked students what they thought of the research about professors giving evidence of an ongoing process in a personal relationship with God and these excerpts were subjected to LSA, which was not a part of Graham's dissertation.

As with the previous four studies in our programmatic research, all data in our final report were collected in a double blind fashion such that the identities of students, researchers, and other faculty members were unobtainable. Research was approved by university ethics committees for research with human participants.

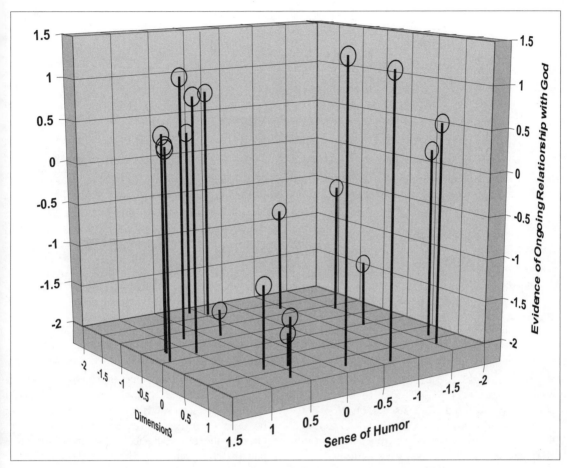

Figure 1. Eighteen George Fox University Professors in three-dimensional space. Numbers on axes represent actual dimension weights.

Results

Compared with factor analysis, MDS tends to produce fewer dimensions (typically the number of variables divided by six), and the value of .2 for model stress, although an arbitrary threshold, has proven a good balance between parsimony and dispersion accounted for.[2] In the GFU data, a three-dimensional model (stress = .206, accounting for 75% of the dipsersion) best fit the .2 criterion, the "elbow" in the scree test, and the expected number of dimensions (18 / 6 = 3). Dimension 2 correlated most strongly with Integration (r = .520), Dimension 1 less so (r = .344), and Dimension 3 least of all (r = -.115; p < .01 for all). As in the previous studies, the professor's Evidence of an Ongoing Process in a Personal Relationship with God loaded highly (.877) on the dimension most correlated with Integration. Other variables that also loaded on this dimension were Secure (.829), Socially Conscious

(.675), and Transparent (.556). A new variable for the GFU sample, Calling (.895), loaded even a little higher than the Evidence variable on Dimension 2. Humor (.799) was the sole variable to load on Dimension 1, which was the next most significant dimension for Integration. Dimension 3, which had the weakest connection with Integration, had no criterion variables load most highly on it, and thus was not interpreted. The 18 GFU professors are represented in three-dimensional space in Figure 1. On the graph in Figure 1, those professors who are highest on the Evidence dimension, and to a lesser extent, to the left on the Humor dimension, are the ones students deemed most helpful for integration. As with the previous Rosemead and Fuller studies, GFU students readily concurred that they learned integration the same way from professors, and that professors' capacities varied in this regard.

SEM showed that the relational model from the Rosemead and Fuller studies (Staton, Sorenson, &

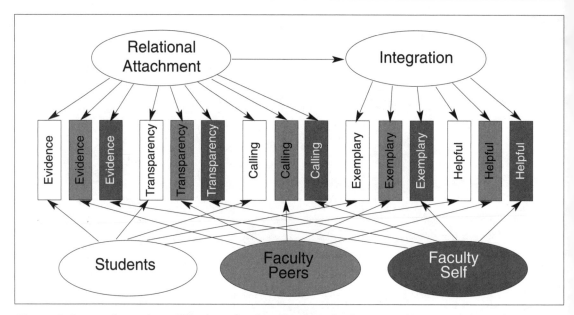

Figure 2. Structural equation application of multitrait-multimethod matrices. Traits are Relational Attachment causing Integration. Methods are perceptions of faculty by Students, Faculty Peers, and Faculty Self. CFI = .950, average off-diagonal absolute standardized residuals = .0452, N = 342. Error terms for dependent variables (measured or latent) are not depicted in graph.

Vande Kemp, 1998, p. 348, Figure 4) also fit the current GFU data (CFI = .968, average off-diagonal absolute standardized residuals =.0314, N = 790). Because Humor loaded on a separate dimension that correlated less strongly with Integration in the GFU data, and Calling loaded even more highly on the same dimension as Evidence, we adjusted the model slightly by replacing Humor with Calling and tested this revised model on the combined data from GFU, Wheaton, and a new Rosemead sample. This model fit the data very well (CFI = .997, average off-diagonal absolute standardized residuals = .0187, N = 1574), indicating that students at all four schools learn integration the same way, through a relational process with their professors. In the revised model, Evidence loaded most highly on faculty relational attachments (.866), followed by Calling (.764) and Transparency (.662).

An SEM application for MTMM is depicted in Figure 2. The latent factors are ovals and the measured variables are rectangles. The trait factors are the two ovals on the top of the graph that model how faculty relational attachments account for students' integration, irrespective of ratings' sources. The method factors are the three ovals on the bottom of the graph that represent: (1) students assessments of faculty members; (2) what faculty think students think of faculty peers, and (3) what faculty think students think of the professors themselves. The full

model includes causal traits and oblique methods (χ^2 = 208.404, 71 df, CFI = .950). A second model having only method factors and no trait factors can be seen as a nested version of the full model because the two trait factors and their respective paths are now removed. This second model (methods only and no traits) fit the data less well (χ^2 = 403.380, 87 df, CFI = .886), and the difference Chi-Square ($\Delta\chi^2$ = 194.976, 16 df, p < .001) indicates that the second model is significantly worse than the first. A third model that assumes causal traits only and no method factors fits the data even worse (χ^2 = 1617.097, 89 df, CFI = .448), and is significantly worse than the second model ($\Delta\chi^2$ = 1213.717, 2 df, p < .001).[3] Therefore, only the full model that includes both traits and methods (as depicted in Figure 2) is an adequate fit, and models that assume only traits or only methods are inadequate and a significantly worse fit with the data.

The results of the MTMM mean that while there was some convergence between the various sources (student, faculty-peer, and faculty-self), faculty had a hard time guessing what students thought of them. What is more, professors believed that relational attachments with students pertained more to other faculty than to themselves. For example, students saw a strong connection between relational attachment with a professor and how useful that professor was to students' integration (r = .72), and

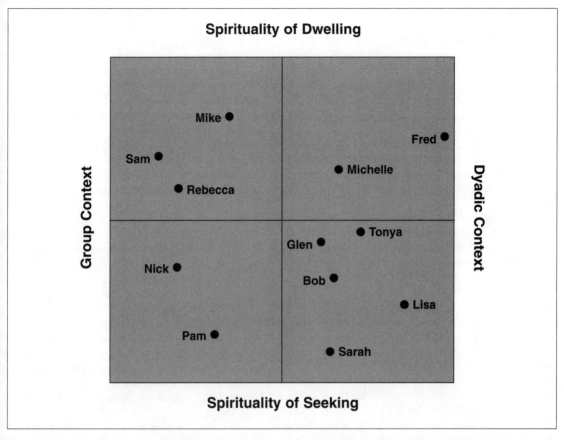

Figure 3. Latent Semantic Analysis of 12 integrative doctoral students' qualitative interviews on what it means for a professor to "give evidence of an ongoing process in a personal relationship with God." Stress = .0469, Dispersion Accounter For = .9531, raw interview data available in Graham (2002, pp. 152-356).

faculty members concurred so long as it involved faculty peers' relationships with students (r = .75), but professors could not see the same connection when it came to their own personal relationships with students (r = .29). What students actually thought of a professor's usefulness to students' integration correlated only .21 with faculty impressions of what they thought students must think of other faculty peers, and just .25 with the faculty member's fantasy of what of students thought of the professor himself or herself. Correlations with what students actually thought of the professor's quality of relational attachment were similarly modest: r = .33 for faculty impressions of peers and r = .26 for self. One account for why faculty had a hard time guessing what students thought of them is that faculty members were excessively humble and could not bring themselves to rate themselves highly. The data do not support this explanation, however. On a scale ranging from 2 to 10 that measured how Exemplary and Helpful faculty members were to

students' integration, the mean student ratings of faculty was almost perfectly at the scale's midpoint: 5.97. By contrast, faculty members rated their faculty peers to be 7.44 on average, and rated themselves even more highly at 7.89. This is a significant difference between the three sources of measurement (student, faculty-peer, faculty-self; ANOVA between groups F Ratio = 41.17, p < .001), and a Scheffé's Test indicates the faculty-self and faculty-peer ratings were significantly higher than student ratings of these same faculty members (p < .05).

LSA generated a similarity matrix which, when subjected to MDS, produced the 2-dimensional solution shown in Figure 3. Inspection of the interview transcripts (Graham, 2002, pp. 152-356) suggests that the horizontal axis pertains to the context (ranging from groups to dyads) in which the professor's evidence of an ongoing personal relationship with God occurred, and the vertical axis relates to the professor's spirituality (dwelling versus seeking). According to sociologist Robert Wuthnow

(1998), a spirituality of dwelling reflects an expression of faith that is more settled and stable, and whose archetype is the cathedral. A spirituality of seeking, by contrast, reflects a faith that is in the throws of doubt, reformulation, and transition that is better symbolized by a tent. Neither style of spirituality is more legitimate or authentic than the other, but people tend to gravitate toward one expression or the other.

Students in the upper left quadrant of the graph like Mike, Rebecca, and Sam appreciate professors whose expression of faith is reassuringly pastoral and typically occurs in group contexts such as leading group prayer in classes, attending a voluntary school chapel regularly, or visible participation in a local church. Students in the upper right quadrant like Michelle value the same spiritual steadiness in faculty members as the previous quadrant, only here its expression occurs in dyadic contexts such as one-on-one interactions in hallways or faculty offices where professors greet students and engage in expressions of faith. (One student, Fred, was so extremely to the right on the graph that his context was barely dyadic to the point of being practically unaccompanied.) Students who identify with a spirituality of seeking tend to learn integration best from professors who are more tortured souls in their faith. In the lower left quadrant, for students like Nick and Pam this takes the form of professors admitting their doubts and struggles in front of groups of students, and in the lower right quadrant it shows up with faculty who are open to one-on-one dialogues with students after hours in a candid fashion that is like a clinical encounter. For example, Lisa, who is located toward the right on this quadrant, appreciated conversations with a professor that "lasted into the wee hours at times … because he would often work in the office late at night" (Graham, 2002, p. 218). Sarah, who was located the farthest toward the spirituality of seeking, and was approximately midway along the continuum spanning dyadic and group contexts, described a professor she admired most as someone who seemed "very inviting, very encouraging" and who offered "a holding environment" that included classroom "disclosure of her personal struggles from life, her relationships with her kids, her husband, everything. It just kind of felt like, gosh, that's integration right there" (p. 336).

Discussion

Data from our 10-year collaborative research indicate three things: (1) students from all over the country—and the world, if international students in integrative programs are representative—learn integration

the same way; (2) faculty have a hard time recognizing what students know in this regard; and (3) although all students' integration is relational, its optimal context and style varies from student to student. The way students learn integration is through relational attachments with mentors who model that integration for students personally. These mentors may be professors, but they don't have to be. They may also be students' therapists, as our two pilot studies and the Rech study found, or other figures. Whoever they are, what counts is that the mentor is affectively and personally present for the student. The word integration comes from the same Latin root from which we get the word integrity. It does not work for the mentor to say, "Do as I say, not as I do." Instead, students want personal access to someone who is modeling integration before them as a living, breathing, flesh-and-blood manifestation of integration-in-process. Students want broad and candid access to integrators so they can see how their mentors think, weigh choices, make clinical judgments, pursue courses of research, and, most importantly, how they interact with themselves and others, including God.[4]

Our research indicates that what is transformative for students is not reducible to Christian belief, not creedal orthodoxy, and not even professorial piety. It's not that students exclaim, "Gosh, Professor X sure does believe that Jesus was born of a virgin!" or "It's obvious that Professor Y believes the Bible is God's Word." Professors X and Y may indeed believe both those things, but that's not the point of our research, and in fact our research includes no measure of Christian belief per se (even though we think it's valuable and important). Instead, our research shows that what is crucial to students' integration is a dynamic, ongoing process that a mentor is modeling before the students' eyes in ways to which students feel they have real access personally, perhaps even as collaborators in the project together. The "gives evidence" part of the most salient variable means that students are saying, "Show me." The "ongoing process" means that it's something that's still in formation and not a completed achievement. And the "personal relationship with God" means this whole process is also something that for students is profoundly theological.

Notes

1. Unlike factor analysis, which assumes that the underlying data are distributed as multivariate normal and that the relationships are linear, MDS imposes no such restrictions and can work with fewer than factor analysis' minimum of 5-to-1 subjects-to-variables ratio. As Kruskal and Wish (1978) affirm, "A rough rule of thumb is that there

should be at least twice as many stimulus pairs as parameters to be estimated, to assure an adequate degree of statistical stability" (p. 34). Our study exceeds this criterion. It also subjects the resulting dimensional structure to replication on a new data set via SEM that employs hundreds of observations.

2. Stress is a measure of how much error there is in the model. The lower the stress value, the less error and greater the dispersion accounted for.

3. In SEM, the higher the Chi-Square and the lower the CFI, the poorer the proposed model fits the data. A rule of thumb is that the CFI must exceed .9 in order for a model to be an adequate fit for the data.

4. An empirical study in preparation on how GFU students learn integration found that 80% of the outcome variance was accounted for by faculty modeling (Bufford, Gathercoal, Williams & Pearson, 2004).

References

American Psychological Association. (2000). *Guidelines and principles for accreditation of programs in professional psychology*. Washington, D.C.: Author.

Bufford, R. K., Gathercoal, K., Williams, A., & Pearson, M. (2004). *Learning integration of psychology and Christian faith: A student's perspective on what counts*. Manuscript in preparation.

Byrne, B. M. (1994). *Application 4: Testing for construct validity: The multitrait-multimethod model. In B. M. Byrne, Structural equation modeling with EQS and EQS/Windows*. Thousand Oaks, CA: Sage Publications.

Campbell, D. T., & Fiske, D. W. (1959). Convergent and discriminant validation by the multitrait-multimethod matrix. *Psychological Bulletin, 56,* 81-105.

Foltz, P. W., Kintsch, W., & Landauer, T. K. (1998). The measurement of textual coherence with Latent Semantic Analysis. *Discourse Processes, 25,* 285-307.

Golding, S. L. (1977). Method variance, inadequate constructs, or things that go bump in the night? *Multivariate Behavioral Research, 12,* 89-98.

Golding, S. L., & Seidman, E. (1974). Analyses of multitrait-multimethod matrices: A two-step principal components procedure. *Multivariate Behavioral Research, 9,* 479-496.

Graham, S. D. (2002). Doctoral clinical psychology students' perceptions of relational interactions that affect the integration of psychology and faith. *Dissertation Abstracts International, 63* (11B), 5516.

Jackson, D. N. (1975). Multimethod factor analysis: A reformulation. *Multivariate Behavioral Research, 10,* 259-275.

Jackson, D. N. (1977). Distinguishing trait and method variance in multitrait-multimethod matrices: A reply to Golding. *Multivariate Behavioral Research, 12,* 99-110.

Jones, S. L., Watson, E. L., & Wolfram, T, J. (1992). Results of the Rech conference survey on religious faith and professional psychology. *Journal of Psychology and Theology, 20,* 147-158.

Kruskal, J. B., & Wish, M. (1978). *Multidimensional scaling*. Beverly Hills, CA: Sage.

Landauer, T. K., Foltz, P. W., & Laham, D. (1998). Introduction to Latent Semantic Analysis. *Discourse Processes, 25,* 259-284.

Landauer, T, K., Laham, D., Rehder, B., & Schreiner, M. E. (1997). How well can passage meaning be derived without using word order? A comparison of Latent Semantic Analysis and humans. In M. G. Shafto & P. Langley (Eds.), *Proceedings of the 19th annual meeting of the Cognitive Science Society* (pp. 412-417). Mawhwah, NJ: Erlbaum.

Sorenson, R. L. (1994a). Reply to Cohen. *Journal of Psychology and Theology, 22,* 348-351.

Sorenson, R. L. (1994b). Therapists' (and their therapists') God representations in clinical practice. *Journal of Psychology and Theology, 22,* 325-344.

Sorenson, R. L. (1997a). Doctoral students' integration of psychology and Christianity: Perspectives via attachment theory and multidimensional scaling. *Journal for the Scientific Study of Religion, 36,* 530-548.

Sorenson, R. L. (1997b). Janusian integration. *Journal of Psychology and Theology, 25,* 254-259.

Sorenson, R. L. (1997c). Transcendence and intersubjectivity: The patient's experience of the analyst's spirituality. In C. Spezzano & G. Gargiulo (Eds.), *Soul on the couch* (pp. 166-199). Hillsdale, NJ: The Analytic Press.

Sorenson, R. L. (2004). *Minding Spirituality*. Hillsdale, NJ: Analytic Press.

Staton, R., Sorenson, R. L., & Vande Kemp, H. (1998). How students learn integration: Replication of the Sorenson (1997a) model. *Journal of Psychology and Theology, 26,* 340-350.

Widaman, K. F. (1985). Hierarchically nested covariance structure models for multitrait-multimethod data. *Applied Psychological Measurement, 9,* 1-26.

Wuthnow, R. C. (1998). *After heaven*. Berkeley: University of California Press.

32

Please Forgive Me: Transgressors' Emotions and Physiology During Imagery of Seeking Forgiveness and Victim Responses

Charlotte vanOyen Witvliet
Thomas E. Ludwig
David J. Bauer
Hope College

We assessed transgressors' subjective emotions and physiological responses in a within-subjects imagery study involving 20 male and 20 female participants. Two imagery conditions focused on the transgressor's actions: participants (1) ruminated about a real-life transgression and (2) imagined seeking forgiveness from the victim. Three imagery conditions focused on the victim's possible responses: participants imagined their victims responding with (1) a grudge, (2) genuine forgiveness, and (3) reconciliation. Compared to ruminations about one's transgression or an unforgiving response from the victim, imagery of forgiveness-seeking and merciful responses from victims (forgiveness and reconciliation) prompted improvements in basic emotions (e.g., sadness, anger) and moral emotions (e.g., guilt, shame, gratitude, hope), and greater perceived interpersonal forgiveness. Perceptions of self-forgiveness increased during forgiveness-seeking imagery, whereas perceptions of divine forgiveness increased during transgression-focused imagery. Imagery of victims' merciful responses prompted less furrowing of the brow muscle (*corrugator* EMG) associated with negative emotion and more smiling activity (*zygomatic* EMG); imagery of forgiveness-seeking affected only *corrugator* activity. Autonomic nervous system measures were largely unaffected by imagery, although skin conductance data suggested greater emotional engagement when victims reconciled with transgressors.

Scientific interest in forgiveness has focused primarily on securing benefits for victims of interpersonal harm rather than for the blameworthy transgressors (e.g., Al-Mabuk, Enright, & Cardis, 1995; Coyle & Enright, 1997; Enright & Fitzgibbons, 2000; Freedman & Enright, 1996; Hebl & Enright, 1993; McCullough, Worthington, & Rachal, 1997). Yet, understanding the transgressor's perspective—in seeking and receiving forgiveness, or having forgiveness denied—is an important topic. As Volf (1999, p. 34) says, "… each of us is both Abel and Cain. In different aspects and at different junctures of our lives, we are both innocent victims and guilty perpetrators. In our innocence, we should not forget our sinfulness, and in our sense of endangerment, we should remember to fear our own dark shadows." We are both victims and perpetrators. We can identify with *both* the Prodigal Son *and* the resentful elder brother (Lk. 15:11-32), with *both* David the innocent victim of Saul's persecution (1 Sam. 19-27) *and* King David the heartless homewrecker (2 Sam. 11).

This article focuses on the role of the transgressor. We empirically investigated the subjective emotions and physiological responses of transgressors as they imagined seeking forgiveness from an individual they had hurt in real life, and as they imagined the victim's possible responses to their forgiveness seeking. To investigate the effects of seeking forgiveness, we assessed transgressors' subjective and physiological responses as they (1) reflected on a real-life transgression in which they had hurt someone compared to when they (2) imagined seeking forgiveness from the victim. To investigate the effects of victims' responses, we assessed transgressors' subjective and physiological responses as they imagined that the victim (1) harbored a grudge, (2) genuinely granted forgiveness, and (3) reconciled in a way appropriate to the nature of the relationship.

Seeking Forgiveness

The Psalmist provides a good model for transgressors: "Then I acknowledged my sin to you and did not cover up my iniquity. I said, 'I will confess my transgressions to the LORD'—and you forgave the guilt of my sin" (Ps. 32:5).[1] But this model is difficult to follow because acknowledging our own culpability runs counter to our self-serving bias. For example, Stillwell and Baumeister (1997) compared the responses of participants assigned to victim and perpetrator roles in a scenario-based experiment. Although all participants engaged in self-serving distortions, perpetrators tended to minimize or exclude information that could motivate them to accept blame or seek forgiveness. In a separate study of personal experiences as victims and as perpetrators, perpetrators' written narratives emphasized apologies and minimized harm done compared to victim accounts (Baumeister, Stillwell, & Wotman, 1990).

Although difficult, seeking forgiveness is an important part of repairing relational damage. It is also central to the life of faith. Christians are called to honestly confess, repent, and seek forgiveness both from others and from God, recognizing that a person "is destroyed only by his sin and can be healed only by forgiveness" (Bonhoeffer, 1954, p. 119).

The very nature of God, as described in Exodus 34:6-7, encourages believers to confess their sins and trust God to forgive: "the LORD, a God merciful and gracious, slow to anger, and abounding in steadfast love and faithfulness, keeping steadfast love for the thousandth generation forgiving iniquity and transgression and sin...." Both the Old Testament and the New Testament connect confession and repentance to blessing (Pr. 28:13, "No one who conceals transgressions will prosper, but one who confesses and forsakes them will obtain mercy." Acts 3:19-20a, "Repent therefore, and turn to God so that your sins may be wiped out, that times of refreshing may come from the presence of the Lord ..."). The failure to confess and repent is linked with suffering (Ps. 32:3-4, "While I kept silence, my body wasted away through my groaning all day long ... my strength was dried up as by the heat of summer. Then I acknowledged my sin to you, and I did not hide my iniquity; I said, 'I will confess my transgressions to the LORD,' and you forgave the guilt of my sin."). The New Testament includes commands to confess our sins to God and to other people, linking confession, prayer, and healing in James 5:16.

Before actually seeking forgiveness, transgressors often imagine confessing, apologizing, and requesting forgiveness. Imagery therefore serves as a useful technique in research, allowing for the assessment of emotional and physiological responses that mirror those that occur during real-world experiences (see Lang, 1979). In the current investigation, we used imagery to assess a variety of research questions about forgiveness-seeking. What sorts of emotions are aroused by imagery of seeking forgiveness compared to ruminations about one's transgressions? Do people feel comparatively better or worse when imagining seeking forgiveness? What facial expres-

sions do transgressors display when contemplating their transgressions or seeking forgiveness? Is physiological stress exacerbated or alleviated by imagining seeking forgiveness?

In their exploration of the benefits of and barriers to expressing repentance, Exline and Baumeister (2000) proposed that repentance may proffer emotional and even physical benefits. They also note that when people express repentance, they are more likely to receive forgiveness from those they have hurt. When transgressors confess (Weiner, Graham, Peter, & Zmuidinas, 1991) and apologize (Couch, Jones, & Moore, 1999; Darby & Schlenker, 1982; O'Malley & Greenberg, 1983; Ohbuchi, Kameda, & Agarie, 1989), victims may be more likely to grant forgiveness, perhaps because apologies promote empathy (McCullough, Worthington, & Rachal, 1997). Given this, might transgressors actually perceive greater forgiveness when they confess and apologize? Might they also *feel* better—experiencing a reduction in negative emotions and an increase in positive emotions?

This possibility was supported by Meek, Albright, and McMinn (1995), who had participants imagine (1) lying to their boss to get time off work, (2) then meeting a coworker who had to work extra hours because of their absence, and finally (3) confessing to the boss. Participants reported feeling less guilt after imagery of confessing to the boss than after the other two types of imagery. These results are consistent with Exline and Baumeister's (2000) theory that "expressions of ... repentance could symbolically erase the roles of victim and perpetrator, placing the involved parties on more equal footing" (p. 138), thereby reducing the negative affect that perpetrators may associate with their culpability.

Similarly, Sandage, Worthington, Hight, and Berry (2000) describe seeking forgiveness as "a motivation to accept moral responsibility and to attempt interpersonal reparation following relational injury in which one is morally culpable" (p. 22). Given Sandage et al.'s emphasis on moral emotions (e.g., guilt, shame, empathy), we assessed participants' ratings of their guilt (behavior-focused), shame (self-focused), empathy for the victim, and the degree of hope they experienced during two types of imagery about their own actions: reliving their transgressions, and seeking forgiveness from their victim. We hypothesized that although both conditions would evoke negative moral emotions, imagery of seeking forgiveness from one's victim (*i.e.*, confessing, apologizing, and asking forgiveness) would reduce guilt and shame, presumably because one is "doing the right thing," which would reduce negative feelings about one's behavior (*i.e.*, guilt) and also about oneself as a person (*i.e.*, shame). Consistent with this, Meek et al. (1995) found that confession imagery reduced guilt in comparison to transgression imagery.

In contrast to the negative emotions of guilt and shame, we hypothesized that seeking forgiveness would increase transgressors' empathy for the victim and their sense of hope. We expected empathy to increase because imagining the acts of confession and apology involve a focus on the possible response of the victim, placing the victim's perspective in a central role. We expected hope to increase because when seeking forgiveness, transgressors take this step in anticipation that the victim may respond favorably.

We also compared participants' perceptions of forgiveness when imagining their transgressions versus imagining seeking forgiveness. We expected transgressors to feel more forgiven by victims when they were seeking forgiveness. This is because seeking forgiveness is a moral response to culpable behavior and moves transgressors closer to the point of being able to receive forgiveness from their victims (who often wait for signs of contrition before forgiving). We also hypothesized that perceptions of forgiveness by God and self-forgiveness would be greater during forgiveness-seeking imagery because the desire for forgiveness is central to this condition.

In addition to influencing moral emotions, transgressors' imagery of committing transgressions and seeking forgiveness may also influence basic emotions, much as imagery of responding to a perpetrator has influenced victims' basic emotions in prior research (Witvliet, Ludwig, & Vander Laan, 2001). We assessed transgressors' sadness, fear, and anger, hypothesizing that sadness and anger would be less potent during forgiveness-seeking imagery, but that fear may be greater because transgressors may be concerned about how their victims will respond (cf. Dorff, 1998).

We also measured the dimensions of emotional valence (negative – positive), arousal, and perceived control. The valence and arousal dimensions of emotion are related to a range of physiological responses, as found by Witvliet and Vrana (1995). Specifically, greater *corrugator* (brow) tension occurs when emotional valence is more negative, whereas greater *zygomatic* (smile muscle) activity occurs when emotional valence is more positive. With increasing levels of arousal, muscle tension under the eye, heart rate, and skin conductance (sweat) are greater. Given these emotion-physiology relationships in prior research (Witvliet & Vrana, 1995), we measured these

physiological responses on-line as participants actively imagined themselves committing the transgression and seeking forgiveness. We hypothesized that both imagery conditions would evoke arousing and negative emotions, but that transgression imagery would be comparatively more negative and arousing than forgiveness-seeking imagery. Hence, we predicted that transgression imagery would elicit greater brow (ie., *corrugator*) and eye muscle (*i.e.*, *orbicularis oculi*) tension, less smile muscle (*i.e.*, *zygomatic*) activity, and the greater physiological stress responses (i.e., higher heart rate and skin conductance level scores). Beyond these emotional measures, we assessed the level of effort transgressors exerted in each type of imagery. We hypothesized that seeking forgiveness would demand more effort than reflecting on one's transgression, although seeking forgiveness would yield greater emotional benefits.

The Impact of the Victim's Responses

The second focus of the study was to assess the emotional impact of having one's forgiveness-seeking behavior met with unforgiving, forgiving, or conciliatory responses from the victim. Bearing the brunt of a harbored grudge or receiving the merciful gift of forgiveness represent the counterparts of previous research on the emotions victims experience when they harbor grudges or grant forgiveness (Witvliet et al., 2001). Witvliet et al. (2001) asked participants to imagine responding to a particular real-life offender in unforgiving versus forgiving ways using a within-subjects repeated measures design. Participants reported significantly higher levels of negative emotion (e.g., anger, sadness) during the unforgiving imagery trials. In contrast, they reported higher levels of positive emotion and greater perceived control during the forgiving imagery conditions. Participants also showed significantly greater reactivity in the cardiovascular (heart rate, blood pressure) and sympathetic nervous systems (skin conductance levels) as well as greater brow muscle (*corrugator*) tension during the unforgiving imagery trials compared to the forgiving imagery trials. Furthermore, the heart rate, sweat, and brow muscle effects persisted after imagery into relaxing recovery periods, suggesting that the effects of unforgiving thoughts were difficult to quell. These results suggest that when people harbor unforgiving responses toward their offenders, they may incur emotional and physiological costs. Instead, when they adopt forgiving responses, they may reduce these costs and accrue psychophysiological benefits, at least in the short term.

Witvliet et al.'s (2001) findings converge with other studies linking victims' forgiving responses to more positive mental health (Al-Mabuk, Enright, & Cardis,

1995; Coyle & Enright, 1997; Freedman & Enright, 1996; Hebl & Enright, 1993; McCullough, Worthington, & Rachal, 1997), and anger/hostility to physical health problems (*e.g.*, cardiovascular disease; Miller et al., 1996). However, research on transgressors' emotional and physiological experiences has not kept pace.

Only one prior study has examined transgressors' emotions during imagery of receiving an unforgiving versus a forgiving response. Meek et al. (1995) asked participants to imagine confessing a transgression to a boss who responded either with forgiveness or unforgiveness. Participants who imagined receiving the forgiving response reported feeling significantly better than those who imagined receiving an unforgiving response.

The current study was designed to build on this research base by assessing a range of emotional and physiological responses evoked by imagining forgiveness denied or granted. We hypothesized that transgressors would experience similar emotional and physiological effects as victims did in Witvliet et al.'s (2001) study of unforgiveness and forgiveness, primarily because we expected unforgiving imagery to prompt negative, arousing emotion, and forgiving imagery to prompt more positive, less arousing emotion. Consistent with this, we anticipated that transgressors would feel less sad, angry, and fearful, but more in control in the forgiveness imagery condition compared to the condition in which victims refused to grant forgiveness and held a grudge. We also hypothesized that when transgressors imagined receiving the gift of forgiveness, they would feel more forgiven by the victim, and more grateful. Although interpersonal forgiveness is distinct from divine forgiveness and self-forgiveness, we anticipated that transgressors would show higher levels of perceived forgiveness by God and oneself along with higher levels of forgiveness by the victim. We also hypothesized that transgressors would feel less guilt about their behavior, less shame about themselves as people, more empathy for their victims, and more hope during the imagery of receiving forgiveness— because this gift of mercy would blot out much of the negative affect transgressors felt and would increase their sense of resolution of the problem and anticipation of good experiences in the future.

Along with the subjective emotional shifts, we hypothesized that in the forgiveness condition, participants would show lower *corrugator* (brow) EMG tension (associated with reductions in negative emotion) and higher *zygomatic* (cheek) EMG activity (associated with more positive emotion), and lower heart rate, skin conductance levels, and *orbicularis*

oculi EMG tension (all associated with lower levels of arousal; cf. Witvliet & Vrana, 1995). We hypothesized that reconciliation imagery would evoke differences in dependent measures similar to those evoked by forgiveness as compared to grudge imagery because reconciliation would involve resolution of the interpersonal problem and the negative affect associated with it, whereas bearing the brunt of a grudge would involve exacerbation of the problem.

By separately studying the conditions of receiving forgiveness and of reconciling with the victim, this study follows in the tradition of distinguishing forgiveness from reconciliation (*e.g.*, Enright & Coyle, 1998; Smedes, 1996; Worthington, 1998). In prior work, theorists and therapists have drawn this distinction primarily for the benefit of victims who may choose to forgive an offender in the absence of an ongoing relationship—perhaps because the transgressor has died, has been abusive, or is likely to cause harm again. As Smedes (1996, p. 27) framed it, "We can forgive even if we do not trust the person who wronged us once not to wrong us again. Reunion can happen only if we can trust the person who wronged us once not to wrong us again."

Method

Participants

Forty introductory psychology students (20 male, 20 female, age 18-22) voluntarily participated in this experiment, and were given credit in their classes for participation. The participants included 39 whites and one Latino. Heart rate data for one participant and *zygomatic* data for another participant were unusable due to errors in data acquisition.

Procedure

This study used a standard within-subjects emotional imagery paradigm (Vrana & Lang, 1990; Witvliet & Vrana, 1995, 2000). Each participant was tested individually in a two-hour session. Initially, the participant identified an incident in which he or she was to blame for significantly hurting the feelings of another person, and completed a questionnaire about the nature of the offense, the victim's responses, and his or her own responses. Then the participant completed eight imagery trials of each of the five different imagery conditions, with orders counterbalanced across participants. In each condition, all participants followed a script designed to prompt that type of imagery related to the interpersonal offense. Following the technique of Witvliet et al. (2001), the imagery scripts encouraged participants to consider the thoughts, feelings, and physical responses that would accompany each imagery condition.

Two conditions used imagery scripts focusing on the transgressor's actions: the participant (1) ruminated about the transgression (recalling the feelings associated with hurting the victim) and (2) imagined seeking forgiveness from the victim (confessing the wrong, genuinely apologizing to the victim, and asking for forgiveness). Three conditions used imagery scripts focusing on the effects of three possible victim responses: (3) refusing forgiveness and holding a grudge, (4) genuinely forgiving the transgressor, and (5) reconciling in a way appropriate to the nature of the relationship.

The imagery portion of the study was broken down into blocks of imagery trials, with two types of imagery trials in each block. Acoustic tones (high, low) were used to signal exactly when the participant was to imagine each type of imagery. Medium tones signaled participants to engage in a relaxation task, thinking the word "one" every time they exhaled (e.g., Vrana & Lang, 1990; Witvliet & Vrana, 1995, 2000).

Physiological Measurements. On-line physiological monitoring allowed us to measure the immediate psychophysiological effects of participants' responses as they occurred. (See Note 2 for a description of the equipment and settings used.)[2] During each trial, the participant's heart rate was measured on a heartbeat-to-heartbeat basis, and cardiac interbeat intervals were converted off-line to heart rate in beats per minute for each imagery period. Facial EMG and SCL data were measured on a second-to-second basis. Within each type of imagery condition, the physiology measures were averaged over the 8 trials for that condition. Each trial consisted of an 8-s baseline (relaxation) period, 16-s imagery period, and 8-s recovery (relaxation) period. Each period was divided into 4-s epochs. During the imagery and recovery periods, the physiological data for the 4-s baseline epoch immediately before the imagery period were subtracted from each of the 4-s epochs for the imagery and recovery periods. This approach was used so that the directional effects of the conditions on each physiological measure (e.g., increases or decreases) can be conceptualized clearly.[3]

Self-Report Ratings. Following each block of imagery trials, participants rated their feelings during the preceding two types of imagery. They did so privately and were encouraged to be completely honest. Using a standard computerized technique, they manipulated a joystick to register their ratings of the effort they had expended during imagery, their emotional valence (negative – positive), arousal, perceived control, sadness, fear, anger, guilt, shame, gratitude, hope, empathy for victim, and perceived for-

giveness from the victim, from God, and from themselves. As a manipulation check, participants also rated the vividness of their imagery. Using a standard approach, all ratings were converted to numerical form using a scale that ranged from 0 to 20 (e.g., Witvliet & Vrana, 1995; Witvliet et al., 2001). (See Note 4 for a description of the ratings technique.)[4]

Results

Transgression Questionnaire Data

The most common transgressions involved breaking someone's heart by ending a relationship (40%), breaking someone's trust (22.5%), and saying something hurtful in the heat of the moment (17.5%). The most common victims of these transgressions were romantic partners (40%), parents (30%), and friends (25%). Most victims were female (62.5%). All transgressions were identified as emotional—rather than physical—offenses. Most transgressions reportedly occurred within a year prior to the study (60%). The majority of the participants had apologized to their victims (85%), and most had repaired relationships with the victims (82.5%) prior to the study.

Nearly half (47.5%) of the participants rated their offenses as highly severe (ratings were considered high if they were 6 or 7 on the 7-point scale). Over half of the sample reported high levels of guilt about their transgression behavior (52.5%) and felt shame about themselves as transgressors (55%). Most of the participants felt highly forgiven by the victim (62.5%), and—of the 92.5% of the participants who reported belief in God—the majority felt highly forgiven by God (75%). Of the 62.5% of participants who felt they had *not* received "complete" forgiveness from the victim, 68% had a high desire for forgiveness. The vast majority of participants (90%) reported valuing forgiveness highly.

Seeking Forgiveness

Self-Report Ratings. (See Table 1) Paired-samples *t*-tests (two-tailed) were also conducted to assess whether self-reported emotions differed for the imagery conditions. Significant differences occurred for almost every rating, with the exceptions of level of perceived control, fear, empathy, and the manipulation check for comparable vividness of imagery [all *t*s ≤ |-1.74|, all *p*s ≥ .09].

Compared to the transgression imagery condition, imagery of seeking forgiveness prompted participants to exert more effort [$t(39) = 6.43$, $p = < .001$], but to feel less negative Valence [$t(39) = -3.07$, $p < .01$] and less aroused [$t(39) = 3.30$, $p = .002$]. Specifically, they reported less sadness [$t(39) = 3.85$, $p < .001$], less anger [$t(39) = 4.46$, $p < .001$], less guilt about the transgression [$t(39) = 2.16$, $p < .05$] and less shame about

Table 1

Means and (Standard Deviations) of Self Report Ratings

	Seeking Forgiveness		Victim Responses		
Measure	Reliving Transgression[t]	Seeking Forgiveness[s]	Holding Grudge[g]	Offering Forgiveness[f]	Experiencing Reconciliation[r]
Effort	6.00 (4.73)	11.53^{ts***} (5.15)	8.43 (4.20)	11.79 (5.18)	11.03^{gf**,gr*} (4.87)
Valence	3.75 (2.57)	6.36^{ts**} (4.83)	4.33 (3.59)	17.10 (2.73)	13.26^{gf***,gr***,fr***} (5.16)
Arousal	14.55 (3.48)	11.33^{ts**} (4.83)	14.55 (5.11)	10.99 (6.93)	10.70$^{gf***,gr**.}$ (6.59)
Control	6.88 (5.02)	8.43^{ns} (4.20)	6.00 (4.73)	11.03 (4.87)	11.53^{gf***,gr***} (5.15)
Sadness	16.14 (2.95)	13.40^{ts***} (3.72)	14.65 (4.00)	4.33 (3.43)	3.94^{gf***,gr***} (4.61)
Fear	10.11 (5.48)	9.80^{ns} (4.80)	10.01 (6.04)	2.91 (2.79)	3.51^{gf***,gr**} (4.25)
Anger	10.10 (5.85)	5.75^{ts***} (5.46)	12.93 (5.64)	2.11 (3.01)	2.21^{gf***,gr***} (3.14)
Guilt	16.21 (3.01)	15.14^{ts*} (3.01)	13.49 (4.34)	9.01 (5.33)	7.61^{gf***,gr***} (5.74)
Shame	15.78 (3.76)	13.78^{ts***} (4.34)	14.26 (3.84)	8.25 (5.28)	6.76^{gf***,gr***} (5.68)
Gratitude	3.48 (2.94)	7.58^{ts***} (4.51)	2.98 (2.96)	16.65 (2.91)	15.86^{gf***,gr***} (3.09)
Hope	4.88 (3.22)	10.71^{ts***} (4.65)	5.10 (3.56)	16.60 (2.93)	16.04^{gf***,gr***} (3.37)
Empathy	15.36 (4.09)	15.74^{ns} (3.56)	10.93 (4.87)	13.90 (3.83)	13.36^{gf***,gr*} (4.65)
Victim-Forgiveness	4.33 (3.59)	13.26^{ts***} (5.16)	6.36 (4.83)	15.56 (3.70)	17.10^{gf***,gr***,fr*} (2.73)
Self-Forgiveness	3.68 (5.10)	6.11^{ts**} (7.19)	4.53 (5.86)	7.39 (7.81)	7.14^{ns} (7.56)
Divine Forgiveness	14.55 (5.11)	10.70^{ts**} (6.59)	11.33 (4.83)	9.78 (7.16)	10.99^{ns} (6.93)
Vividness	15.03 (4.05)	14.54^{ns} (3.87)	14.36 (3.89)	15.60 (2.82)	16.03^{ns} (2.72)

Note. Ratings were made on a 0-20 scale. For valence, 0 = negative and 20 = positive. For arousal, 0 = calm/relaxed to 20 = aroused/excited. For all other measures, 0 = "not at all" and 20 = "completely." Statistical significance of each comparison is indicated in the last column for each set of paired samples t-tests (two-tailed): $p < .05^{ns}$, $p \leq .05^{*}$, $p \leq .01^{**}$, $p \leq .001^{***}$.

themselves [$t(39)$ = 3.65, p = .001]. Conversely, seeking forgiveness prompted more gratitude [$t(39)$ = -6.21, p < .001] and more hope [$t(39)$ = -8.05, p < .001]. Participants' perceptions of forgiveness by the victim [$t(39)$ = -8.46, p < .001] and themselves [$t(39)$ = -3.01, p = .005] were greater when seeking forgiveness from the victim, but their perceptions of divine forgiveness were greater when they focused on their transgressions [$t(39)$ = 3.06, p = .004].

Physiology. (See Table 2) To assess differences in physiological reactivity for the two imagery conditions, we conducted paired-samples t-tests (two-tailed). *Corrugator* EMG was significantly higher (i.e., greater furrowing of the brow muscle occurred) during the transgression imagery than during the forgiveness-seeking imagery [$t(39)$ = 2.01, p = .05]. No other significant physiological differences occurred between the transgression and forgiveness-seeking conditions during imagery periods [all ts ≤ |1.03|, all ps ≥ .31] or recovery periods [all ts ≤ |1.43|, all ps ≥ .16].

The Impact of the Victim's Responses

Because there were three types of imagery about the victim's possible responses, we analyzed the ratings and physiology data for the three imagery conditions in one-way repeated-measures *ANOVA*s using the SPSS multivariate approach as recommended by Maxwell and Delaney (1990). We interpret the results using the multivariate tests because they do not assume sphericity (cf. Green, Salkind, & Akey, 2000, p. 213). The F statistic equivalent for Wilks' *Lambda* is reported for each self-report rating and physiology measure (during imagery and recovery periods). For significant effects, planned paired-samples t-tests (two-tailed) were conducted to test our predictions concerning grudge-forgiveness and grudge-reconciliation differences, and to explore differences between forgiveness and reconciliation.

Multivariate Analyses of Variance

Participant ratings are presented in Table 1. Significant effects occurred for level of effort expended [$F(2,38)$ = 6.16, p < .01], valence (positive-negative) [$F(2,38)$ = 120.94, p < .001], arousal [$F(2,38)$ = 6.13, p < .01], perceived level of control (dominance) [$F(2,38)$ = 28.10, p < .001], sadness [$F(2.38)$ = 77.18, p < .001], fear [$F(2,38)$ = 30.63, p < .001], anger [$F(2,38)$ = 63.90, p < .001], guilt [$F(2,38)$ = 13.30, p < .001], shame [$F(2,38)$ = 35.10, p < .001], gratitude [$F(2,38)$ = 160.15, p < .001], hope [$F(2,38)$ = 120.07, p < .001], empathy [$F(2,38)$ = 5.48, p < .01], and forgiveness from the victim [$F(2,38)$ = 66.14, p < .001]. No significant effects were found for ratings of self-forgiveness, forgiveness by God, or the manipulation check for comparable imagery vividness [all Fs ≤ 2.22, all ps ≥ .12].

Physiological data are presented in Table 2. During the imagery periods, no significant effects of imagery condition occurred for the physiology measures [all Fs ≤ 2.15, all ps ≥ .09]. However, a trend occurred for *corrugator* EMG [$F(2,39)$ = 2.77, p = .075]. This trend is reported because planned paired-samples t-tests were performed and significant effects found. During recovery conditions, skin conductance [$F(2,93)$ = 4.52, p < .05], zygomatic EMG [$F(2,37)$ = 4.53, p < .05] and *corrugator* EMG [$F(2,38)$ = 5.06, p < .05] differed significantly across imagery conditions. No significant effects occurred for heart rate or orbicularis oculi EMG under the eye during recovery conditions [Fs ≤ .76, ps ≥ .48].

Grudge-Forgiveness Comparisons

Ratings. Interestingly, participants reported expending more effort during their imagery of receiving forgiveness compared to having a grudge held against them [$t(39)$ = -3.25, p < .01]. Yet, imagery of receiving forgiveness prompted ratings of more positive (valence) emotion [$t(39)$ = -15.62, p < .001], less arousal [$t(39)$ = 2.89, p < .01], and greater perceived control [$t(39)$ = -6.41, p < .001].

During the grudge imagery condition, as compared to the forgiveness imagery condition, participants felt greater levels of sadness [$t(39)$ = 12.00, p < .001], fear [$t(39)$ = 7.85, p < .001], anger [$t(39)$ = 11.18, p < .001], guilt [$t(39)$ = 4.00, p < .001], and shame [$t(39)$ = 6.62, p < .001].

During the forgiveness imagery condition, as compared to the grudge imagery condition, participants felt greater gratitude [$t(39)$ = -17.88, p < .001], hope [$t(39)$ = -15.70, p < .001], empathy [$t(39)$ = -3.22, p < .01], and forgiveness from the victim [$t(39)$ = -8.43, p < .001].

Physiology. Follow-up analysis of the *corrugator* trend during imagery showed that—as predicted—participants had greater increases in *corrugator* EMG (brow muscle tension) during the grudge imagery than during the forgiveness imagery [$t(39)$ = 2.18, p < .05], and during the grudge recovery period than during the forgiveness recovery period [$t(39)$ = 2.79, p < .01]. Post hoc analysis also indicated a marginal effect for *zygomatic* change scores in the predicted direction. Participants showed greater *zygomatic* (smile muscle) activity when they imagined being forgiven by their victims compared to when they imagined having a grudge held against them [$t(39)$ = -1.94, p = .059]. (Because we predicted this directional difference in *zygomatic* change scores based on the emotion and psychophysiology literature, we note that for the one-tailed paired-samples t-test p =

Table 2

Means and (Standard Deviations) of Physiological Measures

	Imagery				
	Seeking Forgiveness			**Victim Responses**	
	Reliving Transgression	Seeking Forgiveness	Holding Grudge	Offering Forgiveness	Experiencing Reconciliation
Measure	Imagery[r]	Imagery[s]	Imagery[g]	Imagery[f]	Imagery[t]
Corrugator EMG	.93 (2.85)	.71[ts*] (2.35)	.74 (1.90)	.10 (.45)	.01[gr*,gr*] (.28)
Zygomatic EMG	.30 (.98)	.33[ns] (1.59)	.33 (1.18)	1.02 (3.31)	.94[gr+,gr+] (3.14)
Orbicularis Oculi EMG	.50 (.89)	.38[ns] (.68)	.50 (.85)	.57 (1.03)	.73[ns] (1.20)
Skin Conductance	-.08 (.08)	-.09[ns] (.12)	-.08 (.07)	-.06 (.09)	-.05[gr+] (.10)
Heart Rate	1.24 (1.97)	1.27[ns] (2.36)	1.48 (2.22)	1.32 (1.81)	1.35[ns] (2.43)

	Recovery Period				
	Seeking Forgiveness			**Victim Responses**	
	Reliving Transgression	Seeking Forgiveness	Holding Grudge	Offering Forgiveness	Experiencing Reconciliation
Measure	Recovery[c]	Recovery[s]	Recovery[g]	Recovery[f]	Recovery[t]
Corrugator EMG	0.62 (1.69)	0.43[ns] (1.05)	0.48 (1.10)	0.07 (0.56)	0.10[gf**,gr**] (0.73)
Zygomatic EMG	0.13 (0.48)	0.14[ns] (0.53)	0.13 (0.56)	0.40 (.096)	0.50[gf**] (2.08)
Orbicularis Oculi EMG	0.06 (0.78)	0.078[ns] (0.43)	0.08 (0.73)	0.21 (0.66)	0.22[ns] (1.07)
Skin Conductance	-0.17 (0.17)	-0.18[ns] (0.20)	-0.17 (0.20)	-0.16 (0.16)	-0.09[gr**,fr+] (0.22)
Heart Rate	1.30 (2.75)	1.41[ns] (3.45)	1.43 (3.20)	1.58 (2.54)	1.45[ns] (2.58)

Note. All values represent the average change from the baseline relaxation period immediately preceding *each* 16-second imagery trial and 8-second recovery period. *Corrugator, zygomatic,* and *orbicularis oculi* EMG was measured in microvolts. Skin conductance levels were measured in microsiemens. Heart rate was measured in beats/min. Statistical significance of each comparison is indicated in the last column for each set of paired-samples *t*-tests (two-tailed): $p > .07^{ns}$, $p \leq .07+$, $p \leq .05^{*}$, $p \leq .01^{**}$, and $p \leq .001^{***}$.

.03.) Consistent with this, participants continued to show higher *zygomatic* EMG activity during the forgiveness recovery period than during the grudge recovery period [$t(39)$ = -2.90, p < .01].

Grudge-Reconciliation Comparisons

Ratings. As predicted, the grudge reconciliation comparisons paralleled the grudge-forgiveness results. Participants reported expending more effort during the reconciliation imagery than during the grudge imagery [$t(39)$ = -2.43, p < .05]. Despite the effort associated with reconciliation, participants reported feeling more positive (valence) [$t(39)$ = -8.46, p < .001], less arousal [$t(39)$ = 3.06, p < .01], and greater perceived control [$t(39)$ = -6.43, p < .001].

During the grudge imagery condition, as compared to the reconciliation imagery condition, participants felt greater levels of sadness [$t(39)$ = 10.17, p <001], fear [$t(39)$ = 6.90, p < .001], anger [$t(39)$ = 10.90, p < .001], guilt [$t(39)$ = 5.20, p < .001], and shame [$t(39)$ = 8.21, p < .001].

During the reconciliation imagery condition, as compared to the grudge imagery condition, participants felt more gratitude [$t(39)$ = -16.45, p < .001], hope [$t(39)$ = -13.74, p < .001] , empathy [$t(39)$ = -2.26, p < .05], and forgiveness from the victim [$t(39)$ = -11.47, p < .001].

Physiology. As predicted, participants had greater *corrugator* EMG tension associated with negative emotion during the grudge imagery than during the reconciliation imagery [$t(39)$ = 2.34, p < .03] and during grudge recovery periods than reconciliation recovery periods [$t(39)$ = 3.22, p < .01]. Follow-up analyses of the *zygomatic* EMG data indicated that smiling activity was marginally greater during reconciliation imagery compared to grudge imagery, as predicted, $t(39)$ = -1.856, p = .07. (Because we predicted this directional difference in *zygomatic* change scores based on the emotion and psychophysiology literature, we note that for the one-tailed paired samples, t-test p = .036). However, *zygomatic* EMG activity did not differ after grudge compared to reconciliation imagery [$t(39)$ = -1.44, p = .16].

The skin conductance data were counter to our predictions: levels were lower after grudge imagery than after reconciliation imagery, indicating greater habituation after grudge imagery [$t(39)$ = -3.02, p < .01]. We had hypothesized that imagery of having one's victim hold a grudge would be more stressful and arousing than receiving forgiveness—prompting higher skin conductance levels—and that these effects would linger after imagery (cf. Witvliet et al., 2001). Given this unexpected result, we also conducted a post-hoc analysis of skin conductance levels during the imagery periods. Consistent with the

recovery period data, we found that skin conductance change scores tended to be lower during grudge imagery than during reconciliation imagery [two-tailed $t(39)$ = -1.89, p = .066].

Forgiveness-Reconciliation Comparisons

Ratings. Only two differences occurred in the ratings assigned to imagery of receiving forgiveness versus imagery of reconciling with the victim. In the forgiveness imagery condition, as compared to the reconciliation imagery condition, participants experienced more positive emotion [$t(39)$ = -4.68, p < .001]. In the reconciliation imagery condition, as compared to the forgiveness imagery condition, participants felt more forgiveness from the victim [$t(39)$ = 2.54, p < .05].

There were no significant differences between the forgiveness and reconciliation imagery conditions ratings of effort, arousal, control, sadness, gratitude, fear, anger, guilt, shame, hope, or empathy [all ts ≤ |-1.82|, all ps ≥ .08].

Physiology. Follow-up analyses indicated that forgiveness and reconciliation conditions did not differentially affect *corrugator* EMG or *zygomatic* EMG during imagery [both ts ≤ |-1.26|, ps ≥ .21] or recovery periods [both ts ≤ |0.51|, ps ≥ .61]. A marginal effect was found for skin conductance level change scores, which were higher during recovery from reconciliation than forgiveness imagery, [$t(39)$ = 1.88, p = .068].

Discussion

Seeking Forgiveness

Imagining oneself seeking forgiveness carried a range of emotional benefits. Compared to the ruminations about one's transgression, imagery of seeking forgiveness mitigated negative emotion and brought emotional arousal down to moderate levels. Specifically, participants felt less sad and angry, less guilt about the transgression, and less shame about themselves during forgiveness-seeking compared to transgression-focused imagery. Still, the actual ratings values indicate that both conditions were associated with relatively high levels of guilt (transgression = 16.21; forgiveness-seeking = 15.14; 0-20 scale) and shame (transgression = 15.78; forgiveness-seeking = 13.78; 0-20 scale) as predicted. The experience of moderately high guilt and shame is not surprising because even though forgiveness-seeking imagery involved taking an active step to repair relational damage, participants still focused on their culpability. This likely emphasized both regret over past behavior (*i.e.*, guilt) and an awareness of one's failings as a person (*i.e.*, shame). Exline and Baumeister (2000) have argued that acts of confession—especially when public—are likely to evoke feelings of shame. We found this to be the case even when acts of confession were contained in imagery rather than overtly carried out in the presence of the victim. Still, levels of shame—and guilt— were significantly reduced during forgiveness-seeking imagery compared to transgression imagery.

Three findings illuminate some reasons people may resist seeking forgiveness despite its emotional benefits. Specifically, transgressors' fear and perceived control were *not* significantly improved by imagery of seeking forgiveness. In his analysis of obstacles to seeking forgiveness, Dorff (1998) identified that part of the difficulty in asking forgiveness from another person—as compared to God—is that openness from the victim cannot be assured, and "the offender has every reason to fear that the victim will shun him or her" (p. 32). Another obstacle to seeking forgiveness may be the greater effort that accompanied contemplating this action versus reflecting on one's transgression. This heightened effort may reflect the challenges that accompany humbling oneself and acknowledging one's own culpability (Dorff, 1998)—acts that work against self-serving bias. Despite these obstacles, imagery of seeking forgiveness prompted significant increases in hope, likely because forgiveness-seeking is inherently goal-directed.

Consistent with their greater hope, participants reported feeling more forgiven by their offenders and themselves when seeking forgiveness than when focusing on the transgression incident. In contrast (and contrary to our hypothesis), participants reported feeling significantly more forgiven by God when they focused on their transgression than when they imagined seeking interpersonal forgiveness. While ratings of perceived forgiveness by others and God do not indicate *actual* forgiveness granted or received, they reflect participants' perceptions.

Self-forgiveness can be a thorny issue both for logistical and moral reasons (Smedes, 1996). In tackling the difficult nuances involved in self-forgiveness, Smedes (1996) claims "none but the contrite has a right to forgive himself [or herself]. Remorse is a price we pay to forgive ourselves" (97). He also notes that people can only engage in self-forgiveness for "wrongful things that we deserve blame for doing" (p. 99). Consistent with these elements, participants in the current research were asked to identify a real-life situation in which they felt that they were to blame for significantly hurting the feelings of another person. The participants reported higher levels of self-forgiveness when they imagined the forgiveness-seeking behaviors of confessing to the victim, apologizing sincerely, and asking for forgiveness—behaviors that parallel some of the issues Smedes (1996) has raised.

In contrast to self-forgiveness, transgressors reported feeling greater divine forgiveness only when they focused on their transgression rather than on seeking forgiveness directly from the victim. This inward focus on one's transgression has some parallels to the act of confessing one's sins to God, an act closely linked with the assurance of pardon in worship. This result may indicate that people are freer to perceive God's forgiveness when they are more focused on honestly acknowledging their culpability and less focused on receiving forgiveness from others. It may also be that because participants reported feeling significantly lower levels of interpersonal and self-forgiveness during transgression imagery, they emphasized divine forgiveness to compensate for lack of forgiveness from others and oneself.

In victims, empathy for the transgressor is strongly linked with granting forgiveness (e.g., McCullough, Worthington, & Rachal, 1997; McCullough, Rachal, Sandage, Worthington, Brown, & Hight, 1998). However, in our study of transgressors, empathy ratings did not differ across conditions, despite significant differences in forgiveness ratings. Although we had hypothesized that participants would feel more empathic toward their victims during forgiveness-seeking imagery, empathy ratings during transgression imagery may have been as high as those during forgiveness-seeking because the imagery was inherently focused on the other as a victim of one's actions.

In terms of physiology, only one statistically significant difference occurred. Consistent with our hypothesis rooted in prior research (Witvliet et al., 2001; Witvliet & Vrana, 1995), transgression-focused imagery was perceived as more emotionally negative and prompted greater increases in *corrugator* (brow) muscle tension than forgiveness-seeking imagery. However, no other physiological differences occurred during imagery or recovery periods. This may be due to the relationships between valence and arousal ratings for the two imagery conditions. Considering the 0-20 scale, the actual valence ratings for the two conditions (transgression = 3.75; forgiveness-seeking = 6.36), and the actual arousal ratings (transgression = 14.55; forgiveness-seeking = 11.33) were more similar than in other research with significant physiological differences (e.g., Witvliet & Vrana, 1995).

In sum, despite the effort involved during forgiveness-seeking compared to transgression imagery, participants experienced significant improvements in basic and moral emotions, as well as their perceived forgiveness by the victim and themselves. This complex of subjective emotional benefits may offset the obstacles to forgiveness-seeking and motivate transgressors to actually seek forgiveness.

The Impact of the Victim's Responses

The current results suggest that—to a large extent—transgressors' subjective emotions parallel the emotions of victims during unforgiving and forgiving imagery (cf. Witvliet et al., 2001). The current study found that transgressors expended more effort and felt higher levels of arousal, sadness, fear, anger, guilt, and shame when they imagined a real-life victim bearing a grudge against them. By contrast, transgressors felt more positive emotion, control, gratitude, hope, empathy, and forgiveness from the victim when they imagined receiving forgiveness or reconciling with the victim.

Despite the findings that both granting forgiveness (cf. Witvliet et al., 2001) and receiving forgiveness (the current study) carry subjective benefits, receiving forgiveness may not be as physiologically beneficial as granting forgiveness (cf. Witvliet et al., 2001). The current study generally failed to observe the predicted differences for heart rate and skin conductance (as well as orbicularis oculi EMG). This may be related to participants' similar arousal ratings across conditions. Compared to basic emotion research (Witvliet & Vrana, 1995) and research on victims using the same ratings methodology (Witvliet et al., 2001), arousal ratings in the current study were quite similar across conditions (forgiveness = 11, reconciliation = 10.7, grudge = 14.6; the range of 0-20 corresponds to calm/relaxed – aroused/excited). Emotional arousal, in particular, is linked with heart rate and skin conductance levels in emotional imagery paradigms (Witvliet & Vrana, 1995). In their research of victims, Witvliet et al. (2001) found significantly higher arousal ratings for the unforgiving (15.3) than forgiving imagery (7.2), and corresponding significant differences between heart rate, blood pressure, and skin conductance in these conditions. In addition, all measures but blood pressure continued to show significantly higher scores during recovery periods after unforgiving than forgiving imagery. (Note that the current study did not measure blood pressure.) Simple examination of the self-report means in this study also suggests that having forgiveness denied by a victim may be more sadness-inducing than anger-arousing, which is consistent with the relative lack of physiological effects. This contrasts with Witvliet et al.'s (2001) data, which indicate that bearing a grudge against a perpetrator is more anger-arousing than sadness-inducing.

The current study of transgressors indicated a trend in which grudge imagery stimulated greater tension at the corrugator muscle region (i.e., brow) than either forgiveness or reconciliation imagery. Notably, corrugator reactivity continued to be significantly higher during the recovery period after grudge imagery—when participants tried to clear their minds and relax —than after either forgiveness or reconciliation imagery. These corrugator data are consistent with the more negative ratings participants assigned to their grudge imagery compared to either the forgiveness or the reconciliation imagery. This association between corrugator tension and negative emotion is consistent with findings from research on victims (Witvliet et al., 2001) and basic emotion research (e.g., Witvliet & Vrana, 1995).

In general, zygomatic (smile muscle) EMG showed a pattern opposite to corrugator (brow muscle) EMG, as predicted. Zygomatic EMG was higher during forgiveness imagery and recovery periods compared to grudge imagery and recovery periods. Participants also tended to have higher zygomatic EMG during reconciliation imagery than grudge imagery. Prior research links zygomatic activity with positive emotion (e.g., Witvliet & Vrana, 1995), which may have persisted after imagery of receiving forgiveness from or reconciling with the victims of the participants' transgressions.

The final physiological effects indicated that skin conductance levels tended to be lower during grudge imagery than reconciliation imagery, and were significantly lower in the grudge recovery periods than the reconciliation recovery periods. Skin conductance is often considered an indicator of sympathetic nervous system activity, and responsive to emotional arousal. We had hypothesized that skin conductance would be higher during and after the more arousing grudge imagery. Instead, the data suggest that sympathetic nervous system activity was lower during grudge imagery, and especially when grudge imagery was discontinued. It may be that participants became more engaged in the reconciliation imagery, dwelling on their relationship with the victim, and finding it more engaging and difficult to halt these thoughts in comparison to thoughts of having a grudge held against them. Interestingly, participants reported that they expended more effort during the reconciliation (and forgiveness) condition than the grudge condition. Complementing this view, it may be that when forgiveness-seeking is met with refusal, transgressors may feel deflated and withdraw their emotional investment rather than expending effort to rectify the relationship. Alternatively, receiving merciful responses of reconciliation may run counter to transgressors' implicit expectations of how they should be treated after behaving wrongly, stirring arousal.

An additional aim of this study was to investigate possible differences in the emotions induced by imagery of receiving forgiveness versus reconciling with the victim. The results are striking primarily for the absence of significant differences in all but two ratings measures. In particular, transgressors rated forgiveness imagery as more positive than reconciliation imagery. The other difference was a tendency for transgressors to feel even more forgiven by victims during reconciliation imagery than forgiveness imagery. This finding suggests that—in the minds of transgressors—reconciliation implied that forgiveness was granted and took the additional convincing step of repairing the relationship. Marty (1998) has observed that the distinctions between forgiveness and reconciliation may be somewhat artificial, noting their linkage throughout the New Testament. The current data suggest that forgiveness and reconciliation may not only be difficult to separate in practice—especially in the context of otherwise healthy relationships—but that imagining each experience stimulates similar feelings.

Conclusions

We see this research as congruent with the biblical themes relating forgiveness not only to one's relationship with God, but with blessing and healing. Psalm 103:3 identifies the Lord as the one "who forgives all your iniquity, who heals all your diseases." The Psalms also connect forgiveness with blessing (Psalm 65:3, "When deeds of iniquity overwhelm us, you forgive our transgressions." Psalm 32:1, "Happy are those whose transgression is forgiven, whose sin is covered."). When Jesus healed the paralytic man, as recorded in Mark 2:1-12, he both forgave him and enabled him to stand up, take his mat, and walk. In addition to divine forgiveness, Scripture also calls us to interpersonal confession and links it with healing (James 5:16, "Therefore confess your sins to one another, and pray for one another, so that you may be healed"). Whether this healing is meant to be spiritual, emotional, and/or physical, Scripture connects confession and forgiveness with wholeness.

In combination with prior work, this research suggests that forgiveness may similarly benefit the subjective emotions of victims and perpetrators, but that forgiveness has greater physiological effects and potential health implications for victims (cf. Witvliet et al., 2001). Both the victims in Witvliet et al.'s (2001) research and the transgressors in the current study experienced more positive emotion, greater perceived control, and less negative emotion (as well as lower *corrugator* EMG scores) during imagery of forgiveness granted compared to forgiveness refused. However, only victims experienced less physiological stress (as indicated by heart rate, blood pressure, and skin conductance) when they were agents of forgiveness compared to unforgiveness (Witvliet et al., 2001); transgressors did not show significant differences in heart rate or skin conductance when they imagined having their victims grant or withhold forgiveness in the current study.

We hope that future research will refine our understanding of whether and how transgressors may benefit emotionally from seeking forgiveness, receiving forgiveness, and reconciling. Additional work is also needed to determine whether the physiological benefits of forgiveness and costs of unforgiveness are more potent for victims who are agents, rather than for transgressors who are recipients of forgiveness. It may be that when it comes to forgiveness and physiology, it is more blessed to give than to receive.

Notes

1. All Scripture passages are taken from the New Revised Standard Version.

2. A Dell 486 computer timed the experimental events and collected on-line physiological data (using VPM software by Cook, Atkinson, & Lang, 1987). Imagery and relaxation trials were signaled by auditory tones at three frequencies—high (1350 Hz), medium (985 Hz), and low (620 Hz). The tones were 500 ms long and 73 dB[A]. They were generated by a Coulbourn V85-05 Audio Source Module with a shaped-rise time set at 50 ms. The tones were presented through Altec Lansing ACS41 speakers located 2.5 feet to the left of the participant's head during the instructions, and through Optimus Nova 67 headphones during data collection.

Facial EMG was recorded at the *corrugator* (i.e., brow), *zygomatic* (i.e., cheek), and *orbicularis oculi* (i.e., under the eye) muscle regions using sensor placements suggested by Fridlund and Cacioppo (1986). Facial skin was prepared using an alcohol pad and Medical Associates electrode gel. Then miniature Ag-AgCl electrodes filled with Medical Associates electrode gel were applied. EMG signals were amplified (X 50,000) by a Hi Gain V75-01 bioamplifier, using 90-Hz high-pass and 1-kHz low-pass filters. The signals were rectified and integrated by a Coulbourn multifunction V76-23 integrator (nominal time constant = 10 ms).

Skin conductance levels (SCLs) were measured by a Coulbourn V71-23 isolated skin conductance coupler using an applied constant voltage of 0.5 V across two standard electrodes. Electrodes were filled with a mixture of physiological saline and Unibase (Fowles et al., 1981) and applied to the hypothenar eminence on the left hand after it was rinsed with tap water. A 12-bit analog-digital converter sampled the skin conductance and facial EMG channels at 10 Hz.

Electrocardiogram data were collected using two standard electrodes, one on each forearm. A Hi Gain V75-01 bioamplifier amplified and filtered the signals. The signals were then sent to a digital input on the computer that detected R waves and measured interbeat intervals in milliseconds.

3. We wish to thank an anonymous reviewer for the suggestion to analyze the raw physiological data using each condition's baseline as the covariate for each dependent variable. With this approach to analysis, we found that only three of the 20 analyses differed in terms of statistical significance from the approach reported here. Specifically, the trend for corrugator EMG to differ across the victim responses of grudge, forgiveness, and reconciliation became significant, and the non-significant zygomatic EMG differences became significant. In the recovery period, the significant zygomatic differences after grudge, forgiveness, and reconciliation imagery failed to reach significance.

4. Four of the ratings commonly measured in the emotion and physiology literature are emotional valence (negative-positive), arousal (low-high), perceived control/dominance (low–high), and vividness of imagery, assessed with Hodes, Cook, and Lang's (1985) technique of manipulating the expressions of an androgynous figure. Using a joystick, participants could choose any point along a continuum from an extreme frown to an intense smile replete with dimples (valence), from a relaxed/peaceful/sleepy looking figure to an aroused/excited one that jumped up and down (arousal), and from a tiny to a huge figure (perceived control/dominance in the imagined situation). Vividness of imagery was rated by manipulating the image of a 3-D box from completely clear and vivid to completely fragmented and unidentifiable. To register the other single-item emotion ratings, participants used the joystick to place a cursor along a continuous line anchored by "Not At All" on the far left, "Moderately" in the middle, and "Completely" on the far right. For each of the following ratings, participants were asked, "How much did you feel _____ during your imagery?": "anger," "sadness," "gratitude," "fear," "bad about your behavior" (guilt), "bad about yourself as a person" (shame), "hope," "empathy for the victim," "you forgave yourself," "forgiven by the victim," and "forgiven by God."

References

Al-Mabuk, R. H., Enright, R. D., & Cardis, P. A. (1995). Forgiveness education with parentally love-deprived late adolescents. *Journal of Moral Education, 24,* 427-444.

Baumeister, R. F., Stillwell, A. M., & Wotman, S. R. (1990). Victim and perpetrator accounts of interpersonal conflict: Autobiographical narratives about anger. *Journal of Personality and Social Psychology, 59,* 994-1005.

Bonhoeffer, D. (1954). *Life together.* (J. W. Doberstein, Trans.). New York: Harper.

Cook, E. W., III, Atkinson, L., & Lang, K. G. (1987). Stimulus control and data acquisition for IBM PC's and compatibles. *Psychophysiology, 24,* 726-727.

Couch, L. L., Jones, W. H., & Moore, D. S. (1999). Buffering the effects of betrayal: The role of apology, forgiveness, and commitment. In J. Adams & W. H. Jones (Eds.), *Handbook of interpersonal commitment and relationship stability.* New York: Kluwer Academic/Plenum Publishers, 451-469.

Coyle, C. T., & Enright, R. D. (1997). Forgiveness intervention with postabortion men. *Journal of Consulting and Clinical Psychology, 65,* 1042-1046.

Darby, B. W., & Schlenker, B. R. (1982). Children's reactions to apologies. *Journal of Personality and Social Psychology, 43,* 742-753.

Dorff, E. N. (1998). The elements of forgiveness: A Jewish approach. In E. L. Worthington, Jr. (Ed.) *Dimensions of forgiveness.* Philadelphia, PA: Templeton Foundation Press, 29-55.

Enright, R. D., & Coyle, C. T. (1998). Researching the process model of forgiveness within psychological interventions. In E. L. Worthington, Jr. (Ed.) *Dimensions of forgiveness.* Philadelphia, PA: Templeton Foundation Press, 139-161.

Enright, R. D., & Fitzgibbons, R. P. (2000). *Helping clients forgive: An empirical guide for resolving anger and restoring hope.* Washington, DC: American Psychological Association.

Exline, J. J., & Baumeister, R. F. (2000). Expressing forgiveness and repentance: Benefits and barriers. In M. E. McCullough, K. I. Pargament, & C. E. Thoresen (Eds.), *Forgiveness: Theory, research, and practice.* New York: Guilford Press, 133-155.

Fowles, D. C., Christie, M. J., Edelberg, R., Grings, W. W., Lykken, D. T., & Venables, P. H. (1981). Publication recommendations for electrodermal measurement. *Psychophysiology, 18,* 232-239.

Freedman, S. R., & Enright, R. D. (1996). Forgiveness as an intervention goal with incest survivors. *Journal of Consulting and Clinical Psychology, 64,* 983-992.

Fridlund, A. J., & Cacioppo, J. T. (1986). Guidelines for human electromyographic research. *Psychophysiology, 23,* 567-589.

Green, S. B., Salkind, N. J., & Akey, T. M. (2000). *Using SPSS for Windows: Analyzing and understanding data.* Upper Saddle River, NJ: Prentice Hall.

Hebl, J. H., & Enright, R. D. (1993). Forgiveness as a psychotherapeutic goal with elderly females. *Psychotherapy, 30,* 658-667.

Hodes, R. L., Cook, E. W., & Lang, P. J. (1985). Individual differences in autonomic response: Conditioned association or conditioned fear? *Psychophysiology, 22,* 545-560.

Lang, P. J. (1979). A bio-informational theory of emotional imagery. *Psychophysiology, 16,* 495-512.

Marty, M. E. (1998). The ethos of Christian forgiveness. In E. L. Worthington, Jr. (Ed.), *Dimensions of forgiveness.* Philadelphia, PA: Templeton Foundation Press, 9-28.

Maxwell, S. E., & Delaney, H. D. (1990). *Designing experiments and analyzing data: A model comparison perspective.* Belmont, CA: Wadsworth.

McCullough, M. E., Rachal, K. C., Sandage, S. J., Worthington, E. L., Jr., Brown, S. W., & Hight, T. L. (1998). Interpersonal forgiving in close relationships II: Theoretical elaboration and measurement. *Journal of Personality and Social Psychology, 75,* 1586-1603.

McCullough, M. E., Worthington, E. L., Jr., & Rachal, K. C. (1997). Interpersonal forgiving in close relationships. *Journal of Personality and Social Psychology, 73,* 321-336.

Meek, K. R., Albright, J. S., & McMinn, M. R. (1995). Religious orientation, guilt, confession, and forgiveness. *Journal of Psychology and Theology, 23,* 190-197.

Miller, T. Q., Smith, T. W., Turner, C. W., Guijarro, M. L., & Hallet, A. J. (1996). Meta-analytic review of research on hostility and physical health. *Psychological Bulletin, 119,* 322-348.

O'Malley, M. N., & Greenberg, J. (1983). Sex differences in restoring justice: The down payment effect. *Journal of Research in Personality, 17,* 174-185.

Ohbuchi, K., Kameda, M., & Agarie, N. (1989). Apology as aggression control: Its role in mediating appraisal of and response to harm. *Journal of Personality and Social Psychology, 56,* 219-227.

Sandage, S. J., Worthington, E. L., Jr., Hight, T. L., & Berry, J. W. (2000). Seeking forgiveness: Theoretical context and an initial empirical study. *Journal of Psychology and Theology, 28,* 21-35.

Smedes, L. B. (1996). *The art of forgiving: When you need to forgive and don't know how.* Nashville, TN: Moorings.

Stillwell, A. M., & Baumeister, R. F. (1997). The construction of victim and perpetrator memories: Accuracy and distortion in role-based accounts. *Personality and Social Psychology Bulletin, 23,* 1157-1172.

Volf, M. (1999). Original crime, primal care. In L. B. Lampman & M. D. Shattuck (Eds.), *God and the victim: Theological reflections on evil, victimization, justice, and forgiveness.* Grand Rapids, MI: Eerdmans, 17-35.

Vrana, S. R., & Lang, P. J. (1990). Fear imagery and the startle-probe reflex. *Journal of Abnormal Psychology, 99,* 189-197.

Weiner, B., Graham, S., Peter, O., & Zmuidinas, M. (1991). Public confession and forgiveness. *Journal of Personality, 59,* 281-312.

Witvliet, C. V. O., & Vrana, S. R. (1995). Psychophysiological responses as indices of affective dimensions. *Psychophysiology, 32,* 436-443.

Witvliet, C. V. O., & Vrana, S. R. (2000). Emotional imagery, the visual startle, and covariation bias: An affective matching account. *Biological Psychology, 52,* 187-204.

Witvliet, C. V. O., Ludwig, T. E., & Vander Laan, K. L. (2001). Granting forgiveness or harboring grudges: Implications for emotion, physiology, and health. *Psychological Science, 12,* 117-123.

Worthington, E. L., Jr. (1998). Empirical research in forgiveness: Looking backward, looking forward. In E. L. Worthington, Jr. (Ed.), *Dimensions of forgiveness.* Philadelphia, PA: Templeton Foundation Press, 321-339.

Being a Good Neighbor: Can Students Come to Value Homosexual Persons?

Rodney L. Bassett
Marike van Nikkelen-Kuyper
Deanna Johnson
Ashley Miller
Anna Carter
Julia P. Grimm
Roberts Wesleyan College

Attitudes toward gay/lesbian persons and behavior were initially assessed among Christian college students. Students with either uniformly positive or negative attitudes toward homosexual persons and behavior were then exposed to psychological and spiritual interventions designed to help them see more clearly the value of homosexual persons. Attitudes toward homosexual persons and behavior were then reassessed immediately after the intervention and one month later. Generally, the intervention improved attitudes toward homosexual persons. The picture for attitudes toward homosexual behavior was more complicated. With students who were uniformly rejecting, the intervention made their attitudes toward homosexual behavior less rejecting. However, with students who were uniformly accepting, the intervention diminished their acceptance of gay/lesbian behavior.

Christ was clear, when making the Good Samaritan (Luke 10:30-37) prototypic for being a "good neighbor," that people of faith should value everyone. In the Kingdom of God, there is no "colored section." Yet, in our culture, when it comes to the issue of sexual orientation, it can be argued that homonegativism and perhaps homophobia are pervasive (e.g., Kite & Whitley, 1996). Even within many Christian cultures, the issue of sexual orientation has become emotionally loaded and divisive (Olson & Cadge, 2002; Tapia, 1993). Often, Christians claim to make the distinction between valuing homosexual persons while rejecting homosexual behavior. Yet, some Christians are simply prejudiced when it comes to gay and lesbian persons (Bassett, et al., 2000). The label of "gay" or "lesbian" seems to blind them to the value of some persons. Attempting to be faithful to Christ's commands about "good neighbors," is it possible to encourage prejudiced Christians to be better neighbors toward gay and lesbian persons?

Becoming good neighbors for prejudiced individuals will require a change in attitude. One factor that may help to reduce prejudice toward gay and lesbian persons by heterosexuals is simple contact. Span and Vidal (2003) reported that among undergraduate students the number of homosexual friends was inversely related to levels of homophobia. Admittedly, as the 'friendship' measure and

contact theory (Farley, 1982) suggest, simple contact may not be sufficient to reduce prejudice. The conditions of contact may require such things as equal status or working toward common goals for the reduction of prejudice (Lance, 2002).

Researchers have considered other factors that seem to reduce prejudice against gay and lesbian persons. Embracing biological explanations for homosexuality (Altemeyer, 2001; Landen & Innala, 2002), attending human sexuality classes (Cerny & Polyson, 1984; Serdahely & Ziemba, 1984), listening to a class guest speaker who is identified as homosexual (Pagtolun-An & Clair, 1986), exposure to a peer panel of gay and lesbian students (Nelson & Krieger, 1997), and watching films addressing issues of prejudice in general and homosexuality in particular (Goldberg, 1982) have all been shown to reduce prejudice against gay and lesbian persons. For example, the film intervention by Goldberg consisted of showing a film addressing prejudicial issues across a variety of groups, a film of a homosexual clergyman discussing issues related to homosexuality, or two films presenting sexually explicit behavior between same-sex couples. Goldberg reported that students who watched the general film and the film of the homosexual clergyman self-reported greater tolerance toward homosexuality than students who watched the sexually explicit films.

But, understanding and treating prejudice towards gay and lesbian persons may be more complex than the above discussion implies. One consideration in understanding the issue of prejudice against gay and lesbian persons is the issue of religiousness. Apparently, traditional or conservative Christian beliefs predict homonegativism or homophobia (see Hinrichs & Rosenberg, 2002; Plugge-Foust, 2000). Yet, some have argued that this type of finding may be misleading (Bassett, et al., 2000; Bassett, et al., 2002). Measures of prejudice may not take into consideration distinctions that are commonly made in the Christian community when considering the issue of homosexuality. Typically, Christians feel called to affirm the value of all persons. However, when people act in ways that violate perceived Christian values, a common position embraced by many Christians is to affirm the value of that person but reject the value of the behavior. In other words, the Christian will "love the sinner, but hate the sin." Measures of attitudes that gloss over this distinction between persons and behavior for homosexuality may distort how Christians really feel about gay and lesbian persons.

Adding another wrinkle to the issue of prejudice against gay and lesbian persons may be individuals' desire to control prejudicial reactions toward gay and lesbian persons. In the context of racial prejudice, Fazio and his colleagues (Fazio, Jackson, Dunton, & Williams, 1995) developed an instrument to measure this desire to control prejudicial reactions. Bassett, Angelov, Mack, Monfort, & Monroe (2003) have reported an effort to modify this scale to assess the desire to control prejudicial reactions toward gay and lesbian persons. The product of this effort was an instrument that seemed to tap three basic factors: (a) desire to control prejudicial reactions toward gay and lesbian persons, (b) intolerance for gay and lesbian persons, and (c) valuing gay and lesbian persons. It is obvious these three factors may moderate the impact of any efforts to modify prejudicial attitudes toward gay and lesbian persons.

In an effort to combine all of the above issues, we designed a pretest/posttest study. The pretest included a measure of attitudes toward gay and lesbian persons. This measure made it possible to assess attitudes toward homosexual persons separate from attitudes toward homosexual behavior. We used this measure to identify students who were accepting of homosexual persons and behavior and students who were rejecting of homosexual persons and behavior. In addition, we included in the pretest the Bassett et al. (2003) measure designed to assess motivation to control prejudicial attitudes toward gay and lesbian persons. We then introduced interventions designed to enhance attitudes toward gay and lesbian persons that were based upon psychological and spiritual concepts. We followed these interventions with the same measures that were used in the pretest (immediately following the intervention and about one month later). Our prediction was that the intervention would enhance attitudes toward homosexual persons but not homosexual behavior for those students who were initially rejecting of both.

METHOD

Participants

Students were recruited from a variety of psychology classes at a Christian liberal arts college. Those students who were invited to participate in the study were those who had indicated on an earlier questionnaire that they rejected homosexual persons and homosexual behavior (e.g., *universally rejecting*), or that they accepted homosexual persons and homosexual behavior (e.g., *universally accepting*). Of those students invited to participate, 56 signed-up for a one-hour session where they understood they would be watching video clips and reading scripture that addressed issues like sexual orientation. Of these students, 48 (86%) actually attended one of the sessions. Of the individuals that attended, 38 students were included in the final sample for the study. The reduction in sample size from 48 to 38 was a function of two things: (a) not all the students who signed-up for the study met the criterion of being *universally rejecting* or *universally accepting* (see below for the criteria), and (b) some students were randomly dropped from the sample to create an equal n for both groups.

The 38 students included in the final sample, had the following characteristics: (a) average age = 19.6 years; (b) 22 (57.9%) were female; and (c) 20 (52.6%) were first year students, 12 (31.6%) were sophomores, 5 (13.2%) were juniors, and one student did not indicate class status. In addition, in response to the statement, "I am a Christian," the average response was 7.8 on a 9-point scale (9 = "strongly agree").

Questionnaire

At the beginning of the semester, a questionnaire containing several randomly ordered surveys was given to students in a variety of psychology classes at a Christian liberal arts college. Students received a small amount of class extra credit for anonymously responding to the questionnaire. One of the surveys included within the questionnaire was the Sexual Orientation and Practice (SOAP) scale. The SOAP scale largely reflects the work of Rod Bassett and

Christopher Rosik (see Bassett et al., 2003). The instrument contains three subscales: (a) attitudes toward single homosexuals who are sexually active (*sexually active homosexuals*), (b) attitudes toward single homosexuals who are voluntarily celibate (celibate homosexuals), and (c) attitudes toward single heterosexuals who are sexually active (*sexually active heterosexuals*). Each subscale contains 5 items that have participants evaluate the target person in a particular context. For example, "I would attend the performance of a person whom I knew was a sexually active homosexual." Participants respond to each item on a 9-point Likert-type scale (1 = "strongly disagree" and 9 = "strongly agree"). Bassett et al. reported respectable Cronbach's *alphas* for the three subscales ranging from .75 to .84. Comparison of the homosexual and sexually active subscale with the homosexual and celibate subscale makes it possible to differentiate between the valuing of homosexual persons and the valuing of homosexual behavior.

Another survey within the questionnaire was the Motivation to Control Attitudes scale developed by Bassett et al. (2003). This survey represents a modification of the Motivation to Control Prejudiced Reactions Scale (Dunton & Fazio, 1997). The original scale was designed to measure someone's desire to control prejudicial racial attitudes. The modification by Bassett et al. changed the focus of the scale to sexual orientation. The resulting modification produced a 19-item scale with a Likert-type 9-point response format (1 = "strongly disagree" and 9 = "strongly agree"). Principal components analysis with a Varimax rotation revealed the items tapped three basic factors: (a) desire to control prejudicial reactions toward gay and lesbian persons, (b) intolerance for gay and lesbian persons, and (c) valuing gay and lesbian persons.

Procedures

About two months after responding to the initial questionnaire, some students were invited to participate in the intervention study. The invitation to participate was a function of how students responded to the SOAP scale. A median-split was performed on the distribution of average scores for the subscale measuring attitudes toward single homosexual individuals who were sexually active and the subscale measuring attitudes toward single homosexual individuals who were voluntarily celibate. A group of students who were identified as universally rejecting had average scores that were above 3.2 on the sexually active subscale and above 4.6 on the celibate subscale (1 = greatest acceptance, 9 = greatest rejection). Another group of students were identified as universally accepting who have average values below the medians for both subscales. On the original questionnaire, students had also indicated their mother's maiden name and their own birthday. That information was included for both student groups on sign-up lists that were circulated through the classes that had responded to the original questionnaire. Those students identified by their mother's maiden name and their birthdays were then invited to sign-up for the intervention phase of the study. Participation in this phase produced a small amount of class extra credit.

Up to six students could sign-up for a particular one-hour time slot. On the sign-up sheet, students provided their first name and a phone number where they could be reached. Students were called the night before their scheduled participation to remind them of the time and location for the study. When students arrived for the study, they were greeted by one of four student researchers who were not aware of whether the students were universally rejecting or accepting of homosexuals (a mixture of students from both groups signed-up for each session). As students arrived, they were invited to take seats at a large conference table where it would be difficult for them to observe the written work of others.

When all of the students arrived for a particular session, the researcher began by thanking them for participating in the study. The researcher then explained that the first activity would involve watching four scenes from the movie, *As Good as it Gets* (Brooks & Andrus, 1997). The researcher would provide the background for each scene and then the students would simply watch that scene. The scenes included: (a) a gay man (Simon) being brutalized by burglars, (b) Simon talking with friends in the hospital as he realized the extent of his injuries, (c) Simon discussing with two friends a childhood experience that lead to estrangement from his father, and (d) Simon encouraging his roommate (Melvin) to develop a relationship with a female friend. These particular video segments were selected because they tended to emphasize the humanness of Simon (the gay character in the film). These judgments were made by the researchers (four undergraduate students, a social psychologist, and a counseling psychologist). The total time spent watching the video clip (along with the brief descriptions of the context for each video clip provided by the researcher) was about 10 minutes.

The second activity involved the students reading passages of scripture and then writing out their reactions to those passages. The specific instructions on the cover page were as follows:

Jesus showed love and great concern for people who thought and acted differently. On the following pages are passages of scripture. After reading each set of passages please write down your personal reflections in the space provided. Please expand on your thoughts as much as possible. In your reflections think about how the passages can be applied to your actions and attitudes toward people who are gay or lesbian.

The following three pages were randomly ordered for each student and consisted of a title/theme and passages of scripture (passages were taken from *The Message* [Peterson, 2002] translation of the Bible) at the top with room for written responses on the rest of the page (students were encouraged to continue their thoughts on the back of the page if needed). The three pages were: (a) *Living Love* (1 Peter 4:8; Matthew 5:46-47; Matthew 25:35, 37-38, 40; and John 13:34), (b) *Living Acceptance* (Matthew 9:10-12; John 4:7,9; John 8:3-4, 7, 10-11; and Romans 14:10), and (c) *Living Peaceably* (Titus 3:1-5).

The final activity involved students responding to the SOAP scale. With all of the written materials, the only identifying information was the student's mother's maiden name, the student's birthday, and a participant number. This information allowed us to connect information from each student while protecting the identity of the student.

The intervention phase of the study took a week to complete. About a month later, all students from the various psychology classes were invited to anonymously respond to the SOAP scale (the only identifying information on the survey was mother's maiden name and student's birthday along with basic demographic information like gender and year in school). This allowed us to determine the endurance of any effects from the intervention phase of the study. Thirty (15 from each group) of the original participants responded to this second post intervention measure.

Results

Because only thirty of the 38 participants in the intervention process responded to the second post intervention measure, the attitude (SOAP) data was analyzed using a series of mixed model ANOVAs. For each attitude object (*celibate homosexuals, sexually active homosexuals,* and *sexually active heterosexuals*) two mixed model ANOVAs were performed. The 2 x 2 ANOVAs considered attitudes for *universally accepting* and *universally rejecting* students at the

pretest and the initial posttest. The 2 x 3 ANOVAs added the second posttest to the analyses. The means for all these analyses are presented in Table 1.

Looking at attitudes toward *celibate homosexuals*, a 2 x 2 mixed model ANOVA (n = 19 for both groups of students) revealed a main effect for student group, $F(1, 36) = 88.85$, $p \leq .001$. *Universally rejecting* students had more negative attitudes than *universally accepting* students (5.82 vs. 2.69). There was also a main effect for testing time, $F(1, 36) = 15.28$, $p \leq .001$. Attitudes before the intervention were more negative than attitudes immediately following the intervention (4.67 vs. 3.85). However, both main effects were qualified by a significant interaction, $F(1, 36) = 6.75$, $p \leq .05$. There was a tendency for all students to be more accepting of *celibate homosexuals* following the intervention. But, this trend was more dramatic for universally rejecting students than for *universally accepting* students (see Table 1).

Adding the second posttest to this data created a 2 x 3 ANOVA (n = 15 for both groups of students). Again, the main effect for student group was significant, $F(1, 28) = 55.14$, $p \leq .001$. *Universally rejecting students* still had more negative attitudes than *universally accepting* students (5.60 vs. 2.83). There was also a main effect for testing time (Linear: $F[1, 28] = 6.56$, $p \leq .05$; Quadratic: $F[1, 28] = 11.12$, $p \leq .01$). Attitudes became more positive immediately after the intervention (4.78 vs. 3.87) but then shifted back toward the original position with the second post measure (3.99). Again, these main effects were qualified by a significant interaction (Quadratic: $F[5.27] = 5.27$, $p \leq .05$). This tendency, across measurement times, to become more positive and then somewhat drift back, was more dramatic for *universally rejecting* students than for *universally accepting* students (see Table 1).

Considering attitudes toward *sexually active homosexuals*, a 2 x 2 mixed model ANOVA (n = 19 for both groups of students) revealed a main effect for student group, $F(1, 36) = 70.17$, $p \leq .001$. *Universally rejecting* students had more negative attitudes than *universally accepting* students (4.48 vs. 2.18). However, this main effect was qualified by a significant interaction, $F(1, 36) = 6.24$, $p \leq .05$. Following the intervention, *universally rejecting* students showed increased acceptance of sexually active homosexuals while *universally accepting* students showed decreased acceptance (see Table 1).

Adding the second posttest to the design for this data produced a 2 x 3 mixed model ANOVA (n = 15 for both groups of students). Again, there was a significant main effect for student group, $F(1, 28) = 28.00$, $p \leq .001$. Generally, *universally rejecting*

Table 1

*Mean Attitude Scores of Participants Who Were Universally Accepting
and Universally Rejecting of Homosexual Individuals*

	Attitudes Toward Celibate Homosexual Individuals		
	Pretest	1st Posttest	2nd Posttest
Universally Rejecting	**6.51**(6.56)	**5.15**(5.03)	(5.23)
Universally Accepting	**2.83**(3.00)	**2.56**(2.72)	(2.76)

Mean values could range from 1 to 9 with 9 indicating greatest rejection. The participants who responded to only the pretest and the initial posttest produced bold values. Participants who responded to all three measures produced values in parentheses.

	Attitudes Toward Sexually Active Homosexual Individuals		
	Pretest	1st Posttest	2nd Posttest
Universally Rejecting	**4.77**(4.77)	**4.19**(3.89)	(4.24)
Universally Accepting	**2.03**(2.13)	**2.33**(2.47)	(2.92)

	Attitudes Toward Sexually Active Heterosexual Individuals		
	Pretest	1st Posttest	2nd Posttest
Universally Rejecting	**4.00**(3.79)	**3.76**(3.34)	(3.20)
Universally Accepting	**2.89**(2.81)	**2.57**(2.61)	(2.47)

students had more negative attitudes toward sexually active homosexuals than *universally accepting* students (4.30 vs. 2.51). There also was a significant interaction between student group and time of measurement (Linear: $F(1, 28]$ = 9.21, $p \leq$ .005). *Universally accepting* students demonstrated diminished acceptance across the three measurement times. *Universally rejecting* showed diminished rejection following the intervention and then a return to greater rejection with the final measurement (see Table 1).

Looking at attitudes toward sexually active heterosexuals, a 2 x 2 mixed model ANOVA (n = 19 for both groups of students) only revealed a main effect for student group, $F(1, 36)$ = 8.50, $p \leq$ .01. Universally rejecting students had more negative

attitudes than universally accepting students (3.87 vs. 2.73). Expanding the design by adding the second posttest and creating a mixed model 2 x 3 ANOVA (n = 14 for the universally rejecting students and 15 for the universally accepting students), again produced only a significant main effect for group, $F(1, 27)$ = 4.48, $p \leq$ .05. Universally rejecting students were less accepting of sexually active heterosexuals than universally accepting students (3.44 vs. 2.64).

Finally, the design of the study allowed for the consideration of the role of participants' motivation to control prejudicial attitudes toward gay and lesbian persons at three points in the intervention process (pretest, 1st posttest, and 2nd posttest). The scale designed to assess this motivation was included in the initial questionnaire and contained three subscales: (a) desire to control prejudicial reactions toward gay and lesbian persons (*desire to control*), (b) intolerance for gay and lesbian persons (*intolerance*), and (c) valuing gay and lesbian persons (*valuing*). Comparison of the *universally rejecting* and the *universally accepting* students on these three subscales revealed some interesting patterns. A one-way ANOVA revealed significant differences between the two groups of students (*n* = 18 for *universally rejecting*, *n* = 19 for *universally accepting*) for the subscale measuring *desire to control* prejudicial reactions toward gay and lesbian persons, $F(1, 35) = 12.52$, $p \le .001$. *Universally rejecting* students showed less of a *desire to control* than *universally accepting* students (means = 5.86 vs. 7.08 with greatest desire to control prejudicial reactions = "9"). In addition, a one-way ANOVA revealed another difference between the two groups of students (*n* = 19 for both groups) regarding *intolerance* for gay and lesbian persons, $F(1, 36) = 28.27$, $p \le .001$. *Universally rejecting* students showed greater *intolerance* than *universally accepting* students (means = 6.32 vs. 3.58 with greatest intolerance = "9"). However, there was no difference between the two groups of students regarding the *valuing* of gay and lesbian persons (means = 7.64 and 7.37).

Looking at the relationship between the subscales for the Motivation to Control Attitudes Scale and the SOAP scales the researchers calculated correlations across all three measurement opportunities. Those correlations are presented in Table 2. Considering this table, several general trends stand out. First, *desire to control* prejudicial reactions predicted diminished rejection for *celibate homosexuals, sexually active homosexuals*, and *sexually active heterosexuals*. Albeit, the trend seemed most clear for *celibate homosexuals*. Second, *intolerance* for gay and lesbian persons predicted increased rejection for both categories of homosexual individuals. Again, this trend was stronger for *celibate homosexuals*. Third, *valuing* gay and lesbian persons did not predict any of the SOAP measures. Finally, the trends for *desire to control* and *intolerance* seemed to be muted by the intervention (the correlations were smaller for the 1st posttest).

To consider the connection between the three Motivation to Control Attitudes subscales and the effectiveness of the intervention, change scores were calculated. For each student, the posttest attitude score toward celibate homosexuals was subtracted from the pretest attitude score. As a result, larger positive change scores indicated increased acceptance after the intervention. Larger negative change scores indicated increased rejection after the intervention. In the same manner, change scores were calculated for attitudes toward sexually active homosexuals. Collapsing together all the students who participated in the intervention, correlations were calculated between the three subscales and the two change scores. Between the subscales and the change scores, there were two significant correlations. There was a significant inverse relationship between desire to control prejudicial reactions and the change in attitude toward celibate homosexuals, $r(36) = -.38$, $p \le .05$. Higher levels of desire to control prejudicial reactions toward gay and lesbian persons predicted increased rejection of celibate homosexuals following the intervention. There was a significant direct relationship between intolerance for gay and lesbian persons and change in attitude toward celibate homosexuals, $r(37) = .38$, $p \le .05$. Higher levels of intolerance predicted greater acceptance of celibate homosexual individuals following the intervention. Looking within the two groups of students suggested that both these trends were more characteristic of the universally rejecting students (desire to control, $r[17] = -.57$, $p \le .05$; intolerance, $r[18] = .37$, n.s.) than the universally accepting students (desire to control, $r[18] = .25$, n.s.; intolerance, $r[18] = .00$, n.s.). There were no significant correlations between the three subscales and change in attitude toward sexually active homosexuals. However, when all the students were combined there was a significant direct relationship between the change scores for attitudes toward celibate homosexuals and the change scores for attitudes toward sexually active homosexuals, $r(37) = .47$, $p \le .01$.

Discussion

Students who rejected homosexual persons and behavior and students who accepted homosexual persons and behavior participated in an intervention. The intervention consisted of: (a) exposing students, in a salutary fashion, to a gay man through the medium of film, and (b) having students contemplate passages of scripture that emphasized the value of persons regardless of those persons' behaviors. This intervention was then followed by two posttests that allowed students to differentiate between the value of homosexual persons and homosexual behavior.

Immediately following the intervention attitudes toward homosexual persons (*celibate homosexuals*) became more positive. This trend was most dramatic for those students who were initially *universally rejecting*. About a month later, there was somewhat of a trend for these attitudes to drift back to their original position, but for *universally rejecting* students this shift back was quite minimal.

Table 2

Significant Correlations Between the Motivation to Control Attitudes Subscales and the SOAP Subscales

SOAP Subscales	Desire to Control	Intolerance	Valuing
Pretest			
Celibate Homosexuals	-.61***	.70***	
Sexually Active Homosexuals	-.58***	.60***	
Sexually Active Heterosexuals	-.42**		
1st Posttest			
Celibate Homosexuals	-.45**	.57***	
Sexually Active Homosexuals	-.46**	.46**	
Sexually Active Heterosexuals	-.42**		
2nd Posttest			
Celibate Homosexuals	-.57***	.62***	
Sexually Active Homosexuals		.38*	
Sexually Active Heterosexuals			

*Significant at $p \leq .05$ **Significant at $p \leq .01$ ***Significant at $p \leq .001$

Following the intervention, attitudes toward homosexual behavior (*sexually active homosexuals*) showed very different patterns for the two groups of students. *Universally rejecting* students showed increased acceptance of homosexual behavior while *universally accepting* students showed decreased acceptance of homosexual behavior. About a month later, this decreased acceptance for *universally accepting* students continued while the increased acceptance for *universally rejecting* students leveled off.

Apparently, the intervention worked. But, how it worked depended upon the group of students and the attitude object. With *universally rejecting* students, the intervention produced less negative attitudes toward homosexual persons and homosexual behavior. Albeit, the change in attitude toward homosexual persons was more than double the change for homosexual behavior. With *universally accepting* students, the intervention seemed to have more of an effect upon attitudes toward homosexual behavior than homosexual persons. The trend, across both post measurement times, was diminished acceptance of homosexual behavior. The students who attend the college where this study was conducted often come from conservative Christian backgrounds. It may have been that the scriptural inter-

vention reoriented some of those students to a more traditional Christian view of homosexual behavior.

An evaluation of how *well* this intervention worked really hinges on two issues: (a) did the intervention have an effect?, and (b) was the effect in the desired direction? From the above conclusions, the answer to the first issue seems to be "yes." However, the answer to the second probably depends upon what is perceived as "ideal." If ideal means making a distinction between the value of homosexual persons and homosexual behavior, then the intervention seems to have worked well for both groups of students. But, if ideal is perceived as a greater openness to the value of homosexual persons and homosexual behavior, then the intervention worked less well (especially for the *universally accepting* students and homosexual behavior).

The trends for subscales from the Motivation to Control Attitudes Scale were also interesting. Generally, desire to control prejudicial attitudes toward gay and lesbian persons predicted less rejection of homosexual persons and behavior. Intolerance toward gay and lesbian persons generally predicted the exact opposite pattern. However, for both subscales these tendencies (especially toward the value of homosexual persons) were dampened immediately after the intervention.

Apparently, the intervention moderated the predictive value of *desire to control* and *intolerance* in regards to attitudes toward homosexual persons.

The nature of the relationship between the two subscales (*desire to control* and *intolerance*) and the attitude change scores (pretest vs. initial posttest) is more complicated. The positive correlation between the change in attitude for *sexually active homosexuals* and the change in attitude for *celibate homosexuals* makes sense if changes in attitude toward homosexual persons were related to changes in attitude toward homosexual behavior. And, the positive correlation between *intolerance* and change in attitude to homosexual persons makes sense if the intervention (which included contemplating scripture) was especially effective with students who were intolerant of homosexual persons because of religious reasons. However, what made less sense was the negative correlation between *desire to control* and change in attitudes toward homosexual persons. Why would students who initially reported a greater desire to control prejudicial reactions toward gay and lesbian persons demonstrate less improvement in their attitudes toward homosexual persons (more acceptance and/or less rejection) after the intervention? Perhaps the answer lies not in students who were high in *desire to control* but in those students who were low in *desire to control*. For those students who were initially high in *desire to control,* our intervention may have been akin to "preaching to the choir." However, for those students who were initially low in *desire to control,* our interventions may have opened their eyes to the value of homosexual persons. Thus, the significant negative correlation may have been more a function of people low in *desire to control* being affected by our intervention than people high in desire to control resisting our intervention. Consistent with this line of reasoning was the tendency for this pattern to be most robust for the *universally rejecting* students (the ones for whom we most hoped to open their eyes to the value of homosexual persons).

Another curious finding was the tendency on the pretest for *sexually active homosexuals* to be more accepted than *celibate homosexuals*. A repeated measures ANOVA across both groups of students revealed that this trend was statistically significant, $F(1, 37) = 37.29$, $p \leq .001$. Both groups of students initially viewed *sexually active homosexuals* in a more positive light (mean = 3.40) than *celibate homosexuals* (mean = 4.67). This was somewhat confusing since the descriptions for these categories indicated that the decision for celibacy was anchored in ethical considerations. Presumably, people who anchored their decisions about sexual behavior in ethical considerations would have been perceived in a more positive light than other people of the same sexual orientation for whom ethical considerations were not mentioned. Yet, our choice of the term "celibate" may have had an unintended consequence for some of our students. In the last few years, the Catholic Church has struggled with accusations that some priests have violated their vows of celibacy by having same-sex relations with young parishioners. These accusations have received widespread publicity. Could it be that, for some of our students, using the term "celibate homosexuals" created an unintended connection with this priestly scandal within the Catholic Church? If so, then perhaps our intervention was even more powerful than we anticipated. Not only did it work for "average" individuals, but it also worked for individuals who have been stigmatized in the media.

When considering future research directions, several possibilities come to mind. First, our methodology left unresolved the question of what was the active ingredient that made the intervention work. Was it watching the film segments? Was it contemplating the passages of scripture? Or, was it some combination of the two? Second, our methodology could be easily exported. Would the intervention work with other age groups? Would the intervention work with other branches of the Christian family tree (our students were largely conservative Protestants)? Third, what effect would our intervention have upon people who were *selectively accepting*? Some individuals respond to the SOAP scale in such a way as to indicate relative rejection of homosexual behavior but relative acceptance of homosexual persons. Would their response to the intervention be like that of *universally rejecting* students, *universally accepting* students, or would they plot their own course in response to the intervention? And finally, our project focused upon the impact of our intervention upon explicit attitudes toward homosexual persons and behavior. However, the current popularity of dual-process models in social psychology (see Chaiken and Trope, 1999) raises the issue of implicit attitudes. In addition to affecting thoughtful conscious reactions toward homosexual persons and behavior, would our interventions also affect reactions that are more automatic and unconscious?

References

Altemeyer, B. (2001). Changes in attitudes toward homosexuals. *Journal of Homosexuality, 42*, 63-75.

Bassett, R. L., Angelov, A. B., Mack, W. J. A., Monfort, K., & Monroe, J. (June, 2003). *Spontaneous and deliberative attitudes toward gay and lesbian persons among Christian college students.* Paper presented at the annual meeting of the Christian Association for Psychological Studies, Anaheim, CA.

Bassett, R. L., Hodak, E., Allen, J., Bartos, D., Grastorf, J., Sittig, L., & Strong, J. (2000). Homonegative Christians: Loving the sinner but hating the sin? *Journal of Psychology and Christianity, 19,* 258-269.

Bassett, R. L., Baldwin, D., Tammaro, J., Mackmer, D., Mundig, C., Wareing, A., & Tschorke, D. (2002). Reconsidering intrinsic religion as a source of universal compassion. *Journal of Psychology and Theology, 30,* 131-143.

Brooks, J. L. (Producer/Director), & Andrus, M. (Writer). (1997). *As Good as it Gets* [Motion picture]. United States: Gracie Films & TriStar Pictures.

Cerny, J. A., & Polyson, J. (1984). Changing homonegative attitudes. *Journal of Social and Clinical Psychology, 2,* 366-371.

Chaiken, S., & Trope, Y. (Eds.). (1999). *Dual-process theories in social psychology.* New York: The Guilford Press.

Dunton, B. C., & Fazio, R. H. (1997). An individual difference measure of motivation to control prejudiced reactions. *Personality and Social Psychology Bulletin, 23,* 316-326.

Farley, J. (1982). *Majority-minority relations.* Upper Saddle River, NJ: Prentice-Hall, Inc.

Fazio, R. H., Jackson, J. R., Dunton, B. C., & Williams, C. J. (1995). Variability in automatic activation as an unobtrusive measure of racial attitudes: A bona fide pipeline? *Journal of Personality and Social Psychology, 69,* 1013-1027.

Goldberg, R. (1982). Attitude change among college students toward homosexuality. *Journal of American College Health, 30,* 260-268.

Hinrichs, D. W., & Rosenberg, P. J. (2002). Attitudes toward gay, lesbian, and bisexual persons among heterosexual liberal arts college students. *Journal of Homosexuality, 43,* 61-84.

Kite, M. E., & Whitley, B. E. J. (1996). Sex differences in attitudes toward homosexual persons, behaviors and civil rights: A meta-analysis. *Personality and Social Psychology Bulletin, 22,* 336-352.

Lance, L. M. (2002). Heterosexism and homophobia among college students. *College Student Journal, 36,* 410-414.

Landen, M., & Innala, S. (2002). The effect of a biological explanation on attitudes towards homosexual persons: A Swedish national sample study. *Nordic Journal of Psychiatry, 56,* 181-186.

Nelson, E. S., & Krieger, S. L. (1997). Changes in attitudes toward homosexuality in college students: Implementation of a gay men and lesbian peer panel. *Journal of Homosexuality, 33,* 63-81.

Olson, L. R., & Cadge, W. (2002). Talking about homosexuality: The views of mainline protestant clergy. *Journal for the Scientific Study of Religion, 41,* 153-167.

Pagtolun-An, I. G., & Clair, J. M. (1986). An experimental study of attitudes toward homosexuals. *Deviant Behavior, 7,* 121-135.

Peterson, E. H. (2002). *The message: The bible in contemporary language.* Colorado Springs, CO: Navpress.

Plugge-Foust, C. (2000). Homophobia, irrationality, and Christian ideology: Does a relationship exist? *Journal of Sex Education & Therapy, 25,* 240-244.

Serdahely, W., & Ziemba, G. J. (1984). Changing homophobic attitudes through college sexuality education. *Journal of Homosexuality, 10,* 109-116.

Span, S.A., & Vidal, L.A. (2003). Cross-cultural differences in female university students' attitudes toward homosexuals: A preliminary study. *Psychological Reports, 92,* 565-572.

Tapia, A. (1993, November 22). Homosexuality debate strains campus harmony: Homosexuals at Christian colleges press for acceptance. *Christianity Today,* pp. 38-40.

Postscript: What's Next?

As we conclude our retrospective of key integrative scholarship over these last five decades, it seems natural to cast our gaze forward. Our celebration encompasses the work and joy of what has been and what will be.

In many ways, the psychology/theology integration movement reflects the historical developments which have occurred over the past 50 years in the disciplines of psychology, theology, and philosophy, but it has also had its own unique historical contexts, challenges, and focal points. The initial 1954 gathering of a few pastors, theologians, and mental health practitioners, all representing a single theological tradition, has expanded worldwide to encompass the interests of Christian psychologists and psychologically-minded scholars from multiple theological traditions. The current state of the integration enterprise is, at best, a loosely organized body of scholarship. It describes the process for relating the knowledge derived from the scientific study of psychology with the knowledge derived from theological methods and the Scriptures. Although we see much progress in these past 50 years, there is still much work to do.

Now we look ahead. Making predictions about the future is as popular as creating lists of the "greatest" or "best" in any field. A Google search of "the next 50 years" produced over 247 million entries. Narrowing the search to "the next 50 years in psychology" produced over 16 million entries and a search of the "next 50 years in theology" produced just under 5 million entries. *The Journal of Clinical Psychology* and *Christianity Today* produced special issues with predictions for the future in psychology and theology, respectively.

Before getting too caught up in speculating and predicting developments for the next 50, let us remember some of the broad cultural predictions made 50 years ago at the time CAPS started. In 1950, *Popular Mechanics* (February, 1950) published a special issue identifying some of the miracles we would see in the next 50 years. They predicted correctly that we would be cooking meals in minutes and shopping over the television via phone lines. But they incorrectly predicted that we would all be commuting to work in our private helicopters and that houses would be cleaned with a hose because they would be completely made out of plastic.

With this moderate track record of accurate predictions in mind, accompanied by appropriate humility and trepidation, some trends are reasonably predictable about the future of integration. Gathering invited comments from our Advisory Board and from authors in the winter 2006 Anniversary Issue of the *Journal of Psychology and Christianity*, we venture to speculate about a number of external and internal trends that will be influential on integration's course.

External Influences on Integration

Postmodernism

Perhaps the most powerful and least fully defined influence on the future will be postmodernism. Jim Olthuis (1999) identifies several characteristics of postmodernism including these: a move away from grand unified theories toward more particularistic-individualist models, from seeking closure and assuming finitude to accepting open-ended ambiguity, from uniformity and sameness to diversity and difference, and from expert knowledge to more inter-subjective and relational ways of knowing. In assessing the effects of postmodernism for integration, John Ingram (1995) suggests there will be more local, small scale, and interpersonal models of integration, a greater acceptance of multi-perspectival analysis and procedures, and an increase in the plurality of voices, especially from those who have been marginalized and disenfranchised. For the future of integration this means there will be an increasing focus on working to unite a psychological modality with a theological tradition. It also requires a developing awareness of the cultural embeddedness of integration, and through this, a greater acceptance of multiple definitions, processes, and perhaps even language for integration. Lastly, Ingram suggests that an increasingly pervasive postmodern mindset will lead to a more personal, embodied integration with a greater focus on faith/praxis and personal/experiential integration (e.g. practicing spiritual disciplines and spiritual formation).

Multiculturalism

The role of culture in model-making and psychological understanding is recognized now not only as a part of the broader postmodern view, but it is also a given in the social science disciplines. From its roots in a group of Caucasian, male, Dutch, Reformed, academicians, the integration enterprise has broadened considerably. Still, it remains a body of literature largely shaped and guided by Caucasian, male, Protestant, North American clinicians and academicians. In the 25th anniversary issue of the *Journal of Psychology and Christianity* published in December, 2006, Yangarber-Hicks, Behensky, Schwer Canning, Gibson, Plante, and Porter continue a dialogue begun in a special issue of the same journal in 2001, which attempts to give voice to those underrepresented in the integration literature. The future of integration ought to include a greater range of voices from women, cultural minorities, non-clinicians, and international perspective to avoid the irony of tolerating separate silos of thought in a literature labeled integrative. Hopefully, this will lead to a greater acceptance and tolerance of dialogue that engages our differences rather than splinters integration into imperialistic or isolated divisions.

Developments in Theology

In the October 2006 issue of *Christianity Today*, their 50th anniversary special edition, they asked 114 ministry leaders and theologians "What's Next?" with regard to evangelical priorities for the coming 50 years. Among the issues that they identify are: the impact of the exploding growth of Christianity south of the equator and the concordant rise of interest in non-western theologies; the challenge of religious pluralism; the increasing rejection of religious authority; and the desperate need for theology to move out of the ivory tower and to make itself relevant to the life of the church and personal spiritual development. Some of these trends, such as an increased interest in relational theology, spiritual formation, and pastoral care, are already being reflected in the growing integration literature. One clear evidence of this trend in the last several years is the section, *Christian Spirituality and Mental Health*, published twice a year in the *Journal of Psychology and Christianity*. It is dedicated to giving voice to scholarship addressing research and thought about spirituality and spiritual formation.

Developments in Psychology

Psychology continues to be a rapidly developing discipline. Aided by new technologies, the frontiers of cognitive neuroscience, biopsychology, genetics, and psychopharmacology have exploded in recent years. As we develop an ever more detailed understanding of the human genome and brain, the effect and interplay of life experience on the expression or suppression of genetic predispositions and neural networks has made understanding the mind/body relationship ever more complex. For example, research on the development of mirror neurons seems to parallel previous ideas of Freud and Bowlby. The future of psychology appears to be not only more physiological and cognitive neuroscientific, but also one in which the modernistic assumptions of mechanistic determinism and dichotomous division between brain and mind begin to break down. The implications for the integration project are huge, as it leads to a more holistic, personalistic, and nondeterministic science of psychology that was called for long ago by Evans (1977) and Collins (1977). Our training programs must keep up with these trends by designing progressive curricula that meet the standards of a changing discipline and changing mental health delivery systems.

A second trend is the Positive Psychology movement that identifies the strengths and virtues which enables individuals and communities to thrive. With an underlying belief that people want to lead meaningful and fulfilling lives, they focus on how to enhance love, work, and play. The positive psychologists are researching such topics as contentment, happiness, hope, courage, compassion, resilience, creativity, integrity, moderation, self-control, and wisdom. Institutionally they are concerned with justice and responsibility (see http://www.ppc.sas.upenn.edu). Christian values and scriptural truth have something to say about each of these. Along with the existing research on gratitude and forgiveness, these should be exciting topics for future integrative research.

A final trend in the field of clinical psychology is the increasing emphasis on empirically-based and validated treatments. Integration's future, we firmly expect, will include increased reports of research on the effectiveness of integrative clinical interventions, following the lead of researchers like Worthington and his colleagues (Worthington & Sandage, 2002; Wade, Worthington, & Vogel, 2007).

Internal Influences on Integration

Expansion of the Religion and Science Interface

In the last decade, supported by funding from the Templeton and Lilly foundations, there have been increasing dialogue, research, and publications in the broader interface of religion and science. As this body of literature expands, it will impact our understanding of the religion/science interface and in turn, have the potential to broaden our conceptualization of integration and move us beyond the current clinically focused nature of the field. There will likely be new doctoral programs established for specialties other than clinical and counseling psychology.

Increased Integration Research

As identified in the introduction to section seven of this volume, there has been a lack of empirical or even solid qualitative research in integration. To date, much of the research on integration has tended to be survey research with the weaknesses inherent in that approach. The need for solid integration research will only grow in the coming years. This research will need to engage such issues as assessing the outcomes of integrated clinical approaches and exploring the themes of positive psychology (Myers, 2000), cognitive neuroscience (Jeeves, 2006), and biopsychology (Boivin, 2002) from a Christian perspective.

Increased Focus on Embodied Integration

A final trend, which relates to many of those previously mentioned, will be a greater focus on integration at the personal experiential level and of faith praxis. This trend of moving away from the abstract, meta-perspectives to integrated living and practice has already begun. McMinn (1996), Sorenson (1996a, 1996b), Moon (1997) and Langberg (2006), have all clearly identified the importance of the integrationist's character formation and journey with God to the future advancement of the integration movement.

Final Remarks

It has been a fruitful and exciting 50 years since CAPS was founded. The next 50 years hold the promise of unimagined advances in psychology, theology, and philosophy. Although many of the trends identified here appear to have already begun, the history of psychology would show that these trends may not hold course. Perhaps some of these predictions will appear archaic, from the perspective of hindsight, yet perhaps by 2050, we *will* be able to commute to our jobs in our personal helicopters. For now, however, we can be confident in anticipating that the integration enterprise will have an exciting future. As we look forward to the decades ahead, we must commit ourselves to producing sophisticated integrative scholarship that will impact the discipline of psychology at large and that reflects our collective Christian mind. Such a commitment extends from the original mission of CAPS and the broader biblical mandate to seek a fuller, deeper, and more unified understanding of God's creation.

References

Boivin, M. J. (2002). Finding God in prozac or finding prozac in God: Preserving a Christian view amidst a biopsychological revolution. *Christian Scholar's Review, 32*, 159-176.

Collins, G. R. (1977). *The rebuilding of psychology: An integration of psychology and Christianity*. Wheaton, IL: Tyndale.

Evans, C. S. (1977). *Preserving the person: A look at the human sciences*. Downers Grove. IL: InterVarsity Press.

Hansen, C. (2006). What's next: Theology. *Christianity Today, 50*, 75-76.

Ingram, J. A. (1995). Contemporary issues and Christian models of Integration: Into the modern/postmodern age. *Journal of Psychology and Theology, 23*, 3-14.

Jeeves, M. (2006) *Human nature: Reflections on the integration of psychology and Christianity*. Chicago: Templeton Foundation Press.

Journal of Psychology and Christianity, 25(4), December, 2006, 25th anniversary issue.

Kaempffert, W. (1950). Miracles you'll see in the next fifty years. *Popular Mechanics, 2*, 112-118, 264, 266, 270, 272.

Langberg, D. (2006). The spiritual life of the therapist: We become what we habitually reflect. *Journal of Psychology and Christianity, 25*, 258-266.

McMinn, M. R. (1996). *Psychology, theology, and spirituality in Christian counseling*. Wheaton, IL: Tyndale.

Moon, G. (1997). Training tomorrow's integrators in today's busy intersection: Better look four ways before crossing. *Journal of Psychology and Theology, 25*, 284-293.

Myers, D. G. (2000). The funds, friends, and faith of happy people. *American Psychologist, 55*, 56-67.

Olthuis, J. H. (1999). Dancing together in the wild spaces of love: Postmodernism, psychotherapy, and the spirit of God. *Journal of Psychology and Christianity, 18*, 140-152.

Seligman, M. E. P. (2006). *Positive Psychology Center*. Retrieved December 1, 2006, from http://www.ppc.sas.upenn.edu/

Sorenson, R. L. (1996a). Where are the nine? *Journal of Psychology and Theology, 24*, 179-195.

Sorenson, R. L. (1996b). The tenth leper. *Journal of Psychology and Theology, 24*, 197-211.

Wade, N. G., Worthington, Jr, E. L., & Vogel, D. L. (2007). Effectiveness of religiously tailored interventions in Christian therapy. *Psychotherapy Research, 17*, 91-105.

Worthington, E. L. Jr., & Sandage, S. J. (2002). Religion and spirituality. In J. C. Norcross (Ed.), *Psychotherapy Relationships that Work*. New York: Oxford University Press.

Yangarber-Hicks, N., Behensky, C., Canning, S. S., Fanagan, K. S., Gibson, J. S., Hicks, M. W., Kimball, C. N., Pak, J. H., Plante, T., and Porter, S. H. (2006). Invitation to the table conversation: A few diverse perspectives on integration. *Journal of Psychology and Christianity, 25*, 338-353.

Index

Adams, Jay 26, 251, 252, 258
Adler, Alfred 6
"All truth is God's truth" (see also Truth)
"All truth is God's truth"...........................60, 61, 75
....76, 84, 185, 197, 228, 261
Allison, Steve...14
Allport, Gordon 4, 172, 174
American Psychological Association
    ethics code.......................................286, 312-313
    two cultures..114-115
American Psychologist...113, 117
Anthropology (see also Human beings; Human beings'
    consitituent elements; Human nature; Humanity)
Anthropology.....................................64-65, 72-73
    biblical...122
    competing views 111
    fundamental questions...........................159-160
    scientific..104
Aquinas, Thomas 48
Aristotle..294
Augustine..224
Authority of Scripture 197-198, 263
Bandura, Albert...98, 174
Barbour, Ian..138
Barkman, Paul..23
Basinger, David.......................................327, 330-341
Bassett, Rod..........................327-328, 330-341, 366-374
Bauer, David...352-365
Baumeister, Roy 353, 360-361
Beck, James..18, 75-81
Behavioral theory of personality.....................162
Behaviorism...162
Benner, David...............................239, 244-248, 253-254
Bergin, Allen...277
Berkhof, Louis...70-71
Bhaskar, Roy...130-132
Bible
    as a defense...309-311
    in therapy...285
Biblical counseling 53, 75-76, 197, 210-211
Blamires, Harry 37
Boisen, Anton...24, 25
Bouma-Prediger, Steve 178, 187-195, 261
Braybrooke, David 137-138
Browning, Don...145
Buber, Martin...164
Bufford, Rodger 240, 250-260, 327, 342-351
Byrne, G. L..181
Calvin, John...79
Capitulatory position...................................105-106
Carter, Anna...366-374

Carter, John.............................4, 36, 197, 208-216
    sacred and secular models 205
Cartesian assumptions 99-100
Causality...103
Character..258-259
Christian Association for Psychological Studies
    (CAPS)...2, 180
    Dutch reformed tradition 7, 8
    early history...58-59
    ethics code..286
    evangelical influences...................................7-8
    history 7-13
    publications..63
    stages of development................................8-13
Christian counseling (see Psychotherapy, Christian)
Christian living 191-192
Christian worldview...6
Christianity
    convictions for psychology....................224-225
    dialogue with psychology 218
    tensions with science.............................102-112
Church and culture (interaction) 218
Church, Christian
    analogous to culture 219-221
    critique of culture & psychology 218-219
    dialogue with culture..............................223-224
    early apologists 76-78
    evangelical..25
    fears of psychology...................................26-28
    historical development................................24-27
    liberal vs. conservative 24
    relationship with psychology 21
    response to culture 217
    translates culture 221-223
    witness to culture..................................224-225
Church, Roman Catholic (councils)...............78-80
Clement of Alexandria...................................77-78
Client-centered therapy 25
Clinical integration
    breadth...273-279
    ethics 285-287
    foundations...279
    increased efficacy..279
    spiritually-oriented goals........................279-285
    values in..280-281
Clinical integration ethics
    competence 286
    effectiveness of therapy.........................286-287
    respect for beliefs...286
Clinical theology 283
Clore, D. 181

Collins, Gary..................17, 33-37, 39-40, 182, 198, 231
.................................232, 233, 235, 253-254, 262
Common grace 47, 220
Compatibilism 97, 100
Comte, Auguste 103
Confession 353
Consequentialism
    ethical egoism.....................................334-335
    utilitarianism 334
Constructive relationship between psychology and
    religion 146-152
Constructive relationship between psychology and
    religion (foundations).............................146-152
Contemplative prayer....................................284
Control beliefs 225
Conversion..29
Cosgrove, Mark 233
Council for Clinical Pastoral Training...............24
Counseling (see also Psychotherapy)
Counseling
    defined..250-251
    mental health.................................251, 257
    spiritual 251, 257
Counseling, Christian (see Psychotherapy, Christian)
Counseling, consecrated.............................257-259
Counseling, mental health (see Psychotherapy)
Countertransference...................281, 304-305, 307
Covenant...225
Crabb, Larry...34, 233
Creation 170
Creation (of man) 160
Creation grace...47, 52-54
Criticism of social sciences (responses) 104-109
Deception (see also Deception in research)
Deception
    arguments against.................................332-333
    as a character flaw 336
    as a research tool....................................330-331
    benefits..331-332
    prohibited by Scripture...........................336, 337
    Scriptural argument for necessity...............337
Deception in research (see also Deception)
Deception in research
    conclusions 338-339
    participant suspicion.............................332-333
    philosophical perspective 333-335
    psychological perspective......................331-333
    theological perspective 335-338
Delimitation..97-98, 100
Derflinger, Kimberly 327, 342-351
Descartes, Rene.............................99-100, 107
Determinism...105, 118, 163
    fear of...26, 29
Discipleship...224-225
Division 36 (of APA) 5, 136, 150, 208
Doctrine 263
Dorff, Elliot...361
Dualism...107, 172-173
Dueck, Al..206, 217-226
Durkeim, Emile 102

Ebersole, Myron 222
Eck, Brian........................227-237, 241, 312-325
    paradigms of integration..........................196-197
Egan, G. 250
Ellens, J. Harold (Hal) 10, 11, 12, 18, 58-67, 235
    books 63
Ellis, Albert 292-302
    sense of humor 300-301
Ellison, Craig 11
Emotions, fear of..27
Empathy...354, 361
Empiricism..93, 103, 326
Empiricism
    alternatives..137
    usefulness of psychology...........................133
Epistemic values...120
Epistemology...93-94, 141
Epistemoloigcal relativism 130-131
Equanimity, RET vs. Christian virtues...............297
Erikson, Erik..8
Ethical ideals 272-274
Ethics
    applied 274
    based on science..270-271
Ethics, Christian...268-276
    applied to psychotherapy...........................272-274
    educational goals......................................274
    motifs 271-272, 273
Evangelicalism...34
Evans, C. Stephen................93, 102-112, 121-122, 124
.................................125, 156, 170-175, 232
Existentialiam 25
Exline, Julie 353, 360-361
Fairbairn, W. R. D. 246
Farnsworth, Kirk......................132-133, 197, 232, 235
Fechner, Gustav 71
Finch, John 188
Finney, John R. (Jack) 284
Forgiveness (see also Forgiveness seeking)
Forgiveness..328, 352-365
    emotional benefit 363
    from God 353
    of the self...361
    seeking...352-354
    victim response 354-355, 362-363
Forgiveness seeking (see also Forgiveness)
Forgiveness seeking..360-362
    emotional response 355
    physiological response..............................362-363
Fosdick, Harry Emerson 24
Foster, James D. 132-133
Frank, Jerome..244
Free will..172
Freud, Sigmund 102, 162-163, 174, 223
General revelation 39, 212, 263
    value of..60
Gergen, Kenneth.......................................114, 118
Glock, Charles Y. 315
God, foundation for integration.........................263
God concept..343

Gregg, Douglas 201
Grimm, Julia P. 366-374
Gruender, Hubert...69
Guntrip, Harry...174
Guy, James D., Jr...18,38-41
Hall, M. Elizabeth Lewis.....................241,277-291
Hall, Todd W.................................241,277-291
Harmonizing...97-98,100
Hiemstra, William..9
Hill, Peter....................................12,13,94,126-135
Hillman, James...72
Holmes, Arthur, metaphysical perspectives 105
Homophobia
    among Christians.....................................366-367
    effects of intervention 372-373
Homosexuality 328,336-374
Homosexuals, attitudes toward..............................369-370
Houts, Arthur...113-115,123
Howard, George S. 120-121
Human beings (see also Anthropology; Human beings
        constituent elements; Human nature; Humanity)
Human beings
    apex of creation 161
    as children of God 160
    as objects 164
    essential characteristics................................156,160-268
    god-like and animal-like...................................170-171
Human beings' constituent elements (see also
    Anthropology; Human beings; Human nature;
    Humanity)
Human beings' constituent elements.......................166-168
    body and soul 167
    flesh and spirit...167-168
    unity and duality..166-167
Human nature (see also Anthropology; Human beings'
    constituent elements; Humanity)
Human nature..46-47,53-54,96
    dichotomous view..70-71
    fallen 166
    relational 246-247
    trichotomous view 70-71
Human reflexivity...120-121
Humanism 113
    fear of 25,26
    in anthropology...109
    in sociology 109
Humanity (see also Anthropology; Human beings; Human
        beings' constituent elements; Human nature)
Humanity
    biased...47
    rebellious 43
    telos..54
Humanizers of Science position 108-110
Image of God..160-161,246-247
Immortality 165
Incarnation 161,244,245
    in psychotherapy...247-249
Ingram, John..375
Inner healing prayer 284

Integration (see also Integrative thinking;
        Models of integration)
Integration
    applied..239
    as mutual illumination 60-62
    attitudes for success....................................31
    building blocks..263-266
    Christian resistance.....................................23
    clinical..241,262,277-287
    concept of 2,187-189
    coursework...344
    data 227-228
    deficiencies...23
    definition of 34,38,170,188,196,227
    development...96
    depth model 73
    early efforts 22,59
    embodied...377
    evaluation of models 212-215
    Evangelical efforts 60
    experiential..179,193,261
    external influences 375-376
    faith-praxis...178,191,193,261
    future directions 375-377
    goal...227
    impact of professors....................................344-350
    implicit vs. explicit...................................199,279
    interdisciplinary...............178,189-190,261,338-339
    internal influences 377
    intradisciplinary..............178,190-191,261-266
    learning...327,342-351
    levels of 177,180-185
    living 350
    markers 6,7
    meta-models 227
    methods..6,35,97-98
    models..................4,41,205-206,227,231-235,261
    multilingual..262
    paradigms 206
    personal.................170,196,198,200-201,343-350
    personal efforts and commitment.........................30,31
    personal relevance 37
    philosophical concerns 126-134
    practical 192,240
    principled...196-199
    process..228,293
    professional...196,199-200
    qualitative research 350
    reinterpretation 183-184
    research.........................29-30,180,185,327-328,377
    research methods 198
    sacred models..209-212,214
    second to submission to God 51
    secular models...208-209,210
    secular resistance 23-24
    shortcomings...252
    steps for 52
    tasks of 5,6,38-41,182-183
    terminology..187
    theological problems 60-61

Integration (continued)
  theoretical 170, 175
  types 177, 189-193
  use of Scripture 75-76
  virtues approach 292-302
  vs. psychology of religion 4
  within the self...193
Integration processes (see also Integration; Integrative
    thinking; Models of integration)
Integration processes 228-235
  correlates process..233-234
  reconstructs process 231-232
  rejects process 231
  transforms process 232-233
  unifies process...234-235
Integrative paradigms 228-235
  manipulative paradigm 228, 231-233
  non-integrative paradigm..228, 231
  non-manipulative paradigm 228, 233-235
Integrative thinking (see also Integration; Integration
    processes; Models of integration)
Integrative thinking
  biases of...1
  data collection 7
  data interpretation...7
  plurality of ideas 1
  principles of...1
Interaction between religion and the science of
    psychology...147-150
  constructive mode...148-149
  critical-evaluative mode 147-148
  dialogical mode...149-150
Interface of psychology and theology......................................58-67
Interface of scientific and operational disciplines,
    levels of 63-64
Intradisciplinary integration, methods 261-262
Irrationality 163
I-Thou 164
James, William 59, 69
Jerusalem & Athens 217
Jesus Christ, lordship over psychology 42-57
Johnson, Deanna...366-374
Johnson, Eric L. 18, 42-57
Jones, Stanton L. 94, 136-154
Joseph, deception in Genesis..337
Journal of Consulting and Clinical Psychology,
    empirically supported therapy 198
Journal of Psychology and Christianity
    ....5, 7, 11, 17, 58, 63, 375-376
  sola scriptura (special issue)..197
  special issues 13
Journal of Psychology and Theology,.......5, 17, 33-37, 180, 261
  assumptions 35
  diversity in publication 34
  goals...34
  objectives and goals..21-32
  self/soul (special issue)...198
  special issues 36
  the creation of...21-32
  theology 34

Jung, Carl..231
Justification and Wesley's doctrine of perfection.............87
Kant, Immanuel 55-56, 335
Kierkegaard, Søren 25, 293, 297, 301
Kimble, Gregory...113-114, 123
King, Robert, Jr. (Bob)...12
Kingdom living..196
Kingdom of God, and psychology 44-57
  Christians' responses...48-55
  qualities of..43-44
  returning 43-44
Kotesky, Ronald 339
Krasner, Leonard 113-115, 123
Kuhn, Thomas..103, 128-129, 139-141
Kuiper, Klaire 8
Künkel, Fritz...2
Kuyper, Abraham...8, 50
Larzelere, Robert 177, 180-186
Latent semantic analysis 346
Lay counselors..200
Ledbetter, Mark F. 132-133
Leech, Kenneth 247
Limiters of Science position 106-108
  Perspectivalism.......................................107-108, 110-111
  Territorialist..106-107
Livermore, Paul 327, 330-341
Locus of control 52
London, Perry 144-145, 150
Long, Edward L. 271-272, 273
Ludwig, Thomas..352-365
Luther, Martin..78-80, 87-88, 223
MacKay, Donald M. 108, 118-119
Malony, Newton H. 19, 59, 82-91, 178, 187, 188, 196,
    ....280-281, 284
Manicas, P. T...130-132
Marcel, Gabriel...108
Martyr, Justin 77
Marx, Karl..102
Maslow, Abraham...52-53, 56, 109
McDonald, H. D. 156, 159-169
McDougall, William 6
McMinn, Mark..............................258, 286, 327, 342-351
Meehl, Paul 147, 212, 274
Melanchthon, Philip...78
Mental health, factors 251
Meta-models of integration 231-235
Methodists 86-87
Milgram, Stanley..330
Miller, Ashley..366-374
Miller, Geraldine...281
Mind-body problem...215
Mind-brain relationship 117
Miracles..29
Models of integration (see also Integration; Integration
    processes; Integrative thinking)
Models of integration
  content 205
  limitations...205
  nature of the disciplines 205
Moral emotions 353-354

Morality 165
Motivation to Control Attitudes Scale 368, 371
Mowrer, Hobart 25
Multiculturalism 376
Multidimensional scaling 344, 345-346
Multitrait-multimethod matrices 346
Muscle activity and emotion 354
Mutual illumination 60-63, 65
    principles of...61-62
Myers, David 222, 234
Narramore, S. Bruce 17, 21-32, 36, 205, 241, 280, 303-311
Naturalism, fear of 26, 28
Neumann, Erich 69-70
Niebuhr, H. Richard 205-206, 215, 217-218, 223, 224, 268
Niebuhr, Reinhold 4, 12
Nonconsequentialism...335
Object relations theory 174, 246
Objectivity, myth 129-130
Oden, Thomas C. 199, 220, 245
O'Donohue, William T. 145, 270-271
Olthuis, Jim...375
Omnipotence, God's 45-46
Overspecialization 189
Paradigms, scientific perspective 128-129
Paraklasis 214
Pastoral care 136-137
Pathology, psychological vs. spiritual 71-72
Paul (apostle) 28, 42, 107, 249, 296
    flesh and spirit...167-168
    levels of knowledge..49
    man's dichotomous nature 167
    on morality 165-166
Personality 163-164
Personhood, as a reality....................................164-165
    biblical perspective 155
    implications..164-165
    psychological perspectives 155
    scientific perspective......................................159
    self vs. soul...165
Perspectivalism...................107-108, 110-111, 118-119
    doctrine of creation..119
    doctrine of human nature..............................119
    doctrine of sanctification 119
Philosophy, Greek..76-78
Philosophy, moral...78
Plantinga, Alvin 55, 149
Plato 55
Pluralism 224
Plurality...40
Polanyi, Michael...129-130, 134
Popper, Karl 100
Positive Psychology 377
Positivism 113, 126, 138-139
    scientific perspective.....................................128
Postmoderism...375-376
Postpositivism, philosophy of science..............139-141
    rejection of induction......................................139-140
Powlison, David 252
Prayer, in therapy...284

Prejudice, controlling reactions to 367
    the effect of contact.......................................366
Pride..173
Priesthood of believers.....................................225
Proof-texting...211
Psychoanalysis 24, 25
Psychoanalytic theory of personality 162-163
    benefits..163
    conflicts with Scripture 163
Psychologists, religious preferences 136
Psychology
    as a science 126-134, 139, 198
    concept of the self 170-171
    dialogue with Christianity..............................218
    evangelical interest..208
    objectivity..42
    personality theories.......................................168
    politics...115-116
    positive..377
    recent developments......................................376-377
    relationship to philosophy 126-127, 133
    tension with theology.....................................68-74
    trends 36
    values in 113, 115, 116
Psychology of religion 4, 136, 198, 232
Psychology, Christian..22-23
    anthropology..98-99
    Christ's lordship...42-43
    context in which it operates 45-57
    correlating vs. integrating 213
    cultures 113-125
    dependence on God.......................................45
    development...51, 171
    failures...23
    interdisciplinary integration 190
    multilingual...221-222
    plurality 174
    response to positivism...................................132-133
    response to reductionism 171
    response to science.......................................104-105
    response to self-deification 171
    sources of data 182
    theological differences..................................118
    third culture 117
    training programs...150-151
    unique challenges...29-31
    use of empiricism..93
    use of Scripture 47-48, 75
Psychology, secular
    anti-religious attitudes...................................45
    attitude toward integration 23-24
    contended by Christians 51
    determinism..96
    isolated from Christianity...............................28-29
    naturalistic bias...173-174
Psychotherapist, and the *imago dei*................239
    impact on personal integration 343
    as ethicist..268-276

Psychotherapist, Christian, dilemma 304-305
    personal calling 257
    personal faith..257,259
    tasks and roles...253
    spiritual techniques 283-284
Psychotherapy
    addressing spiritual issues 315-316
    agents of change..244
    as a moral enterprise 144-145
    Biblical insights 62
    common elements...254
    curative factors 244-245,248
    ethics 240
    ethics training...150
    goals...264-265
    methods 264-265
    prescriptive 145
    religious concerns 278
    religious resistances 241,303-311
    religious silence...314
    spiritual disciplines..241
    spiritual interventions 312,314-318
    spiritual issues 281-282
    theoretical orientation 244
    treatment goals..240
    value-laden 151
    values in 54-55
Psychotherapy, Christian 35
    branches...252
    building blocks...263-266
    content 266
    content and context 253
    cross-cultural issues..200
    defenses 307
    distinctives 200,239-240,250-259
    emergence 251-252
    history 251
    Holy Spirit's ministry in 199
    outcomes 30
    spiritual growth...283
    use of Scripture 264
    use of spiritual disciplines...................................312-321
    using God's understanding..54
Psychotherapy, secular, virtues 241
Rational Emotive Therapy, virtues.............292-302,295-296
Rational Emotive Therapy, virtues
    equanimity...295-297
    mutuality..295
    rationality...295
    responsibility 295
    self-acceptance 295,298-300
    self-transparency..295
    sense of humor 295-296,300-302
Realism, critical 139
    goals of social science 131-132
    key features 130-131
    ontological 129-130
    research model...131-132
    scientific model 130-132
    scientific perspective..129-132

Realist theory of science 94,126,133
Reductionism..170-171
Reformation, Protestant 78-80
Reformation, radical..79-80
Regan, Paul..13
Relationship between psychology and religion
    implications..150-151
Relativism..334
Religion, as an object 137
Religion,
    cognitive-declarative dimension...............................138
    commonalities with science..............................141-143
    dialogue within science 377
    in psychotherapists...151
    interacting with clinical psychology 144-145
    interacting with the science of psychology.......143-144
    psychological benefits..209
    relationship with science 138-146
Religious beliefs, impact on therapy 280
Research, importance of theory....................................134
Resistance (in therapy)
    defined...303-304
    developmental fears...304
    modification...305-306
    religiously reinforced 304
Resistance (in therapy), religiously reinforced
    modification...306-307
    use of biblical language...307
    use of Scripture 306,309-311
    vignette 308-309
Richardson, F...145-146
Roberts, Robert..241,292-302
Rogers, Carl..25,26,101,245
Role playing, as a research tool...................................333
Russell, Bertrand 129
Sacred models of integration
    Christianity *against* psychology 210-211
    Christianity *integrates* psychology 212
    Christianity *of* psychology 211
    Christianity *parallels* psychology 211
    evaluation 212-215
    isolation vs. correlation...211
Sampson, Edward 116
Sanctification, and therapy..88
    and Wesley's doctrine of perfection 87
Sanders, Randolph K. 12,13
Sanua, Victor 30
Science, alternative perspectives............................128-132
    commonalities with religion 141-143
    defined...110
    dialogue with religion...377
    interacting with religion.....................................143-144
    progressed by theories..141
    relationship with religion...................................138-146
    tensions with Christian beliefs 102-111
Scientific inquiry
    data level 181, 185
    general proposition level...........................181, 182-183
    hypothesis level..................................181, 184-185
    linkage level 181, 183

Scientific inquiry (continued)
　　six levels 181-185
　　specific proposition level 181,183-184
　　worldview level...181,182
Scientific method
　　criticism...14
　　in psychology and theology 58-60,63
　　influenced by values..140
　　unity in 105
Scientific theory, natural vs. social 121
Scientism..93,104
Scientist-practioner model...................................270,274
Scripture, authority of..................................31,75-81
Secord, P. F. 130-132
Secular models of integration
　　against religion...208-209
　　of religion 209
　　psychology integrates religion..................................209
　　psychology parallels religion..................................209
Secularization 192
Self
　　in Christian psychology 173
　　in clinical practice 174
　　concept in psychology................................172
　　dualistic view...172-173
　　freedom objection 172
　　homonculus problem................................172
　　objections to the concept 172-173
　　selfism 173
Self-acceptance
　　biblical..299
　　vs. self-esteem 298
Self-actualization 52-53
Self-deification..170-171
Self-evaluation, biblical...............................299
Serrano, Neftali..14
Sex, fear of 27
Sexual Orientation and Practice Scale (SOAP)..367-368,369
Shafranske, Edward 280-281
Simon, Herbert...143-144
Sin
　　as psychopathology 212-213
　　God's solution 245-246
　　noetic effects 47,50
Skinner, B. F. 98,101,102,117
Smedes, Lewis 193
Social constructionism 116
Sola scriptura...75-81
Sorenson, Randall Lehmann......................327-328,342-351
Soul
　　absence from psychology..............................68-70
　　defined..69
　　relationship to body and spirit...........................70-71
Special revelation....................................40
Sperry, Roger...117,137
Spiritual disciplines
　　behaviorally oriented 318-320
　　cognitively oriented................................318
　　for therapists...................................200-201

Spiritual disciplines (continued)
　　in therapy 199,312-321
　　interpersonally oriented.....................................320-321
Spiritual disciplines in therapy
　　client issues..314-315
　　clinical context 313-314
　　ethical concerns..312-313
　　future directions.....................................321
　　guidelines for us.................................317-318
　　nature of 317
　　research..318,321
　　therapist issues 315
　　use of 318-321
Spiritual interventions 257-258
Spiritual issues in therapy
　　client assessment..............................315-316
　　clinical setting assessment 316
　　therapist assessment...........................316
Stevenson, Daryl H....................................1-15
Stoiker, Hendrick 46
Structural equation modeling.....................343,344-346
Submission, to Christ..................................42
Tan, Siang-Yang.....................178,196-203,258,279-284
Territorialism, (see Limiters of Science)
Territorialism..107
Tertullian 66,76-78,217-218
Theocentricity..45
Theology
　　recent developments.................................376
　　tension with psychology..............................68-74
Theory, hypothesis testing 184-185
Therapeutic alliance....................................245,248
Thorne, Frederick 209
Thymotology 68-69
Tjeltveit, Alan 240,268-276
Tolman, E. C. 6
Toulmin, Stephen.......................................103
Tournier, Paul...342
Tradition, authority of...................................79-80
Transgressors, experience of forgiveness.............352-365
Truth (see also "All truth is God's truth")
Truth
　　available to non-Christians 212
　　for the unbeliever 50
　　God as source 38
　　implications of knowing................................40-41
　　knowledge of 39-40
　　revelation 38
　　through scientific inquiry...............................105
Ulavnov, Ann and Berry 69,72,73
Unger, Rhoda..115-116
Values
　　defined..269-270
　　in therapy......................268-269,273-274,278,305,314
　　intellectual basis 269-270
　　self-awareness.......................................280
Van Leeuwen, Mary Stewart 94,113-125,132,188
van Nikkelen-Kuyper, Marike 366-374
VandeKamp, Hendrika...................18,68-74,127,131

Virtue
    grammar 293-295
    Christian 292
    defined 292
Virtues approach to integration 292-302
Von Rad, Gerhard 49
Watson, John B. 127, 162
Wertheimer, Max 35
Wesley, John 82-91
    lessons for psychology 82
    practice of medicine 89
    response to science 83-85
    salvation 82-83, 85-86
    sanctification and "sinlessness" 87-88
    social justice 88
    use of electricity 84-85

Western Association of Christians for Psychological
    Studies (WACPS) 11, 12
Willard, Dallas 317-318
    spiritual disciplines 200-201
Winch, Peter 109
Witvliet, Charlotte vanOyen 352-365
Wolterstorff, Nicholas 93, 96-101, 191, 225
Woolfolk, R. 145-146
Worldview 257, 259
    biblical 170
    Christian 180
    naturalistic vs. Christian 156
Worthington, Everett L., Jr. 227, 240, 253-254, 261-267, 278
Wundt, Wilhelm 126-127